Everyone Can Write

Everyone Can Write

Essays Toward a Hopeful Theory of Writing and Teaching Writing

PETER ELBOW

New York   Oxford

Oxford University Press

2000

Oxford University Press

Oxford   New York

Athens   Auckland   Bangkok   Bogotá   Buenos Aires   Calcutta
Cape Town   Chennai   Dar es Salaam   Delhi   Florence   Hong Kong   Istanbul
Karachi   Kuala Lumpur   Madrid   Melbourne   Mexico City   Mumbai
Nairobi   Paris   São Paulo   Singapore   Taipei   Tokyo   Toronto   Warsaw

and associated companies in
Berlin   Ibadan

Copyright © 2000 by Peter Elbow

Published by Oxford University Press, Inc.
198 Madison Avenue, New York, New York 10016

Oxford is a registered trademark of Oxford University Press

Library of Congress Cataloging-in-Publication Data
Elbow, Peter.
Everyone can write : essays toward a hopeful theory of writing and teaching writing /
Peter Elbow.
p.   cm.
Includes bibliographical references.
ISBN 0-19-510415-3; ISBN 0-19-510416-1 (pbk.)
1. English language—Rhetoric—Study and teaching.   2. Report
writing—Study and teaching.   I. Title.
PE1404.E42   2000
808'.042'07—dc21   99-20987

9 8 7 6 5 4 3 2 1

Printed in the United States of America
on acid-free paper

For my family—who make everything possible.

Acknowledgments

"Being a Writer vs. Being an Academic." Peter Elbow. *College Composition and Communication*. Reprinted with permission from the National Council of Teachers of English.

"Breathing Life into the Text." Peter Elbow. In *When Writing Teachers Teach Literature: Bringing Writing to Reading*. Ed. Art Young and Toby Fulwiler (Boyton/Cook, a subsidiary of Reed Elsevier Inc., Portsmouth, NH, 1995). Reprinted by permission.

"Closing My Eyes as I Speak." Peter Elbow. *College English*. Copyright © 1987. Reprinted with permission from the National Council of Teachers of English.

"Collage: Your Cheatin' Art" Writing on the Edge, 9.1 (Fall/Winter 1997–1998). Reprinted by permission.

A Community of Writers, 2E, 1995. Peter Elbow and Pat Belanoff. The McGraw-Hill Companies. Reprinted by permission.

"In Defense of Private Writing" Written Communication, Vol. 16 (2). Peter Elbow. Sage Publications, Inc./Corwin Press, Inc. Reprinted by permission.

"Foreword." Peter Elbow. In *Portfolios: Process and Product*. Ed. Pat Belanoff and Marcia Dickson (Boyton/Cook, a subsidiary of Reed Elsevier Inc., Portsmouth, NH, 1991). Reprinted by permission.

"Foreword: Expressive Academic Discourse." Peter Elbow. *Pre/Text* 11.1–2 (1990). Reprinted by permission.

Freewriting and the Problem of the Wheat and the Tares. Peter Elbow. Copyright © 1997. Reprinted by permission of Rowan and Littlefield, 2E.

"To Group or Not to Group: System Leads to Narrow Definition of Intelligence." *Amherst Bulletin* 25.50, 7 January 1994. Reprinted by permission.

"Illiteracy at Oxford and Harvard." Peter Elbow. *Reflective Stories,* also *Encyclopedia of English Studies and Language Arts*. Copyright © 1997. Reprinted with permission from the National Council of Teachers of English.

"Introduction: Voice and Writing." Peter Elbow. *Voice and Writing*. Reprinted with permission from Hermagoras Press, now owned by Erlbaum.

"Making Room for the Mother Tongue: Beyond 'Mistakes,' 'Bad English,' and 'Wrong Language.'" (Summer 1999). Reprinted with permission from the *Journal of Advanced Composition*.

Mimesis: The Representation of Reality in Western Literature. Erich Auerbach. Copyright © 1953, renewed 1981. Reprinted by permission of Princeton University Press.

Contents

Introduction

Note to General Readers

In most of the pieces gathered in this book, I am speaking to teachers of writing and members of the academic field of composition or writing. Other readers—general readers who want to explore the nature of writing and language—will find all the essays clear and direct, I think, but they should probably start with the following pieces: the first half of this introduction, "Illiteracy at Oxford and Harvard," "Freewriting and the Problem of Wheat and the Tares," "Collage, Your Cheatin' Art," "Wrongness and Felt Sense," "Form and Content as Sources of Creation," "Voice and Literature," "Silence: A Collage," and "Tracking Leads to a Narrow Definition of Intelligence." Teachers resistant to exploration of theory might start with "Using the Collage for Collaborative Writing," "Breathing Life into the Text," "The Benefits and Feasibility of Liking," "Getting Along Without Grades—and Getting Along With Them Too," "A Map of Writing in Terms of Audience and Response," "The War Between Reading and Writing—and How to End It," "Separating Teaching from Certifying," and "The Shifting Relationships Between Speech and Writing."

A Hopeful Vision

A skeptical reader might say that this book is just a collection of unrelated essays—and worse yet, "academic"—and not be wrong. Yet there is more to say. Yes, the book is largely a selection of separately written essays that have already appeared in various books and journals since my last collection in 1986 (*Embracing Contraries: Explorations of Learning and Teaching*, Oxford).

But I have selected among essays and parts of essays, and done some rewriting of what I've chosen, in order to get them to work together more coherently in a single book. Most of all, everything here is driven by a single vision of writing that I've summed up bluntly in my title: everyone can write. Let me spell it out more fully:

(a) Most people have had bad experiences with writing. They have come to dislike it or fear it and usually they avoid it. Few people write by choice. Nevertheless, though good writing takes hard work and skill, I insist on some hopeful truths:

- It is possible for anyone to produce a lot of writing with pleasure and satisfaction and without too much struggle.
- It is possible for anyone to figure out what he or she really means and wants to say, and finally get it clear on paper.
- It is possible for anyone to write things that others will want to read. When people manage to say what they really mean and to get themselves into their writing, readers tend to have the experience of making contact with the writer—an experience that most people seek.

(b) Anyone can take various steps to make the experience of writing easier and better:

- Our own habits and feelings often seem to hinder our writing. And we often feel external forces (e.g., teachers, schools, institutions, society) trying to impede us or even shut us up. Nevertheless, if we understand certain important features of the writing process, we can take charge of ourselves and learn to prevent any of these things from stopping us.
- The most important thing to understand is the need for two different mentalities or frames of mind for writing: a fertile, inventive, yea-saying mentality that will help us come up with lots of words and ideas; and a critical, skeptical, nay-saying mentality that will help us critique, cut, and revise what we have. These two mentalities get in each other's way because they push against each other, but if we make separate arenas for them, they can each flourish on their own and even reinforce each other. Thus, we can learn to be more fruitful in our early drafting and exploratory writing if we take on a noncritical, accepting mentality—just writing what comes to mind, not worrying about quality and correctness, and learning to relinquish control. Similarly, we can learn to revise, strengthen, and correct our writing more effectively if—after we have freely generated lots of rich material—we take on a critical and skeptical mentality, pondering, thinking about readers, rearranging, and crossing out in a tough-minded, suspicious mood.
- We have selves that are individual and to some degree unique (though not simple, unitary, or unchanging), and it helps our writing to honor our self and voice. In particular, we can ask ourselves questions like these: What voices do I use most? What voice or voices feel most like me? What voices don't get much chance to speak? What are the voices of others that

I have internalized or taken on—or that have controlled me most? What are the voices of others that I can play with or try out in order to get things written?

- It helps to trust ourselves and our experiences. Our experiences are ours and often differ from those of others. No one else gets to deny or belittle our experience—our sense of what we see and feel. No one gets to interpret or "explain" our experience unless we invite them to do so.
- It also helps to trust our similarities with others and our connections to them, and to find links between our experiences and theirs. Indeed, it helps enormously to work with others—actually writing companionably together with them (with tea and cookie breaks), and sharing and responding to each others' writings in an atmosphere of trust and support. We can come to experience writing as a social, almost communal activity, rather than essentially lonely.

(c) As teachers we can empower our students. We can help them like to write. We can help them trust themselves, work with others, find voices, and be more forceful and articulate in using writing in their lives. We can help make their school experience liberating rather than deadening or oppressive. Indeed, we can help students be better people and help make a more just society.

———————————

But are these essays "merely academic and theoretical?" Well, yes. And no. Let me give a longer answer—which is a story.

When I wrote previous books (most notably *Writing Without Teachers* and *Writing With Power*, Oxford 1973 and 1981) I certainly was an academic, but those books didn't feel academic or theoretical—to me or to readers. I was not writing *as an academic but rather as a writer and a teacher*. I was not writing to academics but rather to everyone and anyone who has ever tried to write. When I wrote most of the essays collected in *Embracing Contraries* (Oxford 1986), I was trying to write to anyone who has ever tried to teach or learn.

During the period when I wrote those earlier books, I wasn't really a participating member of the *discipline* of English or composition. There were seven years of teaching at M.I.T. (in two separate stretches), two years at Franconia College, and nine years at Evergreen State College, but none of those institutions even *had* a department of English, and virtually all my teaching was decidedly interdisciplinary or nondisciplinary. (At M.I.T. I taught mostly Western Civilization courses; at Franconia and Evergreen I taught mostly intensive interdisciplinary programs such as "Words, Sounds, and Images," and "Science and Humanities.") It's true that I had a Ph.D. in English during the last thirteen of those eighteen years, and I wrote a dissertation on Chaucer and even revised it into a published book—a book in which I *was* trying to speak as an academic to academics. But while I was writing those books, I was giving my main time and attention to teaching, not to the profession or the discipline. I didn't even define myself as a teacher of writing. My teaching of writing was always part of some other teaching enterprise—usually interdisciplinary. During these eighteen years, I never taught a freshman writing course—indeed, none of the institutions even had such a course.

However, during the more recent period as I was writing the essays and fragments you hold in your hand, I *did* feel myself a member of the profession and the scholarly discipline of English and composition studies—and I *was* writing to and thinking about the profession. In 1981 I started directing a large first-year writing program at the State University of New York at Stony Brook, eventually directing graduate students interested in composition as a scholarly field. I started subscribing to the National Council of Teachers of English journals for literature and composition, I joined the Modern Language Association, and I started going to professional conferences and giving talks and papers and workshops at them. As I wrote many of these essays, I was indeed trying to prove myself a scholar and member of a discipline—not just someone writing to writers, students, and teachers.

This new writing situation created a problem for me. I don't mean the problem you might first guess, namely, trying to *sound* scholarly and clogging up my prose with footnotes, jargon, and learned quotations from sources. Some scholars don't consider even my recent essays as works of scholarship.

No, I had a different problem. I began to feel that I was writing to an audience that was hostile to my whole approach to writing and teaching writing—the vision I described above that had animated all my writing. That is, starting in the early '80s, as I moved from interdisciplinary teaching at Evergreen to the English Department and Writing Program Directorship at Stony Brook, this vision of mine began to be labeled "expressivist," "romantic," and "individualist," and characterized not just as passé, but as deeply flawed from an intellectual and political point of view. It's probably fair to say that by the late '80s, I was seen as a prime exemplar of a theory and philosophy of writing judged to be suspect or even wrong-headed by most of the dominant scholars in the important scholarly journals. For example, most graduate students experienced it as a problem if they said or wrote something that someone could characterize as "expressivist" or as "defending an approach like Elbow's."[1] And yet, interestingly enough, many classroom teachers did not share this distrust of so-called expressivism, and I could usually count on a sympathetic audience of teachers when I gave a talk or a paper. This split between scholars and teachers bears pondering.

Because of this situation I was faced with the difficult task of trying to follow one of my own main pieces of advice: don't write to enemies who disagree with you and who think you are crazy or stupid; write to friends and allies who are eager to know what you have to say; then after you have gotten your ideas clear the way you like them, you can turn to the job of making adjustments for the enemy.

---

1. It fueled my fears when I discovered in MLA's volume, *Introduction to Scholarship in Modern Languages and Literatures,* that one of the most prominent and least partisan scholars in composition had written an ambitious historical introduction to the field, with a Works Cited list of more than two hundred items, and assumed that none of my work constituted "scholarship" (Lunsford).

But it's hard to follow one's own advice; worse yet when it tells you to ig-nore a hostile audience. As students, we notice our bad grades more than our good ones; as writers, we notice the critical responses more than the approv-ing ones. And as teachers, we are often so distracted by absent students that we can't give our full attention to the students who are sitting right there in front of us. ("You students better be more careful about attendance," we growl to the ones who actually made it to class.) I was probably falling into the same trap in writing the essays collected here: trying to persuade people who didn't agree with me when probably my only readers were those who did.

For of course I did have supportive readers. That's probably what kept me writing. But now as I gather these essays together, I notice a kind of double rhetoric: I am fighting and not fighting my audience. That is, I am often writ-ing *from* an adversarial stance *toward* a nonadversarial goal. It's a tricky dance. In some essays I start right off with my dukes up, fighting the enemy in defense of the underdog ("We need careless writing, wrong words, bad writing! Down with quality!"), and then having done that, I climb to higher ground and build a larger argument on the principle of balance and fairness and nonexclusion ("Of course, we need to strive for quality, care, criticism. I myself spend far more time revising than generating.") In other essays I start with a dispassionate large view ("all audience and response situations are helpful and welcome; let's sometimes pay attention to readers and sometimes ignore them"), and then I slide from this catholicity into impassioned cheer-leading for what most teachers and students neglect ("We need private writ-ing! To hell with readers!").

It's interesting to look at this double rhetoric through different lenses:

- With respect to space, I'm trying to stand in two places at once: crouching down in the trenches as I fight for one position, yet also standing above on a lofty promontory and affirming all positions.
- With respect to oppositional thinking, I'm partisan for one side; yet I'm also affirming all sides equally.
- With respect to rhetoric or discourse, I'm arguing, fighting, and raising my voice against the enemy—for in truth I'm mad (of course trying to maintain good taste at all times!); yet I'm also feeling a sense of acceptance of opposite views and feeling no malice. I'm eager to be close and friendly with all sides.
- With respect to time, I'm immersed in a particular moment in the linear se-quence of time passing as I battle the one-sidedness of a particular moment or era or conversation; yet I'm also trying to step outside of time into pure logic in order to try to see the whole picture in its largest dimensions.

I've been emphasizing conceptual complexity here, but I can also explain my double rhetoric with a fairly simple story: I'm fighting for one side against another, but in doing so I'm only trying to right a balance, I'm only fighting for my space on the bed—trying to make room for multiple views. The only view I'm fighting *against* is the view that my view must be eliminated—not the *positive* content of other views. My goal is to include more points of view and to avoid either/or thinking and zero-sum games. (Some titles found on the cutting room floor: "Fighting For—Not Against," "Rocking the Boat to Get an Even Keel," "Throwing Sand to Level the Playing Field," "Foaming at the Mouth for Civil Discourse.")

An Underlying Vision

In the concluding section of this Introduction I want to explore an underlying but equally hopeful vision of how the academic and scholarly field of composition and rhetoric might look, and how the people in such a field might talk and write to each other.

The field. Because of the peculiarly rich and interdisciplinary nature of composition and rhetoric, we have a chance to forge a model for what a scholarly field could be. It looks to many outsiders as though we are just a motley, "undisciplined" conglomeration of folk thrown together by historical accident for merely pedagogical reasons. The end of World War II brought on large new enrollments and produced a much-expanded call for the teaching of writing in colleges and universities. This need grew even stronger in the '60s with open admissions. If the goal is only pedagogical, academics tend to feel there can be no scholarly center. (I remember a conversation with the chair of an English department who seemed to confuse the words "composition" and "pedagogy.")

Composition does not have its own "discipline" as that word is normally understood. Nor do we have any single theory, methodology, paradigm, or point of view. The National Endowment of Humanities does not recognize composition as a field of scholarship, and therefore no one can take part in NEH activities or get any NEH support for scholarly work in the field of composition. Similarly, when *The Chronicle of Higher Education* lists "New Scholarly Books" every week, it doesn't include books in composition. The editor and compiler of the list told me that they only list "research in the disciplines" (phone conversation with Nina Ayoub, 1/28/98). We are not seen as a discipline partly because we lack any theoretical center and partly because we are tainted by a strong focus on the *teaching* of writing. The *Chronicle* does have the category "rhetoric" in its weekly listing—where one can find books about Aristotle and about the rhetoric of the modern environmental movement. Rhetoric is a scholarly discipline. Composition is not.

In the absence of our own discipline, we call on a conglomeration of existing ones: rhetoric (classical and modern), linguistics, literary studies, history, philosophy, psychology, education, and others. Nor do we have any single, preferred, or dominant methodology. Instead, different members of our field use existing ones: historical investigation, quantitative research, qualitative/ethnographic research, and textual studies (hermeneutic and theoretical) of the sort traditionally practiced in English and philosophy.

And yet composition is not a new upstart any more. Using this grab bag of disciplines and methodologies, people in the field have built up an impressive body of scholarship, both empirical and theoretical. In a historical situation like this, it's not surprising to see strong moves by scholars in the field trying to prove that we *are* a bona fide discipline that deserves the respect and legitimacy of a true discipline—like others recognized as legitimate by the NEH and the *Chronicle*. But since even the academics in composition tend also to assume that we can't be a real and respectable discipline in our present mongrel condition, we have recently seen more scholarly jousting and competition in our field for theoretical dominance—more arguments that certain ideas and approaches are wrong or harmful or misguided. It's easy to assume without reflection that the best way to become a bona fide discipline is to clean house. But my goal is to question that assumption—to fight this kind of fighting. And in truth I think more people in composition are beginning to realize that the strength of our field is in its intellectual pluralism and multidisciplinary dynamic. We are in a good position to demonstrate a *model for what a healthy discipline could be.*

The discourse. If we want the kind of rich and inclusive discipline that I think composition potentially is, we need to develop a way of talking and writing to each other that will nourish it and keep it healthy. The struggles for dominance in recent years have given rise to a discourse that is strikingly more contentious than in the past. Authors of books and articles in our field have been spending more energy in recent years on arguing why opposing views are *wrong, mistaken, misguided*—rather than just arguing why their views are right and helpful. This exclusionary rhetoric fits a more traditional and unified discipline, but we need a more inclusive rhetoric of arguing as hard as we can *for* our position and giving reasons why it makes sense, instead of arguing against other positions as wrong: arguing for, not against.

Scholars often engage in scholarly discourse as a zero-sum game. It is unfortunately common to start off any persuasive or argumentive essay by looking at competing views and showing why they are wrong—as if the only way I can be right is if you are wrong. But this common assumption is misleading. Views or positions can be contradictory and also right—at least in certain respects. The two competing positions might be poorly framed or articulated so that it only *looks* as though they are logically incompatible. After all, the habits and conventions of debate often tempt people into framing two different views as more contradictory than they need to be. With more sophisticated framing or analysis, we can often see how both sides might be valid. The contradiction between the two positions might even result from the limitations of logic as it applies to empirical situations or phenomena.

If we keep in mind that the goal of argument is to get others to listen seriously to our views and perhaps even be persuaded (or as Burke puts it, to induce cooperation), we will see that the refutational model of argument, the debate habit, is often counterproductive. I can usually do better at getting you to listen to my view if I refrain from starting with a message that says, "You cannot take on my view of things until you first admit that you are wrong or stupid."

Arguing for, not against. Nonrefutational argument. What I am proposing may seem utopian. For it's much harder to get people to change *how* they express their thoughts than it is to get them to change *what* they actually think.

(What's the point in suffering through a Ph.D. if you can't publish an essay that *slams* those you disagree with?) But I will end this introduction by giving my reasons for hope. I will list the obstacles that stand in the way of developing a more nonadversarial rhetoric, and then try in each case to show why I think we can make genuine progress against those obstacles.

- Obstacle. There is a powerful tradition of adversarial, zero-sum behavior that is visceral for evolutionary reasons, and that predates even our species. Lots of behavior, from the playground to the battlefield, is driven by the assumption that I can't win or even be safe unless I make you roll over and bare your throat. I don't have to kill you, just make you surrender. This behavior taps into a pervasive sensitivity to *status* and the feeling that only one person or team can be dominant; others must be submissive.
  - Reason for hope. What's important to notice here is not how common this behavior is (how could it not be common given our history and ancestry?), but rather how widely it is beginning to be recognized for what it is: just *one* way to deal with conflict rather than the only way. In many realms of society we now see accelerating moves toward other ways to deal with conflict. It is especially striking to see how mediation and other modes of alternative dispute resolution are growing fastest in the very realm we associate with cut-throat competition: business. Businesses are discovering that mediational modes are cheaper and more effective than litigation—precisely because of the adversarial, zero-sum nature of litigation. (We are also benefiting from exploring the relationship between this zero-sum behavior and gender roles. The determining link between males and adversorial competition may lie not so much in gender itself but rather in a history of dominance by males. That is, only a dominant group finds it advantageous to settle conflicts in an adversarial way. Progress and creativity in nonviolent and nonadversarial methods tends to come from *nondominant* groups.)
- Obstacle. There is a long *scholarly* tradition of refutational argument. Our legal system is built on the principle that the best way to discover the truth is through win/lose adversarial contest and refutation. (Note, however, an opposite principle in the jury process: an acceptable verdict comes only through group consensus.)
  - Reason for hope. Nevertheless, an excitingly wide range of people and groups in our field and in many others are beginning to explore various kinds of nonadversarial discourse. Burke gives us a better understanding of sound argumentation when he talks about rhetoric as "identification": "True, the rhetorician may have to change an audience's opinion in one respect; but he can succeed only insofar as he yields to that audience's opinions in other respects" (Burke 56). Even Aristotle's emphasis on the enthymeme in argument is an emphasis on finding common ground or shared premises. (I append a bibliography of interesting recent work on nonadversarial rhetoric.)

- Obstacle. Probably the strongest intellectual tradition to survive the pure positivism of the nineteenth century is the kind of *disconfirmation model* widely associated with Karl Popper. This model or view emphasizes that even though hypotheses can never be proved right, at least they can be proved wrong or *disconfirmed* by counterevidence. From this powerful tradition (and no doubt from other sources too) we inherit a feeling that we have no real leverage in argument unless we are disproving or contradicting. If we give only positive reasons for our beliefs it feels as though we are doing nothing but wimpish and ineffectual flailing.

  - Reason for hope. There is growing recognition that the disconfirmation model does not comfortably fit a field like ours—that we work in realms where genuine disproof or disconfirmation is seldom really possible. Disproof only works, for example, on extreme and totalizing empirical claims such as, "*all* swans are white," or "*every* freewriting (or grammar) exercise will improve a student's writing" or "*every* writer has an audience in mind when writing." One black swan, or one unsuccessful exercise, *proves* a totalizing claim to be false. More reasonable claims such as that "*most* swans are white" or that "*most* writers have an audience in mind as they write" *are not subject to disproof.* They are subject only to arguments about evidence and distribution—and to *interpretation* about what is meant by "white" or "audience" or "in mind." Similarly, there is no such thing as disproof when it comes to the kind of theoretical or definitional claims that have recently become meat and potatoes in our journals. For the claim that "all language is social," there is no disproof—only argument about definitions of *language* and *social.* Of course disproof works in *pure logic*, but there is always slippage between pure logic and any particular point of view or position or case. Yes, if we discover a logical flaw in someone's argument, we have certainty about their error in logic. But we have no certainty about the wrongness of their position, and we are not safe in dismissing their point of view.

    If we can't really *disprove* positions, then all we have is persuasion, and for persuasion we usually get more leverage if we argue for rather than against. We create less resistance.

My argument for a change in habits of argument or discourse is ultimately epistemological. It is an argument that contrasting and even conflicting positions can be right; and that we should be suspicious of totalizing claims like "X is *always* Y" or "*all* X's are Y (e.g., "identity is always [already] socially constructed"; "All individuals have a unique voice".) Claims framed this way are essential and exclusionary and function to rule out divergent thinking and minority positions. In my essay on private writing in Part IV of this volume, I think I show that totalizing claims of this sort are usually inflated and misguided forms of claims that can be valid only if framed in more limited ways ("in a sense . . .").

Finally, I need to acknowledge that any argument for nonadversarial argu-

ment would be foolish or hopeless if it were a call for doctrinal purity. My argument is *against* purity. Purity is almost always exclusionary. In particular,
let me point to two kinds of purity I am not seeking.

First, purity of attitude and emotion. Nonadversarial argument is usually felt
as completely "soft" and "wimpy." Mr. Rogers, elder and younger. "Don't
fight, just listen, try to believe, don't argue, be nonviolent, go limp, accept
everything." Even though I do in fact value a kind of nonadversarial extrem-
ism or "going all the way" (see my essay on the believing game in *Writing
Without Teachers* and on methodological belief in *Embracing Contraries*), nevertheless, the kind of nonadversarial "arguing for" that I am advocating here
can be loud, assertive, vociferous, even aggressive. In arguing-for-not-against,
we don't need to give up all the trappings and emotional feelings connected
with struggle, agon, and argument. No need to be unrelievedly sweet and always turn the other cheek. We can shout, scream, make a fuss, rock the boat,
and throw sand as long as it's *for* our position, not against theirs. People won't
find it so hard to give up pounding the table and shouting, "You are wrong,
you idiot," if they can still pound the table and shout, "Listen to what I'm
saying, damn it. Pay better attention!" Or to translate this into academic discourse, I don't think academics will find it so hard to give up writing,
"Smith's position is wrong for the following seven reasons," if they can still
write, "In the following seven ways, Smith has misunderstood or misinter-
preted what I wrote." I want to acknowledge that in the end, this is a fighting
book.

Second, pure consistency in avoiding adversarial behavior. If I am arguing
against either/or thinking or zero-sum games, I must not try to make a blanket, totalizing case against *ever* doing it. It's not a reasonable goal. But it *is* a
reasonable goal to build up a strong *custom* or *tradition* of nonadversial argument in composition and rhetoric. Since we are a profession devoted to
the study of discourse, it wouldn't take so much to give up the widely held
assumption that argument is only forceful (manly?) if it is refutational. It
wouldn't take so much—indeed, I think we are already well on the way—to
build up a tradition where people felt it was *normal* to argue for-but-not-
against. In such a culture, people could still sometimes choose the refutational
model of argument, but if they did so they would feel some onus to acknowledge that they were making a *rhetorical choice* for certain specific goals, and
not just using the only right, orthodox, default mode. We need to pay particular attention to the argumentative rhetoric we require in Ph.D. dissertations. (The first chapter "review of the literature" often slips into being an argument why all others are wrong.) It's more and more clear that many mature
scholars and graduate students in our profession would *like* to use a less adversarial rhetoric if it were more widely sanctioned.[2]

---

2. Nor can *I* claim consistency of behavior. Readers will no doubt notice places in these essays where I argue merely *against* another view as wrong or bad. Not often, I hope. I hadn't
worked out this rhetorical principle when I was writing most of these essays. My nonadversarial
approach was mostly a matter of instinct and temperament.

The biggest incentive for less adversarial argument lies in our collective sense of our field. Adversarial, zero-sum, refutational discourse may have increased in recent decades, but I think it has peaked. I sense a widespread awareness among the widest spectrum of members—in our professional meetings and publications—that we mustn't lose our heritage as an intellectually pluralistic discipline. I sense a growing awareness that the tradition of multiple disciplines, methodologies, and theories in our profession is a strength rather than a weakness. Latent in that awareness is a sense that we have to learn to talk more productively with each other.

The underlying goal of this book, then, is to encourage a more welcoming conversation in the field of composition and rhetoric and a more inclusive community. So I want to make sure I am clear that I am not claiming that this book provides the *one true* theory or vision. What I hope is that I have made progress at trying to argue nonadversarially in such a way as to keep our theory larger, and that I have suggested some paths toward a profession where multiple visions can prosper.

About the texts gathered here. In the period since my collection of essays published in 1986, *Embracing Contraries*, I discover I have written far too much to gather into one book. I've left out a number of essays and—resorting to a kind of collage approach—included fragments from a number of others.

Where I felt I could make my thoughts clearer, I've made changes from what was originally published. I've done a great deal of rephrasing, a fair amount of cutting, and a bit of restructuring. I reworked extensively my essay on binary thinking. But I didn't change the points or arguments in any essays.

I couldn't have produced these pages without lots of help and support from many sources—more than I can name here. I am much blessed to have been given it. I am especially grateful to my wife Cami and my daughter Abby for their insightful editorial help; to John Wright, literary agent, for his friendship and support; and to Susan Chang and MaryBeth Branigan, editors at Oxford University Press, for their wise counsel and generous understanding through many vicissitudes.

Works Cited

Burke, Kenneth. *A Rhetoric of Motives*. Berkeley: U California P, 1969.
Lunsford, Andrea. "Rhetoric and Composition." *Introduction to Scholarship in Modern Languages and Literatures*. 2nd ed. Ed. Joseph Gibaldi. New York: MLA, 1992. 77–100.

Starting Bibliography on Nonadversarial Rhetoric

Brent, Doug. "Young, Becker and Pike's 'Rogerian' Rhetoric: A Twenty-Year Reassessment." College English 53.4 (April 1991): 452–66.

Burke, Kenneth. *Rhetoric of Motives*. Berkeley: U of California P, 1969.

Clark, Gregory. *Dialogue, Dialectic, and Conversation*. Carbondale IL: S Illinois UP, 1990.

Elbow, Peter. "Methodological Doubting and Believing: Contraries in Inquiry." In *Embracing Contraries*. NY: Oxford UP, 1986.

———. "The Doubting Game and the Believing Game—An Analysis of the Intellectual Enterprise." In *Writing Without Teachers*. NY: Oxford UP, 1973.

———. "The Uses of Binary Thinking." *Journal of Advanced Composition* 12.1 (Winter 1993): 51–78.

Frey, Olivia. "Beyond Literary Darwinism: Women's Voices and Critical Discourse." *College English* 52.5 (September 1990): 507–26.

Jarratt, Susan. "Feminism and Composition. The Case for Conflict." *Contending With Words: Composition and Rhetoric in a Postmodern Age*. Eds. Patricia Harkin and John Schilb. NY: MLA 1991. 105–23

Lamb, Catherine. "Beyond Argument in Feminist Composition." *College Composition and Communication* 42.1 (February 1991): 11–24.

Lassner, Phyllis. "Feminist Responses to Rogerian Argument." *Rhetoric Review* 8.2 (Spring 1990): 220–31.

Lynch, Dennis A., Diana George, and Marilyn M. Cooper. "Moments of Argument: Agonistic Inquiry and Confrontational Cooperation." *College Composition and Communication* 48.1 (February 1997): 61–85.

Moulton, J. "A Paradigm of Philosophy: The Adversary Method." *Discovering Reality: Feminist Perspectives on Epistemology, Metaphysics, Methodology, and Philosophy of Science*. Eds. S. Harding and M. Hintikka. Boston: D. Reidel, 1983.

Ong, Walter. "Agonistic Structures in Academia: Past to Present." *Interchange* 5:4 (1975): 1–12.

———. *Fighting for Life: Contest, Sexuality, and Consciousness*. Ithaca: Cornell UP, 1981.

O'Reilley, Mary Rose. *The Peaceable Classroom*. Portsmouth NH: Heinemann, Boynton/Cook, 1993.

Pratt, Mary Louise. "The Arts of the Contact Zone." *Profession 91*. New York: MLA, 1991: 33–40.

Ruddick, Sara. *Maternal Thinking: Towards a Politics of Peace*. NY: Ballantine, 1989.

Smith, Janet Farrell. "A Critique of Adversarial Discourse: Gender as an Aspect of Cultural Difference." *Defending Diversity*. Ed. Lawrence Foster and Patricia Herzog. Amherst, MA: U of Mass P, 1994. 57–82.

Teich, Nathaniel, ed. *Rogerian Perspectives: Collaborative Rhetoric for Oral and Written Communication*. Norwood NJ: Ablex, 1992.

Tompkins, Jane. "Fighting Words: Unlearning to Write the Critical Essay." *Georgia Review* 42 (Fall 1988): 585–90.

Trebilcot, Joyce. "Dyke Methods or Principles for the Discovery/Creation of the Withstanding." *Hypatia* 3 (1988): 1–13.

Wyche-Smith, Susan. *Beyond Winning or Losing: A Rhetoric for Survival*. Under contract with Allyn and Bacon (part of Simon and Schuster).

Part I

PREMISES AND FOUNDATIONS

In this section I try to lay out what I see as the premises and foundations underlying the essays in this book. In the first essay I explore a central personal experience underlying my work in writing. In the second essay I explore my core principles for the teaching of writing. In the third essay and the concluding fragment, I explore the central theoretical and epistemological structure that could be said to underlie my thinking.

So, Peter, You're going to introduce your real, true, foundational self? Express it?

Why not? "My name is Peter Elbow. I live at 3 Audubon Place. I have a big sister and brother. I like snow and swimming and picnics. My phone number is . . ." (It's sad: I can't remember that original, almost defining number that came so readily to a child's lips.)

I grew up in a small suburban New Jersey town. My father ran a small men's clothing store and my mother was an amateur but skilled artist. The most powerful personality in our family was a black woman, Estelle Jones, who was just as much my mother.

And now I'm a college professor. When I was a child, I saw college professors seeming to have their summers free. My mother was particularly jealous—given my father's strict two week limit. Is this why I became a professor? I also liked school. It's certainly important that my parents loved to talk about ideas—especially my father. They both admired thoughtful, civilized, sophisticated conversation. Norman Thomas once came to dinner, and my parents voted for him all the many times he ran. Yet when Vietnam happened, they couldn't believe the government had lied to us.

———————

The first essay in this section is autobiographical and it shows how the roots of my interest in writing—obsession, really—come from my experience of being unable to write as I started graduate school. I explore this experience through two different lenses, and I create a kind of collage by voyaging out on six digressive but related reflections.

My sense of who I am as an academic is probably shaped most deeply by my having had to quit graduate school with a feeling of total failure because I couldn't write my papers. I tend to identify *in opposition to* academics or *away from* the academy. And yet I am academic through and through. Once I finally came back to the academy, after feeling I'd been kicked out, I've never wanted to leave it. My mission in life is to change the academy: to make it more supportive to students, more open to more people, and more hospitable to a larger part of the human creature.

The second essay is about teaching. In it I explore the two factors that seem to me most central in most experiences of writing: audience and response. Who do we feel as our audience? What kind of response do we get or expect to get from them? I have recently found my whole pedagogy developing from an analysis of audience and response.

I'm asking the third essay and the concluding fragment to serve as an

introduction to my theoretical foundations—and the emphasis is on epistemology or the nature of knowing. In the scholarly writing of recent years, it
has become somewhat fashionable to look at someone's publications and to
infer their epistemology or theory of knowledge as a way of seeing what they
are "really" doing or are "really" like. (I've had my epistemological cards read
in various ways.) The premise seems to be that your epistemology is the most
real and important part of you. But when I read such essays, I usually feel that
someone's conscious or unconscious theory of knowledge is less real and important than how they act, and especially how they *behave* toward their students and colleagues and staff. So my deepest theoretical foundations are
probably psychological rather than philosophical.

Nevertheless, it's useful and interesting—especially in the present academic context—to try to lay out one's theoretical and philosophical foundations.
The third essay, on binary thinking, explores my tendency to see binary
pairs: generating/criticizing, reading/writing, teaching/research. I wrote this
essay as I began to notice how widely binary thinking had come to be con-
demned, sometimes in a knee-jerk fashion. True enough, binary thinking
tends to foster oversimplification and the habit of always seeing things in
terms of good guys vs. bad guys. But my argument is that we will benefit if
we learn to handle binary oppositions *differently*, non-simplistically—so as to
affirm both sides equally. I try to show that this approach actually helps us
avoid the very problems in thinking and rhetoric that people want to avoid
when they condemn binary thinking.

I can easily translate my epistemology into psychological terms. I seem to
be a person who is always torn between conflicting and contradictory points
of view. I tend to feel persuaded by almost every attractive idea I encounter—
odd ones especially. I often find myself drawn toward ideas that contradict
what I know I believe. More than once I've been critized for what I want to
claim as a perverse compliment: that I give a better argument against my position than for it.

It might be that the believing game underlies everything else. I wrote
about it at length more than twenty-five years ago as the appendix essay to
Writing Without Teachers. I explored the idea more fully and in a more scholarly way fourteen years ago in *Embracing Contraries*. Just recently, I wrote the
fragment that ends this first section as part of my new introduction to the reis-
sue of *Writing Without Teachers*. Yet since I also love doubting, criticism, and
logic, binary thinking may lie deeper than the believing game.

1

Illiteracy at Oxford and Harvard

Reflections on the Inability to Write

What got me interested in writing was being unable to write. First at Oxford, then at Harvard. First, I will tell the story straight—as I experienced it—and see what we can learn. But I've rethought this story—reexperienced it really—and now I also want to go on to *retell* it, crooked perhaps, and draw more reflections. But this is not just an exercise in story telling; I will be working for insights about writing, teaching, and learning. In the end, I'll have two versions of the story and six ruminations. Thus my structure is a kind of collage—a collage in which I am also trying to show that there need be no conflict between academic writing and personal writing.

First Version

I enjoyed writing in the last few years of school. Because my older sister and brother left home for college and I was lonely by myself, because I wanted to ski and was stuck in New Jersey, and because my grandmother had left money for education, I went to boarding school for my last three years. Proctor Academy was then an undistinguished school in New Hampshire. My English teacher, Bob Fisher, was just beginning his career as a teacher. He was excited about reading and writing and learning, and he had us writing about Dostoevsky and truth and the meaning of life—and writing fairy tales too. I loved writing and I decided I wanted to become a high school English teacher like him.

This essay was published in 1998 in *Reflective Stories: Becoming Teachers of College English and English Education*. Eds. H. Thomas McCrackin and Richard L. Larson, with Judith Entes. Urbana IL: NCTE. 91–114. But I've added here the third reflection.

In college, my experience of writing was the experience of being knocked down, but then stubbornly picking myself up, dusting myself off, and finally succeeding. On my third essay for freshman English, my teacher wrote, "Mr. Elbow, you continue your far from headlong rise upward"—and the grade was D. The teachers I met in 1953 at Williams College were sophisticated and I was naive. But I was eager to do well and I worked hard at it—and by the end of my first year had begun to do so. Indeed, I gradually found myself wanting to enter their world and be like them—a college professor, not just a teacher. I wanted to be a learned, ironic, tweedy, pipe-smoking, professor of literature.

As for writing, I took no particular pleasure in it. I wrote when assigned. I no longer experienced any imaginative element in the writing I did; it was all critical. I found it difficult, but I sometimes got excited working out a train of thought of my own. Toward the end of my four years, however, I began to notice out of the corner of my consciousness, an increase in the "ordeal" dimension of writing papers: more all-nighters; more of them the night *after* the paper was due; more not-quite-acknowledged fear. But still I got those As.

And with them, a scholarship from Williams to go to Oxford. I wish I'd been as smart as my predecessor from Williams, Price Zimmerman: smart enough to study a *different* subject at Oxford from what I planned to study in graduate school. But I was too earnest and chose English. My Oxford tutor was another teacher in his first year of teaching: Jonathan Wadsworth, the grand nephew of the poet. My experience with him was, in a way, like the one I had at college, but more so. He played harder. Again I was knocked down—but it felt like I was knocked out and when I gradually staggered to my feet, the grogginess wouldn't go away. I thought I'd become sophisticated and critical at college, but this experience showed me I was still the same old tender, naive boy who wanted to be liked and praised. I thought I'd learned a lot about irony from my college professors, but Jonathan brewed a tougher English strain. (Interesting that I eventually wrote my Ph.D. dissertation on double and triple irony and the relinquishing of irony in Chaucer.)

Tutorials were conducted in the tutor's rooms. Once a week, I'd knock on the oak door and come in and read my essay to him, and be instructed, and then at the end he'd say something like, "Why don't you go off and read Dryden and write me something interesting." My first essay was on Chaucer and he was pretty condescendingly devastating. ("What are we going to do with these Americans they send us?" Interesting again that Chaucer was my Ph.D. topic.) During one tutorial, he cleaned his rifle as I read my essay to him. On another occasion, as I pronounced the title of a poem by Marvell in my broad-vowelled American accent, "On a Drohp of Doo," he broke in with his clipped Oxford accent, "On a Drup of Djyew," and remarked, "Maybe that's why you don't understand poetry, Elbow. You don't know what it sounds like." Before the end of the fall term, I was coming in every week saying, "I don't have an essay for you. I tried as hard as I could, but I couldn't write it." And I really had tried hard, spending the whole week writing initial sentences, paragraphs, and pages and throwing them all away.

Eventually, I changed tutors and limped through my second year. I took a lot of Valium as exams approached. For in fact, it turned out that the Oxford degree didn't depend at all on any of these essays written for tutors over two years. They were nothing but practice for the nine three-hour exams you took during your last four-and-a-half days. I was terrified, but it turns out that the exams didn't throw me as much as the essays had done: in each exam there were only three hours for at least three essays and there wasn't time to agonize—even to revise. I survived with acceptable results (an "undistinguished second")—and very grateful too. "Pretty much what we expected," was Jonathan's comment on the card on which he mailed me my results.

With all that education, you'd think I'd have learned a few simple things— for instance that I needed a break from school. And in fact, I spent the last weeks in August looking for a teaching job in schools. But none turned up and, ever earnest, I started on my Ph.D. in English at Harvard. I still wanted to become a professor, and people kept telling me to "just get the degree out of the way"—like having a tooth pulled or an injection before going on a trip. But, of course, in our American system, the graduate seminar papers count for everything. I had a terrible time getting my first semester papers written at all, and they were graded unsatisfactory. I could have stayed if I'd done well the next semester, but after only a few weeks I could see things were getting worse rather than better. I quit before being kicked out.

My sense of failure was total. It wouldn't have been so bad if I had been less invested or hadn't tried so hard. But I'd long announced my career commitment to my family and relatives, my friends, and my teachers—and I'd tried my damnedest. I'd defined and staked my identity on this business of getting a Ph.D. to become a college professor. And I'd also defined myself—to others and to myself—as "successful," particularly at school. So when I quit, I felt ruined. I felt I never wanted to have anything to do with the world of books and teaching again.

First Reflection: On the Experience of Failure

I realize now that much of the texture of my academic career has been based in an oddly positive way on this experience of complete shame and failure. In the end, failing led me to have the following powerful but tacit feeling: "There's nothing else they can do to me. They can't make me feel any worse than they've already done. I tried as hard as I could to be the way they wanted me to be, and I couldn't do it. I really wanted to be good, and I was bad." These feelings created an oddly solid grounding for my future conduct in the academic world. They made it easier for me to take my own path and say whatever I wanted.

In subsequent years, I've noticed that lots of people's behavior in schools and colleges is driven by the opposite feelings—sometimes unconscious: "Uh-oh. They could really hurt me. I *must* do this or I'll fail. I *couldn't* say that or they'd kick me out. To fail or be kicked out is unthinkable." When you live with these feelings—as I had certainly done through all the years before I failed—you sometimes notice a faint impulse to say or do something unacceptable (for example, to skip an assignment, or to do it in a way that the teacher would find unacceptable, or to stand up to the teacher with some kind of basic disagreement or refusal). But you scarcely notice this impulse because acting on it would be unimaginable; insupportable. I realize now that the most unsuccessful students are often the most adventuresome or brave or mentally creative. They operate from the feeling of, "They can't hurt me any worse. What the hell!" That feeling can be empowering. In truth, the most successful students are often the most timid and fearful. They have the most at stake in getting approval. They do the most cheating in school; they have the most suicides.

On with the First Story

Do I seem to celebrate failure here? Am I sounding smug? ("Look at me. They couldn't kill me.") Am I implying a kind of tough-guy Darwinism? ("It's good to fail students; it toughens 'em up.") I don't mean that. I went back and succeeded because I was stubborn and hungry, yes, but I probably wouldn't have been able to overcome my experience of failure without a foundation of privilege (good schools and lots of support I could take for granted) and *luck*. And in fact, it was the old-boy network that got me into the academic pond again by way of a job I never would have sought: an instructorship at M.I.T. They needed bodies in the middle of July because of a departmental feud and a bunch of resignations—an old college teacher of mine was doing the hiring. (And instructorships were much easier to get in 1960 than they are now.)

I was terrified to take this job, but I needed work. I stayed scared as I started teaching Homer, Aeschylus, Thucydides, and Plato with these M.I.T. first-year students, but I gradually woke up to the fact that I was having a good time. I gradually realized that teaching was much more fun than being a student. I *liked* to read and talk about books when it wasn't for the sake of taking tests or writing papers. I loved the change of agenda that teaching brings. No longer, "Do I understand well enough for *them?*" but rather, "Can I find something to do with this book that students will find worthwhile?" No longer, "Do I love this book enough and in the right way?" but rather, "We're stuck with this book; how can we make it useful in our lives?"

Second Reflection

Since that time in my life, I've often reflected on a curious fact: If you can't write, you can't be a student. But the inability to write doesn't get in the way of teaching at all. Of course, I couldn't have gotten tenure without writing, but my teaching went well. I was an excited teacher and learner. If I'd taught in the schools or at some college, like Evergreen, that doesn't require publication, no one would have ever thought to define my nonwriting as a problem.

I don't know what to make of this asymmetry between being a student and a teacher. On the one hand, I think it's dumb to require people to publish if they want to teach—at least as publication is presently defined. On the other hand, it's sad to define teachers as people who read, not as people who write. (This asymmetry between being a student and a teacher recalls another one: Teachers can't teach without students, but students can learn perfectly well without teachers.)

Finishing the First Story

After three years at M.I.T., I joined the founding faculty at Franconia College, an experimental college in New Hampshire. This was 1963. My three years at M.I.T. gave me more college teaching experience than the other four members of the faculty. My M.I.T. years had been, in a sense, about the rehabilitation of reading for me. These next two years at Franconia were the beginnings of a re-habilitation of writing. For I discovered that I enjoyed writing when I was no longer writing as a student. It was no longer, "Here is my writing. Is it accept-able?" Now it was, "I have some ideas about Socrates that excite me and I think I can make them useful to you in your teaching." I remember writing into the night—long memos on purple dittos—writing out of an excited con-nection with the material and with my colleagues, who were all teaching the same course.

After this total of five years' teaching, I was hit with two strong reasons to reenter graduate school. First, it looked as though Franconia might fold in its second year, and I found I couldn't get another job without a Ph.D. Second, my experience of moving from highly successful students at M.I.T. to highly unsuccessful students at Franconia convinced me that something was deeply wrong with how education worked. For it became clear to us that these stu-dents whom everyone defined as failures were very smart, and they did good work when given good learning conditions. I wanted to speak out about higher education, but I realized that unless I got a Ph.D., people would say, "You just don't like it because you couldn't do it."

My first impulse was to get my degree in psychology or education—the two subjects that really interested me at this point. But I discovered that I could get my degree much more quickly if I stuck with English. So I climbed up on the same horse I'd fallen off of five years earlier. I wasn't worried that I had no commitment to literature, indeed, I found it enormously enabling as a student to have a completely pragmatic motivation. Instead of worrying, "Am I committed enough to literature?" (a question I had worried about in my first go round), I felt, "I don't care whether I like it or it makes sense. I'll do what-ever damn thing you ask. I just want a degree." Under the protection of this psychological umbrella, I gradually discovered how much I loved literature.

But I *was* worried. About writing. Would I get stuck again when I tried to do school writing? I was *so* scared that I set myself a personal deadline for every paper. I forced myself to have a full draft for myself a full week before every real deadline. No matter how bad the writing was, I had to produce the requisite number of pages that I could hold in my hand. Then I had a week to try to improve it. This regime forced me to do something I'd never been able to do before, namely, to write out sentences and paragraphs and pages I knew were no good, to write garbage, and to say, "What the hell." The key was my crassly pragmatic frame of mind.

In addition, I encouraged myself to write little notes to myself about what was happening as I wrote. In particular I wrote notes at stuck points ("How did I get into this swamp?"). And when I finally got my writing or thinking functioning again, I tried to remember to stop for a few moments to explore how I'd managed to do so. Often these were just scrawled notes on little scraps of paper, but I put them all in one folder. After I finally got myself employed again (back at M.I.T.), and I'd finished my dissertation on Chaucer (and even revised it for publication), I did what I'd been wanting to do for a couple of years: pull out that folder of notes to myself and see what I could figure out about writing. I knew there were ideas there that I wanted to figure out. This resulted in *Writing Without Teachers* in 1973. But it wasn't until I had written *Writing with Power* in 1981 that I would call writing "my field."

Retelling the Central Story

A number of years after it happened, I began to think again about this story of my inability to write: not just because I was beginning to have a professional interest in the writing process, but also because my life was coming apart. My first marriage was breaking up. This difficulty led me to a lot of writing in a diary and talking in therapy. So, in fact, I didn't just *think about* my writing difficulty; in this writing and talking I would sometimes touch on these earlier events and feelings and begin in a sense to reexperience. I've always enjoyed watching cows and other ruminants with two stomachs chew their cud—somehow attracted to the idea of rechewing one's food at leisure afterward. That's what I started doing.

In my first chewing for my first stomach—that is, during my original experience of struggle and inability with writing—I experienced myself trying as hard as I could to do what I was supposed to do, but failing. In retrospect a number of years later, however—as this experience of struggle passed on to my second chewing for my second stomach—I gradually got hints of a different story. In my diary writing and talking therapy during this later period of struggle in my life, I began to get whiffs of an underfeeling: a feeling that maybe I didn't *really* want to give those teachers the papers they were asking for. Maybe I *didn't* want to be such an earnest, diligent, compliant student. What I originally experienced as an inability, I now began to sense as perhaps resistance; in fact, *refusal*.

I'd always been so obedient. I'd never really understood my friends who goofed off or didn't do what they were supposed to do. I'd always experienced myself as simply *wanting* to do what I was supposed to do. I never felt any gap between my duty and my desire. I suppose you'd say that in my formative years I'd badly wanted praise and affirmation and learned that school was a good place to get it. And I'd become skilled at it, become hooked on that role, if you wish. I was the paradigm good student—just what you'd want in your class. For I wasn't just a fawning yes-man; I engaged in sophisticated independent thinking of my own. After all, that's what my best teachers wanted and I wanted to do what they wanted me to do. But now I began to sense an underside to the story.

The essays I wrote in college were often ambitious and thoughtful, but they were almost always muddy and unclear. Teachers were always writing comments to me or telling me straight out: "Why don't you just *say* directly what you mean? Why do you wander and digress and beat around the bush so much? Why so tangled?" But I was struggling as hard as I could to say what I meant—to be clear. If they had described me to a third party, they probably would have said, "He's a smart kid, but when he writes he ties himself in knots." And tying myself in knots is what I now think I was doing.

That is, in retrospect, I think I was playing a game with those teachers: they thought they were putting me to the test, but really I was putting them to the test—the following test: "I'm smart. I'm terrific. If you can understand my paper and see through my paper to how good I am, you pass the test. If you can't, you fail. It's my job to write the paper, but it's your job to recognize my brilliance." It strikes me now that maybe I didn't *want* my meaning to be so clear.

Third Reflection: On Brilliance

"It's your job to recognize my brilliance." Oh dear, that sounds so arrogant. Why do people seem so unlikable when they let on that they think they're brilliant? The problem is that we can't imply or feel "I am brilliant" without also implying—and probably feeling—"I am better than everyone else, different from the herd." Brilliance *means* being different and superior. To be brilliant *and* like everyone else would be a contradiction in terms. We have a scarcity or zero-sum or competitive model of brilliance.

What if we tried out a nonscarcity, nonzero-sum, noncompetitive model: *everyone* is brilliant? Consider babies and tiny children. It's not so hard to think of them all as brilliant. It's not so hard to be impressed by how many mental connections and inferences every undamaged child constantly makes—the breadth and imaginative reach of those connections and inferences, and also the speed. Consider most of all the tireless love of learning and figuring out that every child displays.

But could we possibly think of all grown ups as brilliant? It sounds outrageous. But it wouldn't mean saying that everyone *functions* brilliantly. We all know the difference between getting something wrong and getting it right. More to the point, a few people seem to get it right easily, and some seem to screw up all the time. Performances can indeed arrange themselves along that infamous bell curve. The hypothesis here is that everyone *is* brilliant, but that they *function* badly or well according to how clouded or shut down they are—or how much their brilliance is given a chance to flourish. (Or how much their brilliance fits the realm where they are functioning. See Gardner on multiple intelligences and my fragment on "tracking" in Part VI of this volume.)

What an idealistic or utopian idea. How hard to believe. But in fact we already accept lots of ideas like that—for example, this one: Any body in motion will continue in motion—forever—and never even slow down! How could anyone have ever thought up such an outrageous idea? It's never happened on Earth in anyone's normal experience that a body has *ever* continued in motion for ever and ever—at the same speed. It took idealistic utopian thinking to come up with this way of looking at bodies. Galileo had to imagine the movements of *heavenly* bodies (completely unlike earthly bodies) moving in *ideal* space (completely unlike earthly space; see E. A. Burtt). Once he and others got their minds around this odd idea of bodies moving forever and ever at the same speed, they found they could apply it to earthly "sublunar" bodies, and it turned out to be true. That is, even though common sense or "realistic" experience tells us that a moving ball *wants* to slow down, in truth it *wants* to keep going, and only slows down if something gets in its way. Slowing down looks normal because we don't *notice* all the hindrances and obstructions (mostly friction).

What a helpful image this is for a better model of intelligence: people only "slow down" if something gets in their way. There are lots of other truths we cannot see unless we look *through* everyday appearance to idealistic, utopian models: The sun isn't really going around the earth; no physical matter ever disappears, even when a house burns up (except for that pesky exception where they change the tiniest *speck* of matter into a nuclear bomb); people have feelings they can't feel and memories they can't remember.

So maybe it's worth looking past everyday appearance and experience when it comes to human intelligence and considering all humans as brilliant. (I sometimes sense that people are less nervous about seeing how smart all animals are than seeing how smart all humans are.) Just as I often now see traces of the utopian law of inertia in bowling balls and bicycles and sliding boxes, I often now see traces of everyone's brilliance once I look more closely:

- In families and classrooms, I think I see smartness hiding behind wrong answers and even stupid behavior. I notice the child "who can never remember things" actually remembering an astounding quantity of certain kinds of information—usually in some realm that doesn't threaten or cause anxiety as school often does. Our conception of intelligence tends to imply speed and the use of words ("slow" means stupid—as does "dumb"), but I notice the wisdom in much behavior that is nonverbal or slow and in certain wrong answers. Many grammatical "mistakes" are applications of correctly learned rules where the speaker forgot or didn't learn the exceptions—for example, "she fighted all afternoon." ("Ninety percent of the sentences uttered by the average 3-year-old are grammatically correct" according to the valid grammatical rule the child just learned [Brownlee].)

- I think I see brilliance getting clouded over when someone is hurt or anxious—and sometimes reemerging when the fear or threat goes away. I notice myself unable to think clearly when I'm scared. When I'm sight-reading music in a quartet and I get flustered, I can't even read the simplest notes or rhythms.

- I think I see students being smarter, thinking more deeply, and handling words better when teachers look for their brilliance, treat them as smart, and support them in dealing with what is trying to cloud them over.

- I think I see adolescents and adults trying to hide their brilliance. They see that the price of brilliance is isolation; they feel they have to choose between being brilliant and being connected to others. (This is related to Carol Gilligan's findings about adolescent girls: that they have to choose between feeling their own experience and being connected to others.) This helps me understand better why so many school-skilled children and their parents hunger for "gifted and talented" classrooms. They hunger for brilliance-as-connection and solidarity instead of brilliance-as-isolation. A good "gifted and talented" classroom gives a glimpse of how things could be if we had a better model of brilliance—a world where students can say, "Yes, I'm brilliant, just like you. We can share and enjoy our brilliance together."

I used to take the scarcity, competitive model of brilliance for granted and so I couldn't see it; it was simply built into the universe. Now I keep seeing it and seeing how it confuses people's thinking. I know an excellent elite college that is going through an illustrative agony because it is getting fewer applicants and therefore ending up with lower entering test scores. The faculty know they are still teaching just as well, but it's almost as though our very language is forcing them to feel the college is losing its excellence. It's hard for them to break out of the habitual model into a new one that says, "We are excellent *because* of the range of students we accept. Our excellence consists of how well we teach them all!" It's hard for schools and colleges to define themselves as excellent, except in terms of the number of students they reject.

Yet only a few people object when kindergarten and first grade teachers treat all their students as smart and special and give all As on their report cards. The brilliance of babies and small children is less threatening; we can still see their intelligence through all the mistakes they make for lack of information or experience. It's harder to see brilliance in an adolescent or adult who makes mistakes, and harder still to deal with them when they tell us something we don't want to hear—especially if they are right. Fear sets in. Nelson Mandela reminds us that

our deepest fear is not that we are inadequate. Our deepest fear is that we are powerful beyond measure. It is our light, not our darkness, that most frightens us. We ask ourselves, Who am I to be brilliant, gorgeous, talented, fabulous? Actually, who are you not to be? . . . We are all meant to shine, as children do. . . . It's not just some of us; it's everyone.

So maybe it wasn't so odd that I felt myself as brilliant. I was sufficiently undamaged. I now sense that most children who have been decently cherished feel their own brilliance. It takes most of them a while to discover our competitive, zero-sum, isolating model of brilliance—and thus to discover that they have to choose between brilliance and solidarity. Thus I played that perverse, competitive, hiding game with my essays for my college teachers.

Back Briefly to the Story Again

So maybe I was playing a game with my teachers and I didn't want my writing to be so clear. Maybe I didn't want them to understand unless that understanding involved the perception that I was brilliant. I was giving but not giving.

Fourth Reflection: Language to Convey, Language to Disguise

There emerges here a curious and pregnant fact: that language can be used not only to convey meaning, but also to disguise it. We characteristically use words so people will understand us; but sometimes we use them so they *won't*—or at least so some people won't. This may seem perverse, but perverse is what I was being—"contrary" with my teachers. I get mad when I feel others using language this way—such as when professionals and academics write not just to communicate their meaning, but to exclude the unwashed.

Yet this "game" of using language to convey-but-also-to-disguise was explicitly celebrated in medieval theology and criticism as a model for poetry. According to this theory, the poem consists of a tough *husk* that hides and protects, and a sweet and tender *kernel* inside. (Petrarch cites Gregory and Augustine in saying that if it is appropriate for scriptural wisdom to be veiled, how much more appropriate for poetry [see Robertson 1963, 62ff.].) The function of a good poem is to convey the kernel of wisdom or sweetness—but only to those worthy of it; and to hide it from the unworthy.

This wasn't just a theory spun by intellectuals and theoreticians. Christ proclaimed it openly in his parables—talking about his very use of parables, and from the Gospels it became common currency. Here is Matthew's version:

> Then the disciples went up to him and asked, "Why do you talk to them in parables?" "Because," he replied, "the mysteries of the kingdom of heaven are revealed to you but they are not revealed to them. For anyone who has will be given more, and he will have more than enough; but from anyone who has not, even what he has will be taken away. The reason I talk to them in parables is that they look without seeing and listen without hearing or understanding." (Matthew 13:10–14, Jerusalem Bible)

He goes on to say this is the fulfillment of a passage in Isiah (6:9–10). This is a hard saying, but he makes it even harder in Mark 4:11–12:

> The secret . . . is given to you, but to those who are outside everything comes in parables, so that they may see and see again, but not perceive; may hear and hear again, but not understand; otherwise they might be converted and be forgiven.

When Christ said that the rich will get richer and the poor poorer, he wasn't so much trying to preach Reagan economics (though he did seem to mean it in all its economic astringency). He was really using money as an analogy or metaphor for his *main* message—which was about the conveyance of meaning through language (see Kermode 1979, 33ff.). It's a disturbingly elitist point whether it's about money or meaning, but there is no denying an element of truthful empiricism too: The best way to make money is to have a fund of previously accumulated money to work with. (See Matthew 25:14ff. for the passage where Christ bawls out people who don't invest their money to make more, but instead settle for mere saving—timidly "burying their talents.") And the best way to understand hard words or ideas is to have a fund of prior understanding or wisdom to build on.

We see this approach to conveying meaning in many mystical traditions. The master purposely makes something hard to understand so that learners have to go through the right process of *nonunderstanding* struggle to get it. Without that nonunderstanding and struggle, they won't "really" get it. A clear conveyance of the "mere meaning" leads to a kind of superficial cognitive understanding that, in fact, functions as a filter against the deeper understanding or full digestion we need. The common theme here is a purposeful use of language to conceal, not just to reveal.

Helen Fox (1994) points out that many traditional, non-Western cultures value this indirect, and often metaphorical, way of conveying meaning and scorn the modern Western value of being direct and literal. Here is an account by Deborah Fredo (1995) of the difference between traditional and modern ways of conveying knowledge in Senegal:

> The [traditional] kind of knowledge that is sought after is that kind which can come from 'minds that bleed best' [the wisest minds]. . . . [I]ndirect thought . . . is more valued than direct thought because what can be attained through direct thought is said to be the kind of knowledge you don't have to work for, the kind that is given to you. Riddles are used as a kind of intelligence test to see if the mind is open enough to 'bleed.'
>
> Being modern, on the other hand, is associated with being direct, a decidedly inferior attribute of the mind. Being true to traditional form means being able to speak in ways which require a listener to decode what you are saying and analyze your meaning. Making meaning, in such a process, always involves some inquiry and analysis but it is the qualities of the person seeking to understand meaning or knowledge that guarantee its acquisition. (66–67)

So even though I resent this use of language (which I think I engaged in with my college teachers) and dislike this parable about parables, I must recognize that language-to-convey-and-to-disguise is not only a venerable tradition but a perennial human impulse. It lies behind much spontaneous and unsophisticated word play. And isn't much, or even most, poetry an attempt, in a way, to slow down comprehension? (The poet Richard Hugo famously remarked, "If I wanted to communicate, I'd pick up the telephone.") Almost everyone loves riddles, which are a central art form in most oral cultures. In short, humans naturally use language to make their meaning more clear and striking; but they also like to use language to make their meaning *less* clear—to use language as a kind of filter or puzzle or game to distinguish among receivers.

So, although I'm not wanting to defend the tangled quality of those old papers of mine, it strikes me that perhaps we shouldn't be so single-minded in our pursuit of clarity. Perhaps Richard Lanham and Winston Weathers are right in resisting the assumption that good writing always means clear writing. Perhaps students would write better and learn quicker if we were more appreciative of their impulse to write things that we *don't* understand.

Back to the Story

This test I was putting my teachers to—this game I was playing with language: I sense it wasn't just an arrogant game, but an angry one. I think I was mad because they weren't willing to try to build my education on who I was. They felt that the only way to educate me was to strip me down; get rid of all my naivete and wrong feelings. *Learning* wasn't enough for them; I had to be made to *unlearn* and then be built up from scratch. They wouldn't accept or respect me unless I stopped being the kind of person I was. I seem to be implying that I was blaming them—and the taste in my second stomach *is* the taste of anger and blame. Yet, there was no taste of blame at the time, and they would be astonished to hear any talk of blame because I so deeply *wanted* to be like them. Perhaps that's why I was mad—and I guess I still am: it wasn't just my behavior that was dancing on their strings, but my very desires.

In knocking on my tutor's door week after week with *no* paper at all, I was being a tacit refuser, an objector. I didn't experience myself as mad at those Williams College teachers (even though I now suspect anger might have been lurking hidden); I kept giving them their papers. But I *knew* I was mad at Jonathan. Still, I couldn't openly refuse. My inability to write was the closest I could come to giving him the finger. I hid my refusal not only from him, but also from myself. Thus, I experienced myself as weak and helpless and trying as hard as I could to be compliant—but now I suspect I was actually angry and stubborn and (in a sense) shrewd. (See Alice Miller on the anger of the "good child.")

Fifth Reflection: Being Wrong about One's Own Feelings?

Of course all this is just hypothesis. I started by telling events; then I told feelings I was having; and now I'm suggesting that I was having different feelings from what I thought I was feeling. One of my published essays ("The Pedagogy of the Bamboozled") is about how I loved these college teachers that I am now saying I was mad at; how I wanted to be like them; and how falling in love with teachers is such an efficient way to learn because it solves all motivation problems. It seems a kind of absurdity to say, "I thought I was feeling X, but really I was feeling Y." What else does the concept *feeling* mean, after all, but "what we are feeling"? Yet there is this perplexing and troublesome fact: we can be mistaken about our own feelings.

"So what else is new?" the sophisticates will answer: "You've never heard of Freud and the unconscious? And how he was only reminding us of what every nursemaid and mother knows."

Yet surely, we must allow people to be the final authority for what they are feeling. I certainly get mad when a psychoanalyst tries to tell me what I *really* feel, or a Marxist tells me I have "false consciousness"—just as mad as the toddler whose mother brushes aside what he just said with, "Oooh, poor dear. You're just tired [or hungry or wet]." When my son wanted to drop the cello because he said he hated practicing, I made no headway at all by saying, "No you don't. You actually like it. When you practice, I hear enthusiastic verve and cheerful singing." Lots of luck, Dad. But the troublesome fact is, we *can* be wrong about our feelings.

What if a wise and deeply trusted friend had come to me back then and said, "Peter, do you think maybe you don't *want* to give them those essays?" Would I have gotten an inkling of those feelings I wasn't feeling? Who knows? Or did I need some play therapy, perhaps with clay? It might have saved a lot of pain if (the Reagans are everywhere) I'd just said no.

Sixth Reflection: Writing as Giving In

My story seems to be about the movement from compliance to resistance. As a good student I had been expert at compliance, at doing what my teachers wanted me to do, but too much compliance got me in trouble. I was so unable to notice or experience any resistance or refusal or anger—so mistaken about my feelings, so unable to find a path for these feelings—that they found their own underground path to short circuit my entire ability to write or even be a student. My story seems to be about the need to learn fruitful or healthy ways to resist rather than ways that undermine oneself.

This is a familiar theme in studies of the learning process (see, for example, Brooke, Felman, Fox, Jonsberg, Lu, Street, Tobin *Writing Relationships*). These commentators emphasize not only how learning leads inevitably to resistance, but also that we can't learn well without resistance. It seems clear that an important goal for teachers is to help students find fruitful or healthy ways to resist. This became my theme too in most of my subsequent writing about writing: I have been a celebrator of writing without teachers, writing that is free, writing that ignores audience.

But at this stage in my autobiographical reflections, I'm noticing something different in the story. Yes, it's about ineffective resistance, but now I'm struck with how it's also about ineffective compliance. When I couldn't write my papers at all, I may not have been resisting very effectively, but I certainly was resisting. What I wasn't doing at all was complying. During the earlier stages of writing this essay, I was noticing my gift for compliance; now I'm noticing my *problem* with compliance. Something tugs at me now to learn more about this side of the authority relationship of a student to a teacher.

Once I open this door, I'm struck at how many ways writing involves complying or giving in. The need for compliance is most obvious in the case of writing in school and college. There is always a teacher and an assignment and criteria to be met. Someone other than the writer is in charge. The writing has to conform to the teacher's criteria or it's not acceptable (Cleary gives us good pictures of this in her interviews with students). But even when scholars write for learned journals, there is often a strong sense of the need to conform to someone else's criteria. The constraints can be even stronger with a supervisor or employer—sometimes, in fact, the obligation to say exactly what the person in charge wants you to say. Thus in many, or even most, writing situations, there is a subtle, or not so subtle, pressure to give in. When we send writing to journals, publishers, and teachers, what is the verb we use? We "submit."

But now I've come to see in writing for *any* audience a subtle but powerful requirement to give in. Babies and toddlers get to say things however they want, to speak the words and ideas as they come—and parents feel it is their job as audience to interpret no matter how garbled the language. But when we write, we can't be like babies and toddlers. That is, in the very act of writing itself—at least if we want to be understood—we have to give in to the code or the conventions. The conventions. To write is to be conventional.

Look at writers who resist the conventions and refuse to give in. There has always been a small but powerful tradition of writers who feel that accepting conventions means losing their integrity. The most obvious cases are avant garde writers who violate the conventions of meaning, structure, syntax, and orthography: Emily Dickinson, James Joyce, and William Blake are now-hallowed examples. To notice the dimension of resistance in their writing—or in the writing of more recent avant garde writers—helps us notice the unspoken but inherent pressure to comply that they are reacting against. Such writers write the way they want or the way they think best; they push aside the needs of readers. They may lose readers, yet a few are so skilled as to win wide readership. James Joyce managed to persuade readers to do the interpretive work that we usually only do for our own children. (He allegedly said that the only thing he wanted from readers was for them to devote their lives to trying to understand his words—what every baby and toddler simply deserves, but a writer has to earn.) French feminists like Kristeva directly link the conventions of language and writing with the oppressive structures of society and culture (the "law of the fathers").

This pressure from writing to make us give in shows itself in a humble but naked way if we consider the process of copy-editing. Good copy-editing is difficult for all of us who are not real editors, and especially for many students, but I'm not talking about ability, I'm talking about compliance. What interests me here is the common phenomenon of people *not* copy-editing—or copy-editing much less than they are capable of. Copy-editing is such a drudgery; we are never done; we always miss mistakes that we *could* find if we just went through it one more time or read it out loud. Is there not a universal tendency to feel, at some level, "I want you to accept my writing just the way it is—just the way I put it down. I don't want to have to exert myself to clean it up just to make it easy for you." (I found an embarrassing number of surface mistakes in a previous draft of this essay that I had, in fact, shared with friends and colleagues.) I now think that a lot of the mistakes we see in student writing are really the result of a reluctance or even a refusal to change their "natural product." "Take me as I am!" If our only hypothesis for bad copy-editing is laziness, we are forgetting to notice an interesting flavor behind the laziness.

We can also notice the pressure to give in if we notice the release from that pressure when we *don't* have to give in—that is, when we write completely privately, perhaps in a diary or in freewriting. Or we notice this release *if* we can permit it—if we can allow ourselves to turn off that pressure from conventions and readers that most of us have internalized. It's not so easy. I've become pretty good at it, yet sometimes I find myself fixing the spelling of words I've written down, even when I know this is a throwaway draft that no one will read—even when it is just a venting that I won't even read *myself.* (Haswell 1991 studied freewriting and was struck at how *obedient* to conventions it tends to be.) But those who can put aside the pressure to comply almost invariably experience a significant release.

The very act of *giving* itself exerts a pressure to give in. We smile at the child who gives his mother a bag of gummy candy for her birthday. Gradually, we learn that we're supposed to figure out what the recipient would like—not what we would like.

Am I being one-sided here and neglecting the importance of resistance? I don't want to do that. After all, perhaps it was my resistance in quitting school (odd as it was—being experienced as shameful failure rather than as resistance) that eventually allowed me to comply. The implication is that students need resistance for the sake of healthy learning because learning so deeply requires giving in.

It's a little frightening to stick up for compliance. Compliance is what repressive schools and teachers have been emphasizing all along: "What kids need to learn is how to go along, to follow directions, to give in, to obey!" My reflex is the opposite: "What kids need to learn is how to resist and maintain their autonomy." But it's not an either/or matter. It *feels* either/or because that's how we tend to experience it: "Will I fight the dirty bastards or cave in?" But we need *both* resistance and compliance. Nothing I say about the importance of compliance diminishes the need also for resistance: we clearly need resistance if we want to do our own thinking and be our own person—to go against the grain, to hang on to our autonomy, integrity, agency.

In short, we have fetched up against a familiar binary pattern—an opposition between necessary but conflicting elements. I think this pattern helps us understand better the complexities of the teaching and learning process—helps us look at the rich variety of students' strengths and weaknesses around us and notice the spectrum of methods students have developed to deal with this conflict between the inherent need in learning both to resist and also to give in. Some methods are more successful than others, but none feel very comfortable or ideal, for in the last analysis the two needs are at odds with each other.

- At one extreme are the compliant students. I was expert at compliance; I wanted to do what my teachers wanted me to do. There is a long tradition of learning by imitation and copying. Probably the most psychically efficient way to learn a lot is to fall in love with your teachers—as I tended to do (see my "Bamboozled," pp. 96–98). Many feminists see girls as traditionally socialized to comply. Girls and women seem to go along more with teachers—to give less back-talk or other kinds of resistance. (See, for example, Gilligan; see Bolker on the "patient Griselda" syndrome in writing. It's worth noting that the word *buxom* originally meant obedient.)
- At the other extreme are the highly resistant students. They fight and sabotage the teacher, they sometimes walk out, and the only thing they give is the finger. Boys and men seem to fall more often into this relation to teacher authority than women do (see Connors; Tobin's "Car Wrecks"). We don't have to be essentialists to see that women often have a harder time with resistance and men have a harder time with compliance. But this is slippery ground: there are plenty of women who resist and plenty of men like me who seem to love doing what their teachers want them to do (not to mention the complexities of complying-but-not-really-complying and resisting-but-not-really-resisting.)
- In between these two extremes we can look for the various ways that students try to serve *both* goals—to negotiate the competing pressures to give in and to resist. Some make a compromise and are sort of resistant and sort of compliant. These are not the excellent students, but rather the middling or passable or mediocre ones. You can't do a very good job if you only sort of go along with the assignment and conventions and needs of readers—and only sort of fight your way to your own thoughts and point of view.
- True excellence is rare because it consists of something paradoxical and hard to explain: the ability to be *extremely* assertive or even resistant while at the

same time managing to comply *very well* with the requirements of conventions, teachers, assignments, and readers. David Bartholomae points to this paradox in saying that a writer learns "by learning to write *within* and *against* the powerful writing that precedes him, that haunts him, and that threatens to engulf him" (1985, "Against" 27, emphasis added). In writing an essay about his own writing process, he emphasizes resistance and titles it "Against the Grain." And yet, he emphasizes how important it was for him not just to be influenced by strong teachers and writers, but in fact to imitate them and even to *copy over by hand* extended passages of their writing.

- And then there is dysfunction. That is, some students feel these conflicting pressures to comply and to resist so strongly that they get tied up in knots and can't write. (Perhaps this is what stopped me when I had to quit graduate school.) Or they struggle but don't turn out much or any work—or it's very bad and they feel terrible about it.[1]

Surely these competing needs to comply and to resist are not just school issues but rather play out in many areas of life—especially in growing up. What I'm exploring here is related to the Piagetian concepts of assimilation and accommodation. I wonder whether eating disorders might not sometimes be about the dilemma of giving in and refusing.

What follows for us as teachers from this way of looking at writing and learning? For one thing, we might look with new eyes at the unclear writing we get. We might consider the possibility that some of it—perhaps much of it—represents not so much a lack of skill as a way of resisting us as readers and wielders of authority. Much of the tangled quality of my writing in college was really a disguised form of resistance and resentment. Instruction in syntax and organization did me very little good. I had good teachers, they worked hard, and so did I. And still my prose stayed tangled. The problem was that I didn't fully *want* to give those teachers my meaning. My syntax never got clearer until I was finally wholehearted in my desire to *give* myself and my meaning to my readers. This never happened until I stopped writing for teachers.

This way of looking at unclear student writing doesn't make it clear. But it helps me say to myself, "Maybe lack of skill is not the main problem here; maybe he or she doesn't really *want* to be clear to me. Maybe this is part of the 'writing process' considered from a wider angle." That doesn't make me want to reward unclear writing when it's supposed to be clear, but it does help me

1. Edward White writes: "Those who have learned to succeed [on multiple choice tests] do so not by asking which answer is correct in the world or under various circumstances, but by choosing the one the test makers are likely to have chosen to fit the needs of the test. The multiple-choice test thus examines—along with its 'content'—the degree to which the student can adapt reality to the needs of authority. This indeed may be the reason that many such scores correlate well with success in college. The required submission to the world of that kind of test may also suggest reasons why minority groups score less well on these so-called objective tests than they do on writing tests" (1995, 34–45).

say, "this is very unclear to me" with better grace, more charity—and less discouragement. I find I can sometimes look *through* that unclear writing to unused capacities for clarity and force. Most of all, it helps me ask myself, "Am I giving my students enough occasions where the writing can be as unclear or problematic as can be?"

I think my teaching benefits when I recognize that I am faced with conflicting goals: helping students find ways to comply, yet still maintain their independence and autonomy; and ways to resist, yet still be productive. We can't remove the conflict, but we can at least understand it. Thus, I believe it helps our teaching to realize that it is possible ideally for resistance and compliance somehow to reinforce each other. Resistance gives us our own thinking and the ownership over ourselves that permit us to do the giving in we need for learning; compliance fuels resistance and gives us the skills we need for better resistance.

But I believe we should also recognize how difficult and paradoxical this trick is—how neither we, nor our students, can expect to pull it off consistently. We can acknowledge that students are, in fact, doing very well if they manage to career back and forth a bit between complying and resisting—and not stay stuck in one mode. (I make a similar analysis of the dialectical relationship in the writing process between generating and criticizing, being credulous and skeptical. See pp. 52–54.)

Finally, I want to suggest some concrete teaching practices that have become even more important to me now that I think about this paradox of resistance and compliance. The main thing is the helpful contrast between high-stakes and low-stakes assignments. High-stakes assignments foster compliance: When we raise the amount of credit that an essay carries, we raise the pressure on students to comply. Low-stakes assignments allow more space for resistance or rebellion: When we assign work but structure it so it doesn't count for so much, we make it easier for students to resist or refuse—for example, by writing what they know we hate, or writing in a way that we hate.

But now, I'm struck with how low-stakes writing helps with compliance too—not just resistance:

- *Private writing.* Look at the interesting mixture of occasions for compliance and resistance. When I assign private journal writing I am asking for a certain minimum but real compliance with the demands of the teacher: to produce writing at a certain time or lose credit. But since neither I nor any other outside reader sees it, there is no need to comply in any other respect. The writing doesn't have to conform to *any* criteria. I just ask students to flip the pages for me. Thus students can even cheat on this if they want to badly enough. When we do private writing in class, a few students sometimes just sit there not writing. I used to try to pressure them in some way, but now I don't fight them—seeing it as an important occasion for saying no—as long as they don't disrupt others.

  What I hadn't figured out until now is that private writing doesn't just make it easier for students to resist. It also makes it easier for them to comply. Students can decide to *give in* without anyone seeing it—without a shred of teacher-pleasing or caving in to institutional pressure.

- *Writing merely to share.* I assign a good amount of writing that I ask students only to share with each other—no feedback—and which I read but do not respond to or grade. Because this writing is shared, most students feel more pressure from audience and conventions than they do with private writing. But because there is no response, students are freer to resist any of these quiet but perhaps powerful pressures, and to frustrate or even annoy readers with no explicit penalty.

  But here too I am now realizing that mere-sharing-no-response can help with compliance too—not just resistance. It's sometimes easier to comply with conventions or readers' desires when one doesn't *have* to comply.

- We see this same dynamic with the extensive publication of student writing. (At UMass Amherst, every teacher in the first year course publishes a class magazine four or five times a semester—paid for with a lab fee.) Students can thumb their nose at readers; or go along with reader needs. The fact of publication—seeing all your classmates holding in their hands a copy of a class magazine that contains your writing—increases the pressure from peer readers. But by the same token, it helps put teacher standards into more perspective. It helps students think a bit more explicitly about the question, "Are the teacher standards the ones I really care most about?"

- *A grading contract.* I now tend to use a contract for grading. I promise students a B if they comply with an extensive set of requirements (see "Getting Along Without Grades" in Part VI). A contract shakes up the normal resistance/compliance dynamic of the writing classroom—or rather clarifies it. The contract makes the pressure to comply more concrete and explicit. This in itself is a relief compared to the indirectness of conventional grading. But it may be more important that the contract asks for things that are clear and external—rather than a matter of quality and interpretation. My request for compliance is not an attempt to reach inside their head—or to get them to fit themselves into what's inside my head. I think I can have a bigger effect on my students with the contract than with conventional grading by letting my reactions be personal and unrelated to the grade. Thus the contract makes it easier for students to resist; even on major assignments they can write what they know I will hate or write in a style they know I don't like—with no penalty. But in the end, I think the contract makes it easier to comply because they don't have to. They are not caving in; they have more choice.[2]

---

2. Bruce Bashford of SUNY Stone Brook points out that many teachers learn to shape assignments in such a way that the emphasis is on the "demand encountered within the activity" itself, in the problem—rather than on the demand to conform to a teacher's authority. "[A] task can have an integrity of its own, can contain its own criteria of success—what John Dewey had in mind when he said the solution is in the problem" (correspondence 3/9/95). Related here is the recent growth of interest in public service activities in writing courses. Students aren't just writing for the teacher but for outside tasks and people.

If writing is an act of giving in, it seems to me that one of the most practical goals for us as teachers is to help students fall in love with their own ideas and their writing. Then they are stuck with the compliance problem in a productive way instead of a destructive way. Yes, they still have to give in to conventions and to audience—that's hard and it can hurt—but it is easier to put the resentment to one side and get yourself to give in because you love what you've created and you want others to get it, understand it, and appreciate it. It helps if *we* also love what our students write (see my "Ranking, Evaluating, and Liking"). The trouble with most school writing is that students have to comply not only to the conventions of written language, good thinking, and reader needs; they usually feel most strongly of all the need to comply with the teacher, the assignment, and the authority of the institution. This raises the stakes of compliance and makes it harder to give in. For students in this situation, giving in carries a higher price.

I've been describing this difficulty from our point of view as teachers. But it's fruitful to reframe it from the students' blunt point of view: "How can I be a good student without 'sucking up' or being a 'brownnose?'" (Anyone who resists a psychoanalytic view need only reflect on the ubiquity of these metaphors among students.) Sadly, for many students the dilemma seems impossible. But let's turn the question around and use it as a framework for structuring our teaching: How can *we* conduct our teaching to maximize the opportunities for students to be good without experiencing themselves as "teacher pleasers?" Again, it's not easy. We need new thinking and shrewd suggestions.

Researchers have begun to think about this general issue as it is faced by adult nonliterates and by students coming from a minority culture that identifies away from school: how to learn without giving up one's identity or one's culture. Researchers have begun to notice better the inevitable *loss* that goes along with any learning.[3]

Let me conclude with a brief thought about the relationship of my whole story with issues of race, class, gender, and sexual orientation. I imagine someone reading what I have written here and muttering, "What a whiner! A privileged and successful white boy is making such a big drama out of his struggles with the system. Shit, man! It's *his* system." What if I were a differ-

---

3. Arlene Fingeret writes of how "Illiterate adults . . . identify a risk connected to learning to read and write"—a risk of having to "separate themselves from their communities" and social networks (1983, 144). She speaks of the "findings of other researchers that nonreading adults would like to know how to read but that they have been unwilling to tolerate the profoundly disrespectful environment of most educational programs" (1989, 13). Mary Savage speaks of the need to learn to *mourn* "for the way schools teach us how to separate the 'us' from the 'them'" (1990, 25); for "how the academy rearranged people and knowledge in hierarchies and isolated us in agonistic relations" (1990, 27); and for "students who disappeared and relationships which ended and families which became strained and distant" (1990, 36). These are all costs of giving in.

ent color or culture or gender or class? How much harder I would find it to negotiate a fruitful and productive way to comply with a culture that I see as devaluing or even destroying my culture! Given who I am, perhaps I should just laugh at my struggles and brush off my resentments since they are so minor in comparison.

Yet my struggles and resentments were real—and they may be instructive. There's something to be learned from seeing how a culture tries to prepare people in privileged institutions. When looking from the outside at the fit between me and these elite institutions, one is apt to notice how much I seemed to *belong* because of my comfortable mainstream background. But when looking from the inside—from the point of view of my experience at the time— what strikes me most is my completely opposite feeling: my sense that I *didn't* belong and didn't fit in at Williams, Oxford, or Harvard. But, perhaps more important, how badly I *wanted* to belong—how deeply undermining it felt not to be "right"—and thus how high a price I was willing to pay to get that precious feeling of belonging. In a genuine sense it was "my system"—but it seems as though the way my system functions (except perhaps for deeply secure people) is to make it feel as though it *isn't* my system unless I give up on part of what is central to me and go along with it. Perhaps this is how structures of power and elitism function.

It's true that Oxford and Harvard and other elite institutions are, in significant ways, more tolerant of resistance and idiosyncrasy than less elite schools are (at least for those students with unflappable confidence). But in other ways, elite institutions exact the *most* compliance and elicit the most "buying in." If we doubt that, we need only look at how such institutions react to the possibilities of significant change in the educational process—or look at their alumni magazines to see how much graduates have "bought in."

On the one hand, I was the *best* kind of student: just the kind you'd want in your classroom. But I was also the worst: a failure who couldn't do the work and quit and never wanted to have anything to do with books and learning again. My goal in this essay is to complicate our notions of best and worst student. Many of our "best" students may be paying too high a price in their compliance and preventing themselves from doing lasting good work— or complying but not complying and sabotaging themselves. And many of our "worst" students, our refuseniks, might potentially be some of our best, but they are in the same dilemma: we haven't managed to help them find fruitful or productive ways to comply.

Works Cited

Bartholomae, David. 1985. "Inventing the University." *When a Writer Can't Write*, ed. Mike Rose. New York: Guilford Press, 134–65.
———. "Against the Grain." 1985. *Writers on Writing*, ed. Tom Waldrep. New York: Random House, 19–30.
Bolker, Joan. 1979. "Teaching Griselda to Write." *College English* 40.8 (April): 906–8.
Brooke, Robert. 1987. "Lacan, Transference, and Writing Instruction." *College English* 49.6 (October): 679–91.

———. 1991. *Writing and Sense of Self: Identity Negotiation in Writing Workshops*. Urbana IL: NCTE.

Brownlee, Shannon. "Baby Talk. *U.S. News & World Report*, June 15, 1998: 48–55.

Burtt, Edwin A. *The Metaphysical Foundations of Modern Physical Science*. Rev. ed. Garden City NY: Doubleday, 1954.

Cleary, Linda Miller. 1991. *From the Other Side of the Desk: Students Speak Out about Writing*. Portsmouth, NH: Boynton/Cook Heinemann.

Connors, Robert J. 1996. "Teaching and Learning as a Man." *College English* 58.2 (February): 137–57.

Elbow, Peter. 1987. "Closing my Eyes as I Speak: An Argument for Ignoring Audience." *College English* 49.1 (January): 50–69.

———. 1998. "Changing Grading While Working with Grades." *Theory and Practice of Grading Writing: Problems and Possibilities*, ed. Chris Weaver and Fran Zak. Albany NY: SUNY Press.

———. 1986. "The Pedagogy of the Bamboozled." *Embracing Contraries: Explorations in Learning and Teaching*. New York: Oxford University Press, 87–98.

———. 1993. "Ranking, Evaluating, and Liking: Sorting out Three Forms of Judgment." *College English* 55.2 (February): 187–206.

———. 1993. "The Uses of Binary Thinking." *Journal of Advanced Composition*. 13.1 (winter): 51–78.

———. 1981. *Writing With Power: Techniques for Mastering the Writing Process*. New York: Oxford University Press.

Felman, Shoshana. 1982. "Psychoanalysis and Education: Teaching Terminable and Interminable." *Yale French Studies* 63: 21–44.

Fingeret, Arlene. 1983. "Social Network: A New Perspective on Independence and Illiterate Adults." *Adult Education Quarterly* 33.3 (spring): 133–46.

———. 1989. "The Social and Historical Context of Participatory Literacy Education." *Participatory Literacy Education*, ed. A Fingeret and P. Jurmo. New Directions for Continuing Education, no. 42. San Francisco: Jossey-Bass. (summer).

Fox, Helen. 1994. *Listening to the World: Cultural Issues in Academic Writing*. Urbana IL: NCTE.

Fredo, Deborah. 1995. *Women's Literacy, Indigenous Form and Authentic Co-Learning: A Research Approach to Participatory Training for National Language Literacy in Rural Senegal*. Diss., U Mass Amherst.

Gardner, Howard. *Frames of Mind: The Theory of Multiple Intelligences*. NY: Basic Books, 1983.

Gilligan, Carol. 1991. "Joining the Resistance: Psychology, Politics, Girls and Women." *The Female Body: Figures, Styles, Speculations*, ed. Laurence Goldstein. Ann Arbor: University of Michigan Press, 12–47.

Haswell, Richard H. 1991. "Bound Forms in Freewriting: The Issue of Organization." *Nothing Begins with N: New Investigations of Freewriting*, ed. Pat Belanoff, Sheryl Fontaine, and Peter Elbow. Carbondale, IL: Southern Illinois University Press, 32–69.

Jonsberg, Sara Dalmas. 1990. "Learning Requires Resistance." *PRE/TEXT* 11.1–2, (spring/summer): 41–45.

Kermode, Frank. 1979. *The Genesis of Secrecy: On the Interpretation of Narrative*. Cambridge: Harvard University Press.

Lanham, Richard A. 1974. *Style: An Anti-Textbook*. New Haven: Yale University Press.

Lu, Min-Zhan. 1987. "From Silence to Words: Writing as Struggle." *College English* 49 (April): 437–48.

Miller, Alice. 1981. *The Drama of the Gifted Child*. Trans. Ruth Ward. New York: Basic Books.

Murphy, Ann. 1989. "Transference and Resistance in the Basic Writing Classroom: Problematics and Praxis." *College Composition and Communication* 40 (May): 175–87.

Robertson, D. W. 1963. *A Preface to Chaucer*. Princeton University Press.

Savage, Mary C. 1990. "Mourning into Dancing." *PRE/TEXT* 11.1–2 (spring/summer):

23–38.

Street, Brian. 1985. *Literacy in Theory and Practice*. New York: Cambridge University Press.

Tobin, Lad. 1996. "Car Wrecks, Baseball Caps, and Man-to-Man Defense: The Personal Narratives of Adolescent Males." *College English* 58.2 (February): 158–75.

———. 1993. *Writing Relationships: What Really Happens in the Composition Class*. Portsmouth, NH: Boynton-Cook Heinemann.

Weathers, Winston. 1980. *An Alternate Style: Options in Composition*. Rochelle Park, NJ: Hayden Book Co.

———. 1976. "The Grammars of Style: New Options in Composition." *Freshman English News* (winter).

White, Edward M. 1995. "An Apologia for the Timed Impromptu Essay Test." *College Composition and Communication* 46.1 (February): 30–45.

2

A Map of Writing in Terms
of Audience and Response

There are many good ways to map the universe of writing: by genres (e.g., poetry, fiction, nonfiction); by modes (e.g., narration, description, argument); by elements in the writing process (e.g., generating, revising, copy-editing); by parts of rhetoric (e.g., invention, arrangement, style); by purposes (e.g., persuading, informing, entertaining); or even by topics or themes (e.g., science writing, religious writing, technical writing). Whatever the map, the same simple useful moral emerges: writing is not just one thing or activity or experience. Writing poetry does not feel like writing nonfiction prose—nor freewriting like revising, nor science writing like diary writing.

But there's another way to map the universe of writing that I now find particularly useful: in terms of *audience* and *response*. Audience and response seem to me the most "writerly" dimensions of writing. Therefore, the following map has become my main foundation—both theoretical and practical—for thinking about the writing process and for planning my teaching.

With four horizontal rows, I indicate four kinds of audience we write for. With three vertical columns I indicate three kinds of response those readers might give.

The twelve dots indicate twelve intersections of audience and response: twelve sites of writing. For example, the upper left-hand dot represents writing that a student gives to a teacher, where the teacher simply reads it and does not respond. The lower right-hand dot represents writing that is only for one's own eyes, but writing that one reads in a critical or evaluative frame of mind. Just as our experience is likely to be different depending on whether we are writing poetry or writing prose nonfiction, so too our experience is likely to be different depending on whether we are writing for a teacher, a friend, or ourself alone, and whether we are expecting criticism or just an ap-

This essay has not appeared elsewhere.

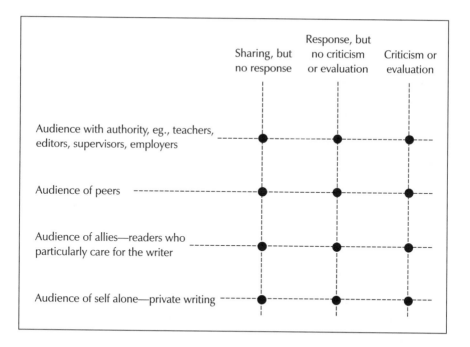

preciative hearing. Yes, occasionally we are so wrapped up in our writing that our experience is unaffected by the readers we are writing for or the kind of response we expect from them. But this is rare. For most of us—and especially for most students—audience and expected response have a huge influence on the experience of writing.

My map or model may raise some nagging questions: How can you share writing and not get *some* response? How can there be a response that is not evaluative? What is an ally reader? I will address these questions in due course.[1]

My point in this long essay is a simple one: that writing prospers most when we have the richest range of experiences with audience and response—when we are well traveled on the map and often visit the many sites where

---

1. I am trying to keep the model simple, so I treat only four kinds of audience. Let me note here three additional interesting and important audience dimensions:

- Are we writing to readers we know or to readers we don't know?
- Are we writing to a large group or a small group or just one reader?
- Are we writing to absent readers or to readers who are present with us as we write?

These variables probably affect our experience of writing as much as the ones in my map. For example, will my essay get judged only by the teacher I know or by an unknown teacher? Am I reading my essay to my buddy, my small group, the whole class—or even allowing it to go into a larger publication? Do I feel the presence of my readers vividly because they are sitting right next to me and we've just been talking about this topic—as often happens in writing classes and writing groups, and as happens when we speak? Or are my readers so far away that I sometimes forget about them?

writing goes on. Yet most people have had the opposite experience. Many students have experienced only one of the twelve sites of writing on the map: they have given their writing *only* to teachers and *only* got an evaluative response. Even teachers with too many students usually feel obliged at least to circle a few mistakes, star a few good points, or give some kind of grade. I believe this impoverished diet helps explain why so many of our students have such a hard time writing and sometimes write so oddly.

Even when students get a bit of peer feedback, it is usually evaluative—so this makes for only two out of the twelve writing experiences. Some teachers ask for a bit of freewriting or journal writing. This makes for three sites— except that many of these teachers *collect* freewriting and journals, sometimes even putting a few evaluative comments on them—which puts us back to two sites again, or just one.

Notice how much more varied a *speaking* diet most people have had in comparison to their writing diet. From the earliest age we have spoken to all four audiences (including lots of self-talk by babies), and we often get no evaluative response—sometimes no response at all, just listening. We speak in all contexts, but writing is something most people learn only in school. My analysis, then, makes me want to see students get a richer experience of *all* the sites of writing. And as a consequence I find myself a cheerleader for the most neglected sites of writing—in effect, the left-hand column (no response) and the bottom two rows (audience of allies and self). I am arguing for a balanced diet.

But a peremptory voice interrupts at this point:

> All you've done is draw a map and then pretended that whatever you've drawn there is necessary. When are you going to give us some reasons?

I'll give my reasons by exploring each of these audience and response relationships in more detail. I will start with those kinds of audience and response that are most widely accepted and most often used. I can treat them briefly because everyone sees them as crucial. I will argue at more length for the neglected and disputed kinds of audience and response. I'll move from the right side of my map to the left; and then from the top to the bottom.

Three Kinds of Response

1. *Evaluative response.* Could anyone ever argue against *all* evaluation? Sheepishly, I raise my hand. On some days I want to wave a magic wand and wipe all assessment off the face of the earth forever. I get discouraged at the obsession with grading and evaluation that permeates our classrooms and indeed our culture. Sometimes it seems as though evaluation is the only thing that students, educational institutions, legislators, and the general public care about. But one of the virtues of my map is that it helps me out on these bad days and shows me that the problem is not evaluation in itself but the fact that so many students get *nothing but* evaluation. The map helps me realize

that if we get a full range of other responses, then evaluation has every chance of being helpful and productive.

2. *Nonevaluative response.* Probably there is no response without *some* tinge of evaluation in it. Nevertheless, we can choose whether or not to *tell* a writer about our evaluative response. Furthermore, we have the power to choose whether to *have* a response that is primarily evaluative or a response where evaluation plays only a small part. That is, our very responses themselves will be different depending on whether we try as hard as we can to *evaluate* a paper, or try as hard as we can to *describe* it without talking about quality or values. When we evaluate, we ask questions like these:

What are the paper's strengths and weaknesses?
How could it be improved?
How good is the paper?
What grade or score shall we give it?

If we want to give a nonevaluative response, we ask questions like these:

What does the paper say? Imply?
What is the writer's point of view or stance?
What does the writer assume?
How does the paper ask me to see the world?
What is the organizational structure?
Describe all the genre and rhetorical features we see.

One of the main nonevaluative responses readers can give is simply to tell *their* views about the topic of the paper. It is a mark of respect to students when we take *what* they write seriously enough to reply with our thoughts on the topic—instead of just making metacomments about how well they have written. And remember, if our views are opposed to those in a paper, this carries no necessary implication of a negative evaluation. We often disagree with papers we think are excellent and agree with papers we think are terrible.

It's no good dismissing nonevaluative response on theoretical grounds just because it doesn't exist in a pure test-tube state. In truth, it is not hard to give useful nonevaluative responses; it just *seems* hard in most academic settings. Nonevaluative response simply takes a bit of training and discipline—and above all good faith. Teachers and students can fairly easily get quite good at it. Once we open this door—once we make a good faith effort to describe a text and respond to it in nonevaluative terms rather than evaluate it—a rich range of response options opens up. (Think about letters. Yes, respondents often say how much they enjoyed our letter, and occasionally how nicely it was written. But if someone replies to our letter by evaluating its strengths and weaknesses, we feel immediately that something has gone awry in the communicative transaction.)

The goal of nonevaluative response is to show writers that they have been *heard and understood*: Isn't this what makes us and our students want to continue to write? To be understood is more rewarding than to be praised. Being understood makes us want to take the trouble to try to articulate more of what is on our minds—and almost on our minds. Thus the most valuable feedback is often to take what is *least* clear in a paper and just rearticulate it back to the student in our own words—and go on to give some of our own thoughts on the same issue.

Of course, students sometimes complain when they get nonevaluative response. Many of them have slid into assuming that the point of writing is not to communicate what is on your mind but rather to be evaluated. Yet students can usually come to appreciate evaluation without response—as long as there is some system to help them feel secure about grading (see my "Getting Along Without Grades—and Getting Along With Them Too" in Part VI of this volume). Where evaluative responses impose the reader's values on the writer, nonevaluative responses give the writer some space to try to work out his or her own sense of what is better or worse. And they lower the stakes.

3. *No response at all—mere sharing.* When I wrote *Writing Without Teachers* in 1973, I was struck with how little response we usually get from teachers. I wanted *more*: more response and more kinds of response, such as nonevaluative response and movies of what was going on in readers' minds as they were reading. And I wanted more private writing—words that didn't even get to the reader. I never imagined the possibility of this odd in-between site: actually sharing one's writing with an audience but getting no response at all. Then one evening I was sitting in a tiny auditorium listening to a few poets and fiction writers read from their work. It finally dawned on me: this is a no-feedback situation.

Here again, a theoretical objection pops up: "Don't be silly. Those writers were listening for where the applause was loudest—and for the laughs and the attentive silences and the bored coughing." True enough. So just as there is no response without *some* evaluation, so too there is no reading without *some* response. I've caught myself, when someone is silently reading what I've written, peering intently at the muscles in their face.

Nevertheless, the response situation that evening was radically different from the normal classroom one. The writers were not asking for any response other than the ritual of applause. They would have been insulted if I had stood up and said, "Let me tell you about a few fascinating weaknesses I noticed"—or even, "Let me explain to you what you did right." These people were "writers" in what may be the most crucial sense of that term (something we would do well to teach our students): they knew that response to their text is something they should get *only if they ask for it.* And they knew the value of not asking for it. They as writers and we as audience had mutually, if tacitly, defined our response relationship to each other as follows: "You get to read, we get to listen and enjoy."

Of course, in an academic setting it often feels odd and even awkward for someone to read what they've written and for others simply to listen and not respond. But the fate of most writing in the world is no response at all. When people write books, stories, poems, newspaper articles, and memos, the words go out and that's pretty much it. If readers read the words at all, the writer is lucky. Occasionally, you get a note back in your mail box, "Good memo."

More often criticism. Sometimes books get a review; most do not. Magazine articles and newspaper stories, virtually never. Friends may give you responses, but often they are nervous to do so.

It's worth noticing, then, that even though most of us write with the expectation of response—usually with the expectation of criticism—nevertheless, the norm for most texts in the world is no response. Of course we may create response and criticism by asking for it from friends and colleagues—and surely we are *sometimes* wise to do so. And of course it's hard to get words out to many readers without the evaluative Yes or No from the editor or supervisor. However, it's amazing how often the editor or supervisor says only Yes or No—and gives no other response. Thus it's sobering to reflect that for most texts in the world, no response is the default mode. (Letters, as we saw above, are an interesting exception: the default mode for letters is a response—but a nonevaluative response.)

I've found it useful to bring into the classroom this more worldly transaction between text and readers: to have students read and others listen—in pairs, small groups, and in the arena of the whole class; to publish magazines of student writing for everyone's edification and pleasure—not response; and to collect some of my students' writing and just read it and scrawl "thanks" at the bottom. Of course I need to explain to students ahead of time that I will just read and not respond. Most first- and second-grade teachers regularly put up student writing on the wall and set up sharing circles where students take turns reading to the class what they've written. (For notable nonacademic uses of sharing without response, see Progoff, Schneider.)

There is usually some awkwardness when one person reads and others listen but don't respond. The writer inevitably feels, "Was it okay?" and the listener feels, "Oh dear, I've *got* to say something." I've developed rituals to help people through this awkward space. If it is a reading to the whole class, we have quick ritual applause; and I always say, "Thank you." If it's a reading in a small group or pair, I get the listeners always to say, "Thank you"—and then go on to the next reader. These rituals are not just pragmatically useful. "Thank you" turns out to be exactly the correct message. Indeed, perhaps I shouldn't label this audience relationship as "no response." For what I am talking about is *appreciative, attentive listening*. I expend some effort in my teaching to emphasize this supportive spirit. In any case, with these guidelines, students soon come to experience mere sharing as natural and pleasurable; awkwardness dissipates.

Sharing without response is not just easy, pleasant, and nonthreatening. It also improves writing. I think mere sharing may produce more improvement with less effort and discomfort than any other activity. When students read their words out loud, they feel them in their mouths and hear them in their ears. They get a palpable feeling for when their words work and don't work. They stumble in saying a problem sentence; they often stop and reword it or explain what they really meant to say. They can hear when the thread of an argument gets lost. Often they didn't notice it while writing and so now they often stop and say, "What I'm getting at here is. . . ." No one had to say,

"This sentence is awkward" or "I don't understand." And they get similar benefits from listening to the writing of their fellow students. They can hear when the words get roundabout or overly abstract or boring or pretentious. This is the most efficient teaching we can do: it's all learning and no teaching. Many good writers testify that the mouth and ear are the main organs for learning to write. Sharing without response also heightens students' experience of the social dimension of writing.

For all these reasons, I try to give equal emphasis to this third response relationship: that is, to make sure that students get not only evaluative responses, not only *non*evaluative responses, but also sometimes no response at all—as long as it is appreciative listening or reading. This process seems to me to improve my relationship to teaching or instruction and to my students. I love the experience of reading their writing and not responding—just jotting "thanks." I can enjoy their writing better when I don't have to think about how to respond or evaluate. I get to notice that they can improve without my help. They can enjoy it more when they don't have to worry about my response.

Four Kinds of Audience

1. *Audience with authority over the writer.* Who could ever argue against teachers as audience? (Who could ever call a book *Writing Without Teachers*?) Some of my best friends are teachers. But the simple fact is that teachers as audience often *do* undermine students' ability to write with satisfaction or even to write at all. Yet here again my map comes to the rescue. The problem is not teachers as audience but rather teachers as the *only* audience.

When students write for teachers, they are writing "uphill" in the authority dimension: instead of having the normal language-using experience of trying to communicate "across" to others in order to tell them what's on their mind, they are having the experience of trying to communicate "up" to someone whose only reason for reading is to judge the acceptability of what they wrote and how they wrote it. (In content courses like history or biology, students have the experience of trying to say what they *don't* know so well to a reader who knows it better.) Therefore, when students write *only* to teachers, they often end up writing not as the act of *communicating to people* but as *performing for a grade*—an exercise in being judged or trying to get approval (see Cleary for rich and compelling accounts by students of their experiences of this situation). If you never play the violin except for your teacher, you will probably find it unrewarding before long, but if you are also playing for yourself and others, playing for the teacher is helpful and rewarding.

2. *Audience of peers.* Peer readers can be a problem. Tom Newkirk points out that they often praise writing that we don't want praised, or worse, say "That sucks" about passages and pieces we want them to admire and emulate. And students sometimes care more about peer opinion than about our carefully considered professional judgment. Yet Newkirk does not conclude, "So

let's not use peer readers." Most teachers now agree that an audience of peers is useful in the teaching of writing.

For when students write to peers, they have a better chance of experiencing writing the way that most language functions in the world: as the act of communicating what's on your mind to others who might be interested—rather than to readers whose only purpose in reading is to judge. It seems clear to me now that when I had to quit graduate school because I couldn't write, my problem was that I wrote only for teachers, the response was always evaluation, and the stakes had become very high. During my early years of teaching at Franconia College, writing finally became feasible to me because I was writing to students and also to fellow teachers in a new core course we were developing together. I actually wanted to tell them things.

3. *Audience of allies—or readers who care for the writer.* Sometimes a teacher or peer will take on a special role and function as an *ally.* The simplest definition of an ally reader is someone who cares more about the writer than about the writing—who cares more about helping and being a friend than about improving the writing. I think of an ally as someone who sees that I am smart even when I write something stupid; who sees that I am good even when I write something that reveals selfishness or meanness or limited vision. When an ally reader notices these things in what I've written, he or she may point them out—if I ask for critical feedback—but I can always feel the feedback as only a part or a subset of caring for me and seeing my goodness. Ally readers are precious and should be cherished. To have one ally is a lot; I've had long periods with none.

And yet perhaps ally readers are not so rare as we might think, and they don't have to be described in such superlative terms. That is, most teachers naturally slide into being ally readers when a student hands in a piece of writing that is a serious call for help or a cry of pain. When we respond to this writing, we don't usually ask ourselves, "How can I help the writing?" We ask, "How can I help this person?" Indeed, as some feminists have been reminding us (see Noddings, Schweickart), it is *not* so rare to read as a person who cares about, cares for, values, or even loves the writer. We often read the work of friends we care about. After a semester is half over, we often discover we have come to care about many of our students—which is one more reason why grading is so difficult. And the converse principle is important: it's easier to read as an ally when we don't have to grade the writing. (By the way, when we read more and more books by one author, it may not so much be a matter of *judging* the quality of this writer but of having come to *like* this writer. Much of our reading for pleasure is of writers we have come to care about.) In short, from a purely theoretical point of view, there is a problem with the implicit, conventional model of the reader as a disinterested evaluator (like the problem in economics with the conventional model of humans as rational calculators).

We all know that children cannot prosper without caregivers who actually care about them. Why should writers prosper without the same thing? I don't think that students and other potential writers learn to be brave and direct in exploring some of their most deeply felt views—or in using their own language or voice—unless they have the experience of caring ally readers.

Because of my interest in ally readers, I no longer try to separate friends when I get students to do peer work. Where I used to say, "How can I get students into pairs and groups so they'll stay on task and not schmooze with buddies about baseball or parties?" now I see a different goal: "How can I get students who schmooze as buddies and friends *also* to share their writing and help each other with it?" For one of my larger teaching goals is to get my students to feel that it's natural to use their close friends when they are writing.

Teachers frequently complain when students are reluctant to give each other substantive or critical feedback, but the students are understandably trying to keep a class activity from undermining their relationships with each other. My goal, therefore, is not to keep friends apart but rather to try to help friends give each other substantive and useful feedback—and still stay friends. For this crucial goal, *nonevaluative* feedback is particularly useful. I now take it as a central goal of a writing course that sharing and responding to writing get all tangled up with friendship and chatting about yesterday's game and tonight's party.

But let me sound again the larger theme of this essay: I am not arguing that allies constitute a *better* audience. I'm just arguing that they are a *necessary* audience—among other necessary audiences. So in my teaching I also try to get nonbuddies to work together in peer groups. Thus I often create groups of four by pairing pairs of friends. This way, students have nonbuddy readers—but they still have an ally or friend in the group.

4. *Audience only of self—private writing.* By private writing I mean something simple and concrete. When I explain it to students I say something like this: "Please treat this writing as something for your eyes only—not for me, not for fellow students. Of course you can decide *later*, if you wish, to take this private writing and adapt it for an audience—or even give it to readers as it is. But *while* you are writing, please insist that this is just for you, not for anyone else. Assume that you won't share it unless *later* conditions make you change your mind." Thus I tell them frankly that *one* of the reasons I like private writing is that it gives me good material for public writing—better material than I can usually get when I start out writing for an audience. But I don't get this benefit unless, *during* the act of writing, I really treat my words as only for me, and invite myself to write things I wouldn't share with others.

In earlier versions of this essay and map, I put private writing into the vertical dimension. I mistook private writing for zero-response writing because there was no chance for *audience* response. I wasn't paying enough attention to responses from the self. Of course the self is very much an audience, and the self naturally responds in all three modes that the map illustrates. That is, sometimes we have an evaluative response to our own writing ("What a stupid idea I had here!"). Sometimes, however, we respond in a nonevaluative way ("I wonder what would happen if I took this idea further?"). And sometimes, especially as we are in the act of writing, we just hear our words and move on and have virtually no response at all.

I used to give pep talks or sermons to students about the benefits of private writing, but not many of them made much use of it. To many people, private writing seems like a waste of time. So I've come to use my authority as teacher to push the experience of private writing on students in the following ways:

- At the beginning of class I often take ten minutes for private freewriting, on any topic, or perhaps on something we will take up in class.
- If a discussion has gone dead in the middle of a class or we are turning to a new topic, I often take ten minutes for private writing about the topic.
- At the end of a class I sometimes ask students to write for themselves about what they learned or noticed from the class—or to get started on something they'll have to continue at home.
- In writing courses I usually require the use of a journal—asking students to write entries almost daily and put in at least an hour a week. I sometimes suggest topics, but make it clear that what they write is entirely up to them.
- I sometimes set a due-date for a *private* first rough draft of an essay that I will ask them to revise later for sharing with me and others in a second and often even a third draft. On the due date, I will invite students to *talk* to each other in pairs or small groups (and sometimes even in a whole-class discussion) about the issues they have written about or about their experience of writing—but not share their writing. This is particularly useful when the topic is slippery, vexed, or controversial. I can invite students to let fly in their private writing with whatever opinions or feelings they find coming to mind—without having to worry about whether they might offend others or even whether they ultimately believe these first thoughts. This helps students get a little perspective on the contents of their minds and feelings— but in a position of safety.

Enforcement is an interesting issue when writing is private. I can't *make* people write during in-class private writing times. I used to try to cajole the resisters, but now I feel I do better by simply setting a good example and losing myself in my own private writing. So if they really want to resist, they can just sit there. All I insist on is that they not bother the rest of us with whispering. But it's usually more boring for them to sit there not writing. I find it rare for people to resist for long, and most students come to appreciate the quiet time with their own thoughts. The stakes are a bit higher for me when it comes to my requirement of keeping a journal or of doing an exploratory draft by a certain date. For the journal, I ask students three or four times a semester (usually in conference) to flash their pages before my eyes—even letting me see some of the dates at the top of the page. And on due dates for private drafts, I wander through the classroom asking students to hold up their draft for me to see.

Thus cheating is possible. Students can refuse to write in class; they can flash fake journal writing for me or hold up fake drafts. Or on the occasions when I want them to do their private writing *about* a certain topic in order to help us have a better discussion, they can write about something else. But I've become comfortable with these loopholes. After all, the main experience of school for many students is the experience of having to do what teachers tell them to do—to follow orders. I think everyone benefits when students get a chance to disobey orders in ways that cause little or no harm.

My main goal in teaching writing is a simple but radical one: that my students will write by choice after the course is over. I don't think they will do this—indeed, I don't think anyone long persists in writing by choice—unless they get recurring tastes of that interesting experience of *surprise*: of finding themselves writing something they didn't expect to write. "Oh, I'd forgotten that." "Oh, I never looked at it that way before." "Oh, I didn't realize I felt that way about it."

In order to get this experience one has to learn a subtle balance of energy: concentrating-but-not-worrying; exerting-but-not-clenching. Private and shared writing are the perfect sites for learning this subtle ability to expend energy yet still relinquish some control—to let the words themselves lead you on. I find it helpful to do a tiny bit of coaching during the early sessions. I say, "What do you *need* to write today?" or, "What do you need to write about this topic?" But I also invite some relinquishing of agency: "Try letting go of the steering wheel." Or, "What needs to be written?" Or, "Let the words take you where *they* want to go." I am trying to encourage risk taking in a protected space—to invite contributions from various corners of the self—or various selves. This can set a good example for later writing that will be responded to and evaluated. That is, students get a sense that adventurous exploration and risk taking are not just possible but can lead to interesting thinking and good writing.[2]

The Practical, Writerly Benefits
of Private Writing

But does private writing improve normal or regular writing for an audience? Most people assume—whether they are teachers, students, or members of the general public—that writing for school should always go to readers other than self (and in fact should even get an evaluation of some sort). I want to fight that assumption. I tend to slide into a more partisan or even argumentative tone when I fight for what is most neglected and undervalued: no response (the left-hand column on my map) and no audience but self (the bottom row). Therefore, I want to emphasize the larger nonpartisan stance of my

---

2. When I have a new class that I feel might be reluctant to do private writing or get themselves to take it seriously, I start with lots of writing to *share* but without response: some written in class and some for homework, some for me and some for peers. By making them do this public but low-stakes writing, I am giving them an experience of writing where they have to take it *somewhat* seriously—but they don't have to worry much about what they say or how they say it. This helps them learn that precious knack of concentrating-but-not-worrying, and they learn that this writing mentality often leads them somewhere interesting. After a number of these sessions of writing for sharing only, they are more open and productive when I finally say, "Now let's do some writing that is fully private. I won't collect it or ask you to share it with anyone."

essay as a whole: nothing I write here is an argument *against* the use of other responses or audiences—just an argument *for* the value and importance of these two neglected ones in addition.

To defend private writing I need to speak to the most concrete and practical objection: that private writing doesn't help students write better for an audience and so isn't worth using in our writing courses. There are other more theoretical objections to private writing, such as the claim that there is no such thing as private writing and that the concept itself represents a misunderstanding of the nature of discourse or a category confusion. I speak to theoretical points in a different essay in Part IV of this volume, "In Defense of Private Writing." In what follows I will discuss the many reasons why private writing, though of course it does not give students practice in addressing the needs of readers, *does* nevertheless help them to improve their writing.

- *Quantity*. People don't improve their writing much unless they do a great deal of it—much more than we can ever read and respond to. Private writing (along with writing only for sharing) vastly increases the *amount* of writing that we can require of students. We can get them to write things we don't see and yet their writing will improve.
- *Full attention*. Most students have never had the experience of writing with their minds focused wholeheartedly on their topic or meaning while they are writing for a teacher. Usually, they are putting considerable attention on the question of how the teacher will evaluate or grade it and on correct usage. Imagine never having concentrated entirely on your topic. Imagine how much our writing would suffer if some of our attention were always bleeding away onto matters of correctness of surface features—wondering what the teacher was going to call wrong—trying to avoid mistakes or wrong language. How can writing go well without full attention on one's thinking?
- *Fluency*. In private writing, students can gradually learn to turn off a common feeling that is damaging to fluency and satisfaction in writing: the feeling that writing means giving primary attention to avoiding mistakes, faults, and weaknesses—to avoiding criticism. Private writing helps students come to experience the act of writing to be as natural and fluent as talking. Many teachers are very skeptical about this possibility because they themselves have never experienced it. But it's no fair objecting to something just because you haven't experienced it—especially if many others have, and it is not so hard to learn.
- *Safety*. Most students, indeed most people, feel that speaking is safer than writing. But this is just an accident of the very imbalance of audience and response relationships that this essay aims to correct. It is a kind of accident that people use speech in lots of trivial, low-stakes, "chatty" ways—but tend to use writing only for discourse that feels more important or high stakes ("putting it down in black and white"). Most people assume that writing should be criticized. But, in truth, *writing can be safer than speaking*. That is, when we speak, we are almost always in the presence of a listener, and so once we utter something, it is heard and we can never take it back.

When we write, on the other hand, our words are seldom immediately read. Writing turns out to be the ideal medium for exploring our thoughts or feelings so no one else will hear them. With writing we can change what we have written or hide it or rip it up or delete the file. Students can easily learn to explore freely—can learn, as it were, to "think onto paper." Of course this privacy also invites carelessness, but it makes students less afraid and self-conscious about writing. Not worrying allows them to enjoy writing more.

- *Ownership.* Students often don't feel much ownership of the writing they do in school. What they write often feels to them as though it is "someone else's": it is for someone else's assignment and designed to meet someone else's criteria. Students often feel that the reader has more power than the writer to define whether the writing has any value or not. When students give us writing, they often say, "Is this what you were looking for?" With private writing, however, their words are completely their own and they get to decide what they want and what has value.

- *Voice.* I think I see private writing helping students develop a more comfortable, fluent, and often livelier voice in their writing—and eventually, a stronger, more inhabited voice. But I can't give this claim the weight it deserves unless I explore a bit of complication here.

I often ask students to look back and compare the voices they hear in their private and public writing. They sometimes see what I sometimes see in my own writing too (and what Fulwiler writes about): that their public writing has a more lively, prominent voice. When we write for others, there is often more sense of "address" in our words. Having the audience in mind makes us "speak up" or "speak out" a bit more.

But this isn't the whole story about voice and audience. That is, while the public voice may be more lively, it is also often more self-conscious, sometimes a bit "put on" or artificial, sometimes even slightly "off" or uncomfortable. If we are not comfortable with the people we are writing to (and many students are not comfortable writing to the teacher), we may well "put on" a voice to deal with them. We may have to pretend a bit to create that voice and "address" them. Think of the lively but seriously "off" voices we often find in our departmental mailboxes when English teachers take on the slippery task of writing to other English teachers. Students too often put on a pretentious or jocular or fake-confident voice—or vacillate a bit from voice to voice.

The voices in our private writing, by contrast, are often more humdrum and nondescript—we're just mumbling, ruminating, or even list-making to ourselves. But at least we are not pretending. So when our private writing does get more animated and "felt" (as of course it sometimes does), these loud or striking or even odd voices often feel much solider or closer to our sense of "who we are" than the lively public voice we used for an audience.

For all these reasons, then, I don't feel bad about pushing for some private writing, even for students who find it useless or boring. I want to give them occasions when they have to talk but there's no one to talk to but themselves. Most students soon appreciate these times.

Before concluding this section, let me make a final and surprising point about private writing. In contrast to the rather extreme theoretical view that declares that there is no such thing as private writing, I'd like to proffer a view that's almost as extreme and perhaps not so theoretical, namely, that *most writing is in fact private*. I invite you to notice that much or even most of what most thoughtful writers write is *never* seen by anyone except themselves. That is, almost no one writes anything and hands it to readers as it is, especially since the coming of computers. People read back over what they've written and virtually always make a few changes—often lots of changes. That first draft (or second or third draft) was in fact private—for their eyes only. Yet people write those drafts *as though* readers were going to break down the door and snatch the words out of their hands before they get a chance to improve them. So even though in one sense this is not private writing because the writer is intending the words for readers, nevertheless, in a simple factual sense the writing *is* private. This may sound like a theoretical quibble, but actually there is a very practical consequence. From an experiential point of view, the writers are not getting any of the benefits of this privacy. When I realized that my early drafts were in fact private, my process of producing them changed, becoming much more adventuresome and productive—much less anxious.

What This Map Can Tell Us About the Shape of Our Teaching: Some Progressions

The map suggests a general movement from the left to right—from zero response to critical response; and a general movement from lower to upper—from audience of self to audience with authority. This implies starting off a course with writing only for sharing and only for the self. These two kinds of writing work together well at the start. If I start with private writing alone, many students find it too boring and pointless; they can't concentrate or take writing seriously if it's not for an outside audience. In effect, they need the experience of audience—but under the safest and most supportive conditions—in order to learn to appreciate and enjoy writing for an audience only of self.

1. The map implies a progression from safety to risk—from low stakes to high stakes. Obviously, risk tends to increase as we move from no response to nonevaluative response, to evaluative response; and also as we move from an audience of self, to ally readers, to peer readers, and finally to readers with authority over us.

We want students to take risks; it's hard to learn well unless you are willing to take risks. But notice the dialectical relationship here: the best way to *help* people take risks is to build a foundation of safety. If someone objects, "But there's no real risk-taking in any action that depends on safety," I reply, "But there's also no risk-taking in any action that depends on pressure." That is, if you hold a gun to my head to get me to jump off a high diving board, I'm not taking a risk, I'm reducing a risk. The only way to get me genuinely to take a risk is to help me build up a foundation of trust and safety—probably by getting me to start with low diving boards and gradually encouraging me higher and higher—step by step.

In short, we can't *pressure* students to risk themselves, we can only set up conditions that increase their willingness to do so. To most students, writing feels like an inherently high risk, high-stakes activity, but that's just because they have been conditioned to associate writing with certain audiences and responses. We can change their attitude to writing by building in a lot of safety at the beginning of a course.

I need to pause here for an important qualification. It is an oversimplification to say that the audience of self is always the safest. Many people find an audience of self the most critical audience of all. When people write only for themselves, they hear internal critical voices saying, "Unclear" or "Awkward" or "Wordy" or "Stupid" or "This is no good." Indeed, it was reflection on this experience of the fierce self-critic that led me to the concept of "ally reader." The audience of self derives from the internalization of external audiences. So when people find it painful to write for themselves alone because of the harshness of the inner critic, it is the experience of writing for *ally* or *caring* readers that helps them gradually learn to internalize a more supportive reader. Most of my students come before long to feel safe in their private writing when I set up supportive conditions and explain my goals.

2. The map implies a progression not only from safer to riskier but also from easier to harder. As students move from left to right and bottom to top, the writing tasks become more difficult. And each stage paves the way for the following one.

Plain sharing leads to better responding. It helps writers become more comfortable reading their writing outloud because they don't have to worry about the response from listeners. Plain sharing also helps listeners become more comfortable and adept at listening to writers read their work because they don't have to worry about how to respond. They get crucial practice in listening, noticing, and reflecting to themselves on their reactions to texts— all without pressure.

We see the same benefit at the next stage: nonevaluative responding paves the way for better evaluative responding. It helps writers listen openly and nondefensively to responses from readers because there is no worry about criticism. Nonevaluative responding also helps responders be more willing to give feedback because they don't have to worry about criticizing their fellow students. And because nonevaluative questions are primarily *descriptive* (e.g., "What do you hear as my main point? What do you hear as my other points? What structure do you see? What voice or voices do you hear?" and so forth), they train both writers and responders to be closer and more observant readers.

Of course, many students *want* peer evaluation and even criticism from the first day. But they are seldom skilled at giving or receiving it until after they have had these other experiences of just sharing for a while and then using nonevaluative questions. Much of the training we give students in peer responding works more quickly and effectively if we move from left to right on the map of responses.

We see the same progression in the vertical or audience dimension. Writing for self and for allies makes students more fluent, comfortable, resilient, and adventuresome in their writing—and thus readier for the tougher audiences of peers and readers with authority over them.

3. For *teachers* too, the map suggests a progression from what is safer and easier to what is harder and riskier: the more we move rightward and upward on the map, the greater the demands on us as teachers. That is, it takes neither skill nor time on our part to get students to write privately (though it's just as well to use some class time for private writing in order to honor and dignify the activity). When we get students merely to share their writing with each other or with us, it takes only a bit of time but no skill at all from us or from our students (though the process asks us and our students to learn to listen respectfully—and invites us all to learn how to listen supportively). Peer sharing takes very little class time compared to peer responding. And for us as teachers, it's a remarkably positive experience to read student writing when we've made it clear that we will give no response at all. We can read out of curiosity and for pleasure, and they can write just to say what they think.

Putting this another way, the further we move rightward and upward on the map, the more our teaching can misfire. We can scarcely go wrong with private writing and mere sharing: students' writing almost inevitably improves and they become more confident. But when we respond to student writing and get students to respond to each other—especially if the response is evaluative—things can easily go wrong. After all, students are unskilled responders, and they often give responses that are thoughtless or based on a misreading. And we (expert as we are!) must often respond under poor conditions: we give single readings to large stacks of papers late at night and give fast, unrevised comments. We know that we often end up giving criticisms or suggestions that run counter to those that would be given by respected colleagues. And even when our responses are sound and *ought* to be helpful, they can still misfire for the particular student, given his or her personality and history. If we obliged ourselves to live by the principle physicians are supposed to follow, we would use only private and shared writing: "at least do no harm."

4. Just as the map suggests how safety can pave the way toward risk taking and easier tasks pave the way for harder ones, so too does privacy pave the way toward sociability. We can see this dynamic most clearly on a small scale in discussion classes. Students are braver about speaking up in class about a given question or topic if we give them a couple of minutes of private freewriting first. In a discussion, students often feel, "I have this thought or feeling on the topic, but I don't want to *say* it because I'm not sure I'm clear on it, and I'm not sure it really makes sense." But if students get a chance to write out the thought quickly, they often feel, "Sure I can share my thought now. I understand it better and I can see that it makes sense." I see the same dynamic in meetings among colleagues.

Because I've noticed this progression, I'm more conscious now of trying sometimes to start my courses with some privacy. During the first class I have more private writing than shared writing, and only quick introductions. Sociability is my goal: sharing, community, collaboration, collegiality. But I now see students getting there more easily when I explicitly provide some protected private time to figure out who they are or want to be in this course, how they want to present themselves, and what the course is about for them—without so quickly having to find a public voice or persona for the situation. In a sense I am giving them a chance to be "alone with themselves" for a little while in this public classroom in this course—before they have to put on a face or come outdoors and work with others. Of course, not all students need this private space; some students are confident being fully sociable from the first moment. But many are not, and the confident students are not held back by a slightly slower progression into sociability. (Some of the confident ones, when given a bit of time, discover that their most practiced identity is not the one they really want to lead off with.)

When I reflect on this dialectic between the private and the social, I notice that the old fashioned, conservative classroom gives us the *worst* of all worlds. When all writing goes to the teacher and none to peers, it means that writing is *never* private, always public; and yet the public dimension is impoverished since "public" consists of only this one reader who is experienced not so much as a real person or genuine audience with whom they are engaging in public discourse, but rather as a kind of semiprivate "judge-function."

5. Finally, the map suggests a progression from what we call elementary or immature or undeveloped or "developmental" to what we call advanced or complex or developed or mature. Or does it? It suggests this impression to the unwary; it did to me. But in fact this final progression is a seductive trap that I now want to label with a red flag. It is certainly true that the progression *is* from what is simple, basic, elementary, and foundational to what is richer, more complex, difficult and, in a sense, advanced. For that reason it may *look* as though the first stages are immature or babyish, and that the goal is to move *beyond* them to more important and "mature" ones. When I assumed this, I assigned lots of private and shared writing at first and then gradually abandoned them and moved on to the more "mature," or "advanced" kinds of response and audience.

But no more. It's true that private writing and mere sharing are enormously *simple*. But simple is not the opposite of mature, valuable, or important. In an earlier draft, when I was listing "advanced" characteristics like "difficult" and "complex," I threw in the word "sophisticated." But that word helped me see the seductive trap here. Shaker furniture is simple, basic, elementary, and foundational—yet deeply sophisticated. Private and merely shared writing are simple but deeply sophisticated.

Let's pause for a moment over these words: "simple," "basic," "elementary," "foundational." Notice that *all* have become code words or euphemisms for what is immature, remedial, and retarded. We see here a deep problem in our mental and linguistic conceptions of learning and education—in one set of metaphors we live by. Yes, I love complexities, especially the complexities of response to text; nevertheless, it's finally clear to me that we need more of these sophisticatedly simple kinds of writing and response. They may be literally simple to engage in, but we need to realize that they invite slow maturational growth, and thus their "pay off" is not quick.

Thus, even though I always *start with* the left-hand column (merely sharing with various audiences) and the two bottom rows (writing for self and allies), and then gradually move rightward and upward, I now make sure that I *maintain* these simpler activities throughout the semester. They are deeply valuable in themselves. I think I sometimes see students getting their greatest benefit from mere sharing and private writing toward the *end* of the semester.

In the last analysis, I would insist that when we move from left to right and from bottom to top, we are actually moving from what is *more* important to what is less important—from the indispensable to the dispensable. Let's look at the matter from the point of view of priorities. The most important thing is writing. Getting a response from readers tells us more than mere sharing; it adds richness, it is a plus. But if responses start to make a student hate writing and avoid it (and this can happen), then perhaps we should look for a way to slow down the progression. Similarly, evaluation tells more than nonevaluative response; it too is a richness and a plus. But if evaluation makes a student avoid responses at all, or stop hearing them or taking them in (and this often happens too), perhaps we can look for ways to hold off evaluation for a little while. Think of all the people who have tried a writers group and dropped out—and all the writers groups that have folded: usually it was because evaluation was killing the desire for response or response itself was killing the desire to share one's writing.[3]

We see the same priorities on the vertical dimension. Writing is the most important thing, and writing for the audience of self and ally is usually the best way to encourage it—especially in combination with the activities of the left-hand column—simply sharing with other audiences. Moving from an audience of self and ally to an audience of others is a plus because it usually helps students notice things in their own writing that they didn't notice when it was only for self or ally; thus it helps them be more careful and thoughtful with their writing. But if writing for other audiences stops students from writing or makes them hate it, then perhaps it's worth trying to find ways to slow down the progression.

Concluding Comment

For all these reasons I have fallen into the custom of "jump starting" my writing courses by beginning with two or three weeks of writing only for sharing,

---

3. When I just said that evaluation is richer or tells us more than nonevaluative response, I was granting something for the sake of argument that is often not true. When readers give an evaluative response to a piece of writing, they often tell us much less than when they describe it and give other nonevaluative reflections on it.

and also lots of private writing. This is a way to get students to write up a storm. I can get more writing out of them because they don't have pressure from evaluation or even response. I don't ask for much revision. I'm looking for lots of starts and sketches and drafts. And it's easy on me. They have lots of safety, yet I get to read lots of their writing, and they get to hear and read lots of each others' writing. But *no one* has the work of responding—or listening to responses. I sometimes refer to it as an "orgy" of writing.

In this period (at first I experimented with just one week), they develop much more confidence and pleasure in writing and often develop a lively voice—or two or three. And when the assignments get harder and stakes get higher, and the writing sometimes falls apart or gets tangled and knotted, I don't have to panic that some of them have a "language deficiency" or a cognitive problem. I just point back to the lively and clear writing they did at the start. I say, "*My* writing often falls apart too when I'm working on something hard. It's natural. But it's not so hard to fix this problem. I need to push you to revise your draft into that lively clear language you used earlier in the semester. Get the sound of that language and voice back into your ear and the feel of it back into your mouth."

After these opening weeks, I move beyond private and merely shared writing, but I still keep them alive throughout the semester. I tend to continue the practice of beginning classes with ten minutes of freewriting; I require a private journal; I often ask for simple sharing of early exploratory drafts; and the celebratory sharing of final published drafts. I think I see students making better use of privacy and mere sharing as the semester goes on.

In addition, I make a big deal of the following announcement during the first or second class—and I usually repeat it a couple of times in the first few weeks: "I care more that you write what is important or true for you than that you write what you are willing to share or what is pleasing to me or to other students. Please push for what is important or true. If in that pursuit, you find yourself writing something you cannot share with other students or with me—or if you write something that you can share but don't want any response on—let me know. There will no problem if this happens a couple of times. If it happens more often, we'll have to sit down and figure out some procedures, but I am sure we can find a way to respect your privacy here." This offer is invoked very rarely—about twice for me so far. Yet I think it helps the climate of the course by building a foundation of safety and respect.

Finally, let me reiterate my overall point. Even though I spend more time in this essay arguing for certain audiences and responses, I do so because they are neglected, not because I think they are superior. Please revisualize my opening map and remember that my main theme is the need for a more equal balance among *all* audiences and responses.

Works Cited

Cleary, Linda Miller. *From the Other Side of the Desk: Students Speak Out About Writing.* Portsmouth NH: Boynton/Cook Heinemann, 1991.

Fulwiler, Toby. "Looking and Listening for My Voice." *College Composition and Communication* 41.2 (May 1990): 214–19. (Reprinted in *Voice and Writing*. Ed. Peter Elbow. Davis CA: Hermagoras, 1994.)

Newkirk, Thomas. "Direction and Misdirection in Peer Response." *College Composition and Communications* 35 (October 1984): 300–11.

Noddings, Nel. *Caring*. Berkeley: U of California P, 1984.

Progoff, Ira. *At a Journal Workshop*. New York: Dialogue House, 1975.

Schneider, Pat. *The Writer as an Artist: A New Approach to Writing Alone and with Others*. Los Angeles: Lowell House, 1993.

Schweickart, Patrocinio P. "Reading, Teaching, and the Ethic of Care." *Gender in the Classroom: Power and Pedagogy*. Eds. Gabriel & Smithson. Chicago: U of Illinois P, 1990.

3

The Uses of Binary Thinking

There is an ancient tradition of binary or dichotomous thinking—of framing issues in terms of opposites such as sun/moon or reason/passion. G. E. R. Lloyd speaks of "the remarkable prevalence of theories based on opposition in so many societies at different stages of technological development." He goes on to give these reasons:

> [M]any prominent phenomena in nature exhibit a certain duality: day alternates with night; the sun rises in one quarter of the sky and sets in the opposite quarter; in most climates the contrast between the seasons (summer and winter, or dry season and rainy season) is marked; in the larger animals male and female are distinct, and the bilateral symmetry of their bodies is obvious. . . . Antithesis is an element in any classification, and the primary form of antithesis, one may say, is division into *two* groups—so that the *simplest* form of classification, by the same token, is a dualist one. (80)

This tradition of binary thinking is still strong and forms a kind of foundation for the many varieties of structuralism. We see this tradition illustrated, for example, in Lévi-Strauss's classic structuralist title, *The Raw and the Cooked*.

But in recent years, especially with the deconstructive reaction against structuralism, we have seen strong criticism of binary thinking. Hélene Cixous is one of many voices arguing that wherever there are polar oppositions, there

---

I have revised this essay more than a little from its original form in *The Journal of Advanced Composition* 13.1 (Winter 1993). I've worked at trying to make it clearer and more rewarding to read by fiddling some with the organization and quite a lot with wording. But there are no substantive changes in my larger or smaller points.

is dominance: some classic terms are day/night, sun/moon, reason/passion—and of course lurking behind all of these pairs is usually gender: male/female. According to this critique, binary thinking almost always builds in dominance or privilege—sometimes overtly and sometimes covertly. (For a strong example of this critique, see LaCapra 23–24).

Even when people try to overturn or reverse the traditional dominance in a polar opposition—proclaiming for example that dark is better than light, passion than reason, female than male—it just means that the underdog is redefined as overdog, and we are still left with thinking in terms of dominance or hierarchy. One side is privileged. Furthermore (so goes this critique), we don't get away from the problem even when we avoid giving victory to one side and instead work out a compromise or a Hegelian synthesis into a new, third term. When the Hegelian bulldozer pushes toward "higher" order or unity—even if the compromise is really "fair" and the synthesis doesn't favor either the thesis or antithesis—*difference and diversity are eliminated*. Jonathan Culler neatly pinpoints this large critical position in his summary of Paul de Man's thinking:

> Deconstruction seeks to undo all oppositions that, in the name of unity, purity, order, and hierarchy, try to eliminate difference. (278)

Even though Culler and de Man are complaining about binary thinking and I am defending it, I want to take this quotation as a kind of foundation for my essay. For I am defending only one *kind* or *mode* of binary thinking. I think I can show that binary thinking, if handled in the right way, will serve as a way to *avoid* the very problems Culler and de Man are troubled by: "purity, order, and hierarchy." That is, binary thinking can serve to encourage difference—indeed, encourage nondominance, nontranscendance, instability, disorder.

In making this point, I'm also calling on a venerable tradition. For there are really *two* traditions of binary or dialectical thinking. The better known is the Hegelian tradition. It uses binary thinking as a motor always to press on to a third term or a higher category that represents a transcendent reconciliation or unity: thesis and antithesis are always harnessed to yield synthesis. Since Hegel, the ancient and broad term *dialectic* has tended to be narrowed to connote this three-termed process.

The lesser noted but older tradition of binary thinking that I am calling on used the term "dialectic" long before Hegel. This tradition sees value in accepting, putting up with, indeed seeking the *nonresolution* of the two terms: not feeling that the opposites must be somehow reconciled, not feeling that the itch must be scratched. This tradition goes as far back as the philosophy of yin/yang. In the West we see it in Socrates, Plato, and Boethius. This tradition of the "coincidence of opposites" was strong in the Middle Ages (Peter Abelard, *Sic et Non*). Perhaps the most common recent champion of this approach is Jung with his emphasis on paired forces in the collective unconscious and the need always to strengthen the weaker in any pairing. Coleridge rides this tradition a bit: how the poet "brings the whole soul of man into activity" with "opposite or discordant qualities" such as sameness/difference, idea/image, general/concrete, manner/matter (II, 12).[1]

Boethius, operating in the Neo-Platonic tradition, believed that unity or truth often exists in a form that human reason cannot grasp with logic or language—and that the closest we can come to the highest knowledge is to try to hold in mind propositions that are irreconcilable: "What God has set such conflict between these two truths? Separately each is certain, but put together they cannot be reconciled" (V, Met 3). Chaucer drew on Boethius, and I learned this tradition of binary thinking during my work on Chaucer (see my *Oppositions in Chaucer;* also Reed). Since then I've learned to notice oppositions or conflicts, even to seek them, but to leave them unresolved. I've learned that when we encounter something difficult or complicated that tangles people into endless debate, we are often dealing with an opposition that needs to be made more explicit—and left unreconciled. (See my *Embracing Contraries: Explorations in Learning and Teaching.*)

Why Dichotomies?

I hear an obvious objection at this point.

> You say you are interested in complexity, but it sounds as though your real goal is to save binary thinking. If you want complexity, why keep everything in neat pairs?

Yes, two is not a very large or complex number. Having three or more options is lovely. Nothing in this essay argues against framing issues in terms of more than two sides. *As long as there's more than one!* Seeing three or five sides is fine, but it is often just a way to talk about one of them as right and the others as wrong. The argument against binaries and for multiplicity is often a

---

1. Here are some formulations deriving from this tradition:

BLAKE. "Without contraries is no progression." "Opposition is true Friendship."

KEATS. ". . . capable of being in uncertainties, mysteries, doubts, without any irritable reaching after fact and reason." (Letters)

BAKHTIN. "Not a dialectical either/or, but a dialogic both/and" (Clark and Holquist 7).

DEWEY. "Mankind likes to think in terms of extreme opposites. It is given to formulating its beliefs in terms of *Either-Ors*, between which it recognizes no intermediate possibilities" (17). Dewey could be said to structure his whole philosophy around the rejection of either/or thinking and the development of both/and thinking.

NIELS BOHR. "The opposite of a correct statement is a false statement. But the opposite of a profound truth may well be another profound truth."

YEATS. "No mind can engender until divided into two."

F. SCOTT FITZGERALD. "The test of a first-rate intelligence is the ability to hold two opposed ideas in mind at the same time, and still retain the ability to function."

MARY BELENKY et al: "[Constructed knowers] show a high tolerance for internal contradiction and ambiguity. They abandon completely the either/or thinking . . . [and] recognize the inevitability of conflict and stress. . . ." (137). (See Perry.)

cover for letting one side be the real winner—in short for hierarchy and singleness of truth. Thus my deeper goal in this essay is not to preserve pairs or binaries in themselves so much as *to get away from simple, single truth*: to have situations of balance, irresolution, nonclosure, nonconsensus, nonwinning.

So multiplicity may be fine, but I focus on the problem of binary thinking because in fact there is no hope of getting away from it in some form or another. Binary thinking is the path of least resistance for human perceiving, thinking, and for linguistic structures. To perceive is to notice a category over against difference, and the simplest path is in terms of simple opposition. The easiest way to classify complex information is to clump it into two piles. Indeed, the most instinctive and tempting clumps to use for complex data are the old favorites: ours/theirs, like/don't like, right/sinister, sheep/goats. This is why dichotomies tend to come packaged with positive and negative poles (see Herrnstein-Smith 122). It may be that the very structure of our bodies and our placement in phenomenal reality invite us to see things in terms of binary oppositions, for example, right/left, up/down, front/back, near/far, male/female (see Lakoff and Johnson). The very same poststructuralists who are so unhappy about too many binary oppositions in structuralism seem to invite far more of them into their very model for how human language and meaning function:

> [E]lements of a text do not have intrinsic meaning as autonomous entities but derive their significance from oppositions which are in turn related to other oppositions in a process of theoretically infinite semiosis.
>
> . . .
>
> To speak of the concept of 'brown,' for example, is, according to semiotics, a way of referring to a complex network of oppositions which articulates the spectrum of colors on the one hand and the spectrum of sounds on the other. (Culler, *Signs* 29, 41)

The question, then, is not *whether* to deal with dichotomies but *how* to deal with them. We have five basic options:

1. Choose one side as right or better. This is "either/or" thinking.
2. Work out a compromise or a dialectical synthesis, that is, find a third term.
3. Deny there is any conflict (e.g., "There is no difference between form and content" or "There is no conflict between teaching and research").
4. Affirm both sides of the dichotomy as equally true or necessary or important or correct. This is the approach I argue in this essay.
   4a. Take the same approach but put an emphasis on mystical unity in the duality.
5. Reframe the conflict or analyze it in more detail so there are more than two sides. This is of course another good path. It is not the focus of this essay, but it is exactly the method I use in making this list. And it is the central intellectual tool I use in my two most ambitious pieces here: my essay about voice (10 in Part III of this volume) and my essay about private writing (12 in Part IV).

The first three options are the most common and habitual ways we deal with dichotomy or conflict because humans seem to be uncomfortable with what is unreconciled or incompatible. When we are presented with conflicting data, our organism itself seems to want somehow to find *some* kind of harmony or unity. Psychologists can explain the most diverse range of human thinking, feeling, and behavior in terms of our instinctive resistance to "cognitive dissonance." Even in the simplest act of visual perception, the retina and brain are presented with swiftly, constantly shifting inputs or data, but what we "see" is virtually always a stable object or category (see Peckham).

In short, even though binary oppositions tempt people to oversimple, black/white thinking, binary oppositions also present us with uniquely valuable occasions for balance, irresolution, nonclosure, nonconsensus, nonwinning. So I will celebrate and explore here the approach to binary oppositions that seems to go against the human grain and that requires some conscious discipline: affirming both sides of a dichotomy as equally true or important, even if they are contradictory.

I'm not going so far as to say that we should balance *every* dichotomy we encounter. Sometimes one side is right and the other is wrong. Indeed, when we *need* to make difficult value judgments or sort out slippery distinctions, pairings are an enormous help. Opticians harness this process to help us figure out which lens is best when there is a multiplicity of subtle choices to make. You could sum up this whole essay as an exercise in saying, "There are two kinds of binary thinking, the good kind and the bad kind." In truth, *all five* ways of dealing with oppositions that I just listed above are valid and useful methods in one situation or another. But I write this essay because I see a need for more effort in noticing the many situations where the easy, good/bad distinction gets us in trouble and where the multiplicity of options is a cover for simply trying to win—and where instead we need balance and nonresolution.

Binary Thinking in Action: Seven Cases

I will apply this balancing kind of binary thinking to a diverse set of cases: writing, teaching, thinking/learning, teaching/research, form/content, reading/writing, private/social. I hope to show that this kind of thinking has useful explanatory power in these realms.

Writing

To write well we need to call on two opposite abilities or activities: generating and criticizing. That is, on the one hand we need to come up with lots of words and thoughts—something that is easiest if we adopt a noncritical, nonevaluative mentality of welcoming yea-saying. But on the other hand, we can't write well unless we evaluate, criticize, and reject—something that is easiest if we adopt a mentality of tough-minded, skeptical, nay-saying.

In recent years, some people have called this view an outmoded piece of dichotomous thinking, arguing that the opposition between generating and criticizing breaks down:

> There is no difference between generating and criticizing or rejecting. To gener-
> ate one word is to reject a host of other words we could have put down. Every piece
> of generating is by the same token also a piece of criticizing. The dichotomy be-
> tween generating and criticizing is an accident of words—a case of being fooled by
> our categories.

This objection is a logical quibble. Even though generating X may seem the same as rejecting Y and Z in the realm of *logic*, the two acts are crucially different in the realm of human *experience*. Yes it *can* happen that in generating X, I also rejected or criticized Y and Z, but if so, it means that I actually *generated* all three: X, Y, and Z all came to mind. But often enough when we generate X, it's the only thing that comes to mind; Y and Z are nowhere in mind to be re-jected or criticized. What I'm pursuing here is the difference between two dif-ferent experiences or abilities, generating and criticizing. What's important about them is that they are both *variables*. At any moment of writing, we may be generating a great deal or not very much; at any moment we may be *criti-cizing* a great deal or not very much.

The same criticism can be framed in terms of *criticizing*: *Every act of criticism is simultaneously an act of generating or creating*. Here again, this *can* happen: the act of criticizing X causes Y to pop into mind. And here again my model in-sists that both mental events occurred: criticizing and generating. Excellent. But far too often it works the other way: criticizing X makes nothing at all pop into mind. Generating and criticizing are variables that can occur together, but they often occur apart. Most commonly, they occur more vigorously in each others' absence because they tend to get in each other's way.

If we honor the binary opposition between generating and criticizing, we get a model with considerable explanatory power. By noticing how generat-ing and criticizing get in each other's way, we can see some of the difficulties of writing more clearly, and understand why the scenarios often play out as they do. People's characteristic way of getting things written often represents their way of negotiating the conflict between generating and criticizing.

- When writing goes very badly, we may be tied in knots by trying to be generative and critical at the same time. Some writers are characteristically
  blocked. Their writing method is the famous one of staring at the paper till
  blood breaks out on their foreheads.
- When writing goes passably but not very well, it is usually because we are
  having to *negotiate a compromise* between these conflicting mentalities. Sometimes *generating* gets the upper hand. We manage to pour out a lot of material
  but we cannot prune and shape it well for lack of cogent criticism. Writers
  who habitually fall into this path tend to produce work that is rich but undisciplined. In contrast, sometimes *criticizing* gets the upper hand. Then we end
  up with a good result but very little of it, because we saw so many faults in
  every thought and sentence we were trying to write. Writers with this habit

produce work that is cramped or tight. (Because *editors* specialize in vigilant criticism, many of them have difficulty writing themselves. Teachers often have the same problem since they spend so much time criticizing student writing.)

- When writing goes *very* well (as it occasionally does), we seem able to reach out for just the right word and yet at the same moment (seemingly without effort or even awareness), we put aside countless possibilities that aren't just right. Generating and criticizing are going on simultaneously. A few excellent writers have learned to operate this way consistently; they have learned magic integration.

Commentators have always had a hard time explaining what it is that wonderful writers do—ascribing it to genius or magic or the muses or whatever. Writers themselves give remarkably contradictory accounts of what they're doing: "It's all inspiration!" "It's all perspiration!" "It's all system!" "It's all magic and serendipity!" This is just what we can expect if people are trying to explain a complex skill which they happened to have learned, but which violates normal patterns of thinking. Their skill represents the ability to be magically extreme with opposing skills. Transcendence is probably the right word and it is a worthy goal to keep in mind. But somehow it's not very helpful advice to say, "If you want to write well, just transcend opposites." Note, however, that many odd but in fact traditional pieces of advice for writing are really aids in transcendence—for example, take walks, wait humbly, abnegate the self, pay homage to the muses, relinquish agency and control, meditate— or drink!

Note the social dimension that often lies behind these patterns. When we are more critical, it is often because we have a particularly critical audience in mind. When we are particularly generative or even magically integrated, it is often because of a particularly inviting or facilitative audience (see Section IV of my *Writing With Power*).

The path to really good writing, then, is seldom the path of compromise or the golden mean. If we are only *sort of* generative and *sort of* critical, we write mediocre stuff: we don't have enough to choose from, and we don't reject ideas and words we ought to reject. We need extremity in both directions. Instead of finding one point on the continuum between two extremes, we need as it were to occupy two points near both ends.

There's a second way to argue against the dichotomy between generating and criticizing:

> Sure, of course there's a difference between them, but spare us all your advice about separating them. That puts us back to the dark ages—back to the rigid "stage" theory of writing: prewriting/writing/rewriting. No writers do that. Haven't you heard of all the research showing that writing is recursive?

I'm not trying to deny that writing is often recursive—or even usually so. Of course, generating and criticizing are often going on more or less together, all mixed up; that's the default mode for lots of people. My point is that they don't *always* go on at the same time, and that in fact it's helpful sometimes consciously to separate them since they get in each other's way. In short, it can pay to learn to make writing less recursive.

Notice that I am introducing the dimension of time. What is paradoxical in logic—"being both generative and critical—occupying two spots on a single continuum"—is ordinary in the realm of time. Thus the easiest and most practical way to negotiate the conflict between generating and criticizing is temporally to separate them and engage in them one at a time. It may seem natural to try to *find* words and thoughts and *scrutinize* them at the same time to see if they are the right ones; but we can get skilled at doing these two things one at a time—thus separating the two mentalities. (Notice, for example, how in most speaking situations, we don't put much energy into scrutinizing the words as they come to mind or to mouth. And on those occasions when we do scrutinize our words as we speak, for example in a job interview, our speaking tends to be more halting and tangled.) And in fact many writers have gradually learned to pour down words and thoughts helter-skelter and then come back to work on them later in a specially vigilant, detached, and critical frame of mind—that is, to hold off revising and editing till the end. The time dimension helps us *heighten* the conflict, not minimize it—permitting us to clear an arena in which each side can operate unhampered to an extreme.

This, then, is the approach to heightening and separating opposites that I gradually learned—and I find I can teach it to students and teachers with helpful results. It is a skill. People often have an easier time taking risks, turning off all criticism, and thereby coming up with words and thoughts they didn't know they had, when they know they will have a time later to be wholeheartedly critical and get rid of foolishness. And people often have an easier time being fiercely critical if they have first had a chance to generate too many ideas and hypotheses. (I have found it helpful, by the way, to notice a link between this generating/criticizing dichotomy and two others: planning/not planning, and controlling/relinquishing control. Writers commonly talk about the need for periods of relaxed planning or control.)

Teaching

The same kind of conflict lies at the heart of the teaching process. Good teaching calls on two conflicting abilities or stances: positively affirming and critically judging. That is, on the one hand, we benefit if we can function as allies and supporters to students—welcoming them and all their thinking— assuming they *can* learn, that they *are* intelligent, that they *have* what it takes. (Teachers' expectations about student abilities, positive or negative, probably have more influence on how well students learn than actual differences in teaching techniques. See Rosenthal and Jacobson.) Yet, on the other hand, we also need to be on guard—to judge, scrutinize, evaluate, examine, and test. We have a loyalty not only to students but also to the body of knowledge we are teaching and to society. We have to evaluate and to criticize what is wrong, reject what is unsatisfactory. In short, to teach well we need skill as host and bouncer, as ally and adversary. Teaching, like writing, may often be recursive, but it is a recursive blending or alternation of two conflicting dimensions: opening the gate wide and keeping the gate narrow.

This conflict explains some of the difficulty most of us experience in teaching, but the difficulty is unavoidable because, again, compromise or reconciliation is not the answer. Look at the options. A happy medium is pretty sad: being only *sort of* helpful or inviting to students and only *sort of* vigilant as to whether they do decent work. Similarly, it's no good *only* welcoming students and never critically examining their work; nor *only* criticizing wrong answers and never praising their weak starts or welcoming their risk taking. Thus most teachers are stuck at one point along a continuum that students know so well: at one end are the "tough teachers" and at the other end are the "easy teachers"; in the middle are "so-so teachers" and "inconsistent teachers." Inconsistency is understandable since any single position is so unsatisfactory: most teachers find themselves muttering these two different phrases to themselves at different times: "Oh, dear, I must have been too harsh" and "From now on, no more Mr. Nice Guy."

This conflict between contrary teaching roles or mentalities is illustrated in the way students often skitter ungracefully between confiding in us as allies and guarding against us as adversaries. And they are right; we are usually both. Notice how these two teaching roles are sometimes institutionalized into separate people. The tutor's function, for example in a writing center, is to be wholly ally, and the examiner's function is to be wholly judge or adversary. Since the Middle Ages, Oxford and Cambridge, like many European universities, have institutionalized the roles of teacher/tutor and examiner.

But really skilled teachers somehow find ways to do justice to these opposed binaries in all their irreconcilability. Again we see two ways to do this. The harder and rarer path is one of mysterious finesse or transcendence. That is, a few remarkable teachers are extremely tough and inviting *at the same time*—remarkably welcoming to students yet remarkably discriminating in saying, "I won't take anything but the best."

The easier and more ordinary path to good teaching involves finding ways to separate the two stances: choosing certain times to be inviting and encouraging, and choosing other times to be especially discriminatory and vigilant. We tend to be more inviting at the beginning of a course or in our opening explorations and explanations of something, and more vigilant at the ends of courses and as we test. Somewhere toward the middle or end of a course, students often feel, "Hey, what happened? I thought this teacher was my friend." Individual conferences can function as a time for being particularly supportive—though also, occasionally, a time for reading the riot act. (More on this whole issue in my "Embracing Contraries in the Teaching Process.")

Thinking and Learning—Doubting and Believing

We see the same contradiction at the heart of the intellectual process itself: a conflict between doubting and believing. The centrality of doubting is obvious. The ability to find flaws or contradictions has been foundational in the development of logic and in the critical tradition running from Socrates through Descartes and undiminished to the present. Criticism and skepticism are usually identified with intelligence itself. People tend to assume that real thinking or good thinking is critical thinking.

Less noticed, however, is the central need in the intellectual process for skill in believing: the ability to enter into, experience, or try on ideas or points of view different from the ones we presently hold. Since "credulity," the tendency just to go along with whatever seems attractive or appealing or persuasive, is often a *problem* in the thinking of children or unsophisticated adults—and since schooling and careful thinking seem to consist of the process of *giving up* credulity in favor being more critical minded or skeptical—people have tended to see belief as a problem in the intellectual life. Intellectuals and academics often overlook the fact that few people are genuinely skilled at thinking and learning unless they are also skilled at entering into and even believing ideas and points of view that are different from what they are used to. In short, we need skill both at doubting even what looks right, and at believing even what looks crazy or alien. This is one reason why good thinking and learning are so hard.

Of course most thinking involves some kind of combination or recursive intertwining of these mental activities, and it feels artificial to most people to try to separate them. But that feeling misleads us. It stems from the dominance of criticism in our culture's model of thinking and learning. In fact, we are all perfectly accustomed to *one* form of trying to separate doubting and believing: trying to remove all credulity or believing in order to clear a space for unimpeded, dispassionate criticism or doubting. But intellectuals are not accustomed to trying to remove all doubting and criticism in order to clear a space for unimpeded, focused entering in or believing.

So here is the same kind of dichotomy I've applied to the activities of writing and teaching. Intellectual skill represents skill at opposites: both accepting and rejecting, both swallowing and spitting out, both letting oneself be invaded and keeping oneself intact. And similarly, at moments of consummate skill in thinking, we seem to be able to manage what is paradoxical: we can take on what is alien, odd, and unknown—yet we are acute in our discriminating rejections.

Let me summarize these three cases before going on to others. I'm arguing the benefits of one *kind* of binary thinking for a better understanding of writing, teaching, and thinking: the process of heightening opposites but holding them unresolved—giving equal affirmation to both sides. This model explains much of the difficulty of these three activities, and the natural patterns of distribution of skills in them. Most commonly, people negotiate a kind of zero-sum compromise between conflicting skills or mentalities: they are strong at generating, being open, and believing and correspondingly weak at the opposite side; or strong at criticizing, being on guard, judging, and doubting, and weak at the opposite side; or else middling at both. Excellence is difficult because it requires doing justice to conflicting demands—somehow getting out of the zero-sum economy. Meeting those demands *simultaneously* is especially rare—and mysterious. What's easier and more feasible is to meet the conflicting demands one at a time, though this leads to a process that is less seamless and graceful—more bumpy, back and forth, and artificial. It is thus a recursive process. However, if we switch back and forth too rapidly, we often find it harder to become productively extreme at one mentality or the other.

In these three examples I have been emphasizing oppositions or conflicts that are often *unnoticed* or overlooked. I turn now to dichotomies that are *much-noticed*—binaries that are traditional and prominent.

Teaching vs. Research

"No conflict. Teaching and research reinforce each other." This is the latest doctrine—and a prime case of unclear, wishful thinking. Of course, research *can* help teaching and vice-versa—just as generating *can* reinforce criticizing if handled well. Research can improve teachers by making them more intellectually lively. (But what about the deadly dull teachers who do a lot of research?) Teaching can improve researchers (this is a bit of a stretch) by helping them be more aware of the relationships between what they are investigating and how most people see and learn things. But it is weak thinking to slide from there into the ever-recurring pious doctrine that there is no conflict between teaching and research.

The two activities conflict in the most obvious and concrete way by competing for our time, attention, and loyalty. The extensive time I'm spending on this essay is time I cannot spend on my teaching. I get completely preoccupied as I am writing it and find myself putting off the preparation or reading I ought to do for my classes. When I'm engaged in a piece of writing and research, I tend to think about it in my free time. When I'm not so engaged, I tend to think about my students and my teaching in my free time. What I do in my research may make me a smarter more thoughtful teacher, but I can scarcely *apply* this work to my teaching, even though this essay has remarkably strong links to teaching. Few faculty members can bring their research directly into their undergraduate teaching.

But it's not just a matter of wishful thinking. When people claim that there is no conflict between teaching and research, they are usually, consciously or not, papering over a deeply entrenched hierarchy or dominance of research over teaching at universities and most four-year colleges. Teachers and administrators at two-year colleges and in the schools don't seem so tempted to proclaim that there is no conflict between teaching and research.

Because this has become a political matter, it's particularly important to try to think carefully about it. Yes, it is a benefit if teachers also research and researchers also teach. But it is simply wrong to say that people can't do one well without doing the other. Nevertheless, I am not arguing that people can teach well without *relief*—without time for reading, thinking, and discussion with colleagues. Teaching is an intellectually and personally draining process of *putting out*. To teach well requires time for *taking in* and reflecting. But it's sloppy thinking to assume that research is the only way for teachers to think and reflect and intellectually renew themselves.

The important point illuminated by my model is this: teaching and research don't *need* each other. It's only *a certain model of being an academic* that needs both teaching and research. Let me illustrate this structural point from the previous topics I've treated.

- To write well requires skill in both generating and criticizing; but people are perfectly capable of developing either skill alone. Generating and criticizing in themselves have no need of each other.
- To teach well requires skill in both supportively affirming and critically judging; but affirming and judging can flourish separately and have no need of each other.
- To think well requires skill in both doubting and believing, but those two activities do fine on their own.

Thus teachers can be outstanding without doing research—just as researchers can be outstanding without teaching. Before World War II, relatively few academics did much writing or research, nor was it expected of most. Only the few research universities of the era demanded research. Since then, the research university model has been spreading throughout all of higher education.

So what does this model of binary thinking tell us about how to improve the relationship between teaching and research? We can follow the same principles here as above. A few really gifted people can make teaching and research work together simultaneously. But most people need to take steps to keep the two from getting in each others' way—which usually means finding times to give *full* attention and commitment to each one separately. Full attention is important because what we want is extremity in both sides. We don't want half-hearted teaching and half-hearted research, we want deeply committed teaching and research. Some people can give full attention to research for a few hours each day and switch their full attention to teaching for the rest of the day. Most people can't switch back and forth so quickly and need longer periods to commit themselves to one or the other. The most pressing question now is how to nurture what is usually the weaker or shadow side of the dichotomy, teaching. We'll never improve it by blithely proclaiming that there is no conflict, and that research always helps teaching—meanwhile, continuing to give most incentives to research and few to teaching. We have to decide whether we are willing to give the incentives to teaching without which it can never thrive.

But there is a larger and trickier question lurking here. Should we preserve and enshrine the research university model for all academics? Should we insist that people cannot be academics unless they teach *and* do research? The model of binary thinking does not give an answer to this essentially political question. A promising suggestion, however, comes from the Carnegie Foundation (Boyer): a conception of "research" that isn't so much at odds with teaching because it doesn't necessarily involve conventional competitive publication. The essential point here is to allow "research" to involve input and reflection, and not require it always to mean output in the form of competitive publication.

Form vs. Content

Form and content are indissoluble. We can't distinguish them or judge one apart from the other. Surely you don't want to be associated with old fashioned schoolteachers who give split grades!

This view is intriguing in light of the history of fashion in English studies. In recent years, there's been a kind of bandwagon attempt to disown everything connected with New Criticism, yet this view represents a New Critical doctrine that has somehow stayed enshrined.

Of course, form and content are *linked*—indeed, they are often *functions* of each other: change in one often entails change in the other. But mathematicians would be startled to hear anyone claiming that we cannot distinguish between entities that are functions of each other. The idea that we cannot distinguish or even evaluate form and content separately also flies in the face of careful thought—not to mention common sense and common practice.

It's the same here as with the other contraries: opposites *do* fuse or magically interact when everything is going perfectly. That is, in the ideal poem, form and content function just as the doctrine proclaims they should: we *can't* tell the dancer from the dance. But in ordinary sublunary texts, we have no trouble telling which is the dancer. The reason the text is not magical is that dancer and dance *don't* perfectly realize each other. When we look at imperfect texts or texts in progress or nonliterary texts—for example, student texts and our own texts and most published texts as opposed to Keats's best poems—we can usually tell that the content is working better than the form, or vice versa. Most of what we say about texts implies a recognition of the difference between form and content, and most of the changes we make in any text are changes we make *because* we can palpably feel how the form and content don't work as well together as they should.

When people deny an opposition or distinction that exists, we need to ask if the denial serves to mystify something. In the realm of grading, when people say, "I can't distinguish between content and form," they are often refusing to name or figure out—or be consistent in—the hidden criteria that determine their grades. In the realm of literary studies, the doctrine that form and content are indistinguishable has often served to give special honor to *form*—to enshrine the superiority of poetry over prose, and the inferiority of texts that are easily paraphrased or summarized compared to those that are not.

Reading vs. Writing

Reading and writing would seem to marry nicely and reinforce each other without conflict. And this is exactly the case when all is going optimally— just as teaching and research *can* reinforce each other. Input can serve output, and vice-versa. We want our readers to be writers and our writers to be readers. But the idea that there is no conflict here is a classic case of doctrine shielding the privilege of one spouse over the other. (This is a large subject that I have treated at length in my "War Between Reading and Writing," printed in Part IV of this volume.) What could be more different than the two root processes: trying to fit your mind around and take in words someone else chose, and trying to choose your own words and put them out and get others to fit their minds around them? What interests me are the differences in agency and control for the learner in both processes.

Between readers and writers, there is an obvious conflict of interest about who gets to decide the meaning and interpretation of a text. It's in the interest of writers that they should decide what their own text means; it's in the interest of readers to say that only they can decide. There's no right solution to the conflict. Either/or, zero-sum arguments are a trap. Both points of view must be given full or even extreme validity. At the present critical moment (a moment that has lasted rather a long time), dominance rests more with readers than writers. Most critical work assumes that readers get the last word about the meaning of texts—and indeed that writers must not be trusted on the matter.

At the most material and political level, we see the dominance of readers in the vastly superior working conditions given to teachers of reading or literature in higher education compared to conditions for teachers of writing (Slevin). As a writing program director, most of the talk I hear about the harmony between reading and writing and their mutual need for each other is used to support proposals for scrapping what is virtually the only writing course in college (first year writing), in order to change it into a reading-and-writing course. Meanwhile, virtually all the other courses in the curriculum are tacitly invited to remain as they are, namely, committed primarily to reading. In sum, reading and writing can and should reinforce each other from a position of parity, but talk about happy harmony can be viewed with suspicion if it masks the current dominance of reading.

If we look back at the earlier dichotomies I explored, we can see the same dynamic. When people claim that there is no real conflict between teaching and research, they are reinforcing an imbalanced status quo. When people say there is no dichotomy between generating and criticizing in writing, or between believing and doubting in thinking and learning, they are reinforcing the present dominance of criticism and critical thinking in the academic or intellectual realm. They are reinforcing the prevailing set of assumptions that tell us that it is a good thing to clear space for nonstop, unrelieved criticism or doubting while people write or think; but it is a bad thing to clear space for nonstop, unrelieved generating or believing or making a mess. Periods of extreme planning and control are currently felt to be fine, but not periods of nonplanning or relinquishing control. Extremity in doubting is fine, but extremity in believing is bad. This attitude toward belief is so ingrained in our academic and intellectual culture that people don't realize that what they are afraid of—namely, fanaticism or closed-mindedness—represents not extremity of belief but poverty of belief: the ability to believe only one thing.

Private vs. Social

My theme here—and throughout this essay—is to beware happy harmonies and mystical unions; look out for declarations of no conflict. For my last case or example, however, I turn to an opposition that the field of rhetoric and composition has highlighted or foregrounded—almost to the point of hypnosis. Yet this too is a case of a binary that tends to enshrine hierarchy—in this case the dominance of the social. The problem again is either/or thinking.

Clearly humans are both inherently connected and intertwined with others and also inherently separate. We can focus on either dimension of human existence. When we look from a distance we can see that everything we say or write comes from outside—we don't make up words. But when we look from close up, we can see that every word we speak and write comes to our lips and our pens from the inside.

If we take the trouble to step outside the doctrinal bickering, we can easily see that it is a good thing to be *more than usually social*—but also to be *more than usually private*. The more we connect and communicate with others, the more . . . well, who needs to argue this point these days? But a moment's thought will also show us that we are clearly better off the more we can hold commerce with ourselves, pursue trains of thought through inner dialogues, even if no one else is interested, resist or tune out the pressures of others, keep our selves separate. (Pascal: ". . . all the unhappiness of men arises from one single fact, that they cannot stay quietly in their own chamber" *Pensée* 139.) We have good reason to value social discourse—and see social interrelatedness everywhere, even where we don't notice it at first; but we have equally good reason to value the cultivation of private, desert-island discourse and individuation.

So again, my argument is for affirming both sides equally—not a compromise but a push for extremity in both directions—*and* to resist attempts at priority or hegemony by either side. The best way to achieve this goal, to fight clear of the trap of partisans on each side fighting to stamp out the other, is to remember what rhetoricians sometimes forget though it was Aristotle's favorite phrase (not so much in the *Rhetoric*, however): "*There is a sense in which* . . . ." There is a sense, currently much emphasized, in which all language is social. This was part of what Aristotle meant in saying humans are "social animals": an entirely unconnected human is not a human; an entirely solipsistic mind is not a mind. But just as clearly, there's another sense in which all language is private. Nothing that anyone says or writes can ever be understood by others in the full senses in which it is experienced or intended. Not either/or but both/and. (For more on this issue, and on the implications for theory of the concept "in a sense," see my "In Defense of Private Writing" in Part IV of this volume.)

When both/and is the goal, it follows that the weaker or neglected dimension needs to be strengthened. Thus, it's obviously a problem when persons are *only* private and always hold themselves apart and unrelated to others and don't know how to connect or function socially. But it's equally problematic when people are *only* social and can only think and use language when there are others around to interact with, and can only think thoughts that others are interested in or agree with. Such people are too subject to peer pressure; we use the expression, they "have no mind of their own."

As with the other binary oppositions I've considered, when all goes well the opposed sides *can* work together and reinforce each other. The more of a social life one has, the richer one's private life can be. As Vygotsky and others point out, our private life is often a folding in of what was first social. But it goes the other way too: the more private life one has, that is, the more one is able to have conversations with oneself and follow thoughts and feelings in different directions from those of people around oneself, the more richly *social* a life one can have. Putting it yet another way: someone with no private life at all is in one sense completely social—is *nothing but* social; but in another sense this person is *less richly* social for bringing less of her own mental amalgam to the colloquy. As Dewey puts it: "The very idea of education is a freeing of *individual* capacity in a progressive growth directed to *social* aims" (98). Interpreting Bakhtin, Clark and Holquist write: "And unlike other philosophies that oppose radical individualism in the name of the greater primacy of socially organized groups, Bakhtin's philosophy never undercuts the dignity of persons. . . . Inasfar as we are all involved in the architectonics of answerability for ourselves and thus for each other, we are all authors, creators of whatever order and sense our world can have" (348).

The Epistemology of Experience vs. the Epistemology of Propositions

The *kind* of binary thinking I'm advocating here—an approach that tries to heighten dichotomies yet maintain the balance and affirm both sides equally— involves, it seems to me, a special link or even commitment to experience. There is a phenomenological bias; perhaps even a bias toward narrative.

My own story is paradigmatic. That is, I came to this approach through my *experience* of writing—primarily an experience of perplexity or even bafflement. I quit graduate school when I got so blocked I couldn't write. When I finally came back five years later, I was scared and self-conscious about writing, so for four years I scribbled notes to myself—short ones and long ones— about what was happening to me as I wrote—especially when things went particularly badly or well. It was from these experiential, often narrative notes that I developed the hypothesis that writing was hard because of the conflicting needs to generate-yet-criticize, control-yet-relinquish-control, say yes-and-no. My thinking grew out of a process of trying to be true to my experience and to find a theory that didn't violate it.

I've come to think that this approach to dichotomies honors the complexity of experience and the wandering narrative of events. The approach invites experience to precede logic. And here too, of course, there is a tradition: an empirical, inductive, pragmatic tradition that favors Aristotle's science over Plato's, Bacon over Descartes—and that we see in William James and John Dewey.

You can't say what I've just said, however, without someone quickly objecting,

> But there is no such thing as experience without theory. That's naive American Romanticism. Theory is always already in everything we do. No act can be innocent of theory.

But here again this claim—and it has become a doctrinal chant—papers over another binary distinction: theory vs. practice. (Boethius pictures Dame Philosophy with two prominent letters embroidered on her robe, Theta and Pi.) The claim that there is no dichotomy or conflict between theory and practice is a slip in thinking that tends to champion theory over practice.

Of course it's true that no act is innocent of premises and implications. But it is a failure of clear thinking to let that fact blind us to a crucial difference— especially in the realm of experience: the difference between coming at an experience with a conscious and explicit theory in mind vs. coming at it as openly as possible—making an effort to try to hold theory at bay and trying to notice and articulate what happens.

It is true that we open ourselves to self-deception when we try to hold theory at bay and not articulate our tacit theories: the theories we "find" are liable to be the ones we are already predisposed to believe. But when people spend all their time wagging their finger at this danger, they tend to miss a crucial intellectual opportunity. We increase our chances of seeing more *complexity* and contradiction in our experience—and finding *new* theories or theories that surprise us—if we make an effort to honor and attend to experience as closely as possible and hold off theorizing for a while. This process can even lead us to theories we are predisposed *not* to believe—theories we don't like. We can notice these two approaches in two ways of going about research. In classroom research, for example, one can start with a position or hypothesis and consciously look at everything through that lens; or one can try to take notes about what one is seeing and feeling from moment to moment, and wait to see what concepts or gestalts emerge.

Donald Schön has recently articulated and celebrated the tradition of research that starts by trying to pay as close attention as possible to one's experience. He talks about "reflective practice" in a movement from practice to theory—an approach with a debt to Dewey and Lewin. Developed even more carefully, this tradition has become the discipline of phenomenology, involving the attempt to "bracket" or hold to one side the preconceptions derived from language or theory. One can never fully succeed in this attempt, but one can get better at it. Like the discipline of holding off critical thinking or holding off awareness of audience, people mustn't say it can't be done just because they haven't learned how to do it. If we want to get better at attending to experience, it helps to notice the competing demands of theory and logic.

Let me stress again that my enthusiasm for experience and induction is not a claim that they are superior or prior or privileged. I don't claim that induction is better than deduction, Aristotle than Plato, Bacon than Descartes,

Dewey than Derrida. I am simply resisting a *counter*claim of priority, an assumption of privilege. I'm simply jostling for fifty percent of the bed. I am trying to maintain a balanced and unresolved opposition in order to prevent *either* side from being slipped into the margin by means of a haughty denial of oppositional thinking.

In fact, I acknowledge that the very position I am arguing for in this chapter has attained such a degree of generality as to become a theoretical bulldozer itself. To the degree that I fall in love with my theory of opposites, I'm liable to use it to bludgeon experience. But I don't shrink from this recognition. I have no hesitation about turning around and celebrating theory too. Sometimes it is only by bludgeoning experience—for example, through being obsessed with something—that we can make experience give up secrets that we don't get by innocent observation. (See Burtt for the classic account of how the advances of modern science depended on the ability to bludgeon experience.) Therefore, to the degree that I am committed to experience, then I will struggle *sometimes* to hold off my preoccupation with binary thinking and try to keep my eyes and pores open to experience that doesn't fit on the saddle of my hobbyhorse.

I want to call attention to a connection between this emphasis on experience and the work of some of the earlier figures in the field of composition: Macrorie, Britton, Murray, myself, and others. What these figures had in common—and what seems to me to characterize that moment in the history of composition—was a burgeoning interest in the *experience* of writing. There was a mood of excitement about talking about what actually *happens* as we and our students write. Thus, there was lots of first person writing and informal discourse. And thus the overused term for the movement: the "process approach." People wanted to talk about their experience of the process of writing—not just about the resultant text or product. "Process" means experience.[2]

---

2. It had become more or less commonplace in rhetoric of the 18th and 19th centuries to say, "We can't really teach invention. We can't fathom the mystery of where words and ideas come from. We must remain tacit about that. But we can teach about the other dimensions of rhetoric." These latter were matters of product (e.g., style and arrangement). But starting in the nineteen sixties people began to say, "Well let's *do* talk more about invention. We *can* say something about the experience of finding words and ideas and what it's like when we write."

More recently those figures in composition (Britton et al.) have begun to be referred to as "expressive" or "expressionists." That term seems to me a problem and I sometimes wonder if it is not hostilely motivated. For the prime originators and theorists who use the term (e.g., James Berlin and Jeanette Harris) have tended to use it as a term of disapproval. None of the "expressionists" use the term "expressive" with any centrality, except Britton—and the term does not well describe or sum up his views or his work. I rarely see the term used, except by people who identify themselves as *not* expressive. I don't recall using the term, and I'm not comfortable with it—partly because of its negative connotations, but especially because I can't get it to stand still and mean something definite and useful. If we define it narrowly—"writing that expresses how I feel"—it's fairly clear, but no one seems to use it that narrowly any more. If we define it more broadly to mean "writing that expresses what I feel—and see and think," then suddenly it is indistinguishable from any other kind of writing. Thus it seems thankless to try to defend "expressive writing." Chris Burnham is one of the few scholars who has shown himself willing to take on the job. See his "Expressive Rhetoric: A Source Study."

I see a correlation between this emphasis on the experience or process of writing and a willingness to articulate contraries and leave them unresolved. To be open and honest about experience leads to unresolved and conflicting propositions. This opening period of the "process" movement in composition corresponds, I'd say, to the moment when literary critics were interested in reader response criticism: "Let's try to tell what actually happens to us as we read." (I called this "giving movies of the reader's mind" in *Writing Without Teachers* in 1973). But since then, scholars in both literature and composition (with the notable exception of some feminists) have tended to back away from this interest in talking honestly and personally about their own experience. An autobiographical openness about one's own experience doesn't seem to fit comfortably with our current model of academic scholarship.

Thus I call the approach to binaries that I'm talking about an epistemology of experience, whereas an insistence on logical coherence is more an epistemology of propositions.

Epistemology and Rhetoric

The kind of binary thinking I am celebrating here seems to suggest an epistemological skepticism: a distrust of language and of the possibilities of knowing (see Gibson for a good collection of pieces about the limitations of language). But actually, I think the epistemological picture is a bit more sunny. For this tradition of binary thinking actually suggests a world of things outside us and our language that we can have a *kind* of commerce with—even though our minds and language and our system of logic are not ideally fitted to them. If we can learn to balance irreconcilable propositions in our minds (at least if they are helpful propositions), and not rush for closure, dominance, or hierarchy, we can make some sort of *approach* to knowledge of a complex world that exists outside our minds.

There is an important link here between binary thinking and metaphor. Just as new metaphors are always created out of a conflict or contradiction (a contradiction between how the word or phrase is being used and the right or literal meaning of the word or phrase), and just as new metaphors often *point at* something that is not yet signified by words (see my "Nondisciplinary Courses" 22–32), so too a well-maintained, unresolved opposition can point at something that cannot be or has not yet been otherwise articulated. The physicists have gotten used to this sort of thing with their conclusion that light must unavoidably be described as *both* wave and particle. Both models or descriptions must be upheld despite their mutual contradiction.

What interests me for this essay is the paradoxical relationship between this epistemology of contradiction and *rhetoric*. Even though I'm arguing throughout for more difference, more contradiction—more of what Boethius called "war" between truths—I think I'm opening a door to a rhetoric that is less warlike or adversarial.

Look at how rhetoric and persuasion and argument usually work. When people argue and call each other wrong, they tend to assume that only one side can be right. Or putting this the other way around (as Graff does), when people assume that only one answer can be right, they tend to engage in more conflict: they are struggling for a single prize in a win/lose arena.

But if we celebrate binary thinking of the sort I've been describing, there's every chance of discovering that *both parties to the argument are right*— despite their disagreement. Their two claims, even though completely contradictory, might *both* be valid and useful views of a complex phenomenon that doesn't neatly fit our language or our minds. If they were more open to the epistemology of contradiction, they might come closer to a full description and understanding of the complex issue by affirming and entering into each others' propositions (without having to give up allegiance to their own). After all, none of the blind men in the fable were wrong when they gave contradictory descriptions of the elephant. But their views were seriously flawed by narrowness of perspective. In the tradition of binary thinking, there is less need to try to force people to agree. Thus John Trimbur's essay, celebrating dissensus or the limits of consensus, has been extremely fruitful and influential in the profession—coming as it does out of the tradition of Bruffee and his consensus-based model of social construction.

My interest in affirming oppositions, then, connects with my interest in nonadversarial, nonviolent, nonoppositional rhetoric: rhetoric as believing game (see my "Methodological Doubting and Believing"). More and more people are noticing the problems with either/or rhetoric: the assumption that in order to argue *for* a position, we must argue *against* the contrary position as wrong. Lakoff and Johnson, in their exploration of the tacit "metaphors we live by," show how deeply enmeshed our culture is in the assumption that "argument equals war."

This assumption of warfare tends to backfire on psychological grounds as well as epistemological grounds. If I want you to consider my point of view, I will have a harder time if I first try to get you to confess you are stupid or mistaken for holding yours. And I'll increase my chances of success if I, in turn, am able to see the truth of your view.

Many conditions in the world have conspired to help us see more clearly than ever the limits of an either/or model for dealing with conflict. Even in the highly adversarial realms of warfare and litigation, it turns out that mediation and negotiation are more and more sought out. In rhetoric itself then, we should not be surprised to find more explorations of alternative models for handling conflict. (See the extensive exploration of "Rogerian rhetoric," for example, in Brent and Teich. For feminist explorations of nonadversarial rhetoric, see Frey and Lamb. Also Ong has a fascinating exploration of the long history of the adversarial and irenic traditions in our culture.) It's my contention, then, that the kind of binary thinking I describe here—an epistemology of contradiction—will help people get unstuck from either/or, zero-sum, adversarial models of rhetoric.

At this point, some readers will be itching to accuse me of not practicing what I preach. For if I am so interested in nonadversarial rhetoric and the believing game, why am I *fighting* so hard in this essay—using the the very kind of good/bad binary thinking that I profess to be against? And why in my career have I so often seemed to take partisan stands?

For I have certainly been partisan. I've always written more excitedly about generating than revising and been preoccupied if not obsessed with freewriting. I've certainly celebrated private writing and the ability to turn off awareness of audience during certain points in the writing process. I've made more noise about teachers as allies than as critical, evaluative adversaries. And I've campaigned my whole career for the believing game.

But there are two goals for fighting: fighting for the sake of being heard vs. fighting for the sake of keeping the other person from being heard; fighting to create dialogue vs. fighting to insist on monologue. I am fighting here to make a case for binary thinking in a climate that considers it a cardinal sin. I'm not fighting to wipe out the sometimes necessary practice of good/bad binary thinking or to prevent the often useful practice of framing issues in terms of *multiple* positions. And as for the practice of fighting itself, here is a case where I want to break out of binary thinking. That is, it's not an either/or choice between fighting and not fighting—between trying to exterminate the enemy and her position or else going into a kind of nonviolent limpness. There is an important third option. We can fight with someone to try to get them to listen to us or to consider our view—fight hard—and yet nevertheless, not press them at all to give up their view. (Of course, it sometimes seems as though the enemy's only "view" is that *our view* must be stamped out—and so we feel we have no choice but to try to stamp out theirs. But mediators and negotiators have learned to be skilled in this situation: helping people to articulate the *positive* goals or views or needs that lie behind their merely negative goal of wiping out the enemy's goal.)

I've always made it clear that my partisan behavior was grounded in my epistemological commitment to binary thinking. Because there has been such a one-sided tradition in the teaching of writing—a tradition that says, "Always plan, maintain vigilance, use critical thinking"—I've seen a clear need to make a louder noise for periods of nonplanning, generating, freewriting, and holding off critical consciousness. But in all of my fighting for the generative, I've never argued against critical consciousness, doubting, criticism, or radical cutting—only for an equal emphasis on both sides—a stronger contradiction—what D. H. Lawrence called the "trembling instability of the balance" (172). I've always been explicit about my commitment to subject matter and even evaluation in teaching; and to doubting in thinking and learning. And when it comes to the opposition between the private vs. the social dimension in writing, I would claim some credit (with my *Writing Without Teachers* in 1973) for helping the profession become interested in the social and collaborative dimension of writing in the first place.

Thus I would invite readers to compare the rhetorical shape of my writing with that of people who are extremely critical of my work (e.g., James Berlin and Jeanette Harris). I may permit myself unabashed enthusiasm and open partisanship; they use more modulated tones of alleged judiciousness. But compare the rhetorical goals to see who is trying to silence and who is trying to sustain a dialogue.

In fact, what really needs explaining is why there has been such a tendency to see me as one-sided and extreme—to see me as someone only interested in generating, making a mess, and the private dimension—to be blind to my support for critical thinking, revising, doubting, and the social dimension in writing—when I preach over and over this theme of embracing contraries and of trying to get opposites into unresolved tension with each other. That is, I'm criticized for being narrow or one-sided, sometimes on epistemological grounds, but really the criticism itself represents an epistemological poverty of thinking. It is fashionable now to celebrate indeterminacy and epistemological doubt, yet even radical theorists often fall into assuming that if anyone argues in favor of feelings, private discourse, or the relinquishing of control, she must by definition be against thinking, analysis, logic, and the social dimension—whatever they say to the contrary. I can't help believing, then, that an epistemology grounded in the tradition of binary thinking highlighted here can lead to a larger mindedness.

So how do we learn or develop this kind of epistemology or this habit of dialectical thinking? One important way we learn it is through interaction with others: through dialogue. After all, that's the original link that Socrates and Plato had in mind in their original conception of "dialectic": bring people into conversation in order to create conflict among ideas. Dialogue leads to dialectic.

So just as we learn to talk privately to ourselves by internalizing social conversation with others (as Mead and Vygotsky tell us), so we can learn this useful kind of binary or dialectical thinking from conversation. That is, our greatest source of difference and dichotomy is when people of different minds come together. So in addition to calling for an "epistemology of contradiction," I could also call it an "epistemology of dialogue" or (to be fashionable) a "dialogic epistemology." But it's not enough to have dialogue between opposing views if the dialogue is completely adversarial. The dialogue we need comes when participants can internalize *both* views—can enlarge their minds and their assumptions—instead of just digging in and fighting harder for their own view. So it's a question of what kind of dialogue we have. The views may clash, but can the parties cooperate or collaborate in the dialogue? We learn rhetorical warfare from dialogue with rhetorical warriors, but we learn dialectical large mindedness from dialogue with people who have learned an epistemology of dialogue or contradiction.

The epistemology that tends to be dominant today among scholars and academics in the humanities is dialectical in one sense: It says, in effect, "I believe X and you believe Y, and there is no real truth or right answer in the back of the book to tell us who is right. So we can keep on fighting." What I'm looking for is a dialectical epistemology that is more generous and hopeful—an epistemology that says, "I believe X and you believe Y, yet by gum we may well *both* be right—absolutely right. If we work together, we might well get a richer understanding than either of us so far has."

Notice finally, then, two different relationships here between epistemology and rhetoric. In the dominant tradition, we have eternal warfare between *people* (rhetoric), because the people don't maintain eternal warfare between *concepts* inside their heads (epistemology). It's possible to have it the other way around: eternal warfare between concepts in the head, resulting in more cooperation and less zero-sum warfare between people.

Dialectic and Rhetoric

In the previous section, I focused on the role of people and rhetorical structures. In this final section I will focus on language. I will suggest that there is a realm of language use or discourse that is a particularly useful site for encouraging the kind of binary thinking that helps concepts and ideas to live in fruitful tension. I see this realm as different from rhetoric and I suggest that we might call it *dialectic*. Dialectic and rhetoric represent contrasting if not absolutely conflicting uses of language.

The dichotomy between dialectic and rhetoric was central to Plato and Aristotle, but now it is widely neglected or denied—mostly because dialectic is enormously unfashionable and rhetoric is the dominant term. Some say indeed that rhetoric covers *all language use* (see Eagleton for a prominent instance). I wonder if there might be links between three current attitudes I am seeing in many rhetoricians and literary critics: a knee-jerk criticism of dichotomies and dichotomous thinking, a neglect of dialectic as a realm or category of language use, and an attraction to rhetoric as the master term.

To deny the dichotomy between rhetoric and dialectic represents yet again the papering over of a power imbalance—an aggrandizing move by rhetoric. When people say everything is X (e.g., all language use is rhetoric), they are making a move to push difference and opposition off the map: no conflict. I would sound the warning again: beware proclamations of no conflict. My aim is to show the fruitfulness of a conflict between dialectic and rhetoric as two uses of language.

The easiest way to dismiss dialectic and claim that everything is rhetoric is to deny the grounds Plato and Aristotle gave for the distinction between the two realms of discourse. Plato saw dialectic as the realm of truth and correct reasoning, and rhetoric as the realm of deception. Aristotle saw dialectic as the realm of certain knowledge, and rhetoric as the realm of probable knowledge. (They too, of course, were making a power play and claiming superiority for dialectic.) But now, since "everyone" agrees that there is no such thing as truth or certain knowledge (do we have certainty about the lack of certainty?), it would seem obvious that there is nothing left but rhetoric. All language use is interested or partisan—and thus ultimately an act of persuasion.

It's not easy to fight this claim; in a sense I agree with it. Yet I think I can argue usefully, if speculatively, for a realm of language use called dialectic that differs from rhetoric. What is "rhetoric"? The term is rubbery, but I think it's fair to define it as language designed to have an effect on an audience. More traditionally and narrowly, it has been defined as language to persuade. And "dialectic"? I am not defining it as the realm of truth or certain knowledge, but rather as the realm of language whose goal is *not* to persuade or not even for the sake of having an effect on an audience. Putting it positively, dialectic is the use of language where the prime goal is to *make* meaning rather than deploy that meaning toward an effect: to get meanings, concepts, and words to interact with each other in order to see where they go; to "figure out" or "figure." (With the term "figure" I am thinking of the activity of doing calculations with numbers. Would aggrandizers for rhetoric claim that all mathematical calculations are rhetoric?) We might even think of dialectic as the realm of language as play—language for its own sake rather than for pragmatic effect. The central thing, then, is that we are using language in such a way that there is not the *pressure* of trying for an effect on an audience—the pressure of rhetoric.

In the present critical climate, this is a slippery and controversial notion. And there is overlap between the categories (more about that below). So it will help to give some examples:

(a) There is a clear contrast in the realm of law between a legal *brief* and a legal *memorandum* (or more precisely an *office memorandum*). A brief lies squarely in the realm of rhetoric: its goal is to persuade the court; to win. In contrast, an office memorandum sits squarely in the realm of language use that I call dialectic. A legal dictionary defines the office memorandum as "an informal discussion of the merits of a matter pending in a lawyer's office; usually written by a law clerk or junior associate for the benefit of a senior associate or partner" (Gifis 296). The "benefit" spoken of here is *not* to argue or persuade or plead for one side, but rather to figure out everything that can be said on *both* sides or—as some people put it—to figure out how a perfect judge or a legal God would rule. The difference between rhetoric and dialectic is intriguingly highlighted by a material or procedural ruling: under the law, an office memorandum is legally "*protected* from discovery" (296) so that the other team cannot see it. The fact that the memorandum is legally "private" helps it be an act of figuring out rather than an act of rhetoric.

(b) I think we most often use language for dialectic in a more private way—writing or talking or verbally thinking *for ourselves*. I'm not claiming that all private discourse is dialectic. As Burke and others point out, we often address language to ourselves for the sake of having an effect or being winning toward that audience of "me." Still, privacy is a realm that at least *invites* dialectic: not trying to have an effect on ourselves but to explore or follow a train of thought.

For example, when I am dealing with an issue where I have a position and disagree with others, I find I have a better chance of understanding the issue if I leave the rhetorical realm, stop addressing them, take myself out of their hearing, and speak to myself in private. ("What if I'm wrong? Let's see what happens if I consider such and such evidence more seriously. Could I admit that I'm wrong?") Someone might object that this kind of private language for making meaning or figuring something out is nevertheless language designed to have "an effect" on my audience of self—namely, the effect of clarifying my thinking or my position. But this is clearly not what Burke or most of us mean when we talk about "language designed to have an effect on an audience." To stretch the word rhetoric to cover all discourse—by definition—is to lose the word.

When I am engaged in the rhetorical task of writing to persuade and I get confused or stuck, I've learned sometimes to take a fresh sheet or open a temporary file and start exploring my perplexity for myself. "What am I really trying to say here? I think X but I feel Y" and so on. Up till that point I had been addressing my language to readers for the sake of making a point or having an effect. But in order to make this move into the realm of dialectic, a crucial internal event must happen. I have to make a little act of letting go and giving up full commitment to my position—to my hunger to persuade. Of course I reserve to myself the right to go back afterward and battle for X—no matter what I discover in my little fishing trip. Indeed, as an incentive to practice dialectic or binary thinking, I can even console myself on pragmatic or rhetorical grounds: "I'll probably do better at fighting for X and increase my chances of 'winning' if I take this detour into the realm of dialectic and figure out whether the position I want to win with is right or wrong." I've got to write myself a little office memorandum.

(c) When naive scientists say they stay objective and write nothing but facts, current critics and theorists reply, "Haven't you read Thomas Kuhn? There *is* no objectivity or factuality—even in science. All language is interested and biased." But that reply again papers over an important distinction in the interests of a power play, and it is a move that explains why so many scientists, even very sophisticated ones, resist the uses that many humanists and social scientists make of Kuhn. Of course most scientists know that genuine objectivity, truth, or factuality is *not* attainable: certainty cannot be had. Yet for some pieces of discourse—even some very public pieces—they nevertheless and unabashedly measure their success by how *close* they come to exactly those goals: objectivity, truth, factuality, even certainty! Even though the goal is unattainable, it is still possible to measure the value of discourse by how close one gets to it. In short, there is a crucial difference between using language to have an effect or make a case and using language to try to *come as close as possible* to objectivity or facts.

This is a complex and controversial issue, and I don't mind admitting that I am trying to work it out for the first time here. It seems to me that this is an issue where we need to be smart enough to use Aristotle's formulation, "In a sense, . . ." That is, in one sense—or through one lens or to some degree or another—all language is addressed and for an effect: all language has a rhetorical dimension. But in another sense, all language is meaning-making, figuring out, or the play of meaning: all language has a dialectical dimension. This way of talking helps us call attention to a *spectrum* of language uses. At one end are discourses in which the rhetorical use predominates. Rhetoric was developed in response to speech making and public writing—language uses where there is a natural emphasis on persuading an audience. But there is another end to this spectrum where we find discourses in which the dialectical use predominates. Much of our private writing and verbal thinking is discourse of this sort.

Therefore, it is not only helpful to use both terms; it would be a distortion and an oversimplification (and a power play) to restrict ourselves to just one term or "sense" or lens for observing and describing the whole spectrum of language use. At this cultural moment when the rhetorical lens is in the ascendant, I see a need to pay attention to those times when we use language with more open curiosity, more interest in mere figuring out, more willingness to let things turn out any which way. It might be that most of our language use is heavily rhetorical—addressed and for effect; it might be that the rhetorical is the path of habit. But it makes no sense to call all language rhetorical just because there's always a trace of pressure or effect, or because one hasn't learned to use (or notice using) language in a more dialectical fashion.

And of course these pieces of "figuring-out" discourse produced under the goals of dialectic can often be developed into passages that serve rhetorical goals: as address to audience for an effect. (Sometimes they can even be used as they are.) It seems to me that some of my forays into the dialectic uses of language in the process of writing this essay have helped me create some of the rhetoric here.

Let me close by trying for a quick summary overview of this ambitious essay. I am exploring and celebrating one kind of binary thinking: the affirmation or nonresolution of opposed ideas. I'm arguing that this kind of thinking often yields a better model for understanding complex activities like writing and also vexed oppositions like teaching/research. If we sophisticate our epistemology by recognizing that contrary claims can both be right or valid, we can encourage a less adversarial rhetoric. We can invite people to emphasize positive arguments for their position and deemphasize negative arguments against the opposed position—since it may also be valid or correct. In short, we can encourage more productive warfare in our heads and less destructive warfare between people. Finally, we will probably do better at encouraging productive binary thinking if we acknowledge a realm or motive of language use that particularly invites it, namely, dialectic as opposed to rhetoric.

I am very grateful to Charles Moran, John Trimbur, Robin Varnum, and Elizabeth Wallace (among others) for helpful responses and suggestions on this essay.

Works Cited

Belenky, Mary, Nancy Goldberger, Blythe Clinchy, Jill Tarule. *Women's Ways of Knowing.* NY: Basic Books, 1986.
Berlin, James. "Contemporary Composition: The Major Pedagogical Theories." *College English* 44 (1982): 765–77.

————. *Rhetoric and Reality: Writing Instruction in American Colleges, 1909–1985*. Carbondale: Southern Illinois UP, 1987.

Blake. *Marriage of Heaven and Hell*. Oxford: Oxford UP, 1975.

Boyer, E. L. *Scholarship Revisited: Priorities of the Professoriate*. Princeton NJ: Carnegie Foundation for the Advancement of Teaching, 1990.

Brent, Doug. "Young, Becker and Pike's 'Rogerian' Rhetoric: A Twenty-Year Reassessment." *College English* 53.4 (April 1991): 452–66.

Burke, Kenneth. *A Rhetoric of Motives*. Berkeley: U California P, 1969.

Burnham, Chris. "Expressive Rhetoric: A Source Study." *Perspectives on Twentieth Century Rhetoric: Essays Toward Defining the New Rhetorics*. Eds. Theresa Enos and Stuart Brown. Los Angeles: Sage, 1992.

Burtt, Edwin. A. *The Metaphysical Foundations of Modern Physical Science*. Rev ed. Garden City NY: Doubleday, 1954.

Clark, Katerina and Michael Holquist. *Mikhail Bakhtin*. Cambridge: Harvard UP, 1984.

Coleridge, Samuel Taylor. *Biographia Literaria*. Ed. John Shawcross. Oxford: Oxford UP 1907, 2 vols.

Culler, Jonathan. "Paul de Man's Contribution to Literary Criticism and Theory." *The Future of Literary Theory*. Ed. Ralph Cohen. NY: Routledge, 1989. 268–79.

————. *The Pursuit of Signs: Semiotics, Literature, Deconstruction*. Ithaca: Cornell UP, 1981.

Dewey, John. *Democracy in Education*. NY: Macmillan, 1919.

Eagleton, Terry. *Literary Theory: An Introduction*. Minneapolis: University of Minnesota Press, 1983.

Elbow: *Oppositions in Chaucer*. Middletown CT: Wesleyan UP, 1975.

————. *Embracing Contraries: Explorations in Learning and Teaching*. NY Oxford UP, 1986.

————. "Embracing Contraries in the Teaching Process." *College English* 45.4 (April 1983). Also in *Embracing Contraries*.

————. "In Defense of Private Writing: Consequences for Theory and Research." *Written Communication*. 16.2 (Spring 1999): 139–70.

————. "Methodological Doubting and Believing: Contraries in Inquiry." In *Embracing Contraries*.

————. "Nondisciplinary Courses and the Two Roots of Real Learning." In *Embracing Contraries*.

————. "The War between Reading and Writing." *Rhetoric Review* 12.1 (Fall 1993): 5–24. Reprinted in *Critical Theory and the Teaching of Literature: Politics, Curriculum, Pedagogy*. Eds. James F. Slevin and Art Young. Urbana IL: NCTE, 1996. 270–91.

————. *Writing With Power*. NY: Oxford UP, 1981.

————. *Writing Without Teachers*. NY: Oxford UP, 1973.

Frey, Olivia. "Beyond Literary Darwinism: Women's Voices and Critical Discourse." *College English* 52.5 (September 1990): 507–26.

Gibson, Walker, ed. *The Limits of Language*. NY: Hill and Wang, 1962.

Gifis, Steven H. *Law Dictionary*. 3rd ed. NY: Barron's Educational Series, 1991.

Graff, Jerry. *Professing Literature: An Institutional History*. Chicago: U of Chicago P, 1987.

Harris, Jeanette. *Expressive Discourse*. Dallas: Southern Methodist UP, 1990.

Kuhn, Thomas. *The Structure of Scientific Revolutions*. Chicago: U Chicago P, 1962.

LaCapra, Dominick. *Soundings in Critical Theory*. Ithaca: Cornell UP, 1989.

Lakoff, George and Mark Johnson. *Metaphors We Live By*. Chicago: U Chicago P, 1980.

Lamb, Catherine. "Beyond Argument in Feminist Composition." *College Composition and Communication* 42.1 (February 1991): 11–24.

Lawrence, D. H. "Morality and the Novel." *Study of Thomas Hardy and Other Essays*. Ed. Bruce Steele. Cambridge: Cambridge UP, 1985.

Lévi-Strauss, *The Raw and the Cooked*. Trans. John and Doreen Weightman. NY: Harper and Row, 1969.

Lloyd, G. E. R. *Polarity and Analogy: Two Types of Argumentation in Early Greek Thought*. Cambridge: Cambridge UP, 1966.

Mao Tse-Tung. "On Contradiction." *Four Essays on Philosophy*. Peking: Foreign Language Press, 1968.

Mead, George H. *Mind, Self, and Society From the Standpoint of a Social Behaviorist*. Ed. Charles W. Morris. Chicago: U of Chicago P, 1934.

Ong, Walter. *Fighting for Life: Contest, Sexuality, and Consciousness*. Ithaca: Cornell UP, 1981.

Peckham, Morse. *Man's Rage for Chaos: Biology, Behavior and the Arts*. NY: Schocken, 1967.

Perry, William. *Intellectual and Ethical Development in the College Years: A Scheme*. NY: Holt, Rinehart and Winston, 1970.

Reed, Thomas. *Middle English Debate Poetry and the Aesthetics of Irresolution*. U Missouri P, 1990.

Rosenthal, Robert and Lenore Jacobson. *Pygmalion in the Classroom*. New York: Holt Rinehart Winston, 1968.

Schön, Donald A. *The Reflective Practitioner. How Professionals Think in Action*. NY: Basic Books, 1983.

———. *Educating the Reflective Practitioner*. San Francisco: Jossey-Bass, 1987.

Slevin, James. "Depoliticizing and Politicizing Rhetoric and Composition." *The Politics of Writing Instruction*. Eds. Richard Bullock and John Trimbur. Portsmouth, NH: Boynton/Cook Heinemann, 1991. 1–22.

Smith, Barbara Herrnstein. *Contingencies of Value: Alternative Perspectives for Critical Theory*. Cambridge MA: Harvard UP. 1988.

Teich, Nathaniel, ed. *Rogerian Perspectives: Collaborative Rhetoric for Oral and Written Communication*. Norwood NJ: Ablex, 1992.

Trimbur, John. "Consensus and Difference in Collaborative Learning." *College English* 51 (October 1989): 602–16.

The Believing Game

A Challenge after Twenty-Five Years

As I was working on *Writing Without Teachers*, I felt an accusation forming in the minds of intellectuals and academics who might read it:

> In your book, you are jettisoning the very foundations of learning and knowing. You invite the student to get along without any teacher—without anyone who can bring to bear greater training, knowledge, wisdom, or authority. In the place of a teacher, you propose nothing but other students. You do propose a process too, but it is a process devoid of critical thinking, logic, debate, criticism, or doubting. It is a flabby, unintellectual process: trying to listen, to appreciate, to understand, and to experience—and sometimes merely to tell the writer about that experience.

Just this year the editor of the leading journal in composition studies (*College Composition and Communication*), writing a history and analysis of the teaching of writing, made the same charge:

> For there is an odd way in which the students in [Elbow's] workshops, like those in Schultz's, do not seem to be *held answerable to each other as intellectuals*. Readers are simply asked to say what they felt about a text, not to *offer a convincing case* for their readings of it; writers need only respond to those questions about their work that strike them personally as interesting or useful. Students in such a class serve more as sounding boards than as interlocutors. (Harris 31, my emphasis)

He is right that I had removed the *responsibility to argue*. (Though he is wrong to use the phrase "simply say what they felt" as a summary for what I lay out as a disciplined process of trying to articulate the events that go on in one's mind as one reads a text.) But nonargument was my whole point. I was struck then—as I still am—with the *limitations* of argument, doubting, debate, and criticism. I was trying to show the power of a disciplined and methodological use of believing, listening, affirming, entering in, attending to one's experience, and trying to share one's experience with others. I think I see students and writers learning to make their writing work better for readers when they just listen to themselves read it out loud and listen to the "movies of the minds" of different readers who do *not* answer back, argue, or defend.

This is a short section from my Introduction to new a edition of *Writing Without Teachers,* 1998

I wanted to address these objections but I didn't want my theoretical analysis to get in the way of practical people using the book in practical ways. So I made it an appendix ("The Doubting Game and the Believing Game—An Analysis of the Intellectual Enterprise"), and put it into smaller type.

In this appendix essay, I was enormously ambitious. I expanded the scope of enquiry from the realm of writing to epistemology itself—the foundations of knowing. I will briefly summarize my argument here because now, twenty-five years later, I want to invite some specific response.

The argument is about how to get trustworthy knowledge. There are two main things we have to do if we want trustworthy knowledge: we have to *get* ideas and *test* ideas. And whether we are getting or testing ideas, we have two main tools or intellectual methods to use: *doubting* and *believing*. "Doubting" is my shorthand for criticizing, debating, arguing, and trying to extricate oneself from any personal involvement with ideas by means of using logic. "Believing" is my shorthand for listening, affirming, entering in, trying to experience more fully, and restating—understanding ideas from the inside. I argue for the believing game because it is so undervalued and underused—and because the doubting game is so overvalued and overused. Nevertheless, I am not arguing to get rid of the doubting game—only to supplement it.

Let's briefly compare how the two tools or methods work:

For getting ideas. Of course doubting can lead us to new ideas, but the believing game (listening, affirming, trying to see what's right) is also effective, coaxing more ideas out of our own minds and the minds of others we work with. The believing game is particularly useful for eliciting and understanding ideas that are at the limits of what we can imagine or explain—ideas that the doubting game usually sees as completely dubious.

For testing ideas. For this activity, the doubting game (criticizing, debating, and using logic) is widely felt to be preeminent. After all, the goal in testing is to avoid credulity and sloppy thinking. If we are trying not to be sucked into accepting ideas that we love or that serve our interests, what could be more appropriate than doubting, and what could be worse than just listening, believing, and trying to see what's good?

But the core of my appendix is an argument for the counterintuitive idea that we can *also* test ideas effectively with the believing game. But only if we make use of a group and have a disciplined method (the method I worked out in the teacherless class). If we want to use the believing game to test an idea—for example, a particular proposal—we need to proceed as follows. First, bring the proposal to a group and invite everyone to suggest as many different or competing proposals as possible. (Since participants know that we will be playing the believing game with all suggestions, they will give us far more competing proposals to choose from than if we were going to play the doubting game with them and try to criticize or debate or find flaws in their suggestions.) Then choose the proposals that seem to be the most fruitful competitors to the proposal we are trying to test, and play the believing game with each of them: listen and try to experience each one and enter into it. This means harnessing the resources of the group to try to see the maximum number of benefits or advantages of each proposal in turn; seeing what the world looks like through the lens of each competing proposal. On the basis of this process, decide which proposal is most trustworthy or valid. Do any of the competing proposals surpass the one we are trying to test—or show crucial limitations in it?

Notice how the two testing processes (doubting and believing) have different gears or teeth. Where the doubting game tests an idea by helping us see its weaknesses and shortcomings, the believing game tests an idea by helping us see the strengths of competing ideas. Both intellectual processes are valuable, but sometimes we can't see the weakness in an idea or proposal by simply looking for weaknesses. The weaknesses don't show up until we look for strengths in competing ideas. And yet we don't see those strengths until we play the believing game. The doubting game often leaves us stuck in the mental frame of reference of what we are trying to doubt. The best way to get out of our original frame of reference is by playing the believing game with some very different ideas—ideas which at first may appear odd or threatening.

Thus the believing game takes a more roundabout route toward testing: searching out competing ideas and seeking strengths in them—instead of looking directly for weaknesses in what is to be tested. Yet this roundabout path is helpful since the crucial mental event in getting rid of a tempting but bad idea is probably not so much the seeing of flaws but the ability to change one's way of seeing by entering into a variety of contrasting ideas.

Of course neither epistemological game is foolproof; for that reason both games are desirable. But when loyalists to the intellectual status quo want to exclude the believing game from our intellectual armamentarium because it is not critical enough, I cannot resist pointing out how ineffectual the doubting game often is for getting even good critical thinkers to abandon bad ideas that they love—however much they hold themselves "answerable to each other as intellectuals." Since the doubting or arguing process invites people merely to *criticize* ideas they don't like, it permits them to stay insulated against any *experience* of alternative thinking.

Not surprisingly, there was a personal dimension behind my abstract argument. I had had excellent training in the doubting game, but at a certain advanced point in my education (Harvard on top of Oxford on top of Williams!), I found myself no longer able to function as an intellectual. I found eventually that I could only learn to develop and express my ideas when I learned to play something like the believing game with myself and my own words and thoughts.

I don't mean to say that no one can flourish without the believing game. Harvard and Oxford are full of people who flourish using only the doubting game. But I am tempted to believe that the *really* smart and intellectually productive people actually *do* make use of the believing game in their functioning, but that this dimension of their thinking is little noticed because our *conception* of the intellectual process is so dominated by critical thinking. If we had a fuller and more accurate picture of what good thinking looks like, we would see that the intelligence of intelligent people is not just acuteness of critical thinking. And many people who don't *now* look smart or successful in education would be seen as smart, and hence would flourish intellectually.

Finally, I want to call attention to the relationship of doubting and believing to the social dimension. A group is the engine of the believing game. Without other people to work with, we have no strong tool for coming up with competing ideas—which is our leverage for testing. And we have no strong tool for entering into alien or foreign ideas, except by having other people tell us about them and describe the view from inside them. Without others, the believing game is crippled. This parallels the argument in the rest of *Writing Without Teachers*: we can get along without teachers, but only if we make primary use of a group of people sharing their experiences with each other—using a process that invites the maximum multiplicity or divergence of views and asks participants not to quarrel with what looks odd or alien but to try to experience and enter into it.

The doubting game, on the other hand, has a strong and trustworthy tool for getting and testing ideas, even if we are all alone: logic. Logic provides a set of rules for testing ideas and for generating new ideas as consequences of the ones in hand—rules that we can use and trust even if we have no help from other people.

A challenge. I dedicated my book to "people who actually use it—not just read it," and I put my theory in an appendix because I didn't want readers to bog down in my theorizing. My strategy worked: lots of people have used the writing process, and teacherless groups are now widely assumed as standard practice in the teaching of writing. There's been a steady stream of research, scholarship, and reflection on teacherless groups, how they function, and how to use them in the teaching of writing. (Of course, teacherless groups lose some of their essence when teachers require students to take part in them. And yet there is still something radical about teachers giving an important function to activities in which they take no part.)

But *now*, in writing this introduction, I am looking for people in the field of composition and rhetoric to engage me at the theoretical level too. In twenty-five years, I don't know anyone who has ever really done so—despite an incredible flowering of theory, much of it epistemological, and despite plenty of criticism of me. In the field of women's studies and human development, Mary Belenky, Nancy Goldberger, Blythe Clinchy, Jill Tarule made notable use of the concept of belief in their important book, *Women's Ways of Knowing* (and Clinchy further in their follow-up collection of essays). But I don't know anyone in my field who has actually engaged the substance of the argument about the epistemological strengths of the doubting and believing games—even with my fuller and more scholarly analysis of doubting and believing in 1985, "Methodological Doubting and Believing: Contraries in Inquiry."

Of course a number of people have criticized my general approach as unintellectual and invalid *because* it avoids argument, debate, and critical thinking (e.g., Harris, Hashimoto). But by merely criticizing me for leaving out argument and criticism, they simply evade my argument itself, namely, that the believing game *can* have epistemological bite or leverage even though it dispenses with critical argument.

James Berlin does write briefly of my epistemology, but it's hard to believe that he looked carefully at what I wrote. For he says that I'm a Platonist who believes that knowledge is totally private, whereas I make it clear that both the teacherless class and the epistemology of the believing game can only function as group processes, and that their validity derives only from people entering into each others' diverse and conflicting experiences. I argue specifically that the very meaning of any spoken or written discourse is entirely dependent on groups and communities (see page 156 of *Writing Without Teachers*). The teacherless class and the believing game are completely undermined if one tries to function solo. (Berlin summarizes my epistemology as follows: "It is . . . only the individual, acting alone and apart from others, who can determine the existent, the good, and the possible" [486].)

Wayne Booth wrote a seminal and important study of doubting and believing (*Modern Dogma and the Rhetoric of Assent*), but so far from challenging my argument, he moves in exactly the same direction. (He didn't make quite as strong an epistemological claim as I did, and in fact he centered his argument more in rhetoric than in epistemology.) He didn't mention my book but that's not surprising, since his came out the year after mine did, and mine was virtually unnoticed for a number of years.

So now I have a chance to show that I mean it when I say I also value the doubting game and critical thinking. I wish someone would try using them on my argument to see what we can learn.

Works Cited

Belenky, Mary, Nancy Goldberger, Blythe Clinchy, Jill Tarule. *Women's Ways of Knowing*. NY: Basic Books, 1986.

Berlin, James. "Rhetoric and Ideology in the Writing Class." *College English* 50.5 (Sept 1988): 477–94.

Booth, Wayne. *Modern Dogma and the Rhetoric of Assent*. Chicago: U of Chicago P, 1974.

Clinchy, Blythe. "Separate and Connected Knowing." *Knowledge, Difference, Power: Essays Inspired by Women's Ways of Knowing*. Eds. Nancy Rule Goldberger, Blythe Clinchy, Jill Tarule, and Mary Belenky. NY: Basic Books, 1996.

Elbow, Peter. "Methodological Doubting and Believing: Contraries in Inquiry." *Embracing Contraries: Explorations in Learning and Teaching*. NY: Oxford UP, 1986.

Harris, Joe. *A Teaching Subject: Composition Since 1966*. Upper Saddle River NJ: Prentice-Hall, 1997.

Part II

THE GENERATIVE DIMENSION

Peter, why are you so hung up with writing as mystery—as though the writer must emulate God and create *ex nihilo,* and singlehandedly? Why won't you accept the fact that sometimes writing doesn't require any new thinking; that most of what we write is really borrowed; that some writers do better not to start with chaos? The fact is that some writers need a tight careful outline and they need to stick to it carefully in order to do their best work—especially if they have a deadline. And some writers don't want to close their eyes and put the reader out of mind. Why won't you accept writing as a matter of skill, rationality, and craft, rather than as playing God or jumping into the unknown? Not everyone is a romantic you know.

I guess my preoccupation with writing as mystery comes from my formative experience with writing: I *had* skill, rationality, and craft, and yet I still found myself unable to do it. Yet even though the experience behind my attitudes was singular and personal, I've found my preoccupations useful—and not just for me but for others too. I think the mystery is actually there. Perhaps that makes me a romantic. I'll accept that—as long as you don't define romantics as self-centered, blind, asocial creeps.

I can't let go of the sense that the central mystery in writing is the business of trying to fish words and ideas from your head. So all the essays in this section deal with this process. Where do ideas come from? How can we think of things we've never thought of before? Why is it that sometimes we can find words and thoughts and sometimes we cannot? (In *Writing With Power* I wasn't so one-sided.)

We don't have to role-play God to write, but if we want to do our best work, I think we do need to cultivate *daring, courage,* and *belief in oneself.* Putting this the other way around, I keep discovering that most people's central experience in writing is *difficulty, fear,* and *anxiety*—and that's true for many skilled and successful writers.

But like any good romantic, I resist the need for an either/or choice between writing as mystery and writing as rationality and craft. Courage and belief in oneself are not the opposite of craft and rational control. In fact, in these essays I'm trying to bring conscious craft, planning, and control *to bear* on the mystery of writing. I think we can get better at learning to control our generative process. Thus I'm trying for a more sophisticated technology or larger rationality—even though it may not *look* rational compared to conventional notions of rationality and control. In order to be as deeply rational as I am trying to be, I have learned to give hostages to irrationality, noncontrol, garbage, and chaos.

In traditional rhetoric, this process of generating was called "invention." Aristotle was interested in invention and had a lot of good suggestions to help speakers come up with ideas. But after the waning of classical rhetoric, invention tended to be neglected. Perhaps understandably, people tended to shy away from trying to formulate principles for where ideas come from and how to find them. But the beginnings of the modern field of composition in this century can perhaps be characterized as a time when people (myself included) found themselves saying, "Well let's *do* talk about where ideas and words come from." More about this in the fragment at the end of this part, "The Neglect and Rediscovery of Invention."

Certainly, in my history as a writer, generativity or invention was key. After my writing broke down in graduate school, I didn't learn to get things written till I learned two crucial principles for generating.

The first is the need for inviting chaos. I couldn't even produce a draft till I learned to think of writing as inevitably making a mess: just putting down words as they come and not worrying about the disorder of it. Freewriting turns out to be the easiest way to learn how to do this. It has rational rules, it provides a kind of control: just write without stopping—but only for ten minutes, and it's private, and don't worry about quality or correctness or even whether it makes sense.

There are two essays about freewriting in this section. The first is a fairly brief practical essay published for professionals and academics outside of composition who want to be more productive in their own writing. The second is a long essay written to people in composition, in which I try to use some of my own writing and experience to analyze both the rationality and the mystery of freewriting. Readers may find this too much about freewriting, but I never tire of trying to understand what seems to me the central and also the most rewarding experience in writing: coming to think of something you hadn't thought of before. How can something as crudely simple as freewriting be endless in its usefulness and implications?

Implicit in freewriting is the *second* essential principle for generating words and ideas: ignoring the audience. Thus the essay here, "Closing My Eyes as I Speak." Stop thinking about readers, about what others will think, about potential criticism. Yes, there are exceptions. It can help to think about readers while you write *if* your readers are inviting and supportive or somehow bring out your best, or *if* they annoy or infuriate you in just the right way. But because most advice to writers and students is to keep their readers in mind, I want to work overtime to peddle a larger and more accurate principle: try thinking of readers and see if it helps; usually, especially in the beginning, you will find it helpful to put readers out of mind for a while.

In the end, of course, we have to think about readers. No matter how wonderful our ideas are, we want to make them work *for* readers. We see here something interesting about the culture of writing: most traditional advice grows out of a *neglect* for generating or invention. "Keep readers in mind." "Make an outline." "Stay in control." These are great pieces of advice for revising. But they tend to be bad advice for generating or invention.

There is a *third* principle central to generating that I only learned much later from Sondra Perl, and it is perhaps the most fruitful—certainly the most mysterious: consult "felt sense." I describe this process in the fragment here, "Wrongness and Felt Sense." This process builds on the connection between writing and the *body*. We sometimes forget that language, and even writing itself, probably derive from gesture. The meanings and potential meanings in our mind are almost invariably implicit in our body. We don't often enough notice a central process in most successful writing: a process of constantly moving our attention back and forth between the words in our minds and our *nonverbal sense* of meaning and intention in our bodies and feelings. Implicit in the recognition of felt sense is the recognition famously formulated by Polanyi in his term "tacit meaning": *we always know more than we can put into words*. Yet if we manage ourselves well (here is craft and control again), we can in fact get more of that tacit knowledge into words and conscious awareness.

4

Freewriting and the Problem of Wheat and Tares

Many people think that freewriting is only for young or unskilled writers: a babyish artificial exercise that would never benefit professionals. Freewriting *is* an artificial exercise—and it seems too easy—but I've found it continues to be of enormous help to me and to other professionals and skilled writers.

But first, what is freewriting? It is simply private, nonstop writing. Freewriting is what you get when you remove most of the constraints involved in writing. Freewriting means

- not showing your words to anyone (unless you later change your mind);
- not having to stay on one topic—that is, freely digressing;
- not thinking about spelling, grammar, and mechanics;
- not worrying about how good the writing is—even whether it makes sense or is understandable (even to oneself).

One constraint remains, however—which is the most imperious constraint of all: having to put words on paper and indeed to put them down without stopping. Notice the paradoxical, double-pronged emphasis here: on the one hand, freewriting seems to remove all risk by removing all the constraints we associate with writing; yet on the other hand, it also *adds* risk by asking us in effect to blurt continuously. Putting it the other way around, freewriting asks us to do the most frightening thing of all, write nonstop—but in a vacuum of unusual safety.

What follows from this definition of freewriting is that there is no such thing as freewriting well or badly. One has freewritten *perfectly* so long as one

This essay was published in 1992 in *Writing and Publishing for Academic Authors*. Ed. Joseph Moxley. NY: University Press of America, 1992. 33–47. 2nd ed., Lanham MD: Rowman & Littlefield, 1997. 35–47.

has written constantly. This functional or process-centered definition clarifies the status of variations on freewriting that result from reimposing certain constraints:

- Focused freewriting asks us to stay on one topic.
- Public freewriting asks us to share our words with others.[1]

Most people learn and practice freewriting in "freewriting exercises" of ten or fifteen minutes of nonstop writing. As with any exercise, the presence of someone in charge and fellow writers taking part can help us break out of accustomed habits and reflexes (such as the reflex to stop and weigh choices in mid-course). But plenty of people manage to learn freewriting alone. As we get comfortable and practiced at freewriting exercises, the process begins to affect much of our early exploratory writing, and we can move in and out of the freewriting mode at various moments in the writing process. It can be especially helpful at moments of blockage and confusion.

———————

I became interested in freewriting because of my own difficulties with writing. During my first year of graduate school I gradually lost the ability to get my papers written, and I had to quit before getting kicked out. When I returned five years later, I discovered that the only way I could count on writing papers was to force myself to *blurt* onto paper pages and pages of exploratory thinking and musing and perplexity—a full week before the deadline. Once I had at least ten pages of messy, wandering, first thoughts more or less about the topic, I found I could write my ten-page paper without undue difficulty.

In this chapter I present four important benefits of freewriting.

The first benefit of freewriting is crudely practical. Freewriting gets you going, gets you writing, makes it much easier to begin. With freewriting, "starting to write" means just blurting out first thoughts, musings, and perplexities, starting anywhere—not trying to write a draft. For me and many others, the most dispiriting thing about writing is not having written yet, and the most empowering thing is simply to *have* lots of raw material already down to work with—even if it's not very good.

Thus, regular freewriting exercises help us develop a "freewriting muscle": the capacity to just *let* words come to mind and immediately write them down, the ability to follow the path those words suggest, to follow the path of the mind as it wonders and wanders. With this muscle we can then benefit from *focused freewriting*: exploring a particular topic or issue, finding lots of things to say, finding words for them, and filling up lots of sheets of paper.

1. This description is adapted from the introduction to *Nothing Begins with N: New Investigations of Freewriting,* a collection of interesting essays about freewriting edited by Pat Belanoff, Peter Elbow, and Sheryl Fontaine; Southern Illinois University Press, 1991.

In other words, the mind is a mess but writing must be neat, and it's too difficult for most of us to leap in one bound from a messy mind to neat writing. But freewriting serves as a helpful intermediate platform: messy writing. We can get the contents of the mind down on paper—even if incoherent and messy. Oddly enough, it is much easier than most people realize to shape messy freewriting into clear, coherent thinking—easier than revising and reshaping a careful draft. The careful draft has cost so much time and effort that changing it is painful; furthermore, the careful draft is intricately wired together with lots of complexity, and so making one change mucks up everything else. A freewritten draft, on the other hand, is crude and rough and easy to cut, add to, and rearrange.

The second benefit is that freewriting doesn't just get words on paper, it improves thinking. I'm convinced it's the no-stopping rule that has this effect. When we have to keep on writing even when we run out of things to say or have second thoughts or change our mind, we naturally drift into writing *metadiscourse:* "Wait a minute, what I just wrote doesn't make sense" or "I just realized that such-and-such contradicts what I just wrote." Under normal conditions we stop writing when we have thoughts like that. But when freewriting leads us to write such thoughts down instead of just thinking them, the process improves and enriches our thinking. The nonstop exploratory process usually encourages us to continue and to articulate *why* our thoughts don't make sense or *what* our dilemma is, and that articulation on paper is the best leverage for sound thinking and new ideas. This benefit has something to do with *dialogue* as the most generative and fruitful form of discourse for thinking. Freewriting encourages us to have dialogues with ourselves.

Third, freewriting puts life into our writing: voice, energy, presence. That is, even though freewriting can lead to incoherence or even garbage, freewritten language is usually livelier than our careful writing because freewriting leads us to *speak on paper.* We can later get rid of the garbage and change the structure and still *use* many of the phrases, sentences, and even longer passages of what we have written—and thereby carry that verbal energy over into a carefully structured and revised piece. In addition, regular freewriting gradually and subtly brings more voice even into the sentences that we labor over. I now revise my careful prose with the sound of live speech in my ear.

Voice and energy are rare qualities in prose, and they are hard to achieve with our usual efforts to improve our writing. We've all tried to remedy a clogged or dead piece of writing. We've struggled to rewrite its sentences, to activate passives, and to cut adjectives and clauses; and we've improved it. But *still* the piece is heavy and wooden. Freewriting, on the other hand, tends to put life into our language with no effort or struggle.

Certain writers have a "voice" in their writing—a spring in their step. When we read their words we hear them. We sometimes hear a voice in our informal writing, such as our letters. But lively voiced writing doesn't have to be informal. Freewriting helps us get that voice into our more careful writing. We can keep the voice and still have a text that is tight, disciplined, and carefully crafted.

The fourth benefit is even more subtle—but perhaps most important. Most of us do not think of ourselves as "writers." *Finally* I do. Few of us make our living from writing, and the concept of *writer* tends to carry all sorts of cultural baggage, like creative genius and suffering. But if we write regularly, we *are* writers. I've found that students and adult professionals who write get a big boost by acknowledging that they are writers—a surprisingly mysterious and difficult inner adjustment of the mind and feelings. The fourth benefit of freewriting is that it can help us *experience* ourselves as writers in certain deeply transformative ways. That is, freewriting doesn't just help us get a lot of useful words on paper. It helps us find some enjoyment in writing. Because it takes much of the struggle out of putting down words, we find ourselves coming up with words, thoughts, and memories that surprise us. We find writing as an occasion of discovery and of getting to know and appreciate our own mind.

Freewriting can give us little temporary visits into the place of "being a writer" in an interesting additional sense. It can give us little visits into a closet where, temporarily and with almost no penalties, we can allow our mind and our feelings complete free rein. This is a door into realms of intuition, insight, and intelligence that we can seldom tap in careful writing or in speech. In short, freewriting is a way to have little bite-sized bits of nonsublimation. And this is the region where we are smartest and most creative—and where our language is most alive.

Perhaps I make all this sound too simple and automatic. Of course freewriting can lead to some uncertainty and struggle. It makes some people nervous. You have to *let go* a bit. (But not so much: after all, there is no need to write about deep dark secret feelings—just keep the mind and the hand on task. And in conditions of safety.) And freewriting is a new "gear" for writing. When people really start to use it, sometimes there are some grinding noises as they shift back and forth. Sometimes at first there is a temptation to lurch into too much informality. (Though I can't resist an intriguing question here: Too much for what? For in the last decade or so, we have been seeing a gradual but steady movement toward informality in professional and academic writing.)

It is one thing to understand what freewriting is, and perhaps even to suspect that it might be useful. It's probably more valuable to get a feel for it in action. Therefore, I include next a long piece of freewriting I did to get myself started on this essay (though I had already jotted down a note to myself suggesting three main ideas). Note that what follows is *focused* and *public* freewriting, not "pure" freewriting. That is, I operated under two constraints: first, I kept my writing confined to one topic—stopping myself from making the digressions I often make in freewriting. Second, I felt exposed while I was writing since I already had the idea of perhaps using the freewriting itself in my essay as an illustration of the process. Because of these two constraints, what you see here is less incoherent and unbuttoned than my fully private freewriting. Nevertheless, it is freewriting: I never stopped for more than three or four seconds, and I haven't changed anything here except to fix spelling and punctuation and add a few words in brackets.[2]

> I've got to get going. How late can I get? I've got to get going. Where to start. I did have an idea for a structure. First pragmatic reasons and arguments: fw [freewriting] gets you going, gets you the main thing you need—words on the page—the end of a blank sheet—getting going. (It didn't seem to succeed in making me start on time, however.) Second. Second. What was it? Something medium—yes, now I remember, voice. It gets a voice into the language. Makes the language be alive, not dead. Makes it so that readers feel some energy or some life in the language. Careful writing is so often dead and horrible to read. What I like to say: I've never met a piece of freewriting I couldn't understand—and I've met LOTS of careful writing that I couldn't understand. Though understanding is not the same as life. But I care so much about both. But VOICE is the theoretical issue that's closest to my life. There's something so pleasing about reading words on a page where you hear a SOUND come up off the paper; where you sense there's someone HOME inside there—where you knock it and it gives off a solid sound; where you can hear a bit of the drama of the mind at work. (A crucial distinction: the difference between words that are the record of a mind having been at work—the summary of PAST action; vs. words that are the dramatization or enactment of a mind AT WORK [IN THE PRESENT]. Of course there's a trade-off: the reasons for using writing for a record of past activity is that it can be cleaned up and made neat—that the mind at work is not a pretty thing—messy and confusing; yet on the other hand there is an energy and drama that comes

[interruption; household duties for more than an hour].

> where was I

> energy and drama that comes from reading words that—from words that follow the mind on its journey. And it's possible to save the energy and life and drama—and still clean up and clarify the structure.) What else, what else. I've lost the thread. Yes what's the third idea. This is a more "far out" idea but close to my heart; triggered by a graduate student's paper. Freud says that repression is necessary for civilization—that we can't live with the id steering; and that writing and art in particular are areas that reflect repression (like dreams?). But (as Dix McComas points out)—(What's his name—at Yale) [Harold Bloom] argues that writers REFUSE and RESIST repression. That writing is a place where we can let the id off its leash a bit—let it run around and romp and make a mess. Writers are people who refuse to stay out of touch with the desires and hungers that reality won't accommodate—people with hungers and visions that they refuse to become numb to. (Does this ex-

2. Also, about half a dozen times I deleted a word I'd just written and immediately wrote another. For example, near the end, I remember writing "saying" and changing it right away to "arguing." (Because I was writing on a computer, there is no visual record.) Should we call these lapses from real freewriting? Who knows? I encourage people not to make changes, but it seems too purist to forbid them altogether—especially if one doesn't stop, there is no rereading, and the essential motion is forward.

plain why there is a lot of tortured and destructive behavior by writers? All that alcoholism.) I think this is a bit hyperbolic about writing in general—though a tempting and attractive theory. But it fits freewriting to a T.

I just realized that if I use this freewriting for my article, I'll have to start with a concrete simple description and explanation of freewriting. Yes; and I've got to do a bit of freewriting here about whom I'm writing for.

Freewriting is a place where there is maximum safety and maximum invitation for the buried places of the mind and the emotions to have a little space—to come out into the sunlight and look around and blink their eyes and for us to see what they have to say to us. I think I won't have much of that kind of thing in this freewriting since it is public freewriting, not private freewriting as freewriting normally is. I've been conscious all along of the possibility of using this freewriting for my article. Is it too much of a gimmick? Maybe. But I want people to see what it's like. Nothing much gained from theoretical talk, abstract talk, statements of principles. Will I let myself change things? I don't know.

What I like about freewriting (that last sentence reminds me) is that it's a chance to talk to yourself. I keep coming across people who say that there is no such thing as private writing, all writing is social. I guess in some theoretical (and I guess important) way that is true, but I find it very precious that when I really get going in freewriting, I talk to myself. And in doing so, I get clear of hangups or pressures of audience. Talking to myself often gives me my best ideas. And it's a fairly rare gift: the ability to genuinely talk to yourself. I call it "desert island discourse": especially hard for young people. Yet I want to call it a prerequisite to genuine intelligence and good quality thinking: the ability to carry on a dialogue with yourself and not need the "right" or "good" others to talk to. You often can't find a good partner for dialogue about some issue you are trying to figure out—but ONESELF is always a good partner if I can simply be honest with myself, nondefensive, open. And that's not so hard when I know it's private writing. I guess I don't have trouble believing it because I've done it many times and it's succeeded in giving me good thoughts.

What next, what next, what next. I guess those three [main overarching] ideas would do—would serve as a structure for a short article.

Let me think for a moment about audience. I've written about freewriting in books for students and writers, but this is, Joe tells me, for professionals and academics. I was tempted to turn down the assignment because I've got too many things I've been trying to write—too busy—but I DO want to talk to this audience about this issue. That is, it makes me so mad when people assume in a condescending way that freewriting is good for kids and for incompetent basic writers—it's a "baby" exercise—that no mature and skilled [writer] would want to use it. And yet, though it IS good for struggling nonwriters, it's BEST for skilled adults and professionals. When I use it with teachers and good writers, then the freewriting is really appreciated most and leads to wonderful stuff. (Though they have to be willing; some refuse to give it a try because it feels too "babyish" or "artificial" to them.)

So how do I talk to professionals and academics? I can't be too missionary and preachy. That's a tone I naturally want to fall into; and I feel missionary about it. My instinct is that freewriting is the single best help to anybody's writing. (Like patent medicines: good for snake bite, measles, flu, menstrual cramps—and also for cleaning the family silver.) How do I talk? I want to be pragmatic. I sense the danger is not only if they see me as preachy—but also if they see it as too "arty" or "poetic" or "personal" or "emotional." Yet on the other hand, there's a danger in projecting an image of them [readers] as [nothing but the] hard-assed, closed, rigid people whom I've sometimes encountered: the dangers of writing to the enemy. What is their situation? Like mine: having lots of things to write; always being behind, being skilled at words and even at writing—but (here this differs from how I now feel) being skittish and even scared about writing. Having mostly unpleasant experience at writing.

Yes. Where could I talk about this: that the main experience that makes writing POSITIVE and REWARDING is the experience of surprise: steaming along and finding yourself writing something you didn't "know" before: "Oh, I didn't know I felt that way" or "Oh, I'd forgotten all about that memory or that book I once read" or "Oh, I never thought of looking at the problem this way" (put this last [example] first). That's so gratifying: finding that there are things in your head you didn't know were there; or finding that your head can "grow" new ideas, new angles, new points of view all by itself. (And I'm sure it's the principle of dialogue that does this: the activity of things interacting with each other—back and forth—that is generative.) Yes, it is the generativity of the mind that is so exciting, and what makes freewriting useful is that it heightens or unleashes the generativity of the mind more than anything else I know.

Yes, perhaps that sums up the two first sections: generativity and voice.

Notice here (I'm thinking about the audience reading this) how what I've just done illustrates how freewriting often works: that what I END UP WITH is clarity and sharpness: a single word to sum up each of my [first two] main points [generativity and voice]. I don't start with clarity; I use writing to achieve clarity. That's how writing is supposed to work, and freewriting heightens it.

I guess I'll stop here. I set my stop watch to be able to say how long this took me, but I forgot to turn it on again after my first interruption.

[A final bit of freewriting—after a pause.] Reading over (fixing spelling and adding minor bits in brackets) there's another thing I want to stress; it especially pertains to private writing. Freewriting is a place where one's private or scary feelings can come out—where one can find words for feelings you are not sure of or feel timid about. It's much safer than talking—since when you talk, there's always someone who has heard you. Fw is really private [—genuinely safe], just rip it up. But I don't mean so much to stress here the "therapeutic" dimension—a place to "deal with feelings" (though why must I run away from that if [I'm] writing for professionals? They are just as battered by their emotional life as the rest of the population). I want to stress how our best "professional" and "academic" thinking is all mixed up with feelings. That my reasons for arguing X or Y tend to be a mixture of personal and professional. I have feelings about why I like X as an idea—or hate Y—or the same thing with persons that are involved in an issue, and those personal feelings may not be appropriate for a professional piece of writing. But if I try to keep them out of my exploratory writing, it makes me write in a more halting way; constantly [holding back, or] stopping and seeing whether what I just wrote is perhaps not appropriate—often leaving out a thought that just occurred to me. Yet I think all that stuff is important for my thinking. I think I do better at trying to think straight when I leave them all mixed up and leave till later the idea of sorting them out. (Just made me think of the parable of the wheat and the tares: someone sowed weeds in among the good seed and Christ—or is it just the character in the parable?—says, well leave them all in together, let them grow together; if we tried to remove the weeds we harm the wheat. Let them all come to harvest—and then at harvest time we'll take them all—but keep only the wheat and put the others into the fires of destruction. Rather a grim and apocalyptic analogy—but it does say exactly what I mean: that if we try to root out unsuitable words and thoughts when they are all tender seedlings, it screws up the good stuff. Indeed—and this isn't in the parable—we can't TELL at early seedling time WHETHER something is weed or wheat.)

Let's stop there. I wonder if that would make a title "Freewriting: A Way to Deal with Wheat and Tares." A little obscure, but pleasingly "toney." Do I really want a biblical allusion in the title? Freewriting will bring you to heaven and if you don't, you'll go to hell? Like I said, avoid preaching at all costs!

Before you say, "Freewriting can't make that much difference for me," ask yourself, "Have I ever experienced it? Have I done writing that is genuinely private—that I really don't plan to show to anyone; writing that is genuinely nonstop; and for ten minutes? And have I actually done this three times?"— since the first two times may simply feel too odd.

So try it. Set yourself up with paper or the computer.[3] Look at the clock and give yourself ten minutes. Start writing. Just start with some issue or question you would like to think about. Or start with whatever happens to be on your mind at the moment. Or start by describing your day or the room. Let yourself digress, but don't let yourself stop. When you run out or get confused, change the subject or write, "My mind is blank" or "I'm confused" or "Damn" or "Where shall I go next?"

It's important to realize that of course our fingers cannot keep up with our minds and we are not trying for some perfect psychoanalytic or novelistic stream of consciousness. Freewriting is fine if it is completely orderly and nonpersonal. There is no kind of writing that constitutes better or right freewriting. If you write without stopping, you have freewritten just right. If you feel that freewriting is not leading you to "lively personal writing," don't worry. The whole point of freewriting is to accept anything, to trust it, to trust your mind. Even if you write "I have nothing to say" over and over for ten minutes—and do this for three or four sessions in a row, that is fine. It happens. The goal is not a product but a process. When you allow freewriting to create an arena of trust, there is no telling what kind of writing will emerge. Things change and that is one of the main benefits of freewriting.

3. Computers, by the way, permit an interesting freewriting variation that some people find helpful: "invisible writing." Turn down the screen so you can't see what you are writing. This feels odd at first, but it gets you to focus your concentration more intensely upon the point of your own emerging thinking *in your head*—rather than upon your words. What often stops us in our writing is our awareness of the completed words on the page or screen.

5

Closing My Eyes as I Speak

An Argument for Ignoring Audience

> Very often people don't listen to you when you speak to them. It's
> only when you talk to yourself that they prick up their ears.
>
> John Ashberry

When I am talking to a person or a group and struggling to find words or
thoughts, I often find myself involuntarily closing my eyes as I speak. I realize
now that this behavior is an instinctive attempt to blot out awareness of audience when I need all my concentration for just trying to figure out or express
what I want to say. Because the audience is so imperiously *present* in a speaking situation, my instinct reacts with this active attempt to avoid audience
awareness. This behavior—in a sense impolite or anti-social—is not so uncommon. Even when we write, alone in a room to an absent audience, there
are occasions when we are struggling to figure something out and need to
push aside awareness of those absent readers. As Donald Murray puts it, "My
sense of audience is so strong that I have to suppress my conscious awareness
of audience to hear what the text demands" (Berkenkotter and Murray 171).
In recognition of how pervasive the role of audience is in writing, I write to
celebrate the benefits of ignoring audience.[1]

This essay was published in 1987 in *College English* 49.1 (Jan): 50–69.

1. There are many different entities called audience: (a) The actual readers to whom the text
will be given; (b) the writer's conception of those readers—which may be mistaken (see Ong;
Park; Ede and Lunsford); (c) the audience that the text implies—which may be different still (see
Booth); (d) the discourse community or even genre addressed or implied by the text (see Walzer);
(e) ghost or phantom "readers in the head" that the writer may unconsciously address or try to

It will be clear that my argument for writing without audience awareness is not meant to undermine the many good reasons for writing *with* audience awareness some of the time (for example, that we are liable to neglect the audience because we write in solitude; that young people often need more practice in taking into account points of view different from their own; and that students often have an impoverished sense of writing as communication because they have only written in a school setting to teachers). Indeed, I would claim some part in these arguments for audience awareness—which now seem to be getting out of hand.

I start with a limited claim: even though ignoring audience will usually lead to weak writing at first, to what Linda Flower calls "writer-based prose," this weak writing can help us in the end to better writing than we would have written if we'd kept readers in mind from the start. Then I will make a more ambitious claim: writer-based prose is sometimes better *as it is* than reader-based prose. Finally, I will explore some of the theory underlying these issues of audience.

A Limited Claim

It's not that writers should never think about their audience. It's a question of when. An audience is a field of force. The closer we come—the more we think about these readers—the stronger the pull they exert on the contents of our minds. The practical question, then, is always whether a particular audience functions as a helpful field of force or one that confuses or inhibits us.

Some audiences, for example, are *inviting* or *enabling*. When we think about them as we write, we think of more and better things to say—and what we think somehow arrives more coherently structured than usual. It's like talking to the perfect listener: we feel smart and come up with ideas we didn't know we had. Such audiences are helpful to keep in mind right from the start.

Other audiences, however, are powerfully inhibiting—so much so, in certain cases, that awareness of them as we write blocks writing altogether. There are certain people who always make us feel dumb when we try to speak to them: we can't find words or thoughts. As soon as we get out of their presence, all the things we wanted to say pop back into our minds. Here is a student telling what happens when she tries to follow the traditional advice about audience:

> You know _____ [author of a text] tells us to pay attention to the audience that will be reading our papers, and I gave that a try. I ended up with-

---

please (see Elbow, *Writing With Power* 186ff. Classically, this is a powerful former teacher. Often such an audience is so ghostly as not to show up as actually "implied" by the text). For the essay I am writing here, these differences don't much matter: I'm celebrating the ability to put aside the needs or demands of *any* or all of these audiences. I recognize, however, that we sometimes cannot fight our way free of unconscious or tacit audiences (as in b or e above) unless we bring them to greater conscious awareness.

out putting a word on paper until I decided the hell with _____ ; I'm going to write to who I damn well want to; otherwise I can hardly write at all.

Admittedly, there are some occasions when we benefit from keeping a threatening audience in mind from the start. We've been putting off writing that letter to that person who intimidates us. When we finally sit down and write *to* them—walk right up to them, as it were, and look them in the eye—we may manage to stand up to the threat and grasp the nettle and thereby find just what we need to write.

Most commonly, however, the effect of audience awareness is somewhere between the two extremes: the awareness disturbs or disrupts our writing and thinking without completely blocking it. For example, when we have to write to someone we find intimidating (and of course students often perceive teachers as intimidating), we often start thinking wholly defensively. As we write down each thought or sentence, our mind fills with thoughts of how the intended reader will criticize or object to it. So we try to qualify or soften what we've just written—or write out some answer to a possible objection. Our writing becomes tangled. Sometimes we get so tied in knots that we cannot even figure out what we *think*. We may not realize how often audience awareness has this effect on our students when we don't see the writing processes behind their papers: we just see texts that are either tangled or empty.

Another example. When we have to write to readers with whom we have an awkward relationship, we often start beating around the bush and feeling shy or scared, or start to write in a stilted, overly careful style or voice. (Think about the cute, too-clever style of many memos we get in our departmental mailboxes—the awkward self-consciousness academics experience when writing to other academics.) When students are asked to write to readers they have not met or cannot imagine, such as "the general reader" or "the educated public," they often find nothing to say except cliches they know *they* don't even quite believe.

When we realize that an audience is somehow confusing or inhibiting us, the solution is fairly obvious. We can ignore that audience altogether during the *early* stages of writing and direct our words only to ourselves or to no one in particular—or even to the "wrong" audience, that is, to an *inviting* audience of trusted friends or allies. This strategy often dissipates the confusion; the clenched, defensive discourse starts to run clear. Putting audience out of mind is of course a traditional practice: serious writers have long used private journals for early explorations of feeling, thinking, or language. But many writing teachers seem to think that students can get along without the private writing serious writers find so crucial—or even that students will *benefit* from keeping their audience in mind for the whole time. Things often don't work out that way.

After we have figured out our thinking in copious exploratory or draft writing—perhaps finding the right voice or stance as well—*then* we can follow the traditional rhetorical advice: think about readers and revise carefully to adjust our words and thoughts to our intended audience. For a particular audience it may even turn out that we need to *disguise* our point of view. But it's hard to disguise something while engaged in trying to figure it out. As writers, then, we need to learn when to think about audience and when to put readers out of mind.

Many people are too quick to see Linda Flower's "writer-based prose" as an analysis of what's *wrong* with this type of writing and miss the substantial degree to which she was celebrating a natural, and indeed developmentally enabling, response to cognitive overload. What she doesn't say, however, despite her emphasis on planning and conscious control in the writing process, is that we can *teach* students to notice when audience awareness is getting in their way—and when this happens, consciously to put aside the needs of readers for a while. She seems to assume that when an overload occurs, the writer-based gear will, as it were, automatically kick into action to relieve it. In truth, of course, writers often persist in using a malfunctioning *reader-*based gear despite the overload—thereby mangling their language or thinking. Though Flower likes to rap the knuckles of people who suggest a "correct" or "natural" order for steps in the writing process, she implies such an order here: when attention to audience causes an overload, start out by ignoring them while you attend to your thinking; after you work out your thinking, turn your attention to audience.

Thus if we ignore audience while writing on a topic about which we are not expert or about which our thinking is still evolving, we are likely to produce exploratory writing that is unclear to anyone else—perhaps even inconsistent or a complete mess. Yet by doing this exploratory "swamp work" in conditions of safety, we can often coax our thinking through a process of new discovery and development. In this way we can end up with something better than we could have produced if we'd tried to write to our audience all along. In short, ignoring audience can lead to worse drafts but better revisions. (Because we are professionals and adults, we often write in the role of expert: we may know what we think without new exploratory writing; we may even be able to speak confidently to critical readers. But students seldom experience this confident professional stance in their writing. And think how much richer *our* writing would be if we defined ourselves as *in*expert and allowed ourselves private writing for new explorations of those views we are allegedly sure of.)

Notice then that two pieties of composition theory are often in conflict:

(1) Think about audience as you write (this stemming from the classical rhetorical tradition).
(2) Use writing for *making new meaning,* not just transmitting old meanings already worked out (this stemming from the newer epistemic tradition I associate with Ann Berthoff's classic explorations).

It's often difficult to work out new meaning while thinking about readers.

A More Ambitious Claim

I go further now and argue that ignoring audience can lead to better writing—immediately. In effect, writer-based prose can be *better* than reader-based prose. This might seem a more controversial claim, but is there a teacher who has not had the experience of struggling and struggling to no avail to help a student untangle his writing, only to discover that the student's casual journal writing or freewriting is untangled and strong? Sometimes freewriting is stronger than the essays we get only because it is expressive, narrative, or descriptive writing and the student was not constrained by a topic. But teachers who collect drafts with completed assignments often see passages of freewriting that are strikingly stronger *even* when they are expository and constrained by the assigned topic. In some of these passages we can sense that the strength derives from the student's unawareness of readers.

It's not just unskilled, tangled writers, though, who sometimes write better by forgetting about readers. Many competent and even professional writers produce mediocre pieces *because* they are thinking too much about how their readers will receive their words. They are acting too much like a salesman trained to look the customer in the eye and to think at all times about the characteristics of the "target audience." There is something too staged or planned or self-aware about such writing. We see this quality in much second-rate newspaper or magazine or business writing: "good-student writing" in the awful sense of the term. Writing produced this way reminds us of the ineffective actor whose consciousness of self distracts us: he makes us too aware of his own awareness of us. When we read such prose, we wish the writer would stop thinking about us—would stop trying to "adjust" or "fit" what he is saying to our frame of reference. "Damn it, put all your attention on what you are saying," we want to say, "and forget about us and how we are reacting."

When we examine really good student or professional writing, we can often see that its goodness comes from the writer's having gotten sufficiently wrapped up in her meaning and her language as to forget all about audience needs: the writer manages to "break through." The Earl of Shaftesbury talked about writers needing to escape their audience in order to find their own ideas (Cooper 1:109; see also Griffin). It is characteristic of much truly good writing to be, as it were, on fire with its meaning. Consciousness of readers is burned away; involvement in subject determines all. Such writing is analogous to the performance of the actor who has managed to stop attracting attention to her awareness of the audience watching her.

The arresting power in some writing by small children comes from their obliviousness to audience. As readers, we are somehow sucked into a more-than-usual connection with the meaning itself because of the child's gift for more-than-usual concentration on what she is saying. In short, we can feel some pieces of children's writing as being very writer-based. Yet it's precisely that quality which makes it powerful for us as readers. After all, why should we settle for a writer's entering our point of view, if we can have the more powerful experience of being sucked out of our point of view and into her world? This is just the experience that children are peculiarly capable of giving because they are so expert at total absorption in their world as they are writing. It's not just a matter of whether the writer "decenters," but of whether the writer has a sufficiently strong focus of attention to make the *reader* decenter. This quality of concentration is what D. H. Lawrence so admires in Melville:

> [Melville] was a real American in that he always felt his audience in front of him. But when he ceases to be American, when he forgets all audience, and gives us his sheer apprehension of the world, then he is wonderful, his book *[Moby Dick]* commands a stillness in the soul, an awe. (158)

What most readers value in really excellent writing is not prose that is right for readers but prose that is right for thinking, right for language, or right for the subject being written about. If, in addition, it is clear and well suited to readers, we appreciate that. Indeed, we feel insulted if the writer did not somehow try to make the writing *available* to us before delivering it. But if it succeeds at being really true to language and thinking and "things," we are willing to put up with much difficulty as readers:

> [G]ood writing is not always or necessarily an adaptation to communal norms (in the Fish/Bruffee sense) but may be an attempt to construct (and instruct) a reader capable of reading the text in question. The literary history of the "difficult" work—from Mallarmé to Pound, Zukofsky, Olson, etc.—seems to say that much of what we value in writing we've had to learn to value by learning how to read it. (Trimbur)

The effect of audience awareness on *voice* is particularly striking—if paradoxical. Even though we often develop our voice by finally "speaking up" to an audience or "speaking out" to others, and even though much dead student writing comes from students not really treating their writing as a communication with real readers, nevertheless, the opposite effect is also common: we often do not really develop a strong, resonant voice in our writing till we find important occasions for *ignoring* audience—saying, in effect, "To hell with whether they like it or not. I've got to say this the way *I* want to say it." Admittedly, the voice that emerges when we ignore audience is sometimes odd or idiosyncratic in some way, but usually it is stronger. Indeed, teachers sometimes complain that student writing is "writer-based" when the problem is simply the idiosyncrasy—and sometimes in fact the *power*—of the voice. They would value this odd but resonant voice if they found it in a published writer (see "Real Voice," Elbow, *Writing with Power*). Usually, we cannot *trust* a voice unless it is unaware of us and our needs and speaks out in its own terms (see the Ashberry epigraph). To celebrate writer-based prose is to risk the charge of *romanticism:* just warbling one's woodnotes wild. But my position also contains the austere *classic* view that we must nevertheless *revise* with conscious awareness of audience in order to figure out which pieces of writer-based prose are good as they are—and how to discard or revise the rest.

To point out that writer-based prose can be *better* for readers than reader-based prose is to reveal problems in these two terms. Does *writer-based* mean:

(1) That the text doesn't work for readers because it is too much oriented to the writer's point of view?

(2) Or that the writer was not thinking about readers as she wrote—although the text *may* work for readers?

Does *reader*-based mean:

(3) That the text works for readers—meets their needs?

(4) Or that the writer was attending to readers as she wrote—although her text may *not* work for readers?

In order to do justice to the reality and complexity of what actually happens in both writers and readers, we need to acknowledge *four* possible conditions in any passage of writing:

(1) The writer was not thinking about readers and the words don't work for them—don't meet their needs.

(2) The writer was not thinking about readers, yet nevertheless the words *do* work for them.

(3) The writer *was* thinking about readers and the words work for them.

(4) The writer *was* thinking about readers, yet nevertheless the words don't work for them.

Two Models of Cognitive Development

Some of the current emphasis on audience awareness probably derives from a model of cognitive development that needs to be questioned. According to this model, if you keep your readers in mind as you write, you are operating at a higher level of psychological development than if you ignore readers. Directing words to readers is "more mature" than directing them to no one in particular or to yourself. Flower relates writer-based prose to the inability to "decenter," which is characteristic of Piaget's early stages of development, and she relates reader-based prose to later more mature stages of development.

On the one hand, of course this view must be right. Children do decenter as they develop. As they mature they get better at suiting their discourse to the needs of listeners, particularly to listeners very different from themselves. Especially, they get better at doing so *consciously*—thinking *awarely* about how things appear to people with different viewpoints. Thus much unskilled writing is unclear or awkward *because* the writer was doing what it is so easy to do—unthinkingly taking her own frame of reference for granted and not attending to the needs of readers who might have a different frame of reference. And of course this failure is more common in younger, immature, "egocentric" students (and also more common in writing than in speaking since we have no audience present when we write).

But on the other hand, we need the contrary model that affirms what is also obvious once we reflect on it, namely, that the ability to *turn off* audience awareness—especially when it confuses thinking or blocks discourse—is also a "higher" skill. I am talking about an ability to use language in "the desert island mode," an ability that tends to require learning, growth, and psychological development. Children, and even adults who have not learned the art of quiet, thoughtful, inner reflection, are often unable to get much cognitive action going in their heads unless there are other people present to have action *with*. They are dependent on live audience and the social dimension to get their discourse rolling or to get their thinking off the ground.

For in contrast to a roughly Piagetian model of cognitive development that says we start out as private, egocentric little monads and grow up to be public and social, it is important to invoke the opposite model that derives variously from Vygotsky, Bakhtin, and Mead. According to this model, we *start out* social and plugged into others and only gradually, through learning and development, come to "unplug" to any significant degree so as to function in a more private, individual, and differentiated fashion: "Development in thinking is not from the individual to the socialized, but from the social to the individual" (Vygotsky 20). The important general principle in this model is that we tend to *develop* our important cognitive capacities by means of social interaction with others, and having done so we gradually learn to perform them alone. We fold the "simple" back-and-forth of dialogue into the "complexity" (literally, "foldedness") of individual, private reflection.

Where the Piagetian (individual psychology) model calls our attention to the obvious need to learn to enter into viewpoints other than our own, the Vygotskian (social psychology) model calls our attention to the equally important need to learn to produce good thinking and discourse *while alone*. A rich and enfolded mental life is something that people achieve only gradually through growth, learning, and practice. We tend to associate this achievement with the fruits of higher education.

Thus we see plenty of students who lack this skill, who have nothing to say when asked to freewrite or to write in a journal. They can dutifully "reply" to a question or a topic, but they cannot seem to *initiate* or *sustain* a train of thought on their own. Because so many adolescent students have this difficulty, many teachers chime in: "Adolescents have nothing to write about. They are too young. They haven't had significant experience." In truth, adolescents don't lack experience or material, no matter how "sheltered" their lives. What they lack is practice and help. Desert island discourse is a learned cognitive process. It's a mistake to think of private writing (journal writing and freewriting) as merely "easy"—merely a relief from trying to write right. It's also hard. Some exercises and strategies that help are Ira Progoff's "Intensive Journal" process, Sondra Perl's "Guidelines for Composing," or Elbow's "Loop Writing" and "Open Ended Writing" processes (*Writing With Power* 50–77).

The Piagetian and Vygotskian developmental models (language-begins-as-private vs. language-begins-as-social) give us two different lenses through which to look at a common weakness in student writing, a certain kind of "thin" writing where the thought is insufficiently developed or where the language doesn't really explain what the writing implies or gestures toward. Using the Piagetian model, as Flower does, one can specify the problem as a weakness in audience orientation. Perhaps the writer has immaturely taken too much for granted and unthinkingly assumed that her limited explanations carry as much meaning for readers as they do for herself. The cure or treatment is for the writer to think more about readers.

Through the Vygotskian lens, however, the problem and the "immaturity" look altogether different. Yes, the writing isn't particularly clear or satisfying for readers, but this alternative diagnosis suggests a failure of the private desert island dimension: the writer's explanation is too thin because she didn't work out her train of thought fully enough *for herself.* The suggested cure or treatment is *not* to think more about readers but to think more for herself, to practice exploratory writing in order to learn to engage in that reflective discourse so central to mastery of the writing process. How can she engage readers more till she has engaged herself more?

The current emphasis on audience awareness may be particularly strong now for being fueled by *both* psychological models. From one side, the Piagetians say, in effect, "The egocentric little critters, we've got to *socialize* 'em! Ergo, make them think about audience when they write!" From the other side, Vygotskians say, in effect, "No wonder they're having trouble writing. They've been bamboozled by the Piagetian heresy. They think they're solitary individuals with private selves when really they're just congeries of voices that derive from their discourse community. Ergo, let's intensify the social context—use peer groups and publication: make them think about audience when they write! (And while we're at it, let's hook them up with a better class of discourse community.)" To advocate ignoring audience is to risk getting caught in the crossfire from two opposed camps.

Two Models of Discourse: Discourse as Communication and Discourse as Poesis or Play

We cannot talk about writing without at least implying a psychological or developmental model. But we'd better make sure it's a complex, paradoxical, or spiral model. Better yet, we should be deft enough to use two contrary models or lenses. (Bruner pictures the developmental process as a complex movement in an upward reiterative spiral—not a simple movement in one direction.)

According to one model, it is characteristic of the youngest children to direct their discourse to an audience. They learn discourse *because* they have an audience; without an audience they remain mute, like "the wild child." Language is social from the start. But we need the other model to show us what is also true, namely, that it is characteristic of the youngest children to use language in a *nonsocial* way. They use language not only because people talk to them but also because they have such a strong propensity to play and to build—often in a *non*social or nonaudience-oriented fashion. Thus although one paradigm for discourse is social communication, another is private exploration or solitary play. Babies and toddlers tend to babble in an exploratory and reflective way—to themselves and not to an audience—often even with no one else near. This archetypally private use of discourse is strikingly illustrated when we see a pair of toddlers in "parallel play" alongside each other—each busily talking but not at all trying to communicate with the other.

Therefore, when we choose paradigms for discourse, we should think not only about children using language to communicate, but also about children building sandcastles or drawing pictures. Though children characteristically show their castles or pictures to others, they just as characteristically trample or crumple them before anyone else can see them. Of course sculptures and pictures are different from words. Yet discourse implies more media than words; and even if you restrict discourse to words, one of our most mature uses of language is for building verbal pictures and structures for their own sake—not just for communicating with others.

Consider this same kind of behavior at the other end of the life cycle: Brahms staggering from his deathbed to his study to rip up a dozen or more completed but unpublished and unheard string quartets that dissatisfied him. How was he relating to audience here—worrying too much about audience or not giving a damn? It's not easy to say. Consider Glenn Gould deciding to renounce performances before an audience. He used his private studio to produce recorded performances for an audience, but to produce ones that satisfied *himself* he clearly needed to suppress audience awareness. Consider the more extreme example of Kerouac typing page after page—burning each as soon as he completed it. The language behavior of humans is slippery. Surely, we are well advised to avoid positions that say it is "always X" or "essentially Y."

James Britton makes a powerful argument that the "making" or poesis function of language grows out of the expressive function. Expressive language is often for the sake of communication with an audience, but just as often it is only for the sake of the speaker—working something out for herself (66–57, 74ff). Note also that "writing to learn," which writing-across-the-curriculum programs are discovering to be so important, tends to be writing for the self or even for no one at all rather than for an outside reader. You throw away the writing, often unread, and keep the mental changes it has engendered.

I hope this emphasis on the complexity of the developmental process—the limits of our models and of our understanding of it—will serve as a rebuke to the tendency to label students as being at a lower stage of cognitive development just because they don't yet write well. (Occasionally, they *do* write well—in a way—but not in the way that the labeler finds appropriate.) Obviously, the psychologistic labeling impulse started out charitably. Shaughnessy was fighting those who called basic writers *stupid* by saying they weren't dumb, just at an earlier developmental stage. Flower was arguing that writer-based prose is a natural response to a cognitive overload and indeed developmentally enabling. But this kind of talk can be dangerous since it labels students as literally "retarded" and makes teachers and administrators start to think of them as such. Instead of calling poor writers *either* dumb or slow (two forms of blaming the victim), why not simply call them poor writers? If years of schooling haven't yet made them good writers, perhaps they haven't gotten the kind of teaching and support they need. Poor students are often deprived of the very thing they need most to write well (which is given to good students): lots of extended and adventuresome writing for self and for audience. Poor students are often asked to write *only* answers to fill-in exercises.

As children get older, the developmental story remains complex or spiral. One model invites us to notice how adolescents must struggle to decenter and become more social. The other model invites us to notice how adolescents must continually learn to master this solitary, desert island, poesis mode better. Thus we mustn't think of language only as communication—nor allow communication to claim dominance either as the earliest or as the most "mature" form of discourse. It's true that language is inherently communicative (and without communication we don't develop language), yet language is just as inherently the stringing together of exploratory discourse for the self—or for the creation of objects (play, poesis, making) for their own sake.

In considering this important poesis function of language, we need not discount (as Berkenkotter does) the striking testimony of so many witnesses who think and care most about language: professional poets, writers, and philosophers. Many of them maintain that their most serious work is *making*, not *communicating*, and that their commitment is to language, reality, logic, experience, not to readers. Only in their willingness to cut loose from the demands or needs of readers, they insist, can they do their best work. Here is William Stafford on this matter:

> I don't want to overstate this . . . but . . . my impulse is to say I don't think of an audience at all. When I'm writing, the satisfactions in the process of writing are my satisfactions in dealing with the language, in being surprised by phrasings that occur to me, in finding that this miraculous kind of convergent focus begins to happen. That's my satisfaction, and to think about an audience would be a distraction. I try to keep from thinking about an audience. (Cicotello 176)

And Chomsky:

> I can be using language in the strictest sense with no intention of communicating. . . . As a graduate student, I spent two years writing a lengthy manuscript, assuming throughout that it would never be published or read by anyone. I meant everything I wrote, intending nothing as to what anyone would [understand], in fact taking it for granted that there would be no audience. . . . [C]ommunication is only one function of language, and by no means an essential one. (Qtd. in Feldman 5–6.)

It's interesting to see how poets come together with philosophers on this point—and even with mathematicians. All are emphasizing the "poetic" function of language in its literal sense—"poesis" as "making." They describe their writing process as more like "getting something right" or even "solving a problem" for its own sake than as communicating with readers or addressing an audience. The task is not to satisfy readers but to satisfy the rules of the system: "[T]he writer is not thinking of a reader at all; he makes it 'clear' as a contract with *language*" (Goodman 164).

Shall we conclude, then, that solving an equation or working out a piece of symbolic logic is at the opposite end of the spectrum from communicating with readers or addressing an audience? No. To draw that conclusion would be to fall again into a one-sided position. Sometimes people write mathematics *for* an audience, sometimes not. The central point in this essay is that we cannot answer audience questions in an a priori fashion based on the "nature" of discourse or of language or of cognition—only in terms of the different *uses* or *purposes* to which humans put discourse, language, or cognition on different occasions. If most people have a restricted repertoire of uses for writing—if most people use writing only to send messages to readers—that's no argument for constricting the *definition* of writing. It's an argument for helping people expand their repertoire of uses.

The value of learning to ignore audience while writing, then, is the value of learning to cultivate the private dimension: the value of writing in order to make meaning to oneself, not just to others. This involves learning to free oneself (to some extent, anyway) from the enormous power exerted by society and others, to unhook oneself from external prompts and social stimuli. We've grown accustomed to theorists and writing teachers puritanically stressing the *problem* that writing tempts us to neglect the needs of readers because we usually write in solitude. But let's also celebrate this same feature of writing as one of its glories: writing invites disengagement too, the inward turn of mind, and the dialogue with self. Though writing is deeply social and though we usually help things by enhancing its social dimension, writing is also the mode of discourse best suited to helping us develop the reflective and private dimension of our mental lives.

"But Wait a Minute, ALL Discourse Is Social"

Some readers who see *all* discourse as social will object to my opposition between public and private writing (the "trap of oppositional thinking") and insist that *there is no such thing as private discourse*. What looks like private, solitary mental work, they would say, is really social. Even on the desert island I am in a crowd.

> [B]y ignoring audience in the conventional sense, we return to it in another sense. What I get from Vygotsky and Bakhtin is the notion that audience is not really out there at all but is in fact "always already" (to use that post-

structuralist mannerism . . .) inside, interiorized in the conflicting languages of others—parents, former teachers, peers, prospective readers,
whomever—that writers have to negotiate to write, and that we do negotiate when we write whether we're aware of it or not. The audience we've got
to satisfy in order to feel good about our writing is as much in the past as in
the present or future. But we experience it (it's so internalized) as *ourselves*.
(Trimbur)

(Ken Bruffee likes to quote from Frost: "'Men work together, . . . / Whether
they work together or apart'" ["The Tuff of Flowers"]). Or—putting it slightly
differently—when I engage in what seems like private nonaudience-directed
writing, I am really engaged in communication with the "audience of self."
For the self is multiple, not single, and discourse to self is communication
from one entity to another. As Feldman argues, "The self functions as audience in much the same way that others do" (290).

Suppose I accept this theory that all discourse is really social—including
what I've been calling "private writing" or writing I don't intend to show to
any reader. Suppose I agree that all language is essentially communication directed toward an audience—whether some past internalized voice or (what
may be the same thing) some aspect of the self. What would this theory say to
my interest in "private writing"?

The theory would seem to destroy my main argument. It would tell me that
there's no such thing as "private writing"; it's impossible *not* to address audience; there are no vacations from audience. But the theory might try to console me by saying not to worry, because we don't *need* vacations from audience. Addressing audience is as easy, natural, and unaware as breathing—and
we've been at it since the cradle. Even young, unskilled writers are already
expert at addressing audiences.

But if we look closely we can see that in fact this theory doesn't touch my
central practical argument. For even if all discourse is naturally addressed to
some audience, it's not naturally addressed to the *right* audience—the living
readers we are actually trying to reach. Indeed, the pervasiveness of past audiences in our heads is one more reason for the difficulty of reaching present
audiences with our texts. Thus even if I concede the theoretical point, there
still remains an enormous practical and phenomenological difference between
writing "public" words for outside persons to read and writing "private"
words meant only for the folks inside my head.

Even if "private writing" is "deep down" social, the fact remains that, as
we engage in it, we don't have to worry about whether it works on outside
readers or even makes sense. We can refrain from doing all the things that
audience-awareness advocates advise us to do ("keeping our audience in mind
as we write" and trying to "decenter"). Therefore, this social-discourse theory
doesn't undermine the benefits of "private writing" and thus provides no
support at all for the traditional rhetorical advice that we should "always try
to think about (intended) audience as we write."

In fact, this social-discourse theory reinforces two subsidiary arguments I have been making. First, even if there is no getting away from *some* audience, we can get relief from an inhibiting audience by writing to a more inviting one. Second, audience problems don't come only from *actual* audiences but also from phantom "audiences in the head" (Elbow, *Writing With Power* 186ff.) Once we learn how to be more aware of the effects of both external and internal readers and how to direct our words elsewhere, we can get out of the shadow even of a troublesome phantom reader.

And even if all our discourse is *directed to* or *shaped by* past audiences or voices, it doesn't follow that our discourse is *well directed to* or *successfully shaped for* those audiences or voices. Small children *direct* much talk to others, but that doesn't mean they always *suit* their talk to others. They often fail. When adults discover that a piece of their writing has been "heavily shaped" by some audience, this is bad news as much as good: often the writing is crippled by defensive moves that try to fend off criticism from this reader.

As teachers, particularly, we need to distinguish and emphasize "private writing" in order to teach it, to teach that crucial cognitive capacity to engage in extended and productive thinking that doesn't depend on audience prompts or social stimuli. It's sad to see so many students who can reply to live voices but cannot create productive dialogue with voices in their heads. Such students often lose interest in an issue that had intrigued them—just because they don't find other people who are interested in talking about it and haven't learned to talk reflectively to *themselves* about it.

For these reasons, then, I believe my main argument holds force even if I accept the theory that all discourse is social. But, perhaps more tentatively, I resist this theory. I don't know all the data from developmental linguistics, but I cannot help suspecting that babies engage in *some* private poesis—or "play-language"—some private babbling in addition to social babbling. Of course Vygotsky must be right when he points to so much social language in children, but can we really deny *all* private or nonsocial language (which Piaget and Chomsky see)? I am always suspicious when someone argues for the total nonexistence of a certain kind of behavior or event. Such an argument is almost invariably an act of definitional aggrandizement, not empirical searching. To say that *all* language is social is to flop over into the opposite one-sidednesses that we need Vygotsky's model to save us from.

And even if all language is *originally* social, Vygotsky himself emphasizes how "inner speech" becomes more individuated and private as the child matures. "[E]gocentric speech is relatively accessible in three-year-olds but quite inscrutable in seven-year-olds: the older the child, the more thoroughly has his thought become inner speech" (Emerson 254; see also Vygotsky 134). "The inner speech of the adult represents his 'thinking for himself' rather than social adaptation. . . . Out of context, it would be incomprehensible to others because it omits to mention what is obvious to the 'speaker'" (Vygotsky 18).

I also resist the theory that all private writing is really communication with the *"audience of self."* ("When we represent the objects of our thought in language, we intend to make use of these representations at a later time. . . . [T]he speaker-self must have audience-directed intentions toward a listener-self" [Feldman 289].) Of course, private language often *is* a communication with the audience of self:

- When we make a shopping list. (It's obvious when we can't decipher that third item that we're confronting *failed* communication with the self.)
- When we make a rough draft for ourselves but not for others' eyes. Here we are seeking to clarify our thinking with the leverage that comes from standing outside and reading our own utterance as audience—experiencing our discourse as receiver instead of as sender.
- When we experience ourselves as slightly split. Sometimes we experience ourselves as witness to ourselves and hear our own words from the outside— sometimes with great detachment, as on some occasions of pressure or stress.

But there are other times when private language is *not* communication with audience of self:

- Freewriting to no one: for the *sake* of self but not *to* the self. The goal is not to communicate but to follow a train of thinking or feeling to see where it leads. In doing this kind of freewriting (and many people have not learned it), you don't particularly plan to come back and read what you've written. You just write along and the written product falls away to be ignored, while only the "real product"—any new perceptions, thoughts, or feelings produced in the mind by the freewriting—is saved and looked at again. (It's not that you don't experience your words *at all* but you experience them only as speaker, sender, or emitter—not as receiver or audience. To say that's the same as being audience is denying the very distinction between 'speaker' and 'audience.')

  As this kind of freewriting actually works, it often *leads* to writing we look at. That is, we freewrite along to no one, following discourse in hopes of getting somewhere, and then at a certain point we often sense that we have *gotten* somewhere: we can tell (but not because we stop and read) that what we are now writing seems new or intriguing or important. At this point we may stop writing; or we may keep on writing, but in a new audience-relationship, realizing that we *will* come back to this passage and read it as audience. Or we may take a new sheet (symbolizing the new audience-relationship) and try to write out for ourselves what's interesting.
- Writing as exorcism is a more extreme example of private writing *not* for the audience of self. Some people have learned to write in order to get rid of thoughts or feelings. By freewriting what's obsessively going round and round in our head we can finally let it go and move on.

I am suggesting that some people (and especially poets and freewriters) engage in a kind of discourse that Feldman, defending what she calls a "communication-intention" view, has never learned and thus has a hard time imagining and understanding. Instead of always using language in an audience-directed fashion for the sake of communication, these writers unleash language for its own sake and let *it* function a bit on its own, without much *intention* and without much need for *communication,* to see where it leads—and thereby end up with some intentions and potential communications they didn't have before.

It's hard to turn off the audience-of-self in writing—and thus hard to imagine writing to no one (just as it's hard to turn off the audience of *outside* readers when writing an audience-directed piece). Consider "invisible writing" as an intriguing technique that helps you become less of an audience-of-self for your writing. Invisible writing prevents you from seeing what you have written: you write on a computer with the screen turned down, or you write with a spent ball-point pen on paper with carbon paper and another sheet underneath. Invisible writing tends to get people not only to write faster than they normally do, but often better (see Blau). I mean to be tentative about this slippery issue of whether we can really stop being audience to our own discourse, but I cannot help drawing the following conclusion: just as in freewriting, suppressing the *other* as audience tends to enhance quantity and sometimes even quality of writing; so in invisible writing, suppressing the *self* as audience tends to enhance quantity and sometimes even quality.

Contraries in Teaching

So what does all this mean for teaching? It means that we are stuck with two contrary tasks. On the one hand, we need to help our students enhance the social dimension of writing: to learn to be *more* aware of audience, to decenter better and learn to fit their discourse better to the needs of readers. Yet it is every bit as important to help them learn the private dimension of writing: to learn to be *less* aware of audience, to put audience needs aside, to use discourse in the desert island mode. And if we are trying to advance contraries, we must be prepared for paradoxes.

For instance, if we emphasize the social dimension in our teaching (for example, by getting students to write to each other, to read and comment on each others' writing in pairs and groups, and by staging public discussions and even debates on the topics they are to write about), we will obviously help the social, public, communicative dimension of writing—help students experience writing not just as jumping through hoops for a grade but rather as taking part in the life of a community of discourse. But "social discourse" can also help private writing by getting students sufficiently involved or invested in an issue that they finally want to carry on producing discourse alone and in private—and for themselves.

Correlatively, if we emphasize the private dimension in our teaching (for example, by using lots of private exploratory writing, freewriting, and journal writing and by helping students realize that of course they may need practice with this "easy' mode of discourse before they can use it fruitfully), we will obviously help students learn to write better reflectively for themselves without the need for others to interact with. Yet this private discourse can also help public, social writing—help students finally feel full enough of their *own* thoughts to have some genuine desire to *tell* them to others. Students often feel they "don't have anything to say" until they finally succeed in engaging themselves in private desert island writing for themselves alone.

Another paradox: whether we want to teach audience awareness or the ability to ignore audience, we must help students learn not only to "try harder" but also to "just relax." That is, sometimes students fail to produce words that work for readers because they don't *try* hard enough to think about audience needs. But sometimes the problem is cured if they just relax and write *to* people—as though in a letter or in talking to a trusted adult. By unclenching, they effortlessly call on social discourse skills of immense sophistication. Sometimes, indeed, the problem is cured if the student simply writes in a more social *setting*—in a classroom where it is habitual to share lots of writing. Similarly, sometimes students can't produce sustained private discourse because they don't try hard enough to keep the pen moving and forget about readers. They must persist and doggedly push aside those feelings of, "My head is empty, I have run out of anything to say." But sometimes what they need to learn through all that persistence is how to relax and let go—to unclench and just follow their nose.

As teachers, we need to think about what it means to *be an audience* rather than just be a teacher, critic, assessor, or editor. If our only response is to tell students what's strong, what's weak, and how to improve it (diagnosis, assessment, and advice), we actually *undermine* their sense of writing as a social act. We reinforce their sense that writing means doing school exercises, producing for authorities what they already know—*not* actually trying to say things to readers. To help students experience us as *audience* rather than as assessment machines, it helps to respond by "replying" (as in a letter) rather than always "giving feedback."

Paradoxically enough, one of the best ways teachers can help students learn to turn off audience awareness and write in the desert island mode—to turn off the babble of outside voices in the head and listen better to quiet inner voices—is to be a special kind of private audience to them, to be a reader who nurtures by trusting and believing in the writer. Britton has drawn attention to the importance of teacher as "trusted adult" for school children (67–68). No one can be good at private, reflective writing without some *confidence and trust in self*. A nurturing reader can give a writer a kind of permission to forget about other readers or to be one's own reader. I have benefited from this special kind of audience and have seen it prove useful to others. When I had a teacher who believed in me, who was interested in me and interested in what I had to say, I wrote well. When I had a teacher who thought I was naive, dumb, silly, and in need of being "straightened out," I wrote badly and sometimes couldn't write at all. Here is an interestingly paradoxical instance of the social-to-private principle from Vygotsky and Mead: we learn to listen better and more trustingly to *ourselves* through interaction with trusting *others*.

Look for a moment at lyric poets as paradigm writers (instead of seeing them as aberrant), and see how they heighten *both* the public and private dimensions of writing. Bakhtin says that lyric poetry implies "the absolute certainty of the listener's sympathy" (113). I think it's more helpful to say that lyric poets learn to create more than usual privacy in which to write *for themselves*—and then they turn around and let *others overhear*. Notice how poets tend to argue for the importance of no-audience writing, yet they are especially gifted at being public about what they produce in private. Poets are revealers—sometimes even grandstanders or showoffs. Poets illustrate the need for opposite or paradoxical or double audience skills: on the one hand, the ability to be private and solitary and tune out others—to write only for oneself and not give a damn about readers—yet on the other hand, the ability to be more than usually interested in audience and even to be a ham.

If writers really need these two audience skills, notice how bad most conventional schooling is on both counts. Schools offer virtually no privacy for writing: everything students write is collected and read by a teacher, a situation so ingrained that students may complain if you don't collect and read every word they write. Yet on the other hand, schools characteristically offer little or no social dimension for writing. It is *only* the teacher who reads, and students seldom feel that in giving their writing to a teacher they are actually communicating something they really want to say to a real person. Notice how often they are happy to turn in to teachers something perfunctory and fake that they would be embarrassed to show to classmates. Often they feel shocked and insulted if we want to distribute to classmates the assigned writing they hand in to us. (I think of Richard Wright's realization that the naked white prostitutes didn't bother to cover themselves when he brought them coffee as a black bellboy because they didn't really think of him as a man or even a person.) Thus the conventional school setting for writing tends to be the least private and the least public—when what students need, like all of us, is practice in writing that is the most private and also the most public.

Practical Guidelines about Audience

The theoretical relationships between discourse and audience are complex and paradoxical, but the practical morals are simple:

1. Seek ways to heighten both the *public* and *private* dimensions of writing. (For activities, see the previous section.)

2. When working on important audience-directed writing, we must try to emphasize audience awareness *sometimes*. A useful rule of thumb is to start by putting the readers in mind and carry on as long as things go well. If difficulties arise, try putting readers out of mind and write either to no audience, to self, or to an inviting audience. Finally, always *revise* with readers in mind. (Here's another occasion when orthodox advice about writing is wrong—but turns out right if applied to revising.)

3. Seek ways to heighten awareness of one's writing process (through process writing and discussion) to get better at taking control and deciding when to keep readers in mind and when to ignore them. Learn to discriminate factors like these:

a. The writing task. Is this piece of writing *really* for an audience? More often than we realize, it is not. It is a draft that only we will see, though the final version will be for an audience; or exploratory writing for figuring something out; or some kind of personal private writing meant only for ourselves.

b. Actual readers. When we put them in mind, are we helped or hindered?

c. One's own temperament. Am I the sort of person who tends to think of what to say and how to say it when I keep readers in mind? Or someone (like the author) who needs long stretches of forgetting all about readers?

d. Has some powerful "audience-in-the-head" tricked me into talking to it when I'm really trying to talk to someone else—distorting new business into old business?

e. Is *double audience* getting in my way? When I write a memo or report, I probably have to suit it not only to my "target audience" but also to some colleagues or supervisor. When I write something for publication, it must be right for readers, but it won't be published unless it is also right for the editors—and if it's a book it won't be much read unless it's right for reviewers. Children's stories won't be bought unless they are right for editors and reviewers *and* parents. We often tell students to write to a particular "real-life" audience—or to peers in the class—but of course they are also writing for us as graders.

f. Is *teacher-audience* getting in the way of my students' writing? As teachers we must often read in an odd fashion: in stacks of 25 or 50 pieces all on the same topic; on topics we know better than the writer; not for pleasure or learning but to grade or find problems (see Elbow, *Writing with Power* 216–36).

To list all these audience pitfalls is to show again the need for thinking about audience needs—yet also the need for vacations from readers to think in peace.

I benefited from much help from audiences in writing various drafts of this piece. I am grateful to Jennifer Clarke, with whom I wrote a collaborative piece containing a case study on this subject. I am also grateful for extensive feedback from Pat Belanoff, Paul Connolly, Sheryl Fontaine, John Trimbur, and members of the Martha's Vineyard Summer Writing Seminar.

Works Cited

Bakhtin, Mikhail. "Discourse in Life and Discourse in Poetry." Appendix. *Freudianism: A Marxist Critique*. By V. N. Volosinov. Trans. I. R. Titunik. Ed. Neal H. Bruss. New York: Academic, 1976. (Holquist's attribution of this work to Bakhtin is generally accepted.)

Berkenkotter, Carol, and Donald Murray. "Decisions and Revisions: The Planning Strategies of a Publishing Writer and the Response of Being a Rat—or Being Protocoled." *College Composition and Communication* 34 (1983): 156–72.

Blau, Sheridan. "Invisible Writing." *College Composition and Communication* 34 (1983): 297–312.

Booth, Wayne. *The Rhetoric of Fiction*. Chicago: U of Chicago P, 1961.

Britton, James. *The Development of Writing Abilities, 11–18*. Urbana: NCTE, 1977.

Bruffee, Kenneth A. "Liberal Education and the Social Justification of Belief." *Liberal Education* 68 (1982): 95–114.

Bruner, Jerome. *Beyond the Information Given: Studies in the Psychology of Knowing.* Ed. Jeremy Anglin. New York: Norton, 1973.

———. *On Knowing: Essays for the Left Hand.* Expanded ed. Cambridge: Harvard UP, 1979.

Chomsky, Noam. *Reflections on Language.* New York: Random, 1975.

Cicotello, David M. "The Art of Writing: An Interview with William Stafford." *College Composition and Communication* 34 (1983): 173–77.

Clarke, Jennifer, and Peter Elbow. "Desert Island Discourse: On the Benefits of Ignoring Audience." *The Journal Book.* Ed. Toby Fulwiler. Montclair, NJ: Boynton, 1987.

Cooper, Anthony Ashley, 3rd Earl of Shaftesbury. *Characteristics of Men, Manners, Opinions, Times, Etc.* Ed. John M. Robertson. 2 vols. Gloucester, MA: Smith, 1963.

Ede, Lisa, and Andrea Lunsford. "Audience Addressed/Audience Invoked: The Role of Audience in Composition Theory and Pedagogy." *College Composition and Communication* 35 (1984): 140–54.

Elbow, Peter. *Writing With Power.* New York: Oxford UP, 1981.

———. *Writing Without Teachers.* New York: Oxford UP, 1973.

Emerson, Caryl. "The Outer Word and Inner Speech: Bakhtin, Vygotsky, and the Internalization of Language." *Critical Inquiry* 10 (1983): 245–64.

Feldman, Carol Fleisher. "Two Functions of Language." *Harvard Education Review* 47 (1977): 282–93.

Flower, Linda. "Writer-Based Prose: A Cognitive Basis for Problems in Writing," *College English* 41 (1979): 19–37.

Goodman, Paul. *Speaking and Language: Defense of Poetry.* New York: Random, 1972.

Griffin, Susan. "The Internal Voices of Invention: Shaftesbury's Soliloquy." Unpublished. 1986.

Lawrence, D. H. *Studies in Classic American Literature.* Garden City: Doubleday, 1951.

Ong, Walter. "The Writer's Audience Is Always a Fiction." *PMLA* 90 (1975): 9–21.

Park, Douglas B. "The Meanings of 'Audience.'" *College English* 44 (1982): 247–57.

Perl, Sondra. "Guidelines for Composing." Appendix A. *Through Teachers' Eyes: Portraits of Writing Teachers at Work.* By Sondra Perl and Nancy Wilson. Portsmouth, NH: Heinemann, 1986.

Progoff, Ira. *At A Journal Workshop.* New York: Dialogue, 1975.

Shaughnessy, Mina. *Errors and Expectations: A Guide for the Teacher of Basic Writing.* New York: Oxford UP, 1977.

Trimbur, John. Letter to the author. September 1985.

———. "Beyond Cognition: Voices in Inner Speech." *Rhetoric Review* 5 (1987): 211–21.

Vygotsky, L. S. *Thought and Language.* Trans. and ed. E. Hanfmann and G. Vakar, 1934. Cambridge: MIT P, 1962.

Walzer, Arthur E. "Articles from the 'California Divorce Project': A Case Study of the Concept of Audience." *College Composition and Communication* 36 (1985): 150–59.

Wright, Richard. *Black Boy.* New York: Harper, 1945.

6

Toward a Phenomonology
of Freewriting

A scene. I am leading a workshop for teachers. I introduce freewriting as
merely a first thing: easiest, lowest level, not very complicated—good for getting started. I don't allocate much time: ten minutes for writing, ten for brief
reactions. This is all just warming up and going on to other more complicated
activities in teaching writing, activities that will take more time to try out and
discuss. But as we talk about it we tangle. Some love freewriting. A few even
get what I would call too enthusiastic, going overboard, developing a reactive
revulsion at all the planning and care they'd always associated with writing:
breaking out, spontaneity is all, "free at last." But others are deeply distrustful, disturbed, critical. Freewriting touches some nerve. We fight. Finally, I
get tired of the fighting and defending—or suddenly realize how much time
has gone by. "Let's move on, this is not the main thing, it's just one of many
kinds of writing: options, spectrum, no big deal."

After this happened a number of times I began to sense the pattern and finally realized it wasn't just *they* who were getting caught up in it. "No big
deal," I say, so I can extricate myself from the tangle—but finally I realize that
it is a big deal for *me*. I must admit to myself and to others that freewriting
may be what I care most about in writing and teaching writing. I learn most
from it. I get my best ideas and writing from it. I get my best group and community work done that way. I feel most myself when I freewrite. I think
freewriting helps my students more than anything else I show them, and they
usually agree with me over the years in formal and informal evaluations (and
often I get the same response from teachers I work with). I'm bemused that I

This essay was published in 1989 in *The Journal of Basic Writing* 8.2 (fall): 44–71. It was
reprinted in *Nothing Begins with N: New Investigations of Freewriting*. Eds. Pat Belanoff, Peter
Elbow, and Sheryl Fontaine, Southern Illinois UP, 1991.

work so hard teaching complicated ideas and procedures, yet at the end they say they learned most from what I taught them in the first half hour of the first class (though I use it extensively throughout the term).

But when I do workshops for teachers I sometimes forget about the depth of my personal connection to freewriting, how much I've cathected it, because I want so badly to be sensible and pragmatic: it's "just a tool"—useful to one and all, no ideology attached.

In this chapter, then, let me try to tell why freewriting is not just a handy-dandy tool but something at the center of what I do as a writer and a teacher. I started out writing a considerably different chapter, more impersonal and analytic. It got soggy and I gradually sensed I should focus on how I use and experience freewriting. But I'll also try to draw conclusions.

Freewriting Without Knowing It: Desperation Journal Writing

What may have gotten me most personally involved with freewriting was, perhaps fittingly, my use of something like freewriting for my own personal life. There was a long period of struggle in my life, almost a decade, when, intermittently, I felt at the end of my tether. When I experienced myself as really stuck, nothing I did seemed to help me or diminish the pain. But I'd kept a kind of diary for a while, and so at really stuck times I took to simply sitting down at the typewriter and trying to *say* or *blurt* everything and anything I could. I remember sometimes sitting on the floor—I'm not sure why, but probably as a kind of bodily acting out of my sense of desperation. I could type fast and I learned that I could just let my hands go and, as it were, "utter" words onto paper with a kind of intensity. When I felt myself shouting I used all caps. This process seemed to help more than anything else, and in this way I drifted into what I now take as the experiential germ of freewriting, the "freewriting muscle": don't plan, don't stop, trust that something will come—all in the interest of getting oneself "rolling" or "steaming along" into a more intense state of perception and language production. I don't think this was a conscious methodology, just a vague awareness that it helped.[1]

This writing was very private. I've never shared it and won't share more than a few short passages here. But the fact that I can do so after twenty-five years—you will not have failed to notice—shows that I saved it. It felt precious to me.

There were all kinds of writing jumbled up in these hundreds of single-spaced typed pages. Anyone who has kept a diary in hard times can imagine what's there. For me the characteristic move was to start from feelings and

---

1. This started before I knew of Ken Macrorie and learned the name and the self-conscious technique from him, and also before an MIT colleague brought back from a summer's teaching in a rural Southern college a different but comparable writing exercise: fill up a legal-sized sheet with nonstop writing; write as small or large as you wish. Here too was the essential germ: a task or even "ordeal" but with extenuating circumstances to guarantee success.

seek relief in trying to figure things out: "I'm being driven out of my mind by ————. What power can I gain over it by this process. Maybe the fact that it is exceedingly hard to get myself to sit down and deal with it on typewriter is clue that it will be effective—ie, that the demons inside don't want me to do this."

But there was more naked blurting too. I began one long entry like this: "Please let me be able to face up to what it is that is bugging me and face it and get through it and come out on the other side."

In this passage I seem to be tacitly using the genre of prayer or supplication—I'm not sure to whom. Prayer was a usable if leftover genre for me since it had been an important part of my life, and I hadn't been above asking for personal favors.

Sometimes in desperation I ranted and raved. Toward the end of a very long entry—in effect, working myself up over three or four pages into a frenzy—I wrote:

AND LESS THAN THAT I WILL REFUSE! LESS THAN THAT IS UNSATISFAC-
TORY! LESS THAN THAT IS WORTHY OF HATE! LESS THAN THAT I WILL
REFUSE. AND I WILL BE ANGRY. AND I WILL ACCEPT NOTHING FROM THIS
UNIVERSE: I WILL ACCEPT NOTHING. I WILL ACCEPT NO WARMTH, NO
COMFORT, NO FOOD, NO GIFT, NO ANYTHING UNTIL . . . [going on and
on and ending with] I HATE EVERYBODY."

Two things strike me (besides the purple theatricality—which I didn't experience that way at the time). First, I was using this private writing to allow myself kinds of discourse or register I couldn't otherwise allow myself (my public language being rather controlled). The basic impulse was to find words for what I was experiencing; somehow it helped to blurt rather than to try to be careful. Second, even in this ranting I see a kind of drive toward analysis that the reader might not notice: by letting myself rave, I helped myself catch a glimpse I hadn't had before of the crucial pattern in my inner life—helped myself admit to myself, "I *insist* on cutting off my nose to spite my face. And I refuse to do otherwise."

In the following excerpt I explore the writing-thinking-discovery process itself (in a passage coming on the fourth single-spaced page of a very long entry):

—There is a moral in what I've done tonight and also last Sunday most of
the day. On both occasions I was bothered by feelings, but didn't know
what they were. I felt helpless both times. Tended to vacilate and wander
around and do nothing. Same thing had happened an infinite number of
times in the past and resulted in hours or days of compulsive wandering
and brooding and being in irons and getting nowhere—ending only when
fortuitous circumstances jolted me out of it. BUT these two times I somehow
had the determination to sit down with the typewriter. And the fact seems
to be that once I do that, and once I begin simply to line up the data—my
feelings and actions—I start to see and sense functionalities and see rela-

tionships. And that produces both insights and even new feelings. BUT THINKING AND BROODING NEVER WORKED: IT SEEMS TO REQUIRE THE WRITING OF THEM OUT. Like writing papers—once one can get writing, things—and *big* things—begin to come. REMEMBER ALSO THAT IT TENDS TO BE DEAD END TO TRY TO WRITE OUT INSIGHTS. WHAT IS TRULY PRODUCTIVE IS AE ATTEMPT SIMPLT TO LINE UP THE DATA AND SEE THEN SEE WHAT EMERGES. WRITING STARTING OUT WRITING UIP INSIGHTS SIMPLY TRAPS ME IN OLD FAILURE PATHES OF THINKING + NO NEW INSIGHTS THAT WAY.

—Thus, it may be that the new element in my life is the determination to apply the seat of the pants to the typewriter. Not determination, really, but somehow I did it, WHEN IN THE PAST I DID NOT DO IT. WHY? WHY? SOMEHOW A SENSE THAT I COULD GET RESULTS.

I could be (read "am") embarrassed by the endless pages of self-absorption in these journals. And I'd happily trade in much of it now, ten cents on the dollar, for some concrete descriptions: where was I, what was I doing, whom was I with, who said what—in short for "good writing." Nevertheless, I hold fast to a charitable view and remember how important this continual churning process was for my survival, *and also,* it now strikes me, for making writing a deep part of me.

What also strikes me is how analytic it is, however driven by feelings and full of descriptions of feelings in loose and often emotional language. Indeed, the hunger to figure things out led to *so much* analysis as finally to show me the limits of analysis—to show me that "expression" or "blurting" was often more useful than insight.

Finally, I see a drive toward honesty here. I felt stuck in my life. I was willing to write things I couldn't tell others and, indeed, didn't want to tell myself, in hopes that it might make things more bearable. I still feel this at the root of freewriting: that it invites a *personal* honesty even in academic writing and thus helps me pursue feelings or misgivings about my thinking that are not possible when I'm writing a draft for the eyes of others.

Freewriting as Incoherent

As I let myself career around in my inner life, I let my journal writing be careless and digressive and unformed. But I never let it be actually incoherent. I was, after all, a graduate student or a teacher for all these years. My motivation was to "figure things out." It wasn't till I had actually worked out a theory of freewriting (thanks to Ken Macrorie and to my experience as a returning graduate student who was now stuck in his writing, not his living) that I consciously adopted the principle that I should sometimes keep on writing even if it led to nonsense.

Freewriting as nonsense happens to me most characteristically now when I am feeling some responsibility about being in charge of a class or workshop. I often find it easier to freewrite coherently and productively when I'm alone or in someone else's class or workshop and can concentrate on my own work and not worry about people I'm responsible for. When I'm feeling nervous about being in charge, I sometimes cannot enter into my words or even very much into my mind. Here is an example of the nervous static I produced just the other day at the start of my 8 A.M. freshman writing class:

> Freewriting. where does my pen take me. Heck Keep the pen going. And keep your pen moving. Whats happening. Whats heppening. Whats happening. I don't know whats happening. I feel sleepy and down. I get more cheerful in their presence. I feel more cheerful when they're here. [Seeing the students be sleepy and grumpy made me overcome my similar feelings.] I feel more sleepy—no happy—when they're here. Whats happening. Whats happening. Whats happening. Whats happening. Whats happening. Whats happening. Whats happening. Whats happening. Whats happening. Whats happening. Whats happening. Whats happening. Whats happening.
>
> Whats happening. Whats happening. Whats happening. Whats happening. Whats happening. Whats happening.
>
> I don't know whats happening to me. I don't want to write. I don't know what I want to write. I don't know what I want to write. I don't know what I want to write. I don't know what I want to write. I don't know what I want to write. I don't know what I want to write. I don't know what I want to write. I don't know what I want to write. [Written by hand]

Is this a *use* of freewriting? Or an abuse or a nonuse? Am I using it to avoid what's bothering me? With all my talk about honesty, why can't I explore what's on my mind in the safety of this private writing? Was I nervous? I don't know. It would have been easier if I hadn't been sitting there facing the class. This whole question still perplexes me.

But this kind of freewriting helps me identify with a certain proportion of the *student* freewriting I've seen (private freewriting that I've been allowed to see later): sometimes nervousness (or something else) prevents students too from entering in or giving their full attention to their writing. A touching irony here: I'm nervous because I'm in charge and wondering whether I'm doing the right thing; they're nervous because they're in this required class with some guy making them write without stopping. In addition, students sometimes produce this mere "noise" or "static" freewriting for the opposite reason: it feels to them too boring and inconsequential to write words on paper that the teacher won't grade and *no* one will read. The moral of the story is that even though freewriting usually helps us concentrate better and enter more fully into our words (not pausing to reconsider our words or worry about reader reactions), it cannot *ensure* safety and involvement even for an experienced writer like me.

In the end, however, my deep sense of *safety* with freewriting depends crucially on my being allowed to "abuse" it this way. It feels crucial to be able to say that the freewriting I quoted earlier is just right: that I've freewritten *perfectly* as long as I didn't stop my pen. If I had to be honest or meaningful or coherent all the time ("Did I do a good job this time?"), it would create a burden that would undermine what I experience as central to freewriting.

Freewriting for Unfocused Exploring

Unfocused exploring is probably my main use of freewriting: I have a thought, perhaps out of the blue or perhaps in the midst of writing something (even while writing something else), and I give myself permission to pursue it on paper in an uncontrolled way wherever it wants to go, even if it digresses (as it usually does). This kind of freewriting is precious to me because my mind seems to work best—at the level of ideas as well as syntax—when I allow it to be uncontrolled and disorganized. I cannot find as many ideas or perceptions if I try to stay on one track or be organized. And the not-stopping seems to build mental momentum, helps me get wound up or get rolling so that more ideas come.

Here is a long example. It is most of a single piece of freewriting (asterisks and all) that provided important germs for two different published essays (on voice and on audience). I'd been reading one evening and I found two passages I wanted to save. The next morning I was merely copying them down on my computer when more thoughts came and I followed the train of associations:

> Perfect example of "constructed" syntax from Ronald S. Crane, famous sentence in "Critical Monism," quoted by Bialostosky, 1 3rd through his "Dialogics of the Lyric": "a poet does not write poetry but individual poems. And these are inevitably, as finished wholes, instances of one or another poetic kind, differentiated not by any necessities of the linguistic instrument of poetry but primarily by the nature of the poet's conception, as finally embodied in his poem, of a particular form to be achieved through the representation, in speech used dramatically or otherwise, of some distinctive state of feeling, of moral choice, or action, complete in itself and productive of a certain emotion or complex of emotions in the reader." (p. 96)
>
> One can feel him building. Perhaps this extreme version is characteristic of a classicist, someone who is immersed in reading Aristotle, Aquinas. (Does he read a lot in original classical languages? Certainly when we are asked to write in Latin or Greek (or some nonnative language in school) we are always CONSTRUCTING. Latin, in particular, seems to lend itself to that—with its free choice word order—invitation to fiddle with placement of words as in a puzzle—there doesn't seem to be a driving force to UTTER words in a particular order. Can it be that the peculiarities of the language's syntax relation to meaning INVITE one, more than in other languages, to, as it were, "formulate a meaning in ones mind first" and then find words for it? Can it be that some languages invite that more than others? Can it be that languages like English—and even more Chinese—where word order is obligatory and carries much of the meaning—invite UTTERANCE more—for

the force of making meaning gives rise to a sequence of words that drives itself forward from the head to the world—the process of FINDING MEANING
in itself implies a word order; whereas in more of a language of free-choice
syntax, there is an invitation to allow a bigger gap between finding meaning
and making words?

* * * * *

The above will make an important footnote in anything I write about
voice/freewriting/utterance &c &c.

* * * * *

Try to find the notes I made about UTTERING and CONSTRUCTING language
while I was teaching 101. The struggle for students in moving from one to
the other. Are they in my "germs" folder? Could there be something in my
101 folders? It was spring 83 that I was noticing it.

* * * * *

Bakhtin evidently says that lyric poetry implies an audience of COMPLETE
trust. Yes? Perhaps. But I suspect its more accurate to say that lyric taps the
impulse to speak TO ONESELF. And is related to the fact that poets, perhaps
more than any other group, are always sticking up for no-audience writing.
To write lyric is to get at TRUSTED, INNER stuff. We do that best when we
have safety and privacy. I suspect lyric poets are often people who learn to
make privacy for selves, write to self, AND THEN LET OTHERS HEAR.

(Thus, it's an instance of my interest in DOUBLE AUDIENCE SITUATIONS.
Good lyric poets are people who learn to write to self, but also to others. Perhaps thats the secret of all writers. Learning to deal with double audience.

DOUBLE AUDIENCE PHENOMENON: THIS IS IMPORTANT POINT. MAY BE
CLOSE TO THE CENTER OF THE PHENOMENON OF GOOD WRITERS. PEOPLE
WHO LEARN TO CREATE PRIVACY FOR THEMSELVES: WHO LEARN TO BE
PRIVATE AND SOLITARY AND TUNE OUT OTHERS, WRITE ONLY FOR
SELVES—HAVE NO INTEREST IN THE NEEDS AND INTERESTS AND PRES-
SURES OF AUDIENCE.

YET, THEY ARE ALSO PEOPLE WHO LEARN TO TURN THAT TO AUDIENCE
INTEREST. MORE THAN USUALLY INTERESTED IN AUDIENCE—HAM,
POSEUR, ACTOR, SHOWOFF.

SO HERE AGAIN, WE HAVE AN ANALYSIS OF COMPLEX DIFFICULT BE-
HAVIOR, PERFORMANCE, SKILL: WHAT MAKES IT DIFFICULT AND COMPLEX
AND SUBJECT TO ARGUMENT IS THAT IT CONSISTS OF ESSENTIAL PARA-
DOX. A GOOD WRITER IS SOMEONE WHO IS MORE THAN USUALLY PRIVATE
AND WRITING ONLY TO SELF YET AT THE SAME TIME MORE THAN USUALLY
SHOWOFFY AND PUBLIC AND GRANDSTANDING AND SELFPANDERING.
THEY SOUND OPPOSITE, YET THATS JUST WHAT WE SEE WITH SO MANY
GOOD WRITERS.

LYRIC POETS; PAUL GOODMAN. WHO ELSE TO NAME?
I'd thought of "double-audience" phenomenon as an interesting anomaly in writing. (It was during one of my writing-to-myself sessions during one of my bard summers. What occasioned it? I must still have the note I wrote then.) BUT REALLY WHAT LOOKS LIKE AN ANOMALY IS REALLY CHARACTERISTIC THE MAIN THING—RIGHT AT THE CENTER OF WRITING. OR AT LEAST GOOD WRITING.

As I look back on this, I don't think I'd have been able to work out these ideas if I'd been trying to stay "on track" or know where I was going.

Freewriting as Sociable

Freewriting is always private—by definition, for the sake of safety. But I have come to feel an intriguing link between freewriting and sociability because I so often do this private writing *in the company of others*—with a class or a workshop. Thus true freewriting "by the book," never pausing, has come in certain ways to feel like a companionable activity: one sits there writing for oneself but hears other people's pens and pencils moving across the paper, people moving in their chairs, sometimes a grunt or sigh or giggle. The effect of using these conditions for freewriting (however private) is to contradict the association of writing with isolation. An even more important effect is the palpable sense of "Look at all these people putting words down on paper without agony. If they can do it, well so can I!" This contradicts a feeling hidden in many of us (not just raw freshmen) that really there's something impossible about putting words down on paper, and when we succeed in doing so it's some kind of accident or aberration, but next time the impossibility will return.

My experience with Ira Progoff's journal approach has also underlined the social dimension of freewriting. His workshops consist of nothing but private journal writing (though he gives powerful prompts for ways to explore one's life), yet after a long writing session he often asks, "Does anyone need to read out loud what he's written?" He stresses that it's not important for others to understand or even listen carefully, and there's *never* any response; he simply suggests that sometimes we feel that the writing is not really "finished" till we've had a chance to read it out loud in the hearing of others. I occasionally use Progoff-like journal writing exercises in my teaching, and though I never invite people to read out loud, there is nevertheless this important experience of doing private work *together*.

But the sociable flavor of freewriting is strongest for me because of the times when, instead of regular freewriting, I've used *public* or *shared* freewriting in a supportive community: "Let's freewrite and then read it to each other." In the first draft of this essay I said I didn't do this very often, but over the course of revising I've realized that's wrong. There are many occasions when I do *some* form of public freewriting. This slowness in my memory is revealing: I'm a bit ambivalent about shared or public freewriting. On the one hand, I tend to avoid it in favor of private writing. For I find most people's writing has suffered because they have been led to think of writing as something they must always share with a reader; thus we need more private writing. On the other hand, I love the sharing of freewriting—for the community of it and for the learning it produces. It's so reassuring to discover that completely unplanned, unstudied writing is often worth sharing. It teaches the pleasure of getting more voice in writing. (And we learn so much by reading out loud—by mouth and by ear.) As a result, I try to find occasions for public freewriting. I find students are often more willing to read something out loud if they've just freewritten it quickly than if they've worked hard revising it.

Let me list, then, the diverse situations where I use public freewriting. (I always make it clear that someone can "pass" if she doesn't want to share.)

- I often start a course or workshop with two short pieces of freewriting, one private and one public, in order to give people a vivid sense of the differences: how seldom they really write privately and what a useful luxury it is to do so. Because of this agenda I sometimes start with the public writing and make the task slightly daunting: "Introduce yourself in writing to the strangers here." Two constraints have been reimposed, namely, that the writing be shown to an audience and that it stay on one topic. Thus the freewriting is both public and focused.
- Process writing. After the opening exercise I just described, I often ask the students or teachers to write about what they noticed during the private and public freewriting—to write as much as they can about simply what happened as they were writing. Here is another case of freewriting that is both focused and public. (Often of course I invite process writing to be private, and sometimes I say, "This is private, but I hope we'll be able to hear a couple of them afterward, or at least talk about what people wrote.") Process writing is interesting for being both very personal and also very task-oriented and cognitive. People are often eager to share what happened to them and hear what happened to others. I make this kind of process writing a staple of my classes throughout the semester, usually asking for a piece of it to accompany each major assignment.
- In my teaching I sometimes ask us all to freewrite on a topic or issue we are working on and then hear many of them. Sometimes this is part of a disciplined inquiry (see Hammond), sometimes it is more celebratory, just writing and sharing on an interesting or enjoyable topic for the pleasure of it.
- My work with the Bard Institute for Writing and Thinking has provided me a particularly important experience of freewriting as sociable. In the summer of 1981 I was given the opportunity to bring together a group of about twenty teachers to teach a three-week intensive writing program for Bard freshmen. It was an exciting but scary adventure into the unknown for all of us, and I needed to ask from the start that we work together as a community of allies. At our first meeting I had us begin by freewriting with the expectation of shar-

ing. This group of teachers has continued this tradition, meeting at least a couple of times a year. (Paul Connolly has been director since 1982 and the group conducts workshops and conferences, in addition to teaching Bard freshmen in the summer.) The freewriting and sharing in this group have been very important for me: a paradigm experience of people working together out of enormous trust, trust in our writing and in each other. The question I used in one of our early meetings is one that is often still used: "What needs to be written?" This question sums up a kind of trust in the group dimension of the Muse. I have very few other groups where I feel I can ask for this kind of open public freewriting with no topic. But the experience remains a touchstone for one way writing can be, and it illustrates a crucial principle: though privacy might seem to be the safest possible condition for writing (since no one will read what you write), the safety is greater when you can share what is private with a full ally—someone who will support you and not condemn you whatever you write. That is, when we write privately we can seldom get away from the condemning judge most of us carry around in our heads, but a really supportive trusting audience can give some relief from that judge. This relates to Britton's emphasis (1975) on the importance of a "trusted adult" as a reader for children. I have occasionally met with a feedback group in which, as a prelude to giving feedback to each other on writing we brought in, we all did a piece of public freewriting and shared it—here too as a way to try to establish openness and trust. I know some feedback groups that do this regularly.

The Difference Between Private and Public Freewriting

Here are examples of both audience modes in freewriting, one written right after the other, that illustrate a difference I've come to notice fairly frequently between my private and public freewriting. The scene was a workshop for English teachers from primary grades through university. The public freewriting came first and the topic was "What do we have in common?":

What do we have in common? Seems to me we're all involved in helping people have *power* over language. And power over themselves. To wh Whether it's kindergarten or graduate school, it's the same struggle—and potentially the same triumph—figuring out what we have to say, what's on our minds, and figuring out how to *say* it to readers.

Then the "Dare to say it," I find myself muttering to myself. Because what so often gets in my way when I'm trying to find my thoughts and find how to say them is a matter of *courage* and *confidence*. Even more for my students. When we I feel brave and trust myself, I am full of good stuff. When I'm scared and doubting myself I am continually tongue-tied and stuck.

And what's interesting is to me is that I have to keep learning that over and over again. I get brave—I was felt brave in getting out WWT [*Writing Without Teachers*]. Yet then over and over again I feel scared or doubt myself. And so I think I see it in my students too. From kindergarten to grad school, we keep having to *relearn* ~~how~~ this lesson.

Why should that be? Perhaps because life continually buffets us. Perhaps because as we learn or get brave ~~we cont inually~~—as we get more slack in the rope—we take on harder scarier tasks.

The topic for the private writing was "What divides us?" but I immediately fell into talking about what I felt during my public freewriting and how different it felt from my private freewriting:

What divides? I was kind of pollyanna as I wrote that. I was on a soap box. It kind of helped me with my syntax: a kind of belly full of air keeping pressure on my diaphragm so that there was more resonance in that writing. I was "projecting" more in my public writing. Making my words kind of push themselves forward ~~over~~ a out and over to readers. Somehow—once I got going—it made it easier to keep writing. In an odd way it *helped* me find words. It was as though I was standing in front of a small group of people listening and I had to keep talking. I couldn't just fall dumb and perplexed. The *pressure* of the audience situation forced ~~me to f~~ words upon me. However they felt a little bit just that—"forced"—a little bit as though I don't trust them.

Odd fact. As I get ~~myself~~ in to this piece of writing—in the middle of the last paragraph—I find myself thinking, "this is interesting." And I'm looking for little bits of process writing ~~for~~ to use in a textbook. I say, "maybe I could use this." And before I know it, I'm feeling the presence of audience and slightly "fixing" or "helping" my words.

You *might* say that shows there's no such thing as really private writing. It's *always* for an audience. And I know there are strong arguments there.

But I still disagree. And even this piece is evidence for me. For I could feel the *difference*. It felt different as I gradually drifted into making my words ready for readers.

I'm not saying I know the words-as-products were different. But *to me*—the process of finding and putting them down was different ~~fo~~ depending on whether I wanted them for just me or for others. [Written by hand]

I hope my public freewriting doesn't always succumb to the slightly "public," tinny quality here, straining for something "meaningful" to say. I was among strangers and nervous, trying too hard. It's different when I feel myself safe among trusted colleagues. But this example illustrates a common effect of audience awareness.

Using Freewriting to Write Responses or Feedback

When I write responses to papers by colleagues and students, I don't freewrite strictly (never pausing), but I sort-of-freewrite. As a writing teacher, I have so much responding to do that I've gradually given myself permission to write quickly. In doing so I've discovered that sometimes I get "steaming along" and a kind of door opens: my perceptions are heightened, my feelings somewhat more aroused, and my language feels more fluid and "at the fingertips"—as though no "translation" is required from mind to paper. I can almost "think onto the paper" with no awareness of language. For me, this condition of "getting rolling" seems a good state for responding. For some reason, this special condition of writing, both more open and more intense, seems to lead to a better condition of reading: a heightened awareness of how the words were affecting my consciousness and more hunches about what was going on for the writer as he or she was writing. Yes, I often write too much and the writing is not judicious, but I do it on a computer so I can delete my worst gaffes. In addition, this somewhat more intense condition makes me write more *to* the writer: makes me talk turkey, not hold back, not tiptoe around. An example, to a first-year student:

Dear Lisa,

This is long and interesting. It has problems as a piece of writing because there is so much in it, but all the things in it are rich.
Here's what I notice:

- I love the way you start out for much of the opening in a mood of *questioning*. Terrific. I say, "Here's an essay/paper that says, I'm baffled, I'm troubled, I want to try to figure something out." And that's a terrific thing to do. Perplexity absorbs the reader. (And of course it's a deep and interesting issue.) And I say to myself, "I hope she doesn't somehow tie it up into some neat tidy package of "wisdom" with a ribbon around it—neater than life.

- But then you drift into a long story of you and Stacy. What's interesting to me here is the change from last time. Last version the mood was primarily "pissed"! Here it's kind of held-back-pissed. It somehow doesn't work for me for much of it. I say, "why doesn't she just admit how mad she is?"

- But then at the end of the story you really do some hard thinking about her and you seem primarily analytic and probing and NOT angry; you are really trying to take hold of it and figure out how to build some stability. And your thinking and probing are convincing and interesting to me.

- So then I finally conclude that the main problem with the story of you and Stacy is just the length and the lost focus: it makes me forget what the paper is really about—or at least I lose track.
So in the end, I feel these things:

- The paper is *trying* very much to be an extended meditation on the question of where do we get stability from—and why instability. And I love that. And I like your thinking about Stacy. But somehow that doesn't solve your larger problem: not everyone has had such a hard life as she has had. (However maybe your generalization would still hold true for the rest of us: I think it really is hard to trust people; and your conclusion is strong. But don't sound so smug and tidy with it. It's only a hypothesis and it may not fit everyone. But if you present it that way, I'd call it interesting and useful.)

Talk to me some week toward the end of the term about perhaps using a week to try another *major* revision of this. There's so much here and you are really trying to deal with something important and hard. I'd like to see you get this bucking bronco under control. Let it rest a few weeks.
    best,
    Peter [On word processor]

There is an important connection between my love of freewriting and my love of giving feedback in the form of "movies of my mind": a narrative of the mind reacting. That is, even though freewriting *can* lead to objective description or to analysis (as it sometimes does for me), it tends to invite an account of the mind reacting. For if you have to keep writing, the only inexhaustible source of material *is* a story of what's happening in your mind at the moment. You can't run out (indeed, like Tristram Shandy, you often fall behind).

Freewriting about Freewriting

I freewrote the following piece in my freshman class in 1987, using a beginning of the class freewriting time to reflect on my perplexity after having recently filled out a questionnaire from Sheryl Fontaine about my use of freewriting. When had I filled out her questionnaire I had been nervous to notice that though I use freewriting a lot in my teaching and in my workshops, I don't so often do *pure* freewriting on my own, by choice.

> Freewriting. Sheryl. You're making me think more self consciously about freewriting. Freewriting. Am I fooling myself about it somehow?
>   Do I not *use* freewriting? Am I guilty of not practicing what I preach?
>   Actually an old story with me. I used to feel that way a lot after WWT [*Writing Without Teachers*] came out. And in truth I *couldn't* [double underline] do, then, what I'd figured out in thinking through that book was a good thing to do. It ie, to relinquish control. It took a year or two. But ~~th~~ it's not so unusual: we the human (mind) often works that way: we figure out in *theory* what we cannot do in *practice*—we learn to "act" with neural impulses acts we cannot yet get our ~~min~~ bodies to do. (Except when it goes the other way around: really clever people learn from their *behavior* and then get the wisdom in their minds. Sometimes
>   But And I even felt it many times after WWP [*Writing With Power*]. Am I a fraud?—is the archetypal question. Will people look beneath my surface to my reality and find out I'm no good—wrong—dishonest?
>   ~~But~~ actually, I think I *do* practice what I preach. (Though I wouldn't be surprised to discover that I ~~preach~~ forget to preach some important things that I practice.)
>   This is like a letter to you—but calling it "fw" gives me permission to be sloppy about it.
>   I forgot to remember that *letters* are another place where I use freewriting. [By hand]

So do I or don't I use freewriting in my own writing? I guess the answer is that I don't use it so often "by the book" or "by the clock" when I'm writing substantive pieces on my own. And I don't do daily freewrites or regular warm-up exercises. But I make journal entries when something is confusing me in my life and I rely heavily on what I like to think of as my "freewriting muscle" in all the ways I describe in this chapter. This "muscle" seems to me in essence to consist of the ability to write in fairly fast and long bursts at early stages of any project—sometimes later stages, too—when I get an idea or hunch (or fruitful doubt): to blurt as much of my thinking on paper as I can. In general, when I am not revising I have learned to lessen control and accept thoughts and words as they come.

Process Writing When I'm Stuck:
Articulating Resistance

As I noted at the start, I drifted into something like freewriting when I felt stuck in my life. One of my most frequent and consistent uses of freewriting is when I feel stuck in my writing. *Writing Without Teachers* grew from little germs of stuck writing. Here is one of the many stuck writings I did while working on this essay. I found myself going back and forth in my head about where to put a projected section about control and noncontrol (and even moving my note about it back and forth in my computer file), *instead of starting to write it*. I freewrite in capital letters here not because I am shouting but because I want to be able to distinguish this metawriting from the rest of my text.

HERE I'M WORRYING ABOUT WHERE TO PUT THIS SECTION ON CON-TROL/NONCONTROL—AND THE UNCERTAINTY IS REALLY GETTING IN MY WAY, AND CAUSING A KNOT IN MY STOMACH AND MAKING ME FEEL BAD BECAUSE I KNOW I'M LOSING TIME AND I'M BEHIND SCHEDULE HERE. WHEN I HAVEN'T EVEN WRITTEN A DRAFT OF THIS SECTION YET. IN THE BACK OF MY MIND I KNOW THAT IF I'D JUST STOP WORRYING ABOUT THE OVERALL RHETORICAL STRATEGY AND JUST PUT MY HEAD DOWN AND START TO WRITE WHAT I WANT TO WRITE, I WOULD NOT JUST FEEL BET-TER ABOUT GETTING SOMETHING WORKED OUT—ALMOST CERTAINLY THE PROCESS OF DOING IT WOULD SOLVE THE STRATEGIC QUESTION OF WHERE IT SHOULD GO OR HOW TO CONSIDER IT. (AM I THINKING OF IT AS PARA-DOX OR AS MY MAIN COMMITMENT?)

WHY IS IT SO HARD TO JUST DO THIS IF I KNOW IT'S THE RIGHT THING TO DO. I CAN FEEL THE ANSWER. THOUGH IT'S MORE EFFICIENT AND SMARTER TO PLUNGE IN, THERE'S SOMETHING THAT HOLDS ME BACK AND THE METAPHOR OF "PLUNGING IN" IS JUST RIGHT FOR "EXPLAINING" WHY: THERE'S SOME KIND OF JUMPING IN TO A DEEP AND SLIGHTLY SCARY ELEMENT THAT'S INVOLVED HERE. [on word processor]

Where there had been intense strain in trying to control my thinking and lan-guage all afternoon, unsuccessful planning and inept steering (leading to awful writing), here was a rush of letting go and just allowing words to take over without much steering. It is a mere blurting, but the effect was to help me see more clearly what was happening and to gain some power over my writing process.

Heightened Intensity

What I value in freewriting is how it can lead to a certain *experience* of writing or *kind* of writing process. The best descriptors of that experience are perhaps the metaphors that have sprinkled this essay so far: "getting rolling," "getting steaming along," "a door opening," "getting warmed up," "juices flowing," or "sailing." These all point to states of increased intensity or arousal or excitement. In these states it feels as though more things come to mind, bubble up, and that somehow they fall more directly into language (though not necessarily better, clearer, or more organized language). And sometimes, along with this, comes a vivid sense of knowing exactly to *whom* I need to say these things.

I know this is dangerous territory I'm wandering into. So many students have talked about how wonderful it *felt* while they were writing something—leaving us the job of telling them how bad the writing was that grew out of that feeling. Excitement doesn't make writing good. But freewriting doesn't pretend to be good. So if we have to write badly, as of course we do, I find it more rewarding to be excited while doing it.

In short, though it is dangerous to defend excitement or heightened intensity or "getting carried away" as conditions we should strive for in writing—and readers will no doubt fear renewed talk about that dangerous concept "inspiration"—I find myself deciding it is time to take the risk. I know I produce a lot of garbage and disorganization when I get wound up in freewriting or freewritinglike extended explorations, but at these times it feels as though I can see more clearly what I'm thinking *about* and also experience more clearly my mind *engaged in* the thinking. They are the times that make it rewarding to write and make me want to return to the struggle of it. I doubt whether many people continue to write by choice, except for the periodic reward of some kind of intensity of this sort. For example, Louise Wetherbee Phelps writes:

> Throughout my daybooks I have tried repeatedly to capture the feeling of the generative moment. It is not a cool, cerebral experience but a joyous state of physical excitement and pure power felt in the stomach and rising up in the chest as a flood of energy that pours out in rapid explosive bursts of language. It is a pleasantly nervous state, like the feeling of the gymnast ready to mount the apparatus who is tuned tautly and confidently to the powers and capabilities of her own body. Ideas compel expression: I write in my daybook of their force shooting and sparking through my fingers onto the paper. ("Rhythm and Pattern in a Composing Life" 247)

Phelps says she is engaged in phenomenology. She is trying

> to approach the level and quality of phenomenological description, which
> involves not only intuiting, analyzing, and describing particulars of com-
> posing in their full concreteness, but also attempting to attain insight into
> the essence of the experience. (243)

The nascent interest in phenomenology in the profession is a good sign: a
respect for the facts of what actually happens in writers. We've had a decade
of protocol analysis and television cameras trained on writers, all fueled by a
devotion to the facts about the writing process. But feelings are facts, and
until this research bothers to investigate the powerful effects that feelings
often have on a writer's thoughts and choices, I will have a hard time trusting
it. (Linda Flower's recent protocols seem to take more account of feelings, e.g.,
"Negotiating Academic Discourse.") My own investigations show me that feelings often *shape* my cognitive choices. When we get more careful phenomenological research, I suspect that one result will be to give us more respect for
this suspect business of being excited, aroused, carried away, "rolling." (For a
few leads into the use of phenomenology and study of feelings in writing, see
Brand *The Psychology of Writing,* Emig "Inquiry Paradigms," Flisser, Gleason,
McLeod, Perl and Egendorf, Phelps, and Whatley.)

A Kind of Goodness in Writing

Because freewriting produces so much careless, self-indulgent, bad writing, I
am nervous about defending it as good, and, as I've just said, it's not for the
product that I value it most. Nevertheless freewriting has come to serve, I
now see, as a model of what seems to me an important *kind* of goodness in
writing. That is, even if I spend much less time freewriting than I spend trying to control and revise, freewriting has come to establish for me a directness
of tone, sound, style, and diction that I realize I often try to emulate in my
careful revising.

For example, freewriting sometimes helps me as it were to break free from
what feels like the heavy mud and clinging seaweed that clog my ability to *say
directly* what I already know. As I was working on the preceding section of
this essay I found myself having written this sentence:

> But it strikes me if we only stop and think about it for a moment, I think
> we'll have to agree that we better take the risk of sounding sophomoric or
> ridiculous in other ways—that is of talking turkey about what it actually
> felt like during the important moments of writing—because that is exactly
> what we haven't gotten much of in fifteen years of people saying they are in-
> vestigating the composing process.

When I looked back and notice what a *soggy* thing I'd just struggled hard to
produce, I was dismayed. In frustration I stopped and forced myself to
freewrite. "Damn it, what am I really trying to *say?*"

WE BETTER RISK TAKING OUR CLOTHES OFF AND DESCRIBING WHAT AC-
TUALLY HAPPENS WHEN WE WRITE—WHAT IT FEELS LIKE—THE TEXTURE
FROM MOMENT TO MOMENT. BECAUSE THAT'S WHAT WE'VE BEEN LACK-
ING FROM ALL THESE YEARS OF PROTOCOL ANALYSIS OF WRITERS.
THEY'VE SUPPOSEDLY GIVEN US PICTURE OF THE WRITERS MIND, BUT
IT DOESN'T LOOK LIKE MY MIND. IT'S TOO SANITIZED. IT LEAVES OUT
FEELINGS.

I GUESS IT'S NO ACCIDENT THAT WE LEAVE THEM OUT. THE FEELINGS
ARE SO SOPHOMORIC OR ODD OR STUPID OR CHILDISH. WRITING BRINGS
OUT FEELINGS THAT MAKE US FEEL LIKE WE'RE NOT GROWN UP, NOT SO-
PHISTICATED. PERHAPS WHAT MAKES SOPHOMORES SOPHOMORES IS THAT
THEY ACTUALLY ADMIT WHAT THEY ARE FEELING.

WHAT I WANT IS MORE PHENOMONOLOGY OF WRITING. PHENOME-
NOLOGY IS PERHAPS JUST A FANCY WORD TO MAKE US ALL FEEL A LITTLE
SAFER ABOUT BEING NAKED—AND FANCIER WORD FOR GOING NAKED.
BUT IF THAT HELPS, SO BE IT. BESIDES, IT'S MORE THAN THAT. THERE IS
THAT ENORMOUS AND COMPLEX DISCIPLINE THAT PHENOMENOLOGISTS
TALK ABOUT—IN THEIR GERMAN JARGON—ABOUT TRYING TO GET PAST
THE OVERLAY OF WHAT IS CULTURALLY OR LINGUISTICALLY DETERMINED
AND HABITUAL. A MESS. BUT WORTH THE EFFORT. LET ME GIVE A FOOT-
NOTE THAT MENTIONS THE PEOPLE I KNOW WHO ARE TALKING ABOUT
FEELINGS AND PHENOMENOLOGY.

I confess I *like* these short bursts of freewriting. They are too careless, too casual, too whatever: I can't "hand them in" that way. (This essay is an excuse to hand in a few pieces "for credit.") But I want to get as much of that quality as I can into my acceptable writing: the energy, the talkiness, the sense of a voice, and the sense of the words' or the writer's reaching *toward* a reader.

Speaking of the effect of feelings on cognition, freewriting somehow seems to elicit more analogies and metaphors, often physical and crass. I find these help my thinking. I've come to call this kind of discourse "talking turkey." My freewriting tends to be more like a speech act and less like the formulation of impersonal truths. Thus even though I can seldom use my freewriting as it is, I think my history with it has put a kind of *sound* in my ear and a *feel* in my mouth, a sound and a feel that guide me in my revising.

Relinquishing Control—Not Striving for Mastery

There is another experience that is central to my involvement with freewriting and that is the sense of *letting go*. This is partly the cause, but also sometimes the effect, of the heightened intensity I've just been talking about. The two condi-tions seem to go along with each other. At any rate, when I am writing carefully or revising I usually experience myself as trying to hold on—to plan or control: to figure out what I want to say, or (knowing that) to *say* what I want to say, or (having done that) to get my words clear or coherent or organized. It feels like trying to steer, to hold things together, to juggle balls. I usually experience this as struggle and strain. When I freewrite I let go, stop steering, drop the balls and allow things to come to me—just babble onto paper. It's the difference between Linda Flower's emphasis on always making a plan and trying to follow it versus plunging along with no plan; between trying to steer versus letting go of the steering wheel and just letting words come.

Not that it's always relaxed. Freewriting often makes for an increased tension of sorts. It's as though writing were a matter of my head containing a pile of sand that has to pour down through a tiny hole onto the paper, as though my head were an hourglass. When I freewrite it feels as though someone has dumped an extra fifty pounds of sand in the top chamber of my head, so the sand is pressing down and coming through that tiny hole in my mind with more pressure, though faster too. (This odd metaphor also came out in freewriting.) But despite the pressure, there is a kind of relief or comfort at the very no-stopping that *causes* the pressure: to see whether I can really bring all that sand down through the small opening.

I sometimes think of it as a matter of *translation*. That is, it feels to me as though the "contents of my mind" or "what I am trying to say" won't run naturally onto paper—as though what's "in mind" is unformed, incoherent, indeed much of it not even verbal, consisting rather of images, feelings, kinesthetic sensations, and pieces of what Gendlin calls "felt sense" [see the piece that follows this one in this volume; also Perl "Understanding Composing"]. Thus it often feels as though writing requires some act of translation to get what's *in mind into writing.* (Some social constructionists like to say that all knowledge is verbal or linguistic. It's hard for me to believe they really believe that, but if it were true we would find it much easier to articulate ourselves.)

Let me put it yet another way. It feels as though my mind is messy and confused and unformed, but that writing is supposed to be clear and organized. Therefore, writing really asks for *two* things: to get my meaning into words *and* to get those words clear and organized. What's really hard here is trying to do the two things in one operation. Freewriting shows me I can do them one at a time: just *get my mind into words,* but leave those words messy and incoherent.

What a relief. For it's not so hard to neaten up those messy words, once they are on paper, where they stay still. For—and this is another central experience for me when I try to write normally or carefully—the words and ideas and feelings in my head won't stay still: they are always sliding around and changing and driving me crazy. Interestingly enough, I find that it's easier to clear up a mess I produced by galloping freewriting than to clean up a mess I produced by careful composing. The freewriting is crudely jointed so that all the sections and elements are obvious, whereas the careful mess is delicately held together by elaborate structures of baling wire, and once I fiddle with it, everything seems to fall apart into unusable or unlinkable elements. (And sometimes, of course, the freewriting is *not* such a mess.)

In fact, I often experience an additional relief in this very messiness and incoherence. That is, sometimes it feels as though there is a primal gulf between my experience and what can be communicated to others: as though I am trapped inside a cavern of feelings, perceptions, and thoughts that no one can ever share; as if I am in a Fellini movie where I shout ineffectually across a windy gulf and no one hears, or in a Faulkner novel where I talk and move my mouth—and no sound comes out. I find great relief in coming up with words that embody or express the very *incoherence* or *unformed* quality of my inner existence. (What I appreciate about reading novels by people like Woolf, Faulkner, and May Sarton is the relief of finding someone who articulates the textures of experience and feeling that sometimes seem trapping.) In short, where everything about the process of normal writing tells us, "Plan! Control! Steer!" freewriting invites me to stop planning, controlling, steering.

I acknowledge that of course we cannot, strictly speaking, get the "contents of mind" onto paper as they are. And, of course, there is probably no such thing as truly unplanned speech or uncontrolled behavior. The human organism seems incapable of randomness. To relinquish conscious control, plans, or goals is to allow for unconscious plans, "unplanned" goals, tacit shapes and rhythms in our thinking—and for more control and inscription by the culture. Nevertheless, there is an enormous difference between the experience of planning one's words and thoughts beforehand (whether carefully planning large chunks on paper in an outline, or just rehearsing phrases and sentences in one's mind before writing them down), and the experience of letting words go down on paper unrehearsed and unforeseen. Obviously, freewriting does not always produce this latter experience, but it does tend in this direction with some reliability: to that undeniable experience of the hand leading the mind, of the emerging words somehow choosing other words, of seeing what comes when one manages to invite the momentum of language or one's larger mind or whatever to take over. Freewriting is an invitation to stop writing and instead to "be written."

Of course, there is a sense in which whenever we write "we are written." But when people are too glib or doctrinaire about this, they obscure the crucial empirical differences between those moments when we have plans, meanings, or intentions in mind and keep to them, and those other moments when we proceed without conscious plans, meanings, or intentions. The difference between these two conditions is something we need to investigate rather than paper over. The most graphic example is surprise. That is, even if there is no such thing as uncontrolled or unplanned writing, there is a huge difference between knowing what one is writing and being startled by it. I'd guess that this kind of surprise is another of those rewards that make people who write by choice continue to do so. Freewriting increases the frequency of surprise. That is, even though it gives scope for one's hobbyhorses and obsessions, it also opens the door to thoughts and feelings that startle and even feel like "not me."

In our culture, *mastery* and *control* are deeply built into our model of writing. From freewriting I learn how writing can, in contrast, involve *passivity,* an experience of nonstriving, unclenching, letting go, or opening myself up. In other cultures people do more justice to this dimension of writing, talking in ways we call superstitious or magical—for example, about taking diction from the Muse or going into a trance. My hunch is that many good writers engage in lots of "wise passivity."

Some writers acknowledge this and talk about consciously trying to relax some control and engage in a process of waiting and listening. (Donald Murray sounds this note eloquently.) For example, distinguished writers often talk about creating characters and then consciously waiting to see what they do. But what's even more touching is the testimony of writers who *try* to stay in control but fail, giving thereby a kind of backhanded testimony to the importance of relinquishing control. Barbara Tomlinson has collected fascinating examples of what she calls the theme of "characters as co-authors" in the phenomenology of writers writing. "[C]haracters 'demand' things (William Faulkner . . . , Reynolds Price, Barbara Wersba), reject things (William Inge, Joyce Carol Oates . . . , Sylvia Wilkinson), insist on speaking (Robertson Davies, Joyce Carol Oates . . . , Harold Pinter), refuse to speak (Paul Gallico, Cynthia MacDonald), ignore authors' suggestions (Katherine Anne Porter), 'resent' what has been written about them (Saul Bellow . . .), confront their authors (Timothy Findley . . . , Margaret MacPherson) and so forth" (Tomlinson 8).[2]

John Cheever is troubled by this kind of talk and insists that "[t]he legend that characters run away from their authors—taking up drugs, having sex operations, and becoming president—implies that the writer is a fool with no knowledge or mastery of his craft (Tomlinson 29)." Surely Cheever is wrong here. Surely a writer *lacks* knowledge and mastery of his craft unless he has the ability to allow himself to develop—even subversively, as it were—the gift for relinquishing control, for example, by unconsciously empowering a character to take over and contradict his conscious plan.

Does it sound as though I am against planning and control in writing? I am not. What is probably the *majority* of my writing time is taken up trying to establish and maintain control, to steer, to try and get the damn thing to go where I want it to go. But my struggle for control rests on a foundation of shorter stretches of time when I manage to relinquish control. And I'm not just saying that my freewriting produces more material or fodder for my planning or control. No, when my writing goes well, it is usually because the plan

---

2. From the many examples from Tomlinson's work, here is Joyce Carol Oates:

[In] general the writing writes itself—I mean a character determines his or her "voice" and I must follow along. Had I my own way the first section of The Assassins would be much abbreviated. But it was impossible to shut Hugh Petrie up once he got going and, long and painful and unwieldy as his section is, it's nevertheless been shortened. The problem with creating such highly conscious and intuitive characters is that they tend to perceive the contours of the literary landscape in which they dwell, and like Kash of Childwold, try to guide or even take over the direction of the narrative. Hugh did not want to die, and so his section went on and on, and it isn't an exaggeration to say that I felt real dismay in dealing with him. (Paris Review 214–15)

itself—my sense of where I'm trying to get my material to go—*came* to me in a piece of noncontrolled writing. Freewriting doesn't just give "content"; it also gives "form."

Dwelling In and Popping Out

Because freewriting is an invitation to become less self-conscious about writing, to stop attending consciously to the choosing and forming of words, it helps me enter more easily and fully *into* my writing and thinking. To use Polanyi's terms, it helps me make writing more a "part of myself" or to "pour myself into" writing. He speaks of writing and language as tools and he is interested in the process by which one "pours oneself into" the hammer while one hammers—focusing attention on the nail rather than on the hammer.[3]

But although this effect of freewriting is important, I am also beginning to notice (with the help of what Pat Belanoff writes) the opposite effect: how often freewriting is not just a pouring myself into my discourse but also popping myself out of it. For some reason, freewriting has the capacity to increase our awareness of what we've written—what we are doing. Notice, for example, in one of my early journal entries how I wrote, "But when I get this down on paper I see that . . .": the act of writing down a feeling made me more aware of it from the outside. Here is a more extended example. My freewriting during a stuck point in writing this essay led me to make a metapoint about the structure of my essay, and then even to reflect on metadiscourse itself:

I SEEM TO BE MAKING TWO POINTS: MORE EXCITING INTENSE STATE; AND RELINQUISHING CONTROL. HOW DO THEY RELATE? DO THEY WORK AGAINST EACH OTHER?

META POINT: FREEWRITING HAS LED ME TO MAKE MORE OF THESE META POINTS AS ABOVE: MORE ARTICULATING MY DILEMMA—TRYING TO PUT THEM INTO WORDS. NOT ALWAYS WRITTEN NONSTOP, BUT USUALLY QUICKLY. BUT IT'S OF THE ESSENCE OF FREEWRITING (FOR ME) TO BE AN ARENA FOR TALKING ABOUT A METAPOINT—A COMMENT ABOUT A DILEMMA—AN ATTEMPT TO FIND WORDS FOR A DILEMMA OR PERPLEXITY.

BEFORE I GOT ACCUSTOMED TO FREEWRITING I DIDN'T WRITE THESE THINGS OUT; I WOULD SIT AND PONDER—PERHAPS WORK OUT NOTES— PHRASES. BUT THESE "FREEWRITING LIKE DISCOURSES" ARE A KIND OF

---

3. "Our subsidiary awareness of tools and probes can be regarded now as the act of making them form a part of our own body. The way we use a hammer or a blind man uses his stick, shows in fact that in both cases we shift outwards the points at which we make contact with the things that we observe as objects outside ourselves. We may test the tool for its effectiveness or the probe for its suitability . . . , but [when we actually use these tools], they remain necessarily on our side . . . , forming part of ourselves. We pour ourselves out into them and assimilate them as parts of our own existence. We accept them existentially by dwelling in them. . . . Hammers and probes can be replaced by intellectual tools" (Polanyi 59). He goes on to talk about language, noting specifically how hyperconsciousness of the language in one's mouth or in one's hand can ruin the smooth use of it.

ACTUAL "TALKING TO MYSELF" IN SPEECH—NOT A MATTER OF BETTER BOILING THINGS DOWN INTO NOTES. THE MOVE TO NOTES IS A MOVE FROM THE TEXT FURTHER AWAY—FROM THE DISCOURSE OF THE TEXT INTO SUMMARY AND ESSENCES—THAT'S THE POINT OF NOTES: THE PERSPECTIVE THAT COMES FROM ESSENCES. BUT THIS MOVE I'M MAKING NOW IS A MOVE FROM THE TEXT IN THE OPPOSITE DIRECTION—MORE TOWARD SPEECH. TALKING TO MYSELF. IT'S MUCH MESSIER—IT DOESN'T HAVE THAT LOVELY PERSPECTIVE OF NOTES AND ESSENCES—BUT SOMEHOW IT OFTEN HAS THE JUICE OR BUBBLING ACTION (ALKA SELZER) TO CUT THROUGH PERPLEXITY THAT I CAN'T WORK OUT WITH NOTES AND ESSENCES. I NEED TO "HAVE A LITTLE CHAT WITH MYSELF"—A KIND OF HUMAN TRANSACTION AS WITH AN UNDERSTANDING AUNT—RATHER THAN TRYING TO DO FREEZE DRIED SUMMARY TRANSACTION WITH ANGELS OR GOD.

When my colleague, Bob Whitney, was trying to help a student who couldn't seem to freewrite because she said "nothing is on my mind," he said *"Nothing* begins with *N."* In saying this he was really popping her out of her stream or plane of thought—which was after all mere emptiness or blankness of mind. For of course no matter how deeply I insist that our minds are never empty, I must admit that we often enough *experience* our minds as genuinely empty. Whitney, then, was coaching her to step *outside* that blankness of mind and to write a phrase such as "Nothing's on my mind" or "Nothing going on here." To write such a phrase is really to *comment upon* one's mental state.

If we reflect for a moment we can see why freewriting invites metadiscourse. When I am writing along in normal conditions I commonly pause: my thought has run out or I wonder about what I've just written or I can't find the word I want. But when I freewrite, the "no stopping" rule won't let me pause. What happens? If I cannot find the next word or thought, the natural next event is to write down a piece of metadiscourse. Indeed, the ticking clock has probably *put* a piece of metadiscourse into my mind ("Oh dear, I've run out" or "I don't know what to say next"). Freewriting also invites metadiscourse because, as blurting, it often leads to something that surprises or dismays us: "That's not the right word" or "Do I really feel that way?" or "What a nasty thought."

It is intriguing that freewriting should help me move in these two directions: on the one hand to "indwell" or pour myself *into* my language, thinking, and feeling; yet on the other hand to step outside or at least *notice* and comment on my language, thinking, and feeling. Yet I don't experience this metadiscourse as a distancing or stepping *outside* my language or thinking. I feel just as "poured into" these pieces of metadiscourse. Indeed, it feels as though the capacity that freewriting has for making writing more a part of myself comes especially from these metacomments, this experience of finding language for these reflections on language. Perhaps the paradigm mental process in freewriting occurs in that moment when Bob Whitney's student uses a word *(nothing)* for what had till then been a nonlinguistic feature of her consciousness (emptiness).

We might be tempted then to argue that freewriting helps us move to "higher" cognitive realms of metadiscourse (and so is particularly important for weak students). But I am reminded of Shirley Brice Heath saying that she refuses to use the term *metacognition* because of its connotations of being something "higher" that only skilled students can do (discussion at the English Coalition Conference in 1987). Pat Belanoff shows that there is more metadiscourse in the freewriting of skilled students than of unskilled students, but she suggests that the unskilled students probably have just as much metadiscourse *in their minds* ("How do you spell that?" "Oh no, I can't write anything intelligent"). Indeed both Perl ("Understanding Composing") and Rose ("Rigid Rules") give good evidence that what gets in the way of unskilled and blocked writers is *too much* metadiscourse. But these weak students don't feel they can bring these metathoughts *into* the text, make them *part* of the dialogue. So instead of saying that freewriting helps move us up to higher cognitive levels, I would argue that it helps us do *in writing* what we can already do perfectly well in our minds.

A Different Relationship to Writing

In conclusion then, freewriting has gradually given me a profoundly different experience of and relationship to writing. Where writing used to be the exercise of greater than usual care and control (especially in comparison to speaking), freewriting has led me to experience writing *in addition* as an arena of less than usual care and control: writing as an arena for putting down words and thoughts in a deeply unbuttoned way. And when I make progress toward something "higher" in writing—toward clarity of thinking or effectiveness of language or toward meta-awareness—I experience this progress as rooted in freewriting, the "lowest" of writing activities.

Works Cited

Belanoff, Pat. "Freewriting as Teacher." In Belanoff, Elbow, and Fontaine.
Belanoff, Pat, Peter Elbow, and Sheryl Fontaine, eds. *Nothing Begins with N: New Investigations of Freewriting.* Carbondale: Southern Illinois UP, 1991.
Brand, Alice. *The Psychology of Writing: The Affective Experience.* Westport, CT: Greenwood P, 1989.
Britton, James. *The Development of Writing Abilities (11–18).* Urbana, IL: NCTE, 1975.
———. *The Web of Meaning: Essays on Writing, Teaching, Learning, and Thinking.* Eds. Dixie Goswami and Peter Stillman. Upper Montclair, NJ: Boynton, 1983.
Emig, Janet. "Inquiry Paradigms and Writing." *College Composition and Communication* 33 (1982): 64–75. Reprinted in *The Web of Meaning: Essays on Writing, Teaching, and Learning, and Thinking.* Ed. Dixie Goswami and Maureen Butler. Upper Montclair, NJ: Boynton/Cook, 1983.
Flisser, Grace. *A Phenomenological Inquiry Into Insight in Writing.* Diss. U of Pennsylvania, 1988.

Gleason, Barbara. "The Phenomenological Study of Composing Experiences." Paper given at *CCCC*, March 1988.

Hammond, Lynn. "Using Freewriting to Promote Critical Thinking." In Belanoff, Elbow, and Fontaine.

McLeod, Susan. "Some Thoughts about Feelings: The Affective Domain and the Writing Process." *College Composition and Communication* 38 (Dec. 1987): 426–35.

Murray, Donald. "The Feel of Writing—and Teaching Writing." *Learning by Teaching*. Boynton, 1982. 42–49.

Perl, Sondra. "Understanding Composing." *College Composition and Communication* 31 (1980): 363–69.

Perl, Sondra, and Arthur Egendorf. "The Process of Creative Discovery: Theory, Research and Implications for Teaching." *The Territory of Language: Linguistics, Stylistics, and the Teaching of Composition*. Ed. Donald McQuade. Southern Illinois UP, 1986. 250–68.

Phelps, Louise Wetherbee. "Rhythm and Pattern In a Composing Life." *Writers on Writing*. Ed. Tom Waldrep. New York: Random House, 1985. 241–57.

———. "Literacy and the Limits of the Natural Attitude." *Composition as a Human Science: Contributions to the Self-Understanding of a Discipline*. New York: Oxford UP, 1988. 108–30.

Polanyi, Michael. *Personal Knowledge: Towards a Post-Critical Philosophy*. New York: Harper, 1958.

Progoff, Ira. *At A Journal Workshop*. New York: Dialogue House, 1975.

Rose, Mike. "Rigid Rules, Inflexible Plans, and the Stifling of Language." *College Composition and Communication* 31 (1980): 389–401.

Tomlinson, Barbara. "Characters Are Co-Authors: Segmenting the Self, Integrating the Composing Process." *The Buried Life of the Mind: Writers' Metaphors for their Writing Process*. Diss. U California, San Diego, 1986.

Whatley, Carol. *Focusing In the Composing Process: The Development of a Theory of Rhetorical Invention Based on the Work in Psychotherapy of Eugene T. Gendlin*. Diss. Auburn U, 1983.

Whitney, Robert. "Why I Hate Freewriting: A Philosophical Self-Study." In Belanoff, Elbow, and Fontaine.

Wrongness and Felt Sense

Once after I led a series of workshops here at UMass, a faculty participant told me sheepishly that some of them had taken to calling me "Write-it-wrong Elbow." He feared I might be insulted, but I wasn't. Let me explore some riches in wrongness.

I start with a germ story of what I learned about giving reactions and feedback to people's writing. I often found myself saying something like this: "Your essay felt to me kind of . . ."—and then breaking off because I couldn't find the word. But in fact I usually *had* found a word. A writer who knew my voice and my way of speaking might even "hear" the word my lips were forming to say: "Your essay felt to me kind of ccch [ildish]. . . ." I stopped not just because I didn't want to insult or annoy the writer, but because I knew that "childish" was not the right word. The essay wasn't childish. Yet my reading and experiencing of the essay brought the word "childish" to my tongue. After I stopped, I would usually fish around for the right word—and usually not find it. Then I would try to explain what I was trying to get at, but my words would become roundabout and vague. The writer couldn't tell what I was getting at, and—here's the central fact—*I* didn't know what I was trying to get at.

I eventually learned an easy solution to this feedback problem, but it only works well if the parties like and trust each other. For this solution, the writer needs to invite me as follows: "Just say the first words that come to mind— even if they are wrong. And then see what other words and thoughts come along." Or even more bluntly: "Exaggerate, allow parody or distortion. What would you say if you were crude and not thoughtful?"

Using this solution, I can even avoid the blunt statement, "Your essay was childish." I can say, "I was *going* to say 'Your essay was childish,' but that's not really right. It's not really childish. But somehow that's the word that came to mind. I wonder what I mean." And then pause quietly and look inside and wait for more words. Usually, more accurate words arise. I might end up with something like, "Yes, your essay isn't childish, but I feel a kind of stubborn or even obsessive quality in it, even though on the surface it seems very clear and reasonable. I feel a refusing-to-budge quality that reminds me of a stubborn child." Till this point, I hadn't really known what I was trying to get at—what my perception or reaction to the writing actually was. But having

This is a section from my Introduction to a new edition of *Writing With Power,* 1998.

said this, I realize, yes, this is what I was noticing and wanting to say. I needed to say the wrong words to get to the right words.

I've been describing a narrow example about feedback—though a pertinent one in a book about writing. But I am using it to introduce a wider meditation on *wrongness* in language. What is it that goes awry when we hold back or push away a wrong word because we know it's wrong—and then stumble around unable to find a better one, end up being mushy and unclear, and finally lose track of what we were trying to get at? And what is it that goes *right* when someone encourages us to use that wrong word and we finally *get to* what we are trying to say?

The key event is this: in pushing away the wrong word we lose track of the *feeling* of what we were trying to get at, the feeling that somehow gave rise to that wrong word "childish"—the *felt* meaning, the felt *sense*. The word "childish" may have been wrong, but it happened to be the only word I had with a string on it leading back to the *important* thing: my actual reaction to the essay, the meaning itself I wanted to express. If I push that word away because it's wrong, I lose my tenuous hold on that delicate string, and hence tend to lose the felt reaction and meaning that I started with.

The larger theme here is mystery in language, but to me at least, this story is finally clear. And for this clarity, I am indebted to an important phenomenological philosopher, Eugene Gendlin. "Felt sense" is the useful term that he coined. What I and others have learned from him is how to make more room for felt sense. As Gendlin points out, people often experience meaning at a nonverbal and even inchoate level. But he lays out a process that is remarkably helpful in finding words for what we sense but cannot yet express:

- Accept the words that just arrive in the mind and mouth. Welcome them.
- But then pause and ask, "Do these words get at what I'm aiming for?" That is, it's important not to ignore or blot out the sense of wrongness and just blunder onward out of a feeling of, "Oh well, I'm just not a verbal, articulate kind of person."
- Pause and pay attention not just to the wrongness or gap but to the felt sense or felt meaning or intention *behind* the wrong words. Try to listen to the felt sense—or more precisely, try to feel it. Gendlin argues that this "sense" or knowledge is ultimately rooted in the body, and when trying to pay attention, it helps to try feel it in the body.
- From this attending or feeling for felt sense, invite new words to come.

It's important to recognize that this process (putting out words, feeling if there is a gap, feeling the gap, pausing to attend to felt sense on the far side of the gap, putting out more words) often needs to go on more than once. Often we don't find the "right" words on the first go around. But if we continue with the process—listening for a wrongness or gap behind the *new* set of words—we often finally find the words that click, that express exactly what we felt. What a miracle to find words for just what we want to say. The real miracle is that they are not so hard to find.

But attitude is crucial here. It's no good noticing that one's words are wrong if the feeling is just, "Oh damn! Wrong words again. Why can't I ever think of the right words?" We need the more hopeful attitude that we get from understanding how the process works: "Of course the words are wrong. That's how it goes with words. But the sense of wrongness is leverage for finding better words—*if* I pause and look to felt sense. Noticing wrongness is a cause for hope, not discouragement." (See Gendlin and Perl for more on felt sense.)

I love the light that Gendlin's insight throws on two common but different forms of inarticulateness: too few words and too many words. Both stem from fear of wrongness. That is, some people come to have too few words because they feel the sense of wrongness so *strongly*. Radically laconic or tongue-tied people push away all these wrong words and often end up with very little they can say. It's easy to see how this can happen.

But in a more roundabout way, fear of wrongness can also lead to too *many* words. That is, some students who have had their words corrected over and over again come to lose all trust in their felt sense: "Why listen to my felt sense if it's just going to lead to mistakes?" So gradually they learn *not to feel* any sense of wrongness. As a result, they no longer judge the words they speak or write in terms of any inner felt meaning—only in terms of *outer standards*. They judge only in terms of their understanding of how language is supposed to go and what they think teachers and others are looking for.

Some of these people who no longer feel the wrongness or felt sense end up producing language that is wildly off base and incoherent, and thus appear to be deeply stupid or operating according to some alien mental gear. But the same deafness to felt sense can lead other people to what looks like successful performance with words: they have learned to spin out skilled and intelligent words and syntax—but the words and syntax are generated *only* by the rules for words and syntax, not by connection with felt meaning. Sometimes it's hard to notice the ungrounded quality to the words—especially if the verbal skill is indeed impressive.

There's actually a *third* kind of inarticulateness that I want to describe, but I have to admit a blatant self-interest. For this is a disability that I suffer from, but I want to redefine it as a good thing! My problem is that I cannot seem to speak in complete sentences or even with coherent syntax. My speech is usually a jumble. And I often speak words that are different from the meaning I intend (for example, saying "after" instead of "before," or "wife" instead of "husband"). But my reflections on the role of felt sense have led me to see my problem in a more generous light. Let me explain.

When people speak or write, they are drawing on two different inner sources: words and nonverbal felt sense. Different situations may tend to lead us to call on one source more than we call on the other. For example, if we are saying something we've already talked about a lot—or heard about and read about—we have lots of ready-made words and phrases sitting there in our heads to use. But if we are trying to say something we've never said before or never figured out, something as yet unformulated in our minds, we have greater need to draw on felt sense.

But some *people* may tend to favor one source more than the other when they speak and write. I think I'm one of that breed of people at one end of the spectrum—people who attend more to felt sense than to words—who often try to speak or write *from* nonverbal felt sense. I think this is the source of syntactic confusion and semantic slips.

This has indeed been a problem for me. I tend to sound like an incoherent bumbler in speaking situations, and I had to quit graduate school because I couldn't write my papers: I couldn't get my thoughts straight. But once I learned to *handle* my disability—to trust my incoherence and wrong words and build patiently from them—I finally learned an amazing and not so common skill. If I work at it and take my time, I can almost always find the *right words* for *exactly* what I feel and mean. Click. This is easiest for me in writing, but I can do it in speech too, if the conditions are unusually safe and I take my time. The words may not be right for readers or right for the rules of language, but they actually say what I want to say. No small blessing. So many people have the sadness of never having expressed exactly what it's important for them to say. So now I conclude that my habitual focus on felt sense is an advantage, despite the verbal incoherence it often leads to.

Am I saying that all incoherence is a good thing? My argument does not logically entail that conclusion. Yet it tickles me to entertain the thought. For of course I have to acknowledge that my argument comes from someone who has always felt resentful of those who are verbally fluent and clear.

Obviously, it is important to make room for felt sense in the process of writing. The germ event in writing—perhaps in thinking itself—is being able to make the move from a piece of *nonverbal felt meaning* to a piece of *language*. And so we see why freewriting is so important. Freewriting is the act of respecting and putting down the words that come to mind and then *continuing* to respect and put down the next words that come to mind. This is why freewriting so often seems repetitive and even obsessive. When we write what comes to mind, we honor the next mental event, which is often, "No, that's not quite it." Whether or not we are quick enough to write down *those* words, we usually write the new words that are produced by the feeling of dissatisfaction. And then often a third and even a fourth way of trying to say what we are trying to get at. Thus freewriting is a particularly apt tool for building bridges between language and felt sense. I should add that Gendlin's insight about honoring felt sense has led me to adjust the way I invite students to freewrite. Instead of just saying, "Please try to write without stopping," I now say, "Try to write without stopping, but that doesn't mean rushing—and in fact you may find it helpful to pause now and then to try to feel inside for what you are getting at."

Works Cited

Elbow, Peter, ed. *Landmark Essays on Voice and Writing*. Davis CA: Hermagoras Press, 1994. (Also distributed by the National Council of Teachers of English.)

Flower, Linda. *Problem-Solving Strategies for Writing*. NY: Harcourt Brace Jovanovich, 1981.

Gendlin, Eugene T. *Experiencing and the Creation of Meaning*. NY: Free Press, 1962.

————. "The Wider Role of Bodily Thought in Sense and Language." *Giving the Body Its Due*. Ed. Maxine Sheets-Johnstone. Albany NY: SUNY P.

Perl, Sondra. "Understanding Composing." *College Composition and Communication* 31.4 (December 1980): 363–69.

————. "A Writer's Way of Knowing: Guidelines for Composing." In *Presence of Mind: Writing and the Domain Beyond the Cognitive*. Eds. Alice Brand and Richard Graves. Portsmouth NH: Heinemann/Boynton-Cook, 1993. 77–88.

The Neglect and Rediscovery of Invention

Let me briefly consider a neglect in the study of writing that is comparable to the neglect of affect or feeling: the neglect of *invention*. If we look to Aristotle's *Rhetoric*, we see that he was interested in invention (if not directly in the psychology of invention, at least in the logic of where to look for all the available arguments about an issue). But after the period of classical rhetoric and especially throughout the flowering of rhetoric during the eighteenth and nineteenth centuries, invention was neglected—and it continued to be neglected for much of this century. Throughout this long forgetfulness it's as though people were saying, "It's too hard to talk about where ideas come from—too messy, too internal, too mysterious. We can only talk clearly about what people *do* with their material once they have it: how they arrange it and what kind of language they use and how they adapt themselves to their audience."

But then a decade or two ago we saw a new interest in invention. People like Young, Becker, and Pike (*Rhetoric: Discovery and Change*) said, in effect, "We've got to stop sweeping invention under the rug and start trying to make sense of it." Research on invention began to take off and this activity seemed to open the door to that resurgence of activity in our profession that came to be called the "process movement" (and which has of course not stopped accelerating even as it changes its character). Indeed, it was this focus on invention—activity-in-time lying behind a text-in-space—that helped give currency to the very concept itself of "process" as opposed to "product."

Now invention no longer seems to be on the front burner in composition studies. I'm curious why. Yet having been established, it will surely remain solidly integrated in the field. No one is likely forget again that any study of the writing process must deal with the crucial question of where writers get

From the Foreword to *The Psychology of Writing: The Affective Experience*, Alice Glarden Brand, Greenwood Press, 1989.

their material.

Interestingly, we can see the same neglect of invention in the study of science. For a long time scientists and commentators on science tended to talk about "scientific thinking" as a logical business of induction or deduction. It's as though they too were saying, "We can't talk about the process of how people come up with ideas; that's too dark and mysterious. We can only talk about the process of checking or verifying ideas. That's rational and systematizable." In truth, only a few people were actually *making* this distinction between the "finding" and the "verifying" of ideas. Most of the trouble came from not realizing how different the processes are: coming up with an idea and figuring out whether the idea is right. To make that distinction was in itself a big step toward starting to realize that scientific thinking is not the logical business we might like to see it as. But then people like George Polya and Jacques Hadamard got interested in the messy processes by which people came up with hunches and teased them out into full-blown hypotheses— hypotheses interesting enough to be worth checking in a more logical fashion. I am drawing here on accounts by people like Peter Medawar and Gerald Holton. Could the interest in invention in our field have been partly spurred by some of this exploration of science? I know that I was drawing on Medawar when I emphasized the difference between the creative-generative process and the critical-verifying process in *Writing Without Teachers*— written while I was teaching at M.I.T.

Work Cited

Hadamard. Jacques. *An Essay on the Psychology of Invention in the Mathematical Field.* Princeton, NJ: Princeton UP, 1945.

Holton, Gerald. *The Scientific Imagination: Case Studies.* Cambridge, England, and NY: Cambridge UP, 1978.

Medawar, Peter. *Introduction and Intuition in Scientific Thought.* Philadelphia: American Philosophical Society, 1969.

———. *The Art of the Soluble.* London: Methuen, 1967.

Polya, George. *How to Solve It; A New Aspect of Mathematical Method.* Princeton, NJ: Princeton UP, 1945.

Form and Content as Sources of Creation

Do you usually start writing by thinking mainly about *what* you want to say or *how* you want to say it? That is, are you thinking about content or form?

This is a "rumination" from Workshop 5 of *A Community of Writers: A Workshop Course in Writing,* a textbook I wrote with Pat Belanoff. Third edition, McGraw Hill, 1999.

Starting with Content

In this textbook we often suggest doing freewriting or exploratory writing without worrying about organization. "Invite chaos," we say; "Worry later about organization or form." In making this suggestion we might seem to be making an interesting and arguable theoretical assumption: that first you create "content" (pure content-without-form, as it were) and then you give it "form."

Even though *Genesis* tells us that God took this approach when He created the heavens and the earth, starting out with "formless" matter, this is only one way to talk about the process of creation. Yet the approach is remarkably helpful to many people in their writing. Whether skilled or unskilled, many people find it a relief when they allow themselves to produce "raw content-without-form"—find it *enabling* to turn out pages and pages of writing without worrying about whether it's organized or fits a certain form.

In Workshops 4 and 5 we may seem even to have *exaggerated* this one-sided approach. In Workshop 4 we asked you to produce, as it were, gallons of formless *content,* and now in this workshop we ask you to pour those gallons into various bottles or forms.

Let us now turn around and look at the *other* way of talking about form and content in the process of creation. In the first place, strictly speaking, all writing has form: there's no such thing as content-without-form. All that writing you produced in Workshop 4 cannot but have *some* form. Perhaps the form is mixed or messy, but that's form too. Besides, what looks messy at first glance is often quite patterned. What you wrote may have a large coherent pattern which is obscured by local clutter, digressions, and interruptions.

For example, if you look carefully at your seemingly chaotic private exploratory writing, you may see that it is shaped by a single narrative flow—or even by a clever flashback narrative pattern. Or perhaps your exploratory writing has a three-step pattern of moving from *event* to *reactions* to the event to *reflective thoughts* about that event and your reactions. Or maybe you'll find the opposite pattern: a movement from reflective thoughts back to the events behind those thoughts. The point is that if you manage to record what's going on in your mind, you are almost certainly recording patterns. Our minds operate by patterns even when we are confused. The human mind is incapable of pure randomness or chaos. Therefore, when you look at your private exploratory writings, don't just respect the chaos as useful and wild (which it is); keep an eye out also for the *order* hiding behind the seeming chaos.

This realization leads to a very practical consequence: there are always organizations and genres *already lurking* in your seemingly messy exploratory writing—organizations and genres that you can discover and prune into shape (like recovering a shapely tree that has become overgrown). Just because you weren't *aware* of writing within a particular genre doesn't mean that you wrote genreless material. When you "organize" your chaotic private writing, you probably don't have to *create* organization from scratch; you can clarify the latent organization that's already there. Or more likely you can choose and develop one of the two or three overlapping organizations that are latent but operating—like overlapping wave patterns caused by two or three pebbles tossed in a pond.

In sum, there's no such thing as "starting with content only"; you can't have a smidgen of content that is not fully formed. But you can *pretend* to start with content. That is, you can put all your attention on following a train of words or thoughts where they lead and totally ignore consideration of form.

Starting with Form

So too, it's possible to start with form. And this too is a very practical approach that can help in writing. That is, it can be helpful to *start with an organization or genre* and look to content afterward. For a genre isn't just a mold to pour unformed raw writing into or a sewing pattern to lay on top of whole cloth to show us where to cut. A genre can serve as a way to *generate* or invent content: choosing a genre will make you think of words and ideas that you might not think of otherwise. For example, if you decide to use narrative as a form, you will not just *arrange* your material in terms of time; you will almost certainly *think* of certain connecting or even casual events you had forgotten. If you are vacillating between a persuasive and an analytic essay, the persuasive genre will cause you to think of reasons and arguments; the analytic genre will cause you to think of hypotheses and causal relationships.

It's not unusual to start by choosing a genre. For example, we may decide to write a letter to someone and not be sure yet what we'll say. Or we may decide to write an essay with a certain organization (for example, a point-by-point refutation of someone else's view). Or someone may choose a genre for us: "Write a persuasive essay on any topic." In Workshop 2, we specified description and narration as the starting points for writing. In loop writing we started with mini-genres (portrait, narrative, letter, and so forth). In this workshop, however, we ask you to think about these genres or types *after* you have done lots of writing.

Because language is inherently both form and content, we can never really have pure or pure form. It is only *our* consciousness which tends, at any given moment, to emphasize one more than the other. If we use process writing to study our tendencies of mind when we write, we will gradually learn when it's helpful to put more attention on form as we write, and when it's helpful to put more attention on content. In this way we can take better control of our process.

Part III

SPEECH, WRITING, AND VOICE

Peter, why are you so obsessed about voice? Can't you stop writing about it? You must have some personal hang-up about it.

Actually, I spend plenty of time not writing about voice. Writing about other things has made this book too damn big. Even in this section, the first and third essays are not really about voice ("The Shifting Relationships Between Speech and Writing" and "Silence: A Collage"). But you're right that there seems to be something personal about me and voice. Indeed, that goes right to the heart of the matter. My view is that there is always a *personal* dimension to any text. When I'm reading, I tend to look for some sense of contact with the person who actually wrote.

I'm not saying this is the best or the right way to read. It's just as valid to read in the pure New Critical way and say, "Forget the actual writer"; or in the deconstructive way and say, "There is no one there"; or even in some kind of subjective way and say, "I'll pretend this text means only what I'd like it to mean" or "I'll use this text for interesting daydreaming about my own experiences." Surely people get to read texts in various ways for various purposes. (For an interesting exploration of reading for contact with the writer, see Gibbons.)

The only thing I really object to is being told I'm *wrong* to read as I do. When critics developed the idea that we should not put our attention on the actual author as we read, they were trying to improve and sophisticate our reading of imaginative literature. And they gave us a helpful corrective. But it needs to be seen *as* a corrective—a suggestion to help us open up texts so we can see things we might miss if we are always trying to make contact with the person writing. But by the same token, paying attention to the person who writes *also* opens up texts for other things we might miss if we give no attention to the actual writer. Ignoring the author is a literary-based model of reading, and it's no good taking that as our only model for all reading.

But you've tricked me into taking a kind of a flat-footed, one-sided statement of my bias. It's not the whole story of my reading. Let me try to tell the story of my reading as it pertains to this section's essays about speech, writing, and voice.

Many years ago I began to notice something as I was reading student papers. Passages that were clearly not "good writing" would often *register strongly*. It struck me that these passages were actually managing to achieve what is difficult and rare in writing of any sort: they struck me, they captured my attention, they *got through*. And these passages weren't memorable because of egregious blunders—though some of them were indeed bad or awkward. What registered strong was the *meaning*. In short, they *worked* as writing. But I didn't have any model for saying why or how they worked. This brought me to think about voice in a text. Most of these strongly registering passages were ones that I *heard* more vividly. Voice was helpful because it pointed at something often neglected in traditional teaching and judging good writing (and I was intrigued by the fact that these passages were hard to call good), yet voice also constitutes something that gives pleasure and that propels the meanings of words forcefully into our heads.

I became enthusiastic about this kind of goodness, and my thinking about it developed into my two chapters on voice in *Writing With Power* (1981). But the enthusiasm of those chapters got me into trouble with a lot of critics and scholars in composition. Here's an example of my enthusiasm:

> [E]veryone, however inexperienced or unskilled, has real voice available; everyone can write with power. . . . [N]othing stops anyone from writing words that will make readers listen and be affected. (304)

For a striking example of a response, there was an essay titled "Voice as Juice: Some Reservations about Evangelic Composition" in which I. Hashimoto lit into me as follows:

> "Voice," then, is something we can't discuss and analyze but can only feel or participate in. . . . "Voice" provides *immediate salvation* if sinners renounce complexity and the evils of over-intellectualizing, return to simple black-and-white ideals, and embrace their primitive, emotive, human selves. . . . The advantage of such vague, emotive description is that salvation becomes a very *personal* affair." (73)
>
>   With a natural voice, students need not worry about content at all. (78)

Now that I think back on this story, both the response and my reaction to it were not surprising. I wrote those chapters before I cared about my membership in the academic field of composition. I was just trying to speak directly to students and writers. But soon after the book came out I moved to SUNY Stony Brook, to the directorship of a writing program, and I began to teach graduate courses in English. I began to want very badly for people in the field to see me as a valid and respectable member. This situation—and my instinct for finessing a fight—made me curb my instinct for writing what is counter, controversial, or unacademic ("writing without teachers"). So I stopped just glorying in the mystery of voice and just emphasizing how different it is from conventional criteria of good writing. I began to exercise another of my instincts: to *analyze* what is complex, troublesome, and mysterious.

Thus it turns out that the essays on voice in this book are really exercises in nonadversarial or mediational analysis. In all this analysis, I am trying to show that most of the controversy about voice has resulted from a failure to notice the quite distinct senses of the term. I argue that if readers, critics, or teachers would look at specific passages, and take care in distinguishing between different *kinds* or *senses* of voice, they would have a good chance of reaching specific agreements.

But having worked so long at trying to avoid unnecessary conflict through careful analysis, I find myself now more willing to begin to fight about the smaller areas of difference. I've been writing an essay from this stance for a while, but I cannot finish it in time for this book. (My editor would shoot me if I said, "How about squeezing in just one more essay.") Let me end with an important point from that essay.

Here is the classic objection to the idea of trying to talk about resonant voice as I try to do.

> Stop talking about the relationship between a text and its actual author. The text is all we can see—nothing but the text. We can't see the writer. Therefore, we have no grounds for making inferences about the relationship between a text in front of us and an invisible, absent writer.

This has seemed like an obvious and common sense objection to many people over many years.

But it's *only* common sense if we privilege the reader's point of view and stay locked in it. For it is *only* the reader who has no view of or contact with the writer. If we were willing to try looking at writing from the *writer's* point of view, we would see that it is perfectly natural and ordinary and rational to talk about the relationship between the text and the writer. As *writer*, we are sitting there in full contact with both the text and the writer. Once we notice this, we realize that as writers, we talk all the time about the relationship or match between the text and our thinking, our intention, our feeling, and who we are. In short, theory changes once we get out of the reader's chair and try sitting in the writer's chair. We would see a similar change in theory if theorists tried looking at things from the teacher's point of view. Theorizing as teachers, we would see that we talk every day in the most ordinary ways about the relationship between texts and their authors.

If we free composition from privileging the reader's point of view and neglecting the writer's point of view, we will find it natural, as theorists, to do what many people and many good readers have always done—namely, to make inferences about the relation between the text and the actual person who wrote it. The more we experience ourselves and our students *as writers*, the more we will find that we cannot get away from an interest in this particular dimension of voice. It is striking, after all, that "writers"—those people who have most clearly taken on the identity of *writer*—have mostly proved immune to a scholarly skepticism about the concept of voice in a text.

Works Cited

Gibbons, Christina. *Shifting Relations: Reading Autobiographers as They Read Their Audiences*, U Mass dissertation, 1993.

Hashimoto, I. "Voice as Juice: Some Reservations about Evangelic Composition." *College Composition and Communication* 38.1 (Feb 1987): 70–79.

7

The Shifting Relationships
Between Speech and Writing

> Paradoxes . . . beset the relationships between the original spo-
> ken word and all its technological transformations. . . . [I]ntelli-
> gence is relentlessly reflexive, so that even the external tools that it
> uses to implement its workings become "internalized," that is, part
> of its own reflexive process.
>
> Walter Ong

We have seen interesting work in recent years on the nature of speech and writing and the mentalities associated with each. The insights from these investigations are extremely valuable, but a dangerous assumption is sometimes inferred
from them: that speech and writing are distinctly characterizable media, each
of which has its own inherent features and each of which tends to foster a particular cognitive process, or "mentality."[1] I am interested in the cognitive
processes associated with speech and writing, but instead of saying that each
medium has a particular tendency, I will argue that each medium can draw on
and foster *various* mentalities. This essay is a call for writers and teachers of
writing to recognize the enormous choice we have and to learn to take more
control over the cognitive effects associated with writing. The essay is in three
parts—each showing a different relationship between speech and writing.

This essay was published in 1985 in *College Composition and Communication* 36: 283–303. It
was given the Braddock Award for the best essay of the year in that journal.

1. See Walter Ong, *Orality and Literacy,* 1982, for a powerful summary of his extensive work
in this area and his wide-ranging citations to others working in it. For welcome warnings about
stereotyping the mentalities associated with orality and literacy, see Cooper and Odell, "Sound
in Composing"; Harste et al., "Assumptions"; Scribner and Cole, *Psychology of Literacy;* Heath,
"Oral and Literate Traditions"; and Robinson, "Literacy." A number of the essays in Kroll and
Vann, *Exploring Speaking-Writing Relationships,* e.g. O'Keefe, also warn against oversimplifying
the contrast between speech and writing as media.

Prologue: A vision of Three Writers

I see a writer clenched over her text, writing very slowly—indeed pondering more than writing—trying to achieve something permanent and definitive: questioning everything, first in her mind before she writes the phrase, then after she sees it on paper. She is intensely self-critical, she tries to see every potential flaw—even the flaws that some unknown future reader might find who is reading in an entirely different context from that of her present audience. She is using the "new" technology of indelible writing that Ong and others speak of and thereby enhancing her capacity for careful abstract thinking by learning to separate the knower from the known. She is learning the mentality of detachment.

I see another writer in a fine frenzy: scribbling fast, caught up in her words, in the grip of language and creation. She is writing late at night—not because of a deadline but because the words have taken over: she wants to go to bed but too much is going on for her to stop. She has learned to relinquish some control. She has also learned to let herself write things she would never show to anyone—at first anyway. By exploiting the ephemeral underside of writing, she learns to promote the mentality of wildness with words—the mentality of discourse as play. And perhaps most important, she has learned to promote the mentality of involvement in her words rather than of detachment or separation. But because that involvement is so totally *of the moment,* she knows she may well write a refutation tomorrow night of what she is writing tonight. She writes to explore and develop her ideas, not just to express them.

I see a third writer at her desk conjuring up her audience before her in her mind's eye as she writes. She is looking *at* them, speaking *to* them—more aware of the sound of her spoken words in her ear than the sight of her written words on paper. She is a writer as raconteur, a writer with the gift of gab. She is not "composing" a text or "constructing" a document in space—she is "uttering" discourse in time; she is not "giving things" to her readers, she is leading readers on a mental journey. She is a bit of a dramatist, using discourse as a way to *do* things to people. She is involved with her discourse through being involved with her audience. Often her audience is a genuine community and her writing grows out of her sense of membership in it.

The Traditional View: Indelible Writing, Ephemeral Speech

Obviously writing is more indelible or permanent than speech. Speech is nothing but wind, waves of temporarily squashed air, waves that begin at once to disperse, that is, to lose their sound. Writing, on the other hand, stays there—"down in black and white." Once we get it on paper it takes on a life of its own, separate from the writer. It "commits us to paper." It can be brought back to haunt us: read in a different context from the one we had in mind—read by any audience, whether or not we know them or want them to see our words.

Where the *intention* to speak usually results automatically in the *act* of speech, writing almost always involves delay and effort. Writing forces us not only to form the letters, spell the words, and follow stricter rules of correctness (than speech); we must also get into the text itself all those cues that readers might need who are not present to us as we write, who don't know the context for our words, and who don't know us or how we speak. In addition to this "contextualizing," we must capture onto the page some substitute for all those vocal and visual cues for listeners that we give without effort or attention in speaking. We can take nothing for granted in writing; the text has to say it all.

In the effort to do all these things as we write, how can we help but pause and reflect on whether what we are engaged in putting down is really right— or even if it is, whether it is what we really wanted to say? If we are going to take the trouble to write something down, then we might as well get it right. *Getting it right* feels like an inherent demand in the medium itself of writing.

Research (see Tannen, "Oral and Literate Strategies") shows that speech tends to carry more "phatic" messages than writing—messages about the relationship between the speaker and the listener or between the speaker and his material (e.g., "I know you're my friend"), even when the ostensible function of the spoken words is purely substantive or informational. Thus writing tends to carry a much higher proportion of "content" messages to absent readers—more permanent messages which are judged for validity and adequacy, not just accepted as social interchange.

This feeling that we must get things right in writing because written words are more indelible than speech is confirmed when we look to the *history* of speech and writing. The development of writing as a technology seems to have led to the development of careful and logical thinking—to a greater concern with "trying to get it *really* right" (see Ong, *Orality,* and his other works; Goody, *Domestication;* Havelock, *Plato*). Ong claims that the development of writing gave us a new "noetic economy," that is, a wholly new relationship to words and knowledge—new habits of shaping, storing, retrieving, and communicating what we know.

We see a parallel argument about the teaching of writing. That is, leading theorists tell us that the poor thinking we see in many of our students stems from their not yet having made that great developmental leap from oral language strategies to written or literate language strategies (Lunsford, "Cognitive Development"; Shaughnessy, *Errors.*) Obviously, students can think better when they can examine their thoughts more self-consciously as a string of assertions arranged in space. The technology of indelible writing permits students in a sense to step out of the flux of time: to detach themselves from oral discourse, from the context in which words are uttered and first thought about, and from the tendency in speech to rely on concrete and experiential modes of discourse. As Havelock emphasizes, writing helps to separate the knower from the known.

This contrast between the two media is reinforced when we turn to the story of how we learn to speak and to write as individuals. We learn speech as infants—from parents who love us and naturally reward us for speaking at all. Our first audience works overtime to hear the faintest intention in our every utterance, no matter how hidden or garbled that meaning may be. Children aren't so much criticized for getting something wrong as praised for having anything at all to say—indeed, they are often praised even for emitting speech as pure play with no message intended.

What a contrast between that introduction to speech and the introduction to writing which most children get in school. Students can never feel writing as an activity they engage in as freely, frequently, or spontaneously as they do in speech. Indeed, because writing is almost always a requirement set by the teacher, the act of writing takes on a "required" quality, sometimes even the aspect of punishment. I can still hear the ominous cadence in my ears: "Take out your pens." Indeed, in the classic case of school punishment the crime is speech and the punishment is writing ("I will not talk in class. I will not talk in class.") Do some teachers still insist, as some of mine did, that ink must be used? The effect was to heighten our sense of writing as indelible, as the act of making irrevocable choices—as though there were something wrong about changing our minds.

I don't mean to imply that these gradgrindish conditions are universal. There is hope that they are not even common. But the school setting in which most people learn to write and have most of their formative writing experiences is just one more reason why we tend to experience writing as more indelible than speaking—and why we tend to experience writing as a medium for getting it right.[2] That first writer in my prologue vision—the writer inscribing so slowly and carefully and with such awareness of future critical readers: she writes in the mentality of writing-as-indelible.

The Opposite View: *Speech* as Indelible, Writing as Ephemeral

As Roland Barthes says, "it is ephemeral speech which is indelible, not monumental writing. . . . Speech is irreversible: a [spoken] word cannot be retracted . . ." ("Death of the Author"). Precisely because speech is nothing but temporary crowdings in air molecules, we can never revise it. If we speak in the hearing of others—and we seldom speak otherwise—our words are heard by listeners who can remember them even (or especially) if we say something we wish they would forget. Once we've said (as a joke), "I've never liked that shirt you gave me," or (in a fight), "Well damn it, that *is* a woman's job," or even (in a seminar, without thinking about what our colleagues might

---

2. It may be, however, that many of the effects we are tempted to ascribe to literacy are really effects of schooling. See Gere, "Cultural Perspective"; Olson, "Languages of Instruction"; and Scribner and Cole, *Psychology of Literacy.*

think of us), "I've never been able to understand that poem"—or once Jesse Jackson refers to Jews in public as "hymies"—once any of these words are spoken, none can be undone.

Speech is inherently more indelible than writing also because it is a more vivid medium. When we speak, listeners don't just see our words, they see us—how we hold and move ourselves. Even if we only hear someone over the phone or on the radio—perhaps even someone we've never met—still we experience the texture of her talk: the rhythms, emphases, hesitations, and other tonalities of speech which give us a dramatized sense of her character or personality. And if we *don't* reveal ourselves more through our speech than our writing, that too is taken as a revelation: someone will say, as of Gary Hart, "he seems a bit cool and aloof."

But perhaps you will reply that *casual speech* is more ephemeral than writing. Yet there are plenty of occasions when we are trying as hard as we can to "get it right" in speech—because our speech is "a speech," or an "oral report," or discourse to strangers; or for some reason we feel we are being carefully judged for our speech, as in a job interview. Perhaps casual speech is more common in our culture—or in literate or print cultures—than in others. In oral cultures such as the Homeric Greek, the Anglo-Saxon, and the Native American, there was scorn for anyone who spoke hasty unplanned words. Perhaps we fall into the assumption that speech is ephemeral because we live in a blabbing culture.

In short, our sense of speech as ephemeral and writing as indelible stems not so much from the nature of speech and writing as media but from how and where they are most often used. (And researched. See Schafer, "Spoken and Written," for a corrective view.) Our paradigm for speech is casual conversation among trusted friends; our paradigm for writing is more formal discourse to a little-known audience or an audience that is likely to judge us on our utterance.

So far from speech being ephemeral, then, the problem with speech is that it isn't ephemeral enough. What we need is a mode of discourse that really *is* ephemeral—we need the luxury of being able to utter everything on our minds and not have anyone hear it until *after* we decide what we really mean or how we want to say it. Interestingly enough, the most indelible medium of all is also the most ephemeral: writing.

However indelible the ink, writing can be completely evanescent and without consequences. We can write in solitude—indeed, we seldom write otherwise—we can write whatever we want, we can write as badly as we want, and we can write one thing and then change our mind. No one need know what we've written or how we've written it. In short, writing turns out to be the ideal medium for *getting it wrong*. (This evanescence of writing is enormously enhanced by the new electronic media where words are just electrical or magnetic impulses on a screen or a disk.)

Perhaps there's nothing new in the idea of writing as ephemeral. Perhaps the phrase from Barthes has tempted me into that Gallic weakness for trying to phrase the obvious as a scandal. In the days of parchment people wrote to last, but now we are flooded with ephemeral temporary documents.[3]

But though we float in a rising tide of ephemeral writing, our writing habits and instincts are dominated by the old assumption that writing is indelible. That is, most people, even when they are writing a draft that no one will read, nevertheless write by habit *as though readers were going to see it*. Do I exaggerate? Plenty of people experiment or make a mess as they write. Yet what do most people do when they are writing along and they suddenly wonder whether they really believe what they are about to write, or whether it holds up on examination, or even whether it is well phrased. Most people stop writing and don't resume writing till they have figured out what they want to say. This *feels* like a reasonable and normal way to behave, but notice the assumption it reveals: that the function of writing is to record what we have *already* decided—not to figure out *whether* we believe it. If we were speaking, we would be much more likely to speak the train of thought as it comes to mind, even though we're not sure of our final opinion—as a *way* of making up our minds. It is almost as though we fear, as we write, that someone might at any moment swoop down and read what we have just written and see that it is rubbish.

Thus writing for most people is dominated by the experience of not writing: of elaborate planning beforehand to decide what to write and frequent pausing in midcourse to search for the right word or the right path. This non-writing behavior is not surprising since *planning* is probably stressed more than anything else in advice to writers. (This advice is stressed not only in traditional textbooks but also in recent ones such as Linda Flower's.) But because of my own difficulties in writing, I have come to notice the enormous cognitive and linguistic leverage that comes from learning to avoid the mentality dominated by the indelibility of writing and learning instead to exploit the ephemeral or "under" side of writing. It feels very different to put down words not as commitment but as trial, or as Barthes and some of the deconstructionists say, as play, *jouissance,* or the free play of language and consciousness. Thinking is enriched. Writing in this mode can produce an *immersion in discourse itself* that doesn't occur when we sit and think—an immersion in language that can entice us into ideas and perceptions we could not get by planning.

Exploiting the ephemeral quality of writing is often a matter of exploiting chaos and incoherence. Often I find I cannot work out what I am trying to say unless I am extremely disorganized, fragmented, and associative, and let myself go down contrary paths to see where they lead. (Note that what

---

3. Literate people like to complain that the telephone and other electronic media have almost destroyed writing by permitting people to do most of their business orally and refrain from writing unless there is some pressing need for "hard" (i.e., indelible) copy. But I suspect that more people write more now than ever before. Engineers are estimated to spend from a quarter to a third of their working time involved in some kind of writing. See Faigley et al., "Writing After College." The spread of radios and phonographs raised fears that people would no longer play musical instruments: the opposite has occurred.

one is *trying to say* is more than what one *has in mind*—see Perl on "felt sense" in "Understanding Composing.") I can't be that incoherent when I start off trying to write it right. I can't even be that incoherent in speech. My listeners are too impatient for sense, for my main point. (Now I know why I often close my eyes when talking about something difficult: it is an instinctive attempt to blot out the audience and their implicit demand that I be clear and come to the point.) So when trying to write it right, and even in speaking, I must usually settle for the short run of *some* coherence—making *some* sense—and abandon the thread (only it's not really a thread because it's so broken) of the long-run, incipient, more complex meaning which has been tickling the back of my mind. But when I write in the ephemeral and fully exploratory mode for myself alone, I can usually find that meaning by inviting myself to wander around it and finally stumble into it. Thus whereas the commonsense view is that planning is more appropriate to writing than to speaking, the opposite is also true: we badly need arenas for *nonplanning* in our discourse, and speech is too constricting. For nonplanning we need private writing.

We think of the mind's natural capacity for chaos and disorganization as the *problem* in writing—and before we finish any piece of indelible public writing, of course, that incoherence must be overcome. But what a relief it is to realize that this capacity for ephemeral incoherence is valuable and can be harnessed for insight and growth. The most precious thing in this kind of writing is to find one contradicting oneself. It guarantees that there will be some movement and growth in one's thinking; the writing will not just be a record of past thoughts or prejudices. (Good teachers, in commenting on student papers, have learned to see contradictions in the text as positive opportunities for mental action and growth, not just as problems.)

But even when we have the safety of knowing that our words are private and ephemeral and that we will revise them into coherence, we often feel there is something dangerous about letting ourselves write down what is wrong or doubtful or ungainly, or even just something we are not sure we believe. To do so seems to violate a taboo that derives from a magical sense that writing is indelible even if no one else ever sees the words. We stop and correct our words or crumple up the sheet because it feels as though if we leave the wrong words there, they will somehow pollute us. Words on paper will "take"—debilitate the mind. Yet we cannot exploit the ephemerality of language unless we are willing to take the risk.

But why not use the *mind* for all this ephemeral work? Would God have given us a mind if He'd wanted us to waste all this paper writing down what's wrong or badly put? But that internal thinking process lacks a dimension which writing provides. When we just think inside our heads, the cycle of language is incomplete; we are prey to obsession. The thoughts, sentences, images, or feelings that play in our heads continue to play round and round. But when we write down those thoughts or feelings, the sterile circle is often broken: they have a place on paper now; they evolve into another thought or even fade away. Writing is a way to get what is inside one's head outside, on paper, so there's room for more.[4] (Of course, speaking too can have this same function—"getting things out"—but sometimes the presence of a listener is a hindrance.)

I come here to what I most want to emphasize: the *mentalities* related to speech and writing. Ong and the others emphasize how the use of writing enhances logical, abstract, and detached thinking. True enough. But there is a very different kind of good thinking which we can enhance by exploiting the underside of writing as ephemeral. And like the effect Ong speaks of, this kind of thinking is not just an occasional way of considering things but a pervasive mode of cognitive functioning. I'm talking about the mentality that gradually emerges when we learn how to put down what's in mind and invite that putting down to be *not* a committing ourself to it but the opposite, a letting go of the burden of holding it in mind—a letting go of the burden of having it shape our mind. Having let it go, our mind can take on a different shape and go on to pick up a different thought.

In this way writing can function as a prosthesis for the mind—a surrogate mind instead of just a mouthpiece for the mind. For the mind is a structure of meaning and so too is a piece of writing. The mind, as a structure of meaning, can grow and develop through stages and so too can a piece of writing. Thus writing provides us with two organisms for thinking instead of just one, two containers instead of just one; the thoughts can go back and forth, richen and grow. We think of writing as deriving meaning from the mind that produces it, but when all goes well the *mind* derives meaning from the text it produces. (Organization, or meaning, or negative entropy, can flow in both directions.)

I don't mean to sound too mysterious here. I am just talking about the common phenomenon of people's ideas developing and changing as a result of their thinking. It often happens as people live and talk and write over months and years. But in truth, people tend to stay stuck in their points of view. They are prevented from growing until they get out of or move past the structure of meaning that *is* their mind. Ong might say that indelible, careful writing enhances such growth. Yes, that's true when all goes well. But the crucial mental event in growth is often the *abandonment* of a position we hold. Ephemeral writing is usually better than careful writing at helping us abandon what we start out thinking. (See Elbow, *Teachers,* Appendix essay.)

Thus the potentiality in writing that I want to highlight here does not just involve generative techniques for getting first drafts written quicker, but rather a genuine change in mentality or consciousness. The original development of writing long ago permitted a new mentality that fostered thinking that was more careful, detached, and logical. But along with it and the indelibility that makes writing valuable came also a mentality that tends to lock us into our views once we have carefully worked them out in writing. In contrast, the cultivation of writing as ephemeral fosters the *opposite* mentality

4. This somatic perspective heightens the paradoxes. Writing is the external indelible medium—yet is the most easily changed. Thinking is the most internal and changeable medium—yet from another point of view it is the most intractable to change: try removing or changing a thought you don't like. Speech, chameleon-like, is in the middle.

whereby we use discourse (and writing in particular) not so much to express what we think but rather to develop and transform it.

Before going on to the next section, I should emphasize that the opposite claims in the first two sections—that writing is both *more* and also *less* indelible than speech—do not really undercut each other. My celebration of writing as ephemeral in no way diminishes the fact that writing is also the best medium for being careful, for getting things right, for "quality." I am unrepentant about insisting that we can have it both ways—if we learn how.

We need writing to help domesticate our minds (the title of Goody's book about the development of literacy is *The Domestication of the Savage Mind*), but we also need writing as a way to unleash some cognitive savagery—which is often lacking in a "literate" world too often lulled into thinking that picking up a pencil means planning and trying to get things right. And speech, being a social medium, seldom leads us to the conceptual wilderness we sometimes need.

For not only is there no theoretical contradiction between the two functions of writing, it turns out that they enhance or reinforce each other. People can be *more* careful and get their final drafts *righter* when they spend some of their time unhooking themselves from the demands of audience and inviting themselves to get it wrong. And contrarily, people can be more fruitful in the mentality of nonsteering when they know they will turn around and shift consciousness—impose care and control and try for indelibility—before their text goes to the real audience.

That second writer in my prologue vision—the writer scribbling fast because she is writing out of hot involvement in the moment, knowing that she gets to make radical changes in the cool of tomorrow: she writes in the mentality of writing-as-ephemeral.

A Third View: Writing as Similar to Speech

Having indicated two ways in which speech and writing are *different* or *opposite* from each other, finally I want to argue how they are or can be essentially similar. I will proceed by focusing on a series of features characteristic of speech, and argue in each case why we should seek to foster them in writing.

To exploit the speech-like qualities of writing as we teach is a way of teaching to strength: capitalizing on the oral language skills students already possess and helping students apply those skills immediately and effortlessly to writing—a way of helping with the crucial process Ong calls the "internalization of the technology of writing."

1. In informal speech situations we can utter our words spontaneously—comfortably, naturally, unselfconsciously—with full attention on our meaning and no attention on how we actually *form* the signs or symbols that convey our meaning. We can come close to achieving this situation in writing through the use of "spontaneous writing" or "freewriting": writing in which we put down whatever words come to mind—without regard to the conven-

tions of forming words and without regard to the quality of the writing. We don't give the writing to an audience—or if we do, the audience merely "listens" to it for the meaning and doesn't respond (see Elbow, *Power,* 13–19). The work of Graves and Calkins shows how much we have tended to overestimate the amount of special knowledge or control of the medium people need for fluent and comfortable writing.

2. Speech is usually social and communal, writing solitary. But we can make writing communal too by having people write together and to each other in ways that are worth spelling out in more detail below.[5]

3. Speech usually responds to a particular occasion and fits a particular context. It's not usually meant to last or be recorded—it's for a particular audience which is right there when the discourse is uttered and hears it right away. We can make all this happen in writing if we have students write in class or in small groups—particularly if they write about some issue or situation in which they are involved—and have them immediately share with each other what they write. The audience is right there and known; the writing is part of the context and the interaction of a particular group on a particular day. In speech, when something isn't clear, the audience asks for clarification right away. We can invite this naturally to happen in response to writing.

4. In speech, the response—immediate, of course—is usually a *reply* to *what* has been said, not an *evaluative comment* on *how* it was said. And the reply is almost invariably an invitation to the speaker to reply to the reply. We can make this happen too in our teaching (though students often need coaching to get out of the assumption that the only way to respond to a text is to criticize it).

For of course the point of speech is often not to be a final or definitive statement but rather to keep the discourse going and produce more discourse in response—to sustain an ongoing dialogue or discussion. We can easily give writing this quality too by making our course a forum for constant writing-in-response-to-each-other's-writing, that is, by stressing the ways in which writing naturally functions as an invitation to future writing or a reply to previous writing—which is how most writing in the world actually occurs. Paradoxically, it turns out that if we invite much of the writing in a course to be more temporary and speech-like (that is, if we relax some of the pretense of chirographic, i.e., formal, definitiveness), students often manage to achieve *higher* levels of text-like definitiveness or indelibility on the fewer pieces where we stress revision and transcendence of local context.

Obviously I am not arguing that we should exploit the similarities to speech in *all* the writing we ask of students. Many of our assignments should stress indelibility—stress the need for tight, coherent, final drafts which are statements that could survive outside the context of local author and local audience. We can decide on how much writing to treat in one mode or the other

5. In enumerating these characteristics of speech I am drawing on Tannen, "Oral and Literate"; see also Emig, "Writing as a Mode of Learning." In describing some ways to provide speech conditions in a writing class, I am drawing on a discussion with members of the fall 1983 teaching practicum at Stony Brook—for whose help I am grateful.

depending on the students we are teaching. For example, if the course is for weak students who are scared or uncomfortable in their writing, I would go quite far in exploiting speech similarities.

Thus the teaching practices I have just described *could* be called condescending strategies: ways to manage the writing context so as to *relax* temporarily some of the inherent difficulties in writing as a medium.[6] But I wish to go on now to stress how writing of the very highest quality—writing as good as any of us could possibly hope to achieve—not only can but also should have many of the essential qualities somewhat misguidedly labeled "inherent in speech."

5. The best writing has *voice:* the life and rhythms of speech. Unless we actively train our students to *speak onto paper,* they will write the kind of dead, limp, nominalized prose we hate—or *say* we hate. We see the difference most clearly in extreme cases: experienced teachers learn that when they get a student who writes prose that is so tied in knots as to be impenetrable, they need only ask the student to *say* what she was getting at and the student will almost invariably speak the thought in syntax which is perfectly clear and lively, even if sometimes inelegantly colloquial. If the student had known enough to "speak the thought onto paper" and then simply cleaned up the syntax, the writing would have been much better than her best "essay writing."

6. Excellent writing conveys some kind of involvement with the audience (though sometimes a quiet nonobtrusive involvement). This audience involvement is most characteristic of oral discourse. The best writing has just this quality of being somehow a piece of two-way communication, not one-way—of seeming to be an invitation to the audience to respond, or even seeming to be a reply to what the audience had earlier thought or said. This ability to connect with the audience and take its needs into account is *not* lacking in most students—contrary to much recent received opinion. Students use this social skill quite spontaneously and well in much of their speech to a present audience, but they naturally enough neglect to use it in much of their writing since the audience is less clear to them. We can easily help students transfer to writing their skill in connecting with an audience by having them write more often in a local context to a limited and physically present audience (as when they talk).

I am speaking here to what I see as a growing misconception about the inability of adolescents to "decenter": a dangerous tendency to make snap judgments about the level of a student's cognitive development on the basis of

---

6. I don't really grant this point, however. Though these procedures are particularly suitable for basic students, they are also the kinds of writing that occur in many workplace settings (for example with a research team, an investigative committee, or any other working group whose members communicate to each other in letters, queries, and rough position papers). Sometimes people who talk about the "inherent difference" between speaking and writing get carried away and ignore the brute fact that much of the writing in the world—perhaps even most of it—takes place in a strongly social or communal context: the writing is in response to an earlier discourse and gives rise to subsequent discourse and is asked for and read by particular people whom the writer knows—people who share a common context and set of assumptions with the writer.

only a text or two—texts which are anything but accurate embodiments of how the student's mind really operates. Teachers and researchers sometimes describe the weakness of certain student writing as stemming from an inability to move past oral language strategies and a dependence on local audience and context.[7] But in reality the weakness of those pieces of writing should often be given the *opposite* diagnosis: the student has drifted off into writing to *no one in particular.* Often the student need only be encouraged to use *more* of the strategies of oral discourse and the discourse snaps back into good focus, and along with it usually comes much more clarity and even better thinking.

7. Commentators like to distinguish speech from writing by saying that speech is reticent: it invites listeners to fill in meanings from their involvement in the context and their knowledge of the speaker. Good writing, on the other hand (so this story goes), must make all the meanings explicit, must "lexicalize" or "decontextualize" all the meanings, and not require readers to fill in. But here too, this talk about the inherent nature of speech and writing is misguided. It is precisely a quality that distinguishes certain kinds of good writing that it makes readers *contribute to* or *participate in* the meanings, not just sit back and receive meanings that are entirely spelled out.

Deborah Tannen, a speech researcher, illuminates this confusion ("Oral and Literate," 89):

> If one thinks at first that written and spoken language are very different, one may think as well that written literature—short stories, poems, and novels—are the most different from casual conversation of all. Quite the contrary, imaginative literature has more in common with spontaneous conversation than with the typical written genre, expository prose.
>
> If expository prose is minimally contextualized—that is, the writer demands the least from the reader in terms of filling in background information and crucial premises—imaginative literature is maximally contextualized. The best work of art is the one that suggests the most to the reader with the fewest words. . . . The goal of creative writers is to encourage their readers to fill in as much as possible. The more the readers supply, the more they will believe and care about the message in the work.

Although we can *maximize* the unstated only in imaginative literature, nevertheless, I believe it is unhelpful to go too far with Tannen's contrast between imaginative and expository writing. Surely it is the mark of really good essays or expository writing, too, that they bring the reader *in* and get him or her to fill in and participate in the meanings, and thereby make those written meanings seem more real and believable. (I think of the expository writing of writers like Wayne Booth, Stephen Gould, or Lewis Thomas.) And even to the degree that imaginative literature is different from expository prose, we must

7. See Lunsford, "Cognitive Development," and Shaughnessy, *Errors.* Instead of just talking about "oral interference" as a problem, I would also use the term in the positive sense: oral skills and habits can "run interference" for writing—knocking down some of the obstacles that make writing difficult.

not run away from it as a model for what gives goodness to good expository prose.

If we accept uncritically the assumption that "cognitive development" or "psychological growth" consists of movement from concrete "oral" modes to abstract "literate" modes, we are left with the implication that most of the imaginative literature we study is at a lower developmental and cognitive level than most of the expository writing turned in by students. I'm frightened at the tendency to label students cognitively retarded who tend to exploit those oral or concrete strategies that characterize so much good literature, namely, narration, description, invested detail, and expression of feeling. I'm not trying to deny the burden of Piaget, Bruner, etc., etc., namely, that it is an important and necessary struggle to learn abstract reasoning, nor to deny that teaching it is *part* of our job as teachers of writing. Again I claim both positions. But there is danger in *over*emphasizing writing as abstract and nonspeech-like. (Even Bruner makes a similar warning in his work "Language, Mind.")

8. Commentators on orality and literacy tend to stress how speech works in time and writing in space. Ong is eloquent on the evanescence of speech because it exists only as sound and thus is lost in the unstoppable flow of time. In speech, past and future words *do not exist* (as they would do if they were part of a text): the only thing that exists is that fleeting present syllable that pauses on the tongue in its journey to disappearance. Speech and oral cultures are associated with narration—which takes time as its medium. Writing and literate cultures are associated with logic—which exists outside of time.

This is an important distinction and people like Ong are right to exploit its remarkably wide ramifications, but there is a danger here, too. In truth, writing is also essentially time-bound. Readers are immersed in time as they read just as listeners are when they hear. We cannot take in a text all at once as we can a picture or a diagram. We see only a few written words at a time. It is true that if we pause in our reading, we can *in a sense* step outside the flow of time and look back to earlier sections of the text, or look forward to later sections; I don't mean to underestimate the enormous contrast here with speech where such "back-" or "forward-scanning" is impossible. Nevertheless, the essential process of reading a text is more like listening than looking: the essential phenomenology involves being trapped in time and thus unable to take in more than a few words at a time.

This point is not just theoretical. The problem with much poor or needlessly difficult writing is the way it pretends to exist as it were in space rather than in time. Such writing is hard to read because it demands that we have access all at once to the many elements that the writer struggled to get into the text. The writer forces us repeatedly to stop and work at finding explanations or definitions or connections which he *gave,* it is true, or *will* give in a few pages, but which he does not bring to our minds now when we need them. (It often feels to the writer as though he's *already* given us the material we need when we are reading page two—even though we don't get it till page six—because he's *already* written page six when he rewrites page two.) Poor writers often assume that because they are making a document rather than a talk, they are *giving us a thing in space* rather than *leading us on a journey through time,* and that therefore they can pretend that we can "look at the whole thing."[8]

One of the marks of good writers, on the other hand, is their recognition that readers, like listeners, are indeed trapped in the flow of time and can take in only a few words at a time. Good writers take this as an opportunity, not just a problem. The drama of movement through time can be embodied in thinking and exposition as naturally as in stories. And the ability to engage the reader's time sense is not a matter of developing some wholly new skill or strategy, it is a matter of developing for writing that time-bound faculty we've all used in all speaking.

9. By reflecting on how writing, though apparently existing in space, is essentially speech-like in that it works on readers in the dimension of time, we can throw important light on the peculiar *difficulties of organizing or structuring a piece of writing.*

In thinking about organization in writing we are tempted to use models from the spatial realm. Indeed, our very conception of organization or structure tends to be spatial. Our *sense* of what it means to be well organized or well structured tends to involve those features which give coherence to space—features such as neatness, symmetry, and nonredundancy. Giving good organization to something in time, however, is a different business because it means giving organization or structure to something of which we can grasp only one tiny fraction at any moment.

A thought experiment. Imagine a large painting or photograph that looks well organized. Imagine next an ant crawling along its surface. How would we have to modify that picture to make it "well organized" for the ant? Since he cannot see the picture all at once, we would have to embed some tiny, simplified reductions or capsule "overviews" of the whole picture at periodic points in his path—especially where he starts and finishes. Otherwise, he could never make sense of the barrage of close-up details he gets as he crawls along; he would have no overall "big picture" or gestalt into which to integrate these details. But if we should make such modifications we would make the picture much "messier" from a visual point of view.

The big picture problem is really a problem of how to get readers to hold in mind a *pattern* or *relationship* among elements while having to focus attention on only one of those elements. Imagine an essay with three major points or sections (as with the present essay). If we think of it "structurally" or "from above"—that is, spatially—we see three emphases or focuses of attention, as so many paintings and photographs are organized triangularly. But what

---

8. This is particularly a problem in certain technical documents and reports, and it is interesting to see how canny readers of such genres have learned to accommodate to the bad treatment they receive: they "read" such documents as though they were looking at a diagram rather than reading a text—namely, by quickly scanning through it, perhaps more than once, trying to develop an overview and a sense of perspective which they know the writer does not provide. Being trained and consenting to read in this way, in a sense they perpetuate the problem.

holds the picture together is the fact that in the realm of vision we can focus on one of the three main areas yet simultaneously retain our view of the other two and our sense of how they relate to the one we are looking at. With an essay, on the other hand, we can read *only* one small part at a time, and so it is hard to experience the *relationship* or *interaction* of the three parts.

Thus the problem of structure in a temporal medium is really the problem of how to *bind time*. Whereas symmetry and pattern bind space (and also bind smaller units of time—in the form of rhythm), they don't manage very well to hold larger units of time together. What binds larger units of time? Usually it is the experience of anticipation or tension which then builds to some resolution or satisfaction. In well-structured discourse, music, and films (temporal media) we almost invariably see a pattern of alternating dissonance-and-consonance or itch and then scratch. Narrative is probably the most common and natural way to set up a structure of anticipation and resolution in discourse.

But how do we bind time with patterns of anticipation and resolution in *essays or expository writing?* Here the tension or itch that binds the words is almost always the experience of some *problem* or *uncertainty* that is somehow conveyed to the reader. Unless there is a felt question—a tension, a palpable itch—the time remains unbound. The most common reason why weak essays don't hang together is that the writing is all statement, all consonance, all answer: the reader is not made to experience any cognitive dissonance to serve as a "net" or "set" to catch all these statements or answers. Without an itch or a sense of felt problem, nothing holds the reader's experience together—however well the text itself might summarize the parts. (This is a common problem in the essays of students since they so often suppose that essays are only for telling, not for wondering.)

When we tell ourselves to "be careful about organization" or to "give good structure" to our text, we tend to think in terms of building blocks laid out in space, but this often fails to give our readers an *experience* of coherence and clarity (however neatly we pattern our blocks). If on the other hand, we think of our structural problem as that of trying to speak a long monologue to a listener in such a way that he or she doesn't get lost and indeed feels a coherent shape in what we are saying, we are more likely to call on crucial organizational skills that we commonly use in speech. Some examples:

- We are more likely in speaking than in writing to give the quick forward- and backward-looking coherence aids that readers need when they are trapped in the linear flow of time. When our listeners are right there in front of us as we speak, we are less likely to put our heads down and forget about their need for help in coherence.
- In speaking, we are more likely as it were to "tell the story" of our thinking. This doesn't necessarily mean turning it into actual narrative (though it's surprising how many good essays use a genuine narrative shape). But we are likely to give it a narrative *feel:* "Where does this thinking *start?* Where is it *going?* What is the *goal?*"

- Discourse is sometimes given coherence in time by the use of recurring phrases, images, metaphors, or resonant examples (not merely decorative or illustrative but structural) which "chunk" or function as microevocations of the whole. Such recurring miniature units are characteristic of oral discourse and music (e.g., the leitmotif). A phrase can continue to ring in the reader's ear even while we are tangled in the underbrush of prose. In revising this essay, I moved my vision of three writers from the end to the beginning in hopes they would function as structural motifs.
- Oddly enough, the *list*, that crudest of all structures, is a remarkably effective way to give structure to discourse in time. Lists are common in oral and epic poetry and also in speech ("Here's another reason why . . ."). As researchers into document design have noticed, written texts are often much more coherent to readers when a connected chain of points is reshaped into a main statement and a *list* of supporting or following items. Lists have an interesting cognitive characteristic: as we take in each item we tacitly rehearse our sense of what that item is an instance *of*. Thus a list is a way of increasing unity by giving readers a reiterated sense of the main point without having to repeat it explicitly so often.

The problems of structure in writing are subtly difficult. Because of the confusion introduced into our very notion of structure by the pervasive metaphor of space, I suspect that we are still waiting for the help we need in showing us the most effective models of good structure in time. We would probably do well to look to studies of the structure of music, film and poetry (see, e.g., Meyer and Zuckerkandl on music).

10. A final reason why writing needs to be like speech. Perhaps it is fanciful to talk of speech having a magic that writing lacks—call it presence, voice, or *pneuma*—but the truth is that we tend to experience meaning somehow more *in* spoken words than written ones. (Socrates and Husserl make this point: see Searle, "The Word Turned Upside Down.")

This vividness of speech is illustrated in academic conferences where people speak written papers out loud. Because we are listening to *writing* presented orally, we may notice in a curiously striking way how it seldom seems as semantically "inhabited" or "presenced" as speech.

Of course, most of us can convey *more* meaning by reading a written essay out loud than by trying to give a speech from notes—more precisely, clearly, and quickly too. Yet the moment-to-moment language of a recited essay (even if more precise) is almost invariably less "full of meaning" than the language of our actual live speech (even if that speech has some stumbling and lack of precision). In short, writing seems to permit us to get *more* meaning into words (get more said more quickly), but speech helps get our meanings integrated more *into* our words.

But why should it be that we seem to experience the meaning more in spoken words than written words? Is it just because spoken words are *performed* for us and so we get all those extra cues from seeing the speaker, hearing how she speaks—all those rhythms and tonalities? That is important, but there's something else that goes deeper: in listening to speech we are hearing mental activity going on—live; in reading a text we are only encountering the record of completed mental events. It's not that the audience has to *receive* the words while the mental activity is going on, but that the language has to be *created* while the mental activity is going on: the language must embody or grow out of live mental events. The important simultaneity is not between meaning-making and hearing, but between meaning-making and the production or emergence of language. The crucial question for determining whether discourse achieves "presence" is whether the words produced are *an expression of something going on* or *a record of something having gone on*.

To speak is (usually) to give spontaneous verbal substance to mental events occurring right at that moment in the mind. Even when we are stuck or tongue-tied we seldom remain silent for long: Billy Budd is the exception. Usually, we say something about our inability to figure out what to say. To write, however, is usually to *rehearse* mental events inside our heads before putting them down. (Someone's speech usually sounds peculiar if he rehearses his words in his head before speaking them.)

My hypothesis then, is that when people produce language *as* they are engaged in the mental event it expresses, they produce language with particular features—features which make an audience feel the meanings very much *in* those words. Here then is an important research agenda for discourse analysis: what are the language features that correlate with what people experience as the semantic liveness of speech? (See Halpern, "Differences," for a start at this job.)

Such research would have very practical benefits for writing theory, since of course writing *can* be as alive as speech. What characterizes much excellent writing is precisely this special quality of lively or heightened semantic presence. It's as though the writer's mental activity is somehow there in the words on the page—as though the silent words are somehow alive with her meaning.

When a writer is particularly fluent, she has the gift of doing less internal rehearsal. The acts of figuring out what she wants to say, finding the words, and putting them down somehow coalesce into one act—into that integrative meaning-making/language-finding act which is characteristic of speech. But even beginners (or writing teachers) can achieve this liveliness and presence when they engage in freewriting or spontaneous writing. It is this semantic presence which often makes freewriting seem peculiarly lively to read. One of the best directions for coaching freewriting is to tell oneself or one's students to "talk onto the paper."

Of course, we cannot usually produce a carefully pondered and well-ordered piece of writing by talking onto paper. In any piece of writing that has been a struggle to produce, there is often a certain smell of stale sweat. And freewriting or spontaneous speech may be careless or shallow (the meaning is *in* the words but the *amount* of meaning is very small). But if we learn to talk onto paper and exploit the speech-like quality possible in writing, we can have the experience of writing words with presence, and thereby learn what such writing *feel* like—in the fingers, in the mouth, and in the ear. This experience increases our chances of getting desirable speech qualities into the writing we revise and think through more carefully.

That third writer in my prologue vision—the one who has conjured up her audience and is seeing them and speaking to them as she writes, who is "uttering" more than "composing" or "constructing": she writes in the mentality of writing-like-speech.

Conclusion

I have argued three contrary claims: writing is essentially unlike speech because it is more indelible; writing is essentially unlike speech because it is more *ephemeral;* and writing is essentially *like* speech. My goal is to stop people from talking so much about the inherent nature of these media and start them talking more about the different ways we can *use* them. In particular I seek to celebrate the flexibility of writing as a medium, and to show that we need to develop more control over ourselves as we write so that we can *manage* our writing process more judiciously and flexibly. Thus, I am not putting my three writers in my prologue vision into competition with each other. None is better than the other. Even though the mentality of writing-as-indelible has caused difficulty and even kept many people from writing at all, writing *is* indelible, and sometimes (not always) we need that painstaking care. There is no single best way to write.

And yet in the end I claim that there *is* a single best way to write, and that is to be able to move back and forth among them. Furthermore, there is a particular mentality which the technology of writing is peculiarly suited to enhance (as speech is not), namely, *the play of mentalities.* We can learn to *be* all three writers imaged above. Writing can show us how to move back and forth between cognitive processes and mentalities which at first may seem contradictory, but which if exploited will heighten and reinforce each other.

Works Cited

Note: For two rich bibliographies on the relation between speech and writing, see the Kroll and Vann volume noted below, and the annotated bibliography by Sarah Liggett in *CCC:* 35 (October, 1984), 334–44.

Barthes, Roland. "Death of the Author." In *Image, Music, Text.* New York: Hill and Wang, 1977.

Bruner, Jerome. *Studies in Cognitive Growth.* Cambridge, MA: Harvard University Press, 1966.

———— "Language, Mind, and Reading." In *Awakening Literacy.* Ed. Hillel Goelman, Antoinette Obeng, and Frank Smith. Exeter NH: Heinemann Educational Books, 1984.

Calkins, Lucy. *Lessons from a Child on the Teaching and Learning of Writing.* Exeter, NH: Heinemann Educational Books, 1983.

Cooper, Charles and Lee Odell. "Considerations of Sound in the Composing Process of Published Writers." *RTE,* 10 (Fall, 1976), 103–115.

Elbow, Peter. *Writing Without Teachers.* New York: Oxford University Press, 1973.

———— *Writing With Power.* New York: Oxford University Press, 1981.

Emig, Janet. "Writing as a Mode of Learning." *CCC,* 28 (May, 1977), 122–128. Reprinted in *The Writing Teacher's Sourcebook.* Ed. Gary Tate and Edward P. J. Corbett. New York: Oxford University Press, 1981.

Faigley, L. et al. "Writing After College: A Stratified Survey of the Writing of College-Trained People," Writing Program Assessment Technical Report No. 1, University of Texas, Austin, 1981.

Gere, Anne Ruggles. "A Cultural Perspective on Talking and Writing." In Kroll and Vann, *Exploring Speaking-Writing Relationships.*

Goody, Jack. *The Domestication of the Savage Mind.* Cambridge, England: Cambridge University Press, 1977.

Graves, Donald. *Writing: Teachers and Children at Work.* Exeter NH: Heinemann Educational Books, 1983.

Halpern, Jeanne, "Differences Between Speaking and Writing and Their Implications for Teaching," *CCC,* 35 (October, 1984), 345–357.

Harste, Jerome C., Virginia A. Woodward, Carolyn L. Burke, "Examining our Assumptions: A Transactional View of Literacy and Learning," *RTE,* 18 (February, 1984), 84–108.

Havelock, Eric A. *Preface to Plato.* Cambridge MA: Belknap Press of Harvard University Press, 1963.

Heath, Shirley Brice. "Oral and Literate Traditions." *International Social Science Journal,* 36 (1984), 41–57.

Kroll, Barry M., and Roberta J. Vann (ed.) *Exploring Speaking-Writing Relationships.* Urbana IL: National Council of Teachers of English, 1981.

Lunsford, Andrea. "Cognitive Development and the Basic Writer." CE, 41 (September, 1979), 38–46.

Meyer, Leonard B. *Emotion and Meaning in Music.* Chicago: University of Chicago Press, 1956.

Olson, D. R. "The Languages of Instruction: The Literate Bias of Schooling." In R. C. Anderson, R. J. Siro, and W. E. Montague (ed.), *Schooling and the Acquisition of Knowledge.* Hillsdale, NJ: Lawrence Erlbaum, 1977.

Ong, Walter J. *Orality and Literacy.* New York: Metheun, 1982. 81.

Perl, Sondra: "Understanding Composing." *CCC,* 31 (December 1980), 363–369.

Robinson, Jay L. "The Users and Uses of Literacy." In *Literacy of Life: The Demand for Reading and Writing.* Ed. Richard W. Bailey and Robin Melanie Fosheim. New York: Modern Language Association, 1983.

Schafer, John C. "The Linguistic Analysis of Spoken and Written Texts." In Kroll and Vann, *Exploring Speaking-Writing Relationships.*

Scribner, Sylvia, and Michael Cole. *The Psychology of Literacy.* Cambridge MA: Harvard University, Press, 1981.

———— "Unpackaging Literacy." In *Variations in Writing: Functional and Linguistic-Cultural Differences.* Ed. Marcia Farr Whiteman. Hillsdale NJ: Lawrence Erlbaum, 1981, 71–87.

Searle, John. "The Word Turned Upside Down." *The New York Review of Books,* 27 October 1983, 74–79.

Shaughnessy, Mina P. *Errors and Expectation: A Guide for the Teacher of Basic Writing.* New York: Oxford University Press, 1977.

Tannen, Deborah. "Oral and Literate Strategies in Spoken and Written Discourse." In *Literacy for Life: The Demand for Reading and Writing.* Ed. Richard W. Bailey and Robin Melanie Fosheim. New York: Modern Language Association, 1983.

Zuckerkandl, Victor. *Sound and Symbol: Music and the External World.* New York: Pantheon Press, 1956, reprinted 1976.

8

Voice in Literature

> A dramatic necessity goes deep into the nature of the sentence.
> Sentences are not different enough to hold the attention unless
> they are dramatic. No ingenuity of varying structure will do. All
> that can save them is the speaking tone of voice somehow entan-
> gled in the words and fastened to the page for the ear of the imagi-
> nation. That is all that can save poetry from sing-song, all that can
> save prose from itself.
>
> Robert Frost, Introduction to *A Way Out*

In the beginning all literature was voice. That is, what we call literature started out in every culture as voiced—as actual speech, song, or chant. But now in our culture, and in many other industrial cultures, literature is silent text, words on a page. Indeed, the very term for what we are discussing, *literature*, means "letters." Thus, "oral literature" is an oxymoron, since there are no letters in oral literature, only voiced sounds.

It's not surprising then, that some of the most influential schools of criticism—semiotics, structuralism, and poststructuralism—emphasize that not only literature but indeed all discourse is nothing but text. Derrida argues that our habit of inferring a voice behind all language is a big mistake, the mistake of "phonocentrism." This textual approach to literary criticism emphasizes "intertextuality," the idea that texts don't come so much from human agency as from language itself, from the operation of semiotic systems, and the idea that texts are not so much about things in the world as about other texts. A semiotic point of view sees everything as text.

Despite these misgivings about voice in texts, the interest in it does not go away. There are three main ways in which many critics and teachers use voice

This essay was published in 1994 in the *Encyclopedia of English Studies and Language Arts*. Ed. Alan Purves. Urbana IL: NCTE.

as a critical term in talking about literary texts: (1) They talk about voice as style. (2) They talk about the voice of a speaker in the text. (3) They talk about the voice of an author behind the text.

We can illustrate these three uses in a short lyric by Emily Dickinson:

> To make a prairie it takes a clover and one bee.
> One clover, and a bee,
> And revery.
> The revery alone will do,
> If bees are few.

Voice as Style

One of the best ways to get at style in language is to describe language in terms of voice. This is especially true in teaching. Thus if we want to describe the style of the Dickinson lyric literally or directly—without reference to voice—we would probably talk about its plain style and simple words, about the repeating of simple concrete nouns *(clover* and *bee),* emphasizing them by rhythmic accent and contrasting them with something as unconcrete as can be *(revery),* and about the lack of a verb in the second sentence adding an informal or even conversational note to the style or diction. The style is almost transparent; an unsophisticated reader might say, "But there is no style here."

But if we call on the concept of voice—if we listen to the words as though spoken—we can make our understanding of style more vivid and human. Readers who listen for voice are likely to notice the following kinds of things. The voice seems to start off in a confident, declaratory, almost oracular voice—though not loud. In the second line the voice seems to become quieter and less oracular, repeating what was said in the first line as though musing. The first line seems to talk to everyone while the next two lines seem to bend closer or speak more softly, intimately, as though to fewer, closer listeners or to oneself. The voice keeps pausing and thoughtfully repeating and reframing what it already said. The opening seems to be declared with full seriousness, while the ending suggests a faint note of irony or the wisp of a smile as it completely takes back what was so confidently asserted in the opening. (This note, however, is so faint that we're not quite sure if there's any element of humor or irony. This laconic possibility of humor is a tone of voice that Robert Frost was expert at, another Amherst/New Englander. Indeed his poem "Fire and Ice" closely echoes even the turn of logic in this one by Dickinson.) Nevertheless, the last two lines could be voiced as more serious, more mystical, than the lines that precede them. *Tone* is a more traditional literary term, and it can be somewhat mysterious and ambiguous in meaning. It becomes clearer and more concrete when we fill in the implied metaphor: We are talking about "tone of voice."

To talk about style is to focus on the actual language and syntax itself. To talk about voice, on the other hand, is to be in a way more roundabout and imprecise, that is, to talk about how the words ask to be performed or spoken. When readers talk about style, they are more likely to sound as though they are making objective interpretations or impersonal statements because they are making literal observations about the language itself. When readers talk about voice, they are likely to sound more subjective and even to use more metaphors. They are also more likely to notice the differences and conflicts among interpretations because they are necessarily talking about the way the language ought to be performed—and it's hard not to notice that it could be performed in different ways.

Nevertheless, students and untrained readers are often more sophisticated in getting at how language works when they talk in terms of voice than when they talk about textual style. Everyone has had more practice in listening for voice quality and describing distinctions between voices than in describing textual style, so most readers can call on more subtle discriminations in terms of voice. These voice-based perceptions and discriminations can then help readers (especially students) be more sophisticated if they want to go on to analyze stylistic and syntactic features.

The Voice of the Speaker in the Text

In their efforts to pay better attention to the voices in texts, influential modern critics have given us important critical terms: Wayne Booth made *implied author* a central term in literary criticism: Yeats gave currency to *mask,* Pound to *persona.* (Note that *persona* comes from a Latin word for the mask that classical actors wore to amplify their voices for the large amphitheater stage they played on: *per* + *sona* meaning something that words "sound through.")

By asking about the voices in texts, critics have been led to questions like: "What kind of person is telling us this story or speaking this poem to us? How does she see things? Do we believe her?" Henry James was one of the first influential modern critics and writers who was particularly interested in the presentation of events through the voice of a narrator with a point of view different from the author's and from that of careful readers. It has been a characteristic of twentieth-century imaginative writers to use slippery voices, or what some critics call unreliable narrators.

By focusing on the voice of the speaker, the New Critics brought out the maximum drama in literary texts. Their approach has helped us get away from treating all poems and stories as sincere statements by actual authors or disembodied statements of universal truth. In effect, New Critics taught us that where there is language, there is drama: someone saying something to someone. (This is also the lesson we learn from speech act theory.)

There is a drama in the Dickinson lyric that we might miss without an emphasis on the voice of a speaker. After all, there is no "I" and the poem is nothing but bare, unattributed sentences or assertions. But if we listen to the words as voiced, we hear a drama: someone's mind at work over time. In the first line, the speaker makes a simple universal pronouncement. He sounds oracular or even Godlike. (Let's call the speaker "he" to show that we are not equating it with Dickinson herself.) Since he is talking about creating a piece of nature, the voice might even remind us of that simple, quiet, but vast voice that God used in Genesis. But once the speaker makes this pronouncement, he seems to pause to savor it in line 2, to linger over the ingredients he just named. This reflective pause leads him to an afterthought in line 3, a realization that his initial confident pronouncement left out an essential ingredient: revery. Yet this afterthought leads him to another one, quietly wry but more radical and paradoxical: that the revery is not just necessary, it is actually sufficient. Thus in the last line, we can hear a wry laconic speaker who makes fun of himself by utterly denying the truth of his original Genesislike pronouncement: Everything that he specified in his opening confident assertion and repeated in subsequent musing is in fact expendable.

The Voice of the Author Behind the Text

It would seem utterly misguided to listen for Emily Dickinson's own voice in her poems. Her actual voice is completely unknown to us, and her character or personality is a celebrated mystery. Critics have often gotten themselves in serious trouble by assuming that writers always write "in their own voice" or from their own point of view. For example, some critics used to date Donne's poems by placing them along a biographical trajectory from young roustabout sinner to aging repentant Christian. They didn't consider the fact that Donne at various times in his life wrote poems from various points of view; most of all, that he wasn't always writing "as himself." Writers often "take on" voices or create dramas.

Nevertheless, there are always two voices or two "authors" for every text. We have just looked at the persona in the text: the implied author. Here we will consider the actual historical author, or the voice *behind* the text. For it is important to realize that readers and critics always have a choice about which author to attend to or emphasize at any particular moment of reading. It is more dangerous, of course, to make inferences about the real author, but it is a human tendency and a critical tradition to do so. For just as we can get a sense of what someone is really like if we listen to her or him speak long enough, critics can get a sense of what writers themselves are really like through reading enough of their work.

Thus, voice is a useful word to use when we want to ask ourselves: "What is this writer like and how does she see things and render experience into language?" For even though Emily Dickinson's poems don't all speak in the same voice or express a similar point of view, many good readers do hear a characteristic voice behind most of her poetry: a voice that is intriguingly intimate yet distant, emphasizing unique personal experience yet somehow abstracting or universalizing it (a voice that is often corroborated in her letters). Many good critics hear this voice as capturing the way Dickinson as a person seemed to see things and put them into words—not just how her personae did. In fact, it is hard not to hear a characteristic voice in many writers—for example, even in John Donne, Henry James, Virginia Woolf—and many critics are interested in making inferences about the writers themselves, not just their personae. Thus if we are interested in *intention* in works of literature, listening for voice can be a useful tool. (The two terms are not the same, however. Intention speaks to the conscious mind; voice tends to answer to the unconscious.)

This dimension of voice is more difficult to talk about in slippery and "dramatic" writers who don't in fact seem to develop a characteristic style or voice. Shakespeare is the paradigm case: a writer who never wrote anything in his own voice, except a few flowery dedications (though a few critics see his sonnets as speaking in his own voice), and about whose life very little is known. Yet even here some critics listen for "voice" in a more metaphoric sense, and read his plays and make useful if debatable inferences about the actual mind and character that was at work rendering the world into language.

Some recent critics, of course, argue that there is no such thing as a self in writers or anyone else, that the self is nothing but a constantly changing collection of roles or "subject positions." It is these critics who are most vociferous against the use of voice as a critical term.

9

Silence

A Collage

Empty, empty, empty. That's the main impulse I feel now. Towards emptiness. I'm tired of words. The tyranny of words. I have a hunger for silence.

It makes me realize how committed to words I've been, how deeply stamped by certain formative experiences. Being inarticulate, unable to write, blocked, stuck—and therefore having to quit graduate school as a failure. And then some years later, being able to write. Losing my tongue, finding my tongue.

Having found I could write, I've kept writing, writing, writing. Afraid I'd lose it again if I stopped? Got to keep talking on paper for dear life? Perhaps a quality of desperation.

And not just the experience of writing but of actually succeeding in saying what I want to say! Despite the struggle. What a miracle! It's left me with an insistent feeling that we can write anything. I get mad at the deconstructive idea that language always fails. No, damn it, we can say anything. Language doesn't fail. A stubbornness. Shrillness? Fear?

But now I think I'm ready to move on. Tired. I think I want to wander now into the place that values silence, emptiness, inarticulateness. To celebrate nonlanguage—silence—not having to write or say all the time.

And in fact perhaps these two impulses—toward language and toward silence—actually go together in some paradoxical way. For I have a sense this morning of my whole life—even my writing life—as a stubborn if underground celebration of inarticulateness and brokenness. That's what I've been fighting for in my writing. I've always been angry at the articulate and fluent people.

This collage is very little changed from what was published in 1993 in *Presence of Mind: Writing and the Domain Beyond the Cognitive*. Eds. Alice Brand and Richard Graves. Portsmouth NH: Heinemann/Boynton-Cook. 9–20.

I wrote those words (slightly more jumbled) in June 1991, during a workshop at Pendle Hill, a Quaker retreat center near Philadelphia. In the last few years, my interest in voice has gradually led me to feel some correlation between powerful or resonant voice and silence. In fact, I've always been interested in people who don't write or talk—the silent ones. *When* they say something, their words often seem remarkably powerful: more umph, more conviction, more presence—their words more "gathered up." I think I see it even in small versions: if we sit in silence for a while, there is apt to be more gathered energy and focus in what we say. Is this really so?

I think of Billy Budd: he stutters, and at the most important moment is utterly silent. Wordsworth praises the speech of country folk. Of course this seems like dubious sentimentality, but isn't it true that something special does happen—or rather *can* happen—when people spend a lot of time locked inside their own heads: talking and listening inside in silence? The old rural, solitary life was apt to enhance this inner life. Freewriting is an attempt to imprison people inside their head.

So with some of these intimations in my head, I was happy to accept the invitation from Pendle Hill to co–direct a weekend workshop on "Voice and Silence."

We wrote and talked a lot. I talked more about voice than about silence, but what figured most in all our conversations and our written reflections at the end was silence: the various periods of silence we had—and particularly the unbroken silence we had both mornings stretching from wake-up through breakfast till the end of "silent meeting" at around ten o'clock.

Charlie Janeway:

> *Breakfast. Eating slowly, carefully. A shy furtive glance at the person next to me, avoiding eyes.*
>
> *Strange sensual intimacy, sitting next to someone and not speaking, knowing that another time and place we might be speaking.*
>
> *[Silent] meeting. Through half closed eyes, people's legs and shoes on the shining waxed floor.*
>
> *Silence. Except for my breathing and the occasional stomach gurgle, only the chattering of the birds outside the Barn.*
>
> *My thoughts run in the silence. . . .*
>
> *Breathing in. Breathing out. One in. One out. Two, three, four. . . .*
>
> *Thoughts slow down, slip away. Calm. Peace.*
>
> *I feel as close to happiness as I can recall. Right now.*

Torrey Reade:

> *Strikes me that there are all kinds of silences. Yesterday's was dreamy, this morning's verged on the prim. The kind I thought I had from laziness really comes from fear. Silence in meeting is a peaceful nonevent or something that vibrates. Here in this group we are on the one hand dealing with the polite silence we've all been bred to, and on another with some deep nurturing thing that emits from its darkness things that turn into words.*

Ardeth Deay:

WORDS WORDS WORDS pouring out and over me, drowning my core, distracting my integrity.

This is the first time I've been able to articulate how painful it is for me when we use words to separate, to disconnect, to ignore each other. To cover up who we are? that we don't know? fear? lack of trust? indifference? pain? power?

What would happen if we all only spoke when we had something to say? Would we go about our lives with the comfortable feeling of connection I felt at breakfast? Lovely silence—opportunity to notice we are here together. Space to feel our spirits overlapping. (see William Johnson)

Diane Cameron:

The silence has helped me hear the voices better, to listen to myself. I feel more connected to myself, more grounded than I have in a long time.

Me:

I was so grateful at breakfast at the realization that we had permission to be with each other without having to figure out what to say—how to be with each other. . . .

In this silence, are we more together or apart? The question gets at the paradox of it. One feels the distance, awkwardness. And yet the communion is deeper too. . . .

[Silence is] a chance to attend to what's inner. Not that chatter in the brain. Actually, of course there is a chatter—for me, most of the time, anyway. It's louder in the silence, but I can sort of peep around the chatter just a bit and wonder what's behind it. Get a few glimpses of something quieter behind it. . . .

For a few moments in the Barn [silent meeting] I had a sense that I might really be able to open the door, still the noises, go into a dark place— scary but somehow desirable. But I got nervous and the door shut and I was back to the distractedness. Still, a lingering sense of feasibility.

The collage form is important here. The force of the collage is the force of embedded silence: asterisks, gaps. Parts don't "flow" in the "logical order" demanded by "good writing." The collage is jagged and broken rather than smooth. What a relief. Parataxis rather than hypotaxis: nonconnection, nonsubordination. And the collage doesn't say what it's saying. It's just a bundle of fragments. (See Weathers 1976 on "crots.")

This explains why I hate sentence combining exercises. They always want you to change *The woman threw the ball. The dog sprang up and ran after it.* into *When the woman threw the ball, the dog sprang up and ran after it* (or some such subordination). There's something wrong with their very *model* of good writing. They assume that everyone wants what I, for one, don't want. Readers may *think* they want smoothness, flow, connection, but I'll bet that's not what affects them most.

James Seitz (1991) points out that we tend to accept fragmentary texts and alternative syntactic structures only in freewriting which doesn't "count" as real writing since it's too "easy" and a "sign of failure" (819). He looks to Barthes who celebrates the fragmentary text as serious and valuable. Also to Woolf, Faulkner, Barthelme, and Paley who "reveal the rhetorical and aesthetic power generated by disruptive discontinuity and disorder . . ." (823).

By using unconnected fragments and putting them in the "wrong" order, the collage sucks the reader in. The reader has to make the connections. Whenever there is silence, the reader must enter in, read in, participate. "Finally, the reader of silence is implicated in the text in a new way in Woolf's novels, for she or he must join with the writer to understand and decipher the silences in the novel: a mode of subjectivity" (Laurence, 217).

Ron Padget writes about *The World of Silence* (Gateway Press):

Max Picard, the author, was a Swiss philosopher whose work is known in this country only by professors of philosophy and aesthetics and by a handful of poets. . . . For years I have recommended this book to friends and colleagues, but because it was out of print for so long . . . and the messianic look in my face as I spoke about it, no one ever seemed to take my advice. Every once in a while, though, the response would be explosive: "You know about The World of Silence? Isn't it the most amazing book you've ever read?" It is an amazing book, hypnotic and almost crazy, partly because the word silence appears in 95% of the sentences. After a while you realize you don't quite know what the author is saying, but by then you have been floated into the mysterious dreamy mental space he has created, and it's wonderful to be there. How can you use this book in the classroom? I don't know. All I can do is urge you to get this strange and beautiful book before it goes out of print again. (see also Forman, Kalamaras)

Silence and felt sense. The foundation of verbal meaning often lies in the silence of what is felt nonverbally and bodily. When writing goes well, it is often because we periodically pause and say, "Is this what I mean to be saying?" It's amazing that we can answer that question: that we can tell whether a given set of words corresponds to an intention. The source of the answer is the feelings and the body—consulted in silence. When writing goes badly, it is often because we don't make these pauses for quiet consultations with felt sense.

Anne Dalke has given me permission to quote at length from her essay "'On Behalf of the Standard of Silence': The American Female Modernists":

> For at least the past fifteen years, my generation of feminist artists and writers has insisted on the dangers and oppressiveness of silence, on the urgent need for women to find an authentic means of expression. They have been entreating women to speak up, to employ whatever language they have available to them. Adrienne Rich has argued that in a world where language is power, a means of changing reality, silence is a state of deprivation, of ignorance. [Dalke also quotes Tillie Olsen, Michelle Cliff, Audre Lorde, and Sandra Gilbert on this theme.]
>
> In the earlier decades of this century, several American women writers [Gertrude Stein, Ellen Glasgow, Willa Cather, Edith Wharton, Zora Neale Hurston, Eudora Welty, and Flannery O'Connor] offered quite another view of silence, a more positive and suggestive one: they described it not as void, but as fullness.

. . .

> The contemporary feminist equation of language with power, of self-expression with self-empowerment, is a relatively new, and relatively one-dimensional, development. The earlier writers do not anticipate the contemporary emphasis on the power and primacy of language. They do not equate silence with disenfranchisement.

. . .

> The texts of these writers chronicle the acquisition but also the inadequacy of language, which often fails to capture the central female experience. . . . [T]hese novelists are modernist both in their denial that language constitutes reality, and in their assumption of a reality of experience, mysterious and inexpressible, which precedes and evades articulation. In their works, language is not only inadequate as expression; it can also be a hindrance, even a falsification. The acquisition of language, they say, is not an unadulterated virtue; it may mean great loss. Several of them celebrate silence as a gift: they suggest that, when we do not speak, we may listen, hear, understand, even communicate in other ways. Silence may function as an altogether alternative means of communication, not dependent on speech for fulfillment.

. . .

In her essay on modernism, "The Aesthetics of Silence," Susan Sontag presents silence similarly as a means for furthering speech. . . . Silence, she argues, has specific uses:

> . . . certifying the absence or renunciation of thought . . . certifying the completion of thought . . . [and] providing time for the continuing or exploring of thought. Notably, speech closes off thought.

. . . Silence keeps things "open." Still another use for silence: furnishing or aiding speech to attain its maximum integrity of seriousness . . . [W]hen punctuated by long silences, words weigh more. . . . Silence undermines "bad speech." (19–20)

. . .

These seven modern women writers question the concept of silence as unnatural, as a prelude only to giving voice, and affirm instead the possibility of quiet revelation. When silence is embedded in our speaking, they suggest, we may better hear what is said, and better give it voice; moreover, silence alone may be fuller, richer, more replete than language can ever be [463–65; 479; for some interesting works that Dalke refers to in other parts of her essay, see the citations in the Works Cited under her name.]

Analogies between silence and freewriting:

- Both are quiet.
- Both encourage you to communicate with yourself.
- Both involve relinquishing control, letting go; thus sometimes fear.
- Both tend to start with jabber, jabber, jabber, noise, static, baloney. Yet both often lead to—or at least clear space for—voice, nonbaloney, and language and thinking that are grounded in actual experience rather than in convention or external authority. If there is a class or meeting or conversation that has gone wrong in some way—even if only very subtly "off"—a period of either silence or freewriting tends to help people both notice the problem and begin to deal with it. ("How come everyone is avoiding the main issue we came here to talk about?" "Why are no women speaking?")
- In silent sitting and freewriting, there is often a feeling of fellowship or companionship—in a "gathered" separateness.
- Both silence and freewriting are hard to classify in terms of "input" vs. "output." Both are times of "producing" but also "waiting for things to arrive."
- Both give relief from logic and linearity.
- Both consist of one part of the self ministering to another part of the self.
- Experienced silence-sitters say they can somehow feel it in the air when the silence in a group is deep, when a meeting is "gathered." I think I can feel the same thing in the silence of a group of people freewriting—when it is deeper rather than resistant or distracted or sullen (as sometimes happens in an exam or when people don't want to write).

Here's a minicollage of passages from Erika Scheurer, *"A Vice for Voices": Emily Dickinson's Dialogic Voice From the Borders.*

Dickinson is saying a lot about silence. First, there are certain things, "Hallowed things," that should not be spoken of aloud, and when people do so it bothers her so much that she secludes herself; second, she wants it clear that her silence is not a sign of ignorance or lack of words—she *chooses* silence as a response to certain situations; and third, silence is central to her poetic project—her work is to enable us to hear, not ordinary sound, but a "noiseless noise": the fullness of silence? it's meaningfulness?

She explains that she shuns society because "they talk of Hallowed things, aloud—and embarrass my Dog. . . ." L[etter]271

L[etter] 572: "Why the full heart is speechless, is one of the great wherefores."

The words the happy say
Are paltry melody
But those the silent feel—
Are beautiful—

　　　　　1750

We have enough from Dickinson on both silence and voice to infer that she did not see them as mutually exclusive either. First, on the qualities of silence and how they relate to voice: the usual opposition we see is of writing/silence/absence and speech/voice/presence. Post-structuralists like to emphasize the division here . . . but I want to say that silence can be as present as voice, that silence is a part of voice, or even maybe *has* voice. The resonance of silence.

The first observation I'd offer to break up the tidy dualism of writing/silence/absence and speech/voice/presence is that silence requires presence to give it meaning. If I am silent and nobody is aware of it as silence—say I'm sitting home all day working on a piece of writing, receiving no calls and making none—that silence doesn't mean much. However, if someone repeatedly tries to reach me, knowing I'm home, and I don't pick up the phone, then that silence has meaning (it could mean any number of things). In this sense, the power of silence is just as wedded to presence and connection as the power of speech.

We talked with each other about each other
Though neither of us spoke—

　　　　　1473

Speech is one symptom of Affection
And Silence one—
The perfectest communication
Is heard of none

　　　　　1681

Communication specialists are now looking at silence in the context of speech as well. In *Perspectives on Silence* (Tannen and Saville-Troike 1985), a collection of articles by linguists and anthropologists, Muriel Saville-Troike points to the increasing attention that silence is getting—that it is no longer considered simply as what surrounds the important thing, speech. She writes, "The significance of silence can usually be interpreted only in relation to sound, but the reverse is also the case, with the significance of sound depending on the interpretation of silence" (3). In other words, silence is an equal part of conversation, not just the space around it. I'm reminded of my discourse-analysis research with collaborative writing groups. One of the groups had turned on the tape recorder's speech-activation mechanism for recording their group meetings, so no pauses in the conversation are recorded, only speech. Listening to this sort of recorded conversation is like listening to one where the speech of one group member has been erased—the conversation is ultimately misrepresented. So the silences within speech are speech acts themselves.

> My will endeavors for its word
> And fails, but entertains
> A rapture as of Legacies—
> Of introspective Mines—
>
> 1700

Dickinson doesn't just express a philosophy about the inexpressible; her writing, with its elided syntax, pervasive dashes, and ambiguous meanings is replete with the inexpressible itself. What are these qualities of her work if not *silences*—places in which she refuses to (or cannot) speak? What happens when we read her work? We speak in the silences. We try—even if we ultimately fail—to fill in the meaning, to figure it out. Often we leave the poem with the meaning just as unclear as when we began, but the silences have a different character after we try to create meaning in them: they become *resonant* silences. I'm wanting to say, odd as it sounds, that this sort of silence has *voice*—it engages us in the act of filling it. We're engaged in dialogue with silence and the words surrounding it. Dickinson's voice comes not only through her words, but through the silences that pervade them.

> L614: "Vocal is but one form of remembrance, dear friend. The cherishing that is speechless, is equally warm."

> If what we could—were what we would—
> Criterion—be small—
> It is the Ultimate of Talk—
> The Impotence to Tell—
>
> 407

How often do we truly feel comfortable with long periods of silence? When we're with strangers, or even casual friends, when the conversation falters, we panic and do anything to fill up the air. At first this seems strange; when we're talking we're revealing ourselves, which you'd think would be more frightening than anything else. Could it be that silence reveals even more than speech does, and that's what we fear? Again, I'm thinking of silence replete with meaning, resonance. And to be willing to share that meaning—not fear it—requires a relationship of some trust.

And this is exactly the same context required for voice, isn't it? To write or speak in a voice that is not put-on from outside, but comes from the person's reality, a reality of perpetually shifting borders, requires the context of trusting relationship.

> My best Acquaintances are those
> With whom I spoke no word—
>
> > 932
>
> When Bells stop ringing—Church—begins—
> The Positive—of Bells—
> When Cogs—stop—that's Circumference—
> The Ultimate—of Wheels.
>
> > 33

From Eva Hoffman's *Lost in Translation: A Life in a New Language* (1989):

I am writing a story in my journal. . . . I make my way through layers of acquired voices, silly voices, sententious voices, voices that are too cool and too overheated. Then they all quiet down, and I reach what I'm searching for: silence. I hold still to steady myself in it. This is the white bland center, the level ground that was there before Babel was built, that is always there before the Babel of our multiple selves is constructed. From this white plenitude, a voice begins to emerge: it's an even voice, and it's capable of saying things straight, without exaggeration or triviality. As the story progresses, the voice grows and diverges into different tonalities and timbres; sometimes, spontaneously, the force of feeling or of thought compresses language into metaphor, or an image, in which words and consciousness are magically fused. But the voice always returns to its point of departure, to ground zero. (275–76)

Here is the last piece I wrote during the Pendle Hill workshop:

I want to bring more silence into my teaching. Here are some things I want to do more:
- *Writing itself brings in silence. It's such a relief to end the yammering in classrooms and sit quietly writing.*
- *Stress freewriting as listening to the voices within—as waiting and receptivity and input—silence—not agency and output and pushing.*

- *Work on listening. Especially by more emphasis on sharing: just hav-ing the writer read and listeners listen in silence. Remember the non-necessity of response—whether to speech or to writing.*
- *Stress how the writer can be a silent listener to her own writing. "Please read your piece out loud. No feedback from listeners or from yourself. Just listen to your own words. Don't try to judge or diagnose or fix your writing, just ask yourself, 'What do I hear? What is this telling me?'" (Thanks to Anne Mullins and her U Mass dissertation for this idea.)*
- *Just as I often ask for five and ten minutes of writing in class, I think I can ask for five and ten minutes of silence now and then. They can't think I'm crazier than they already do. I am always saying, "Write, write, write." I need to have the courage to say (as Don Murray does), "Wait, wait, wait."*
- *Stress silence—and writing—as a way to reach for the unspoken, the meanings that are hard to find or don't want to go into words. Try to ex-plain and exploit felt sense, tacit knowledge; a way (as Dena Muhlenberg wrote) "to get in touch with the parts of the self we often push away."*
- *In this connection: the silence and nonverbal of the bodily as opposed al-ways to the mental.*

From John Cage's "Lecture on Nothing":

```
                                        What we re-quire                    is
silence                    ;         but what silence requires
            is             that I go on talking              .
                                                        Give any one
thought
                    a push                        : it     falls down easily   .
            but the pusher        and the pushed     pro-duce    that enter-
tainment            called                    a dis-cussion              .
            Shall we have one later ?
            Or  we could simply de-cide                 not to have a dis-
cussion.                    .
                                        I have nothing to say
            and I am saying it                                and that is
poetry                              as I need it              .
            This space of time                      is organized
.                    We need not fear these      silences, —
we may love them      .
                                        This is a composed
talk                    ,         for I am making it
      just as I make              a piece of music.        It is like a glass
         of milk      .              We need the          glass
and we need the      milk                    .
```

WORKS CITED

Brown, Marshall. "Unheard Melodies: The Force of Form." *PMLA* 107.3 (May 1992): 465–81.

Cage, John. "Lecture on Nothing." *America a Prophecy: A New Reading of American Poetry from Pre-Columbian Times to the Present.* Eds. Jerome Rothenberg and George Quasha. NY: Random House, 1974. 369–70. Originally printed in *Incontri Musicale*, August 1959.

Dalke, Anne. " 'On Behalf of the Standard of Silence': The American Female Modernists and the Powers of Restraint." *Soundings: An Interdisciplinary Journal* 78, 3–4 (Fall–Winter 1995): 501–19. Following are some works that Dalke cites in other parts of her essay that readers might want to consult. Anderson, Wayne. "The Rhetoric of Silence in the Discourse of Coleridge and Carlyle." *South Atlantic Review* 49 (January 1984): 72–92. Cliff, Michelle. "Notes on Speechlessness." *Sinister Wisdom* 5 (1979): 5–9. Dauenhauer, Bernard. *Silence: The Phenomenon and Its Ontological Significance.* Bloomington: Indiana UP 1980. Lorde. Audre. "The Transformation of Silence Into Language and Action." *Sister Outsider.* Trumansburg, NY: The Crossing Press, 1984. 40–44. Olsen, Tillie. *Silences.* NY: Delta, 1979. Rich, Adrienne. *On Lies, Secrets, and Silence: Selected Prose 1966–87.* NY: Norton, 1979. Sontag, Susan. "The Aesthetics of Silence." *Styles of Radical Will.* New York: Farrar, Straus, and Giroux, 1969. 3–34. Steiner, George. *Language and Silence.* NY: Atheneum, 1967.

Forman, Robert K. C. *The Problem of Pure Consciousness: Mysticism and Philosophy.* NY: Oxford UP, 1990. See especially Forman's Introduction and his essay on Eckhart.

Foucault, Michel. "The Incitement to Discourse." *The History of Sexuality. Volume 1: An Introduction.* Trans. Robert Harley. NY: Pantheon, 1978. 17–35.

Hoffman, Eva. *Lost in Translation: A Life in a New Language.* NY: Penguin, 1989.

Johnson, William. *Silent Music.* NY: Harper and Row, 1979.

Kalamaras, George. *Reclaiming the Tacit Dimension: Symbolic Form in the Rhetoric of Silence.* Albany: SUNY P, 1992.

Kammer, Jeanne. "The Art of Silence and the Forms of Women's Poetry." *Shakespeare's Sisters: Feminist Essays on Women Poets.* Eds. Sandra M. Gilbert and Susan Gubar. Bloomington: Indiana UP, 1979. 153–64.

Laurence, Patricia Ondek. *The Reading of Silence: Virginia Woolf in the English Tradition.* Stanford: Stanford UP, 1991.

Lyotard, Jean-Francis. *The Postmodern Condition: A Report on Knowledge.* Trans. Geoff Bennington and Brian Massurai, 1979. Minneapolis: U of Minnesota, 1984.

Padget, Ron. "Books." *Teachers and Writers* 23.3 (Jan-Feb 1992): 16.

Scheurer, Erika. *"A Vice for Voices": Emily Dickinson's Dialogic Voice From the Borders.* Dissertation, UMass Amherst, 1993.

Seitz, James. "Roland Barthes, Reading, and Roleplay: Composition's Misguided Rejection of Fragmentary Texts." *College English* 53.7 (Nov 1991): 815–25.

Sheerin, Michael. *Beyond Majority Rule.* [A sociologist study of Quaker decision making]

Sontag, Susan. "The Aesthetics of Silence." *Styles of Radical Will.* NY: Farrar, Straus, Giroux, 1969.

Suhor, Charles. "Silence." *The Council Chronicle.* June 1992. (Reprinted from *Education Week.*)

Tannen, Deborah and Muriel Saville-Troike. *Perspectives on Silence.* Norwood NJ: Ablex, 1985.

Weathers, Winston. "The Grammars of Style: New Options in Composition." *Freshman English News.* Winter 1976 [the entire issue].

10

What Is Voice in Writing?

Instead of considering it our task to "dispose of" any ambiguity .
. . we rather consider it our task to study and clarify the resources of ambiguity.

Kenneth Burke

I'm setting out on a long path in this essay so I'd better give an overview of the terrain. In the first section, I describe three major debates about voice. These debates involve large, ideological questions about the nature of self or identity and about the relation of the text to the writer. These debates are all the more troublesome because they tend to be cast in binary, either/or terms. In the much longer concluding section ("Five Meanings of Voice), I respond to these debates by trying to show that we don't need to resolve them in either/or terms. Instead, we can look carefully at the term voice and see that it has some fairly noncontroversial meanings when applied to writing. Thus I devote most of this second section to an extended exploration of a family of five different meanings for the term voice in writing—meanings that make the concept of voice solid and usable in spite of the theoretical debates. I'm not saying that the theoretical, ideological disputes about the nature of self never come up. But they only come up in relatively circumscribed arenas and so don't muddy most uses of the concept of voice in writing. In short, my hope is that I can make descriptive claims about the meanings of voice in writing that people from various ideological camps will be able to agree on.

This is the introductory essay I wrote for a book I edited in 1994 called *Landmark Essay on Voice and Writing*—a collection of already published essays by various authors. It is a volume in the Landmark Essays series, published by Hermagoras Press, now part of Erlbaum. The second section of this essay was also published under the title, "What Do We Mean When We Talk About Voice in Writing?" in *Voices on Voice: Perspectives, Definitions, Inquiry,* edited by Kathleen Blake Yancey, NCTE, 1994.

Three Debates About Voice

The Overarching Debate: Discourse as Text vs. Discourse as Voice

Imagine the following minihistory of music: Once upon a time people just sang and played on drums, flutes, and strings. Then they learned to write down music on paper. Music was always performed, yet composers and editors often wrote it down so as to preserve it and help with performing. A few composers and performers came to be able to look at the written scores and "hear" the music. Slowly, slowly, over a long period of time, more and more people learned to read and enjoy music silently off the page and to write down music out of their heads. Finally, it came to pass that reading and writing music on paper were as normal as singing, playing, or listening. It seemed self-evident that anyone who didn't write music or read it off the page for mental listening was seriously flawed and not a full member of society.

As a history of music, this is fantasy. But it *is* the history of language. In our highly literate culture at least, writing simply *is* as "primary" and "natural" and "foundational" a medium as speech. I treasure many of Ong's insights about orality and literacy, but when he declares that writing is "thoroughly artificial and essentially defective," I have to throw up my hands in dismay ("From Mimesis" 280). When Saussure claims that writing is unnatural and corrupt, how can Derrida (in *On Grammatology*) not make a fuss?

Excesses like these by Ong and Saussure might tempt us to flop over to the other extreme and declare that *writing* is prior or more foundational or essential. But that would be wrong too. Even Derrida (as far as I can tell) is not claiming that writing is metaphysically real while voice is not. I take it that he's simply fighting the claim or assumption that *voice* is metaphysically real while writing is not. If I am right about this, Derrida's "grammatology" is simply the study of discourse *as* "writing"—discourse seen through the lens of "writing."

Even Barthes, declaring the "Death of the Author" and celebrating discourse not as "work" but as "text"—not as an authored or fathered creation but as a free orphan we can play with as we please—text as plural, slippery, and a site for the play of myriad interpretations—even Barthes isn't saying that all discourse *is* text, not even all written discourse. He's saying that we can choose which lens to look through.

In short, we now have a choice about how to think about discourse: as semiotic text or as voiced utterance. Yes, virtually everyone learns to speak before learning to write, and most people remain more comfortable in speech than writing. But we live in a text world just as much as we live in an oral world. In some ways I feel *more* comfortable writing and reading than I do speaking and listening—and this condition is not really so uncommon. Furthermore, the burgeoning electronic media of networked computers, e-mail, and internet are making more and more people feel as easy and fluid with text as with speech. It's surely incontrovertible, then, that in our culture, both speech and writing are completely grounded, natural, authentic, real, primary.

There is no problem, then, with either the voice lens or the text lens. There is a problem only when people try to outlaw one and insist that we are not dealing with two lenses for discourse, two "terministic screens," but rather with a debate between right and wrong. The fact is, we need both lenses. Each one shows us things the other hides.

Insofar as we consider discourse as text or semiosis, it is pure disembodied language; no one is speaking to anyone. The paradigm cases are mathematics and logic. Mathematics is language—and in many ways the best one we've got. An equation is seldom a case of someone saying something to anyone else. It's usually just a set of things-standing-for-things or semiosis. The symbols do nothing but proclaim a relationship: that something is the case or means something or equals something.

If we look at natural language through this lens of text or semiosis, we see important things about it. We strip away the people, the historical drama, the body, the actual person trying to do something to someone else. So stripped, we can see better those root, bare meanings and relationships. The people, the body, the historical drama, and the fact that someone has designs on us when they speak or write these words—all these things muddy the water and often make us confused or mistaken in our reading or analysis of the signs as pure semiosis. Most of us can probably remember examples of trying to listen to mathematics when the voice or embodiment or human relationship got in the way. Perhaps we were so mad at someone that we couldn't understand the train of thought they were explaining. Perhaps we were trying to listen to a math teacher who thought we were dumb. We could have heard the math better from a machine.

I may be going against the current emphasis on the historical and subjective dimension of all discourse (the rhetorical emphasis) in saying that it can be useful to look at even natural language as pure disembodied semiotic meaning. But there's no doubting how much we have learned from this approach in our era. The New Critics made us better readers by teaching us to look at literature not as authors talking to us but as well-wrought urns existing out of time.[1] Semiotics, sign theory, and structuralism in linguistics and literary criticism also changed our reading for ever by showing us how to see highly abstract, geometricized, impersonal patterns in any myth or piece of literature or discourse at all. "Text" and "sign" became the preferred words not only for language but also for anything that carries meaning (e.g., the textuality of clothing or the semiotics of driving). Poststructuralists carried on with this powerful project of helping us not be "fooled" by the writer's character or the music of his language.

But of course it's become obvious in recent years how helpful it is to use the *other* lens and see discourse as always historically situated and always

1. In telling this stripped-down story, I pass over some interesting complications. For example, when New Critics insist that the text is *not* an author or real person talking to us as persons, their favorite word or metaphor was "*speaker.*" They insisted that every text involves a speaker and they ask us to sharpen our ears and hear all literature—indeed, all language—as a drama containing the play of voices (Brower).

coming from persons and addressed to others—that is, to use the rhetorical lens rather than the stripping-away lens. But in taking this rhetorical point of view, not so many scholars use the voice metaphor. The tendency is always to talk in terms of "text" or "discourse" as issuing from historically situated persons—not "utterance" or "voice." It is this fear and avoidance of the term voice that I hope to remove.

After all, Bakhtin—admired on all fronts—insists on voice as the central term (even while acknowledging that discourse *can* be analyzed as disembodied language). Here's one passage:

> Where linguistic analysis sees only words and the interrelations of their abstract factors (phonetic, morphological, syntactic, and so on), there, for living artistic perception and for concrete sociological analysis, relations among *people* stand revealed, relations merely reflected and fixed in verbal material. Verbal discourse is the skeleton that takes on living flesh only in the process of creative perception—consequently, only in the process of living social communication. ("Discourse in Life" 109; emphasis in original).

Bakhtin describes all discourse in terms of "voices" and "speakers" and "listeners." All discourse is part of a "Speech Chain" (the title of one of his essays). "For Bakhtin, words cannot be conceived apart from the voices who speak them" (Emerson 24). (See also Deborah Brandt who argues in an important book that texts are sites of interaction between people, and that in a text we don't just have persona and implied author but the real presence of actual writer and reader [e.g., 71]. Speech act theory is another approach to language that insists on the centrality of who is speaking to whom and also for what purpose.)

It can even be helpful to look at mathematical discourse through this voice lens. *In a sense* (we need this phrase that Aristotle loved, since he saw that understanding depends on the ability to look at something first through one lens and then through another), a set of equations doesn't just sit as a semantic relationship, it can also be seen as someone responding to someone else who wrote different equations.

In short, the pure semiosis *textuality* metaphor highlights how discourse issues from other discourse or for logical relations (seeing all texts as "intertextual"), while the *voice* metaphor highlights how discourse issues from individual persons and from physical bodies. The text metaphor highlights the visual and spatial features of language and emphasizes language as an abstract, universal system; the voice metaphor highlights sound and hearing rather than vision, and it emphasizes the way all linguistic meaning moves historically through time rather than existing simultaneously in space. The textuality metaphor calls attention to the commonalities between one person's discourse and that of others and of the culture; the voice metaphor calls attention to the differences from one person to another. (The same discourse in two human settings is not the same. This is true even of single words: two people's "cat," though similar as text, sound very different as spoken or voiced.) We benefit from both metaphors or lenses and lose out if either is outlawed. In this essay I am openly celebrating the discourse-as-voice lens and the dimension of sound because of my own interests and because it is a kind of underdog in the scholarly world; but I'm not trying to get rid of the discourse-as-text lens or the visual metaphor.

But when we turn from theory and reading to *writing* and teaching writing, it might seem hard to keep up this even handed, dual approach. In putting words on paper, we would seem to have to choose: should we try to use our voice to *speak* and *utter* on paper? Or should we try to deploy textuality to *construct* written discourse? The traditional view in teaching is that we should emphasize writing as the production of *text* and thus heighten the difference between writing and speaking. According to this view, the weakness in many weak writers is their tendency to mistake writing for speaking. (For various versions of this view, see Dasenbrook, Farrell, Lunsford, and Olson.) Brandt would disagree, as would I and others.

Yet even here we can avoid the either/or trap. That is, I notice that I benefit at certain moments in my writing from just playing with meanings or structures—as though I'm doing pure math or playing disembodied games or trying to get musical shapes right—and not trying to *address* or respond to anyone. This is especially true during private, exploratory freewriting. At other moments (sometimes also in freewriting), it helps me to experience myself as an embodied *speaker* trying to reach out palpably with my words toward other embodied readers. And it helps me to move back and forth between these modalities of text and voice.

It's my belief, then, that even in the processes of writing and teaching writing, we do better not to try to declare a winner in the voice/text debate, but instead to make use of both approaches or lenses. (I develop this argument at more length in "The Shifting Relationships Between Speech and Writing," included in this part of the volume?

The Traditional Debate in Rhetoric: Is Ethos Real Virtue or the Appearance of Virtue?

It's worth taking a few pages to show how far back the debate goes between whether we hear the actual author through his or her language—or just hear an adopted role. In an important essay about the history of rhetoric, Nan Johnson writes: "The status of *ethos* in the hierarchy of rhetorical principles has fluctuated as rhetoricians in different eras have tended to define rhetoric in terms of either idealistic aims or pragmatic skills" (105). She shows how Plato and Aristotle each stand at the head of one of these two traditions:

> [For Plato] the reality of the speaker's virtue is presented as a prerequisite to effective speaking. In contrast, Aristotle's *Rhetoric* presents rhetoric as a strategic art which facilitates decisions in civil matters and accepts the appearance of goodness as sufficient to inspire conviction in hearers. (99)

The contrasting views of Cicero and Quintillian about the aims of rhetoric and the function of ethos are reminiscent of Plato's and Aristotle's differ-

ences of opinion about whether or not moral virtue in the speaker is intrinsic and prerequisite or selected and strategically presented. (105)

(This simple opposition between Plato and Aristotle is schematically handy,
but Johnson herself later discusses how Aristotle actually hedges his position
on ethos, and so in fact can almost be said to stand at the head of both traditions. Toward the end of this essay, I explore Aristotle's ambiguity in more
detail.)

Johnson goes on to trace these two traditions in the treatment of ethos
down through the history of rhetoric. For example, in the medieval period,
the *ars praedicandi* or preaching or ecclesiastic rhetoric followed the more idealistic tradition of Plato and Quintillian that emphasized ethos as a reflection
of the *actual author*; the *ars dictaminus* or letter writing followed the strategic
or pragmatic tradition of Aristotle and Cicero that emphasized ethos as *role*.
"A focus on the 'opinion' of the hearers is typical in pragmatic definitions of
ethos; the emphasis is placed much more on the speaker's need to be aware of
audience needs than on the disposition of the intrinsic virtue of the orator.
Ecclesiastical rhetoric, however, emphasizes the importance of the reality
rather than the appearance of virtue" (108).

As these traditions appear in eighteenth- and nineteenth-century rhetoric,
Johnson notes that the pragmatic tradition is more belletristic—and is represented by Whately; the idealistic tradition is essentially epistemological—and
is represented by Channing (109). Thus Channing writes:

> It would not be going too far to say that it is not in all the graces of address,
> or sweetness and variety of tones, or beauty of illustration—in all the out-
> ward and artificial accomplishments of the orator, to equal or even approach
> the power conferred by a good character. Its still eloquence is felt in the
> commonest transactions of life. (quoted in Johnson 110).

Blair and Campbell, she says, try to do justice to both the pragmatic, belletristic tradition *and* the idealistic, epistemological one—according to whether
they are dealing with secular or religious situations.

Matthew Hope, writing in the mid-nineteenth century, brings in a term
that has become a center of modern dispute. "Hope regards the character of
the speaker as potentially having great persuasive force, a force Hope defines
as *'presence.'* Presence, he explains, is 'due to intellectual force, somewhat to
strength of will or purpose or character, somewhat to the spiritual qualities of
the man'" (quoted in Johnson 111; emphasis added).

Johnson describes contemporary rhetoric as dominated by the pragmatic or
strategic tradition (noting Richard Weaver and Wayne Booth as exceptions):

> The marked tendency of modern rhetorical texts to present strategic defini-
> tions of ethos seems to proceed from a widely held Aristotelian-Ciceronian
> view that rhetoric is an art of inventional, compositional, and communica-
> tive competence. . . . Explanations and guidelines for the use of ethos re-
> peat traditional pragmatic advice that writers must create the appearance of
> sincerity in order to persuade. The concept of ethos rarely appears in cur-

rent texts by name. Rather, it is discussed under such varied stylistic head-
ings as "tone," "writer's voice," "personal appeal," "attitude," "persona,"
and "credibility." [She goes on to quote from Maxine Hairston's *Successful
Writing* as a typical textbook treatment.] "When you write you create an
identity for yourself. Using only words—no make-up, no costumes, no
scenery, no music—you have to present yourself to an audience and get its
attention and its confidence. You can . . . by using imagination and trying to develop a sense of tone, learn to present yourself in various ways.
. . . You ask, 'how can I use language to make my audience believe in this
character?'" Modern texts advise students to correlate "persona" with assessments of the reader and the writing situation. Such advice presents
ethos as a skill of stylistic adaptability to mode and audience, and typically
eschews moral implications. (112–13)

This ancient and venerable debate about ethos and virtue leads to, and in a
sense even contains, the modern debate about the relationship between voice
and identity. That is, if persuasion depends on genuine virtue in the speaker,
not just on virtuous-seeming role-playing, then the implication is clear: Plato,
Quintillian, Channing, Hope, and the others in that tradition believe that listeners and readers get a sense of the real speaker and his or her real virtue or
lack of virtue through the words on the page.

The Modern Debate: Is Voice a Function of the Self or of a Role?

Johnson suggests, then, that modern rhetorical studies are dominated by a
"strategic" or "pragmatic" stance on voice: that "we create an identity for
ourselves" when we write, that our written voice is a linguistic creation
rather than any reflection of some "real self," and that in discussions or explorations of textual voice there's no use bringing in talk about the actual character of the writer. Johnson's "pragmatic" tradition becomes in our times what I
think of as the sophisticated, ironic, critical view on voice. In this view, either
there is no "real self," since "self" consists of nothing but the succession of
roles or voices or selves that we create in language; or there is a real self but
it's completely invisible in a text and unavailable to readers; therefore the only
thing worth talking about is the created self on paper.
    But there have always been staunch defenders of the opposite view—
Johnson calls it "intrinsic" or "idealistic"—about the relationship between
voice and identity. This is a view that is commonly called naive nowadays,
and it holds that people do have some kind of identity that exists apart from
the language they use, and that it's worth trying to talk about whether or not
that identity shows in the words they write (or speak). There are various versions of this view: that everyone has a unique and special self—or that only
special geniuses do; that the self is single and unchanging—or developing
and multiplex; that it is difficult to express or embody this identity in

words—or that it's easy if only you speak or write naturally and sincerely instead of artificially. In any event, the phrase "finding one's own voice" has somehow become common and remains so—and not just among self-obsessed sophomores, not just among naive members of the general public, but across a wide spectrum of critics, scholars, creative and imaginative writers, and teachers of writing. Here is Helen Vendler talking about Sylvia Plath: she "had early mastered certain course sound effects," but in her later poetry, "she has given up on a bald imitation of Thomas and has found her own voice" (131). Here is John Simon (anything but loose about language) talking about Ingmar Bergman: "With Barktok and Stravinsky, Braque and Picasso, Rilke and Valéry, Borges and Proust, among others, he is one of the fertile and seminal masters, an artist of many modes and one, unique voice" (7).

Here are two classic grandfather formulations of this kind of thinking about voice and identity. Tolstoy:

> I have mentioned three conditions of contagion in art, but they may be all summed up into one, the last, sincerity; that is, that the artist should be impelled by an inner need to express his feelings. . . . [I]f the artist is sincere he will express the feeling as he experienced it. And as each man is different from everyone else, his feeling will be individual for everyone else; and the more individual it is—the more the artist has drawn it from the depths of his nature—the more sympathetic and sincere it will be. ("What is Art?")

Yeats:

> We should write our own thoughts in as nearly as possible the language we thought them in, as though in a letter to an intimate friend. We should not disguise them in any way; for our lives give them force as the lives of people in plays give force to their words. . . . I tried from then on to write out my emotions exactly as they came to me in life, not changing them to make them more beautiful. "If I can be sincere and make my language natural, and without becoming discursive, like a novelist, and so indiscreet and prosaic," I said to myself, "I should, if good luck or bad luck make my life interesting, be a great poet; for it will be no longer a matter of literature at all." (*Autobiographies*)

Views like these almost cry out for sophisticated critiques—and critiques are not lacking. New Critics talk of the intentional fallacy and say that we cannot talk about sincerity or the real person who wrote the text. Marxist and cultural critics say that "the subject is itself a social construct that emerges through the linguistically-circumscribed interaction of the individual, the community, and the material world" (Berlin 489). Poststructural and deconstructive critics, feeling that New Critics didn't do a thorough enough job, cut loose the text from the author yet again. Plenty of influential critics and sociologists say that the "self" is nothing but a collection of roles. And plenty of writing teachers—*even if* they have conventional views of the self and of sincerity—nevertheless say, "Sure, sure, sincerity is a virtue in writing, but only a minor one. The major virtues are careful thinking, coherent structure, and clear syntax. Let's not kid students into thinking they can get very far with sincerity or self in writing. What they most need to get into their writing is not the self but the craft."[2]

This large dispute about the relationship between voice and identity, then, is the issue of greatest contention in "voice" discussions in composition. Indeed, with Derrida's focus on what he calls the metaphysics of voice and presence, this issue of voice/discourse/identity has become one of the main critical issues in English studies, cultural studies, and critical theory.

At first glance, the debate seems to be between a naive credulity about the power of sincere presence in texts vs. a sophisticated, ironic skepticism—especially when we look at it from our present cultural moment. But I hope I can persuade you not to define the debate in such simplistic terms. On the one hand, the seemingly sophisticated or skeptical position can take many forms, and I find the Amherst version represented by Gibson and Coles to be the most subtle and nuanced—the least merely skeptical. On the other hand, the allegedly naive position can be seen as not so naive. In some formulations it functions as a kind of sophisticated but *not* ironic critique of the sophisticated critique (see, for example, Park and Freisinger). Similarly, when Gilligan, hooks, and Jordan speak as women and/or African Americans, they are not fighting for a single, unchanging, unsocial voice, but they *are* insisting that if your habitual or accustomed or home voice has been devalued or silenced, there is something important and political at stake in being able to use a voice that you experience as *yours*. In short, they are rejecting the ironic, sophisticated view that says, "All voices are just roles, and the relation between your textual voice and who you really are is a naive irrelevance." When people feel that the culture is calling their habitual voice illegitimate or scholars are calling it irrelevant, they are more likely to insist that a piece of their identity is at stake in their textual voice.

---

2. It's worth noting two interesting *curricular* sites where voice in writing was seriously explored. The sophisticated and ironic view of the self as continually created anew from language was reflected in the striking Amherst College first year English course inaugurated and directed by Theodore Baird from 1938 to 1966. Walker Gibson and William Coles both taught in that course, and there is a remarkable list of others who also taught in it or can be argued to have been influenced by it: Rueben Brower, Richard Poirier, Roger Sale, Neil Hertz, David Bartholomae, Gordon Pradl. Robert Frost, with his interest in voice, lurked in the background of this course—with his not infrequent presence at Amherst College. Baird and the others who taught in the course were interested in voice and had some of the best ears around for noticing its nuances. They engaged in what Pritchard called "ear training" in an essay of that title. They were very interested in the self—but a self continually being remade by language. (See Varnum for a fascinating book-length exploration of this course. Also Joseph Harris. The passages from Tolstoy and Yeats, above, came from one of the assignment series for that course—a semester-long series of assignments on the topic of masks.)

A more writerly approach to voice—one that devoted lots of emphasis to exercises with the breath, the physical voice, and even the body—was undertaken at Stanford University in an ambitious program called "The Voice Project." (See Hawkes. The project was influenced by *The Personal Voice*, a text/reader by Albert Guerard, John Hawkes, and Claire Rosenfield.)

Untangling Different Meanings of Voice

The best way to deal with these three debates about voice and writing is to distinguish between *different meanings or senses* of voice. We don't have to figure out winners or losers in these binary and ideological disputes if we define how we are using the term voice with more care and discrimination. In this longer and final section of my essay, I will first explore some of the features of literal, physical voice. Then I will explore five meanings of voice as applied to writing: (1) audible voice or intonation (the sounds in a text); (2) dramatic voice (the character or implied author in a text); (3) recognizable or distinctive voice; (4) voice with authority; (5) resonant voice or presence. By making these distinctions, I think I can confine the ideological dispute to that fifth meaning—the only meaning that requires a link between the known text and the unknown actual author. That is, I think I can show that the first four senses of voice in writing are sturdy, useful, and relatively noncontroversial. And even though the fifth meaning will be a tempting site for ideological dispute, I will argue that the fifth sense of voice is helpful and useable even among people who disagree on the theoretical issues.

Literal Voice: Observations About the Human Voice

When people refer to voice in writing or to someone "achieving voice," for example, in *Women's Ways of Knowing* (Belenky, Clinchy, Goldberger, and Tarule), they are using a metaphor. This metaphor is so common that perhaps it will one day become literal—as "leg of the table" has become a literal phrase. Once you start listening for the word *voice,* it's amazing how often you find it in books and articles and reviews—especially in titles. Sometimes the writer is consciously using the term to make some point about writing or psychology, but more often the term is used only in a loosely poetic or elevated way. When there is so much metaphorical talk about voice, I find it intellectually cleansing to remind myself that it *is* a metaphor and to acquaint myself better with the literal term—and even to immerse myself actually in the experience of the literal thing itself, the human voice. If this were a workshop, it would be good to stop and do some talking, reciting, singing, and other exercises in orality—and see what we notice.

Let me put down here, then, some literal facts about the human voice. These are not quite "innocent facts" since I want them to show why voice has become such a suggestive and resonant term. But I hope you will agree that they are "true facts."

- Voice is produced by the body. To talk about voice in writing is to import connotations of the body into the discussion—and by implication, to be interested in the role of the body in writing.
- Almost always, people learn to speak before they learn to write. Normally,

we learn speech at such an early age that we are not aware of the learning process. Speech habits are laid down at a deep level.

- Speaking comes before writing in the development of cultures.
- Nevertheless, people can become just as comfortable in writing as in speaking, indeed we are sometimes deeply awkward, tangled, and even blocked in our speaking.
- We identify and recognize people by their voices—usually even when they have a cold or over a bad phone connection. We usually recognize people by voice even after a number of years. Something constant persists despite the change. Of course there are exceptions—such as when some boys go through adolescence.
- People have demonstrably unique voices: "voice prints" are evidently as certain as fingerprints for identification. This might suggest the analogy with the fact that our bodies are genetically unique, but our voice prints are less dependent upon genes than our bodies.
- We can distinguish two dimensions to someone's voice: the *basic sound* of their voice and the *manner or style* with which they use their voice. The first is the quality of noise they make, based as it were on the physical "instrument" they are "playing." The second is the kind of "tunes, rhythms, and styles" they play on their instrument.
- Despite the unique and recognizable quality of an individual's voice, we all usually display enormous variation in how we speak from occasion to occasion. Sometimes we speak in monotone, sometimes with lots of intonation. And we use different "tones" of voice at different times, for example, excited, scared, angry, sad. Furthermore, we sometimes speak self-consciously or "artificially," but more often we speak with no attention or even awareness of how we are speaking. The distinction between a "natural" and "artificial" way of talking is theoretically vexed, but in fact listeners and speakers often agree in judgments as to whether someone was speaking naturally or artificially on a given occasion.
- Our speech often gives a naked or candid picture of how we're feeling—as when our voice quavers with fear or unhappiness or lilts with elation or goes flat with depression. People sometimes detect our mood after hearing nothing but our "hello" on the phone. Our moods often show through in our writing too—at least to sensitive readers; but it's easier to hide or fake how we're feeling in our writing; we can ponder and revise the words we put down. Speaking is harder to control, usually less self-conscious, closer to autonomic behavior. Cicero says the voice is a picture of the mind. People commonly identify someone's voice with *who* he or she is—with their character—just as it is common to identify one's self with one's body. (The word "person" means both body and self—and it suggests a link between the person and the sound of the voice. "Persona" was the word for the mask that Greek actors wore to amplify their voices [per + sona]. In an interestingly analogous way, a person's "character" is etymologically linked to their "mark" or handwriting.)

- However, there are good actors, on and off the stage, who can convincingly make their voices seem to show whatever feeling or character they want.
- Audience has a big effect on voice. Partly, it's a matter of *imitating* how those around us talk. Partly, it's a matter of *responding* to those around us. That is, our voice tends to change as we speak to different people—often without awareness. We tend to speak differently to a child, to a buddy, to someone we are afraid of. My wife says she can hear when I'm speaking to a woman on the phone. Some listeners seem to bring out more intonation in our speech (see Bakhtin on "choral support" in "Discourse in Life").
- Though voice is produced by the body, it is produced out of *air* or *breath*: something that is not the body and which is shared or common to us all—but which issues from inside us and is a sign of life. This may partly explain why so many people have been tempted to invest voice with profound or even spiritual connotations.
- Voice involves sound, hearing, and time; writing or text involves sight and space. The differences between these modalities are profound and interesting. (To try to characterize these modalities as deeply or essentially as Ong and Ihde do, however, is speculative, so I must resort briefly to parentheses here. Sight seems to tell us more about the outsides of things, sound more about the insides of things. Evolutionarily, sight is the most recent sense modality to become dominant in humans—and is dealt with in the largest and most recent parts of the human brain. Sight seems to be most linked to rationality—in our brain and our metaphors—for example, "idea" and "do you see?" But there are crucial dangers in going along with Ong and Havelock in making such firm and neat links between certain *mentalities* and orality and literacy—especially for the teaching of writing. (For warnings against such linking, see Brandt, Tannen, and my essay here, "Shifting Relationships Between Speech and Writing .")
- Spoken language has more semiotic channels than writing. That is, speech contains more channels for carrying meaning, more room for the play of difference. The list of channels is impressive. For example, there is volume (loud to soft), pitch (high to low), speed (fast to slow), emphasis (present to absent), intensity (relaxed to tense). And note that these are not just binary items, for in each case there is a full spectrum of subtle *degrees* all the way between extremes. In addition, there are many patterned sequences: for example, tune is a pattern of pitches; rhythm is a pattern of slow and fast and accent. Furthermore, there is a wide spectrum of timbres (breathy, shrill, nasal); there are glides and jumps; there are pauses of varying lengths. Combinations of *all* these factors make the possibilities dizzying. And *all* these factors carry meaning. Consider the subtle or not so subtle pauses we make as we speak, the little intensities or lengthenings of a syllable—and all the other ways we add messages to the *lexical* content of our speech. (For a masterful and scholarly treatment of all dimensions of intonation in speech, see Dwight Bolinger's *Intonation and its Parts: Melody in Spoken English*. See also Hoddeson.)

It's not that writing is poverty stricken as a semiotic system. But writing has to achieve its subtleties with fewer resources. A harpsichord cannot make the gradations of volume and attack of a piano, but harpsichordists use subtle cues of timing to communicate the *kind* of thing that pianos communicate with differences in volume and attack. Mozart had fewer harmonic resources to play with than Brahms, but he did quite a lot with his less. To write well is also to do a lot with less. If we are angry, we sometimes press harder with the pen or break the pencil lead or *hit* the keys harder or write the words all in a rush, and our speech would probably sound very angry; but none of these physical behaviors shows in our writing.

Consider the many ways we can say the sentence, "Listen to me"—from angry to fondly—or in fact with a whole range of modes of anger. With writing, our options are comparatively small. We can underline or use all caps; we can end with a comma, a period, a question mark, an exclamation mark. We can create pauses by using the ellipsis sign. There are other textual resources of course—such as varying the spacing, sizing, or color of letters and words, playing with the shaping of letters and words, and so forth—but these are considered "informal" and inappropriate to "literate" writing. Perhaps the main resource in writing is word choice: choose different words, put them in different orders, set a context by what comes before or afterward to affect how readers will "hear" any given sentence. These are the ways we convey significations in writing that we convey effortlessly in speech. In writing, we must do more with fewer channels. (For an exploration of how poets add to the resources of written language by the use of meter, line, and stanza, see Brower).

Voice in Writing: A Family of Five Related Meanings

People have voices; radios, telephones, TV sets, and tape recorders have voices. Texts have no voices, they are silent. We can only talk about voice in writing by resorting to metaphor. It's my argument that this is a metaphor worth using, but we can't use it well unless we untangle five related meanings that have got caught up in it: audible voice, dramatic voice, recognizable or distinctive voice, voice with authority, and resonant voice or presence.

1. Audible Voice or Intonation in Writing. All texts are literally silent, but most readers experience some texts as giving more sense of sound than others—more of the illusion as we read that we are hearing the words spoken. Robert Frost insists that this is not just a virtue but a necessity: "A dramatic necessity goes deep into the nature of the sentence. . . . All that can save them is the speaking tone of voice somehow entangled in the words and fastened to the page for the ear of the imagination."

How is it, then, that some texts have this audible voice? We have to sneak up on the answer by way of two facts I cited in the previous section: that most people have spoken longer and more comfortably than they have written, and that speaking has more channels of meaning than writing. As a result of these two facts, most people, when they encounter a text—a set of words that just sit there silently on the page with no intonation, rhythm, accent, and so forth—automatically *project aurally* some speech sounds onto the text. Given how conditioning and association work, most people cannot help it. Our most frequent and formative experiences with language have involved hearing speech.

In fact, people are virtually incapable of reading without nerve activity in the throat as though to speak—usually even *muscular* activity. We joke about people who move their lips as they read, but such movement is common even among the sophisticated and educated—and many poets insist that it is a travesty to read otherwise. (Have researchers checked out the *hearing* nerves while people read? I'll bet the circuits are busy.) Silent reading must be learned and is relatively recent. St. Augustine tells in his *Confessions* how amazed he was to see Ambrose reading without saying the words outloud.

In short, hearing a text is the norm. We are conditioned to hear words, and the conditioning continues through life. Thus the fruitful question is not why we hear some texts but rather why we don't hear them all.

There are two main things that prevent us from hearing written words. The most obvious barriers come from the text itself: certain texts resist our conditioned habit to hear. The writer has chosen or arranged words so that it is hard or impossible to say them, and as a result we seem to experience them as hard to hear. This further illustrates the mediation of voice in written language: for of course, strictly speaking, we *can* hear any word at all. But when written words are easy to say, especially if we have frequently heard these phrases or cadences because they are characteristic of idiomatic speech, we tend to hear them more as we read; when written words are awkward or unidiomatic for speech, we tend to hear them less.

People produce unsayable writing in many ways. Some poets, for example, want to block sound and exploit vision (as in concrete poetry, some poems by e. e. cummings, and some L=A=N=G=U=A=G=E poetry). Much legal and bureaucratic writing is unidiomatic and unsayable and thus tends to be less hearable since the writers so often create syntax by a process of "constructing" or roping together units (often jargon or even boiler plate units) in a way that has nothing to do with speech. Some scholarly writing is unsayable for various reasons. (A certain amount of technical and difficult terminology may be unavoidable; and consciously or not, scholars may want to sound learned or even keep out the uninitiated.) And of course many unskilled writers also lose all contact with the process of speech or utterance as they write: they stop so often in the middle of a phrase to wonder or worry about a word, to look up its spelling, or to change it to one that sounds more impressive, that they lose their syntactic thread and thereby produce many jumbled or unidiomatic sentences.

But we can't blame inaudible writing only on awkward language or ungainly writers. There is a larger reason—culturally produced—why we often don't hear a voice in writing. Our culture of literacy has inculcated in most of us a habit of working actively to keep the human voice out of our texts when we write.

Notice, for example, the informal writing of children and adolescents or of people who are just learning the conventions of writing. Notice how often they use the language of speech. In, addition they often use striking textual devices that are explicitly designed to convey some of the vividly audible features of speech—some of the music and drama of the voice: frequent underlining—sometimes double or triple; three or four exclamation marks or question marks at once; frequent all-caps; oversized letters; colors; parenthetical slang asides "(NOT!!)". (I'm sure I'm not alone in using too many underlinings in my rough drafts—as I'm trying to speak my emphases onto the page—and so I'm always having to get rid of them as I revise and try to find other means to give the emphasis I want.)

What interests me is how unthinkingly we all go along with the assumption that these textual ways to simulate voice are wrong for writing. That is, most of us are unconscious of how deeply our culture's version of literacy has involved a decision to keep voice out of writing, to maximize the difference between speech and writing—to prevent writers from using even those few crude markers that could capture more of the subtle and not so subtle semiotics of speech. Our version of literacy requires people to distance their writing behavior further from their speaking behavior than the actual modalities require. So when Derrida tries to remove connotations of voice from writing, (though he's not saying, "Stop all that informal language and that underlining and putting things in all caps!"), he is nevertheless giving an unnecessary fillip to a steamroller long at work in our version of literacy. (And yet, perhaps Derrida attacks voice so vehemently because he is living at a cultural moment when the old antipathy to voice in writing is beginning to fade, and writing is beginning to be invaded more and more by voice. What McLuhan and Ong call "secondary orality" is surely taking a toll in writing. Even academic writing is much more open to informal oral features.)

Thus it is *not* lack of skill or knowledge that keeps an audible voice out of the writing of so many poor writers. It's their worry about conforming to our particular conventions of writing and their fear of mistakes. Unskilled writers who are *not* worried—usually unschooled writers—tend to write prose that is very audible and speechlike. Here is a small writer (a first grader) writing a large story:

> One day, well if there was a day. There was sand and dust and rocks and stones and some other things. And it was a thunderclaps! And a planet began to rise. And they called it Earth. And do you know what? It rained and rained and rained for thirty days in the big holes. And see we began to grow. And the first animal was a little dinosaur. . . . Don't listen to the newspaperman, all that about the sun. Don't be afraid because the sun will last for ever. That's all there is. (Calkins 49. Of course this is a corrected version of what the child wrote in "invented spelling:" "1 day wel if thar was a day. . . ." And the text was only half the story: it went along with a series of vivid drawings.)

The very term "illiterate writing," as it is commonly used, tends in fact to imply that the writing suffers from being too much like speech. The culture of school and literacy seems to work *against* our tendency to write as we speak or to hear sounds in a text. (Two important exceptions: first, the still-evolving conventions for writing on email—even scholarly writing—seem to be inviting more oral and voiced qualities into writing or literacy. Second, our culture sanctions more audible voice in poetry and fiction and literary nonfiction—perhaps because of the stronger or more recent links to orality in these forms.)

So far I have been focusing on the question of how speech intonation gets into writing. But we mustn't forget the important prior question: how does intonation get into speech in the first place? For of course sometimes our speech *lacks* intonation. Sometimes we speak in a monotone; some people put more "expression" into their speech than others. Bakhtin focuses on intonation in his essay, "Discourse In Life and Discourse in Art." He argues that intonation often carries the most important meaning in any discourse—meaning that may not be carried by the lexical, semantic meaning. As he says, "In intonation, discourse comes into contact with life. And it is in intonation above all that the speaker comes into contact with the listener or listeners—intonation is social par excellence." He points out further that we often lose intonation in our speaking if we lack "choral support" from listeners—that is, if we have an audience that doesn't share our values. But it doesn't always work that way. In the face of an unsupportive or adversarial audience, we sometimes rise to the challenge or even lose our temper, and thus *raise* our voice and increase our intonation.

I sense even a gender issue here. Do not women in our culture tend to use more expression or intonation in their speech than men—more variation in pitch, accent, rhythm, and so forth—men tending on average to be a bit more tight lipped and monotone? A recent extensive study shows that even in writing, women use more exclamation marks than men (Rubin and Greene 22). Perhaps the culture of literate writing is more inhospitable to women than to men. (I wonder if I am right in my impression that native speakers of non-mainstream dialects of English, such as Black English or Hawai'ian "Pidgin," tend to use more intonation in speech than native speakers of the mainstream dialect.)

Despite the two formidable barriers to audibility in writing (frequently unsayable writing and a culture that wants to keep speech qualities out of writing), most humans come at writing with echoes of speech in their ears. We hear a text if it gives us half a chance. The onus is on people who resist the idea of voice in writing to show that hearing the words *isn't* a pervasive fact of reading.

Thus, "audible voice" is a necessary critical term because it points to one of the main textual features that affects how we respond to writing. Other things being equal, most readers prefer texts that they hear—that have audible voice. After all, when we *hear* the text, we can benefit from all those nuances and channels of communication that speech has and that writing lacks. Admittedly, people sometimes find it useful to produce a voiceless, faceless text—to give a sense that these words were never uttered by a human being but rather just exist with ineluctable authority from everywhere and nowhere ("All students will . . .")—and thus try to suppress any sense that there might be a voice or person behind them.

Naturally, not all readers *agree* about whether a text is audible. But there is at least as much agreement about the audibility of a text or passage as there is about the "structure" or "organization" of it—and we assume the usefulness of those critical concepts. A fruitful area for research lies here: What are the features of texts that many readers find audible? How much agreement do we get about audibility of texts—and among what kind of readers? (In an interesting study, Crismore points out that passages of "metadiscourse" in writing tend to be heard as more voiced, for example, "Let me now turn to my second point." But I think her insight is really part of a larger point: it's not just metadiscourse that creates audibility, but rather the signaling of any *speech-act*. "I disagree" is not metadiscourse, but as with any speech act, it highlights the presence and agency of a writer. For more about audible voice, see the fragment on that topic later in this section.)

2. Dramatic Voice in Writing. Let me start again from a fact about literal voice. We identify people by their spoken voices—often even when we haven't talked to them in years. In fact, we often identify someone's voice with what they are like. I don't mean to claim too much here. I'm not yet touching on voice and identity; I don't mean that we always believe that someone's voice fits their character. After all, we sometimes say of a friend: "He always sounds more confident than he really is." My point is simply that we do tend to read a human quality or characteristic into a voice. Even in that example, we are reading *confidence* into a voice in the very act of deciding that the person is *not* confident.

The same process occurs even with people we've never met before. When we hear them talk for more than a few minutes, we tend to hear character in their way of speaking. Again, the negative case clinches my point: we are struck when we *cannot* hear character: "She spoke so guardedly that you couldn't tell anything about what she was like" or even, "She sounded like a guarded kind of person."

Therefore, it would be peculiar—habit and conditioning being what they are—if people *didn't* hear character or dramatic voice in written texts since they so habitually hear it in speech. And in fact I've simply been trying in the last two paragraphs to sneak up by a pathway of everyday empiricism on what has become a commonplace of literary criticism—at least since the New Critics and Wayne Booth: that there is always an implied author or dramatic voice in *any* written text. New Critics like to describe any piece of prose in terms of the "speaker." Where there is language, they insist, there is drama. Of course, the speaker or implied author may not be the real author; in fact, the New Critics brought in this terminology in order to heighten the *distinction* between the character implied by the text and the actual writer. (See Park for a careful and surprising historical analysis of this change in critical attitude.)

My point is this: when we acknowledge that every text has an implied author, we are acknowledging that every text has a character or dramatic voice. Indeed, students usually do better at finding and describing the implied author in a text when we use instead the critical term *dramatic voice* and invite them to use their ears by asking them, "What kind of voice or voices do you hear in this essay or story or poem?" The New Critics, the people in the Amherst tradition (e.g., Gibson and Coles), and those in the Stanford Voice Project (Hawkes) tended to use voice in this way. In the Amherst tradition, students were always asked, "What kind of voice do you hear in your writing?" and "Is that the kind of person you want to sound like?" But in asking this question, they weren't identifying the textual voice with the student's "real" voice.

Of course, the dramatic voice in the text may be hard to hear. For example, we may read certain wooden or tangled texts and say, "There's *no one* in there." But these good listeners among New Critics trained us to look again—listen again—and *always* find a speaker. It may just be "the bureaucratic speaker" hiding behind conventional forms, but it is a speaker. And Bakhtin continues this training—helping us hear *multiple voices,* even when it looks at first like monologue.

Let me illustrate dramatic voice with a passage where D. H. Lawrence is talking about Melville:

> The artist was so *much* greater than the man. The man is rather a tiresome New Englander of the ethical mystical-transcendentalist sort: Emerson, Longfellow, Hawthorne, etc. So unrelieved, the solemn ass even in humour. So hopelessly *au grand serieux* you feel like saying: Good God, what does it matter? If life is a tragedy, or a farce, or a disaster, or anything else, what do I care! Let life be what it likes. Give me a drink, that's what I want just now.
>
> For my part, life is so many things I don't care what it is. It's not my affair to sum it up. Just now it's a cup of tea. This morning it was wormwood and gall. Hand me the sugar.
>
> One wearies of the *grand serieux.* There's something false about it. And that's Melville. Oh, dear, when the solemn ass brays! brays! brays! (157–58)

Lawrence's dramatic voice here is vivid: the sound of a brash, opinionated person who likes to show off and even shock. If we are critically naive we might say (echoing Lawrence himself), "And that's Lawrence." If we are more critically prudent we will say, "Notice the ways Lawrence constructs his dramatic voice and creates his role or persona. We sense him taking pleasure in striking this pose. It's a vivid role but let's not assume this is the 'real' Lawrence—or even that there *is* such a thing as a 'real' Lawrence." (Of course, in saying this we would also be echoing Lawrence—in his dictum, "Never trust the teller, trust the tale.")

Compare the following passage by the Chicago critic, R. S. Crane:

> . . . a poet does not write poetry but individual poems. And these are in-
> evitably, as finished wholes, instances of one or another poetic kind, differ-

entiated not by any necessities of the linguistic instrument of poetry but primarily by the nature of the poet's conception, as finally embodied in his poem, of a particular form to be achieved through the representation, in speech used dramatically or otherwise, of some distinctive state of feeling, of moral choice, or action, complete in itself and productive of a certain emotion or complex of emotions in the reader. (96)

Crane has a less *vivid* dramatic voice here than Lawrence, but anyone who is following and entering into this admittedly more difficult prose (and such a short snippet makes it hard to do that) can sense a character here too. I hear a learned builder of distinctions, careful and deliberate and precise—and someone who takes pleasure in building up syntactic architecture. But because his prose sounds less like a person talking—the syntax is more "constructed" than "uttered"—readers may disagree more about the character of the speaker than in the case of Lawrence. Such disagreements do not, however, undermine the well-ensconced critical notion of an implied author in any text.

Let me try to sharpen *dramatic voice* and *audible voice* as critical terms by comparing them in these two samples. For most readers, Lawrence's words probably have more audible voice than Crane's. Notice in fact how Lawrence heightens the audible or spoken effect by embedding bits of tacit dialogue and minidrama. He says, "You feel like saying: . . ." so that what follows ("Good God, what does it matter?" and so forth) is really a little speech in a different voice, and thus in implied quotation marks. Similarly, when he writes "Hand me the sugar," he's setting up a mini *scene-on-stage* that dramatizes the mood he's evoking.

Crane's passage is not without audible voice. He starts out with a crisply balanced pronouncement (something pronounced): "a poet does not write poetry but individual poems." And the second sentence begins with a strikingly audible interrupted phrase or "parenthetical" ("And these are inevitably, as finished wholes, . . ."). But as he drifts from syntactic utterance to architectural construction, I find his words increasingly unidiomatic and difficult to say and hear.

So, whereas a text can have more or less audible voice, shall we say the same of dramatic voice? Yes and no. On the one hand, the critical world agrees that every text is 100 percent chock full of implied author. Even if the dramatic voice is subtle or hard to hear, even if there are multiple and inconsistent dramatic voices in a text, the word from Booth to Bakhtin is that the text is nothing but dramatic voices. But common sense argues the other way too, and this view shows itself most clearly in the everyday writerly or teacherly advice: "Why do you keep your voice or character so hidden here? Why not allow it into your writing." (Palacas shows how parenthetical insertions heighten dramatic voice or the sense of an implied author. The fact that these parentheticals also increase audible voice shows that the different kinds of voice that I am working so hard to distinguish often blend into each other.)

So I would assert the same conclusion here as I did about audible voice. Just as it is natural and inevitable to hear *audible* voice in a text unless something stops us, so too with *dramatic* voice: we hear character in discourse unless something stops us. We need dramatic voice as a critical term.

3. Recognizable or Distinctive Voice in Writing.   Like composers or painters, writers often develop styles that are recognizable and distinctive. And it is common for both popular and academic critics and writers themselves to go one step further and not just talk about a writer finding "a" distinctive voice but finding "*her*" voice.

There is nothing to quarrel with here. After all, writing is behavior, and it's hard for humans to engage repeatedly in any behavior without developing a habitual and thus recognizable way of doing it: a style. Perhaps the most striking example is the physical act of writing itself: handwriting (thus the force of one's literal signature or mark or "character"). And we see the same thing in walking, toothbrushing, whatever. We can often recognize someone by how they walk—even how they stand—when we are too far away to recognize them by any other visual feature. If our walking and handwriting tend to be distinctive and recognizable and usually stable over time, why shouldn't that also be true of the kind of voice we use in our writing?

Of course, if we seldom walk, and always with conscious effort, we probably don't develop a habitual, recognizable, distinctive walking style. Early toddlers haven't yet "found their own walk." So it is natural that inexperienced writers often have no characteristic style or "signature" to their writing.

But it's worth questioning the positive *mystique* that sometimes surrounds the idea of "finding one's voice." It's surely wrong to assume, as so many people do, that it is necessarily better to have a recognizable, distinctive voice in one's writing. It is just as admirable to achieve Keats's ideal of "negative capability": the ability to be a protean, chameleonlike writer. If we have become so practiced that our skills are automatic and habitual—and thus characteristic—we are probably pretty good, whether as walker or writer. But a *really* skilled or professional walker or writer will be able to bring in craft, art, and play so as to deploy different styles at will, and thus not necessarily have a recognizable, distinctive voice. Don't we tend to see Yeats as more impressive than Frost (not necessarily better)—Brahms than Elgar—for this ability to use a greater variety of voices?

Notice how I am *still* not broaching any of the sticky theoretical problems of self or identity that haunt arguments about voice in writing. If I have a "recognizable voice," that voice doesn't necessarily *resemble* me or imply that there is a "real me." Recognizable or distinctive voice is not about "real identity." We may *recognize* someone from their handwriting or their walk, but those behaviors are not necessarily pictures of what they are like. For example, we might find ourselves saying, "He has such a distinctively casual, laidback walk, yet his personality or character is very uptight."

So if we strip away any unwarranted mystique from the term "recognizable, distinctive voice in writing," it has a simple and practical use. We can ask about any author whether he or she tends to have a characteristic style or recognizable voice; and if so, whether a particular text displays that style or voice—whether it is characteristic or different from how that author usually writes. And we can ask our students to develop comfortable fluency and to notice if and where they seem to develop a distinctive style—and whether that style seems to be helpful for them. But I tend to discourage students from *lusting* after their own "distinctive voice," since that so often leads to pretension and overwriting.

So look again at our example from D. H. Lawrence: it may not be a picture of the "real" Lawrence (if there is such a thing), but it *is* vintage Lawrence criticism—not just a nonce style or voice he used in this essay.

4. Voice with Authority—"Having a Voice."   This is the sense of voice that is so current in much feminist work (see, e. g., Belenky, Clinchy, Goldberger, and Tarule in *Women's Ways of Knowing*). But the sense is venerable too. Indeed, the phrase "having a voice" has traditionally meant having the authority to speak or wield influence or to vote in a group. ("Does she have a voice in the faculty senate?")

As readers we often have no trouble agreeing about whether a text shows a writer having or taking the authority to speak out: whether the writer displays the conviction or the self-trust or gumption to make her voice carry. As teachers, we frequently notice and applaud the change when we see a timid writer finally speak out with some conviction and give her words some authority. We often notice the same issue in our own writing or that of our colleagues. One of the problems people face in revising dissertations for publication is a deferential, questioning, permission-asking, tone—a lack of authority in the voice. It would be an interesting research project to try to figure out the textual features that give readers a sense of the writer's authority. One source of authority is to bring in others who have written about one's topic and address their thoughts with some assurance—even "taking on" or "making one's own" their words and voices, in Bakhtin's sense (see Bialostosky).

Notice that this sense of voice, like all the previous ones, does not entail any theory of identity or self, nor does it require making any inferences about the actual writer from the words on the page. When we see this kind of authority in writing, or the lack of it, we are not necessarily getting a good picture of the actual writer. It's not unusual, for example, for someone to develop a voice with strong authority that doesn't match their sense of who they are— or our sense of who they are. Indeed, one of the best exercises for helping students find authority or achieve assertiveness of voice is to ask them to role-play and write in the voice of some "invented character" who is strikingly different from themselves. We see this in simple role-playing exercises where the timid person "gets into" strong speech. And we see it in the complex case of Swift. He exerted enormous authority in the person of Gulliver and all his other ironic personae, and never published anything under his own name. (Ironically, he wielded excoriating judgmental authority through personae that were nonjudgmental and self-effacing.)

Let's look at our examples again. Clearly D. H. Lawrence had no trouble using a voice with authority and making it heard in print. Some feel he over-did it. R. S. Crane uses a quieter voice but achieves a magisterial authority nevertheless. An authoritative voice in writing need not be loud; it often has a quality of quiet, centered calm. We see this in speech too: schoolchildren often talk about "shouters"—teachers who shout a lot because they lack authority.

As teachers, most of us say we want our students to develop some au-thority of voice, yet many of our practices have the effect of making students more timid and hesitant in their writing. In the following passage Virginia Woolf writes about voice as authority—that is, about the struggle to take on authority in a situation where she was expected to be deferential:

> Directly . . . I took my pen in my hand to review that novel by a famous young man, she slipped behind me and whispered, "My dear, you are a young woman. You are writing about a book that has been written by a man. Be sympathetic; be tender; flatter; deceive; use all the arts and wiles of our sex. Never let anybody guess that you have a mind of your own. . . ." And she made as if to guide my pen. . . . [But in doing so] she would have plucked the heart out of my writing. (83)

We may write elegantly and successfully, she implies, but if we don't write with authority, with a mind of our own that is willing to offend, what we pro-duce scarcely counts as real writing (the heart is plucked out of it).

5. *Resonant Voice or Presence.* Here at last is trouble—the swamp. This is the meaning of voice that has made the term such a site for dispute. This is the arena where we find people bringing in notions like "authenticity," "pres-ence," sincerity, identity, self, and what I called "real voice" in *Writing With Power*.

Before wading in, let me pause to emphasize what I have gained by holding back so long—carefully separating what is solid from what is swampy. For my main argument in this essay is that there is little reason to question voice as a solid critical term—a term that points to definite and important qualities in texts that cannot easily be gainsaid: audible voice, dramatic voice, recogniz-able or distinctive voice, and voice with authority. That is, even if we are com-pletely at odds about the nature of selves or identities, about whether people even have such things, and about the relation of a text to the person who wrote it, we have a good chance of reaching agreement about whether any given text has audible voice, what kind of dramatic voice it has, whether it has a recognizable or distinctive voice, and whether the writer was able to achieve authority of voice. Similarly, even if teachers disagree completely about the nature of self and identity and about the value of sincerity in writ-ing, they can probably agree that students would benefit from exploring and attending to these four dimensions of voice in their writing. And so I, too, with these meanings secure, feel more authority to enter the arena of diffi-culty and conflict.

Indeed, I can begin my account of resonant voice by showing that the ground is not as swampy as we might fear. That is, even though the concept of resonant voice or presence is arguable because it involves making inferences about the relation between the present text and the absent writer, it does *not* assume any particular model of the self or theory of identity. In particular, it does not require a model of the self as simple, single, unique, or unchanging. I can illustrate this point by describing resonant voice in contrast to *sincere voice* (something that enthusiasts of voice have sometimes mistakenly celebrated).

We hear sincere voices all around us. Lovers say, "I only have eyes for you"; parents say, "Trust me"; teachers say, "I am on your side." Even salesmen and politicians are sometimes perfectly sincere. Surely Reagan was sincere much of the time. But sometimes those sincere words, *even in their very sincerity*, ring hollow. Genuine sincerity can itself feel cloyingly false. Even the celebrations of sincerity by Tolstoy and Yeats (quoted in the first section) will grate on many teeth. Yet we mustn't flip all the way over to the cynical position of people who have been burned too often by sincere words, and declare that sincerity *itself* is false ("never trust a guy who really thinks he loves you"), or to the sophisticated position of some literary folk ("sincere art is bad art"). *Sometimes* we can trust sincere words. Sincere discourse is not always tinny.

What is a sincere voice? When we say that someone speaks or writes sincerely, we mean that they "really really believe" what they are saying. This means that they experience no gap at all between utterance and intention, between words and available thoughts and feelings. But what about gaps between utterance and *unavailables* or *unconscious* thoughts and feelings?

Resonant voice is a useful concept because it points to the relationship between discourse and the *unconscious*. When we hear sincerity that is obviously tinny, we are hearing a *gap* between utterance and unconscious intention or feeling. Self-deception. Sensitive listeners can hear very small gaps. Thus, correspondingly, they are also likely to be sensitive to the resonance that occurs when discourse *does* fit larger portions of the speaker—those precious moments in life and writing when a person actually does harness words to fit more than conscious intention—those words which seem to "have the heft of our living behind them" (Adrienne Rich's phrase, cited below).

Such words are of course rare. For a discourse can never *fully* express or articulate a whole person. A person is usually too complex and has too many facets, parts, roles, voices, identities. But at certain lucky or achieved moments, writers or speakers *do* manage to find words which seem to capture the rich complexity of the unconscious; or words which, though they don't *express* or *articulate* everything that is in the unconscious, nevertheless somehow seem to *resonate with* or *have behind them* the unconscious as well as the conscious (or at least much larger portions than usual). It is words of this sort that we experience as resonant—and through them we have a sense of presence with the writer.

Notice now how the concept of resonant voice opens the door to irony, fiction, lying, and games; indeed, it positively *calls for* these and other polyvocal or multivalent kinds of discourse. If we value the sound of resonance—the sound of more of a person behind the words—and if we get pleasure from a sense of the writer's presence in a text, we are often going to be drawn to what is ambivalent and complex and ironic, not just to earnest attempts to stay true to sincere, conscious feelings. Can two million New Critics be completely wrong in their preoccupation with irony? The most resonant language is often lying and gamey. Writing with resonant voice needn't be unified or coherent; it can be ironic, unaware, disjointed.

Any notion of resonant voice would have to include Swift's strongest works; even Pope's "Rape of the Lock" where he makes fun of the silliness and vanity he also clearly loves. When Lawrence says of Melville, "The artist was so much greater than the man," he is talking about lack of resonance in Melville's sincere sentiments compared to the power in those parts of his fiction that express his larger darker vision—writing that resonates with more parts of himself or his vision or his feelings than he was sincerely, consciously able to affirm. In effect, Lawrence is saying that Melville "the man" has plenty of audible dramatic, distinctive, and authoritative voice ("And that's Melville. Oh dear when the solemn ass brays! brays! brays!"). But he lacks resonant voice ("But there's something false")—except where he functions "as artist" and renders more of his unconscious knowledge and awareness. It's no accident that the resonance shows up most in his discourse "as artist": that is, we tend to get more of our unconscious into our discourse when we make up things, tell stories, use metaphors, and exploit the sounds and rhythms of language.

Once we see that resonance comes from getting more of ourselves behind the words, we realize that unity or singleness is not the goal. Of course, we don't have simple, neatly coherent, or unchanging selves. To remember the role of the unconscious is to remember what Bakhtin and social constructionists and others say in different terms: we are made of different roles, voices. Indeed, Barbara Johnson (discussing *Their Eyes Were Watching God*), asserts a link between voice and *splitness* or *doubleness* itself—words which render multiplicity of self:

> [T]he very notion of an "authentic voice" must be redefined. Far from being an expression of Janie's new wholeness or identity as a character, Janie's increasing ability to speak grows out of her ability . . . to assume and articulate the incompatible forces involved in her own division. The sign of an authentic voice is thus not self-identity but self-difference." (238–39)

Keith Hjortshoj (exploring relations between writing and physical movement) makes the same point in a different context:

> Cohesion, then, isn't always a cardinal virtue, in [physical] movement or writing. . . . To appreciate fully the freedom, flexibility, and speed with which young children adapt to their surroundings, we have to remember that

they continually come unglued and reassemble themselves—usually several times a day. They have wild, irrational expectations of themselves and others. They take uncalculated risks that lead them to frustration, anger, and fear. In the space of a few minutes they pass from utter despair to unmitigated joy, and sometimes back again, like your average manic-depressive. (8)

Selves tend to evolve, change, take on new voices, and assimilate them. The concept of resonant voice explains the intriguing power of so much speech and writing by children: they wear their unconscious more on their sleeve, their defenses are often less elaborate. Thus they often get more of themselves into or behind their words. This is what we mean when we call them so expressive.

One of the advantages that writing has over speech—and why writing provides a rich site for resonant voice or presence—is that writing has always served as a crucial place for trying out parts of the self or unconscious that have been hidden or neglected or undeveloped—to experiment and try out "new subject positions" (see Jonsberg).

When we see that the central question then for this kind of power in writing is not "How sincere are you?" but "How much of yourself did you manage to get *behind* the words?" we see why voice has been such a tempting metaphor. That is, the physical voice is more powerful when it can get more of the body resonating behind it or underneath it. "Resonant" seems a more helpful word than "authentic," and it is more to the point than "sincere," because it connotes the "resounding" or "sounding-again" that is involved when distinct parts can echo each other (thus Coleridge's figure of the aeolian lyre). Just as a resonant physical voice is not in any way a *picture* of the body, but it has the body's resources behind or underneath it, so too resonant voice in writing is not a picture of the self, but it has the self's resources behind or underneath it. The metaphor of voice inevitably suggests a link with the body and with "weight," and this is a link that many writers call attention to. After all, the body often shows more of ourselves than the conscious mind does: our movements, our stance, our facial expressions often reveal our dividedness, complexity, and splitness.

Here is a striking passage where William Carlos Williams sounds this theme of a link between writing, voice, and the body:

> So poets . . . are in touch with "voices," but this is the very essence of their power, the voices are the past, the depths of our very beings. It is the deeper . . . portions of the personality speaking, the middle brain, the nerves, the glands, the very muscles and bones of the body itself speaking.

Roland Barthes is particularly intriguing on this theme. He celebrates "the grain of the voice" as more powerful than the "dramatic expressivity" of opera or than mere "personality"—more powerful, in effect, than mere sincerity:

> Listen to a Russian bass (a church bass—[since] opera is a genre in which the voice has gone over in its entirety to dramatic expressivity . . .): some-

thing is there, manifest and stubborn, (one hears only *that*), beyond (or before) the meaning of the words, their form . . . , the melisma, and even the style of execution: something which is directly in the cantor's body, brought to your ears in one and the same movement from deep down in the cavities, the muscles, the membranes, the cartilages, and from deep down in the Slavonic language, as though a single skin lined the inner flesh of the performer and the music he sings. The voice is not *personal*: it *expresses nothing of the cantor and his soul* [emphasis added]; it is not original . . . , and at the same time it is individual: it has us hear a body which has no civil identity, no "personality," but which is nevertheless a separate body. . . . The "grain" is that: the materiality of the body speaking its mother tongue. (181)

Adrienne Rich uses the figure of *weight* to talk about poetry that matters. She imagines:

> Even if every word we wrote by then
> were honest   the sheer heft
> of our living behind it
> > not these sometimes
> lax indolent lines[3]

---

3. The whole poem is worth providing. It seems to me itself an example of resonance.

Poetry: III

Even if we knew the children were all asleep
and healthy   the ledgers balanced   the water running
clear in the pipes
> and all the prisoners free

Even if every word we wrote by then
were honest   the sheer heft
of our living behind it
> not these sometimes
lax indolent lines
> these litanies

Even if we were told   not just by friends
that this was honest work

Even if each of us didn't wear
a brass locket with a picture
of a strangled woman   a girlchild sewn through the crotch

Even if someone had told us, young: *This is not a key
nor a peacock feather*
> *not a kite nor a telephone*
This is the kitchen sink   the grinding-stone

would we give ourselves
more calmly over   feel less criminal joy
when the thing comes   as it does come
clarifying grammar
and the fixed and mutable stars—?

Of course, I'm not saying that writing with resonant voice *must* be ironic or split—cannot be sincere or personal. The Rich poem is surely sincere and personal. Nor that the self does not characteristically have a kind of coherence and even persistence of identity over time. I'm just insisting that the notion of resonant voice or presence in writing does not require these things.

Examples of resonant voice? I venture the Adrienne Rich poem itself. But examples are hard to cite because we cannot point to identifiable features of language that are "resonant"—as we can point to features that are audible, dramatic, distinctive, or authoritative. Rather, we are in the dicey business of pointing to the *relation* of textual features to an inferred person behind the text. Of course, this inferred presence can only come from other features of the text. It's as though—putting it bluntly—any sentence, paragraph, or page can be resonant or not, depending on the context of a longer work or oeuvre.

Look, for example, at our passages from Lawrence and Crane. I hear so *much* voice in the Lawrence: audible, dramatic, distinctive, authoritative. So much vividness and noise; I can't decide whether I hear resonance. The passage is gamey, tricky, show-offy—a pose. But of course that doesn't disqualify it either. I'm not sure; I'd have to read more.

Crane? Again we cannot decide from such a short passage. It is not so rich as the Lawrence passage in the kind of audible and dramatic voice that Robert Frost asked for (the "speaking tone of voice somehow entangled in the words and fastened to the page for the ear of the imagination"). But that's not the point with resonant voice. If we read more we might indeed hear in this somewhat forbidding prose the "sheer heft of his living," and experience a powerful resonance or presence in the passage.

For, of course, assertions about resonant voice will always be much more arguable than assertions about other kinds of voice. Not only because we are dealing with subtle inferences rather than pointing to particular linguistic features, but also because our main organ for listening to resonance is our own self. That is, we are most likely to hear resonance when the words resonate with *us*, fit *us*. This is enough to make some people insist that the only resonance we can talk about is between the text and the reader, not the text and the writer. (Bakhtin uses a metaphor of *literal* resonance between speaker and listener when he says that we lose intonation in our speech unless we have "choral support" from sympathetic or like-minded listeners ["Discourse in Life"]. Don Bialostosky, drawing on Bakhtin, coins the term "well-situated voice" for writing that "situates itself in the conversation" we are trying to enter. To achieve "well-situated voice," Bialostosky says the writer needs to "take on" the voices that make up the conversation.)

I acknowledge that when we hear resonance, we are always likely to be hearing a resonance of the words with our own predilections, tastes, obsessions—our temperament. But something more than this is happening, surely, when readers of many different temperaments hear resonance in the same piece of writing—even a very idiosyncratic piece. And most of us have occasionally had a teacher or editor who is peculiarly good in possessing the ability to "hear around" her own temperament and predilections—to hear resonance even when it doesn't fit her. This is the ability to love and feel great power in a piece while still being able to say, "But this is not my kind of writing—it doesn't really fit me"—and still help the writer revise her piece in a direction different from one's own predilections or taste. To put it another way, this kind of reader is expert at listening for resonance, even when it involves what is "other" or "different" from herself. Garcia Marquez illustrated this kind of listening when he said of Borges: "[H]e is a writer I detest. . . . On the other hand, I am fascinated by the violin he uses to express his things" (Coetzee 80).

The Relationship Between the Text and the Actual Author

The concept of resonant voice or presence may not entail any particular ideology of self or identity, but it does entail something else controversial: that we can make inferences about the relation between the voice in a text and the actual unknown, unseen historical writer behind the text—on the basis of the written text alone. We can have audible, dramatic, distinctive, and authoritative voice without any sense of whether the voice fits or doesn't fit the real author. Not so here with resonant voice or presence.

Although it may seem peculiar to say that we can sense the fit between the voice in a text and the unknown writer behind it (especially in the light of much poststructural literary theory), in truth people have an ingrained habit of doing just that: listening not only *to* each others' words but also listening *for* the relationship between the words and the speaker behind the words. To put this in a nonstartling way, we habitually listen to see whether we can trust the speaker. Such judgments are natural and nonproblematic if we know the speaker: "Alice, your words make a lot of sense, but they just don't sound like you."

But we sometimes make the same judgments about the discourse of people we *don't* know. When we hear an announcer or public speaker or we begin to converse with a stranger, we sometimes conclude that they sound unbelievable or fake, even when *what they say* is sensible and believable in itself. Something is fishy about the voice and we feel we don't trust this person. Sometimes the speaker sounds evasive, halting, awkward. But as often as not, on the contrary, we are bothered because the speaker seems too glib or fluent—as in the case of certain overzealous salesmen or politicians. Sometimes the speaker sounds insincere, but sometimes something sounds "off" even when the person sounds sincere.

Sometimes we are relying on visual cues from the speaker before our eyes. Yet we go on making these judgments without visual cues—when strangers speak over the phone or on the radio. Even when there is nothing but literal voice to go on, we sometimes conclude nevertheless that there is something untrustworthy about the politician or radio announcer or salesman. It's not that we necessarily distrust the message; sometimes we believe it. But we distrust the speaker—or at least we distrust the fit between the message and the speaker.

How do we make these judgments about whether to trust someone when all we have is their language? Doubtless we go on auditory cues of intonation and rhythm: literal "tone of voice." But tone of voice is nothing but a "way of talking," and when we only have *writing by a stranger*, we still have a "way of talking" to go on—that is, his or her way of writing. Even though we can't see or hear the writer, and even though writing provides fewer semiotic channels for nuance, we still draw inferences from the writer's syntax, diction, structure, strategies, stance, and so forth.

Obviously, these inferences are risky. But my point is that we've all had lots of training in making them. Repeatedly in our lives we face situations where our main criterion for deciding whether an utterance is true is whether to trust the speaker. When we take our car to a mechanic, most of us don't base our decision about whether the carburetor needs replacing on data about carburetors but rather on a decision about trustworthiness of voice. We often do the same thing when we take our body to a doctor—or decide to trust *anyone* about a matter we don't understand. We mustn't forget how practiced and skilled most of us have become at this delicate kind of judgment just because we remember so vividly the times we judged wrong. And it's clear that some people are better than others at figuring out whether someone can be trusted. They must be reading something. The practice of counseling and therapy depends on this kind of ear. Skilled listeners can sometimes hear *through sincerity*: they can hear that even though the speaker is perfectly sincere, he cannot be trusted. There must be real cues in discourse—readable but subtle—about the relationship between discourse and speaker. Because we are listening for relationships between what is *explicit* in the text and *implicit* cues about the writer that somehow lurk in the text, we can seldom make these kinds of judgments unless we have extended texts—better yet two or three texts by the same writer.

Because our inferences about resonant voice are so subtle, they are seldom based on conscious deliberation: we usually make these inferences with the *ear*—by means of how the discourse "sounds" or "feels" or whether it "rings true." We use the kind of tacit, nonfocal awareness that Polanyi addresses and analyzes so well. Oliver Sacks describes a scene where aphasics are watching Reagan give a talk on TV. Because aphasics are unable to understand the propositional content of his speech,

> they have an infallible ear for every vocal nuance, the tone, the rhythm, the cadences, the music, the subtlest modulations, inflections, intonations, which can give—or remove—verisimilitude to or from a man's voice. In this, then, lies their power of understanding—understanding without words what is authentic or inauthentic (76).

Notice that this peculiar skill—evaluating the trustworthiness or validity of utterances by *how* things are said because we cannot evaluate *what* is said— often does not correlate with "school learning." Schools naturally emphasize texts, and when we are learning how to deal with texts, and especially when our culture becomes more text oriented or literate in the ways described by

Olson and Ong and so many others, we are learning how to pay more attention to the relationship between words and their meanings and referents—and less attention to the relationship between words and their speakers or writers.

In a sense, we've stumbled here upon the very essence of schooling or literacy training: learning to attend better to the meaning and logic of words themselves and to stop relying on extratextual cues such as how impressive or authoritative the author is or how you feel about her. School and the culture of literacy advise us to this effect: "Stop listening for tone of voice and interpreting gestures. These are the tricks of illiterates and animals—evaluating speech on the basis of what they think of the speaker because they can't read or judge the message for itself." Sometimes the successful student or scholar is the *least* adept at this kind of metatextual reading—at what we call "street smarts."

I'm really making a simple claim here—and it's the same claim that I made earlier about audible and dramatic voice: that our primary and formative experiences with language were with words that emerged audibly from physically present persons—and most of us continue to encounter this kind of language as much as we encounter silent texts, if not more. For this reason, we can scarcely prevent ourselves from hearing the presence of human beings in language and making inferences about the relationship between the language and the person who speaks or writes it. Conditioning alone nudges us to do this, but more important, much of our functioning in the world depends on this skill. Many school practices blunt this skill—allegedly for the sake of literacy training. But Brandt argues intriguingly that these practices are based on a mistaken model of literacy. Good teachers of literacy, whether in first grade or college, learn to *integrate* street smarts with book smarts or literacy training. Instead of making students feel that their skill at reading the person behind the discourse is a hindrance for school, they help students harness this ability toward increased sophistication with purely silent, textual language.

If we pause for a moment to explore Aristotle and the process of persuasion, we can find more corroboration for the nonstartling claim that humans naturally listen to discourse for cues about the actual person behind it. Aristotle defines *ethos* as a potent source of persuasion, but scholars argue about what he meant by *ethos*.

Sometimes he emphasizes the actual "personal character of the speaker," saying "We believe good men more fully and more readily than others" (*Rhetoric* 1356a). But sometimes he emphasizes how speakers can fool listeners and persuade them with just dramatic voice or implied author. Aristotle talks about the ability to "make ourselves *thought to be* sensible and morally good." (1378a, my emphasis). And he notes that this is a matter of skill, not character:

> We can now see that a writer must disguise his art and give the impression of speaking naturally and not artificially. Naturalness is persuasive, artificiality is the contrary; for our hearers are prejudiced and think we have some design against them. (1404b)

Scholars fight about Aristotle's ambiguity in his *Rhetoric*, but the fight would disappear if they simply realized that by affirming *both* positions, he is in fact taking the most commonsense view: "It's nice to *be* trustworthy; but if you're skilled you can fake it."

When Aristotle says that we can persuade people by creating a dramatic voice that is more trustworthy than we actually are—when he says, in effect, that a good rhetor can sometimes fool the audience—he is talking about the inevitable gap between discourse and the actual speaker, that is, between implied author and real author, between dramatic voice and resonant voice.

Because he's writing a handbook for *authors*, he's telling them how they can hide this gap if they are skilled. They can *seem* more trustworthy than they are, but in order to do so they must fool the audience into not seeing the gap. If he'd been writing a handbook for *audiences* rather than authors (writing "reception theory" instead of "transmission theory"), he would have looked at this gap from the other side. He would have emphasized how skilled listeners can *uncover* the gap that speakers are trying to hide. He would have talked about how skilled listeners can detect differences between the implied author and the real author—can detect, that is, dishonesty or untrustworthiness even in a sensible message or a fluent delivery. In short, by arguing in the *Rhetoric* that skilled speakers can seem better than they are, he is acknowledging that there is a gap to be detected, and thereby also implying that good listeners can make inferences about the character of the speaker from their words.

Since readers and listeners make these perceptions all the time about the trustworthiness of the speaker or writer on the basis of their words alone, any good rhetorical theory must show how persuasiveness comes from *resonant voice* or *communicated presence* as often as it comes from merely dramatic voice or implied author. Aristotle clearly implies what common sense tells us: we are not persuaded by implied author as such—that is, by the creation of a dramatic voice that has a skillfully trustworthy *sound*; we are only persuaded if we believe that dramatic voice *is* the voice of the actual speaker or author. We don't buy a used car from someone just because we admire their dramatic skill in creating a fictional trustworthy voice. If ethos is nothing *but* implied author, it loses all power of persuasion.

But How Does the Ideology Play Out When We Write or Teach Writing?

So far, I have been trying as hard as I can to dodge ideological dispute. I have been claiming that none of these five senses of voice assumes any particular theory of identity. People can have various ideological positions about the nature of the self and talk productively together about texts using the various senses of voice. They will have as good a chance of agreeing with each other about the presence or absence of various kinds of voice as they do in trying to apply many more traditional concepts such as *structure* or *irony*. Even resonant voice accommodates conflicting ideological positions. But so far I've talked from the point of view of readers and critics who are exploring voice in texts produced by *others*. Once we set out to *write*, however, or to teach writing, it seems hard to dodge the ideological dilemma.

For there is an asymmetry between reading and writing. As readers we usually have access only to the text, not to the writer, but as writers we have access to *both*. When I write, I can listen for the sound of my text and I can also listen for the sound I experience as "me."

There are many occasions when it seems clear that the voice that we feel as "ours" is clearly wrong for this task or audience. Students sometimes put the situation bluntly: "Can I just write this comfortably in my own language or do I have to sound proper and detached and academic?"

We can respond to this common dilemma with two ideologically opposite pieces of advice (whether we are talking to ourselves as writers or to our students). At one extreme, the "sentimental" position echoes Tolstoy and Yeats and says,

> Hold fast to your true "you" at all costs. Don't give in and write in the voice "they" want. Your voice is the only powerful voice to use. Your true voice will conquer all difficulties.

At the other extreme, the "sophisticated" position says,

> Your sense of "you" is just an illusion of late Romantic, bourgeois capitalism. Forget it. You have no self. You are nothing but roles. Write in whatever role works best for this topic and these readers.

But even here, if we emphasize pragmatism rather than ideological theory, we can dodge the ideological choice. In practice we don't have to choose between such extreme positions. It is far more helpful to move somewhat back and forth between some version of them. That is, we can usefully come at the activity of writing itself from both sides of the identity fence.

First, let's take the "sentimental" approach. Suppose I'm a student who has to write about Thucydides or quantum mechanics for a reader who wants a very restricted academic voice or register—a reader who is not just uninterested in my "presence" but who will in fact be put off if she feels too much contact with "me." Nevertheless, I don't have to try to write my paper in that "proper" or detached voice that feels alien to me. I can write in whatever voice feels most comfortable and habitual and try to figure out my thinking about Thucydides or quantum mechanics—for exploratory, early, and perhaps even midstage drafts. For then it turns out that it's not so hard for me to take a midstage or late draft, written comfortably in this wrong voice, and revise it into the register or voice (and of course the structure) that the audience demands. When I do this, the *underlying plasma* of my prose still feels to me as though it is me, my own voice; and yet I have managed pretty well to make my text seem distant and impersonal and thus fit the voice needs of my readers.

Consider a trickier case involving more personal senses of self. Suppose I've become convinced from repeated feedback that my characteristic voice—the voice that feels like me or mine—is a problem: too angry, say, or too emotional or too insecure. My most habitual or natural voice repeatedly undermines my writing—at least for many audiences. Again, I don't have to try to write in a voice that feels alien and uncomfortable. I can use whatever voice feels comfortably mine for early drafts, and again, in revising, adjust or get rid of the worst pieces of anger or emotionality or tip toeing.

This is an unsurprising strategy for getting more comfort into the writing process. It is nothing but what many teachers apply when they emphasize drafting and revising (at least those teachers who invite comfortable writing on early drafts). But the strategy has interesting implications with regard to voice-and-self. In the *long run*, when I use the voice or voices that I experience as mine—such as they are and with all their limitations—use them a lot for exploratory and private and early draft writing and try them out on myself and others—listening to them and even appreciating them—these voices tend to get richer and develop. That is, the more I write about Thucydides or quantum mechanics in my comfortable voice, the more my voice will stretch and expand. Of course I won't suddenly write in the voice of a physicist, say, but one of the qualities of a physicist's voice is *comfort in talking about quantum mechanics*, and I'll begin to get some of that. And to say this is to say that I will be learning to get more of the resources of my self into discourse about physics—as physicists do.

Turning to the more personal example, I can use the same strategy. I can let the "wrong voice" have free reign, and then in late drafts adjust or get rid of the offending bits but keep the energy. Yet as I use this strategy over time, the more I allow myself to use my angry voice, the more my writing can stretch and develop. I can slide or bounce *comfortably* into other moods instead of trying consciously to adopt them when they don't feel comfortable. The more I use my insecure voice, the more I can write myself into passages of confidence; as I use my emotional voice more, I write myself into more passages of calmness and control. It's not that I give up the original voices, but I develop more options. Gradually, I find I have more flexibility of voice—more voices that feel like me.

So much for the allegedly sentimental approach. It's equally helpful to work from the "sophisticated" side of this identity issue. Suppose I think of all discourse as nothing but the taking on of roles or the using of others' voices. I can take on the approach that Auden celebrated in his lovely poem, "The Truest Poetry is the Most Feigning." I can consciously practice role playing, ventriloquism, and heteroglossia. Role playing and irony and make-believe often get at possible or temporary dimensions of the protean self that are important and useful but unavailable to conscious planning and control. To take a concrete example, people who are characteristically timid, quiet, self-effacing—who have a hard time getting heard or putting any force into their writing—often come up with a powerfully angry voice when they let themselves *play* that role. (It's as though they have an angry voice in their unconscious.) When this angry voice gets hold of the pen, the resulting language is often very powerful indeed—if hard to control at first. And though the voice may feel uncomfortable to start with, people often gradually take to it and get some control.

Notice that in both the sentimental and sophisticated approaches, we see the same crucial process: a gradual development and enrichment of voice. In one case it is a matter of using, trusting, and "playing in" (as with an unplayed violin) a voice that feels like one's own—and seeing it become more ample and flexible. In the other case it is a matter of trusting oneself to use unaccustomed or even alien voices in a spirit of play and noninvestment—and seeing those voices become more comfortable and skilled. In both cases one is getting more of the self—or the shifting temporary roles that constitute the nonself of the moment—behind, under, or into the text.

And whichever ideological position or strategy one uses, it helps to emphasize the strategy that was central to the Stanford Voice Project: helping students learn better to *hear* voices in their own and others' writing. At Stanford they got students to do lots of speaking and reading out loud of their own writing, and they used lots of live and taped readings of speech and writing by students and professionals. Many unskilled writers don't think of their writing as *having* a sound or a voice.

Bakhtin provides us with a good example of someone trying to do justice to *both* ideological positions. All the while he is arguing that every word we speak or write comes from the mouths and voices of others, he never stops being interested in the process by which we take these alien words and "make them our own":

> The importance of struggling with another's discourse, its influence in the history of an individual's coming to dialogical consciousness, is enormous. One's own discourse and one's own voice, although born of another or dynamically stimulated by another, will sooner or later begin to liberate themselves from the authority of the other's discourse. ("Discourse in the Novel" 348; see also 343)

William Coles and Walker Gibson provide two more examples of straddling on the issue of voice and identity. They might resist my reading them this way, for they both repeatedly insist that they are not interested in the real writer at all, only in the textual voice; they insist that we create ourselves anew every time we speak or write. Yet the test they often use for language is not only whether it is strong in itself or well suited to the audience but also whether it carries a certain sense of authenticity. Here is Coles writing about the textual voice in a letter by Nicola Sacco (of Sacco and Vanzetti): "for me there's no 'facade' here, not any more than Sacco is 'behind' anything. That language of his so far as I'm concerned, he's in. He's it. And it's him" (135). When they criticize a textual voice, they often call it "fake"; Coles sometimes even calls it "bullshit." If we create ourselves anew every time we speak or write, how can our creation ever be anything but real?

Here is another example of Coles doing a kind of justice to both sides of the voice/identity issue in two adjacent sentences. He is talking about revising his book and the unavoidable process of "rewriting" himself. In one sentence he says he is doing "no more than trying to solve a writing problem." But in the next sentence he says his revising is "a way of seeing what it could mean to belong to one's self." (276). I sense an ambivalence in Coles and Gibson—an ambivalence I also sense in the culture of the Amherst College course they both taught in: on the one hand, an insistence that voice is nothing but a phenomenon restricted entirely to the text; yet on the other hand, a continual, intuitive listening for how textual voice reverberates in relation to a person behind the page. Gibson's *Tough, Sweet and Stuffy* seems to me one of the best books around about voice and writing.

In short, I'm arguing that we can finesse the knotty theoretical questions of self, even when we are sitting in the lap of the self in question—that is, when we are engaged in writing. We can learn (and help teach our students) to move flexibly back and forth between using and celebrating something we feel as our own voice, and operating as though we are nothing but ventriloquists playfully using and adapting and working against an array of voices we find around us.

Conclusion

I hope I've made it clear why voice is such a useful metaphor for this related family of dimensions in a text—dimensions that are so important to how we read and how we write. Of course voice is a lightning rod that attracts ideological dispute, but I hope I've provided the kind of analysis needed to make voice a practical critical tool that we can *use* rather than just fight about. We may not agree about the presence or absence in a particular text of audible, dramatic, distinctive, or authoritative voice, but we can agree about what these terms mean. Even for resonant voice, we don't have to agree on the nature of self.

In order to stabilize and solidify the concept of voice in writing, I think we need to distinguish the five different kinds of voice I have spelled out here—or work out more accurate distinctions. But once we have had our careful critical conversation about the different dimensions of voice, I don't think we'll always have to be so fussy about distinctions. We'll be able to say to a friend or student, "I hear more voice in these passages; something rich and useful and interesting is going on there; can you get more of that?" and not necessarily have to make careful distinctions between audible, dramatic, distinctive, authoritative, and resonant voice. There are substantive differences between them, but more often than not they go together. And surely what holds them together are the richly bundled dimensions and connotations of the human voice.

Works Cited

Aristotle. *Rhetoric*. Trans. Rhys Roberts. *Aristotle: Rhetoric; Poetics*. NY: Random House, 1954.
Bakhtin, Mikhail. "Discourse in Life and Discourse in Art (Concerning Sociological Poet-

ics)." Appendix to *Freudianism: A Marxist Critique*. V. N. Volosinov. Tr. I. R. Titunik. Ed. Neal H. Bruss. NY: Academic Press, 1976. (Holquist's attribution of this work to Bakhtin is generally accepted.)

———. "Discourse in the Novel." *The Dialogic Imagination: Four Essays*. Ed. Michael Holquist. Trans. Caryl Emerson and Michael Holquist. Austin: U of Texas P Slavic Series, no. 1, 1981. 259–422.

Barthes, Roland. "Death of the Author." *Image, Music, Text*. Trans. Stephen Heath. NY: Hill and Wang, 1977.

———. "The Grain of the Voice." *Image, Music, Text*. Trans. Stephen Heath. NY: Hill and Wang, 1977.

Belenky, Mary Field, Blythe McVicker Clinchy, Nancy Rule Goldberger, Jill Mattuck Tarule. *Women's Ways of Knowing: The Development of Self, Voice, and Mind*. NY: Basic Books, 1986.

Berlin, James A. "Rhetoric and Ideology in the Writing Class," *College English* 50.5 (Sept 1988): 477–94.

Bialostosky, Donald. "Liberal Education, Writing, and the Dialogic Self." *Contending with Words: Composition and Rhetoric in a PostModern Age*. Eds. Patricia Harkin and John Schilb. NY: MLA, 1991. 11–22.

Bolinger, Dwight. *Intonation and its Parts: Melody in Spoken English*. Stanford: Stanford UP, 1986.

Brandt, Deborah. *Literacy as Involvement: The Acts of Writers, Readers, and Texts*. Carbondale: Southern IL P, 1990.

Brower, Reuben Arthur. *The Fields of Light: An Experiment in Critical Reading*. NY: Oxford UP, 1962.

Burke, Kenneth. *A Grammar of Motives*. Berkeley: U California P, 1969. xix.

Calkins, McCormick Lucy. *The Art of Teaching Writing*. Portsmouth NH: Heinemann, 1986.

Coetzee. J. M. "Borges's Dark Mirror." Rev. of *Collected Fictions*, by Jorge Luis Borges. *New York Review of Books* (22 Oct. 1998): 80–82.

Coles, William E. Jr. *The Plural I—And After*. Portsmouth NH: Boynton/Cook Heinemann, 1988.

Crane. R. S. "The Critical Monism of Cleanth Brooks." *Critics and Criticism: Ancient and Modern*. Chicago: Chicago UP, 1951. 83–107.

Crismore, Avon. *Talking With Readers: Metadiscourse as Rhetorical Act*. NY: Lang, 1989.

Dasenbrook, Reed Way. "Becoming Aware of the Myth of Presence." *Journal of Advanced Composition* 8 (1988): 1–11.

Derrida, Jacques. *Of Grammatology*. Trans. Gayatri Spivak. Baltimore: Johns Hopkins UP, 1976

Elbow, Peter. "The Shifting Relationships Between Speech and Writing," *Conference on College Composition and Communication* 36.2 (Oct 1985): 283–303.

———. *Writing With Power: Techniques for Mastering the Writing Process*. NY: Oxford UP, 1981.

Emerson, Caryl. "The Outer Word and Inner Speech: Bakhtin, Vygotsky, and the Internalization of Language." *Critical Inquiry* 10 (December 1983): 21–40.

Farrell, Thomas J. "IQ and Standard English." *College Composition and Communication* 34 (December 1983): 470–84.

Freisinger, Randall. "Voicing the Self: Toward a Pedagogy of Resistance in a Postmodern Age." *Voices on Voice: A (Written) Discussion*. Ed. Kathleen Blake Yancey. Urbana, IL: NCTE, 1994. 242–74.

Frost, Robert. *A Way Out*. NY: Seven Arts, 1917.

Gibson, Walker. *Tough, Sweet, and Stuffy: An Essay on Modern American Prose Styles*. Bloomington: Indiana UP, 1966.

Gilligan, Carol. "Letter to Readers, 1993." *In A Different Voice: Psychological Theory and Women's Development*. 2nd ed. Cambridge MA: Harvard UP, 1993. xv–xxvi.

Harris, Joseph. "Voice." *A Teaching Subject: Composition Since 1966*. Upper Saddle River NJ: Prentice Hall, 1997. 23–45.

Havelock, Eric. *The Muse Learns to Write: Reflections on Orality and Literacy from Antiquity to the Present.* New Haven: Yale UP, 1986.

Hawkes, John. "The Voice Project: An Idea for Innovation in the Teaching of Writing." *Writers as Teachers: Teachers as Writers.* NY: Holt Rinehart and Winston, 1970. 89–144.

———. *The Voice Project, Final Report.* Stanford: Stanford UP, 1967. ERIC ED 01844.

Hjortshoj, Keith. "Language and Movement." Unpublished MS.

Hoddeson, David. "The Reviser's Voices." *Journal of Basic Writing* 3.3 (Fall/Winter 1981): 91–108.

hooks, bell. "'When I Was A Young Soldier For the Revolution': Coming to Voice." *Talking Back: thinking feminist, thinking black.* Boston: South End Press, 1984.

Ihde, Don. *Listening and Voice: A Phenomenology of Sound.* Athens OH: Ohio UP, 1976.

Johnson, Barbara. "Metaphor, Metonymy, and Voice in Zora Neale Hurston's *Their Eyes Were Watching God.*" Ed. Mary Ann Caws. *Textual Analysis: Some Readers Reading.* NY: MLA, 1986: 232–44.

Johnson, Nan. "Ethos and the Aims of Rhetoric." *Essays on Classical Rhetoric and Modern Discourse.* eds. Robert J. Connors, Lisa Ede, and Andrea Lunsford. Carbondale: Southern Illinois UP: 1984. 98–114.

Jonsberg, Sara. "Rehearsing New Subject Positions: A Poststructuralist View of Expressive Writing." Presentation at Conference on College Composition and Communication, April 1993, San Diego.

Jordan, June. "Nobody Mean More to Me than You: And the Future Life of Willie Jordan." *On Call: Political Essays.* Boston: South End Press, 1985. 123–39.

Lawrence, D. H. *Studies in Classic American Literature.* NY: Doubleday, 1951.

Lunsford, Andrea. "The Content of Basic Writers' Essays" *College Composition and Communication* 31 (October 1980): 278–90.

Olson, David. R. "The Languages of Instruction: The Literate Bias of Schooling." *Schooling and the Acquisition of Knowledge.* Eds. R. C. Anderson, R. J. Siro, and W. E. Montague Hillsdale, NJ: Lawrence Erlbaum, 1977.

———. "Writing: The Divorce of the Author from the Text." *Exploring Speaking-Writing Relationships: Connections and Contrasts.* Ed. B. M. Kroll and R. J. Vann. Urbana IL: NCTE, 1981. 99–110.

Ong, Walter. "From Mimesis to Irony: Writing and Print as Integuments of Voice." *Interfaces of the Word: Studies in the Evolution of Consciousness and Culture.* Ithaca: Cornell UP, 1977. 272–304.

———. *Orality and Literacy: The Technologizing of the Word.* NY: Methuen, 1982.

Palacas, Arthur L. "Parentheticals and Personal Voice." *Written Communication* 6.4 (Oct 1989): 506–27.

Park, Clara Claiborne. "Talking Back to the Speaker." *Hudson Review* 42.1 (Spring 1989): 21–44.

Polanyi, Michael. *Personal Knowledge: Toward a Post-Critical Philosophy.* NY: Harper and Row, 1958.

Pritchard, William. "Ear Training." *Teaching What We Do.* Amherst MA: Amherst College P, 1991.

Rich, Adrienne. "Poetry: III." *Your Native Land, Your Life.* NY: Norton, 1986. 68.

Rubin, Donald L. and Kathryn Greene. "Gender-Typical Style in Written Language." *Research in the Teaching of English* 26.2 (Feb 1992): 7–40.

Sacks, Oliver. "The President's Speech." *The Man Who Mistook His Wife for a Hat: and Other Clinical Tales.* NY: Summit Books, 1987. 76–80.

Simon, John. Rev. of *Images: My Life in Film* by Ingmar Bergman, *New York Times Book Review* (30 Jan 1994): 7–8.

Tannen, Deborah. "Oral and Literate Strategies in Spoken and Written Discourse." *Literacy for Life: The Demand for Reading and Writing.* Eds. Richard Bailey and Robin Fosheim. NY: MLA, 1983.

Varnum, Robin. *A Maverick Writing Course: English 1–2 at Amherst College, 1938–66.* Urbana IL: NCTE, 1996.

Vendler, Helen. "An Intractable Metal." *New Yorker* (15 Feb. 1982): 131.

Williams, William Carlos. "How to Write." *New Directions 50th Anniversary Issue.* Ed. J. Laughlin. NY: New Directions Publishing, 1936.

Woolf, Virginia. *Between Ourselves: Letters, Mothers, Daughters.* Ed. Karen Payne. NY: Houghton Mifflin, 1983.

On the Concept of Voice

We write not with the fingers but with the whole person.

Virginia Woolf, *Orlando*

It's hard not to talk about writing as though it were speech: in discussing silent texts we talk about the "voice" or "tone of voice"; also about the "speaker" and about what we "hear" a piece of writing "saying." Diverse critics even refer to a writer as having "found her voice."

Influential modern figures have rejected the psychological or metaphysical implications of voice and given us critical terms which seek to separate the "voice" or "character" or "ethos" in a text from the actual author or writer or self behind the text: Pound's "persona," Yeats's "mask," Booth's "implied author." Next come *post*moderns to insist that there is no such thing as a self or author behind the text—either to be revealed *or* concealed by the text. But when these critics kill off the author, they merely inject new life into voice: the text is nothing *but* voices. (Yet all discourse is "writing"!)

. . .

Why do I care so much about voice? I think voice is one of the main forces that *draws* us into texts. We often give other explanations for what we like ("clarity," "style," "energy," "sublimity," "reach," even "truth"), but I think it's often one sort of voice or another. One way of saying this is that voice seems to overcome "writing" or textuality.

That is, speech seems to come *to* us as listener; the speaker seems to do the work of getting the meaning into our heads. In the case of writing, on the other hand, it's as though we as reader have go to the text and do the work of extracting the meaning. And speech seems to give us more sense of contact with the author.

To talk this way gets me in trouble with Derrida, of course: hopelessly phonocentric and a sucker for "presence." For I am a kind of "listening Tom" with a prurient interest in hearing voices in texts. But perhaps Derridians shouldn't be too quick on the trigger since I suspect my analysis might even aid their enterprise. For it could be said that I'm searching for what gives the *illusion* of presence. I'm trying to show how *some* texts give the sense of coming to the reader, of doing the work for the reader, and of producing a sense

All three fragments come from "The Pleasures of Voices in the Literary Essay: Explorations in the Prose of Gretel Ehrlich and Richard Selzer," an essay published in 1989 in *Literary Nonfiction: Theory, Criticism, Pedagogy*. Ed. Chris Anderson. Southern Illinois UP. 211–34.

of genuine and direct contact with the reader—and others do not. After all not much useful critical work gets done by grand epistemological and ontological arguments about whether *all* discourse is essentially speech or essentially "writing." What we need are tools to talk about *differences* among texts. Voice can be a crucial tool for this sort of work.

Audible Voice

How Much Do We Hear the Text?

Robert Frost said that the distinguishing mark of good prose is "the speaking tone of voice somehow entangled in the words and fastened to the page for the ear of the imagination." Even though texts are literally silent, some texts make us hear someone's voice. Admittedly, we can "sound out" any text and thus inject audible voice into it, but texts with audible voice give us the sense of a sound coming up from the page by itself; and they seem to *give* us energy rather than requiring energy of us. I highlight here the uttered dimension of written language as opposed to the constructed or composed dimension: the aural and experienced-in-time dimension as opposed to the visual and experienced-in-space dimension.

Perhaps the best illustration of audible voice is the radical absence of it. The classic examples tend to come from government documents, army manual instructions, bureaucratic memos. This is from a letter from a stock company:

> In connection with the Offer to Purchase for Cash All Outstanding Units of Beneficial Interest of American Royalty Trust (the 'Unit Offer') and the Offer to Purchase All Outstanding Shares of Common Stock, $3.33 Cumulative Convertible Preferred Stock, $2.28 Cumulative Preferred Stock and $1.65 Cumulative Preferred Stock (the 'Stock Offer') each dated August 7, 1986 by FPCO Inc., PETRO-LEWIS CORPORATION (the 'Company'), and, in the case of the Unit Offer, American Royalty Producing Company ('ARPCO') and PLC-ARPC, Inc. ('PLC-ARPC'), by letters dated August 7, 1986 (the 'Recommendation Letters'), have conveyed their recommendations regarding the Unit Offer and the Stock Offer.

But garden-variety inaudible prose is all around us in all the lifeless or tangled writing we cannot avoid having to read.

. . .

It's important to note that something completely different from speech can nevertheless be experienced as audible and have a strong "uttered" or existing-in-time quality—*if* it has the right kinds of rhythms, parallels, and echoes. I'm guessing that most readers would find the following example audible, even though they'd never uttered or heard or spoken such a massively left-branching syntactic structure:

> Because these men work with animals, not machines or numbers, because they live outside in landscapes of torrential beauty, because they are confined to a place and a routine embellished with awesome variables, because calves die in the arms that pulled others into life, because they go to the mountains as if on a pilgrimage to find out what makes a herd of elk tick, their strength is also a softness, their toughness, a rare delicacy. (Ehrlich, *Solace* 52–53)

Musicians say that certain passages "lie under the fingers." They mean that the notes are very playable. However unspeechlike, that passage by Ehrlich is very sayable.

For another source of audibility, consider next two versions of a passage about morning:

> Morning. Blue air comes ringed with coyotes. The ewes wake clearing their communal throats like old men. Lambs shake their flop-eared heads at leaves of grass, negotiating the blade.

> In the morning when blue air comes ringed with coyotes, the ewes wake clearing their communal throats like old men, while the lambs shake their flop-eared heads at leaves of grass, as they negotiate the blade.

I suspect most of us would hear the first version more (and it is Ehrlich's, p. 56). Its short simple sentences seen more speechlike than the long embedded sentence. Yet we don't *speak* poetic sentences of this sort. It's my guess that the real source of audibility is this: Ehrlich's simple sentences give us an experience of mental activity *going on*, whereas the single embedded sentence gives more of an experience of a *completed* thought. (Walter Ong relates oral discourse to "language as event" and written discourse to "language as record.")

Another source of audible voice in texts: textual cues that heighten our sense of the *person in there*—someone at home, someone making that language. Here is an example from Selzer:

> Take Dom Pietro. Eighteen years in a monastery and he has remained a personage. I can see him carried across the Piazza San Marco . . . shedding benedictions on the crowd. Listen . . . [and Selzer goes off on an illustrative anecdote]. (18)

What interests me is "Take Dom Pietro" and "Listen." Yes, those two short sentences are speechlike, but more than that, they call attention to their status as *speech acts*.

Admittedly, all discourse is a speech act—not just a *saying* but a *doing*; not just an assertion in the realm of meaning, but an acting in the realm of people.

Speech act theory shows us that we haven't described discourse if we've just described the meaning or language itself; we've left something out till we've also described who is trying to do what to whom—and in what setting. Nevertheless, *writing*—especially poor writing—has a tendency to be remarkably effective at *seeming* to belie speech-act theory—that is, at *hiding* its status as an act. Writing often suffers from the sense that no one is trying to do anything to anyone, that there's no context, and thus that there's nothing but "language" sitting there asserting meaning under its own auspices.

The paradigmatic example of *non*speech-act language is the grammar-book sentence—for example, "The cat is on the mat." Notice how it becomes audible when we say, "I doubt the cat is on the mat." When prose calls attention to itself as a speech act—language doing, not just saying—it usually heightens our sense of audible voice.

Thus every time an author writes, "Notice that . . ." or "What I'm arguing is . . ." or "Let me now turn to . . ." she is calling attention on the silent page to the speech act she's performing—thus heightening our sense of the writer's presence as a person acting on us. Usually this heightens the audible voice. This effect is stronger if she actually refers to herself or to the reader. And stronger still if she uses first person for herself and second person for the reader. Thus notice the progression here:

Warm clothing will be needed for the trip.
The organizer urges participants to bring plenty of warm clothing.
I urge you to bring plenty of warm clothing.

Metaphors often increase audible voice. Why? Consider these two sentences:

The table is stationary.
The table lurks stationary.

Notice how "lurks" as a metaphor doesn't just animate the table, it animates the writer. It heightens our sense of the *presence* of an active consciousness at work in the text, exerting a force on her material.

The principle here, then, is that audible voice is increased by words which call attention to the presence of the person writing. Thus the second sentence below will probably be slightly more audible because of the mere change of one adjective—a change that signals the feelings of the writer.

The government food was distributed throughout the district.
The hateful food was distributed throughout the district.

And so when Ehrlich writes, "Winter lasts six months here," she is making her sentence more audible than if she had written, "Winter lasts six months in Wyoming." "Here" calls attention to a particular person writing from a particular place and situation. "Winter lasts six months in Wyoming" could be a sentence in an almanac—words as it were from nobody to nobody.

Though I'm obviously celebrating the pleasures of audible voice, I'm not saying it's enough by itself to make writing good. The following sentence may be full of audible voice, but if it were found in a serious essay about the causes of the French Revolution, it would have to be judged bad for not doing the task.

> I'm sitting here looking at the cursor on my screen. It's blinking at me as much as to say, "What *are* the causes of the French Revolution?

Voice in Texts as It Relates to Teaching

I've been trying to rehabilitate the vexed notion of *voice* as a useful critical concept, and thus have sought some precision by analysis or division into various meanings of the term. I have stressed complexities. But the applications of voice to teaching are relatively simple, and I conclude with some concrete suggestions.

Audible voice. When student writing is tangled and dead and without audible voice, we can easily get the student to see the problem—or rather hear the problem—and break through to audible voice. If we get the student to *read the prose out loud*, he can usually hear the tangle with his ear or feel it with his mouth. Often he stumbles. Or we can read it out loud ourselves or have someone else read it. The student can usually hear the deadness with his ear. Then we can ask, "How would you *say* it? *Tell* me what you are getting at!" and usually he cuts through the tangle to clearer diction, stronger syntax, and sometimes better thinking. (All this, note, without "teaching" or advice.)

Dramatic voice. When a student uses an odd or offensive or contradictory stance in her writing, a problematic implied author, we can ask her what kind of voice she hears in there (or get her to ask her peer group to tell her who they hear in her writing). Or if we're writing comments, we can simply describe the problem in terms of voice: "You sound so timid here. [Or arrogant, or angry, or like two different people.] Did you mean to use that voice?" This kind of comment grants the student some safety through distance between herself and her text.

Voice with authority. So much writing by students is timid. This is understandable. For most students, writing is something they do only in school—for teachers—and so their experience of writing is usually the experience of creating something to see if it is acceptable to the person who *authorizes* the writing. Many students don't feel they authorize their words. And yet it is possible for us to help students *take authority* for their words. The concept of "voice with authority" can help us here. We can simply ask students to try rewriting certain passages or papers as though they weren't timid or afraid. When they manage to do so, an enormous range of *other* writing weaknesses tend to disappear. We can help tune their ears to how often fear is tangled up with writing.

Resonant voice. When writing is perfunctory and uninvested we can say, "I find myself doubting whether *you* even believe what you are saying." Or when, in contrast, the writing is desperately sincere but tinny and clichéd, we can say, "I believe you are sincere here, but somehow it seems as though you're *trying* too hard to *be* sincere. Why must you work at it so? In the end I don't quite trust the voice here." ("Methinks she doth protest. . . .") This is in fact a slightly evasive comment. That is, I often suspect pressure from something the student may *not* be aware of, but I don't feel it's fair to say that. Or to put it more positively: I feel it's all right to comment on my sense of the language, but I'm reluctant to bring up any of my speculative inferences about unfelt feelings. I try to make these comments tentatively—so the student can easily reject them. Most of all, I find it helpful to point to contrasting passages and say, "I hear more resonance and solidity in these other spots." (They are usually spots where the student isn't breathing so hard or protesting so much—places where he or she is producing a sound as it were from the diaphragm and not just from the throat.)

Resonant voice is especially important for teaching persuasive writing. As Aristotle points out in the *Rhetoric*, trustworthy *ethos* is a major source of persuasiveness. But he also notes that we are *not* persuaded if we sense that the "trustworthiness" is a matter of "conscious art." He clearly implies that we need to experience that trustworthiness as inhering *in* the actual writer, and that we distrust a writer to the extent that we sense him as a clever creator of personas.

Thus, even though there is not yet any critical consensus about voice, and even though the concept leads us into theoretical brambles, students quickly and easily understand talk about voice in texts. Talking about ineffective writing in terms of voice tends to bring about quicker improvements than talking in terms of, say, heavy nominalization, passive voice, or *ethos*.

Works Cited

Ehrlich, Gretel. *The Solace of Open Spaces*. NY: Viking, 1985.
Frost, Robert. Preface. *A Way Out*. NY: Seven Arts, 1917. Reprinted in *Selected Prose of Robert Frost*. Ed. Hyde Cox and Edward connerey Lathan. NY: Holt, Rinehart and Winston, 1966.
Ong, Walter. *Orality and Literacy: The Technologizing of the Word*. NY: Methuen, 1982.
Selzer, Richard. *Taking the World in for Repairs*. NY: Morrow, 1986.

Part IV

DISCOURSES

You're doing sheep and goats again, Peter. You talk of discourse as though it were all about good guys vs. bad guys. The good guys are human, natural, sincere, and caring, and they speak a natural, lively, down to earth discourse that has lots of voice. The bad guys are institutional, academic, bureaucratic, stuffy, skeptical, and uncaring. They speak a theoretical, professional discourse that is ungrounded in felt human experience and designed to keep people out. At the bottom you are seeing everything in terms of *natural* vs. *unnatural*. But natural is a sentimental fuzzy-minded concept. What you call natural is not natural, it's constructed, it's a convention. Freewriting is just a genre or convention that people learn—like academic discourse or the epic—only sloppier and more personally intrusive. Discourse is always about conventions and about power.

You're probably right. Actually, I prefer goats to sheep. We kept a couple of lovely nubian goats for a number of summers and we milked them morning and evening. I loved them. I've never understood the appeal of sheep. And yes, I am a sucker for seeing complex issues in terms of good guys vs. bad guys. But you pretty much have my number in what you say about natural vs. unnatural. You may want to call my position naive.

Still I defend the term "natural." Surely it's the right word for language that comes to the tongue and mind without effort or planning. I'm not saying that culture doesn't shape what comes naturally to tongue and mind. I'm not saying that the same kind of language will be natural from one person or culture to another. But since we speak long before we write, and most of us speak more than we write, the language that comes most easily to tongue and mind will tend to have features characteristic of speech (though not always). When language is careful and planned, it often sounds different from language that is less planned. Listeners or readers usually hear the planning or effort or lack of ease. It's not surprising that people often remark on language as sounding natural or not.

I'm not saying that natural language is necessarily clear. Nixon was natural in his tapes, but his language was often impenetrable (at least on paper). And I'm not saying that only one style can be natural. Anyone can get so practiced in *any* style (e.g., academic discourse) that they produce it without effort or planning. In such a case, that language is indeed natural, and some readers will feel the ease and naturalness in it—while others will feel it as unnatural since it's so different from what is natural for them.

I'm not even saying that natural language cannot be carefully planned and consciously crafted. But this is a paradoxical formulation that needs explaining. Writers commonly use conscious care and craft to produce language that *sounds* like the language they themselves produce when they relinquish planning, care, or effort. After all it's hard to sound effortless when the thinking and the structure are requiring every ounce of effort and care.

I'm not even saying that natural language is inherently *better* than language that most readers would call highly artificial. I love the high artifice in the syntax and diction of writers like Thucydides, Henry James, Virginia Woolf, and Henry Fowler.

My brief for natural language is limited, but I'll stick by it:

- What makes language good is mostly that it is clear, eloquent, and a good conveyer of good meaning. These qualities have nothing inherent to do with naturalness. But if writers convey meaning clearly and eloquently and make it sound natural *too*, this is an added benefit.
- Natural language is available to everyone. Every human is capable of being enormously eloquent when using the language that comes easily and naturally. Thus, if we are trying to teach people to do good thinking and get it into eloquent writing, it makes sense to help them develop a feel for getting natural language on the page.
- Natural language, because it comes without effort or planning, *often* has a better fit with the thinking it conveys. Of course, the thinking it conveys is often sloppy or minimal. But if we can give people that experience of getting their thinking into writing that fits it—that click that comes when we write something that actually fits what we are trying to say—that experience is *foundational* for learning how to write well. That is, we can go on to help people struggle to improve and complicate their thinking—yet still hang on to the knowledge that they can find written language that comfortably fits this more complex and careful thinking. And when *readers* experience a good fit between language and thinking in a text, they will usually experience the meanings as clearer and more eloquent.

These are not insignificant gains, but I need to be clear that I am not making a simple argument to "shuck off the chains of artificiality." I accept the following blunt dictum: As a writing teacher, I have to try to help my students learn to use discourses that are almost certainly going to be *unnatural* for them—in particular the kinds of academic discourses that their teachers will be looking for. But this blunt dictum actually hides two subtleties that need unpacking.

1. We mustn't jump to conclusions about what teachers are actually looking for. This is an empirical matter and we need more investigation than we now have about the responses and standards of teachers in various realms. In particular, it is helpful to distinguish between what I call "academic discourse" and "school discourse": between the standards academics use when they read work by fellow academics and the standards they use in reading work by students. For students there is good news and bad news here. In some ways, faculty are less demanding of students: they will praise student writing that is simpler and less sophisticated than what they expect from colleagues. But by the same token, they are often more rigid with students than with colleagues—often not accepting adventuresome rhetorical choices from students that they are content to see in academic writing. (How many academics who say "Don't use the first person" expect peers to follow this principle? See Freedman for intriguing research on how teachers marked down students for too much assertiveness.)

2. We can *harness* the use of natural, personal (and private) language in trying to attain the goal of better school discourse—or other discourses that

may feel highly unnatural for students. That is, we have a better chance in pushing students for strong thinking and careful structure if we can invite them not to sweat the language. One less worry. Then when they *have* a draft that is strong in thinking and structure, it's not so hard for them to revise it into good school discourse. In addition, school discourse is often rewarded more highly by teachers if, while conforming to certain rhetorical restrictions, it *also* nevertheless has certain features of natural and personal writing such as the kind of comfortable and easy syntax that fits naturally in the mouth.

One of my goals, then, is to help students get good grades from their other faculty members. In taking this goal, I am agreeing with one of *your* central premises: discourse carries within it the power of society, the sanctions of culture. Yes. But when people in composition and rhetoric talk about "learning the language of power" and "learning academic discourse," they often slide into assuming these two are the same. It strikes me that academic discourse is one of the least powerful discourses in our culture—especially recently. Many academics are strikingly unsuccessful in writing for a larger audience. If we were better at it, we might see less bashing of academics. And when academics want to write for a larger audience or write for government, business, or journalism, their biggest problem is often their academic discourse. When highly successful students take jobs outside the academy, they also usually need to unlearn academic discourse. In academic discourse, better tends to mean longer and more complex, but these qualities are usually vices in the discourse of power. It's my sense that the discourse of power in society is sometimes quite natural and personal.

Up to here, I've been trying to offer naked reasoning. Academic discourse itself has traditionally been characterized as reasoning without special clothing, reasoning without a spin, reasoning that stands on its own two feet. But one of the main theoretical messages in academic discourse itself, these days, is that reasons are never naked. Reasons are always embodied in a human and ideological context. So it strikes me to offer four experiences that were surely formative for my relationship to discourse.

1. I grew up in a comfortable middle class family where my parents cared about good language. But the most powerful rhetorician in the house—in the bedroom next to mine—was Estelle Jones, a woman who never went past third grade and spoke a full, strong, South Carolina black dialect. (This may not be such an untypical linguistic matrix for middle-and upper-class children of my era.) Her speech was the most powerful in the house and she tended to carry the day in any interchange that depended on rhetoric.

2. Throughout my life I've found myself characteristically ineffective in speaking. Not only do I tend to bumble and stumble at the level of syntax, but I also can never even get my thoughts straight. Over and over I have had the experience of trying to explain or persuade people about something that seemed palpably true to me, only to have them not understand me or think my

thinking was foolish or useless. This has been a big incentive for me to use writing. I have had more success speaking my mind on paper.

3. For this reason, however, I vividly notice the occasions when I do manage to be clear and forceful in speech. These are usually occasions of great personal intensity where I somehow blast my thinking and feelings through the interfering static; or occasions (thanks to my writing!) where I find myself speaking to a group of people who think my ideas are dandy and want to hear more of what's on my mind.

4. My first successful communication with the academy was in *Writing Without Teachers*—a book in a decidedly nonacademic discourse. I was not writing to the academy (consciously anyway); I was trying to speak to all humans and trying to use the most universal and human language I could muster. Face it, I was trying to produce what could be called a popular, corny self-help book. And the truth is that I never could have thought and said all the things in there if I'd been trying to write to academics. Even if I *had* been able to think and say it all, my odd message wouldn't have gotten through. I'd already published two essays in *College English* to no particular effect. I can't help concluding that I was heard more by academics because I wrote in the wrong discourse and to a different audience.

If I try to bring the reasoning and the storytelling together, I come up with this. It's hard to be blunt and bald and full of feeling in academic discourse because academics distrust those very qualities. And they should. One of the major and laudable goals of the academy is to *avoid* bald simplification or rhetorical spin. And yet this can be a problem since many students (and many professors!) have trouble *using* their best cognitive, rhetorical, and linguistic powers in academic discourse.

Works Cited

Freedman, Sarah Warshauer. "The Registers of Student and Professional Expository Writing: Influences on Teachers' Responses." *New Directions in Composition Research*. Ed. Richard Beach and Lillian Bridwell. New York: The Guilford P, 1984.

11

Reflections on Academic Discourse

How It Relates to Freshmen and Colleagues

I love what's in academic discourse: learning, intelligence, sophistication—even mere facts and naked summaries of articles and books; I love reasoning, inference, and evidence; I love theory. But I hate academic discourse. What follows is my attempt to work my way out of this dilemma. In doing so I will assume an ostensive definition of academic discourse: it is the discourse that academics use when they publish for other academics. And what characterizes that discourse? This is the question I will pursue here.

As a teacher of freshman writing courses, my problem is this. It is obvious why I should heed the common call to teach my students academic discourse. They will need it for the papers and reports and exams they'll have to write in their various courses throughout their college career. Many or even most of their teachers will expect them to write in the language of the academy. If we don't prepare them for these tasks we'll be shortchanging them—and disappointing our colleagues in other departments. It's no good just saying, "Learn to write what's comfy for you, kiddies," if that puts them behind the eight-ball in their college careers. Discourse carries power. This is especially important for weak or poorly prepared students—particularly students from poorer classes or those who are the first in their families to come to college. Not to help them with academic discourse is simply to leave a power vacuum and thereby reward privileged students who have already learned academic discourse at home or in school—or at least learned the roots or propensity for academic discourse. (Shirley Brice Heath shows how middle-class families instinctively give home training in the skills that teachers want: labeling and defining and so forth. Children from other classes and backgrounds get plenty of language training, but their skills are mistaken by teachers for no skill.) Still, I remain troubled.

This essay was published in 1991 in *College English* 53.2 (Feb): 135–55.

The Need for Nonacademic Writing in
Freshman Writing Courses

I am troubled, first, by the most extreme position—the idea of giving over the freshman writing course entirely to academic discourse. Here are three brief arguments for teaching nonacademic discourse in freshman writing courses. These are not arguments against academic discourse; only for teaching something else in addition.

1. Life is long and college is short. Very few of our students will ever have to write academic discourse after college. The writing that most students will need to do for most of their lives will be for their jobs—and that writing is usually very different from academic discourse. When employers complain that students can't write, they often mean that students have to *unlearn* the academic writing they were rewarded for in college. "[E]ach different 'world of work' constitutes its own discourse community with its own purposes, audiences, and genres. The FDA, for example, produces documents vastly different from those of the air force; lawyers write in genres different from those of accountants" (Matalene vi).

But to put the argument in terms of writing that people have to do is to give in to a deeply unwriterly and pessimistic assumption, held by many students and not a few colleagues, namely that no one would ever write except under compulsion. Why should people assume without discussion that we cannot get students to write by choice? In my view, the best test of a writing course is whether it makes students more likely to use writing in their lives: perhaps to write notes and letters to friends or loved ones; perhaps to write in a diary or to make sense of what's happening in their lives; perhaps to write in a learning journal to figure out a difficult subject they are studying; perhaps to write stories or poems for themselves or for informal circulation or even for serious publication; perhaps to write in the public realm such as letters to the newspaper or broadsides on dormitory walls. I don't rule out the writing of academic discourse by choice, but if we teach only academic discourse we will surely fail at this most important goal of helping students use writing by choice in their lives. I don't succeed with all my students at this goal, but I work at it and I make progress with many. It is not an unreasonable goal.

In a workshop with teachers not long ago I was struck with how angry many teachers got at a piece of student writing. It was not particularly good (it was about falling asleep while writing an assigned essay and waking up on a Greek island with "topless maidens"), but what infuriated these teachers was not really the mediocre quality but that the writer said in a piece of process writing that the piece was easy and fun to write and that he didn't revise it much because most people in his group liked it. I sensed resentment against the most basic impulses that are involved in being a writer: to have fun telling a story and to give pleasure to others. We need to get students to write by choice because no one can learn to write well except by writing a great deal—far more than we can assign and read.

2. I want to argue for one *kind* of nonacademic discourse that is particularly important to teach. I mean discourse that tries to render experience rather than explain it. To render experience is to convey what I see when I look out the window, what it feels like to walk down the street or fall down—to tell what it's like to be me or to live my life. I'm particularly concerned that we help students learn to write language that conveys to others a sense of their experience—or indeed, that mirrors back to themselves a sense of their own experience from a little distance, once it's out there on paper. I'm thinking about autobiographical stories, moments, sketches—perhaps even a piece of fiction or poetry now and again.

I am really asking us to take a larger view of human discourse. As writing teachers our job is to try to pass on the great human accomplishment of written language. Discourse that explains is part of that accomplishment, but discourse that renders is equally great—equally one of the preeminent gifts of human kind. When students leave the university unable to find words to render their experience, they are radically impoverished. We in English recognize the value of rendering experience when we teach reading. That is, most of the texts we teach in English courses are literary pieces that render experience. Yet we hesitate to teach students to write discourse that renders. And if we don't do it, no one else will. For virtually all of the other disciplines ask students to use language only to explain, not to render. It's important to note, by the way, that rendering is not just an "affective" matter—what something "feels" like. Discourse that renders asks for careful observation and often yields important new "cognitive" insights such as helping us see an exception or contradiction to some principle we thought we believed. (For example, a rendering of an evening's struggle with writing might well force us to adjust some dearly loved theoretical principle about the writing process.)

3. We need nonacademic discourse *even* for the sake of helping students produce good academic discourse—academic language that reflects sound understanding of what they are studying in disciplinary courses. That is, many students can repeat and explain a principle in, say, physics or economics in the academic discourse of the textbook but cannot simply tell a story of what is going on in the room or country around them on account of that principle—or what the room or country would look like if that principle were different. The use of academic discourse often masks a lack of genuine understanding. When students write about something only in the language of the textbook or the discipline, they often distance or insulate themselves from experiencing or really internalizing the concepts they are allegedly learning. Often the best test of whether a student understands something is if she can translate it *out* of the discourse of the textbook and the discipline into everyday, experiential, anecdotal terms.

Thus, although we may be unsatisfied unless students can write about what they are learning in the professional discourse of the field—majors, anyway—we should be equally unsatisfied unless they can write about it *not* using the lingo of the discipline. (Vygotsky and Bakhtin make this same point: Vygotsky, when he describes the need for what he calls "scientific" or "formal" concepts to become intertwined in the child's mind with "everyday" or experienced concepts [82ff]; Bakhtin, when he explores the process by which people transform "the externally authoritative word" into the "internally persuasive word" ["Discourse and the Novel" 36ff.].) I'm all for students being able to write academic discourse, but it bothers me when theorists argue that someone doesn't know a field unless she can talk about it in the discourse professionals use among themselves. There are plenty of instances of people who know a lot about engines or writing but don't know the professional discourse of engineering or composition. There's something self-serving about defining people as ignorant unless they are like us. (Besides, much of the talk about students learning academic discourse in their disciplinary courses seems to assume those students are majoring in that subject. But most students are not majors in most courses they take. For example, most students in English courses are nonmajors who never take more than one or two English courses in their career. Do we really expect them to write the academic discourse of English? If so, we must mean something peculiar by "academic discourse.")

Let me repeat that I've made no negative arguments against teaching academic discourse, only positive arguments for teaching something else in addition. The case for teaching academic discourse is usually an argument from practicality, and I insist that it's just as practical to teach other kinds of discourse—given the students' entire lives and even the needs of good academic discourse.

Trying to Make the Problem Go Away

The fact is that we can't teach "academic discourse:" there's no such thing to teach. Biologists don't write like historians. This is not news. Pat Bizzell and Joe Harris, among others, write thoughtfully about the differences among communities of discourse. Linda Flower writes: "there is no Platonic entity called 'academic discourse' which one can define and master" (3). So although some students may need to write like historians or biologists, few of us in English can teach them to do so. To write like a historian or biologist involves not just lingo but doing history or biology—which involves knowing history and biology in ways we do not. In short, we are not qualified to teach most kinds of academic discourse.

But I want to push this further. Suppose we made an empirical study of the nature of discourse in English studies. Think of the differences we'd find—the different discourses in our field:

- The bulldozer tradition of high Germanic scholarship. Give no prominence to your own ideas. Emphasize the collecting and integrating of the ideas and conclusions of others. Of if you want to say something, avoid saying it until you have demonstrated that you have summarized and shown the shortcomings of previous works in the literature. Cite everything—sometimes even your own ideas under the guise of someone else's. (Not such an alien practice, after all: it is a commonplace among journalists that the only way to get your article to say what you want it to say is to quote someone saying it.)

- The genial slightly talky British tradition—which also connects with the rhetorical tradition (e.g., work by people like C. S. Lewis and Wayne Booth). This tradition gives us discourse that is fully scholarly and professional, but it is nevertheless likely to talk to the reader—sometimes even make anecdotal digressions or personal asides. Citations and references tend to be kept to a minimum. We can deride this as a tradition of privilege and authority ("Gentlemen don't cite everything. If you don't recognize the tacit footnotes you're not one of us"), but it is also the tradition of the amateur that welcomes the outsider. (Notice the structural implications that have gotten attached to these two traditions. Most of my teachers in college and graduate school wanted opening and closing paragraphs that provided readers a definite map of what my essay would be about and a definite summary of what it concluded: the voice of the German tradition says "Announce at the border what you have to declare." But I had other teachers who spoke for the British tradition and counted such signposting as a weakness in writing. I can still hear one of them: "Don't talk about what you're going to do, just do it. Just start with the point that belongs first and readers won't need an introduction." The same for transitions: "If you put your points in the right order, they won't *need* explanatory connections or transitions; they'll *follow*. Just think straight.")
- Poststructuralist, continental discourse: allusive, gamesome—dark and deconstructive. Again few footnotes, little help to those who haven't already read what they are alluding to.
- German Critical or Marxist discourse that is heavy on abstraction, special diction and terminology—and very consciously ideological. Practitioners would insist that anything less ideological is a cop-out.
- Psychoanalytic criticism uses its own linguistic and intellectual practices. When *College English* devoted two issues to psychoanalytic criticism in 1987, I heard colleagues complain, "These people write a completely separate language."
- The field of composition is particularly diverse. Some of its discourse is unashamedly quantitative and "social science." Imagine setting yourself the goal of publishing in *Research in the Teaching of English, College Composition and Communication,* and *PRE/TEXT:* you would need three different discourses. Steve North counts seven discourse communities in composition, involving not just different lingos but ways of knowing.
- I think of two Creoles: the Chicago Aristotelian dialect of R. S. Crane and fellows, and the New York intelligentsia dialect of Lionel Trilling and Irving Howe and fellows.
- Notice the subtle difference between the discourse of people who are established in the profession and those who are not—particularly those without tenure. Certain liberties, risks, tones, and stances are taken by established insiders that are not usually taken by the unannealed. Discourse is power.
- Notice finally the pedagogically crucial distinction between how academics

write to each other and how they have come to expect students to write to them as teachers. We see here the ubiquitous authority dimension of discourse. Students must write "up" to teachers who have authority over them—often being assigned to write to experts about a subject they are just struggling to learn. In contrast, academics write "across" to fellow academics—usually explaining what they have worked out to readers who don't know it. (Sarah Freedman did an interesting piece of research in which she had teachers respond to essays by students—only some of the essays were actually written by teachers or professionals. One of her findings was that teachers were often bothered by the writing of the nonstudents—the "grown-ups" as it were—because it wasn't sufficiently deferential.)

- Suppose a student in a literature course asks me whether it's appropriate to bring in her feelings or some event from her personal life as part of the data for the interpretation of a text. There is no clear answer in English: it is appropriate in psychoanalytic and reader response criticism and certain kinds of feminist criticism—but not in many other literary discourses. What about data from the author's life and opinions? Again, for some English courses it's appropriate, for others not. Suppose a student argues against a critic's position by bringing in that critic's class, gender, politics, or sexual affiliations—or professional training. Some English professors call this out of bounds, others do not.

Thus, I can't tell my students whether academic discourse in English means using lots of structural signposts or leaving them out, bringing in their feelings and personal reactions or leaving them out, giving evidence from the poet's life for interpretations or leaving that out, referring to the class, gender, and school of other interpreters or leaving that out—nor finally even what kind of footnotes to use. Even if I restrict myself to composition studies, I can't tell them whether academic discourse means quantitative or qualitative research or philosophical reflection. In short, it's crazy to talk about academic discourse as one thing.

But It Won't Go Away

Not only can't I stop myself from talking about academic discourse in the singular, but I also can't help looking for an academic discourse I could teach in freshman writing courses. Couldn't there be some larger entity or category—academic writing in general—a generic Stop and Shop brand of academic discourse that lies beneath all those different trade names? (I often buy generic.) A certain deep structure or freeze-dried essence of academic discourse that is more universal than what we've looked at so far? A stance or a way of relating to our material that reaches across the differences between disciplines?

What would seem central to such a conception of academic discourse is the giving of reasons and evidence rather than just opinions, feelings, experiences: being clear about claims and assertions rather than just implying or insinuating; getting thinking to stand on its own two feet rather than leaning on the authority of who advances it or the fit with who hears it. In describing academic discourse in this general way, surely I am describing a major goal of literacy, broadly defined. Are we not engaged in schools and colleges in trying to teach students to produce reasons and evidence which hold up on their own rather than just in terms of the tastes or prejudices of readers or how attractively they are packaged?

Thus the conventions of academic discourse may seem difficult or ungainly, but they reflect the diligence needed to step outside one's own narrow vision—they are the conventions of a certain impersonality and detachment all working toward this large and important goal of separating feeling, personality, opinion, and fashion from what is essential: clear positions, arguments, and evidence (see Bartholomae 155; Olson 110). And so this idea of a single general intellectual goal behind the variety of different academic discourses is attractive.

But the very appeal of academic discourse as I have just described it tends to rest on the assumption that we can separate the ideas and reasons and arguments from the person who holds them; that there are such things as unheld opinions—assertions that exist uninfluenced by who says them and who hears them—positions not influenced by one's feelings, class, race, gender, sexual orientation, historical position, etc.—thinking that "stands on its own two feet." In the end, behind this conception of academic discourse in general is a bias toward objectivity or foundationalism—a bias which many of us have come to resist on the basis of work by a host of thinkers from Polanyi to Fish.

Most academics, certainly in English and composition, are more sympathetic to a contrasting *rhetorical* bias—a preference for seeing language in terms of speech acts: discourse is always talking to someone—trying to have an impact on someone. Grammar books and logic books may be full of disembodied propositions that we can think of in terms of disinterested truth value—messages without senders and receivers—but *discourse* as used by human beings is always interested, always located in a person speaking and an audience listening. We've learned that many of our difficulties and disputes and confusions come from falling into assuming that discourse is detached, nonrhetorical, and not a speech act—learned, as Bizzell says, that "an absolute standard for the judgment of truth can never be found, precisely because the individual mind can never transcend personal emotions, social circumstances, and historical conditions" (40).

In short, the very thing that is attractive and appealing about academic discourse is inherently problematic and perplexing. It tries to peel away from messages the evidence of how those messages are situated as the center of personal, political, or cultural interest; its conventions tend toward the sound of reasonable, disinterested, perhaps even objective (shall I say it?) men.

Am I saying that people who write academic discourse pretend to be objective or assume that there are absolute standards for truth? Of course not. (Though some do—such as this professor of physics: "Scientific communication is faceless and passionless by design. Data and conclusions stand bare and unadorned, and can be evaluated for what they are without prejudice or emotion. This kind of impersonal communication has helped science achieve the status of public knowledge, a coinage of truth with international currency. It's like Sgt. Joe Friday used to say: 'The facts, Ma'am, just the facts'" [Raymo 26].) Yet when people use academic discourse they are using a medium whose *conventions* tend to imply disinterested impersonality and detachment— a medium that is thus out of sync with their intellectual stance—a bias toward messages without senders and receivers. I wonder if this mismatch doesn't help explain why the discourse we see in academic journals is so often ungainly or uncomfortable and not infrequently tangled.

Let me illustrate these conventions of detachment by looking at three violations of academic discourse that naive students sometimes commit. First, they overuse the first person, for example, "I'm only saying what I think and feel—this is just my opinion." Second, naive students are liable to use the second person too much and too pointedly, sometimes even speaking directly to us as particular reader ("As you stressed to us Tuesday in class. . . ."). Third, they are apt to refer to Hemingway as "Ernest." What interests me is how these violations *highlight* what the conventions of academic discourse usually disguise: that discourse is coming from a subject with personal interests, concerns, and uncertainties (even professional academics sometimes feel uncertain); that discourse is directed to a reader who is also situated in her subjectivity; and that discourse is about an author who is also asserted to be a person like the writer. (Notice yet another divergence among academic discourses in English: academic biographers get to call Hemingway "Ernest.")

But of course if pure objectivity is discredited, it doesn't mean we must embrace pure subjectivity and bias: "Hooray! I've read Kuhn and Fish and there's only subjectivity. Everyone has a bias, so I don't have to try to interrogate my own." Good academic discourse doesn't pretend to pure objectivity, yet it also avoids mere subjectivity. It presents clear claims, reasons, and evidence—not in a pretense of pure, timeless, Platonic dialectic but in the context of arguments that have been or might be made in reply. Most academics reflect in their writing and teaching a belief that passionate commitment is permissible, perhaps even desirable—so long as it is balanced by awareness that it is a passionate position, what the stakes are, how others might argue otherwise. In short, as academics we don't pretend to write as God from an objective or universal spot of ground immune from history and feelings; nevertheless, we feel it's possible to have a *bit* of detachment with our left eye as it were—a certain part of one's mind that flies up to the seventh sphere with Troilus and sees, "Ah yes, I'm really taking a strong position here—and I've got a big personal stake in this."

This intellectual stance transforms the dichotomy ("killer dichotomies" Ann Berthoff calls them) between subjective and objective. That is, the very act of acknowledging one's situatedness and personal stake invites, and is itself a movement toward, enlargement of view—not that it's a guarantee. Conversely, if someone pretends to be disinterested and objective, she invites smallness of view because she doesn't locate her interest in a larger picture: she tempts herself into believing that her view *is* the larger picture.

Here then, finally, is a definition of generic academic discourse that sounds right. It's essentially a rhetorical definition: giving reasons and evidence, yes, but doing so as a person speaking with acknowledged interests to others— whose interest and position one acknowledges and tries to understand. I'm for this. I try to teach it. I want my students to have it.

But there is a problem. Though this intellectual stance is characteristic of academic discourse at its best, it is also characteristic of much nonacademic discourse—such as that produced by writers like Montaigne, Woolf, Orwell, Paul Goodman, even William Gass or Joan Didion. If I get my students to achieve this admirable stance in their writing, they still might not be producing what most professors would call academic discourse or look for in assigned essays. Indeed, have we not all sometimes sent and received letters that were written even in personal expressive discourse which nevertheless embodied this intellectual stance: in which we made claims, gave reasons and evidence, acknowledged our position—and just as effectively organized our discourse and set our arguments within the context of others who have written on the matter—without writing as we tend to write in our professional publications? (See *PRE/TEXT* 11.1 & 2 [1990] for a collection of personal or expressive writing engaged in the work of academic discourse.) In short, I think I've described a prominent feature of *good writing*—so of course it characterizes good academic writing. It simply doesn't distinguish academic writing from nonacademic writing.

There are other attractive definitions of academic discourse which lead to the same dilemma. Flower writes: "The goals of self-directed critical inquiry, of using writing to think through genuine problems and issues, and of writing to an imagined community of peers with a personal rhetorical purpose— these distinguish academic writing . . ." (28). She further specifies two common "practices" which "stand as critical features of academic discourse which often limit entry and full participation in the academic community. . . . (1) integrating information from sources with one's own knowledge and (2) interpreting one's reading/adapting one's writing for a purpose" (3). Susan Peck MacDonald writes: "[I]t is problem-solving activity that generates all academic writing" (316). (It is interesting to see MacDonald rather than Flower focus on "problem solving," but a moment's thought explains the apparent paradox: Flower "uses up" problem solving by characterizing *all* writing as problem solving.) These too are characteristic features of good academic discourse, but they are no more useful than my earlier definition for distinguishing academic discourse from nonacademic discourse. In short, we must beware of talking as though the academy has a monopoly on a sound intellectual stance toward one's material and one's readers.

Maybe it's not, then, the intellectual stance or task that distinguishes academic discourse but certain stylistic or mechanical conventions—not the deep structure but certain surface features.

Mannerisms: Stylistic Conventions or Surface Features of Academic Discourse

Just as it was interesting to dig for some common or generic intellectual practices behind the variations in different discourses, let me now try to dig for some common or generic surface features of academic discourse. An example will help: a paragraph from James Berlin's essay. "Contemporary Composition: The Major Pedagogical Theories."

> My reasons for presenting this analysis are not altogether disinterested. I am convinced that the pedagogical approach of the New Rhetoricians is the most intelligent and most practical alternative available, serving in every way the best interests of our students. I am also concerned, however, that writing teachers become more aware of the full significance of their pedagogical strategies. Not doing so can have disastrous consequences, ranging from momentarily confusing students to sending them away with faulty and even harmful information. The dismay students display about writing is, I am convinced, at least occasionally the result of teachers unconsciously offering contradictory advice about composing—guidance grounded in assumptions that simply do not square with each other. More important, as I have already indicated and as I plan to explain in detail later on, in teaching writing we are tacitly teaching a version of reality and the student's place and mode of operation in it. Yet many teachers (and I suspect most) look upon their vocations as the imparting of a largely mechanical skill, important only because it serves students in getting them through school and in advancing them in their professions. This essay will argue that writing teachers are perforce given a responsibility that far exceeds this merely instrumental task. (766)

Berlin writes a clean, direct prose. That is, I could have chosen a sentence like this one from the currently fashionable theory laden tradition:

> Now, literary hypospace may be defined as the lexical space which, having been collapsed to exclude almost all referentiality but that generated by verbal echoes alone, glows like an isotope with a half-life of meaning co-extensive with its power to turn its tropes into allotropes or "transformational" (in the Chomskyan sense) nodes, capable of liberating the "deep structures" of metaphoricity from buried layers of intertextuality. (Rother 83)

Or this sentence from R. S. Crane and the venerable Chicago Aristotelian tradition:

> [A] poet does not write poetry but individual poems. And these are inevitably, as finished wholes, instances of one or another poetic kind, differentiated not by any necessities of the linguistic instrument of poetry but primarily by the nature of the poet's conception, as finally embodied in his poem, of a particular form to be achieved through the representation, in

speech used dramatically or otherwise, of some distinctive state of feeling, or moral choice, or action, complete in itself and productive of a certain emotion or complex of emotions in the reader. (96)

It's because Berlin's prose is open and clear that I look to it for some general or common features of the academic style. Berlin has just named what he conceives as the four "dominant theories" or approaches to composition and announced his plans to explore each in detail in his essay. Thus in this early paragraph he is "mapping" or "signposting" for the reader: explaining what he is going to do and laying out the structure. Even though there is a wide range of custom as to the degree of signposting in different academic discourses, signposting is probably the most general or common textual convention of academic discourse. Thus the last sentence of his paragraph—introducing his thesis near the start of his essay—is particularly conventional.

It is the convention of explicitness. That is, only nonacademic discourse is allowed to merely imply what it is saying. A nonacademic piece can achieve marvelous thinking and yet not really work it out explicitly; indeed the effectiveness of such a piece may derive from having the principal claim *lurk* rather than announce itself. Fine. But in academic writing it is a convention always to say what you are saying. Thus there is a grain of truth in the old perverse chestnut of advice: "First say what you're going to say, then say it, then say what you've already said." Academic discourse is business, not pleasure (and so business writing asks for even more explicit signposting than most academic writing).

But there is also a convention of inexplicitness in academic discourse. Look at the first sentence of Berlin's paragraph: "My reasons for presenting this analysis are not altogether disinterested." He is not using this mock-elegant double negative to hide what he is saying, yet the conventions or voice of academic discourse have led him to use a double negative rather than come out and say positively what he is actually saying, namely, "I have a stake in this analysis." And those same academic conventions have led him to write a sentence about reasons with the verb "to be" rather than a sentence about a person with an active verb ("My reasons are not altogether disinterested" rather than, "I have a stake"). Perhaps some readers hear a tone of quiet irony in his phrase, "not altogether disinterested," but I don't hear him actually being ironic; he's just falling into a syntactic commonplace of academic discourse, the double negative combined with understatement. For after this sentence he virtually comes out and says (using a number of "I"s), that his analysis of composition into four theories is designed to show why his theory is best. Indeed, the subtext of the whole article is a celebration of the idea that all discourse is interested or biased—by definition—and that an "altogether disinterested" position is impossible. Yet in an essay that never hides its "I" and in which Berlin takes full responsibility for his interested position, discourse has led him to conclude the paragraph with a sentence about the *essay* arguing rather than about him arguing. It seems to me, then, that in the convention or voice of his academic discourse, there are locutions left over from an intellectual stance of disinterested objectivity: the ideal of conclusions issuing "perforce" from reasons and arguments rather than from the play of interested positions. Somewhere in his book, *Works and Lives,* Clifford Geertz makes a distinction between "author-saturated" and "author-evacuated" prose. The stylistic conventions of academic discourse are the conventions of author-evacuated prose.

Double negatives and irony are both ways of saying something without saying it. I'm not calling Berlin evasive here. Rather I'm trying to highlight the interesting fact that in an extremely nonevasive essay, his use of academic discourse led him into a locution that goes through the motions of being evasive—and a locution whose verbal conventions carry some wisps of former irony. This may sound like a paradox—conventions of both explicitness and inexplicitness—but it is not. Academic discourse tries to be direct about the "position"—the argument and reasons and claim. Yet it tends to be shy, indirect, or even evasive about the texture of feelings or attitude that lie behind that position.

Because Berlin's prose is not pretentious or obscure, it illustrates all the more clearly that academic discourse also leads to a somewhat formal language. I'm not talking about technical terms that are necessary for technical concepts; I'm talking about a tendency simply to avoid the everyday or common or popular in language. For example, academic discourse leads Berlin in just one paragraph to say "full significance of their pedagogical strategies" rather than "implications of how they teach"; "mode of operation" rather than "how they act." It leads to words and phrases like "imparting of a largely mechanical skill," "the dismay students display," "perforce," "merely instrumental task," "far exceeds." This is not difficult or convoluted language by any means; merely language that avoids the ordinary more than he probably would do if he were writing the same thoughts in a memo to the same teachers he is addressing with this article—or in *Harpers* or *Hudson Review.*

Berlin uses a special term, "epistemic," as central to this essay. One might call it a technical term that is necessary to the content (you can't talk about penicillin without the word "penicillin"). But (and colleagues argue with me about this) I don't think "epistemic" really permits him to say anything he couldn't say just as well without it—using "knowledge" and other such words. Admittedly, it is the mildest of jargon these days and its use can be validly translated as follows: "A bunch of us have been reading Foucault and talking to each other and we simply want to continue to use a word that has become central in our conversation." But through my experience of teaching this essay to classroom teachers (the very audience that Berlin says he wants to reach), I have seen another valid translation: "I'm not interested in talking to people who are not already part of this conversation."

Indeed, there is what I would call a certain rubber-gloved quality to the voice and register typical of most academic discourses—not just author-evacuated but also showing a kind of reluctance to touch one's meanings with one's naked fingers. Here, by way of personal illustration, are some examples of changes made by editors of academic journals working on manuscripts of mine that were already accepted for publication. The changes are interesting for being so trivial: that is, there is no reason for them except to add a touch of distance and avoid the taint of the ordinary:

- *who has a strong sense of* changed to *who retains a deep conviction that*
- *always comes with* changed to *is always accompanied by*
- *when I dropped out of graduate school* changed to *when I interrupted my graduate education*
- *I started out just writing to aid my memory* changed to *At first I wanted only to aid my memory*
- [About a teacher I am interviewing and quoting] *he sometimes talks about students as though he doesn't give a damn about them* changed to . . . *as if they meant nothing to him*

I chose Berlin for my analysis because we can see academic discourse leading him into locutions of indirectness and detachment, even vestigial objectivity—when he is clearly taking the opposite intellectual stance. But I also chose Berlin because I want to piggy-back on his main point: "in teaching writing we are tacitly teaching a version of reality and the student's place and mode of operation in it." I agree, but I want to state an obvious corollary: in *using a discourse* we are also tacitly teaching a version of reality and the student's place and mode of operation in it. In particular, we are affirming a set of social and authority relations. Here are four things that I think are taught by the surface mannerisms or stylistic conventions of academic discourse:

1. A version of reality. The convention of explicitness and straightforward organization in academic discourse teaches that we can figure out what we really mean and get enough control over language to actually say it—directly and clearly. I confess I more or less believe this and think it's a good convention to teach. Of course, I also acknowledge what has come to be called the deconstructive view of language and reality, namely, that we can never get complete control over language, that there will always be eddies of subversive meaning and wisps of contrary implication in anything we write, no matter how clear and direct we make it, so that a New Critic or deconstructor can always find gaps *(aporiae)* in what looks straightforward. Indeed, as I insisted in my opening section, we should also try to teach the opposite convention of inexplicitness—teach people to relinquish control over language so that it leads where we never expected it to go, says things we didn't think we had in mind. I am talking about consciously trying to unleash the subversive forces of language (for example in freewriting) instead of trying to keep them in check. This subversive kind of writing is equally valuable and leads to an equally important view of reality. Nevertheless, the convention of explicitness implied in academic discourse is something I affirm and want to teach.

2. Academic discourse also teaches a set of social and authority relations: to talk to each other as professionals in such a way as to exclude ordinary people. That is, in the academic convention of using more formal language and longer and more complex sentences with more subordinate clauses (for example, calling that kind of language "the deployment of hypotaxis rather than

parataxis"), academics are professing that they are professionals who do not invite conversation with nonprofessionals or ordinary people. Many groups act this way. Doctors don't say "thumbbone," and the medical profession went out of its way to mistranslate Freud's *ich, ueber ich* and *es* into *ego, super ego,* and *id*—rather than into the *I, over I,* and *it* that Freud clearly intended with his German (Bettelheim 49–62). It may be common for groups to try to prove that they are professional by means of this kind of exclusionary language, but I wonder if we really want to teach this discourse-stance once we notice the messages it sends: "We don't want to talk to you or hear from you unless you use our language." (Ostensibly the goal is to exclude the hoi polloi, but perhaps there is also some fear of intellectual nonacademics who may be more thoughtful and learned.) Howard Becker is a respected sociologist who argues that there is no need for jargon and exclusionary discourse even in that field. He describes a graduate seminar engaged in revising and untangling someone's essay, where a student suddenly blurts: "Gee . . . when you say it this way, it looks like something anybody could say." Becker's comment: "You bet" (7).

3. I often hear behind the stylistic and textual conventions of academic discourse a note of insecurity or anxiety. Students may deal with their insecurity by saying, "This is just my opinion. . . . Everyone is entitled to their own opinion" and so on. But having led many workshops for students and faculty members, I've noticed that faculty members are usually *more* anxious than students about sharing their writing with each other. Of course, faculty members have greater reason for anxiety: the standards are higher, the stakes are higher, and they treat each other more badly than they treat students. It turns out that the voice and stylistic conventions of academic discourse serve extremely well to cover this understandable anxiety. Think about how we talk when we're nervous: our voice tends to sound more flat, gravelly, monotone, and evacuated. We tend to "cover" ourselves by speaking with more passives, more formal language, more technical vocabulary. We often discover that we sound more pompous than we intended. Bakhtin ("Discourse in Life") explores how meaning is carried by intonation and how our speech tends to lose intonation and thus meaning when we feel unsafe. Even in Berlin's fairly direct language, I hear that characteristically flat tone with little intonation. Not, probably, that he was anxious, but that he availed himself of stylistic conventions that avoid intonation and take a somewhat guarded stance.

4. Finally, I sometimes see in the stylistic conventions of academic discourse an element of display. Despite the lack of intonation, there is often a slight effect of trying to impress or show off (though I don't see this in Berlin). That is, even though academics can write as peers and professionals to colleagues, it is helpful to notice how even grown up, full-fledged academics are sometimes so enmeshed in the rhetorical context of school discourse that they keep on writing as though they are performing for teachers with authority over them. Many academics have never written except to a teacher. We may be three thousand miles away, tenured, and middle-aged, but we are often still writing about the same field we wrote our dissertations on and writing to the

very same teachers we had to impress in order to get tenure. Think about the stylistic stratagems of bright, intellectually excited, upperclass majors who grow up to be professors: How do they deal with that school situation of having to write "up" to readers with more knowledge and more authority—and needing to distinguish themselves from their peers? I believe that the conventions of academic discourse—voice, register, tone, diction, syntax, and mannerisms—often still carry vestigial traces of this authority transaction of trying to show off or impress those who have authority over us and to distinguish ourselves from our peers.

Really, of course, I'm talking about *ethos:* How do academics create authority and credibility when they write to each other? William Stafford thinks we get off easy on this score compared to poets:

> If you were a scientist, if you were an explorer who had been to the moon, if you were a knowing witness about the content being presented—you could put a draft on your hearer's or reader's belief. Whatever you said would have the force of that accumulated background of information; and any mumbles, mistakes, dithering, could be forgiven as not directly related to the authority you were offering. But a poet—whatever you are saying, and however you are saying it, the only authority you have builds from the immediate performance, or it does not build. The moon you are describing is the one you are creating. From the very beginning of your utterance you are creating your own authority. (62–63)

As academics, that is, we have various aids to authority. The most obvious one is to take a ride on the authority of others—and so (naming, finally, the most conspicuous stylistic convention in the genre) academics use footnotes and quote important figures. What we write is not just a neat idea we had that we send out to be judged on its own merits; it builds on Aristotle and echoes Foucault. And our discourse conventions teach us to be learned not only in our quotations and citations but also in the other linguistic mannerisms we use. And so—though we may be modest, open, and democratic as persons—the price we pay for a voice of authority is a style that excludes ordinary readers and often makes us sound like an insecure or guarded person showing off.

Implications for Teaching Freshman Writing

I hope I am not too unkind in my reading of the stylistic conventions of academic discourse, but it helps me understand that I can happily devote a large proportion of my freshman writing activity to the admirable larger intellectual tasks like giving good reasons and evidence yet doing so in a rhetorical fashion which acknowledges an interested position and tries to acknowledge and understand the position of others. (Also Flower's "self-directed critical inquiry . . . to an imagined community of peers" [28]; or MacDonald's "problem-solving.") These are the kinds of intellectual practices I want to teach—and in fact already do. But now I can continue to work on them and not feel guilty or defensive about neglecting academic discourse for merely "sensible" writing. Indeed, my work on these goals should be slightly transformed by my knowledge that in pursuing them I *am* working on academic discourse—which is only one kind of discourse and that, as Berlin implies, it involves a particular reading of the world, and as Bizzell insists, there are "personal, social, and historical interests in academic discourse." And as I see better that these admittedly sensible intellectual tasks are only some among many, I feel more secure in my commitment to spend a significant portion of the course emphasizing nonacademic discourse with other intellectual tasks— discourse that renders rather than discourse that explains.

I want to emphasize here, however, that my reason for isolating the stylistic mannerisms and giving less attention to them is not just a matter of personal distaste. Serious pedagogical consequences are at stake. The intellectual tasks of academic discourse are significantly easier for students to learn when separated from its linguistic and stylistic conventions. That is, it is not alienating for almost any students to be asked to learn to engage in the demanding intellectual tasks of clarifying claims and giving reasons and so forth (however difficult they may be), but it is definitely alienating for many students to be asked to take on the voice, register, tone, and diction of most academic discourse. If we have to learn a new intellectual stance or take on difficult intellectual goals, we'll probably have better luck if we don't at the same time have to do it in a new language and style and voice. (Teachers of English as a second language have learned that students do better on difficult school tasks if they can use the language they find comfortable.)

And as for those students who are sophisticated enough to take on the voice of academic discourse without much trouble, many of them get seduced or preoccupied with that surface dimension and learn only to mimic it while still failing to engage fully the intellectual task. Putting it crassly, students can do academic work even in street language—and indeed using the vernacular helps show whether the student is doing careful intellectual work or just using academic jive.

Besides, learning new intellectual practices is not just a matter of practicing them; it is also a matter of thinking and talking about one's practice. Or, speaking academically, students need metacognition and metadiscourse to help them understand just what these new intellectual practices are that they are being asked to learn. Toward this end, many teachers make heavy use of "process writing," in which students try to describe and analyze what they have written and how they went about writing it (see Elbow and Belanoff).

But everybody does better at metacognition and metadiscourse if he or she can use ordinary language. Flower provides intriguing evidence for this point. She starts with her finding that "students often demonstrated the underlying cognitive abilities to analyze, synthesize, or reconceptualize that would support these high potential strategies, . . . [yet] such strategies do not appear to be live options in their repertoire. Why?" (7). She goes on to note that "metacognition could play a large role in helping students to learn and engage in new types of discourse" (8). Her essay suggests that her research process itself is probably one of the best ways to produce this meta-awareness and task awareness in students. That is, she had the students produce speak-aloud protocols of their thinking and writing, then look at those protocols, and then discuss some of them in class. Here are a couple of examples of metadiscourse or process writing that students had a chance to discuss:

> So anyway. . . . So I wrote five or six pages on nothing, but I included the words "African nationalism" in there once in a while. I thought, why this is just like high school. I can get away with doing this. I got the paper back, and it was a C minus or a C or something like that. It said "no content." And I was introduced to the world of college writing. (9)

> I started with "There are several theories as to the most efficient strategies concerning time management." Which is really bad—And I wrote like a page of this. I just stopped and I went: This is just so bad—and I just said, like—I have to take this totally from my own point of view. (PAUSE) *But first I have to get a point of view.* (12)

Flower doesn't make this point, but it seems to me that the students probably wouldn't think so clearly and frankly about their own thinking and discourse if they weren't using ordinary language. The vernacular helps them talk turkey.

The intellectual practices of academic discourse are not only more appealing to me than its stylistic conventions, they are also more useful. That is, even though there may be differences between what counts as evidence and valid reasoning in various disciplines and even subdisciplines, the larger intellectual activities we've focused on are useful in most academic disciplines—and of course in much nonacademic writing, too. The stylistic conventions, on the other hand, seem more local and variable—and in my view carry problematic intellectual and social implications. No one seems to defend the stylistic conventions themselves—merely the pragmatic need for them. I find many academics dislike them but feel guilty and furtive about it. Richard Rorty put it bluntly in an interview: "I think that America has made itself a bit ridiculous in the international academic world by developing distinctive disciplinary jargon. It's the last thing we want to inculcate in the freshmen" (7). Finally, I suspect students can learn the surface features of academic style better if they have first made good progress with the underlying intellectual practices. When students are really succeeding in doing a meaty academic task, then the surface stylistic features are more likely to be integral and organic rather than merely an empty game or mimicry.

What specific teaching practices does this analysis suggest? I've tried these:

- Ask students for a midprocess draft that summarizes something (for example, a piece of reading, a difficult principle from another course, the point of view of a classmate, or a discussion): pure summary, simply trying to get it right and clear—as it were for God. Then ask them for a major revision so that the material is not just summarized but rather interpreted and transformed and used in the process of creating a sustained piece of thinking of their own—and for a real human audience. Ask also for process writing with each piece and spend some class time afterward discussing the differences between the two intellectual tasks.

- Ask students for a piece of writing that renders something from experience. The test of success is whether it makes readers experience what they're talking about. Then ask them for a different piece of writing that is built from that writing—an essay that figures out or explains some issue or solves a conceptual (rather than personal) problem. I don't ask them to suppress their own experience for this piece, but to keep it from being the focus: the focus should be the figuring out or the solving. The test of success for this piece is whether it does the conceptual job. Again, ask for process writing with each piece of writing and then discuss in class the differences between the two intellectual tasks.

- Ask students to write a midprocess draft of an essay, and then for the next week's assignment ask them to make two revisions of the same draft: one in which they try to be completely objective and detached, the other in which they acknowledge their point of view, interest, bias—and figure out how to handle the rhetorical problems. Again, process writing with each piece and class discussion afterward emphasizing the differences between the two intellectual tasks. This system also speaks to another concern: how to get students to do substantive rather than perfunctory revising—how to insist that revisions be genuinely different, even if not necessarily better.

As for those problematic stylistic conventions of academic discourse: my analysis helps me feel a little better about neglecting them, but I will continue to spend a bit of time on them in my course. The obvious approach would be to describe these stylistic features formally or as a genre. But a form or genre is always an artificial construct that represents a compromise among the actual practices of live writers. If our goal is to tell students what stylistic features are characteristic of the writing in a given discipline, no answer will fit all the particular teachers they will meet—and the answers will be even more out of whack if we are talking about the discourse teachers actually want from students on assignments, because those practices differ even more widely.

- To help students think about style and voice not as generic or formal matters but as audience matters, I use a variation on the process I just described: asking for two revisions of the same midprocess draft, perhaps one for me as teacher and the other for casual friends; or one for people who know a lot about the topic and the other for readers who don't; or one for adults and the other for children; or one for a school newspaper and the other for a teacher.

- Once in the semester I ask for a paper that explains or discusses something students are studying in another course—and again two revisions. One version is for us in this course, considered as amateurs; the other version is for students and the teacher in the other course, considered as professionals. I ask the students to try out both drafts on us and on some students in the other course—and if possible on the teacher in the other course. A rhetorical and empirical approach dictates these procedures, a way of learning by interacting with readers and seeing how they react, rather than by studying forms or genres of discourse.

- I also like to get a teacher from another discipline to visit my class and distribute copies of a couple of essays that she has assigned and graded and to talk about them. I ask her to tell what kind of assignments and tasks she gives, what she is looking for, and especially to talk in some frank detail about how she reads and reacts to student writing. I try to get this colleague to give some movies of her mind as she reads—in effect, an informal speak-aloud protocol of her reading. And there are two issues I bring up if she doesn't do so: How does she react when she finds a vernacular or nonacademic voice in student writing? And does she assign any nonacademic discourse in her course (for example, journal writing or stories or letters or newspaper articles about what they are studying)? I want students to hear how this teacher from another discipline reacts to these issues. I also try to get her to speculate about what her colleagues would say on all these matters.

- In effect, I'm talking about doing a bit of informal ethnography, and this makes me realize that I am the most convenient ethnographic subject. That is, in recent years I have often found myself giving my reactions to students on their papers in a more reflective way: noticing myself as a member of the profession and as an individual and trying to help students interpret my reactions in a more anthropological way. I think more about multiple audiences and find myself making comments like these: "I am bothered here—I'll bet most teachers would be—but perhaps general readers wouldn't mind." Or "I liked this passage, but I suspect a lot of teachers would take it as an inappropriately personal digression—or as too informal or slangy."

The central principle here is this: I cannot teach students the particular conventions they will need for particular disciplines (not even for particular teachers within the same discipline), but I can teach students the principle of discourse variation—between individuals and between communities. I can't teach them the forms they'll need, but I can sensitize them to the notion of differences in form so that they will be more apt to look for cues and will pick them up faster when they encounter them. Or to put it somewhat negatively, I'm trying to protect myself and keep my students from saying to my colleagues in history or psychology, "But my freshman English teacher likes this kind of writing that you failed me for!" What I want my students to go away thinking is more like this: "My freshman English teacher was good at telling us what went on in his mind as he read our papers—what he found strong and weak, what he liked and didn't like. But he set things up so we were always seeing how different members of the class and even people outside the class had different perceptions and reactions and standards and followed different conventions—how other people in other communities read differently. He tried to get us to listen better and pick up quicker on conventions and reactions." (If only we could write our students' evaluations of our teaching!) This inductive and scattered approach is messy—frustrating to students who want neat answers. But it avoids giving them universal standards that don't hold up empirically. And more than that, it is lively, interesting, and writerly because it's rhetorical rather than formal.

A Final Note: "But at my Back . . . "

Don't forget to notice how fast academic discourse is changing—certainly in our discipline and probably in others. And these changes are really an old story. It wasn't so long ago, after all, that Latin was the only acceptable language for learned discourse. Gradually, the other European dialects became acceptable—vernacular, vulgar, and of the people, more democratic, closer to the business of the everyday and to feelings. Yet it seems to me that many academics seem more nervous about changes in discourse—and especially incursions of the vernacular—than about changes in ideas or content or doctrine. Many happily proclaim that there is no truth, no right answer, no right interpretation; many say they want more voices in the academy, dialogue, heteroglossia! But they won't let themselves or their students write in language tainted with the ordinary or with the presence and feelings of the writer.

Yet despite this fear of change, change is what we are now seeing even in the deep structure or central intellectual practices of academic discourse:

- Deconstructionists make a frontal attack on straight, organized prose that purports to mean what it says. They have gotten a good hearing with their insistence that language always means something different from what it says, that seemingly plain and direct language is the most duplicitous discourse of all, and that fooling around is of the essence.
- Bruner and scholars of narrative attack the assumption that thinking is best when it is structured in terms of claims, reasons, warrants, and evidence. Narrative is just as good a form for thinking.
- Some feminists attack the idea that good writing must follow linear or hierarchical or deductive models of structure, must persuade by trying to overpower, must be "masterful."
- Academic discourse has usually focused outward: on issues or data. But now the focus of academic discourse is more and more often on discourse and thinking itself. In effect, much academic discourse is metadiscourse.
- In a host of ways, genres are becoming blurred. It is worth quoting Geertz:

    [T]he present jumbling of varieties of discourse has grown to the point where it is becoming difficult either to label authors (What is Foucault—historian, philosopher, political theorist? What is Thomas Kuhn—historian, philosopher, sociologist of knowledge?) or to classify works. . . . It is a phenomenon general enough and distinctive enough to suggest that what we are seeing is not just another redrawing of the cultural map—the moving of a few disputed borders, the marking of some more picturesque mountain lakes—but an alteration of the principles of mapping. Something is happening to the way we think about the way we think. ("Blurred Genres" 19–20)

Arguments that any currently privileged set of stylistic conventions of academic discourse are inherently better—even that any currently privileged set of intellectual practices are better—for scholarship or for thinking or for arguing or for rooting out self-deception: such arguments seem problematic now.

In the end, then, I conclude that I should indeed devote enough time in my freshman writing course to the intellectual practices of academic discourse; but also work on nonacademic practices and tasks, such as on discourse that renders rather than explains. (And our discussion about the difference between these two uses of language will help both.) Similarly, I should devote a little bit of time to the stylistic conventions or voices of academic discourse; but only as part of a larger exploration of various voices and styles—an exploration centered not on forms but on relationships with various live audiences. Let me give Joe Harris the last word: "What I am arguing against, though, is the notion that our students should necessarily be working towards the mastery of some particular, well-defined sort of discourse. It seems to me that they might better be encouraged towards a kind of polyphony—an awareness of and pleasure in the various competing discourses that make up their own" (17).

Interested readers will want to consult the growing body of empirical research on representative academic texts of different disciplines and on what happens as actual students engage in learning to use academic discourse. I am thinking of the work of people like Bazerman, Herrington, McCarthy, and Myers. Also a note of thanks: I have been trying out various versions of this paper for two years now and I've gotten enormously helpful responses and suggestions from more people than I can mention here. I am very grateful to them.

Works Cited

Bakhtin, Mikhail. "Discourse and the Novel." *The Dialogic Imagination: Four Essays*. Ed. Michael Holquist. Trans. Caryl Emerson and Michael Holquist. Slavic Series 1. Austin: U of Texas P. 1981. 259–422.
——. "Discourse in Life and Discourse in Art (Concerning Sociological Poetics)." *Freudianism: A Marxist Critique*. Trans. I. R. Titunik. Ed. Neal H. Bruss. New York: Academic, 1976. 93–116.
Bartholomae, David. "Inventing the University." *When A Writer Can't Write*. Ed. Mike Rose. New York: Guilford, 1985. 134–65.
Bazerman, Charles. *Shaping Written Knowledge: Genre and Activity of the Experimental Article in Science*. Madison: U of Wisconsin P, 1988.
Becker, Howard, *Writing for Social Scientists*. Chicago: U of Chicago P, 1986.
Berlin, James. "Contemporary Composition: The Major Pedagogical Theories." *College English* 44 (1982): 766–77.
Bettelheim, Bruno. *Freud and Man's Soul*. New York: Knopf, 1983.

Bizzell, Pat. "Foundationalism and Anti-Foundationalism in Composition Studies." *Pre/Text* 7.1–7.2 (1986): 37–56.

Crane, R. S. "The Critical Monism of Cleanth Brooks." *Critics and Criticism: Ancient and Modern*. Chicago: U of Chicago P, 1951. 83–107.

Elbow, Peter, and Pat Belanoff. *A Community of Writers: A Workshop Course in Writing*. 3rd Edition. New York: McGraw-Hill, 1999.

Flower, Linda. "Negotiating Academic Discourse." Reading-to-Write Report No. 10. Technical Report No. 29. Berkeley, CA: Center for the Study of Writing at U of California, Berkeley, and Carnegie Mellon.

Freedman, Sarah, C. Greenleaf, and M. Sperling. "Response to Student Writing." Research Report No. 23. Urbana, IL: NCTE, 1987.

Geertz, Clifford. "Blurred Genres: The Refiguration of Social Thought." *Local Knowledge: Further Essays in Interpretive Anthropology*. New York: Basic, 1983. 19–35.

———. *Works and Lives: The Anthropologist as Author*. Palo Alto: Stanford UP, 1988.

Harris, Joe. "The Idea of Community in the Study of Writing." *College Composition and Communication* 40.1 (February 1989): 11–22.

Heath, Shirley Brice. *Ways With Words: Language, Life, and Work in Communities and Classrooms*. New York: Cambridge UP, 1983.

Herrington, Anne. "Composing One's Self in a Discourse: Students' and Teachers' Negotiations." *Constructing Rhetorical Education: From the Classroom to the Community*. Ed. D. Charney and M. Secor. Carbondale: Southern Illinois UP, 1992. 91–115.

———. "Teaching, Writing, and Learning: A Naturalistic Study of Writing in an Undergraduate Literature Course." *Advances in Writing Research, Vol. 2: Writing in Academic Discourse*. Ed. D. Jolliffe. Norwood, NJ: Ablex, 1988. 133–66.

Hirsch, E. D. Jr. *The Aims of Interpretation*. Chicago: U of Chicago P, 1978.

MacDonald, Susan Peck. "Problem Definition in Academic Writing." *College English* 49 (1987): 315–30.

Matalene, Carolyn B. Introduction. *Worlds of Writing: Teaching and Learning in the Discourse Communities of Work*. Ed. Carolyn B. Matalene. New York: Random, 1989, v–xi.

McCarthy, Lucille. "A Stranger in Strange Lands: A College Student Writing Across the Curriculum." *Research in the Teaching of English* 21 (1987):233–65.

Myers, Greg. *Writing Biology*. Madison: U of Wisconsin P, 1990.

North, Stephen. *The Making of Knowledge in Composition: Portrait of an Emerging Field*. Upper Montclair, NJ: Boynton, 1987.

Olson, David R. "Writing: The Divorce of the Author from the Text." *Exploring Speaking-Writing Relationships: Connections and Contrasts*. Ed. B. M. Kroll and R. J. Vann. Urbana, IL: NCTE, 1981. 99–110.

Raymo, Chet. "Just the Facts, Ma'am." *Boston Globe* 27 February 1989: 26.

Rorty, Richard. "Social Construction and Composition Theory: A Conversation with Richard Rorty." *The Journal of Advanced Composition* 9.1 and 9.2: (1989): 1–9.

Rother, James. "Face-Values on the Cutting Floor: Some Versions of the Newer Realism." *American Literary Realism* 21.2 (Winter 1989): 67–96.

Stafford, William. "Making a Poem/Starting a Car on Ice." *Writing the Australian Crawl: Views on the Writer's Vocation*. Ann Arbor: U of Michigan P, 1978. 61–75.

Vygotsky, Lev. *Thought and Language*. Trans. Eugenia Hanfman and Gertrude Vakar. Cambridge: MIT P, 1962.

12

In Defense of Private Writing

Consequences for Theory and Research

> For so public-spirited they are [writers of memoirs], that they can
> never afford themselves the least time to think in private for their
> own particular benefit and use. For this reason, though they are
> often retired, they are never by themselves.
>
> Third Earl of Shaftesbury

Most of the words written by most people are intended for the eyes of others. Indeed, many people have this intention for everything they write. Still, some people sometimes, and many people occasionally, write words not meant for others to see. Some of this writing seems trivial, as when people make lists and jottings for themselves for day-to-day business; but some of it is far from trivial, as when people write out important thoughts or feelings they don't want anyone else to see. Some of this writing goes in a diary of some sort, but some it is discarded or destroyed soon after it is written.

There is no dispute at all that some people sometimes write in these ways. But there is a rich and interesting dispute about how to *name* and *think about* this kind of writing. I call it by the conventional name, "private writing." The essential feature of private writing, as I see it, is that the writer doesn't intend the words for the eyes of others.[1]

This essay was published in *Written Communication* 16.2 (1999): 139–69.

1. This simple definition is enough for the purposes of this essay, but I can be a little more precise by looking at three cases on the margin. (1) I don't call it private writing when someone writes a letter to someone intimate and doesn't want *others* to see it, even if the writer scrawls "private" on the envelope. (2) I don't call it private writing when people write things for the eyes of others, but which never reach those eyes. Perhaps the writing gets lost or perhaps the

But there is a remarkably widespread view these days that the very concept of private writing is a mistake. This view grows out of a strong version of a social constructionist or cultural studies position. According to this view, because everything that anyone writes is deeply constructed by ideas or discourses that come from outside the mind of the writer, heavily influenced by culture or ideology, it follows that this writing is not really private at all, and need not be named as different in kind from the regular writing intended for the eyes of others. My goal in this essay is to contest this view and persuade our profession to pay closer attention to private writing—and indeed encourage it. But in order to reach this goal, I first need to look more closely at the theoretical grounding behind the claim that writing can never be private. As my title suggests, I think my enterprise will lead to payoffs in theory, in empirical research, and finally in teaching.

I. Addressing the Argument that Private Writing Is Not Really Private

Thomas Mallon writes in his book about diaries that "no one has ever kept a diary for just himself" (xvi). Jeannette Harris, in a book-length critique of "expressive discourse," writes:

> [W]riting-for-self does not exist in any real sense. . . . [U]ltimately all discourse is intended for an audience other than the self who is doing the writing. . . . [E]ven when we are exploring a subject rather than consciously communicating with a reader, we are aware of that eventual audience and attempting to shape a text that he or she will understand. . . . I can conceive of no significant instance in which a writer does not think in terms of a possible audience. Writing, like speaking, is inherently a social act. (66–9)

Ken Bruffee, one of the earliest and most prominent messengers of social constructionism to the field of composition, writes as follows:

> In short, when we go off by ourselves to put pen to paper or to read what someone else has written, we displace into solitude acts that are essentially social and collaborative. Writing is not a private act. It is an aspect of social adaptation. When we write, we return conversation, displaced and internalized as thought, to the social sphere where it originates." *(Short Course* 2)

John Trimbur explicates Bruffee and sums up the strong version of a social constructionist critique of private writing:

---

writer changes her mind. This writing doesn't seem private because it is so phenomenologically different from writing that the writer *doesn't* intend it for the eyes of others. My own experience of public writing (such as for an essay like this) has changed as I've learned to treat early drafts as truly private. (3) I call writing private even if the writer much later changes his mind and shares it with readers. Again, I am emphasizing the *experience* of writing words not intended for the eyes of others.

In this view, the author is no longer the nineteenth-century individualist but rather a social function in a larger system of dependencies. Writing is not so much the personal expression (and property) of the individual author. Instead, Bruffee says, if "thought is internalized conversation, then writing is internalized conversation reexternalized." (99–100. Quotations from Bruffee are from "Collaborative Learning" 641)

Geoffrey Summerfield begins his essay on journal writing: "Let me plunge straight in and argue that every utterance, every text, embodies, enacts, or realizes a social act, a movement toward an other" (33).

Deborah Brandt writes (in correspondence with me, but summarizing a point from her book):

> I can keep a piece of writing in a locked drawer. Whatever that writing is, it stays private. Where I differ with you is that I think that when we are composing and we decide to write something down (rather than just have it in our head) we "go public" to a certain degree and that changes the status of our language. We are now responsible toward it as public language, beyond our selves, in its public domain, its public meaning. Such an experience can occur in journal writing, nay, even in freewriting—even if it stays locked in that drawer.

Let me look more closely and try to figure out with more precision what is really entailed in the claim that all writing is social. In fact, the claim can have distinct meanings:

1. "All writing is social" *could* mean that all writing is eventually read by someone other than the writer. This would be the extreme or limiting claim. It's hard to imagine anyone seriously asserting it. Who could deny that *some* writers *sometimes* manage to keep *some* writing away from the eyes of others?

2. "All writing is social" could mean that all writing is *consciously shaped* for other readers—even when other readers never see it. I might write for my private diary and successfully keep it under lock and key, but really, as I am writing, imagine others reading my words after my death. "They'll see what a wonderful writer I am, what a fine sensibility I had. They'll feel bad they didn't appreciate me when I was alive. They'll see that I was right and my wife was wrong in that argument we had." And as I write in my diary about a trivial dispute over breakfast, I try to do it as well as Cheever did in his diaries that I read in *The New Yorker*. Probably there are no stronger feelings driving us than the feeling of wanting to be appreciated—or perhaps more important still, to be understood. What better way to be really understood than to lay out our most private thoughts and feelings and experiences in a diary and hope that some day others will read it. This kind of behavior must be very common. Yet surely some writers have sometimes managed to write some private bits that they didn't want or intend others to see. Not *consciously* anyway.

3. But unconsciously? That is, "all writing is social" could mean that all writing is at least *unconsciously* shaped for readers. We need to distinguish the following senses of this third claim:

3a. When people write, they are always thinking about future readers in the ways I just described in (2)—but thinking about them unconsciously.

3b. Everything we write is unconsciously shaped for strong readers from the past who now live on as "readers in the head." That is, I might write exploratory thoughts and know I'll discard them before anyone ever sees them—not trying to please any readers at all—yet all the while be busily trying to "avoid passive verbs" and "supply vivid details." I am unconsciously writing to the demands of my powerful tenth grade teacher, Mrs. Lewalski. She may be dead, but she lives on in my head—I have internalized her. We all have readers in the head (my term from *Writing With Power*). I might be tacitly writing to Cheever or some other powerful writer (Bloom). I might be writing to a strong teacher who always rewarded me for a certain kind of tone or stance (ironic, sentimental, idealistic), or for a certain kind of intellectual or interpretive strategy. So when I am writing "only for myself," I am really writing significantly for one of these hidden but powerful past readers.

3c. Everything we write has "textually implied readers." That is, even if I don't consciously or unconsciously address any reader, my words will inevitably *imply* a reader. As Gibson puts it, every text asks readers to adopt certain kinds of roles and not others. Thus every text is more suitable for certain kinds of readers and less suitable for others. "Implied reader" is a widely accepted critical concept (Walker Gibson used the term "mock reader," Gerald Prince "narratee").

3d. Everything we write is shaped by the minds, attitudes, values, and consciousnesses around us—family, institutions, and above all, culture. Here is Bruffee's contention that private writing is always collaborative. I may be writing privately in my successfully guarded diary about my most intimate private feelings, but those feelings turn out to be uncannily like the intimate private feelings of other people around me—and strikingly different from the intimate private feelings of people in different families, institutions, or cultures. This is the provenance of ideology or what I like to call culture-in-the-head: writing as "channeling." *Invention as a Social Act* is a book-length argument that others are always involved in any process of having any ideas (LeFevre).

3e. All writing betrays the shaping effect of society and culture *through the medium of language itself*. That is, even if I destroy what I write as soon as I write it, I am using language, and in doing so, I am using a deeply public, social medium. Natural language itself is a kind of map or recording of all the voices of culture. As parents we classically say to our toddlers as we walk along the street, "Don't put that penny in your mouth. Who knows where it's been!" But one of the main jobs of toddlers is to put words into their mouths that were first in the mouths of countless others. Bakhtin gives the classic formulation: "The word in language is half someone else's. . . . Language is not a neutral medium that passes freely and easily into the private property of the speaker's intentions; it is populated—overpopulated—with the intentions of others" (293).

4. Finally, "All writing is social," could mean that even when people write only for themselves and keep their words from any other eyes, the writing is still "social" in that it is intended for the *audience of self.* As Walter Ong writes, "Every human word implies not only the existence—at least in the imagination—of another to whom the word is uttered, but it also implies that the speaker has a kind of otherness within himself" *(Barbarian Within* 88).

Given all these possible meanings, we simply can't judge the truth of the claim that all writing is social. There are really eight claims or eight senses within this claim. We have to make separate judgments about each subclaim or sense. This complicates things, but it offers hope for greater clarity.

Some senses are clearly false:

1. It's clearly false that *every* text is seen by external readers.
2. It's clearly false that *every* text is written with the *conscious* intention that others read it.

Some senses are clearly true:

3c. Everything we write surely *is* better suited to some readers than to others.
3d. Everything we write surely *is* shaped or affected by the minds, attitudes, values, and consciousnesses around us—family, institutions, and above all culture.
3e. Everything we write surely *is* shaped by the medium of language— which of course is highly social.

And some senses are debatable:

3a. Do we always harbor unconscious hopes or expectations of future readers for *everything* we write?
3b. Do we *always* unconsciously shape our writing for strong readers from the past?
4. Is the self *always* an audience for our writing?

"Always Already?" Alright Already!

I'll return to the debatable senses later, for intriguingly enough, the most important senses to explore are the ones that are clearly true: 3c, 3d, and 3e. They may be "clearly true," but there is something crucially unclear and complicated about them. They are not just clearly true, they are *inevitably* true— perhaps even true by definition. That is, they cannot be denied:

• It is impossible for a text *not* to be easier or more suitable for some readers' tastes and interests than others' (3c).
• It is impossible for humans *not* to be affected by the culture and people they grow up with and live with (3d).

- It is impossible for private writing *not* to be in language, and for language not to be social (barring unique private languages) (3e).

All writing is social in these three senses, that is, by virtue of how we use the operative terms.

It was because theorists became so preoccupied with these inevitably true senses of writing as social that they have so often graced us with the fashionable mantra *"always already."* Of course all writing is "always already social"—it must be so, no matter how the writing is written, and no matter who sees it or doesn't see it—*if* you mean senses 3c, 3d, and 3e. But this is not the case if you mean any of the other five senses. Thus, to say that "all writing is always already social" is to make a claim that is clearly true *in a sense*—indeed, in three out of eight senses.

There is an instructive larger point here about the very nature of language and argument: when people write "always already," they are leaving out the words "in a sense." That is, claims that are "always already" or inevitably true are *lens statements* or "terministic screens" (Burke's term). They are lenses through which we see the world—or screens that filter our view of the world.

There are some interesting but seldom acknowledged features of lens statements:

- It is impossible to have a valid debate about whether a lens statement is *true*—and highly misleading to pretend to do so. One can only validly debate whether a lens statement is *useful* in one situation or another.
- Lens statements pay a heavy price for being always already true. They are, by the same token, in a sense, always already false! That is, they are no "more true" than a host of conflicting or contrary statements which are also "always already true."

It follows then that people are misleading us when they claim that anything is "always already" the case without adding the phrase "in a sense"—that is, without acknowledging that it is only one among many conflicting claims that are *all* "always already true."

Let me illustrate this abstract theoretical point by zeroing in on our case at hand: writing as social. The statement that "all writing is social in senses 3c, 3d, and 3e" *has* indeed been a useful lens. It has helped people overcome any thoughtless temptation to see writing as an exclusively solitary, private, and asocial activity, a function only of isolated individuals in lonely garrets, or to see writing as unconnected to and uninfluenced by others or by culture. This case has been powerfully and effectively made in recent years, and usefully so.

But once we realize that the statement, "all language is social in senses 3c, 3d, 3e" is a lens statement or terministic screen, *not* a matter of "winnable debate," we have a chance to realize that the opposite lens statement is also true: *"all language is always already private."* This statement is also helpful. It highlights an important feature of human language use: every utterance carries a set of connotations, and sometimes even denotations, that no listener will ever fully comprehend. Therefore, nothing that anyone says or writes can ever be understood by others in the full senses in which it is experienced or intended by the speaker or writer. The claim that "all language is always already inherently essentially social" has no more force than the claim that "all language is always already inherently essentially private."

This case has not recently been well made in the composition community, but George Steiner provides a classic formulation:

> No two historical epochs, no two social classes, no two localities use words and syntax to signify exactly the same things, to send identical signals of valuation and inference. Neither do two human beings. Each living person draws, deliberately or in immediate habit, on two sources of linguistic supply: the current vulgate corresponding to his level of literacy, and a private thesaurus. The latter is inextricably a part of his subconscious, of his memories so far as they may be verbalized, and of the singular, irreducibly specific ensemble of his somatic and psychological identity. Part of the answer to the notorious logical conundrum as to whether or not there can be "private language" is that aspects of every language act are unique and individual. . . . Each communicatory gesture has a private residue. The "personal lexicon" in every one of us inevitably qualifies the definitions, connotations, semantic moves current in public discourse. The concept of a normal or standard idiom is a statistically-based fiction. . . . The language of a community, however uniform its social contour, is an inexhaustibly multiple aggregate of speech-atoms, of finally irreducible personal meanings. (46)

(See also my account of meaning as the outcome of a tug of war between the public dialect of a speech community and the individual's private ideolect in *Writing Without Teachers*, 151–57.) Kenneth Burke similarly calls attention to a "generic divisiveness which, being common to all men, is a universal fact about them, prior to any divisiveness caused by social classes. . . . Out of this emerge the motives of linguistic persuasion" (61).

Thus, if writers think that they as individuals are the only ones who have a role in their writing, it's helpful to point out how much they are trapped behind only one lens and how much they need to look through the other lens—the one that shows how all writing and language is inherently social. However, if writers cannot seem to find any of their *own* thoughts or feelings as they write, if they feel that all writing belongs to teachers, if they feel that writing is always just a matter of putting down what experts or authorities have said, if they feel unable to write anything any different from what "everyone" feels and says and thinks, if they can't notice any of their own signature in their experience or thinking or language, then it's helpful to stress the lens that shows how all writing and language is inherently private. We need to remember that more than one thing can be "inherent" and "essential" and "always already true" of something else.

Bruffee, in arguing that all writing is social, likes to quote the last lines of Robert Frost's "Tuft of Flowers":

> "Men work together," I told him from the heart,
> "Whether they work together or apart."

But in quoting only these lines, he leaves out the conceptual basis of the poem. It tells of a farmer who goes out to turn the hay that had been scythed by someone else earlier in the day:

> I looked for him behind an isle of trees;
> I listened for his whetstone on the breeze.
>
> But he had gone his way, the grass all mown,
> And I must be, as he had been,—alone,
>
> "As all must be," I said within my heart,
> "Whether they work together or apart."

The whole force of the poem comes from showing the same scene through *two* contrary lenses, not one. The poem spends most of its energy looking through the lens that shows how people are separate, alone, and unconnected (even when they are together). The lines that Bruffee quotes occur only at the end when Frost switches lenses in order to show how people are nevertheless connected even when apart. The poem only *affirms* the two contradictory propositions; it never *denies* either.

Lens statements, then, are always misleading unless we have more than one. To have only one lens blinds us to what that lens hides, and tempts us to assume that there is only one right view. To have more than one lens helps us look at language and writing through multiple conceptual filters so as to see more dimensions, features, and facts about them. (What Bakhtin loved about the "carnival" dimension of the novel and claimed to be largely absent from epic poetry was this quality of providing multiple lenses.)

It follows that it's a waste of time to argue whether this or that lens statement is true. The only useful arguments are about *when* to use them. To be more precise:

- What does each lens statement help us see, and what does it tend to hide from us?
- Does one lens statement help us see *more* facets than another?
- Under what conditions is a lens statement most useful?
- In *which senses* are various lens statements true?

Certain lens statements may help us see *more* of a given phenomenon or to see it *better* than other lens statements. The social lens *may* show us more about writing than the private lens; or the social lens may be more *useful* now than the private lens. It is not my aim here to dispute these claims (though I have my doubts). My aim is to dispute totalistic discourse—that is, to help us see when people are mistaking lenses for reality. For I'm afraid that discourse in English studies has been considerably damaged by the intellectual naivete of arguments based on "always already" lens statements *as though one could win,* as though these statements could destroy competing claims—as though these were questions of truth or falsehood rather than of competing lenses. (An illustrative example: The essay on invention in *Teaching Composition: 10 Bibliographical Essays,* covering the period from the late 1950s to 1973 treats the use of journals for invention. The follow-up essay, covering the period from 1973 to 1987, does not mention the use of journals for invention [Young].)

But What About Empirical Evidence?

Empirical evidence can only *support* a lens statement, it cannot unseat it. For example, Smith's lens may bring into focus important features or facts about something that Jones's lens ignores or even hides. This is strong evidence in favor of Smith's lens. But it cannot disprove or disconfirm Jones's lens. After all, Jones's lens may well show things that Smith's lens ignores or hides.

If Smith wants to argue against Jones's lens claim, these are the only ways she can do it: she can disprove evidence that Jones brought in favor of his lens (pointing out either logical or empirical flaws); she can bring *so much* positive evidence for her lens that Jones's lens will seem overwhelmed or crowded out; perhaps she can even persuade others that no one could *ever* find good evidence for Jones's lens. But she can never prove or even validly argue that there *is* no good evidence to support Jones's lens. Neither positive nor negative evidence can unseat a lens claim. Someone can always turn up with good but hitherto unknown evidence in its favor—evidence, by the way, that is most likely to be found by people who *believe* in the out of fashion lens. (In the traditional scientific theory of disconfirmation, as famously formulated by Karl Popper, evidence has the opposite role: it can only *unseat,* never confirm. But this principle applies to the realm of empirical hypotheses, not to lens statements. Besides, numerous historians and philosophers of science, in addition to Kuhn, are quick to point out that some empirical hypotheses in science *do* survive negative empirical evidence—when the hypotheses are sufficiently attractive, compelling, or fruitful.)

We need to be explicit about the implication of these principles for discussions about writing as social and private. People have found lots of good evidence and argument *for* the social lens or the social dimensions of language. In doing so, they have bolstered that lens or claim; they have shown that it's an excellent and helpful lens to use. We have benefited. But no amount of evidence that language is social has force to disprove the lens statement that language is also—always already—in a sense—private. Even if people should undermine certain arguments or evidence for the private lens, that would have no force to show that there *is no evidence* for the private nature of language. The only way to damage a lens statement is to point out that no one seems to be able to find any use for it or any valid evidence for it or any senses in which it is true.

Since so much of academic discourse and argument is about lens statements, a wider understanding of their nature would improve the quality of argument and professional discourse. In particular, if more people understood that lens statements and empirical evidence had only positive force and not negative force, they would be quicker to notice when they had slid into an unfruitful either/or argument. This understanding might even temper the hunger for "winning as we know it." If by winning we mean demolishing the enemy view, this is impossible. If by winning we mean making everyone accept our position and feel the opposing one as old fashioned, retrograde, naughty, shameful, or stupid, this *is* indeed possible. We see it all the time. But such winning is really losing, for it restricts our vision and robs the community of the fuller understanding that we need. I fear we may be (or perhaps recently have been) in such a condition among composition scholars: a condition where members had come to feel that the private lens, the sense in which language has a private dimension, was illegitimate or naughty.

There is only one way to "really win"—but "winning" is not a good word for this happy outcome: getting people to see the value of our lens; getting them habitually to try it out when they want to understand something—even people who don't quite like our lens or are not disposed toward looking through it. And surely the best way to get reluctant people to look through our lens is to be willing to look through theirs.[2]

Almost any statement can be a lens statement—always already true or true in a sense. To notice this is to get some good views of the history of English studies. Here are some examples moving backward in time:

---

2. Some examples. Kenneth Burke is a good model of someone who uses totalistic or "all" or "always" propositions with precision and awareness. First, he catches sight of a new and unusual kind of language: "dramatistic" language as opposed to the "regular" ("scientific") kind of language that merely predicates. But once he notices and gets interested and becomes sensitive to dramatistic language, once he really sharpens the focus of this useful lens, it helps him see that in a sense, *all* language is dramatistic: all language has *some* of that dramatistic dimension. But even though he gets a bit carried away over the power of his new lens, he always comes back to noticing that there are distinctions to be made (42) and that it is only *in a sense* that all language is dramatistic.

Sandy Petrey shows a similar sophistication with totalistic or "always" claims in his comparable exploration of speech act theory. First, he notices that some language doesn't describe or predicate, it makes things happen. That is, not all language is "constantive"; some is performative. Like Burke, once he notices and gets interested in performative language, this makes him notice that in a sense, all language is performative. He can see all language through the performative lens. (He chides Austin for stopping short and not applying this lens to all language.) Yet he too always comes back to the realization that this is a lens, and that it is only in a sense that all language is performative. Neither Burke nor Petrey forgets that the only really interesting thing about the ubiquity of dramatistic and performative discourse is the way it exists over against a backdrop of the distinction between two kinds of language or two ways of considering language.

The intellectual sophistication I want to highlight in Burke and Petrey is that they never lose sight of the fact that they are doing "in-a-sense" thinking (Aristotle liked to be very explicit about this), and so they don't throw away distinctions: they don't throw away the competing lenses or competing concepts. They don't let themselves lose sight of the real and useful difference between scientific or constantive language on the one hand, and dramatistic or performative language on the other. How dull and intellectually unproductive it would be just to say, "All language is dramatistic/performative. The end. All scything is social." The conceptual energy comes from enriching concepts, not destroying them.

- "All language can be shown in one way or another to mean the opposite of what it purports to mean." This is why the project of deconstruction has been useful and is always already in a sense true.
- "All texts have multiple meanings." And so the New Critics were usefully always already in a sense right.
- "All texts mean what the author actually intended them to mean." And so common sense folks in the street, as well as many scholars (see Juhl), are also usefully always already in a sense right.

II. Exploring Arguments that Private Writing Exists but Is Misguided

Up to this point I've been addressing arguments against the very *concept* of private writing—writing only for self. I turn now to five arguments that accept the concept and acknowledge private writing as different from public or social writing—*but* that tell us not to encourage students to engage in it.

First argument. *If we ask students to write privately for themselves alone, we are asking them to do something that is not natural—something that goes against the deeply social grain of language.* There can be no doubt that language is inherently social: a creation and reflection of society and culture. It may even begin socially in the life of the infant. For example, I've noticed something interesting on some occasions when I've led first and second graders in an exercise I often use with older students and adults. I invite us all first to write something private; and then afterward something public to share—which we share in pairs or small groups; and then finally we write and talk about how everyone experienced these two writings. The children tend to go along ever so sweetly with everything I ask. But then at the end, many of them raise their hands and ask to read their private writing outloud! This seldom happens with older writers. Vygotsky and Mead, founding authors for the social constructionist perspective, argue that language itself starts out as overt dialogue with others.

But Vygotsky and Mead don't argue *against* the private use of language—especially written language. Vygotsky sees children learning language socially in dialogue with others, but then naturally learning to use it privately with themselves—initially outloud and then gradually internally and silently, and eventually as thinking. "The inner speech of the adult represents his 'thinking for himself' rather than social adaptation" (18). This is an instance of the larger principle that children learn *most* things in a social setting and then internalize that social learning to a private or solitary realm. When Bakhtin champions dialogic rather than monologic language, he is championing a dialogic *dimension* of discourse that can exist in solitary or private language as well as public language. In short, Bakhtin, Vygotsky, and Mead will not serve as witnesses for the claim that private writing is unnatural. As Chomsky notes," [C]ommunication is only one function of language, and by no means an essential one." He goes on to say:

As a graduate student, I spent two years writing a lengthy manuscript, assuming throughout that it would never be published or read by anyone. I meant everything I wrote, intending nothing as to what anyone would [understand], in fact taking it for granted that there would be no audience. (quoted in Feldman 5–6)

Since private writing is no more unnatural than writing itself, we need to go on to more substantive objections about the *harms* that private writing might cause.

Second argument. *If we ask students to write privately for themselves alone, we are reinforcing* "the myth of private authorship" (Spigelman 236), "*traditional notions about the autonomy of the author*" (Trimbur 100), *and the* "*lie*" *that they can be* "*the owners of all that they can say* . . . [*when in fact their writings are*] *the products of their time, politics and culture*" (Bartholomae, "Writing With Teachers" 70).

If we think that every student's entire essay is "channeled" or "plagiarized" as a word-for-word whole from the culture or ideology, then this objection makes perfect sense. But if we think that some students sometimes make a bit of their own individual mixture out of the ingredients they borrow from around them, and if, in particular, we think that a few students on a few occasions have a few thoughts or perceptions that one might call "their own"—then private writing might prove useful. For if we ask students to do some non-careful private writing and then look back at it in comparison to their public writing, they have a greater chance of noticing the furnishings of their minds and comparing what they find to the various cultural influences around them.

Let me illustrate my point with a very practical teaching application. When asking students to write about some controversial or delicate issue (e.g., something that bears on race or class or sexual orientation), I find it helpful to start by asking for a substantial piece of private writing: not just ten minutes of private freewriting (though that can help) but something more extended that explores one's thinking as fully as possible. This is not for sharing with me or with anyone else. When students get a chance to work out and put down their thoughts, feelings, and opinions without the need to share or defend them, they can more easily reflect on the various sources of these feelings and views. (It's helpful to ask them to pause and look back and even write about their private writing after they have done it—not just plunge onward to the public writing.)

This use of private writing (for which I am indebted to Paul Puccio) helps students sort out various influences on them and gives them a bit more space or agency to decide what they want to accept or reject. Indeed, this kind of private writing makes it easier for students to allow their thinking to *change,* since they are not having to defend it. ("Among the ancients . . . it was accounted the peculiar of philosophers and wise men, to be able to hold themselves in talk" (Shaftesbury 113). (For these passages from Shaftesbury, I thank my colleague Jean Nienkamp, who is completing an ambitious book tracing the history of what she calls "internal rhetoric"—discourse in which people address words to themselves in order to clarify their thinking or persuade themselves.) Of course, no amount of private writing can guarantee that students won't fool themselves into thinking that every thought they have is unique and original. But it will at least improve their chances of getting more perspective on the furnishings of their minds—perhaps even of achieving some ideas or perceptions that are more their own. It's my sense that writers who settle most for kneejerk commonplace writing are having trouble dealing with the pressures of audience—as with timid students and airline magazine writers. (In the third section I suggest a way to think more constructively and empirically about this current theoretical question of writers "writing" vs. "being written.")

Third argument. *Private writing reinforces the idea of "private property" and fosters selfishness, capitalism, and the hunger to own things or to have things all to oneself.* Trimbur warns against the danger of thinking that writing is "the personal expression (*and property*) of the individual author" (*100*). Certainly some of the rampant injustice in our society comes from capitalist market forces heightening people's hunger to own things and accumulate wealth. But in our classrooms, private writing turns out to be one of the best ways to subvert the capitalist itch. That is, the greatest *resistance* to private writing comes from students who are the most "capitalist," in that they see writing only as an occasion for competing to accumulate the main "capital" that schools provide: grades. These are students who do indeed confuse writing with accumulation, but private writing represents no accumulation or capital gain. It gives us a way to create one corner of our classroom where students are specifically helped *not* to confuse writing with grades and the accumulation of property.

Material property involves a zero-sum game: whatever property you own I cannot own, and anything I own you cannot have. But writing works the other way: the more you write and share and publish, the more opportunity that gives me to write. Perhaps if students were invited to "accumulate" and "own" as much writing as they wanted, it might even satisfy in a more benign way some of their hunger for ownership.

The Oxford English Dictionary notes that the term *private* comes from the Latin *privatus* which means "withdrawn from public life, deprived of office." From the earliest English use (1380), the word has continued that sense of private-as-withdrawn and contrasted with public. (Wyclife used the word *private* for the order of friars—a group that was in fact communal and that even turned away from private property.) Etymology doesn't prove anything, but it helps us notice that private writing is not so much about *ownership* as about turning away from society and from the observation and control of others. Most people who live with others need *some* areas of thought or experience that others cannot see or control. A paradigm site for privacy is sexuality—hence the term, "private parts."

Fourth argument. *Private writing fosters individualism.* It probably does. It invites people to turn away from others and pay attention to themselves and their own thoughts, and to notice where their experience is like and unlike that of others. But I would invite us not to treat individualism as the dirty word it is sometimes taken to be. Individualism doesn't entail what we could call *pathological* individualism: being *unable* to identify with others or feel solidarity with them and the illusion that one is isolated and invincible. Individualism itself is not the enemy of connection and relationship with others. Self-exploration usually increases people's ability to identify with others. We bring more to relationships as we get a better sense of who we are.

In parallel with a pathological individualism is a pathological connectedness: the lack of any sense of self, deafness to one's own experience and predicament and self-interest, and a tendency only to identify with others. (Where pathological individualism has been described as a trap for men, pathological connectedness has been described as a trap for women.) As Dewey argues, the social and the private are not either/or dimensions; they are dialectically linked. Vygotsky and Mead show how the private realm grows out of the social. It is part of our social adaptation to create some space apart from what is public and social. Compared to most teachers of writing, I find myself pushing in both directions: asking for more private writing and more sharing of writing. The two goals seem to reinforce each other.

A nonpathological individualism is surely something to foster, not inhibit. If we were trying to come up with a list of abilities that characterize wise or well-educated people—qualities we hope to produce in our students—one of the prime candidates would surely be the ability to develop and pursue a line of thinking all by oneself, privately and unaided. Thinking socially and collaboratively with others is a precious goal, but if our students cannot pursue a topic *unless* they have others to do it with, they are crucially deficient in the use of language and their minds. Isocrates notes that, "We call those able to speak to the multitude orators, and we regard as persons of sagacity those who are able to talk things over within themselves with discernment" (*Nicocles,* §8 quoted in Perelman and Olbrechts-Tyteca 41; see also Winnicott's "The Capacity to Be Alone").

Private writing is one of the few simple and effective exercises in helping our students learn this crucial ability to pursue a topic or line of thinking on their own. This is particularly important for adolescents, since they so often find it hard to pursue a topic that their peers are uninterested in or disapprove of.

Fifth argument. *Private writing trains people to cut themselves off from social commerce.* I want to call attention to a puritan flavor in some extreme social constructionist critiques of private writing: a notion that there is something self-indulgent and therefore naughty about retreats from social interaction. For example, when Joe Harris writes about my guidelines for a writing workshop where I urge students to speak their responses to each others' texts but to refrain from answering or arguing with each other, he disapproves of me for encouraging a site where students "do not seem to be held answerable to each other as intellectuals" (31). Though this is not actually a situation of private discourse, Harris is objecting to what is central in private writing: an invitation sometimes to value one's own words and thoughts and not worry about the reactions to them by others.

The puritan undertone needs to be put on the table where it can be coolly assessed. We can't really condemn private writing on the grounds of retreat from social commerce unless we are prepared to condemn something ubiquitous in human functioning. David Burrows, in a study of human music making, points out a simple but important fact: "The greater part by far of the world's music is produced by solitary hummers and whistlers [and singers] for no one's consumption but their own" (34). There is surely a quality of natural pleasure-in-self when people make music for themselves:

> Pendant to whistling in the dark is singing in the shower: in situations that are secure to begin with, self-generated sound may function as self-celebration. . . . [W]ith enhancement of the voice [in the shower] goes enhancement of self-esteem. Especially when no potential critics are visible. (Burrows 35)

Artists and musicians seem to be more comfortable than members of the composition community with the private uses of symbolic activity. It's sad when people think it's more natural to sing, draw, or dance for oneself than to write for oneself. Poets and fiction writers also speak more often than teachers or academics do about putting readers out of mind while they write.

If we decide we should stamp out self-enhancing or self-celebratory performance for the audience of self, we have our work cut out for us. Life presents us with constant threats to our sense of ourselves as valued or good, and humans seem to have an impulse to find occasions for self-celebration. I call the impulse healthy, but even if you call it unhealthy or sinful, you have to acknowledge the ubiquity of people's private commerce with themselves. Writing to oneself is less common than humming and singing or even dancing for oneself, but think for a moment about language use in general: most humans probably address far more language to themselves in their own heads than they address to others.

These five arguments against private writing don't address the most writerly and pedagogically practical objection: that private writing is bad for *writing*. This is the argument that private writing reinforces the tendency in students or inexperienced writers to ignore the needs of readers other than themselves. I deal directly with this objection in an essay that is more directly writerly and pedagogical, "A Map of Writing in Terms of Audience and Response" in Part I of this volume.

III. Opening Up Fruitful Research by Moving From the Theoretical to the Empirical

In the first section of this paper, I treated lens debates—debates that are highly theoretical since they can never be settled or won and are almost inimical to evidence. In the second section, I dealt with debates about private writing and mentality, and these debates also tend to go on interminably when they are framed as theoretical or ideological. In this third section, I want to move the investigation of private writing to a more empirical realm. Indeed, I fear that people have *neglected* empirical research on private writing because the theoretical dismissals have been so prominent. Research is usually inhibited by totalizing claims in terms of "always" and "never," and usually stimulated by more open inquiry in terms of "sometimes" and "when?" and "how much?"

But how can we research private writing? If it's private, we can't look at it. Yet this needn't rule out fruitful research possibilities:

- The most obvious approach is to interview people who enjoy and regularly use private writing. We can find out how they experience private writing in comparison to their other writing—and explore their attitudes and how they go about their different kinds of writing.
- Autoethnography can be helpful here: people can research themselves and their own writing, and of course they have free access to their own private texts.
- For comparison with people who use private writing, we can study people who dislike and avoid it. My hunch is that people who are adept at private writing enjoy writing more and are better at exploratory drafting and substantive revising—perhaps even at changing their thinking. Of course, such results can only reveal correlation, not causation, but correlations can be valuable. (Stover provides a valuable and skilled study of these areas—and describes a powerful exception to my hunch.)
- It might be interesting to see if different *kinds* of writers differ in how much private writing they do, for example, writers of poetry, fiction, and "creative nonfiction," college students who do no creative writing, and professionals who do only on-the-job writing.
- Speculatively, we can even look for differences in the *public* writing of people who use and don't use private writing but are otherwise comparable. We can look at pieces by the two groups, perhaps in response to the same assignments, and compare them for specific differences: for example, complexity of syntax, complexity of organization or reasoning, amount of questioning or perplexity in their essays, asides or parentheticals, plurality of voices, bringing in opposed opinions or speaking to the views of others.

Nevertheless, we *can* I think, validly look at private writing itself. Trust is the issue here. If we go to people we really trust and ask if they will let us look at some examples of writing they did with the unambiguous intention of not showing it to anyone else, I would call their offerings private writing. The results will be most trustworthy if we ask them for writing they did a long time ago. For it's easier to believe that people might now feel more open about allowing a researcher to see writing they experienced a long time ago as completely secret or private. Looking at such writing, we can ask research questions like these:

- Will any interesting features or qualities come to light if we look at a large body of private writing by many people—especially if we compare it to public writing by the same people?
- How about in-depth studies of single writers—looking not only at their writing but also interviewing them extensively? There is a tradition to be built on here of literary researchers investigating and comparing the journals and the published writing of major figures.

Enabling Further Research by Changing "Always" to "Sometimes"

In my initial analysis of the claim that all writing is social, I ended with three subclaims that were debatable. The first one, 3a, asserts that we always harbor unconscious thoughts about future readers whenever we write. This claim strikes me as fairly intractable to empirical research and so I will not consider it further.

But the second debatable claim, 3b, is a different story: We always unconsciously shape our writing for strong readers from the past. If we change "always" to "sometimes," we can change an unhelpful "yes/no" debate into a fruitful "when-and-how-much?" empirical investigation. We can interview writers to learn about past readers they experienced as powerful and influential (e.g., teachers who pushed for concrete details, or who kept asking for poetic adjectives, or who always rewarded a certain point of view or tone or stance.) We can then, with students' help, look for evidence of those readers in their writing. It will be interesting to speculate why some writers have been more deeply shaped than others by strong writers from the past.

Even more fruitfully, we can look for *changes* in people's "readers-in-the-head." We already have some longitudinal studies that track students' writing over time. Perhaps some of these could be helpfully reframed and the data re-examined so as to look for changes in students' internalized readers. It's my hypothesis that frequent private writing—as long as people look back on it and reflect on what they see—would help writers gradually be more aware of past readers-in-the-head, and help them make more conscious choices about whether to continue to write for Mrs. Lewalski—and, in general, which kinds of reader they want to please.

Using this same crucial move—transforming "always" to "sometimes" and asking "when-and-how-much?"—we can actually make some progress on what is probably the most important theoretical issue in this paper, and indeed one of the most important and now somewhat stalled questions in our profession. This is the issue of "ideology" or what I like to call "culture-in-the-head." I formulated this as (3d): Everything we write is shaped by the minds, attitudes, values, and consciousnesses around us—family, institutions, and above all, culture.

Given this wording, the claim is obviously true, indeed necessarily true.

Culture-in-the-head is inevitable. But I hope I've succeeded in showing that a claim in this form is remarkably dull and fruitless—and also ambiguous. That is, culture-in-the-head is only inevitably or always true if we silently add the phrase "in a sense" or "to some degree." The claim only becomes interesting or meaningful if I ask how *much* of my writing is shaped by my culture? Surely very few of even the strongest-minded cultural critics believe that every person's every piece of writing—as an entire unit—is an unchanged "channeling" from outside the writer's head. Many cultural critics probably believe that some students sometimes produce texts that represent their own "mix" of ingredients from the culture around them—and even perhaps that some students occasionally have a thought or perception worth calling "their own."

David Bartholomae is a useful commentator to consider here. Sometimes he allows himself to sound as though he thinks all student writing is nothing but a product of culture—such as when he makes fun of "classrooms where students are asked to imagine that they can clear out a space to write on their own, to express their own thoughts and ideas, not to reproduce those of others" (Writing With Teachers" 64). But in the end, Bartholomae seems to be concerned with something much more interesting, namely, the *degree* to which writers reproduce the commonplaces of their culture: "The key distinguishing gesture of this [student] essay, that which makes it 'better' than the other, is the way the writer works against a conventional point of view, one that is represented within the essay by conventional phrases that the writer must then work against" ("Inventing the University" 152). More productive still, Bartholomae, like most good teachers, shows that he is interested in the possibility of *changing* culture-in-the-head: "If . . . we are going to do anything but preside over the reproduction of forms and idioms, we have to make the classroom available for critical inquiry." ("Writing With Teachers" 66).

In short, we can make the theoretical discussion of culture-in-the-head ("ideological interpellation") much more interesting and useful if we pay more attention, as Bartholomae does here, to the fact that some students' writing seems to indicate that their heads are particularly strongly stamped with the values and opinions of the culture around them; while others look a bit more independent in their thinking—or at least seem able to make more idiosyncratic mixtures of the varied cultural ingredients around them. Instead of just emptily proclaiming that culture-in-the-head is always already present, we could follow the writing of some students over time, and perhaps learn more about the processes by which some of them get more distance or perspective on the culture around them. I can't help hypothesizing that students might gain more of this kind of perspective if they do a lot of non-careful private writing and look back and reflect on what they see.

Readers-in-the-head and culture-in-the-head are obviously subtle and difficult matters to research. But literary critics have long explored the unconscious shaping of literary texts by culture and by other strong "writers-in-the-head" (e.g., Bloom), and they have often come up with results that are useful and interesting, if not definitive.

The Self as Audience

The third debatable subclaim was (4): The self always functions as audience for our writing. Here too we can get rid of the "always," which leads to interminable yes/no debates, and replace it with "sometimes" so as to invite investigation of when and under what circumstances.

Let's start with a limiting case. Presumably there is plenty of *deciding* or even *thinking* that we don't overhear. But do we ever produce inner speech that we don't overhear? Probably. Outer speech? Perhaps now and then. Think about involuntary utterances like "ouch" or "damn" or "oh no," that we produce when we are utterly absorbed in some task. We aren't even aware that we've uttered them. (Here is where speech shades into mere "audible gesture," for example the "uuhhhmmmmmmm" we gradually utter—actually more a breathing out than an uttering—as we're trying to do something difficult with our hands.) We need to investigate people who talk a lot to themselves. But do we ever *write* in such a radically nonself-aware way—with *no* aware registering or overhearing of the words we are writing? Conceivably, but probably not. Yet let's explore limiting cases some more. It will help our thinking and lead us to some practical payoffs.

When Georgie Yeats and the dadaists and others engaged in "automatic writing" induced by a trance state, it would seem as though they were not proprioceptively "receiving" or registering their own writing. I wonder if this kind of thing can't occasionally happen in more everyday circumstances. When I am engaged in private exploratory writing just to figure something out or to sort through my feelings or even just to vent them, it seems to me that occasionally I get so wound up in simply "emitting words" through my fingers that I stop hearing or registering them. (This may depend on my being a fast, habitual typist.) Probably, it's more accurate to say that I'm "sort of registering" them, since I must be sort of or in some sense aware of the words as I put them down. Nevertheless, what's most interesting about these bits of writing is how *little* I register the words and thoughts—how *different* it is from most of my writing with respect to my awareness of my own words.

If it seems too far out to suggest that people occasionally write things they don't even register or overhear, let's not forget an important principle from logic: it's dangerous to assert the *nonexistence* of something. Counterexamples have a habit of turning up. And I'm tempted to add a principle from "psychologic": it is dangerous to assert that there is something that the human mind *never* does. In particular, theorists shouldn't say that something doesn't exist just because they haven't seen it or experienced it—or because they are committed to theories that imply its nonexistence.

My point is this: once we consider and wrap our minds around this unusual concept of language *emitted but not received*—or scarcely received—we will find it fruitful. As I pointed out in the examples from Burke and Petrey, once we catch a glimpse of something that seems odd or rare, and then come to understand it better, we may find that it's not so odd or rare. In effect, it is a matter of trying out an unfamiliar lens that doesn't seem to show much, but then gradually getting it into focus and discovering that it shows a great deal. Here again, the secret to fruitful research will be to move from yes-or-no theoretical debate to "when-and-how-much?" empirical investigation.

Consider the exasperated joke that frustrated writing teachers sometimes blurt: "I just read a paper that had never been seen before by human eyes!" We have all read papers that make us sense that the student never experienced or overheard these words. Almost every writing teacher has learned a simple way to handle this kind of writing: ask the student to read it over outloud in our presence. Almost always, the student immediately experiences the problem, and can often readily fix that incoherent syntax or the tangled meaning. What I want to call attention to here is the fact that the student often has the experience of never really having seen or experienced these sentences before.

What is going on here? How can it be that someone writes something while awake, and yet experiences it as unfamiliar when reading it over? Let me ask the question more fruitfully: What does it mean to experience or be an audience of our own writing? This question will help us notice an enormous range of writing behavior all around us and see a fruitful spectrum: at one extreme, people are writing with rich awareness and consciousness of what they are saying and meaning; at the other end, people are writing and scarcely hearing or registering their words. How can we usefully characterize the different degrees or levels of experiencing one's own writing—degrees or levels of paying attention—from very little experiencing to very full experiencing?

We can make more progress on this question if we notice that there is more than one dimension involved. That is, it's not just a question of *quantity* of experience but also of the *mode* of experiencing; not just a question of how much attention but also how *wide* the beam of attention is. That is, perhaps the students who wrote garbled sentences did indeed experience and overhear every single word or phrase in those sentences—*as words or phrases*. But they probably didn't experience the words *as sentences*. Similarly, the students who wrote tangled paragraphs or longer sections might well have experienced every sentence—as sentence. But not as paragraphs or larger cognitive or semantic "chunks" or units. There are different degrees of *breadth* or *scope* in a writer's attention to his or her own writing. And thus these questions:

- In what ways can we help students to hear or experience their writing more fully? For starters, consider this progression: writing words down in silence; reading them over silently afterward; reading them outloud afterward in solitude; reading them outloud to a listener or a group. There's also the peculiar process of *saying* one's words as one writes them—as in protocol analysis.
- Is it possible or useful to distinguish between *experiencing* one's words and *reflecting on* that experience? As Dewey stresses, experience itself doesn't necessarily lead to learning or growth; it's *reflection* on experience that does the job. I and many other teachers call for this kind of reflection by asking students to write "process letters" or "process logs" with major assignments.

I've used the word "overhear" in a casual and metaphorical way, but now I want to look more carefully at the literal concept:

- Under what conditions do people actually "hear" their words in their inner ear as they put them down? What are the effects of that hearing or not hearing? For example, it seems to me that I hear my words more when I write by hand than when I write on a computer. I have a definite sense that this hearing affects my syntax.
- Sometimes we subvocally *speak* our words as we write them. What leads us to do this or not to do it, and what are the effects? By the way, it would be perfectly feasible to check out nerve activity in the ear and in the throat while people write.
- Are there other modalities besides subauditory hearing and subvocal speaking through which people experience their words as they put them down? Surely gesture can play a role. I've recently been relieved to learn that I'm not the only person who occasionally gestures (or makes noises) as I write. What about deaf writers? Evidently, some of them hear in their mind's ear, and some do not. What about experiencing one's own language in the form of sign language? Vygotsky hypothesizes gesture as the origin of writing—indeed, of language itself.
- If we interviewed and observed writers who seem to experience their own words more and those who experience them less, we could fruitfully explore the differences.

I'm hoping these and related questions can spark fruitful research—and also spark ideas for our teaching. In my own teaching, I have drifted into more and more practices that I now realize are simply ways to help students be better audiences of self—to help them increase their proprioception of their own language. I push them to read their drafts outloud in pairs or small groups (even when I ask them also to share a paper copy); occasionally, I have students read portions or even whole essays to the class; I get each student to read a draft to me every other week in a short conference; we publish a class magazine for every major essay; I have begun experimenting with exercises using gesture and performance. It's my sense that students write better when I push them to be better audiences for their own language. We would all benefit from more research about self as audience—exploring degrees of reception of one's own language.[3]

---

3. One final thought about self as audience for one's own writing. I don't know what to make of it and so I relegate it to this note. Even though the self is always already somewhat an audience for our writing, there is a nontrivial *sense* in which the self is rarely an audience for it. Relatively little of the language we write is actually *addressed* to the self as audience. The self mostly *overhears* what we say or write to others. The fact is that we don't usually use the word "audience" for people who merely overhear words not directed to them. And we can usually feel a palpable difference between the common experience of addressing words to others and the rarer experience of actually addressing words directly *to* ourselves. For example, sometimes I interrupt my drafting of words to others with a passage addressed explicitly to myself where I write something like: "Where am I going? I think this is a blind alley." Or, "Should I move this paragraph to the beginning? It could make a good start for the whole essay?" Whether these notes are short or long, the discourse is quite different for actually addressing the self as audience.

Before I conclude, let me hark back to the first section of this essay about lens statements. We are considering here the lens statement (4): The self always functions as audience for our writing. Now that I am so conscious that lens statements always carry a hidden "in a sense," or "at least to some degree," I realize that the following claim is also always true: "We *never* fully hear or experience the language we emit." In truth, I'm still struggling to *hear fully* this essay that I've been writing for more than two years—and I must hope that publication of it does not have to wait on my fully succeeding.

Conclusion

In this essay, I've tried to help our profession pay better attention to private writing. I've tried to indicate major problems with the totalizing claims that there is no such thing as private writing—showing such claims to be lens statements that are no more true than their opposites. And I've tried to show how a move from totalizing claims about "always" and "never" to empirical claims about "sometimes" and "when-and-how-much?" will open up lots of possibilities for fruitful research about private writing and interesting possibilities for teaching.

In a number of senses, all writing is social and even shot through with the words and thoughts of others. Nevertheless, writers often fit their words better to outside readers when they put those readers out of mind for a while and write privately to try to make sure their words fit themselves and their own experience of things. For us teachers, the most important question may be the political one that students have no trouble asking: *"Are you going to collect this?"* That is, do we collect and read everything our students write? Or do we actively push them to engage in the seemingly peculiar activity of writing some things *not* for our eyes—or anyone else's?

Do we really want to make writing part of the project that Foucault calls the panopticon: the pervasive "surveillance" of us and our consciousness by others with institutional power? (Of course Foucault implies that there's no hope of getting away from this surveillance because everyone internalizes it and becomes his or her own prison guard. But to make this claim is to leave the matter in the realm of black and white and to avoid investigation of when and how much.) As teachers with authority, we can nudge students into spaces where—though they cannot get away from culture—they can operate under less supervision. We can provide them with some crucial time-outs from their experience of the unending oversight and testing of their minds that constitutes schooling. When students write privately, they often notice how much they write for us anyway—and this noticing can give them a bit more awareness of their situation and a bit more space for choice and agency. But we can only make these moves if we bring care and clarity to our theorizing about writing and language—especially about private writing.

Works Cited

Austin, J. L. *How to Do Things With Words*. NY: Oxford UP 1965.

Bartholomae, David. "Inventing the University." *When A Writer Can't Write*. Ed. Mike Rose. New York: Guilford, 1985. 134–65.

———. "Writing With Teachers: A Conversation with Peter Elbow." *College Composition and Communication* 46.1 (Feb. 1995): 62–71.

Bakhtin, Mikhail. "Discourse in the Novel." *The Dialogic Imagination: Four Essays*. Ed. Michael Holquist. Trans. Caryl Emerson and Michal Holquist. Austin: U Texas Slavic Series, no. 1, 1981. 259–422.

Bloom, Harold. *The Anxiety of Influence: A Theory of Poetry*. NY: Oxford UP, 1973.

Bruffee, Kenneth A. "Collaborative Learning and the Conversation of Mankind." *College English* 46 (1984): 635–52.

Burke, Kenneth. *Rhetoric of Motives*. Berkeley: U Cal P, 1969.

Burrows, David. *Sound, Speech, and Music*. Amherst MA: U Mass P, 1990.

Elbow, Peter. "High Stakes and Low Stakes in Assigning and Responding to Writing." *Writing to Learn: Strategies for Assigning and Responding to Writing in the Disciplines*. (A volume in the series, *New Directions for Teaching and Learning*.) Eds. Mary Deane Sorcinelli and Peter Elbow. San Francisco: Jossey-Bass. 1997. 5–13.

———. "A Map of Writing in Terms of Audience and Response." [In Part I.]

———. *Writing Without Teachers*, 2nd ed. NY: Oxford (1973) 1988.

Feldman, Carol Fleisher. "Two Functions of Language." *Harvard Education Review* 47 (1977): 282–93.

Gibson, Walker. "Authors, Speakers, Readers, and Mock Readers." *College English* 11 (Feb 1950): 265–69. Reprinted in Tompkins.

Harris, Jeanette. *Expressive Discourse*. Dallas: Southern Methodist UP, 1990.

Harris, Joseph. *A Teaching Subject: Composition Since 1966*. Upper Saddle River: Prentice Hall, 1997.

Juhl, P. D. *Interpretation, An Essay in the Philosophy of Literary Criticism*. Princeton: Princeton UP, 1980.

LeFevre, Karen Burke. *Invention as a Social Act*. Carbondale: Southern Illinois UP, 1987.

Mallon, Thomas. *A Book of One's Own: People and their Diaries*. NY: Ticknor and Fields, 1984.

Mead, George H. *Mind, Self, and Society From the Standpoint of a Social Behaviorist*. Ed. Charles W. Morris. Chicago: U of Chicago P, 1934.

Nienlcamp, Jean. *Internal Rhetoric*. Forthcoming.

Ong, Walter. *The Barbarian Within: and Other Fugitive Essays and Studies*. NY: Macmillan, 1962.

———. "The Writer's Audience Is Always a Fiction." PMLA 90 (January 1985): 9–21.

Perelman, Chaim, and Lucie Olbrechts-Tyteca. *The New Rhetoric: A Treatise on Argumentation*. Trans. John Wilkinson and Purcell Weaver. 1958. Notre Dame: U Notre Dame P, 1969.

Petrey, Sandy. *Speech Acts and Literary Theory*. NY: Routledge, 1990.

Prince, Gerald, "Introduction to the Study of the Narratee." *Poetique* 14 (1973): 177–96. Reprinted in Tompkins.

Shaftesbury, Anthony Ashley Cooper, Third Earl of. *Characteristics of Men, Manners, Opinions, Times*. Ed. John M. Robertson. Intro Stanley Green. 1711 Indianapolis: Library of LiberalArts-Bobbs-Merrill, 1964. 109, 113.

Spigelman, Candace. "Habits of Mind: Historical Configurations of Textual Ownership in Peer Writing Groups." *College Composition and Communication* 49.2 (May 1993): 234–55.

Steiner, George. *After Babel: Aspects of Language and Translation*. NY: Oxford UP, 1975.

Stover, Andrea. *Resisting Privacy: Problems with Self-Representation in Journals and Diaries*." Dissertation, 1999. U of Mass at Amherst.

Summerfield, Geoffrey. "Not in Utopia: Reflections on Journal-Writing." *The Journal Book.* Ed. Toby Fulwiler. Portsmouth NH: Boynton/Cook Heinemann, 1987.

Tompkins, Jane. *Reader-Response Criticism: From Formalism to Post-structuralism.* Baltimore: Johns Hopkins UP, 1980.

Trimbur, John. "Collaborative Learning and Teaching Writing." *Perspectives on Research and Scholarship in Composition.* Eds. Ben W. McClelland and Timothy R. Donovan. NY: MLA, 1985. 87–109.

Winnicott, D. W. "The Capacity to Be Alone." *The Maturational Processes and the Facilitating Environment.* London: Hogarth Press and the Institute of Psycho-Analysis, 1965. Also in *Collected Papers: Through Paediatrics to Psycho-Analysis.* London: Tavistock Publications. 1958.

Vygotsky, Lev. *Thought and Language.* Trans. Eugenia Hanfman and Gertrude Vakar. Cambridge: M.I.T. Press, 1962.

Young, Richard. "Invention: A Topographical Survey." *Teaching Composition: 10 Bibliographical Essays.* Revised and Enlarged Edition. Ed. Gary Tate. Fort Worth: Texas Christian UP, 1987. 1–43.

———. "Recent Developments in Rhetorical Invention." *Teaching Composition: 12 Bibliographical Essays.* Revised and Enlarged Edition. Ed. Gary Tate. Fort Worth: Texas Christian UP, 1987. 1–38.

13

The War Between Reading and Writing— and How to End It

We tend to assume that reading and writing fit naturally together: love and marriage, horse and carriage. It is a commonplace that the very best thing for writing is to read a great deal—and it seems as though those students who write best are readers. But when we see things in binary pairs, one side usually ends up on top—privileged or dominant: love and marriage, man and woman. I will argue that this is true here too and that reading has dominance over writing in the academic or school culture. But my main point in this essay is that the imbalance is unnecessary. Reading and writing *can* work productively together as equals to benefit each other and the profession. Both parties can be on top. We can create a better balance and relationship between reading and writing. To do so we will need to give more emphasis to writing in our teaching and our curricular structures and use writing in more imaginative ways. When we achieve this productive balance, even reading will benefit.

There are four sections here: (1) Where the war is waged; (2) Who is winning the war; (3) The benefits of reclaiming lost territory; (4) Ways to end the war and create a more productive interaction between reading and writing.

Where the War Is Waged

Gerald Graff wrote a whole book about the conflicts in the English profession and chose to ignore the most striking and problematic conflict of all: that between reading and writing—between literature and composition (Friend).

This essay was published in 1993 in *Rhetoric Review* 12.1 (Fall): 5–24. It was given the James A. Berlin award for the best essay of the year in that journal. It was reprinted in *Critical Theory and the Teaching of Literature: Politics, Curriculum, Pedagogy*. Eds. James Slevin and Art Young. Urbana IL: NCTE, 1996. 270–91.

The conflict of interest between reading and writing shows itself most clearly perhaps in the question of authority. From ancient times on, authors were the source of 'author'-ity—and it was the reader's job to find out what the author intended to say. Someone who could establish himself as "writer" or "author" (and it was usually "he") was felt to be special—even as seer or oracle. People often sought out authors or writers in order to hear their pronouncements on all sorts of matters (thus the phenomenon of "table talk").

In recent times *readers* have battled back successfully to take authority for themselves. The New Critics convinced much of the profession that the author's intention didn't matter. Deconstructive theorists convinced much of the profession that even the concept of meaning in a text is problematic. Roland Barthes speaks of the death of the author giving rise to the birth of the reader; he characterizes the reader as alive and sexy and full of energy, and the "scriptor" as pallid and lacking in juice.

The most specific focus of contention is over who gets authority over the meaning of a text. Take my own text here as an example. I get to decide what I *intended to say*. You get to decide what you *understand me to say*. But as for what I actually *did say*—what meanings are "in" my text—that is a site of contention between us. We see this fight everywhere, from the law courts to literary criticism to the bedrooms: "But I said . . ." / "No you didn't, you said . . ."

So the interests of the contending parties are clear. It's in the interest of readers to say that writers' intentions don't matter or are unfindable, to say that meaning is never determinate, always fluid and sliding, to say that there is no presence or voice behind a text—and finally to kill off the author. This leaves the reader in complete control of the text.

It's in the interest of writers, on the other hand, to say that their intentions are central—to have readers actually interested in what was on writers' minds, what they intended to say. As writers we often fail to be clear, but it helps us if readers have some faith that our authorial meanings and intentions can be found. If I am lost in the woods, you have a better chance of finding me if you think I am actually there. And it goes without saying that writers are interested in not being killed off. (Even critics who celebrate the death of the author are likely to get irritated when readers completely misread what they have written.)

Writers also have interest in *ownership* of the text—and, as with "killing," I want to take this metaphor literally. Writers have a interest in monetary payment for their labor. But of course the figurative psychological meaning is more pervasive. Writers *feel* ownership. People sometimes like to say now that the sense of individual ownership over words is only a recent, modern phenomenon, but even Chaucer in the fourteenth century wrote into his poem a plea to copyists please not to "miswrite" his words in copying the text.

Listen to the dismay of Toni Morrison on this point:

Whole schools of criticism have dispossessed the writer of any place whatever in the critical value of his work. Ideas, craft, vision, meaning—all of them are just so much baggage in these critical systems. . . . The political consequences for minority writers, dissident writers and writers committed to social change are devastating. For it means that there is no way to talk about what we mean, because to mean anything is not in vogue. (Sanders 25)

Here is Scott Russell Sanders commenting on her statement:

Rightly or wrongly, many of us who make novels and stories and poems feel that the net effect of recent theorizing has been to turn the writer into a puppet, one whose strings are jerked by some higher power—by ideology or the unconscious, by ethnic allegiance, by sexual proclivities, by gender, by language itself. We may wade through Derrida and Adorno and de Man, we may read Harold Bloom and J. Hillis Miller and Stanley Fish, or we may simply hear rumors of what they and their innumerable followers are up to; whether at first or second hand, we learn that to regard ourselves as conscious, purposeful, responsible artists is a delusion; we learn that material conditions or neuroses control us; we learn that our efforts at making sense are doomed to failure; we learn that our words, like Zeno's forlorn rabbit, will never reach their destination. (25)

Am I only telling a story of readers privileging themselves over writers? No, writers privileged themselves over readers long before the intentional fallacy was a gleam in the eye of Wimsatt and Beardsley. Writers often say, "What do readers know? My toughest audience—sometimes my main audience—is me. For some pieces, I don't even *care* whether readers understand or appreciate my efforts." So perhaps it's not surprising that readers have finally retaliated with a modern doctrine that says, "What do writers know? We can read the text better than they can. Intention is a will o' the wisp. Never trust the teller, trust the tale." In short, where writers are tempted to think they are the most important party in the transaction, readers and academics are tempted to think they are the most important party (Wallace.)

Just as children think their parents should always have them in mind, many modern readers think that writers should always have them in mind. When readers are teachers (and most teachers think of themselves more as readers than as writers), they tell students, "You must always keep us in mind as you write." And if student writing is weak, they diagnose "writer-based prose!" and assume that the student stopped thinking about them—when in fact the problem was probably that the student was *too* preoccupied with the teacher-reader. When readers are theorists (and most theorists also think of themselves more as readers than as writers), they often completely contradict that teacherly advice and declare, "There is no such thing as writing without readers in mind—no such thing as private writing. If you *thought* you were not thinking about us and just writing privately in your journal for yourself alone, you were fooling yourself. You are never not thinking about us." (See, for example, Harris 66.)

But writers, like parents, tend to insist on time away from the imperious demands of readers. Writers know they need some time when they can just forget about readers and think about themselves. Yes, writers must finally acknowledge the humbling truth that, in the end, readers get to decide whether their words will be *read* or *bought*—just as parents have to accept that, in the end, the child's interests must come first. But smart writers and parents know that they do a better job of serving these demanding creatures if they take some time for themselves.

I hope it's clear that this reader/writer conflict isn't just theoretical. I feel it quite concretely in my teaching—especially in a writing course for first-year students. Yes, ideally I want my students to feel themselves as both writers and readers. But my pressing hunger to help them feel themselves as writers makes me notice the conflict. That is, I want my students to have some of that uppitiness of writers toward readers—to be able to talk back—to say, "I'm not just writing for readers or teachers, I'm writing as much for me—sometimes even *more* for me." I want them to fight back a bit against readers.

Let me point to another conflict of interests between writers and readers: a conflict over the relationship between *language* and *knowledge*. Writers frequently testify to the experience of knowing more than they can say, of knowing things that they haven't yet been able to get into words. Readers on the other hand, (especially when they are also teachers or academics), being mostly on the receiving end of texts, are often tempted to put forth the doctrine that all knowledge is linguistic, that there is nothing we can know outside of language: "If you cannot talk about an experience, at least to yourself, you did not have it" (Emerson 252).

Again, this isn't just theoretical. Paying better attention to the *in*articulate—having more respect for the nonverbal—often leads writers to the articulate. Most of my own progress in learning to write has come from my gradually learning to listen more carefully to what I haven't yet managed to get into words—waiting and trying to feel better my nonverbal feelings and intentions—and respecting the idea that I know more than I can say. This stance helps me be willing to find time and energy to tease into language what the phenomenologist Eugene Gendlin calls my "felt bodily sense." The most unhelpful thing I've had said to me as a student and writer is, "If you can't say it, you don't know it." Not surprisingly, painters, musicians, and dancers are more than a little amused at the odd dogma that all knowledge is linguistic—that if you can't say it in language you don't know it and it doesn't count as knowledge.

I want to call attention to some very central pedagogical implications of this point about language and meaning—a point that writers often understand and readers and academics and teachers often do not. The main thing that helps writers is to be *understood*. Pointing out what we don't understand is only the second need. In my teaching, I find it helpful to assume that I often *can* hear intentions that are not really articulated. Yes, I'll point out where these intentions are badly realized, but if my goal is to make students feel like writers, my highest priority is to show that I've understood what they're saying. It's only my second priority to show them where I had to struggle.

I see a third conflict between readers and writers these days: over whether to trust language. Again let me describe the conflict in terms of my own teaching. If my goal is to get my first-year students to take on the role of reader, I should constantly try to get them to distrust language. For it is a central tenet of intellectual and academic thinking in this century that words are not a clear and neutral window through which we can see undistorted nonlinguistic things.

Of course, I acknowledge the merit in this skeptical view of language. Nevertheless, if I want to help my students experience themselves as *writers,* I find I must help them *trust* language—not question it—or at least not question it for long stretches of the writing process till they have managed to generate large structures of language and thinking. Some people say this is good advice only for inexperienced and blocked writers, but I think I see it enormously helpful to myself and to other adult, skilled, and professional writers. Too much distrust often stops people from coming up with interesting hypotheses and from getting things written. Striking benefits usually result when people learn that decidedly unacademic capacity to turn off distrust of language and instead not to *see* it, to look through it as through a clear window, and focus all attention on the objects or experiences one is trying to articulate. Let me quote the distinguished poet and writer, William Stafford, about the need to trust language and one's experience.

> Just as any reasonable person who looks at water, and passes a hand through it, can see that it would not hold a person up; so it is the judgment of common sense people that reliance on the weak material of students' experiences cannot possibly sustain a work of literature. But swimmers know that if they relax on the water it will prove to be miraculously buoyant; and writers know that a succession of little strokes on the material nearest them—without any prejudgments about the specific gravity of the topic or the reasonableness of their expectations—will result in creative progress. Writers are persons who write; swimmers are (and from teaching a child I know how hard it is to persuade a reasonable person of this)—swimmers are persons who relax in the water, let their heads go down, and reach out with ease and confidence.
>
> . . . [M]y main plea is for the value of an unafraid, face-down, flailing, and speedy process in using the language. (22–23)

For the last site of conflict between reading and writing (and an intriguing one), let's look at what's called "invisible writing." A couple of decades ago, James Britton and colleagues (35ff.) were interested in how important it is for writers to get that literal, short-term feedback of simply *seeing* what they are writing. They demonstrated this by artificially taking it away. That is, they tried writing with spent ballpoint pens so they couldn't see what they were writing (but putting carbon paper and another sheet underneath the page they were writing on). Sure enough, they felt stymied and their writing fell apart. But then Sheridan Blau replicated the experiment many times—and showed in virtually every case that students and professionals were *not* significantly harmed by ten- and twenty-minute stretches of what he called "invisible writing" (despite some initial frustration). Indeed, students often produced better pieces in various modes or genres under these conditions (Blau). His explanation of the phenomenon seems right to me from my own trials of invisible writing: when you can't see what you are writing, you are almost automatically forced into a much greater focus of attention and energy on what you are trying to say—on the meaning and intention in your mind. And you can't stop and worry; you must forge on.

What these experiments show is the odd fact that normal writing is really both-writing-*and*-reading. Invisible writing stamps out the reading we normally do as we write, and forces us to engage in nothing-*but*-writing—with a consequent boost of concentration and intensity of mind. Thus invisible writing is strikingly helpful with a common problem: finding ourselves stalled in our writing and spending most of our so-called *writing* time sitting and reading back over what we have already written. Word processors make invisible writing very easy: just turn down the screen.

Who Is Winning the War?

Most schools and colleges emphasize reading and neglect writing. A (no longer recent) investigation of English classes in secondary schools has found that students spend less than 3 percent of their class and homework time devoted to writing a paragraph or more—and most of the "writing" time in class consists of writing short-answer exercises (Applebee).

In most school and college courses, reading is more central than writing. Even in English departments there is usually only *one* writing course—some kind of "freshman writing." Sometimes there is a sprinkling of creative writing or other advanced writing courses—but even when these are given, they are available to comparatively few students. Other departments (except for journalism) typically have no writing courses.

Of course, writing is *assigned* in a fair number of courses (though some students in large universities learn to avoid much writing for their whole college career). But when writing is assigned, it is traditionally meant to *serve* reading: to summarize, interpret, explain, or make integrations and comparisons among readings. In the last couple of years, there has even been a widespread move to change the first-year writing course into a reading-and-writing course, even though it is usually the *only* writing course—the only place in the entire curriculum where writing is emphasized more than reading. In every other course in the university, reading is privileged, and writing, when used at all, is used to serve reading.

I won't try to analyze here the complicated historical and cultural reasons why we have this imbalance, but I can't resist mentioning one interesting hypothesis (Laurence). If we assign much writing, we find ourselves positively awash in what many people find discouraging or depressing: our students' thinking and feeling—with all its naïvete and immersion in pop culture. Faculty can spare themselves from any real knowledge of extensive student thinking and feeling about their topic if they assign mostly reading, if they use carefully focused topics on the few occasions when they do assign writing, and if they fill up their classes with lectures or carefully controlled discussions. Howard Gardner points out that good teaching and learning seldom happen unless we understand and acknowledge and learn to deal with what is really happening in students' minds.

The dominance of reading has produced some powerful political and economic consequences for higher education. It is fairly common for English departments to "live off" writing teachers—paying them poorly, denying them the possibility of tenure, and providing poor working conditions, in order to give tenure, much better pay, and a lighter teaching load to teachers of reading or literature. People who teach writing are apt to be TAs or nontenure track lecturers or adjunct part-timers who must piece together jobs at two or three institutions, and are often paid less than $1,000 per course—with no benefits. They often don't know if they'll be hired till a month or a week before the term begins—sometimes, in fact, only after the semester has started. (James Slevin lays out these conditions in more detail and makes an interesting argument about the reasons for the imbalance.)

Let me turn from the outward material conditions of employment to the inward premises of our thinking. That is, the relationship between reading and writing in most school and college courses enacts a kind of root metaphor or originary story of our culture: that we hear and read before we speak and write—that input precedes output. This seems a natural story: babies and children seem to hear before they can speak—to listen before they answer. But it's not so simple. Yes, children wouldn't speak unless they grew up in the presence of other speakers, and of course babies and children usually answer when spoken to. But careful observation of children suggests that it works the other way round too: the reason why children *get* input—*hear* language—is often that they *initiate* the "conversation." Even when a baby gives as little as a gurgle or a coo, parents often take it as the initiation of discourse (which it sometimes is), and respond. Babies don't just read the textbook and listen to lectures and then answer questions; sometimes they start the conversation. Babies often "write" before they "read."

I suspect that the child's initiation of speech is as important or more so in learning to talk than the initiation by others. That is, the adult's enabling act is as much listening and understanding and answering as it is starting a conversation. The most productive and generative act by a teacher or parent is often to listen. In short, most parents instinctively know that their job is to get children to start with output, not input—start with writing, not reading.

But the relationship between reading and writing in schools and universities belies this instinctive wisdom of parents. Our very concept of what it is to learn privileges reading over writing because that conception has been shaped by the same root metaphor: *learning is input*—"taking things in"—putting things inside us. People think of the root activities in school as listening and reading, not talking and writing. Of course, when we stop and think about it, we realize that students learn from output—talking and writing—

but we don't naturally think of learning as talking and writing. Notice, for example, how many teachers think of testing as measuring input, not output. Tests tend to ask, in effect, "How well have you learned the ideas of others?" not "What new ideas of your own do you have?"

Even if we grant that, more often than not, input precedes output, and that we usually speak and write in response to what we hear and read, we must still beware the claim that some people make today: that *all* writing is in response to text or textuality. This is not a fair translation of Bakhtin's insight about the ubiquity of voices. When people fixate on a theoretical dictum that all writing is in response to texts, they paper over a concrete and indeed political distinction: the distinction between asking students to write in response to our texts and lectures versus asking them to write in response to their own ideas and experience (even if their ideas and experience are made up of texts and voices already inside their heads). Even if we were to take it as our main goal to show students that what they experience as their own ideas and voices are really ideas and voices from outside them, our best strategy would be to get them to write extensively about something *before* reading any new texts about it. That is the best way to make visible all the voices that are already jampacked inside their heads.

Why is it that our profession stresses so much the *reading* of imaginative writing—fiction and poetry and drama—while neglecting the writing of it? Most of us got into the field not only because we loved to read imaginative writing but also because we liked to write it—often harboring wishes to be writers. But as adult professionals, we tend to run away from it. We seldom write it or ask our students to write it. Can we really say we understand something we never try to engage in? We should surely require Ph.D. candidates at least to *try their hand* at the kind of writing they profess to understand and hope to teach.

I've had an interesting glimpse into the archaeology of this fear of writing in literature professors. Whenever I teach any graduate course in writing, I ask students to write case studies of themselves as writers: to look back through their lives at what they've written and to figure out as much as they can about how they went about writing and what was going on—to try to see all the forces at play. I've noticed a striking feature that is common in literature students that I don't much see in graduate students from other disciplines: a wry and sometimes witty but always condescending tone they take toward their younger selves who were usually excited with writing and eager to be great writers. Behind this urbanity I often see a good deal of disappointment and even pain at not being able to keep on writing those stories and poems that were so exciting to write. But instead of acknowledging this disappointment, these students tend to betray a frightening lack of kindness or charity—most of all a lack of *understanding*—toward that younger self who wanted to grow up to be Yeats or Emily Dickinson. Instead, I see either amused condescension or downright ridicule at their former idealism and visionary zeal. My point is that no one can continue to engage in writing without granting herself some vision and idealism and even naïve grandstanding. Yet these literature students, now that they see themselves on the path to being professors of literature—that is professors of reading—seem to need to squelch any sense of themselves as writers.

Even in MFA programs, which are devoted to writing and which are sometimes even guilty of neglecting reading, we see an odd but powerful ritual that privileges readers over writers: the so-called gag rule. It is standard in workshops that writers must be silent and only readers may speak. That is, writers must refrain from the most natural thing that they might want to do, namely, to specify the kinds of response they need from readers or the issues they want readers to explore. (This pervasive custom seems to derive from the early Iowa workshops, and perhaps has definite gender associations of writers as "tough guys who can take it.")

Notice how the dominance of reading over writing is embedded in our language. The word *literacy* really means power over letters, for example, reading and writing. But as *literacy* is used casually and even in government policy and legislation, it tends to mean *reading,* not writing. Similarly, the word *learning* tends to connote reading and input—not writing and output. Finally, the very words *academic* or *professor* or even *teacher* tend to connote a reader and critic, not a writer. Thus deeply has the dominance of reading infected our ways of thinking.

I can conclude this section by making it clear that I am not arguing *against* reading—against the importance and special value of reading and listening: only against privileging them over writing and speaking. Reading and listening are precious for the very ways they are different from writing and speaking. They are precious because they ask us to step outside our own preoccupations and hear what others have to say, to think in the language of others, to recognize the authority of others without letting it overwhelm us, and above all to relinquish some control. I hope that my long advocacy of the believing game (1973) or methodological belief (1986) will show that I don't slight this side of our intellectual life.

Nor am I trying to imply that students are already good at reading and listening. Far from it. Yes, learning means getting inside someone else's language and thinking, taking in ideas, indeed taking in lists of brute facts—and getting them right. But I suspect that part of students' difficulty with reading stems from the ingrained educational pattern I'm pointing to here: It's always, "Read first and then write to see if you got it right. What *they* have to say is more important than what *you* have to say." Reading and listening might go better if we sometimes said, "Let's start with what *you* have to say. Then we'll see if the reading can respond to it and serve it." I find it common for people to be more interested in a subject and able to take in more new material about it if they first work out their own thinking about it.

Benefits of Reclaiming Lost Territory

What if we undid the imbalance? The benefits would be considerable. If we gave more centrality to writing, it would help out with an important and vexing problem in the teaching of reading itself. That is, we often have difficulty getting students to see how the meaning of a text is actively created and negotiated—not just found as an inert right answer sitting there hidden in the text or in the teacher's mind or in a work of authoritative criticism. "Yes," we say to our students, "the text puts some constraints on our reading. Not any interpretation is acceptable. Nevertheless, the resulting meaning is something that readers have to build and negotiate." This lesson is all the harder to teach because students sometimes flop over into the opposite misunderstanding of reading: "Well this is what *I* think the poem means, and nothing you can say will change my mind. Literature is just a matter of *personal opinion.*"

Reading can learn from writing here. Writing involves physical actions that are much more outward and visible than reading does. As a result, it's easier to see how meaning is slowly constructed, negotiated, and changed in writing than it is in reading. The erasing, crossing out, and changing of words as we write is much more visible than the erasing, crossing out, and changing of words that do in fact go on as we read—but more quickly and subliminally. Students can see evidence of the writing process in the messy manuscripts and revisions even of famous published authors. And we usually *experience* the construction of meaning more vividly, even painfully, when we write than when we read. Most writing teachers now try to set up their classes so that students can experience how written meaning is constructed through a process of thinking, generating trial text, revision, and social negotiation with peers and teachers. It seems to me then that writing is the most helpful paradigm we have for teaching what may be the central process in our profession and what we most want to convey to students: the way meaning in both reading and writing is constructed and negotiated.

By the way, because the reading process is so quick and hidden, it seems less fraught with struggle for people who are skilled. Therefore, literature teachers often fail to experience themselves in the same boat or engaged in the same process as their unskilled students. When it comes to writing, however, almost all teachers experience the common bond of struggle or even anxiety, no matter how good they are. Writing is a leveler.

But students *could* come to see reading as a "process" of cognitive and social construction if only there were a tradition in literature, as there is in writing, of teachers and researchers sharing what we might call "rough drafts of reading": showing or talking about their actual reading process *from the beginning*—for example, by working with colleagues or students on texts they have not seen before; giving an honest protocol or an accurate account of the mental events that go on in one's mind while engaged in creating meaning from a text. I like to call this giving "movies of the reader's mind." If there were more widespread attention to this sharing of our own reading processes, we'd spend more time talking to our colleagues and to our students about how of course we misread and misunderstand an enormous number of words and phrases and sections of a text as we engage in even the most skilled reading. That is, the mysterious innerness of reading isn't just because good readers "revise" and correct themselves so quickly and often subliminally; it's also because there's no tradition of revealing misreadings and wrong takes as there is of sharing early drafts. Where the writing tradition of the last two decades shows teachers how to write with students and share that they produce in its raw crummy state, the literary tradition tells literature teachers that it would be wrong to teach a class on a text that they have not carefully studied and mastered beforehand; and that it would be odd to have a discussion with colleagues about a text they've never seen before. Reading becomes vivid and alive in classes where everyone, even teachers, reveals early rough "readings" in process, and shows how these are adjusted and transformed over time and by means of negotiation through comparison with readings by others.

One of the virtues of reader-response criticism is that if people really engage in it honestly and empirically, it tends to make them braver about the kind of exploring I've just described. It promotes professionalism in the good sense (nondefensive thinking together) and undermines professionalism in the bad sense (trying to hide your struggles and to erase bonds with the unwashed). I'm suspicious of the fact that reader-response criticism has gone so deeply out of fashion in literary criticism. I know there are lots of culturally sophisticated reasons, but frankly, I think a lot of it can be explained this way: critics began to stumble onto a critical method that required giving naked accounts of what was actually happening inside them as they read—and decided to back away from the process.

If writing were more central, it would also help in the *assessment* of reading. The field of composition has managed to convince schools and colleges that testing means testing a practice or a performance, not a content: that if we want to find out how well students write, we've got to get them to write—despite budgetary pressures and the blandishments of cheaper tests of grammar and usage from ETS and ACT. In the case of literature, however, virtually every school, college, and university in the country accedes to ETS and ACT testing of literature and reading by means of multiple-choice, machine-graded tests—many of them tests of correct information. We see some of the same difference between writing and reading if we look at teachers' course exams: it has come to feel peculiar if the final exam in a writing course asks mostly for recall of ideas and information—whereas that does not seem peculiar in many literature courses.

Another benefit of emphasizing writing: it will yield us a better model not just for reading but for learning itself. The dominance of reading at all levels of education reinforces the problematic banking metaphor of learning: the assumption that students are vessels to be filled. But when we give equal emphasis to writing, we are more likely to assume the contrasting metaphor: *learning is the making of meaning.* This metaphor helps explain much that is otherwise paradoxical about the learning process:

- The more we write and talk, the more we have left to write and say. The greater the number of words that come out of us, the greater the number of words we find left inside.
- When students feel empty ("I have nothing to say, nothing on my mind"),

the cause is not insufficient input but insufficient output. What gets more words in their heads is more talking and writing.

• Of course, teachers and politicians love to talk: the more people talk, the more they want to talk.

When we see learning not as input but as the making of meaning and connections, these phenomena become natural, not paradoxical. Notice too that when we stop privileging reading over writing, we stop privileging passivity over activity. Yes, I grant the usefulness of the currently fashionable paradoxes: that the reading is really "writing" (actively creating meaning), and writing is really "reading" (passively finding what culture and history have inscribed in our heads). But in the end I would insist that writing simply does promote more activity and agency than reading:

• Reading tends to imply "Sit still and pay attention," while writing tends to imply "Get in there and *do* something."
• Reading asks, "What did they have to say?" while writing asks, "What do you have to say?" In normal speech listeners usually want to know what the speaker was actually intending to say, and this reinforces the impulse to "look for the right answer" in reading. Similarly, speakers usually have the impulse to say what's on their mind, and this reinforces the impulse for writers to take authority over their own meaning.
• Reading tends to be a matter of the teacher and author choosing the words; writing tends to be a matter of the student choosing the words.
• Reading means consumption, writing means production. Part of the stale passivity of students comes from their being cast always in the role of consumer.
• I would point even to the purely physical dimension. Writing involves more physical movement than reading. Try this experiment: On an occasion when a discussion class goes listless or dead, have everyone stop talking and silently read a helpful piece of text; on another occasion have everyone stop and write something. You'll find that students tend to be more awake and involved after they write—even displaying more tonus in their bodies—than after they read. (Notice also how the physical act of reading out loud—especially with any gesturing—helps the cognitive dimension of reading.)

In short, when we make writing as important as reading, we help students break out of their characteristically passive stance for school and learning. The primacy of reading in the reading/writing dichotomy is an act of locating authority away from the student and keeping it entirely in the teacher or institution or great figure. The privileging of reading over writing has locked schools into sending a pervasive, deep-level message: don't speak until spoken to; don't write your own ideas till you prove that you can reproduce correctly the ideas and information of others; writing *means* responding to authority outside the self; as a student you should be a consumer of knowledge, not a producer.

If we made writing as important as reading, we might begin to feel ourselves as writers too, not just readers. At present, when we take on the role of "academic," we tend to take on the role of reader and critic—and not writer. To make this large change, we'd have to foster and nourish creative risk-taking in ourselves and in the profession. We celebrate the imagination in the authors we study; we would grow as a profession if we celebrated and cultivated it in ourselves too. Just as society or individual relationships lose vitality and intelligence if women or a minority are suppressed, so English is losing vitality and intelligence because writing is suppressed.

Let me end this section by answering a possible objection: "We *must* keep writing in its secondary role—as the medium for responding to reading—or else we will invite romantic solipsism. If you invite students to write out of their own experience rather than in response to texts, you will increase the rampant individualism our culture suffers from —permitting students to disappear into cocoons of solipsistic isolation." This fear rests on a misguided model of individual development—a kind of parody of Freud and Piaget that says children start out as egocentric monads dominated by selfish desires to stay separate and egocentric; and that they cannot become "decentered" or social without a terrible struggle. It's as though we fear that our students are each in their own little bathroom and we must beat on the door and say, "What are you *doing* in there? Why have you been in there so long with the door locked? Come on out and have some wholesome fun with us."

But a very different course of development now seems more believable and generally accepted—a model that derives from thinkers like George Herbert Mead, Bakhtin, and Vygotsky: our children *start out* very social and intertwined. Their little selves are not hermetically sealed atoms but are rather deeply enmeshed or rooted in the important figures in their lives. We don't have to struggle to make children want to connect with others—they are naturally already connected. We don't have to bang on the bathroom door to make them listen, feel part of, and collaborate with the various people and cultural forces around them. They may not want to listen to *us* but that doesn't make them private and solipsistic. (In fact it's usually the private and solipsistic kids that listen best to us teachers.) What this picture of human development shows us is that separateness and autonomy are not qualities that children start out with but rather qualities they only gradually achieve—often with struggle and setbacks throughout adolescence and young adulthood. If we do lots and lots of writing, this is not a move toward solipsism, it's an extremely social practice. Sometimes an emphasis on reading is more solipsistic. The social dimension of writing is particularly vivid when we give students lots of opportunity to hear and read each other's writing.

Ways to End the War and Create a More Productive Interaction between Reading and Writing

There are some specific practices that will help reading and writing reinforce each other better—in both curriculum and teaching.

In curriculum, the important steps are obvious and can be quickly described. First, we need more writing courses. When students are polled, they usually ask for more. Second, we need more of what are called "fifty-fifty courses": half reading and half writing. Here are some good examples in the curriculum at the University of Vermont: "Writing Literary Criticism"; "Reading and Writing Nonfiction"; "Reading and Writing Autobiography"; "Personal Voice"; "Writing the *New Yorker.*" Some campuses have junior level courses in the disciplines ("Writing in Physics" or "Writing in Anthropology") that are really fifty-fifty courses. Such courses are probably the most natural and fruitful place for reading and writing mutually to enhance each other—courses where we go back and forth constantly between reading and writing and neither activity is felt as simply a handmaiden to the other one. A good "writing across the curriculum" or "writing intensive" course is a "fifty-fifty" course, but many fall short.

In teaching, there are various ways that reading and writing can learn from each other. Let me look more concretely now at some teaching practices to see interesting ways in which we can give more emphasis to writing.

The obvious step is to assign more writing, but this leads to an obvious problem: it causes so much more work for us as teachers with all those papers to grade and respond to. But we can largely avoid this problem if we learn to use writing in the varied and flexible ways we use reading.

Notice, above all, that we don't *evaluate* or *grade* all the reading we assign. It feels perfectly normal to assign lots of reading and test or evaluate or grade only some of it. For the rest, we assume that if students don't do it, they'll be less successful at the activities we do grade and evaluate. But somehow teachers tend to assume they have to evaluate or comment on every piece of writing they assign.

For another example, in most courses we have both required reading and supplementary or suggested reading: texts we feel all students must read and texts we expect diligent or interested students to read. We don't ask or expect them all to do it. Yet we seldom take this approach with writing.

In other words, whereas we usually have a spectrum of reading from high stakes to low stakes, most teachers fall unthinkingly into the habit of treating all writing as obligatory, high-stakes work. Writing is usually handled in such a way as to make it an unpleasant ordeal, even a punishment—for students *and* teacher. The flexible and varied uses of reading is a mark of the respect and sophistication with which we treat reading. We need to respect writing with similar flexibility—by also having low-stakes, supplementary, and experimental writing instead of being so rigid and one dimensional about it.

Many breakthroughs in our relation to writing occur when we learn to have a whole spectrum of writing—from high stakes to low stakes:

- A few pieces (as now) that we evaluate and count as important.
- Some more informal pieces that we collect but only grade with a check—or with "check plus" and "check minus." Some of these might function as drafts for evaluated pieces.

- Some pieces that we collect but just read or even just glance over—and that's all.
- Some pieces that are purely private to help students think to themselves about the reading or discussion or lectures. Sometimes we devote some class time to this writing; sometimes we make it a journal assignment to be done as homework, and just check periodically to make sure students are keeping up.
- Some nonrequired pieces that are "supplementary" or "suggested": we read and give a brief comment to those pieces that are done. Even if relatively few students do these pieces, there are striking benefits not only to those students but in fact to the quality of the class as a whole. There is a richer mix of voices in the conversation—some of them much more invested and authoritative.

Many teachers are helping students learn more by getting them to share their writing with each other, for example in pairs or small groups. It takes little time for mere sharing—and a great deal is learned. (It takes more time if we want students to give each other feedback, but that is not crucial. The greatest learning comes from the sharing itself.) In addition, many teachers get students to contribute (say) weekly to a computer conversation about the course material—if only in a low-tech way where students simply go to the computer lab once a week and add a few screens full to a class-conversation disk.

Similarly, teachers are learning flexible ways to publish student writing. We can use a lab fee to pay for class publications; we can ask students to bring in twenty or so copies of something they have written. If I ask for two pages, single-spaced, back-to-back on a single sheet, this is a good sized essay and is very easy to manage, and therefore I can do it a number of times in a semester. Even in a class of one hundred students, we can ask them to bring in just twenty copies of their piece in order to make publications of a more manageable size.

Publication of student writing flushes out some interesting assumptions about reading and writing: we take it for granted that students should shell out money for reading, but some teachers are startled at the thought of asking them to do the same for writing. But such money is well spent, and students usually appreciate the result. And when we realize that students will have to pay for the publication of their writing, we tend to adjust our assignments in a helpful way: "Let's see. How can I frame an assignment that will lead to pieces of writing that other students would actually want to read and benefit from?" This is a question that cuts right to the heart of good pedagogy: how to connect our material to their lives. The publication of student writing helps us here because when students write for publication, *they* find connections we'd never dream of.

If we brought to the evaluation of student writing the critical sophistication we take for granted in literary work, we wouldn't do so much rigid and thoughtless *ranking* or *grading*. That is, in literary study we realize that there is no single correct interpretation of a text, that even the best critics cannot agree, and that it would be laughable to assign quantitative grades to a text (and certainly not one based on one quick reading late at night). Thus literary consciousness would help us get away from assuming that we can immediately grade student writing with quantitative scores of A, B, C, and so forth. Grades of "strong," "medium," and "weak" would suffice. And by the end of the semester, these crude grades, along with a portfolio, would "add up" or at least point clearly to a final grade.

Using writing as a springboard. The conventional practice is almost always to start with reading and then write in response—making the writing serve the reading. But we can turn that around and write first and make reading serve writing. Certain teachers at all levels are slowly learning this approach. For example, teachers get students to write about an intense mental experience and what it feels like inside their heads. They use this as a springboard for reading some poems by Emily Dickinson. The goal is not just to read and appreciate Dickinson better—though of course that happens too—but to take student writing more seriously. Students come at Dickinson more as peers, saying things like, "She used a metaphor in this way, but I decided to do it that way." When I had trouble getting students to connect with Shakespeare—putting him "under glass" as it were—for example, in reading *The Tempest* where Prospero seems both hallowed yet unattractive—I started off by asking my students to write informally about their most long-standing unresolved grudge (fun in itself). When we turned to Shakespeare, students were more invested and skilled in dealing with this difficult Prospero and his grudge and the play. One of the main emphases in the powerful "Writing-across-the-Curriculum" movement is on helping students use writing not just for demonstrating what they have learned but also for the process of learning itself. Indeed, many people call this the "Writing-to-Learn" movement.

Using reading as a springboard. But writing doesn't have to come first to be important. We can have *reading* come first—and still serve writing. That is, we can use the reading as something to reply to, bounce off, or borrow from. In this practice we are not trying to make the writing "do justice" to the reading or "get it right." We are inviting students to use the reading as a springboard to their own writing: to use the theme or structure or spirit or energy of the text to spur their own writing. This, after all, is standard practice by writers (as Harold Bloom and others show): to misread or misuse or distort the works of others as a way to enable your own writing.

This approach is particularly important in getting students to try out imaginative pieces like those they are reading. Students are often nervous about writing poems, stories, or dramatic scenes/dialogues. We can help them by borrowing themes or structures from the reading. For example, a few key words or phrases from a poem can serve as a helpful springboard or scaffold that will help students find a way to write a poem or story of their own. Of course, students need to be invited to treat imaginative writing as an experiment—not necessarily to finish or revise. I don't feel I can grade these pieces, but I can require them. (For more, see chapter 17.)

Making writing more central in what was formerly just a "reading" or literature course causes a major change in the way students come at the reading. They are braver, more lively, and more thoughtful. We read differently when we read like a writer. (See Charles Moran's classic article about this: "Reading Like a Writer.") Students come at purely analytic discussions of texts in a much more shrewd and energetic way when they have had a chance to try out some of the same kinds of writing in an experimental, playful, nongraded way.

Using rough drafts of reading. Students and colleagues would benefit enormously from the kind of workshop activity I described earlier: where students and teacher work together on texts that neither has seen before—periodically pausing during the process of reading to write out how they are perceiving and reacting to the text. This process helps everyone see vividly how reading creates meaning by a process of gradual and often collaborative and transformative negotiation.

None of these teaching practices can be called wild or visionary any more. All are being used by teachers at all levels with all kinds of students. And if we use them more, we will think of more ways to bring reading and writing into a relationship of mutual support.

To close, I'll evoke an image—a corrective paradigm for the relations between reading and writing. Teachers of kindergarten and first grade all around the country are demonstrating that writing is easier and more natural than reading, and that writing is more useful than reading for entrance into literacy. Their practice is based on a fact that is startling but obvious once demonstrated. Tiny children can write before they can read, can write more than they can read, and can write more easily than they can read. For small children can write *anything they can say*—once they know the alphabet and are shown the rudimentary trick of using invented spelling. In fact, the process works even with younger children who don't know the alphabet. Even they can "write" *anything* by just making scribbles. Often they don't need to be taught; just ask them what writing is and they'll do purposeful and meaningful scribbling. They'll call it writing and they'll be able to read back to you what they "wrote" (Harste, Woodward, and Burke).

In many classrooms around the country, kindergarteners and first graders are not just writing stories but "publishing" their own books. Teachers and helpers type up their writing in conventional spelling to go with the pictures that the children draw with their writing, and then these books are bound with cloth covers and become texts for reading. We tend to have been brainwashed into thinking that reading comes first and that reading is easier than writing, but the reverse is true. It has been demonstrated over and over that children get quicker understanding and control of literacy—language and texts—through writing than through reading. Thus output precedes input—and prepares the way for input. (People have done research comparing the stories that children in these classrooms write and read. The stories they write are at a higher level of development and sophistication than the stories they can read.)

Of course, the effects of this approach were obvious once people like Don Graves and Nancie Atwell had the sense to figure it out: it vastly improves students' skill and involvement in *reading*. Students are much more excited and competent when they read what they and their classmates have written than when they read published books from the outside (especially basal readers). They learn reading faster; they have a healthier stance toward reading—a stance that recognizes, "Hey, these things called books are what we write. Let's read books to see what other people like us have written." No longer do children think of books as something written by a corporate, faceless "they"—like arithmetic workbooks.

There is a much-told story of a reporter visiting one of these classrooms where the first graders eagerly offer to show him some of their books. "Have you really written a book?" the reporter asks one child with a tone of condescending surprise. "Haven't you?" replies the child.

Just think how it would be if we and our students were more like those first graders. They are so eager to read and to write; they are the happiest and most invested in their literacy of any students in the whole educational world. We can move decisively in that direction by ending the priority of reading and giving more serious and playful priority to writing—bringing to writing some of the flexible sophistication we use in reading—so that both processes reinforce each other as equals.

Works Cited

Applebee, A. N. *Writing in the Secondary School: English and the Content Areas.* Research Report No. 21. Urbana, IL: NCTE, 1981.

Atwell, Nancie. *In the Middle: Writing, Reading, and Learning with Adolescents.* Portsmouth NH: Heinemann, 1987.

Blau, Sheridan. "Invisible Writing: Investigating Cognitive Processes in Composition." *College Composition and Communication* 34 (1983): 297–312.

Britton, James, et al. *The Development of Writing Abilities (11–18).* Urbana, IL: NCTE, 1975.

Elbow, Peter. "The Doubting Game and the Believing Game." *Writing Without Teachers.* New York: Oxford UP, 1973. 147–91.

———. "Methodological Doubting and Believing." *Embracing Contraries: Explorations in Learning and Teaching.* New York: Oxford UP, 1986. 254–300.

Emerson, Caryl. "The Outer Word, Inner Speech: Bakhtin, Vygotsky and the Internalization of Language." *Critical Inquiry* 10 (1983): 245–64.

Friend, Christie. "The Excluded Conflict: The Marginalization of Composition and Rhetoric Studies in Graff's Professing Literature." *College English* 54 (1992): 276–86.

Gardner, Howard. *The Unschoooled Mind: How Children Think and How Schools Should Teach.* New York: Basic, 1991.

Gendlin, Eugene. *Focusing.* New York: Bantam, 1979.

Graves, Donald. *Writing: Teachers and Children at Work.* Portsmouth, NH: Heinemann, 1983.

Harris, Jeanette. *Expressive Writing.* Dallas: Southern Methodist UP, 1990.

Harste, Jerome, Virginia Woodward, and Carolyn Burke. *Language Stories and Learning Lessons.* Portsmouth, NH: Heinemann, 1984.

Laurence, David. Personal communication.

Moran, Charles. "Reading Like a Writer." *Vital Signs*. Ed. James L. Collins. Portsmouth, NH: Boynton/Cook, 1990. 60–70.

Sanders, Scott Russell. "The Writer in the University." *ADE Bulletin* 99 (1991): 22–28.

Slevin, James. "Depoliticizing and Politicizing Composition Studies." *The Politics of Writing Instructions: Post-secondary*. Ed. Richard Bullock and John Trimbur. Portsmouth, NH: Boynton/Cook, Heinemann, 1991. 1–21.

Stafford, William. *Writing the Australian Crawl: Views on the Writer's Vocation*. Ann Arbor: U of Michigan P, 1978.

Wallace, Elizabeth. Unpublished MS, Department of Humanities, Western Oregon State College.

14

Your Cheatin' Art

A Collage

A TV documentary on cancer. It opens with shots of a funeral—people standing around the side of a grave: a close-up of a widow, and then over to the coffin being lowered. Cut to a sequence of cells under a high-powered microscope—time-lapse so that we see the cells multiplying and going crazy. A voice-over is telling us about how cancer cells behave. Then a man in the docor's office—getting the verdict. Then Ronald Reagan cracking a joke about his colon cancer. Then a young medical student telling how she wants to go into cancer research—why she finds it exciting and all the progress that's being made. We cut from her, bursting with health and enthusiasm, back to a victim, balding and emaciated from the therapy, but walking in the woods—obviously drinking in the scene as though he can't get enough. Then a sequence of someone earnestly giving us statistics: how many cases of this and that; how much more than in the past, but also how there are more successful treatments and cures. Back now to Reagan going about his work. Then the victim trying to explain things to his child. Finally, a sequence of advice about how to avoid cancer.

It's all a hodgepodge—completely "disorganized"—no connectives.

But it works. It's a collage.

I've made a few revisions and additions here to the version that appeared in *Writing On the Edge* in the fall of 1998. I've been writing about the collage for a long time, but I've never made it the center of an essay or chapter till now. (It figured prominently in my chapter on "loop writing" in *Writing With Power* in 1981 and in the first and third workshops in *Community of Writers*. "Silence: A Collage" appears in Part III of this volume.)

[T]wo parts of a piece of writing merely by lying side-by-side, can comment on each other without a word spoken. (John McPhee. quoted in Sims 13).

Directions for writing a collage:

1. Do or gather as much of your writing on your topic as you can. Go fast, don't worry. Freewriting is a good idea. Take thoughts in any order that they come.
2. Go through what you have and choose the best and potentially best bits—freely cutting to find long and short sections.
3. Revise what you have, mostly by cutting, not rewriting. Cut paragraphs and sentences; cut phrases and words. It's amazing what is possible with just cutting.
4. Figure out a pleasing order for the bits: perhaps logical, more likely intuitive and associative—maybe even random.

Another option: add fragments of writing by others—as you'll see I am doing here.

Just as Cubism can take a roomful of furniture and iron it onto nine square feet of canvas, so fiction can take fifty years of human life, chop it to bits, and piece those bits together so that, within the limits of the temporal form, we can consider them all at once. This is narrative collage. The world is a warehouse of forms which the writer raids: this is a stickup. Here are the narrative leaps and fast cuttings to which we have become accustomed, the clenched juxtapositions, interpenetrations, and temporal enjambments. . . . The use of narrative collage is particularly adapted to various twentieth-century treatments of time and space. Time no longer courses in a great and widening stream, a stream upon which the narrative consciousness floats, passing fixed landmarks in orderly progression, and growing in wisdom. Instead time is a flattened landscape, a land of unlinked lakes seen from the air. . . . The point of view shifts; the prose style shifts and its tone; characters turn into things; sequences of events abruptly vanish. Images clash; realms of discourse bang together. Zeus may order a margarita; Zsa Zsa Gabor may raise the siege of Orleans. In a recent *Tri-Quarterly* story, Heathcliff meets Chateaubriand on a golf course. [A writer can create] a world shattered, and perhaps senseless, and certainly strange. (Annie Dillard 20–24)

Dingbats. Blips. Crots. Collage seems to favor the Anglo-Saxon over the Latinate.

Dingbats are the traditional decorative markers that printers use for separations. Placeholders for nothing. Great pleasure from the word and the thing. Asterisks are a sad substitute.

I like to call collage elements *blips*. But Winston Weathers has a more interesting word:

> The *Crot*. A crot (crots, plural) is an obsolete word meaning "bit" or "fragment." The term was given new life by Tom Wolfe in his "Introduction" to a collection of *Esquire* magazine fiction, *The Secret Life of Our Times*, edited by Gordon Lish (New York: Doubleday, 1973). A basic element in the alternate grammar of style, and comparable somewhat to the "stanza" in poetry, the crot may range in length from one sentence to twenty or thirty sentences. It is fundamentally an autonomous unit, characterized by the absence of any transitional devices that might relate it to preceding or subsequent crots and because of this independent and discrete nature of crots, they create a general effect of metastasis—using that term from classical rhetoric to label, as Fritz Senn recently suggested in the *James Joyce Quarterly* (Summer, 1975), any "rapid transition from one point of view to another." In its most intense form, the crot is characterized by a certain abruptness in its termination: "As each crot breaks off," Tom Wolfe says, "it tends to make one's mind search for some point that must have just been made—*presque vu!*—almost seen! In the hands of a writer who really understands the device, it will have you making crazy leaps of logic, leaps you never dreamed of before."
>
> The provenance of the crot may well be in the writer's "note" itself—in the research note, in the sentence or two one jots down to record a moment or an idea or to describe a person or place. The crot is essentially the "note" left free of verbal ties with other surrounding notes.
>
> . . . The crots, of whatever kind, may be presented in nearly random sequence or in sequences that finally suggest circularity. Rarely is any stronger sense of order (such as would be characteristic of traditional grammar) imposed on them—though the absence of traditional order is far more pronounced when the grammar is used in fiction and poetry. The general idea of unrelatedness present in crot writing suggests correspondence—for those who seek it—with the fragmentation and even egalitarianism of contemporary experience, wherein the events, personalities, places of life have no particular superior or inferior status to dictate priorities of presentation.
>
> Nearly always crots are separated one from the other by white space, and at times each crot is given a number or, upon rare occasion, a title. That little spectrum—white space only, white space plus a numbering, white space plus a titling—provides a writer with a way of indicating an increase in separation, discreteness, isolation.

.   .   .

Crots are akin, obviously, to a more general kind of "block" writing—the kind of writing found, for instance, in E. M. Forster's Two Cheers for Democracy and in Katherine Anne Porter's essay "Audubon's Happy Land." In such block writing, the authors have strung together short, fairly discrete units of composition to make whole compositions. Likewise, a series of crots is not unlike a collection of aphorisms—say those of Eric Hoffer who, in a book like The Passionate State of Mind and Other Aphorisms, has brought together brief compositional units, some a sentence long, some several paragraphs long, each quite distinct from the other, yet grouped into a whole composition on the basis of a certain attitude and view of life common to them all. These compositions of "blocks" or "aphorisms" are so much in the spirit of crot writing that they may be considered a part of its development out of a traditional grammar of style into the alternate grammar. The writing of Forster, Porter, and Hoffer—in fiction and nonfiction—gives evidence of the usefulness of something other than the ordered linear procedure of traditional grammar even to writers who would not be identified as especially experimental or stylistically daring. (Weathers 4, 12)

I sit here with seven short pieces of writing scattered around me on the floor. Some as long as a page and a half, some only a paragraph or a sentence. Some printed out, some written by hand. A couple of the blips consist of two smaller pieces taped together. The miracle is that I *like* it all. I want to show all these blips to readers.

How could I like all this writing when I didn't feel I was doing anything particularly good this week—just churning stuff out, writing fast, producing assorted blips and pieces?

I didn't *change* a word. Yet now my pile of writing feels strong and right. The secret is cutting—elimination—absence.

In art, the "collage" *seems* modern, but consider the typical medieval stained glass window. Or the *collection* of stained glass windows in a church or cathedral. The walls and ceiling of the Sistine Chapel are a collage.

Symphonies, concertos, and suites don't feel peculiar but they are collages. Why do music critics look for thematic or structural links between movements? Because most movements in most pieces of music are strongly unrelated.

Poetry is the most natural collage form. Poems often don't say what they are saying, and they jam unlike things together.

Why should the collage be old and natural in art, music, and poetry—but not in prose?

A few crots from what is probably the classic collage of our era, "For the Etruscans":

[T]he woman finds she is irreconcilable things: an outsider by her gender position, by her relation to power; may be an insider by her social position, her class. She can be both. Her ontological, her psychic, her class position all cause doubleness. Doubled consciousness. Doubled understandings. How then could she neglect to invent a form which produces this incessant, critical, splitting motion. To invent this form. To invent the theory for this form.

Following the "female aesthetic" will produce artworks that incorporate contradiction and nonlinear movement into the heart of the text.

An art object may then be nonhierarchic, showing "an organization of material in fragments," breaking climactic structures, making an even display of elements over the surface with no climactic place or moment, since the materials are "organized into many centers."

.   .   .

What we here have been calling (the) female aesthetic turns out to be a specialized name for any practices available to those groups—nations, genders, sexualities, races, classes—all social practices which wish to criticize, to differentiate from, to overturn the dominant forms of knowing and understanding with which they are saturated. (Rachel Blau DuPlessis 278, 285)

Boxes. The shaded box with prose inside—somewhere on the page of a magazine, newspaper, or even of a book. A separate thread of writing, but glued on where it somehow "goes." I remember how startled and pleased I was by Dorothy Dinnerstein's classic early boxes in a serious scholarly work, *The Mermaid and the Minotaur*. Short bits, sweetmeats, to keep us going in a long sustained argument.

Collages are cheating because they permit weak writers to produce strong finished pieces.

What's hardest for writers of essays? Figuring out exactly what they are trying to say. And getting everything well unified and well organized.

What is easiest? Getting some good ideas and some good writing. Weak writers can often produce essays with a number of strong points—points that are definitely related and that throw good light on the overall topic. Yet the points don't quite follow each other coherently and the whole piece doesn't really hang together. And then there are those clunky transitions.

The collage lets us *skip* what's hard. Skip figuring out exactly what we are really trying to say. Skip unity. Settle for a gathering of parts that are all *sort of* related. Skip organization and just put pieces in some intuitive order. And skip transitions altogether.

When we show weak writers how to produce strong collages—and especially when we publish a class magazine with everyone's collage—we have a better chance of getting students to enjoy and care about writing and to work harder at the harder skills.

Here is Erich Auerbach on the difference between *parataxis* and *hypotaxis*.

> The tone [in a passage from St. Augustine] has something urgently impul-
> sive, something human and dramatic, and the form exhibits a predominance
> of parataxes. . . . As we try to trace the impression back, we are reminded
> of certain Biblical passages, which in the mirror of the Vulgate become:
> *Dixitque Deus: fiat lux, et facta est lux* (Genesis 1: 3) [And God said: Let
> there be light, and there was light]; or: *ad te clamaverunt, et salvi facti sunt;
> in te speraverunt, et non sunt confusi* (Ps. 22: 6) [To thee they cried, and were
> saved; in thee they trusted, and were not disappointed]; or: *Flavit spiritus
> tuus, et operuit eos mare* (Exod. 15: 10) [Thou didst blow with thy wind, and
> the sea covered them]; or: *aperuit Dominus os asinae, et locuta est* (Num. 22:
> 28) [The Lord opened the mouth of the ass, and she spoke]. In all of these in-
> stances there is, instead of the causal or at least temporal hypotaxis which
> we should expect in classical Latin (whether with *cum* or *postquam*,
> whether with an ablative absolute or a participial construction) a parataxis
> with *et;* and this procedure, far from weakening the interdependence of the
> two events, brings it out most emphatically; just as in English it is more dra-
> matically effective to say: He opened his eyes and was struck . . . than:
> When he opened his eyes, or: Upon opening his eyes, he was struck . . .
> (61–62)

. . .

> In the classical languages paratactic constructions belong to the low style;
> they are oral rather than written, comic and realistic rather than elevated.
> But here [in the *Chanson de Roland*] parataxis belongs to the elevated style.
> This is a new form of the elevated style, not dependent on periodic struc-
> ture and rhetorical figures but on the power of juxtaposed and independent
> verbal blocks. An elevated style operating with paratactic elements is not,
> in itself, something new in Europe. The style of the Bible has this character-
> istic (cf. our first chapter [above]). Here we may recall the discussion con-
> cerning the sublime character of the sentences *dixitque Deus: fiat lux, et
> facta est lux* [And God said: Let there be light, and there was light] (Genesis
> 1: 3) which Boileau and Huet carried on in the seventeenth century in con-
> nection with the essay *On the Sublime* attributed to Longinus. The sublime
> in this sentence from Genesis is not contained in a magnificent display of
> rolling periods nor in the splendor of abundant figures of speech but in the
> impressive brevity which is in such contrast to the immense content and
> which for that very reason has a note of obscurity which fills the listener
> with a shuddering awe. It is precisely the absence of causal connective, the
> naked statement of what happens—the statement which replaces deduction
> and comprehension by an amazed beholding that does not even seek to
> comprehend—which gives this sentence its grandeur. (95–97)

The principle of negativity; absence. Strength from what's left out, not what's put in. Shaker furniture. Spareness—the flavor of old timers and seasoned professionals. The old tennis pro who scarcely moves—he makes his opponent move. The collage makes the reader move. Silence can be most powerful in music; space in art. Picasso's bare line drawings. If everything there is strong, the observer will put in what's not there. The crashing silences in some of Beethoven's Opus 18 Quartets.

I find it helpful to lay out the spectrum that runs from the tightest essay to the loosest collage. This is a story of gradually loosening ties, slowly diminishing explicitness, unity, focus, connectedness, linearity:

- The school essay. Slam bam thank you ma'am. Say what you're going to say, then say it, then say what you said. No surprises allowed.
- The academic essay. Academics permit themselves striking liberties that they don't permit to students. Still, their essays are supposed to be smoothly connected and to *say* what they are saying. (Actually, the truly learned article—because of its long discursive footnotes—functions as a kind of collage. Nowadays publishers ruin the effect by trying to make the text look seamless and removing all the notes from the page and hiding them together at the end.)
- The essay in the larger tradition of Montaigne. It's supposed to *get around to* saying what it's saying—but sometimes does not. From Montaigne on, this more expansive genre has served as an invitation to see where the mind goes as it explores something—and to welcome the fact that the resulting path is not tightly logical but instead has a lot of surprises and wandering. Nevertheless, the implicit principle of the essay is to *connect* that wandering, to *lead* the reader's mind from point to point, to create bridges. The principle of the collage, on the other hand, is to blow up the bridges and make the reader jump or swim.
- The focused collage. It doesn't say what it's saying—but it implies a definite point.
- The open collage on a specific issue or topic. It doesn't even imply a point. Rather it presents conflicting points and multiple points of view. Many newspaper feature stories and radio and TV documentaries take this form because it's so much easier: no need to choose or decide.
- There are open collages with no topic at all but that hover over a general area. "Sports Roundup." "Medical Breakthroughs in our Lifetime."
- The collage on no topic at all. Sheryl Fontaine and Francie Quaas get their students to make collages at the end of a writing course by simply choosing passages they like from everything in their portfolios. This is an invitation to the centrifuge. Still, there will almost certainly be a lurking theme or issue. As Chaucer says, "The tongue returns to the aching tooth." What else is a

"magazine" but a collage on no topic at all. "Magazine" means a store-house—classically of gunpowder.

In fact, the collage process can provide a quicker and easier way to create a draft for a conventional or logically organized essay, and it usually adds more life and energy to the final product—more raisins in the loaf. Just follow the main steps of quickly writing everything you can think of in any order and choosing the best pieces and cleaning them up a bit. Then arrange in a *logical* order (perhaps with the help of an outline), and then figure out what is missing.

Collages use the simplest but most effective aesthetic principle: put things together if they "sort of go." They need to go—but not too well. Interest and pleasure increase if there is some friction, resistance, difference. A bouquet is a collage, but a good bouquet needs some clash.

But what makes a collage good? Is there anything besides "Use good quality meat and vegetables for your stew, and have some contrast"? I don't know, but here are two good suggestions from recent listeners to a draft:

- Anne Herrington: a sense of craft—of an intentional and shaping consciousness.
- Stephen Clingman: resonance across the gaps.

Just do it! Things go better with collage. TV ads are often microcollages—functioning as unrelated dingbat interrupters of unrelated programs. As creators of non sequitur, they are often more vivid and interesting than the programs they interrupt: often better art, better rhetoric—a more concentrated aesthetic experience.

I dial the phone. I must choose from a menu of choices. Then I'm on hold. Then I hear a short ad for the company. Then I'm thrust into the middle of a sequence of disconnected pieces of music. Then someone answers and we talk. Then she puts me on hold again. And so on.

"Call waiting" creates a collage of phone calls that our children and their friends use to create a collage of conversations.

Everybody's home page. Hypertext. Indeed the internet itself is a vast collage.

They told us life was a connected narrative but it feels more like a collage.

I wonder whether the demand for connected, coherent, logical thinking in the field of philosophy might in itself have prompted Pascal and Wittgenstein to compose important works in the form of the disconnected collage. Perhaps their crotted works are saying, "Stop pretending that you can say what really needs saying and still use valid chains of connected reasoning." An allergy to the pretense of coherence?

This makes me think of the allergy that led to Hemingway's notorious style. He said he was avoiding abstraction and pursuing concreteness—and he was. But he was also avoiding syntactical hierarchy and pursuing syntactical flatness. He went from hypotaxis to parataxis. Short sentences and the proliferation of *ands*.

> There were many words that you could not stand to hear and finally only the names of places had dignity. Certain numbers were the same way and certain dates and these with the names of the places were all you could say and have them mean anything. Abstract words such as glory, honor, courage, or hallow were obscene beside the concrete names of villages, and the numbers of roads, the names of rivers, the numbers of regiments and the dates. (Hemingway 191)

In our struggles to teach and to write well-constructed essays, we are constantly reminded of the mind's tendency to disconnect. But if we spent more time seeking randomness—for example, by constructing collages on no topic at all—we'd notice a much stronger tendency in the human mind—namely, to connect. The human mind is *incapable* of not making sense. It is difficult even to program a computer to produce true randomness.

Drawing together such disparate manifestations as Seurat's pointillism, Muybridge's stop-motion photography, the poetry of Whitman, Rimbaud, and Laforgue, the tone rows of Schoenberg, and the novels of Joyce, the author [William R. Everdell, in *The First Moderns: Profiles in the Origins of Twentieth-Century Thought*] makes an engrossing and persuasive case for his claim that "the heart of Modernism is the postulate of ontological disconinuity" (Holt 65).

The man stepped on the gas. The car surged forward.
The man stepped on the gas and therefore the car surged forward.
After the man stepped on the gas, the car surged forward.
The man having stepped on the gas, the car surged forward.

Sentence combining—an enormous if waning industry—is designed to teach students to create longer and more complex syntactic structures—to combine small sentences (line one) into longer ones (following lines)—to move from parataxis to hypotaxis. The goal is syntactic and semantic hierarchy and subordination: building in transitional words (thus the preoccupation with teaching connectives like "however," "although," "moreover"), so as to rope in larger and larger pieces of linguistic terrain as single units. They call it "syntactic maturity" when students spell out connections between sentences and structure clauses hierarchically. I guess this makes sense. Yet I resist.

I feel naughty in that feeling, and indeed with part of my mind and part of my teaching, I *don't* resist. I concur. I try to teach thinking, and thinking *does* mean figuring out hierarchy and subordination: what are your main points and what are the subpoints and how do they relate? Make it all explicit. After all, the whole point of an essay is . . . no, wait, that's not quite right. The whole point of the *school* essay or *academic* essay is to *say* what you are saying, not to leave it implicit. And complex, hierarchical prose is good to learn and can be lovely. I make no argument against it—only against the notion that it's better, more advanced, and that it is the only goal in teaching writing.

It is *not* always syntactically immature to lay out unconnected sentences or units and let them rub up against each other without connective tissue. There is more energy in unconnected sentences, more drama. They tend to be an enactment of something going on rather than a record of a past event that is conceptually finished. Let the reader feel the energy of the jump. The man stepped on the gas. The car surged forward. *And God said, Let there be light, and there was light.* We need help in remembering that there is, in fact, some mystery in the fact that the car surges forward after the man steps on the gas.

"Things are seen," says Pascal. "Causes are not seen" (*Pensees* #235). Age-old writing wisdom shakes its finger at us and declares, "Don't be vague," but do we always want to nail down the relationship? Naked fragments suggest blessedly that everything is not so simple.

Etymologies. *Hypotaxis*. From the Greek. "Subjection, submission." No wonder I fight it. *Parataxis*. "Setting side by side," indeed, as one dictionary says, "an arranging in order for battle" (*Random House College Dictionary*, revised, 1982).

His first, or nearly first text (1942) consists of fragments, . . . because incoherence is preferable to a distorting order. Since then . . . he has never stopped writing in brief bursts. . . . (Roland Barthes writing about himself in third person. Quoted in Park 394.)

But damn it, first we've got to teach them to be explicit and clear. *Then* we can give them permission to leave things out. If they are going to use the techniques of the collage, they have to do it from a basis of skill with conscious craft—not just because they are lazy or unskilled. Picasso only made those empty and suggestive line drawings *after* he demonstrated that he could draw bulls the way they really look.

Collage and parataxis are important not only because they're easy and lazy—though that's important too. They are also important for the sake of *thinking*. If we ask our beginning students to spell out all their thinking, they often limit themselves to what's dull. If we invite them to use parataxis and collage—however lazy or cheating it may seem—they often capture more *sophisticated* thinking: greater cognitive complexity. And it often comes across too, despite our complaints about "the need for development." Surely, it's preferable—often anyway—and perhaps especially in the beginning—to have sophisticated and complex thinking that is *tacit* and *sort of* there than pedestrian and dull thinking that is well spelled out.

Richard Haswell made a careful and sophisticated study of many graded student essays and discovered a disconnect between the quality of the writing and the level of the thinking. He discovered that the most successful essays were the most primitive and empty in thinking and logical inference. The *poorer* pieces of student writing had much more complex trains of thinking or inference. Yes, the poorer ones were poor as essays and the better ones were better—genuinely more satisfactory to read. But if the price of good clear writing is increased emptiness of thinking (and that's what his study clearly showed), should we not sometimes—and perhaps especially in the beginning—invite parataxis or collage and the complexity of implied logic that is invited by this "looseness"?

I've been working for a long time on a difficult essay. I'm writing to readers who will disagree with me and I've spent hours and hours trying to strengthen and refine these ideas. I care about them. My early writing was exciting to me. I knew I was going in the right direction. But lots was rough.

As I revised I cut, changed, added, and then cut, changed, added—all this over a week or more. I finally felt I was working it out, figuring it out. Then I had to put it aside for a couple of weeks.

I come back to it now with excitement—it's the fruit of so much caring and work. But when I read it through I discover it's *terrible*: muddy, tangled, frustrating to read, unconvincing. How can it be that my best efforts lead to terrible writing? My first raw writing was better—and yet it was no good either.

It's at times like this that I need to remember collages—and how I can produce clear and lively language and interesting ideas without having to agonize. It's *not* that I can't find good thoughts or words. It's just when I worked on *these* thoughts (which are hard), and for *this* audience (which is hard), everything turned to sludge. But I can fix it. My collages and freewriting are there to prove that I *can* find lively, clear language and good ideas.

If I want a good, organized essay on this topic, an essay that spells out everything explicitly, then I've got to keep going and try to work through to coherent, connected clarity. But if I just want a good piece of writing on the topic, I could take an easier route. I could still go back to my early rough writing and take the good bits and make a collage—and it would be better than what I have now.

That reminds me. But I digress.

Collages are built on the principle of association—the mind's gift for thinking of things that are *different* and yet *linked*. Which leads to surprise.

Something I've already written makes me think of something I hadn't thought of—something I would never have thought to link. Something rolls off my pen that I couldn't have planned. *Surprise* is the most important writing experience for me. Surely, not many people write by choice unless they have tasted the pleasure of surprise and are hungry for more of it.

> All there is to thinking is seeing something noticeable which makes you see something you weren't noticing which makes you see something that isn't even visible. (Norman Maclean, A River Runs Through It)

> Grammar B [using crots and other nonlinear devices], with characteristics of variegation, synchronicity, discontinuity, ambiguity and the like . . . is no longer an experiment, but a mature grammar used by competent writers and offering students of writing a well tested "set of options" that, added to the traditional grammar of style, will give them a much more flexible voice, a much greater communication capacity, a much greater opportunity to put into effective language all the things they have to say" (Weathers 2–3).

. . .

> [I]n writing the essay in Grammar B I felt a freedom to comment on Blake's poem that I would not have felt in Grammar A; in fact, I would never have attempted to say such disparate things about the poem in Grammar A. I also discovered that in "gathering my thoughts" and making my "notes," I felt—between the act of invention and the final act of composition—far less distance than I frequently have felt betwixt invention/composition while using Grammar A. (Indeed, I'm convinced that many of us in the academic world linger over our research and our studies, delaying the writing of articles and essays, because we are inwardly, unconsciously resisting having to transform our material into the forms dictated by Grammar A.) And I also

realized, in writing my Grammar B essay, that while I was losing audiences on one side, I might well be making myself accessible to audiences on another. (Weathers 17)

People use the same form, collage, for conflicting goals:

- The modernist goal of creating deeper meaning—meaning beyond language;
- The dadaist and postmodern goal of destroying meaning—creating no-meaning;
- The naughty and journalistic goal of finding a quick and easy way to create something rhetorically pleasing.

"That's just the way it is." The phrase always points to bad news:

- The good die young.
- The wicked prosper.
- No dessert till you eat your salad.

Especially in writing:

- You can't communicate unless you use words as others do.
- You won't be taken seriously unless you conform to Standard Written English.
- People just won't read it if it's boring or unclear.
- Commas and periods go inside the quotation marks, semicolons and question marks outside—except on the other side of the Atlantic.

So let's celebrate the subversive: "just the way it is" can also point to *good news*. Using a collage, we can write a good piece—something people will read—without quite figuring out what we are really trying to say and without figuring out a logical or coherent organization. And let's celebrate all the other ways to cheat in writing and teaching writing:

- Freewrite. Don't plan, don't be careful, don't structure. Invite garbage. It often yields good writing—good ideas and language that's alive.
- Stop writing. Take a walk. Forget about it for a while. Stop struggling. *Not doing* is essential for doing.
- Put readers out of mind. The piece may have to work for them eventually, but think about them later in revising. Writing is often stronger when we say "screw readers."
- Share drafts with others and ask for *no response*. Get everyone simply to listen and enjoy. We improve our writing immensely just by feeling our words in our mouths, hearing them in our ears, and experiencing the presence of listeners. No criticism, no instruction, no suggestions. Just the pleasure and mutuality of sharing.

- Share our drafts with others and ask them *not* for feedback or criticism, but rather for some of *their* thoughts and ideas on the topic that they are willing to give away. Our thoughts will usually trigger good thoughts in them that they are happy to let us have.
- Write *with* others. Meet at someone's house or in a cafe or restaurant or an empty classroom. One or three hours of writing with short breaks for chatting and tea. The presence of others somehow makes writing more feasible and satisfying. Body heat. Companionship. When we write alone, we are often pulled down by a feeling that says, "I can't do this."

Yes, struggle is necessary and inevitable. No danger of forgetting that. The danger is in forgetting that we can sometimes finesse the struggle.

Yes, cheating is unfair. Babies are given everything they need—without earning it. Little children get to play all day. Taking the easy way helps us relax and risk. Shortcuts help our minds to jump.

It seems as though smooth logical prose is "regular" and the collage is odd or deviant. But actually the collage—because it is just a bundle of fragments that don't *say* what they are saying—gives us a better picture of how language really works. Words are nothing but empty balloons unless we blow them up. Words themselves don't "carry" meaning. Meaning must always be supplied by readers or listeners—for all writings not just for the collage.

Thus the collage is the universal paradigm for discourse (like the relativity model), while smooth logical prose (the Newtonian model) disguises how discourse actually works.

I read my collage outloud to a friend. He ends up thinking I have the opposite opinion from the opinion I really have. Is it because I wrote so badly? No, it's not badly written. It's because, as a collage, it doesn't say what it's saying—or even try to say *anything*. It just *presents* material. Yes. And I like that about collages. They can settle for throwing live bits at readers and asking them to *experience* them and make up their *own* mind.

But his "misreading" leads to a subversive thought. Perhaps he's right. Perhaps, now that I look at my collage again, I don't think what I thought I thought. Perhaps my collage allowed me to find words for what I didn't know. My collage—and my reading it outloud to my friend—are making me wonder if I disagree with my old self.

Works Cited

Auerbach, Erich. *Mimesis: The Representation of Reality in Western Literature*. Tr. W. Traske. NY: Doubleday Anchor, 1957. Originally Princeton UP, 1953.
Dillard, Annie. *Living by Fiction*. NY: Harper and Row, 1982.
Dinnerstein, Dorothy. *The Mermaid and the Minotaur: Sexual Arrangements and Human Malaise*. NY: Harper and Row, 1976.
DuPlessis, Rachel Blau. "For the Etruscans." *The Future of Difference*. Ed. Alice Jardine and

Hester Eisenstein. Boston: G. K. Hall, 1981. Reprinted in *Feminist Criticism: Essays on Women, Literature, Theory*. Ed. Elaine Showalter. NY: Pantheon, 1985.

Elbow, Peter. *Writing With Power: Techniques for Mastering the Writing Process*. NY: Oxford University Press, 1981.

Elbow, Peter and Pat Belanoff. *A Community of Writers: A Workshop Course in Writing*. NY: Random House/McGraw Hill, 1989. 3rd ed. 1999.

Fontaine, Sheryl and Francie Quaaf. "Transforming Connections and Building Bridges: Assigning, Reading, and Evaluating the Collage Essay." *Teaching Writing Creatively*. Ed. David Starkey. Portsmouth NH: Heinemann/Boynton Cook, 1998. 111–25.

Haswell, Richard H. "The Organization of Impromptu Essays." *College Composition and Communication* 37 (Dec. 1986): 402–415.

Hemingway, Ernest. *A Farewell to Arms*. NY: Charles Scribner's Sons, 1929.

Holt, Jim. "Infinitesimally Yours." Rev. of *The First Moderns: Profiles in the Origins of Twentieth-Century Thought*. *New York Review of Books* 20 May, 1999: 63–67.

Park, Clara Claiborn. "Author! Author! Reconstructing Roland Barthes." *Hudson Review* 43.3 (Autumn 1990): 377–398.

Showalter, Elaine, ed. *Feminist Criticism: Essays on Women, Literature, Theory*. NY: Pantheon, 1985.

Sims, Norman, ed. Introduction. *Literary Journalists*. NY: Ballantine, 1984.

Weathers, Winston. "The Grammars of Style: New Options in Composition." *Freshman English News* 4.3 (Winter 1976): 1–4, 12–18. Reprinted in Richard Graves' *Rhetoric and Composition: A Sourcebook for Teachers and Writers*. 3rd ed. Portsmouth, NH: Boynton/Cook, Heinemann, 1990. 200–214. Weathers also has a book on the topic: *An Alternate Style: Options in Composition*. Portsmouth, NH: Boynton/Cook, Heinemann, 1980.

Can Personal Expressive Writing Do the Work of Academic Writing?

What is the work of academic discourse? A simple answer is serviceable: academic discourse makes arguments, solves problems, analyzes texts and issues, tries to answer hard questions—and usually refers to and builds on academic discourse. So why can't these jobs be done with personal and expressive writing?

Perhaps you'll say that I've left out the most important job of academic discourse: to be objective or unbiased. But objectivity is passé. Few academics now believe that they can achieve objectivity—or that this view from everywhere-and-nowhere is even a desirable goal. Everyone seems to agree that we can never write anything except from a situated and interested point of view. (What would happen if Alec Guinness stepped out of *The Man in the White Suit* with another new invention: not just a process for making impervious suits but also for making irrefutable truths? I think we'd have to bundle him off again.)

But the death of objectivity has not catapulted academics into publishing personal expressive writing in learned journals. Let me point to four important features in current academic discourse that seem to distinguish it from personal expressive writing. (Perhaps these features are surrogates for objectivity.)

A larger view. Even though academic writers seldom profess true objectivity (at least in the humanities), they tend to try nevertheless for a kind of larger perspective that shows how their position relates to the positions other people have taken or might take on the topic. They don't just say, "Here's my position," but rather, "Here's how my position relates to yours. I'm not objective, but I'm not myopic either. I can see the larger terrain."

Clear thinking. While still not professing objectivity, academic writers nevertheless tend to try for clear thinking. Above all, this means centering on claims, reasons, evidence—argument. Being winning or sincere or even powerfully seductive is not enough.

Logical organization Academics tend to insist on a kind of "bony" structure in their publications; points should follow reasonably from each other, and the skeleton of argument is prominent—heightened by signposts that tell what's ahead and where we've been.

These passages come from the Foreword for a special issue of *Pre/Text* that I edited—an issue devoted to examples of personal and expressive writing doing the work of academic discourse. The issue was Vol. 11 Nos. 1 & 2, dated 1990, but it didn't come out until late in 1991.

Judicious tone. When academics write for publication they usually restrain themselves in style and voice—often achieving a certain impersonality. They tend to avoid much talk about themselves or their feelings; they favor control over abandon.

These seem like four pretty solid differences between academic discourse and personal expressive writing. But do these differences really mean that personal expressive writing cannot do the work of academic discourse? Let me look again at these four differences and try to show how they needn't exclude personal writing from academic work.

Tone? The contrast with personal expressive writing is obvious and decisive. But is it part of the essential job of academic writing to sound judicious, restrained, and somewhat impersonal?—or is that tone just one way of doing the job? Some people say there can be no wedding without morning coats and other formal attire. My hope is that this issue of PRE/TEXT will help convince readers that good academic work can be done in a more personal tone of voice.

Logical organization? Personal expressive writing obviously invites looser, less four-square structures of organization—more intuitive and associative— allowing us to imply more and spell out less. Yet there is nothing in the nature of personal expressive writing that prevents explicitness and a four-square bony organization. Something can be clear and obviously shaped without being stiff—without being any less personal or expressive. In fact, of course, the letters and journal entries we write often make our points more explicitly and clearly than our published articles. The pieces I have gathered here represent a relatively broad range of organizational modes, but none will seem particularly unbuttoned to readers of contemporary critical theory. For the truth is that organizational "standards" have already "broken down" in much academic writing in the humanities. Deconstruction has sanctioned the publication of many pieces that don't even "say" what they are "saying"—on the principle that it is impossible to do so. And if we look concretely back through the annals, we'll see that academics have always managed to depart now and then from conventions of language and organization if their writing was sufficiently interesting—or if they had sufficient prestige.

Clear thinking? Similar conclusion. Personal expressive writing may open the door to blurting and venting—no claims, reasons, evidence, or arguments. But again (as I hope many of the pieces here show) despite the open door, there's nothing in the nature of personal and expressive writing that militates against clear claims, reasons, and evidence. A focused argument doesn't make something less personal or expressive.

Larger view? Many people assume that personal writing tends by its nature to occupy itself only with its own position; and certainly there is plenty of good personal expressive writing that operates this way. But this assumption is a problem. For there is also plenty of personal expressive writing, as you'll see in this issue of PRE/TEXT, that is deeply attentive to the views and positions of others. There's nothing in the nature of personal expressive writing that is at odds with talking about, summarizing, explaining, or building on the writing of others. In fact, personal expressive writing is often more clearly attentive to an audience and its views than what we see in much academic writing—where writers often slide into a glassy-eyed stance of talking to everyone but not really connecting to anyone. We see this particularly vividly in personal writing in the form of letters to colleagues. It is one of the worst clichés of dichotomy-bound thinking to assume that feelings always push us toward solitary unconnected discourse, and that thinking pushes us toward social connection. "Personal" usually involves being personal in relation to others.

My premise, then, in putting together this collection, is not that all personal expressive writing does the work of academic writing: simply that some does; and that more could if we let it. Personal expressive writing happens to be one among many registers of discourses we can use for academic duty. Because personal writing invites feeling does not mean that it leaves out thinking; and because it invites attention to the self does not mean that it leaves out other people and the social connection.

·   ·   ·

What's at Stake?

What I like about personal or expressive writing is how it usually acknowledges what is at stake for the writer. So often, as reader, we only know what is at stake in a larger more impersonal sense (Western civilization or the epistemological premises of various theorists or the reputation of some important author). We often sense that we are not hearing what is actually driving the piece of writing we are reading—why the writer is choosing to take on the burden of Western Civilization at this point and in this way. That is, despite the pious doctrine that meaning is always ideologically situated, people who make that case often fail to situate meanings in terms of the personal stake they have. (They might reply, of course, that the very concept of a 'person' is a fiction, but their prose often betrays a palpable personal stake—even while not quite revealing what that stake is.) Up to now it has seemed inappropriate to include one's own feelings and story in academic discourse. But since the personal dimension has such a big influence on one's position, perhaps we should turn that convention around and say it is inappropriate to publish an argument or take a position unless you tell your feelings and story.

But that would be wrong. I've had it thrown at me: I'm just a privileged person who had trouble with an elite education and my positions are nothing but playings out of my rebellion. No, we deserve to have our arguments taken on their own merits. Even if my ideas are nothing but epiphenomena of my unresolved Oedipal struggle, they deserve to be taken seriously as arguments if they have any possible value. And judgments about my ideas are more secure than those about my inner dynamics. Wayne Booth argues compellingly about the dangers of ad hominem psychologizing argument in his *Modern Dogma and the Rhetoric of Assent*.

Nevertheless, this sincere warning is no argument against my main point in this essay: that we will benefit from *allowing* and even inviting people to write more personally in academic publications if they *want* to. There is no reason to exclude voluntary acts of personal expressive writing. In short, I am all for purely impersonal discourse—good arguments only for their own sake, pure geometry—as long as we grant equal validity to personal discourse that does the job.

. . .

Mara Holt, in this issue, gives a good model for maintaining both sides of the dichotomy about the individual and society. She draws on George Herbert Mead writing more than sixty years ago:

> Human Society . . . does not merely stamp the pattern of its organized social behavior upon one of its individual members, so that this pattern becomes likewise the pattern of the individual's self; it also at the same time gives him a mind, as the means or ability of consciously conversing with himself in terms of the social attitudes which constitute the structure of his self and which embody the pattern of human society's organized behavior as reflected in that structure. And his mind enables him in turn to stamp the pattern of his future developing self (further developing through his mental activity) upon the structure or organization of human society, and thus in a degree to reconstruct and modify in terms of his self the general pattern of social or group behavior in terms of which his self was originally constituted.

It's when people give in to hierarchical thinking and assume that one side of any dichotomy must always win or dominate the other that we get assumptions like those I'm fighting here: that either we have "knowledge" that is social, communal, socially justified etc., etc.—or we have non- or pseudoknowledge that is private, subjective, confessional, and so forth.

Work Cited

Booth, Wayne. *Modern Dogma and the Rhetoric of Assent*. Chicago: U of Chicago P, 1974.
Mead, George H. *Mind, Self, and Society From the Standpoint of a Social Behaviorist*. Ed. Charles W. Morris. Chicago: U of Chicago P, 1934.

Part V

TEACHING

Peter, you're always telling that story of how you quit graduate school and felt you never wanted to deal with books or classrooms again, but then discovered that you liked teaching—that it wasn't books and classrooms you hated, but being a student. Enough already. Don't become an old geezer repeating old stories. This comfy one just masks the old authority game: you hate following orders but you're happy once you can give them.

Well, it's true, I am getting old. And what you call my "comfy" story is precious to me. And it's true that I hate following orders. But as for giving orders, I'm not quite happy doing it. I'm continually perplexed, frustrated, and dissatisfied by teaching—and especially by wielding authority and giving orders. Again and again I come home complaining about how frustrated I was by today's teaching—particularly my first year class. "Face it," my wife says, "you hate teaching freshmen." "No I don't," I reply. But it often makes me feel bad. It's a little embarrassing to have published so many essays—often in a confident voice—about something that mixes me up so much.

Instinctively, I'm probably a pushy teacher, and also someone who wants to put himself into the limelight—even to show off. And yet I'm always fighting that instinct. For my unambiguous goal is (to use an unfashionable word) to empower students. And pushy performative teaching is definitely frowned on in the crowd I hang out with. Indeed, I distrust it myself—though I'm beginning to suspect that I'd be a better teacher if I let myself run with it more.

So I'm perplexed about teacher authority and student empowerment. But I'm sensing it's not an either/or choice. This is easiest to see in one particular realm of teaching—a realm that is central to me: the *workshop* dimension of teaching. This is an important dimension for me because my goal in teaching is not so much to convey things in conceptual or verbal form—not even to have wonderful discussions. Rather I want to give students *experiences*, for example, by getting them to write for ten minutes without stopping and invite whatever comes; to share writing outloud with others and get no response but "thank you"; to give each other certain kinds of response and refrain from giving other kinds of response; and even to try out certain physical performative or gestural activities with words and writing.

I have to use lots of clear, nonambivalent authority if I want to give students experiences like these, and I've grown fairly comfortable doing so. It doesn't take much authority to lecture or to lead a discussion; that's what everyone expects. Workshop situations have the virtue of often getting me on the sidelines while students work with each other. And workshops invite students to figure out their own conclusions. (I have helped a certain number of my students figure out that freewriting is a stupid waste of time.)

Perhaps I can formulate my perplexity about teacher authority best as a binary conflict. On the one hand, I have come to acknowledge more and more the instinctually pushy side of myself, and the need or even inevitability of teachers wielding authority. And yet on the other hand, I seem to have just as strong a *resistance* to making students do things they don't want to do—or to giving answers to questions students didn't ask. The very kind of learning

I'm after is diminished to the degree that I force students to do things. No wonder I'm perplexed.

Recently, I've reached a certain resolution to this perplexity. It comes from teaching annual week-long summer workshops for teachers (with a wonderful colleague, Lucile Burt). We call these workshops "Teachers as Writers." Our premise is that the foundation for being a better teacher of writing is to have a better relationship with one's own writing. So we do lots of writing and sharing and we put aside all talk about teaching. We also invite some peer responding, but not judgmental or critical responses. We're trying to create a setting of unqualified support—indeed, to make a space for bad writing or rather for trying not to think in terms of good or bad. Our sense is that writing cannot otherwise get genuinely good.

I find these workshops very easy teaching and I can exert clear unconflicted authority. But of course the conditions are utopian: the "students" are adults who are interested in writing and are there by choice; I'm not giving judgments or criticism; and I'm giving no grades or credit. Yet these workshops have given me great help with my perplexity and anxiety about my "regular" teaching—even with the first year writing course that students are required to take, and where I am required to give judgment, criticism, a grade, and credit.

Here's how the teacher workshops help me. My main problem in most institutional teaching—especially with the first year course—is that I fear that what I want to do is crazy and that all my anxiety is a result of my own confusions or hang-ups. What the teacher workshops show me (or so I conclude) is that I am *not* crazy. What I *want* to do makes sense; the teaching seems completely natural and highly rewarding for both "students" and teachers. It doesn't bother me that I can't replicate this teaching in my first year course—as long as I get to feel that my instincts and goals are not crazy. I can fairly contentedly set myself this pedagogical problem: How can I come as close as possible in my teaching of first year students to this desirable kind of teaching—even though I have to operate under much more difficult institutional and psychological constraints? With my first year students I have to *require* this and *make* them do that, but in my head I can still be aiming for this other model of teaching that feels right.

I'll end by mentioning three experiences that have probably been central to my teaching:

- I was a diligent good student from an early age.
- I failed as a student—when it mattered most and despite trying my hardest.
- I did lots of my teaching in experimental settings. I was one of the five founding faculty at Franconia College from 1963–65. I was a mentor in "The Experimental Study Group" at M.I.T. from 1969–72 (a program that invites about two dozen freshman to follow their noses for a year and get full credit without having to take any courses). From its second to its tenth year, I taught at The Evergreen State College, a highly experimental institution—but staffed largely by second generation experimenters.

- Most of my teaching at M.I.T. was in an interdisciplinary freshman course, and most of my teaching at Franconia and Evergreen was in programs that were team-planned and team-taught with colleagues from other disciplines. (The Evergreen programs were full credit, full time—that is, programs that constituted the full load for both students and teachers, sometimes for an entire year.) My happiest and I think my best teaching has been when I'm having to learn new material along with the students.

15

Inviting the Mother Tongue

Beyond "Mistakes," "Bad English," and "Wrong Language"

> Every time I say something the way I say it, she correct me until I
> say it some other way. Pretty soon it feel like I can't think. My
> mind run up on a thought, git confuse, run back and sort of lay
> down. . . . Look like to me only a fool would want you to talk in
> a way that feel peculiar to your mind.
>
> Alice Walker

> . . . Alice Walker's . . . subject . . . *writes* herself to a per-
> sonal freedom and to a remarkable level of articulation in the di-
> alect voice in which Hurston's protagonist *speaks*.
>
> Henry Louis Gates, Jr.

> [T]he eradication of one tongue is not prerequisite to the learning
> of a second.
>
> Keith Gilyard

This essay grows out of feeling torn between conflicting goals or obligations. I think most teachers of first year college writing courses also feel this conflict, and I experience it acutely as director of a university writing program. On the one hand, I feel an obligation to invite all my students to use their own language and not to make them conform to the language and culture of mainstream English (see "Students' Rights to Their Own Language" [Committee]). On the other hand, I feel an obligation to give all my students access to the written language of power and prestige.

This essay was published in the *Journal of Advanced Composition* 19.3 (Summer 1999).

The written language of power and prestige. This is not a very precise formulation, and I will use an equally imprecise but common label for it: Standard Written English (SWE). Precision is not possible here. The conventions of SWE, or what is called correct by prestige readers, can vary from one setting to another—from business to journalism to the academy and even within disciplines. (For example, some will say that SWE forbids all run-ons, fragments, split infinitives, or any use of a capital after a colon; others will say such usages are correct if used well.) But for the purposes of this paper I can sidestep such ambiguities and use a highly pragmatic definition of SWE. I say here what I say to my students: "Standard Written English is the usage, grammar, syntax, punctuation, and spelling that will pass muster with most university faculty around here as correct or at least acceptable. Faculty members will differ from each other a bit, but on *most* of these language matters, they will agree."

The most common attitude toward "wrong" language is to want to get rid of it. Citizens of all sorts—whether they are teachers in the schools, college faculty, members of the mainstream general public, spokespersons for culture, or legislators—are likely to agree that a teacher's job is to *"improve"* students' language. And students often feel the same goal for themselves—as we ourselves are likely to feel in relation to our own speaking and writing: if the words that come naturally to our mouth or pen are labeled wrong, we feel ourselves to have a problem.

Historical conditions can intensify these impulses to improve language. There has been a series of influxes into higher education of diverse populations whose native dialect was not the correct or accepted one:

> [T]he push for "proper" grammar and word usage has been shown to coincide with a dramatic change in the demographics of the college population brought on by relatively more open admission policies in the years after the Civil War (Ohmann 234). No longer could the homogeneous student population of the pre-War years be assumed, as more and more young people from non-elite backgrounds came to fill the universities in search of access to the privileges of high socio-economic rank (Berlin 73; Rudolph 151). [from Boyd 57–58]

During this period, as Robert Connors tells us, textbooks emphasized grammar to an unprecedented degree:

> Between 1865 and 1895, such elements of mechanical correctness as grammar, punctuation, spelling, and capitalization, which would never have been found in textbooks before 1850, came to usurp much of the time devoted in class to rhetorical instruction and most of the marking of student writing (Connors 65). [from Boyd 57].

After World War II, returning GIs created another wave of "new students" into higher education. Then came open admissions in the 1960s. And now we live in yet another time of extensive immigration into the country and into higher education. In our college and university classrooms, we find an unprecedented number of speakers of nonmainstream dialects and students for whom English is a second language. In addition, it seems to many college faculty and outside commentators that even the monolingual natives—students who grew up with the mainstream dialect—arrive in college with "bad English." Historical situations like these, then, can fuel desires to preserve the standard or accepted or prestige language intact—to keep it from being misused, debased, corrupted. No wonder we hear strong calls for "English Only."

But I am *not* trying to get rid of what people call wrong language, errors, carelessness, or nonmainstream language. On the contrary, I'm trying to make a safer place for all of it. I may sound perverse to some readers, but my main goal in this essay is to show how the *writing classroom* can be a safer place for such language than most other sites of language use—a place where, for a good deal of the time, students can put out of mind any worries about whether anyone might consider their language wrong or incorrect.

The problem is that students cannot have that crucial experience of safety for writing *inside* our classrooms unless we can also show them how to be safe *outside*—that is, unless we can also help them produce final drafts that conform to Standard Written English. It is because I care so much about making room for the mother tongue and making the classroom safe for what people call wrong that I want to insist that my students learn to produce SWE too. (By "mother tongue" in this essay, I mean dialects of English, not languages other than English.)

How can we possibly pull this off—especially in a one-semester course for first year students? Especially if it's their only writing course, or their only course except for some "writing intensive" courses or a junior year writing course—a common situation in colleges and universities. Before I offer some concrete proposals, I need to explore the two goals themselves: safety inside our classrooms for the mother tongue and language people call wrong, and also the ability to produce correct SWE.

Because the second goal is so clear and simple, let me start with it: correct Standard Written English. Teachers of other subjects sometimes penalize students more for what they call wrong language and surface mistakes than for other weaknesses in their writing. Issues of correctness become even more weighty from the perspective of race. Lisa Delpit is surely right when she criticizes white "liberal" teachers for handicapping students of color by ignoring their need to master the dialects of power:

> To imply to children or adults . . . that it doesn't matter how you talk or how you write is to ensure their ultimate failure. . . . [T]here is a political power game that is also being played, and if they want to be in on that game there are certain games they too must play. ("Silenced Dialogue" 292)

But what about my first goal of safety? It's not that I love language that people call wrong *because* they call it wrong (though my wife thinks I do). What I love is the mother tongue. Most people cannot really feel comfortable or at home writing, and cannot use writing as naturally as speaking, unless they are taught to write in their home voice—that is, in whatever language comes naturally to hand and mouth. People can't learn to write well unless they write a great deal and with some pleasure, and they can't do that unless they feel writing to be as comfortable as an old shoe—something they can slip into naturally and without pinching.

After all, we experience our language or dialect not just as something we use but as a deep part of *us*. Our home language is not just inside us; we are also inside it (see Pierce, Norton, and many of the essays in the volume by Severino, Guerra, and Butler). The metaphor of "mother tongue" is no joke. How do you think I'll feel if you shout at me, "Aaahhh, your mother tongue wears combat boots," or "Your mother tongue spends her life on her back?"

I grew up in the comfortable white middle class. Both my parents went to college and they respected teachers—professors more so. They admired most things intellectual, and along with that, "good" language. Indeed, my mother was a bit disappointed when I came home from two years' study at Oxford with no English accent, thus revealing a not so uncommon feeling that American English is inferior to British English (or rather "good" British English). I also grew up, I should add, with another mother who spoke Black English.

Despite my linguistic blessings, I have come to notice something interesting when I am trying to copy-edit away my mistakes for a final draft: not just that copy-editing is a bother because it takes so much time and trouble. What strikes me more, now that I've come to notice and acknowledge it to myself, is a feeling of resentment against the *actual acquiescence* to correctness. I feel a little sheepish about admitting what seems to be such a childish feeling, but I have a hunch I'm not the only one: "I want you to take me as I *am*."

There is a crucial larger point here: *Standard Written English is no one's mother tongue*. People like me have a mother tongue much closer to SWE than many others do, but there is still a distance. The words and constructions that come naturally to my tongue are often inappropriate for writing. Speech and writing are different dialects. For writing, there is still a need to acquiesce— to "give in."[1]

If *I* feel I have to give in when I write, then what must many of our students be feeling? When students turn in final drafts full of mistakes, we often say, "How careless!" or "How lazy!" But now I'm suspecting that plenty of them may be saying—consciously or unconsciously: "If you won't take me the way I am, then screw you."

What if I'd been raised poor or working class and speaking a nonmainstream dialect? Furthermore, what if it weren't just nonmainstream but *bad*?

---

1. An adult graduate student, teacher of writing, and serious writer (also white and middle class) responded to an earlier draft of this paper with an example that is telling because it is something so trivial that nevertheless still sticks in her craw.

> In an essay, I wrote that my parents were going "down to the store." The teacher lived in our town, our geography, but he corrected the English: "to the store." I was baffled at the time (I can remember this, even though it was 5th grade) because that is exactly the prepositional phrasing my family used and the phrasing matched our physical reality (the store was down hill). But it was also my mother tongue, in a way. Though only a phrase, I felt a bit taken back. I can't even begin to fathom what African American students, say, feel in a composition class. (Alex Peary, written response, 12/3/97)

That is, certain dialects are widely seen as inferior, defective, or broken (e.g., African-American English, Latino or Hispanic English, Puerto Rican English, Mexican-American English, or Hawai'ian Creole English). If I spoke a stigmatized dialect, my speech would be widely experienced as stupid—and I along with it. And I might get this message not only from speakers of mainstream English. Even my mother—whose tongue it is—might call our shared natural speech "bad English" or "trash" talk. Jesse Jackson publicly characterized Ebonics or Black English in just such terms. Yes, his response was blurted, and he later qualified it, but his blurt said a lot. ("[S]ome of the most scornful and negative criticism of AAVE [African American Vernacular English] speakers comes from African Americans" [Lippi-Green 200]. Note that my real mother also harbored the hope that I'd abandon her perfectly respectable dialect for a "superior" one.)

Of course, middle class white speakers may also be told that their mistakes are "bad English" that imply ignorance. But such mistakes are seldom experienced as implying stupidity. Spanish speakers from Spain who are struggling with English will not feel that their dialect is inherently stupid or trash. The mistakes of ESL speakers from an Asian background are often experienced by teachers as poetic and insightful.

I try to imagine what it would be like if I had grown up with a stigmatized dialect. Suppose I found myself a student in your class and you asked me to write in mainstream English (and I wasn't comfortably bidialectal): your request would be problematic. If I went along with you, I would know, consciously or not, that I would have to give in to a culture that thinks my language is defective or bad—or even that a core part of my very self is stupid or bad. Not only that: I would also have to give in to a culture that has been trying to wipe out my culture and what I experience as part of my core self. Besides, some of my best buddies or family members might make fun of me or even disown me if I were to give in and start using your English. (" 'Over at my school, if they—first time they catch you talkin' white, they'll never let it go. Even if you just quit talking like that, they'll never let it go!'" [Lippi-Green 191]. "In the group I most loved, to be fully hip meant to repudiate a school system in which African-American consciousness was undervalued or ignored" [Gilyard 160]. See also Fordham and Ogbu.)

It wouldn't matter how understanding and supportive you were: I'd still be liable *not* to want to give in to mainstream or prestige English—or at least not till I'd done some hard chewing and unpleasant swallowing. Yet if you don't find some way around this problem, you will have no success as my writing teacher. For even if you somehow do get me to write correctly—by carrot or stick—I'll be building anger and resentment into the very activity of writing.

If I were a student in that situation, how might you get me to write without resentment—and write more than the minimal required amount? You would have to try to set up the following conditions:

- You would have to show me that you respect my dialect and accept it as a full, complete, sophisticated language—in no way inferior or defective compared to Standard Written English. Fortunately for you, this is something that most linguists agree on.

- You would have to show me that you see me as smart. And not just smart but linguistically sophisticated. Fortunately for you, there is a simple obvious fact here—though I and others in the class will constantly need to be reminded of it: even though I am less skilled in SWE than most speakers of prestige English, I possess a linguistic sophistication that most of them lack. I have had lots of practice in hearing and understanding *multiple* dialects. In fact, I have probably learned to switch codes quickly and easily. My mainstream classmate speakers are usually less linguistically sophisticated and more blind to some of the social realities of linguistic variation.
- You would have to make your class a place where I can *use* my mother tongue as much as I want. *Or* as little as I want. That is, you have to offer me a real invitation to use my mother dialect, yet you can't come across like bell hooks' teacher and fellow students who told her that her voice was only "true" and "authentic" when she used a Southern black dialect (hooks 11).
- Ideally you would have to set things up so that *other students* see me and my language as fully sophisticated and rich. But let's hope that I would understand that chauvinist, classist, and racist attitudes of some of my fellow students cannot be changed by a teacher in a single course.

I don't mean to imply that all speakers of stigmatized dialects are resistant or angry. Some have internalized the feeling that their mother dialect is indeed inferior or wrong. Such a feeling is understandable for many reasons. Lippi-Green points out that any black student who feels her language to be as good as mainstream English will have to live with "an unresolvable conflict": "'I acknowledge that my home language is viable and adequate' and 'I acknowledge that my home language will never be accepted'" (186, emphasis in the original). Students who have internalized a sense of inferiority about their mother tongue may be compliant and docile, but their internalized prejudice against their own mother tongue is liable to undermine them as strong users of language.

Yet how can I reconcile this goal of a completely safe place in our classrooms for the mother tongue and language that people call wrong with my other goal of producing essays that conform to Standard Written English? I'll give my argument in a minute, but first one more delay—one more reason why I want so much for the writing classroom to be a safe haven for the mother tongue.

Walter Ong repeatedly points to the obvious fact that the mother tongue is more deeply connected to the unconscious than any dialect or language we learn later. When language is in touch with the unconscious and draws on it, that language usually has more force and resonance. Writing gains energy, life, and voice when it is fed by the various linguistic elements that permeate the unconscious, but many of these elements are wrong or incorrect in writing: slang, colloquialisms, childishness, idiosyncratic voice, so-called deviant or nonmainstream dialects—and all the kinds of instinctive and bodily-linked utterances and partial utterances that Julia Kristeva calls "semiotic" rather than "symbolic" discourse.

I'm not arguing that the mother tongue and these elements from the unconscious are the only sources of power and vitality in writing. But they are strong sources, and more to the point, *they are the sources most readily accessible to unskilled writers*—especially writers who grew up using nonprestige dialects of English. It is for all these reasons, then, that I take it as my goal to make the first year writing course (indeed, every writing course) a place where our students' own comfortable and natural language can flourish—the language that comes instinctively to mind, ear, and tongue. (Could we extend this goal to speakers of languages other than English? I've never tried it.)

I've been talking so much about dialects the mainstream culture seems bent on wiping out that perhaps you'll think I have no interest in apple pie mistakes that mainstream speakers produce through carelessness or ignorance of the conventions. Not so. Even if mainstream students don't have the handicap of a nonprestige dialect, they still have a serious disadvantage in writing; they also need safety. That is, very few of them have ever had the experience of writing for a teacher while their minds were *focused wholeheartedly on their meaning, topic, or thinking.* Even mainstream English speakers tend to devote a large amount of their attention to questions of correctness in grammar, spelling, and so forth.

How must our writing suffer if some of our attention is always leaking away from our meaning, our reasoning, and our organizing to matters of correct language—wondering what a reader with authority over us will call wrong? Full attention to thinking and rhetoric is not possible unless we can make the classroom a place that is safe for *all* forms of language considered wrong.

How Can I Achieve Both Goals?

So where am I? I'm seeking safety for all language that comes naturally to the tongue, and yet I know that such language *cannot* be safe, and that the mother tongue cannot flourish, unless we also help our students produce final drafts that conform to the conventions of SWE. In the face of this dilemma, I could simply repeat what people might expect from my past writing: "Just relax about propriety or correctness on early and middle drafts, but then be vigilant about copy-editing at the end. Learn to alternate between opposite mentalities."

This answer is all very well in general, but it's too general to help us in a one semester writing course that is the only one students are likely to get. Too many students are simply incapable of getting their final drafts to conform to what we call SWE—no matter how vigilantly they copy-edit. We could try to *teach* them everything they need for successful copy-editing, but some students don't need this teaching at all while others need more than we can provide even if we did nothing else. (If I were an English teacher in elementary or high school, I would make the teaching of grammar a substantial part of my curriculum, but I would be with my students more hours per week and more weeks per year than I now get in my college course, and I'd also know that they take English in every grade.)

We could also restrict our *regular* one semester first year writing class to those students who don't need instruction in conventions of usage or copy-editing, and put the others in remedial or basic classes devoted to those matters. But if we take that path, we tend to focus the basic course on "error" and send just the wrong message to students who are least skilled at SWE: "If you want to learn to write, you must first concentrate most of your attention on grammar and correctness. Only after you master surface features do you get to concentrate your attention wholeheartedly on the substance of your thinking." Also, segregation on the basis of surface features of language can result in segregation on the basis of race and class. I am not arguing against all basic writing courses, but I am troubled by how they often function. (See Royer and Gilles for a promising approach to placement into basic writing.)

So I'm stuck with the same conflict of goals or obligations I started with, and yet I've dug myself deeper into a hole. By becoming even more committed to safety for the mother tongue, I've made it harder to achieve my goal of giving students power and control over the kind of language that most teachers and most employers will insist on as correct. It seems as though I'll have to give in a bit on correctness. This is, of course, a well-trodden path: simply to become a bit more tolerant of final drafts with grammar, syntax, and spelling that deviates from SWE from speakers of nonprestige dialects. But Delpit's indictment continues to ring in my ears: that white "liberal, middle class" teachers ensure "that power . . . remains in the hands of those who already have it" ("Silenced Dialogue" 285). I want *all* students to produce the language they need in order to avoid stigmatization by other teachers and readers.

Therefore, in this essay I will suggest another path—one that I have begun to follow in my teaching. Instead of relaxing the "tough" goal of successful copy-editing, I can *reframe* it or rethink it. That is, I can demand and try to teach a slightly different writerly ability—one that is both more important yet in fact more teachable than the ability singlehandedly to get all grammar, syntax, and spelling to conform to SWE. I'm talking about the practical ability to take whatever steps are necessary to get the desired grammar, syntax, punctuation, and spelling—*even if that means getting help.*

Whatever steps are necessary. It's surprising how many students can copy-edit successfully if they just focus their wholehearted attention and commitment to the job. They can access knowledge of conventions that they sometimes trick us into thinking they lack. But of course many students cannot get rid of all deviations from SWE no matter how much they care or how hard they try. They will have to call on help. I urge these students to seek help from various sources: spell checkers, grammar programs (admittedly problematic), writing centers, learning labs, roommates, friends, loved ones, and even paid typists or editors. I offer help in copy-editing during my office hours too, though like the writing center, I won't copy-edit for them. We have no qualms about requiring *typed* papers from students, even if that means some of them pay for the job. We don't object when professional writers are given copy-editing by publishers. Why should we object if students also get help? As teachers of writing, we need to recognize that taking whatever steps are needed for successful copy-editing is an important and inherent part of *what it means to be a writer.* (Of course, speakers of a nonmainstream dialect may need more than just copy-editing. More about this later.)

The central thing here is a shift in what we require: not the impossible demand that all our students know enough about English grammar and conventions of usage to do it all without help, but rather the pragmatic and feasible demand that they know how to take charge of their writing process and do what is needed. I now simply make this a required part of my course—like attendance—for the four or five most important essays of the semester.

In one sense, this policy is a move toward *softness*—letting students off the hook. Some will say it condones "cheating." But help in copy-editing is not plagiarizing—unless you want to say that all published authors are guilty of plagiarism. It makes me happy when students figure out how to get the help they need. This is feasible knowledge, and it is crucial for success in future courses and jobs. If I say they have to copy-edit successfully without help, I am setting them up for inevitable failure, no matter how hard I try to teach grammar and spelling.

And as for real or substantive plagiarism, this approach helps prevent it. I can see more easily if students are really writing their own papers when I see early and middle and even late drafts that are very much in their own tongue—for it is inherent in this approach to use at least three drafts on major essays as we move toward an additional copy-edited, "publication draft." I also have them do plenty of informal writing in class and I see lots of that.

But in another sense, this policy is a move toward *toughness*: students who need the most help will often have the fewest friends and loved ones who can copy-edit well—and the least money to buy help. This could be called unfair, but I've reconciled myself to it because I find the alternatives unacceptable: making the class *less* safe for the mother tongue or letting these students turn in final drafts that will undermine their chances of success with other teachers and employers. And as I've begun to use this policy, I've discovered that students who speak a nonmainstream dialect (and also second-language students) are usually more understanding of the need for these copy-editing steps. They can usually manage my requirement with the help of writing centers and friends; a few pay. It's the complacent mainstream speakers who resent the requirement or can't comprehend that they need help. Mainstream speakers also need to know the pragmatic truth about the power and politics of language: You have to turn in correct final drafts if you want to avoid stigma; but you don't have to do all the correcting yourself.

Admittedly, a *few* stickler teachers mark down students on matters of surface mechanics on in-class essay exams where there is no chance for help in copy-editing. But my nonmainstream dialect students will be worse off in such situations if they can't even put their best thinking into comfortable and clear language. There are also a few jobs that demand the ability to copy-edit memos on the spot with no chance for help. But these jobs are pretty rare, and I don't think it makes sense to design a first year, one-semester writing course as preparation for them.

Putting This Policy into Practice

This policy can seem contradictory and confusing to students. Some of them think I don't really care about good copy-editing since I invite the mother tongue and carelessness about surface language on early and midprocess drafts. Others think I am "hung up about correctness" with my blanket demand for conformity to SWE on final drafts. And some students are confused when I push them for good thinking, organization, and clarity on *midprocess* drafts while nevertheless not pushing them on correctness. (If a student really wants feedback on surface features on early drafts, I'll give it, but only if this doesn't deflect attention from thinking, organization, and clarity of meaning.) But few students have trouble understanding the policy when I relate it to the political realities of language use. I make it clear that I'm not calling SWE inherently better than other dialects. I'm emphasizing that they can't have success in most college courses and most job situations without writing that conforms to the conventions of SWE.

More to the point, I engage in some concrete practices that I think are worth spelling out briefly:

- I make this copy-editing demand on only four or five major essays. I assign lots of quickwrites, exercises, and informal assignments that needn't be well copy-edited.
- On major essays, I find it crucial to specify copy-editing as a separate assignment with a separate due-date. On my course calendar I have one due date for the "third and almost final draft" (which does not have to be well copy-edited), and then a due date one or two classes later for the fourth or "publication draft," and this must be successfully copy-edited. When I used to stop with a third draft, I came to realize that I was asking students to do two conflicting cognitive tasks at once: revise for content, organization, and style, *and* copy-edit for surface features. It doesn't bother me that some students will find the copy-editing assignment quite easy. In the second half of the semester, I sometimes ask for a bit of other homework for the same class.
- I find it helpful to define copy-editing as a blunt yes/no requirement rather than something I grade along a continuum. I compare it to the requirement that they come to class, or that they turn in all previous drafts with later drafts, or do process writing. If I "grade" copy-editing, I am treating it as a matter of talent. Yes, good copy-editing *is* a talent, but I'm purposely taking it out of that realm and putting it into the realm of responsibility, diligence, and self-management—something done or not done. That's the message I'm trying to send: "If you want to pass this course you simply have to manage yourself and do the things that writers do—one way or another."

- I try to exploit what seems to me the biggest help in copy-editing: the human voice. Many students have never *heard* what they have written. When they read out loud with any degree of presence and they actually *hear* their words, they make many improvements in the surface features of their words. No, the ear won't help with spelling mistakes or even usually with forms like "would of," but the improvements from reading out loud are extensive—*as long as* I train students to be brave and speak with full intonation and to listen with care (see Chafe). Therefore, I get students to do lots of reading out loud in pairs, in small groups, sometimes to the whole class—and often to me in frequent conferences. I use many short conferences for hearing them read their papers out loud and then responding on the spot (instead of taking the papers home to respond in writing). Of course speakers of non-mainstream dialects don't by any means notice all deviations from SWE by ear, but they do in fact notice and correct a remarkably large number of them, especially problems in punctuation. Much of their knowledge of the mainstream dialect is in their ears.
- In our program we have always used lots of publication. Four or five times a semester every teacher publishes every student's essay in a class magazine. Students have an easier time taking copy-editing seriously when they see their "publication drafts" in a magazine in their classmates' hands. We use a lab fee to pay for photocopying class magazines.
- And of course I try to find as many ways as I can to soften my "hard" requirement with concrete teaching and help:
  - I teach some mini-lessons in usage, grammar, punctuation, occasionally a point of spelling, and we do some exercises in copy-editing a sample paper.
  - I take some class time for discussing ways to get help in copy-editing—just like getting help having papers typed. I talk about what the writing center can and cannot do. I try to help them make better use of spell checkers. (I want to learn how to help them make better use of grammar/style checkers.) We talk about trying to find friends or loved ones who can do a good job, and ways of bartering for help.
  - On their first major essay, when I get their third drafts, I write in copy-editing suggestions for the first page or two, and suggest copy-editing strategies they might need to use for the rest of the paper. I may call in a few students who face a big copy-editing job and give them some help in conference—but I also get them to talk about the steps *they* need to take to get more help.
  - On the days when I return third drafts, I usually set up peer copy-editing teams in class. I wander around a bit, and at the end I try to have some whole-class discussion of specific questions that come up.[2]

---

2. Long ago in the Bard Writing and Thinking Program I experimented timidly with shared responsibility for copy-editing. Small groups were officially responsible, as groups, for the copy-editing of all their members. If any single member's paper was not well copy-edited, none of their papers were acceptable. See Johnson and Johnson, Sharan, and Slavin for more about this dimension of cooperative learning in various school subjects and levels. I would like to explore this kind of sharing again (and would love to hear about successful uses of it for copy-editing).

An Objection to This Approach for Speakers of Nonmainstream Dialects

Your approach may be fine for mainstream students, but you can't invite speakers of other dialects of English to do most of their writing in the mother tongue and then at the end say, "Now just copy-edit out the surface features of the dialect." Dialects consist of more than just different third-person verb endings. A dialect carries deeper habits of rhetoric and organization. Speakers of nonmainstream dialects who write early drafts in their mother tongue will have to rewrite much of the substance and even thinking of their essays at the end in order to have a college essay in Standard Written English. Where does one find a partner or hire an editor for that job? Thought and language are deeply linked, but your proposal implies that they can be handily separated.

This objection connects with the scholarship in contrastive rhetoric that shows how culture is linked with language, rhetoric, thinking, and even modes of identity. There is extensive research about how people in different cultures argue and persuade and present ideas differently. For one example, Arnetha Ball, one of the prime researchers of African American English (AAE), re-searched the modes of organizing and presenting ideas that were used and preferred by a group of African American students and compared them to results for a group of mainstream students. She found that AAE students had a greater tendency to use and to prefer narrative and circumlocutionary modes for presenting their thinking or experience. (For interesting contributions to contrastive rhetoric, see Coleman, De and Gregory, Fox, and Shen. For an ambitious overview of studies in contrastive rhetoric, see Connor.)

This objection also connects with the almost universally accepted advice about learning a new language: "don't *formulate* your thoughts in your home language and then *translate* them into the new language; it's far better to operate *in* the new language so you can learn to get comfortable in it." In short, if culture, language, thinking, and perhaps even identity are deeply linked, it would seem to follow that we shouldn't ask students to write in their home dialect when it carries a different culture of thinking and rhetoric from what they are supposed to end up with.

In response to this strong objection, I want to propose three arguments.

1. *I am not writing about ESL.* Most of the research in contrastive rhetoric about the links between culture and rhetoric, and about the difficulties of students who were raised in one culture trying to write in a new one, involves *different languages.* Helen Fox and others emphasize the difficulty and anxiety for students moving across entire languages. (Arnetha Ball's research on dialects, just mentioned, is an exception; I'll take up her findings below.) In this essay, I am not suggesting that students move from one language to an entirely different one, but rather that they move a much shorter distance from one dialect of English to another.

Yet even though I'm not suggesting that we invite speakers of Japanese or Turkish to write early drafts in their home language, perhaps it's not such a wild idea. Some startling research on total translation from one language to another provides interesting support for my suggestion that students engage in a much milder form of "translation" between dialects of the same language. In a careful research study of forty-eight Japanese university students writing in English, Kobayashi and Rinnert compared the quality of their compositions using two composing processes: writing directly in English, and writing in Japanese and then translating into English. They found that all students produced higher quality compositions through translation—though high English-proficiency students benefited much less:

> In the translation versions, these students developed more ideas with explanations and specifics, which captured the readers' attention, and they also used more sophisticated vocabulary and a greater variety of form. These results suggest that composing initially in the first language allows students, especially those of lower language proficiency, easier and freer discovery of meaning (e.g., as discussed by Zamel, 1982 and Spack, 1984) and support Lay's (1982) and Cumming's (1989) observations about the benefits of first-language use in second-language writing. (201)

2. *The hardest journey may be from oral to literate.* Most nonmainstream or stigmatized dialects of English are oral and not written. Therefore, the journey for speakers of these dialects in writing college essays may not be so much a journey from one language to another, *per se*, nor from one ethnic culture to another, *per se*, as it is a journey from oral modes of thinking and rhetoric to written modes of thinking and rhetoric. Ball writes: "[S]peakers of AAE . . . because of their cultural and linguistic experiences, rely on oral discourse features" and have "vernacular-based preferences in expository patterns" ("Cultural Preference" 520). That is, the changes in rhetoric and thinking needed for writing college essays are difficult not because the home dialect is a *different dialect* but rather because the home dialect is an *oral dialect*.

Therefore, the strategy of asking these students to write out their oral thinking and rhetoric as it comes to the tongue will serve as a helpful midway stage in their journey from oral to written modes of thinking and rhetoric. If we want our students to take on the power of full mainstream literacy, we can never remove the difficulty or even identity anxiety that some of them may experience in having to move past an oral culture (not necessarily to leave it) and take on a culture of literacy. But we can substantially mitigate their anxiety by inviting them to take on *full literacy* in their oral dialect. And let's not forget that *lots* of mainstream students in our first year writing classes have not read or written very much; therefore, they too cannot really be considered to have entered the culture of literacy. Many of them also show the same tendencies toward an oral-based rhetoric of narrative, circumlocution, and indirectness.

3. *Links are not chains.* There may indeed be deep links between language, thinking, culture, and identity, but links are not chains. Even a knowledgeable authority about contrastive rhetoric like Ilona Leki insists that a culture does not consist of just one way of thinking:

Despite a possible resurrection of the Sapir-Whorf hypothesis (see Connor's essay in this volume), contrastive rhetoric cannot show us the thought patterns of another culture. Rhetorical choices are not directly linked to thought patterns; they are made in response to social, political, and rhetorical contexts and histories. . . . [And] yet the findings of contrastive-rhetorical research on a single text type (or a small number of text types) have sometimes been promulgated as discoveries about an entire cultural group's general rhetorical preferences. . . . How many writing teachers of native English-speaking (NES) students would be willing to accept descriptions of English rhetorical patterns based on essays by a randomly selected group of NES freshmen writing in a language other than English, even one as close to English as French, let alone Chinese? (236. Leki is writing in a rich and impressive collection of essays that will probably interest readers of this essay: *Writing in Multicultural Settings*. Eds. Severino, Guerra, and Butler.)

The mere *use* of a dialect or language does not lock someone into one way of thinking or prevent other ways of thinking. Shall we say, for example, that people cannot analyze or think abstractly if they are using AAE? Smitherman is at pains to show otherwise in her *Talkin and Testifyin* and in some remarkable research findings noted below. (See Thomas Farrell for a striking contrary assertion that such links are indeed chains. He argues that Black children get lower IQ scores because their dialect is oral and lacks "the full standard deployment of the verb 'to be' and depends too much on additive and appositional constructions rather than embedded modification and subordination" [481].)

Does mainstream English or SWE "own" certain discourses? Do people have to give up their cultural identity to take on certain rhetorical or intellectual or cognitive tasks? Surely not. I believe we can validly invite speakers of AAE or other dialects and cultures to take on academic tasks and write an academic essay *in* their home dialects—*as* Latinos, African Americans, or Caribbeans. (Note a related case. The discourses of abstraction, analysis, and logic are genuinely and deeply *linked* with white, male, Western culture, yet plenty of women have insisted that they don't have to give up their identity as women to use these discourses. See Nussbaum for a vigorous statement of this position.)

Two Strategies for Changing Thinking

So where are we? I've been trying to address this objection:

We shouldn't ask speakers of nonmainstream dialects to compose in their mother tongue and copy-edit later, because they will have to make substantive changes in their rhetoric and thinking at the end—instead of just copy-editing.

I hope I've given convincing answers to the first part of the objection. That is, I've given reasons why it is valid to invite these students to compose in their mother tongue (though not to force them to do so). But I have not answered the second part of the objection. That is, I fully agree that many of these students will indeed have to make substantive changes in their rhetoric and thinking if they want to end up with strong college essays that conform to the conventions of SWE. Language and thinking are deeply linked or intertwined, and therefore my teaching approach makes special difficulties for students who have strong roots in a nonmainstream culture. Let me describe two teaching strategies that I use to deal with these difficulties. I choose one or the other, depending on the assignment, the student, or the point in the semester.

First strategy. I use this strategy when I am pushing for an essay of fairly standard or orthodox structure—that is, an essay that makes a single main point that is well supported with reasons and evidence. I start by inviting students to write about something they care about and to produce exploratory writing or a draft that follows whatever path comes most naturally or comfortably. From a male African American student I get an initial piece of writing that shows various features, some of which are the ones that Ball talks about: it is short; it is narrative based; it treats a personal situation in a personal, conversational way with lots of first person; it has an angry tone and sometimes drifts into hostile second-person address; and it is indirect in that it implies or suggests an overall point but doesn't really make it. In addition, it uses many surface dialect features of AAE.

As a first step, I get the writer to make it longer by explaining more and by giving more details and examples. But I don't ask for any changes in the surface dialect. Next, on the basis of feedback from me and/or classmates, I ask the student to settle on a main point and give more reasons and argument for it. In addition, I get him to think more about purpose and audience and lead him not to direct his anger *at his reader*, but rather to explain in a less angry fashion to *other* readers why his anger at certain people makes sense. (In doing this I am also teaching him about the genre of academic discourse—where you are supposed to speak in the third person to a group of "general readers" rather than speaking directly in the second person to the people you are actually annoyed at.) Only at the end do I get him to make the changes in surface dialect that are needed to get his final draft to conform to the conventions of correct SWE—giving him *some* help but still leaving a lot of responsibility on his shoulders.

This process raises an intriguing question as to the nature of dialect: as he gradually transforms his essay—first in thinking, rhetoric, and organization and finally in grammar, syntax, and spelling—at what point has he abandoned AAE? I think the answer will be a matter of fruitful debate, but however it is settled, it is clear that I am asking him to make substantive changes in his thinking as he moves his drafts to mainstream or academic or "white" modes of thinking and presentation. And thus I have to acknowledge to him that he might experience some of the difficulty or even anxiety that students sometimes experience as they try to adopt rhetorical modes of a different culture from the one they grew up in.

Nevertheless, I would still be able to emphasize to him that he need not, throughout this difficult work, worry at all about his surface language. As he struggles to change his pattern of thinking and organizing, he is still free simply to put down whatever words, syntax, grammar, and spellings that come to mouth and hand, without having to notice, question, or doubt them. So even though I don't want to *minimize* the task this student faces as he tries to change his larger rhetoric, I would argue that this approach considerably reduces the size of his struggle by postponing one very large battle. For the allegedly "minor" or surface features of our dialect are often the peskiest or even the most disturbing elements to try to change.

Of course, some students will not *want* to start off writing in their home dialect. They've always tried to write in mainstream English and it feels too odd to do otherwise. Some even feel it would "pollute" their home dialect: "If I have to end up with a white essay, I want to start off writing white." Fair enough; I make it clear that this is fine with me. This is the bidialectal path that most speakers of nonmainstream dialects have traditionally chosen: one dialect for speech, another for writing. But I want to show such students that they have a *choice*: they don't *have* to start out with mainstream English if they want to end up with mainstream English. And I suggest to these students that they *try* drafting in AAE on some other occasions—perhaps in low-stakes freewrites or quickwrites. The whole point here is to give students more choice about language and dialect. Till now, most students were obliged always to try to write in the mainstream dialect of English—and made to feel that they had a big problem if they had trouble doing so.

Second strategy. I use this strategy when the final essay doesn't have to follow a strictly conventional academic organization. And this time let me picture a female student, since some argue (Fox in particular) that women in some nonmainstream cultures have special difficulty moving from a rhetoric of indirectness to the full, blunt, hierarchical explicitness that most teachers want in school essays. This could be someone of Latino or Hawai'ian background (or in fact many seemingly mainstream U.S. backgrounds, as De and Gregory point out [122]). In this strategy I encourage her and help her along in writing it "her way"—perhaps beginning with a story or digression, and only gradually circling around to her main point—a point that she finally makes somewhat indirectly and without any oppositional confrontation with contrary views. I try to help her make her essay as good as she can in "her rhetoric." I give her feedback on early drafts to help her make it better, but without trying to get her to change her rhetorical approach.

But then for her final stages of revision, I suggest a way she can try to *fit* this draft to mainstream readers—even academic readers. I show her how she can add a tiny introductory section to this effect:

> In my essay I am making the following point: [and here she needs to state her point directly and briefly]. But I think I can develop and transmit my point most effectively if I work up to it slowly and state it subtly, weaving it together with various suggestive narratives and scenes.

And if the ending seems abrupt or trails off inconclusively—that is, if it doesn't do what we think of as "concluding" in an academic culture—I might suggest adding a comparable blunt note at the end. Of course she might find these opening or closing sentences offensive, clunky, rude, or even difficult to write. But I would suggest to her that this approach is easier than trying to transform the rhetoric of her whole essay. Thus, where the first strategy involves moving step by step away from one's home rhetoric and dialect—first in matters of rhetoric and organization and finally in surface details—the second strategy invites the student to hang on to home thinking and rhetoric till the end.

This second strategy calls attention to a powerful rhetorical principle: the opening of any discourse has a disproportionate effect on the audience. The opening usually determines whether readers are cooperative or resistant as they read the rest of the text. Cooperative readers often appreciate and even praise the very things they would criticize if they were reading in a resistant frame of mind. An explanatory opening like the one I've just described tends to give readers that crucial feeling: "Yes, I'm in safe hands. This writer seems to know what she is doing." When readers have a sense of where the essay is trying to end up, they are less likely to feel lost if the path wanders. (This holds even for surface features: readers are usually much less upset over spelling and grammar problems if they don't see any in the first page or two.) Similarly, the closing of a text often determines how a reader decides on a final evaluation of a text.

In describing this second strategy I also need to insist on an important cultural observation. Not all successful academic or published writing uses the slam bam thank you ma'am style: first tell 'em what you're going to say, then tell 'em what you are saying, and finally tell 'em what you told 'em. (The five paragraph essay is the paradigm of slam bam.) Many teachers are grateful for subtlety, finesse, movement, and even indirection, *as long as* they can see the writer's skill and control, and as long as they get the help necessary for not feeling lost or bewildered. In the last few decades, academic readers have become accustomed to an astounding range of rhetorical strategies that are anything but four-square. And our journals show a number of first year writing faculty and writing-across-the-curriculum faculty describing adventuresome forms for academic writing (see Bridwell-Bowles for a classic statement).

In fact, I look forward to pushing the second strategy even further. That is, I could invite this student to forget about providing any introductory or concluding assistance to mainstream readers and instead go straight to the final copy-editing. Consider the result. She might well end up with an essay that starts with an anecdote or story and circles around digressively to a main point that is only brushed in. This could be viewed as a very nonmainstream or even "non-Western" essay, but, in fact, it wouldn't be very different from much writing published in any number of magazines and literary journals. Remember, this essay will not be "carelessly" nonacademic and nonmainstream. The writer will have worked hard—with the teacher's help—to make it as good as it can be in "her rhetoric." And it will be in impeccably correct SWE. Indirection and subtlety are much valued and published—as long as they are handled well. Students from stigmatized dialects need to know this.

We need to ponder the point that Victor Villanueva makes in looking back at his writing as an undergraduate college student. He points out that his essays were grounded in what he calls a "Sophist" rhetoric—a "Latino sophistic" that neglected logic—yet these essays were highly successful with his teachers because he made his grammar and spelling flawless (87). Citing and analyzing Villanueva, Pat Bizzell argues for opening the door in our college writing classes to "Rhetorics of 'Color'" (her title).

Maybe Speakers of Stigmatized Dialects Don't Have to Change Their Rhetoric

I've been at pains to acknowledge that speakers of nonmainstream dialects will have to change their rhetoric and thinking, not just tweak their grammar and syntax. I like to acknowledge this because it suggests a larger truth about our job as teachers of writing: whether our students are from the mainstream or not, we usually spend most of our energy trying to affect students' thinking and rhetoric—not just their grammar and syntax. But the examples of Villanueva, Bizzell, and Bridwell-Bowles suggest that perhaps there is a bit more room for variation than is sometimes assumed.

For further and more substantive evidence, we can look at research conducted by Geneva Smitherman and a team of readers who analyzed student exams written for the National Assessment of English Proficiency (NAEP). Their main finding was this:

> For 1984 imaginative and 1984 and 1988 persuasive NAEP essays, a team of experienced writing instructors was able to identify a discernible black discourse style [involving rhetorical and structural features—which they distinguished from black grammar and syntax] and establish criteria for rating the "blackness" of student essays. The team achieved a 90 percent agreement for 867 essays. Results indicated that students who employed a black expressive discourse style received higher NAEP scores than those who did not. In the case of primary trait scores, this finding held regardless of the frequency of BEV [Black English Vernacular] syntax. ("The Blacker the Berry" 94)

Smitherman argues that language and rhetorical norms have changed over time. Her team looked at essays from two earlier tests (1969 and 1979), and found that black discourse style did *not* correlate with higher scores then. She concludes:

> As cultural norms shift focus from "book" English to "human" English, the narrativizing, dynamic quality of the African American Verbal Tradition will help students produce lively, image-filled, concrete, readable essays, regardless of rhetorical modality—persuasive, informative, comparison-contrast, and so forth. (95)

One of the important correlative findings by the Smitherman team was that black language and black discourse were *not* necessarily linked. "No correlation was found between a discernibly African American discourse style and the production of BEV syntax" (94).

Of course, Smitherman's is only one study (actually she calls on another one too), and her team did not look at college level writing. Still her results suggest that we shouldn't be too quick to assume speakers of stigmatized dialects must abandon *all* the rhetorical and linguistic habits of their culture. When people like De and Gregory point to rhetorical losses for students from other cultures writing for mainstream teachers, they usually base their findings on texts produced when students were trying to start off writing in "proper English." Indeed, many of their examples are taken from timed exams—surely a poor window into students' language and thinking. Students may well pay a smaller rhetorical price when they actually get a chance to compose in their home dialect.

There is another price that students pay when they start off trying to write in "proper English": what ESL teachers have called "production errors." That is, students create *additional* deviations from SWE because they are stretching for correctness in an unfamiliar dialect—errors that wouldn't show up if they wrote in their home dialect. Of course the home dialect produces its own deviations from SWE, but the important point here is this: the grammar and syntax of a nonmainstream dialect of English in the United States is usually *less* alien from SWE than many students think. Every teacher is familiar with the destructive effects of students stretching for an unnecessary "propriety" in writing.

A Long-Term Goal

My short-term goal is crudely pragmatic: to help speakers of nonmainstream dialects come up with good essays in *correct SWE* as quickly and easily as possible. But my long term goal is probably no secret: to honor and help preserve multiple dialects of English and to legitimize their use *in writing*. Do we really want a world with fewer and fewer dialects? Listen to Toni Morrison:

> The worst of all possible things that could happen would be to lose that language. There are certain things I cannot say without recourse to my language. It's terrible to think that a child with five different present tenses comes to school to be faced with those books that are less than his own language. And then to be told things about his language, which is him, that are sometimes permanently damaging. . . . This is a really cruel fallout of racism. I know the Standard English. I want to use it to help restore the other language, the lingua franca. (quoted in Lippi-Green 185–86)

Linguists tell us that dialects tend to drift toward the dominant language and to die out. I don't think minority dialects can survive and flourish unless they come to be legitimate for writing. Given the growing recognition of English as a *world* language rather than merely the language of the United Kingdom and the United States, however, it's not unrealistic to imagine a future where multiple and very distinct dialects of English *are* legitimate and widely used for writing.

So even in a one-semester writing course, while we try to make sure that all students get the final drafts of most of their major essays to conform to the conventions of SWE, I think we can also honor writing in nonmainstream dialects. We can invite students to leave their exercises and low-stakes writing in the home dialect—helping send the message that nonmainstream dialects don't need to be "corrected" into SWE to be legitimate. And even on major essays, we can invite copy-editing into *two* final drafts: one into correct SWE and one into the best form of the student's home dialect.

Speakers of stigmatized dialects need to know how much good writing is currently being published in these dialects. They need to know about the works of writers like Gloria Anzaldua, Zora Neal Hurston, Earl Lovelace, Darrell Lum, Sapphire, "Sistren," Alice Walker, and Lois-Ann Yamanaka. As Gates and others have noted, nonprestige dialect tends to appear first as reported speech in poetry and fiction. Gradually, it spreads to narrators and to nonfiction. Geneva Smitherman uses African American English even for scholarly and academic writing.

Knowing this, students will be more adventuresome in finding audiences for their writing in nonmainstream dialects—audiences that do exist. They will have friends and peers who will appreciate such pieces, and this kind of work is already starting to be published in some campus literary magazines and even at times in the student newspaper. As teachers we may find, as I have, that *we* enjoy it—particularly because writing in nonmainstream dialects tends to have a stronger and livelier voice. Given how much is now being published in nonmainstream dialects, I see a day when many more mainstream readers will also appreciate it.

Some people say nonmainstream dialects are not meant to be written; orality is their essence. I have heard this even from native speakers of these dialects. But Middle English literature and a good deal of Renaissance literature in English is nothing *but* writing in local, oral dialects that varied widely according to region. And much of this literature was widely published—some of it by means of copying and circulating, some of it actually printed. Only later did *one* of these dialects become "standard" because it happened to be the dialect of the region that became economically and politically dominant. This tradition of publication in the vernacular continued past the Renaissance with writers like Robert Burns and, more recently, James Kelman. I suspect that the same thing happened in other countries. Dante wrote in a vernacular of the people that was looked down on by many academics for that reason. All our modern European languages started out as nonmainstream oral vernaculars.

So the truth about writing in oral dialects is more curved and interesting than we might have thought: it *used* to be common and it is getting common again; but we have been living through a long period—in England and the United States anyway—when writing in nonprestige oral dialects seems to have been relatively rare. Our present situation highlights a question that is coming more and more to the fore—a dominant question that was the focus of the Spring 1997 special issue of *TESOL Quarterly*: "Who owns English?" In the introductory essay, Bonny Norton asks, "whether English belongs to native speakers of English, to speakers of mainstream English, to White people, or to all of those who speak it, irrespective of their linguistic and sociocultural histories" (422).

Brief Responses to Two Other Objections

1. I imagine an objection from even a *champion* of nonprestige dialects. I'm thinking of people like De and Gregory who worry about minority dialects being "colonized," engulfed, or tamed when they interact with English and "Western epistemic practices" (120) and with the "rigors of academic thinking and writing" (123). I can imagine them saying that this colonization process will accelerate if we invite students to compose in their home dialect and then revise into SWE. Perhaps nonmainstream dialects can only be preserved intact by *heightening* their separation—and keeping them oral.

I suspect that the strategy I am describing might lead to more mixing and hybridity; and I admire the pedagogical suggestions De and Gregory offer in their efforts to help students keep the logics of two cultures distinct (they focus more on logic than rhetoric). Still, I suspect that dialects can only survive and prosper if they are widely used—in writing and for various purposes. This will probably result in some change, but I'm worried about the survival of dialects if people try too hard to preserve them in their "pure" or unmixed form. Change is the rule when it comes to language and especially dialect. Standard English itself has changed substantially because of contact with nonmainstream dialects. English, perhaps more than most languages, is itself a hybrid. Pratt argues as a linguist that interaction among languages and dialects is the norm and that linguistic homogeneity is the exception, the "utopia." William Labov (see Fasold, Stevens), studying Black English, and Charlene Sato, studying Hawai'ian Creole English, both observe an interesting phenomenon: even though creoles *tend* to drift toward the dominant language (in this case mainstream English), Black English and Hawai'ian Creole English are halting this drift and resisting being swallowed by the mainstream dialect. When students can write early drafts in home dialect and home rhetoric, I think that both their language and their thinking will be stronger and be more their own—even if not remaining pure.

2. Am I just a "well intentioned white liberal" with a sentimental attachment to other dialects because I already have access to the dialect of power? A friend has called my proposal "lily white." Lisa Delpit criticizes teachers who introduce "dialect readers" into the early grades and who also, in their liberal looseness, veil their authority and offer students too much choice and therefore too little access to the language of power. Such teachers may be well in-

tentioned, she says, but their behavior serves "to prevent the schools from teaching the linguistic aspects of the culture of power, thus dooming Black children to a permanent outsider caste" ("Silenced Dialogue" 285).

The substantive question is not about my color, I hope, but about whether my proposal sufficiently achieves Delpit's goal of offering access to the language of power for students of stigmatized dialects. This is probably the most important question raised by this essay, and I acknowledge that the answer is debatable. For my approach here might seem to involve mixed messages about teacher authority, student choice, and the demand for competence in the language of power. On the one hand, I am offering students a new choice of writing early drafts in their home dialect. And I am also inviting them to get help in copy-editing into SWE rather than trying to insist that they be able to do it without help. Yet on the other hand, I'm insisting that students learn to turn in final drafts in the language of power. In doing so I'm not using what Delpit calls "veiled commands" (289); I make it a blunt requirement. I'm not sure what Delpit would say about this mixed approach, especially since her criticisms seem to be addressed more to teachers in the schools than to teachers in colleges. (It's important to remember that I'm talking about a one-semester first year college course; not full-year, every-year English courses in the schools.) But she recently made a suggestion about the teaching of writing that is not so different from what I am suggesting here:

> Unlike unplanned oral language or public reading, writing lends itself to editing. While conversational talk is spontaneous and must be responsive to an immediate context, writing is a mediated process which may be written and rewritten any number of times before being introduced to public scrutiny. Consequently, writing is more amenable to rule application—one may first write freely to get one's thoughts down, and then edit to hone the message and apply specific spelling, syntactical, or punctuation rules. ("Ebonics and Culturally Responsive Instruction" 7)

Geneva Smitherman makes a similar recommendation:

> I am often asked "how far" does the teacher go with this kind of writing pedagogy. My answer: as far as you can. Once you have pushed your students to rewrite, revise; rewrite, revise; rewrite, revise; and once they have produced the most powerful essay possible, then and only then should you have them turn their attention to BEV grammar and matters of punctuation, spelling, and mechanics." ("The Blacker the Berry" 95)

Arnetha Ball writes that

> students can continue to use their informal language patterns while acquiring competence in new academic registers. These kinds of curricula mandate further research on creating bridges between patterns used in students' home discourse communities and those required for school success. ("Cultural Preference" 525)

Patricia Bizzell has earned her stripes as not-a-white-liberal, and so it is interesting to hear her thinking in this area. In a short paper for a recent conference, she wrote, "It may no longer be necessary, or even accurate, to say that all students must write only in traditional academic discourse and Standard English to satisfy academic expectations" ("The Need for a Common Language: A Constraint on Civic Literacy?"). In a recent full essay she seems to restrict her focus to "Rhetorics of 'Color' " rather than grammar and syntax of color. In her first paragraph, she acknowledges that "we have a responsibility to teach the standard forms" (1), but in the second paragraph, she turns and devotes the rest of the essay to arguing that nevertheless,

> the academy should allow culturally diverse students to retain their home habits of language use and adapt these to academic writing. This means that the academy would have to accept alternative forms of academic discourse, forms that reflect the students' own cultural diversity. (2)

I look forward to more research and conversation as to whether the approach I suggest in this essay provides students of stigmatized dialects enough access to the language of power.

Conclusion

After these excursions into complex and often theoretical matters of dialect and culture, I want to move back to the concrete realm of the classroom. Consider the criteria that most teachers use in judging most essays: sticking to the topic or question or assignment; getting the information or concepts right; having good ideas of one's own; reasoning carefully; giving enough arguments, evidence, and examples; organizing effectively; and making meaning clear at the sentence level. *It is possible to meet every one of those criteria and still use lots of language people call wrong.* Thus it is possible to meet all those criteria before worrying about grammar, syntax, and spelling. (Only a few matters of punctuation will come up in trying to achieve clear meaning at the sentence level.) And thus it is possible to give students feedback on *all* these criteria and help them satisfy every one—and never once talk about surface features of language.

Once a draft has become strong and clear on *all* these substantive criteria, it's usually not so hard to make the changes needed in grammar, syntax, and spelling for conformity to SWE. Students can get better at this job relatively quickly, and get help with it—*after* they've worked on all the other criteria without worrying about surface features (as Smitherman urges). It may be difficult for speakers of nonmainstream dialects to copy-edit final drafts, but not as difficult as trying to write *all* their drafts in SWE. The same goes for "giving in": it may be galling to give in on final drafts to a culture that seems bent on destroying your culture—but not as galling as giving in on all drafts, all writing.

But this approach can put a strain on teachers. It's not uncommon to hear teachers say they can't pay attention to substance if there are too many mistakes; they need to "clean up the language" enough to see the thinking and structure. Here's a comment I recently overheard on a list serve discussion among writing teachers: "Only now can I really address the underlying thinking and understanding problems because previously the writing was so atrocious that I couldn't see them." This is a common reaction—I occasionally feel it myself. But it's a reaction we need to get over. Premature attention to surface correction has created a serious handicap for many students—plenty of them speakers of the mainstream dialect. Over the years, the writing of these students has not improved enough because they have not been pushed hard enough or held accountable enough on the *substance* of their thinking. Their thinking and rhetoric have been too much ignored because their teachers have too often addressed only problems in grammar, syntax, and spelling. Think about the effects of never being pushed about weakness in thinking, organization, or even clarity of explanation and only being pushed about your language.

In short, providing safety about language does not mean discarding standards and evaluation. Carelessness about surface language is not the same as carelessness about meaning, thinking, organization, and clarity. We can make it clear to students that our invitation not to worry about grammar, syntax, and spelling on early drafts is our method of asking them to give *more* attention to meaning, thinking, organization, and clarity. We can give them more feedback and hold them more responsible on these matters of substance if we are not trying to correct grammar and syntax on early and middrafts.

Since I've been trying to cover such a lot of territory in this essay, let me conclude by summarizing my main hypotheses and suggestions:

- It is possible and often beneficial to do most of our writing using all sorts of language that people call wrong and only at the end make changes to get the text to conform to the conventions of Standard Written English.
- Plenty of students will need help in making those final changes, but it is reasonable to invite them to get that help if we are teaching the only writing course they have in college or in their first two years. In teaching such a course, we do not need to take it as our goal that all students know how to make their final drafts conform to correct SWE without help. But we can and should insist that they know how to manage themselves as writers so as to do what is necessary to get their final drafts into SWE—the language of prestige and power.
- Students *can* use nonprestige dialects for whatever cognitive and rhetorical tasks face them. In doing so, they will usually find writing more comfortable and inviting and will usually be able to find more words and ideas and get more force, power, energy, and voice into their writing. This approach might help stigmatized dialects and their cultures to persist and flourish.
- We can make the writing classroom one of the most *hopeful of all sites of language use*: a place where students can learn to put their entire attention on

their meaning and not on surface propriety—and where students can use their mother tongue as much as they want (or as little as they want). We can communicate respect for all dialects and help all students realize that speakers of nonmainstream dialects are usually more linguistically sophisticated than speakers of mainstream English.

I think this last is the most important benefit for speakers of stigmatized dialects. We can show them that *writing* provides a safer site for language use than speaking—easier access to linguistic power. That is, when they *speak* to mainstream listeners they must use correct mainstream English—even down to intonation—or risk stigmatization; but when they write to mainstream readers, they can do most of their work in their mother tongue and still end up with a text in SWE.

Finally, I want to call attention to an underlying principle of great generality. Everything in this essay reflects a recent discovery that will stand as one of the most important and enduring principles of literacy: *Anyone at any time can write anything he or she can say; writing is easier than reading and hence serves as a much more empowering doorway to literacy*. It was only a few years ago that Donald Graves (with the powerful help of people like Nancie Atwell) learned that tiny children could be taught how to write before they could read—if only they were shown how to make use of squiggles and invented spelling. Now, kindergarteners and first graders all over the country are learning that they can put their words on paper as naturally and easily as they speak. Children in these elementary classrooms become literate much more quickly and comfortably when they start by writing in their idiosyncratic dialect. Even their relationship to reading improves. Since virtually everyone is far more linguistically sophisticated in speaking than in writing, we do well to call on speech in order to import that sophistication into writing. Putting it another way, more and more teachers are learning to build more bridges to literacy by blurring the boundaries between speech and writing.[3]

Works Cited

Anzaldua, Gloria. *Borderlands / La Frontera: The New Mestiza*. San Francisco: Spinters-Aunt Lute, 1987.

Atwell, Nancie. *In the Middle: Writing, Reading, and Learning with Adolescents*. Portsmouth NH: Boynton/Cook Heinemann, 1987.

Ball, Arnetha F. "Cultural Preference and the Expository Writing of African-American Adolescents." *Written Communication* 9.4 (1992): 501–32.

———. "Expository Writing Patterns of African American Students." *English Journal* 85 (January 1996): 27–36.

Ball, Arnetha and Ted Lardner. "Dispositions Toward Language: Teacher Constructs of Knowledge and the Ann Arbor Black English Case." *College Composition and Communication* 48 (1997): 469–85.

3. I have shared various versions of these thoughts on various occasions and I am indebted to helpful feedback I have gotten from far too many people to name here. But I would especially thank Marcia Curtis, Diana Eades, and Suzie Jacobs.

Berlin, James. *Writing Instruction in Nineteenth-Century American Colleges*. Carbondale: Southern Illinois UP, 1984.

Bizzell, Patricia. "The Need for a Common Language: A Constraint on Civic Literacy?" Position paper for "New Directions for Programs in Writing, Rhetoric and Composition Studies: Visual and Civic Literacy." Conference at the University of Rhode Island, May 28, 1998.

———. "Rhetorics of 'Color': The Example of *Bootstraps*." *Race, Rhetoric, and Composition*. Ed. Keith Gilyard. Portsmouth NH: Heinemann/Boynton Cook. 1999.

Boyd, Richard. "'Grammatical Monstrosities' and 'Contemptible Miscreants': Sacrificial Violence in the Late Nineteenth-Century Usage Handbook." *The Place of Grammar in Writing Instruction*. Eds. Susan Hunter and Ray Wallace. 1995. Portsmouth NH: Heinemann/Boynton Cook. 54–70.

Bridwell-Bowles, Lillian. "Discourse and Diversity: Experimental Writing within the Academy." *College Composition and Communication* 43 (October 1992): 349–68.

Chafe, Wallace. "Punctuation and the Prosody of Written Language." Technical Report No. 11, Center for the Study of Writing, Berkeley CA and PA, 1987.

Coleman, Charles F. "Our Students Write with Accents." *College Composition and Communication* 48 (1997): 486–500.

Committee of the Conference on College Composition and Communication. "Students' Rights to Their Own Language." *College Composition and Communication* 25 (1974): 1–18.

Connor, Ulla. "Contrastive Rhetoric: Implications for Teachers of Writing in Multicultural Classrooms." In Severino, Guerra, Butler. 198–208.

Connors, Robert J. "Mechanical Correctness as a Focus in Composition Instruction." *College Composition and Communication* 36 (1985): 61–72.

Cook, William. "Writing in the Spaces Left." *College Composition and Communication* 44 (1993): 9–25.

De, Esha Niyogi and Donna Uthus Gregory. "Decolonizing the Classroom: Freshman Composition in a Multicultural Setting." In Severino, Guerra, Butler. 118–32.

Delpit, Lisa. "Ebonics and Culturally Responsive Instruction." *Rethinking Schools 12.1 (Fall 1997): 6–7.*

———. *"The Silenced Dialogue: Power and Pedagogy in Educating Other People's Children."* Harvard Educational Review 58.3 (1988): 280–98.

Elbow, Peter. "The War Between Reading and Writing—and How to End It." *Rhetoric Review* 12.1 (Fall 1993): 5–24.

Farr, Marcia and Harvey Daniels. *Language Diversity and Writing Instruction*. NY: ERIC, 1986.

Farrell, Thomas. "IQ and Standard English." *College Composition and Communication* 34.4 (December 1983): 470–84.

Fasold, Ralph. W. (introd.). Labov, William. "Are Black and White Vernacular Diverging?" *Papers from the NWAVE XIV Panel Discussion. American Speech* 62.1 (Spring 1987).

Fordham, Signithia and John Ogbu. "Black Students' School Success: Coping with the 'Burden of "Acting White."'" Urban Review 18 (1986): 176–206.

Fox, Helen. *Listening To the World*. Urbana IL: NCTE, 1994.

Gates, Henry Louis Jr. *The Signifying Monkey: A Theory of African-American Literary Criticism*. NY: Oxford UP, 1988. 169.

Gilyard, Keith. *Voices of the Self: A Study of Language Competence*. Detroit: Wayne State UP, 1991. 160.

Graves, Donald. *Writing: Teachers and Children at Work*. Portsmouth, NH: Heinemann, 1983.

hooks, bell. "'When I was a Young Soldier for the Revolution': Coming to Voice." *Talking Back: thinking feminist, thinking black*. Boston: South End P, 1988. 10–18.

Hurston, Zora Neal. *Their Eyes Were Watching God; A Novel*. NY: J. B. Lippincott Co. 1937.

Johnson, David W. and Frank P. Johnson *Joining Together: Group Theory and Group Skills*. 2nd ed. Englewood Cliffs: Prentice Hall, 1982.

Jordan, June. "Nobody Mean More to Me Than You: And the Future Life of Willie Jordan." *On Call: Political Essays*. Boston: South End P, 1985. 123–39.

Kobayashi, Hiroe and Carol Rinnert. "Effects of First Language on Second Language Writing: Translation versus Direct Composition." *Language Learning* 42:2 (June 1992): 183–215.

Kristeva, Julia. *Revolution in Poetic Language*. Trans. Margaret Waller. NY: Columbia UP, 1984.

———. "The System and the Speaking Subject." *Times Literary Supplement*, 12 Oct. 1973: 1249–52.

Leki, Ilona. "Cross-Talk: ESL Issues and Contrastive Rhetoric." In Severino, Guerra, Butler. 234–44.

Lippi-Green, Rosina. "The Real Trouble with Black English." *English With an Accent: Language, Ideology and Discrimination in the United States*. London: Routledge, 1997. 176–201.

Lisle, Bonnie and Sandra Mano. "Embracing a Multicultural Rhetoric." In Severino, Guerra, Butler. 12–26.

Lovelace, Earl. *The Wine of Astonishment*. NY. Vintage, 1984.

Lum, Darrell H. Y. *Pass On, No Pass Back*. Honolulu: Bamboo Ridge P, 1990.

Norton, Bonny. "Language, Identity, and the Ownership of English." *TESOL Quarterly* 31.3 (1997): 409–29.

Nussbaum, Martha. "Feminists and Philosophy." Rev. of *A Mind of One's Own: Feminist Essays on Reason and Objectivity*, ed. Louise M. Antony and Charlotte Witt. *New York Review of Books* (20 Oct. 1994): 59–63.

Ohmann, Richard. *Politics of Letters*. Middletown CT: Wesleyan UP, 1987.

Ong, Walter. *Orality and Literacy: The Technologizing of the Word*. NY: Methuen, 1982.

Pierce, Bonny Norton. "Social Identity, Investment, and Language Learning." *TESOL Quarterly* 29.1 (1995): 9–31.

Pratt, Mary Louise. "Linguistic Utopias." *The Linguistics of Writing*. Ed. Nigel Fabb et al. Manchester: Manchester UP, 1987. 48–66.

Royer, Daniel J. and Roger Gilles. "Directed Self-Placement: An Attitude of Orientation." *College Composition and Communication* 50.1 (September 1998): 54–70.

Rudolph, Frederick. *Curriculum: A History of the American Undergraduate Course of Study Since 1636*. San Francisco: Jossey-Bass, 1981.

Sapphire. *Push: A Novel*. NY: Knopf, 1996.

Sato, Charlene J. "Language Change in a Creole Continuum: Decreolization?" *Progression and Regression in Language: Sociocultural, Neuropsychological, and Linguistic Perspecitves*. Eds. Kenneth Hyltenstam and Ake Viberg. Cambridge: Cambridge UP, 1993.

Severino, Carol, Juan C. Guerra, and Johnnella E. Butler, eds. *Writing in Multicultural Settings*. NY: MLA, 1997.

Sharan, Shlomo, ed. *Handbook of Cooperative Learning Methods*. Westport CT: Greenwood P, 1994.

Shen, Fan. "The Classroom and the Wider Culture: Identity as a Key to Learning English Composition." *College Composition and Communication* 40 (1989): 459–466.

Sistren, with Honor Ford Smith, editor. *Lionheart Gal: Life Stories of Jamaican Women*. London: The Women's Press, 1986.

Slavin, Robert E. *Cooperative Learning: Theory, Research, and Practice*. Boston: Allyn and Bacon, 1995.

Smitherman, Geneva. "'The Blacker the Berry, the Sweeter the Juice': African American Student Writers." *The Need for Story: Cultural Diversity in the Classroom and Community*. Urbana IL: NCTE, 1994. 80–101.

———. *Talkin and Testifyin: The Language of Black America*. Detroit: Wayne State UP, 1986.

Stevens, W. K. "Study Finds Blacks' English Increasingly Different." *New York Times,* March 15, 1985, A14.

Troutman, Denise. "Whose Voice Is It Anyway? Marked Features in the Writing of Black English Speakers." In Severino, Guerra, Butler. 27–39.

Villanueva, Victor, Jr. *Bootstraps: From an American Academic of Color.* Urbana, IL: NCTE, 1993.

Walker, Alice. *The Color Purple.* NY: Harcourt Brace, 1982. 183–84.

Yamanaka, Lois-Ann. *Blue's Hanging.* NY: Farrar, Straus and Giroux, 1997.

———. *Saturday Night at the Pahala Theater.* Honolulu: Bamboo Ridge P, 1993.

16

High Stakes and Low Stakes in Assigning and Responding to Writing

As I try to understand my own experience of writing and the experience of my students, and as I try to plan my teaching, nothing has been more useful to me than the simple, crude distinction between high-and low-stakes writing—the question of how much a piece of writing *matters* or *counts*.

High and Low Stakes in Assigning Writing

The goal of low-stakes assignments is not to produce excellent pieces of writing but to get students to think, learn, and understand the course material. Low-stakes writing is usually informal and tends to be graded informally. In a sense we get to throw away the low-stakes writing itself, but keep the neural changes it produced in students' heads. High-stakes assignments also produce learning, but they are more fraught because students know they are writing to be judged—and we have to do the judging.

It's obvious why we need high-stakes assignments in our courses. We can't give trustworthy final grades that reflect whether students actually understand what we want them to understand unless we get them to articulate in writing what they have learned. If students take only short answer tests or machine graded exams, they will often *appear* to have learned what we are teaching, when in fact they have not.

This is a slightly revised version of the essay published in 1997 in a collection of essays written to help faculty in all disciplines use writing more effectively in their teaching: *Writing to Learn: Strategies for Assigning and Responding to Writing in the Disciplines.* Eds. Mary Deane Sorcinelli and Peter Elbow. (A volume in the series, *New Directions for Teaching and Learning.*) San Francisco: Jossey-Bass. The other essays in the collection throw useful light on the issues in this essay.

Am I saying that if students can't explain something in writing, they don't know it? Not quite. That is, I acknowledge that some students can understand something well and yet be hindered from explaining it in writing because of their fear of writing or lack of skill. And we sometimes can't even *say* what we know (much less write it). Nonverbal knowing is most obvious in realms like music, art, and dance (mathematics?) but it can occur in any realm. That is, we can know something at a felt, nonverbal level before we find words for what we know.

Nevertheless, even though students *can* sometimes know things they can't explain in writing, surely good college grades should reflect more than non-verbal and nonwritten understanding, but also in addition the ability to *convey* that understanding in writing. (Conceivably, we should relax this demand in music and art and dance classes. And I hasten to add that my tough position rests on two gentler premises: we should *honor* nonverbal knowing, inviting students to use low-stakes writing to fumble and fish for words for what they sense and intuit but cannot yet clearly say; and if we assign lots of low-stakes writing, students are much less liable to be held back by fear or inability to put what they know on paper when they come to high-stakes writing.)

Students may complain, "But how can you grade on the basis of writing when this isn't a writing course?" We mustn't forget here a basic pedagogical principle: we are not obliged to teach everything we require. We don't teach typing, yet we often require it. We don't teach reading, yet we require it. Besides, if we require students to explain their learning on paper, we will be doing a big favor to our campus writing program and writing teachers. Writing courses only work well if students *need* writing to prosper in their other courses.

The Importance of Low-Stakes Assignments

Writing *feels* like an inherently high-stakes activity—especially because most people learn and use writing primarily in school, where it is virtually always evaluated—usually graded. Writing tends to be used for more serious occasions than speaking. ("Are you prepared to put that in writing?") Speech feels more like a low-stakes activity because we learn it in the home and on the playground and use it casually everywhere. We don't usually think of our speech as being graded.

But speech *can* be used in formal and evaluative settings—as when we are interviewed for a job or give a talk. In fact, if we pause and reflect for a moment, we will realize that our speech is almost *always* evaluated, even if not formally graded. How we talk and what we say are probably the main basis by which people we meet look down on us or are impressed with us.

And writing *can* be used informally, even casually, and in a nonevaluative setting. The fact is that if we are looking for the best possible low-stakes arena for language—for using words to learn, explore, take risks, or commune with ourselves and not have our words be evaluated—writing is much *better* than speaking. Writing permits us to keep our words private or to revise them before showing them to anyone else. Speech on the other hand is riskier because it is almost always heard by someone in its first bloom and it can never be taken back.

Low-stakes writing assignments are typically frequent and informal and designed to make students regularly spend time reflecting in written language on what they are learning from discussions, readings, lectures, and their own thinking. These informal pieces of writing are sometimes done in class and sometimes for homework. These pieces are low stakes because individually they don't have much effect on the final grade. Teachers tend to distinguish these assignments by calling them not essays but quickwrites, letters, freewrites, thinkpieces, inkshedding. (When we require students to turn in a draft of a high-stakes essay a week or more before the final version is due, the draft tends to function as a lower-stakes piece.)

Because we are so habituated to treating writing as a high-stakes activity, especially in schools and colleges, I want to summarize here some of the special benefits of low-stakes writing:

- Low-stakes writing helps students involve themselves more in the ideas or subject matter of a course. It helps them find their own language for the issues of the course; they stumble into their own analogies and metaphors for academic concepts. Theorists are fond of saying that learning a discipline means learning its discourse, but learning a discipline also means learning *not* to use that discourse. That is, students don't know a field until they can write and talk about what's in the textbook and the lectures in their *own* lingo, in their informal, "home," or "personal" language—language that, as Vygotsky says, is "saturated with sense" or experience.
- When students do high-stakes writing, they often struggle in nonproductive ways and produce terrible and tangled prose. When they do low-stakes writing, their writing is usually livelier, clearer, and more natural—often more interesting—in spite of any carelessness and mistakes. They don't tie their syntax in so many knots (or defensively restrict themselves to simple "Dick and Jane" sentences) because they aren't worrying so much about the grade or whether they are writing exactly what the teacher was looking for. I've almost never seen a piece of low-stakes writing I couldn't easily understand. But I've seen *lots* of high-stakes writing that students worked very hard on—and found it impenetrable.
- With frequent low-stakes pieces we ensure that students have *already* done lots of writing before we have to grade a high-stakes piece—so that they are already warmed up and more fluent in their writing. And it's no small help to their high-stakes writing that *we* have seen a number of their low-stakes pieces. For then when they turn in a high-stakes essay that is awkwardly tangled or even impenetrable, we don't have to panic or despair; we can just say, "Come on. You can say all this in the clear lively voice I've already seen you using."

- Low-stakes writing gives us a better view of how students are understanding the course material and reacting to our teaching. We get a better sense of how their minds work. We can see better the interactions between their thinking about course material and their thinking about other realms of their lives, and between their thinking and their feelings. We get better glimpses of them as people.
- Probably the main practical benefit of frequent low-stakes assignments is to force students to keep up with the assigned reading every week. When students put off the reading till an exam or major paper, they learn much less from discussions and lectures. And when only the teacher and a few diligent students have done the reading, the whole course tends to sag.

Responding to Writing

When we assign writing, we can trust that we are helping students learn more and probably even write better. But when we respond or comment, we can't be so confident. The news from researchers is not encouraging. They have discovered how often teacher's comments are not clear; how often comments are misunderstood by students even when they are clear; and how often comments cannot be trusted (for example, the teacher writes, "You should omit this section," or, "You need a comma here," or, "This hypothesis has been discredited," when in fact many equally authoritative colleagues would disagree). Researchers have trouble finding good evidence that our comments on student writing actually help students learn more or write better.

These sobering results are not really so surprising once we stop and reflect on the conditions in which we write our comments and the conditions in which students read them. After all we write comments in great quantity—working slowly down through thick stacks of papers on our desk. It is often late at night and we are usually in a hurry. And truth be told, we are often writing in a discouraged or downright grumpy mood. Writing comments on papers and exams is a *major* portion of the "academic writing" of most academics, yet it's not the writing we really care about. It seldom has much effect on our careers and we seldom look back and revise what we've written. No wonder it is seldom our best writing. And let's face it: it's not feasible to write our comments really slowly and to revise them carefully. We're surely going to continue to write comments fast, late at night, and not always in the best mood. Still we can learn to do it better—thus our efforts in this book.[1]

Even when we write clear, accurate, valid, and helpful comments, our students often read them through a distorting lens of resistance or discouragement—or downright denial. (Don't we sometimes read responses to our own

---

1. It interests me as a writing teacher to note that though our commenting on student papers is undeniably "professional academic" writing, it is often very casual: we often write in incomplete sentences and use lots of "I" and "you." I'm not saying that these features make our writing bad or unprofessional or unacademic. I'm just pointing out that many academics unthinkingly *assume* that casual informal writing is not academic or professional.

articles by professional reviewers through similar lenses?) When students read what we write, they are usually reacting at the same time to all the past teacher comments they have received on their writing. The most obvious example of this is that students tend to take almost *anything* we write as criticism—even if we are just asking them a question or making an observation—or even making a low key statement of mild praise. ("I'm curious how you managed to be so dispassionate on such a controversial issue" or "I was interested that you were able to quote from a book that I didn't assign." "Uh oh, I'll never do those things again.") And when we include a grade with our comment, we increase the likelihood of a distorted reading—sometimes no reading at all!

What discouraging news. But I think we need to hear it. It helps us ask some very practical questions as we are writing a comment: "Am I wasting my time with this comment? What are the chances that it will be understood as I intend it? That it will help?" Perhaps we could adopt the principle of our better paid fellow-professionals: "At least do no harm." When we *assign* writing, at least we do no harm.

A Continuum between High-Stakes and Low-Stakes Responding

In the face of this bleak situation, I call again on the distinction between high and low stakes. But here I am emphasizing a *continuum* with many intermediate points. And it turns out, perhaps not surprisingly, to be a continuum from the shortest to the longest responses.

- *Zero response (lowest stakes).* When I am clear and honest with students about the fact that I need to require more writing from them than I can comment on, they quickly get over any feelings of deprivation or resentment about getting no response. Most students come to appreciate the chance to write with the knowledge that they will be heard but will not have to deal with my response. In fact, many teachers require some low-stakes writing that they don't even read. Students can appreciate and benefit from the freedom of this private writing.
- *Minimal, nonverbal, noncritical response.* We can note effective or strong or correct passages by simply putting a straight line underneath particular words or phrases or alongside longer sections. (Teachers have traditionally used check marks in the margin for this purpose, but straight lines are more accurate, whether one is marking particular words or longer passages.) I can respond in this way virtually as quickly as I can read. Almost every student needs some encouragement, and some students on some occasions need lots. Even in very poor pieces of writing, certain parts are always better than others; students benefit from having them pointed out. To find strong points, even in weak writing, is a skill that will help us improve student learning and writing.
- *Supportive response—no criticism.* There are usually things that students do

well that are hard to point to with simple straight lines (e.g., "You chose a good approach to your topic," or "You write with a clear and lively voice.") Whether we call it "praise" or "positive reinforcement," the fact remains that this kind of response does the most good with the least effort. That is, we are most likely to cause learning and least likely to do harm if the message of our response is, in effect, "Please do more of this thing you are already doing here." We are *least* likely to cause learning and most likely to do harm if we give the message that is all too often implied in critical feedback: "Start doing something you've never done before."

- *Descriptive or observational response.* An example: "You begin with an anecdote from your own experience; then show us how it throws light on your academic topic. Then you make your case—which really rests on a process of definition—showing what fits and what is excluded." One of the hardest things for student writers (all writers!) is simply to see their own text: to understand the logical and rhetorical strategies they have used. Neutral and noncritical observations can be very effective because students don't need to resist them.

- *Minimal, nonverbal critical response.* Just as quickly as we can put straight lines underneath words or alongside passages that we find strong, we can use wavy or wiggly lines for parts that are unclear or problematic or wrong. It's remarkable what a strong sense of our readerly presence and response we can give to students when we note five or six phrases or passages per page with straight and wiggly lines: they get a felt sense of what is working and not working for us as readers.

- *Critical response, diagnosis, advice (highest stakes).* I acknowledge that we often need to give critical response to help with learning and to explain the basis of poor grades. But my premise here is that the higher we go on the continuum, the more we need to ask the crucial pragmatic questions: Is this comment worth it? How much response do I need? How much criticism will be useful? What is the likelihood of my effort doing good or harm?

I don't mean to suggest that we can just mechanically match low-stakes responses with low-stakes assignments and high with high. Obviously, we will often *mix* levels of response—in particular, mixing praise and criticism. Even the *highest*-stakes assignment merits some praise.

Nevertheless, it pays to notice the natural links between levels of assignment and response. That is, the lowest-stakes response (zero response) goes most naturally with low-stakes assignments: when the writing doesn't much matter to the final grade, we can afford to withhold our response or criticism. Similarly, the highest-stakes response (critical response) goes most naturally with high-stakes assignments: if our judgment of a student essay will have significant impact on the final grade, we are obliged to explain any criticism we have. This critical response carries the highest stakes for many reasons: (a) with critical response we have to worry more about whether we are wrong or unsound; (b) critical response is more likely to misfire or do harm because of how it is received—even if it is sound; and (c) critical response costs us more work and more uncertainty. In contrast, low-stakes minimal responding requires the least time and effort from us, requires the least expertise from us, takes the least time, and is least likely to undermine the teaching climate by turning students and teachers into adversaries.

I am not trying to stamp out critical response; just argue that we should use less of it—and use more minimal and low-stakes response and praise. Note for example (and this is another case of mixing) that we can use plenty of low-stakes praise without giving up criticism—without pretending that a piece of writing is better than it is. For example, we can write something like this:

> Your paper doesn't work very well for me because of many confusing sentences. I often couldn't understand you. Nevertheless, you do have plenty of clear sentences and I've marked particularly strong ones with a straight line. To work on your serious problem, try to figure out what was going on when you wrote those strong sentences—and do more of that.

Finding good sentences in a poorly written paper might seem easier than finding examples of good organization in a disorganized paper. But actually it's not so hard once we take on the task. For example, we can write:

> I got lost a lot as I read your paper. It has big problems with organization. But I've put straight lines along several paragraphs that hang together just fine; and also drawn lines *between* several paragraphs where they follow well and your transition works fine. Give us more of that! You've shown you can do it.

It is important for us to realize that we don't need to feel *guilty* if we use lots of low-stakes, minimal, and positive response—especially if we are not teaching a writing course. Assigning more writing, using less response, and using more praise doesn't mean leaving out all criticism or lowering standards. Students need the experience of writing a great deal and getting minimal low-stakes response because they tend to associate writing with criticism and high stakes. If we are not so much teaching writing but rather *using* writing to promote learning, it makes particularly good sense to use lots of minimal and low-stakes response. When we assign a piece of writing and don't comment on it, we are *not not-teaching*: we are actively setting up powerful conditions for learning by getting students to do something they wouldn't do without the force of our teaching.

Conclusion: Seven Concrete Suggestions

1. For high-stakes assignments, it can be very helpful to require a draft at least a week before the final version. Teachers handle drafts in a wide variety of ways depending on their circumstances and styles. Comments on a draft are almost automatically lower stakes even if critical: we can write suggestions for

revising rather than just giving an autopsy. If a class is large it might seem as though it's not possible to require drafts. But requiring drafts may be more feasible than some teachers think:

- We can cut back on the amount of responding on *some* assignments for the sake of giving students at least one experience of feedback on a draft aimed at a revision. If we can only do this once, it's better to do it in the first half of the semester—so students can better internalize some of our responses when they work on later high-stakes assignments without any input from us.
- If we give good responses on a draft, we can make do with a very quick verdict on the revision (perhaps using the kind of grid that I suggest in an essay on grading in chapter 19).
- Even a radical shortcut is surprisingly helpful: require drafts one week before the final due date, but tell students that you can't comment and will just quickly glance over them to make sure they are done with some seriousness. With this system, students don't *have* to revise; they can hand in the same thing again. But usually they see how much better they can make their paper after it's sat for a week.

2. Even when we are commenting on a final version, we can frame our comments in a forward-looking way: instead of saying, "Here's what didn't work," we can say, "Here's what to work on in future papers."

3. I find it easier to comment on important assignments if I get students to turn in a short, reflective "cover letter" or piece of "process writing" with the assignment itself. I invite something informal—even handwritten. I ask them to tell me: what they see as their main points, how they went about writing and what happened, which parts they are most and least satisfied with, and what questions they have for me as reader. Reading the cover letter helps immeasurably in writing my comment. Often I can simply agree with much of what the student has said—sometimes even being more encouraging about the essay than the student was. Students may have difficulty at first with this self-reflective writing, but it is a skill worth working on. It gives them practice in trying to see their own thinking and their own text more clearly.

4. Crucial principle: I can comment *far* more easily and effectively if I force myself to read the whole piece before making any comments—except for straight and wiggly lines. I save lots of time by reminding myself that students can seldom benefit from criticism of more than two or three problems. Therefore, my main decision in commenting is to choose *which* problems to focus on, and I can't make that decision till I read the whole paper through. Most of my bad commenting comes from jumping in with marginal comments as I am reading: I am more likely to waste my time on something that turns out to be a minor issue; or make some passing remark that the student misunderstands; or say something that's actually wrong ("you obviously don't understand x"—when later on it's clear that she does understand x); or get caught up in a little spasm of unhelpful irritation. If I settle for just making straight and wiggly lines, these serve as a map when I glance back over the paper after I've read the whole thing and I am trying to decide what are the few main

things I need to say. (Chris Anson points out an exception here: when we put our comments on a tape cassette we may want to tell the story of our reactions *as* we are actually in the process of reading. See his essay in the Sorcinelli, Elbow collection.)

5. When we return papers to students with our comments attached, it's a great help sometimes to ask students to take five minutes right then and write us a short note telling what they heard us saying and how they are reacting to it. This helps us learn when we are unclear or when students misinterpret our words or react in ways we don't expect.

6. If we are writing comments where the stakes aren't too high, we can save time by waiting till we have two pieces in hand, read them together, and write only one comment on both. The comparison is often pedagogically useful. ("Notice how much clearer your point was on this paper compared to that one [or how much more carefully you argued]. What helped you?")

7. Most students benefit when they feel that writing is a transaction with human beings rather than an "excercise in getting something right or wrong." For this reason, I try to make my comments on students writing sound like they come from a human reader rather than from an impersonal machine or a magisterial, all-knowing God source. Thus:

- Instead of saying "The organization is unclear here," I like to say "I got confused by your organization here."
- Instead of "unconvincing," "I'm unconvinced."
- Instead of "Diction," "Too slangy for me in this context."
- Instead of "Awk," "I stumbled here."

I sum up my essay by repeating that useful principle; at least do no harm. Think how much good we do in assigning lots of writing, especially lots of low-stake writing. But we can only assign lots more writing when we learn to be more strategic and sparing with our response and criticism.

17

Breathing Life into the Text

For a long time after college, I thought that "holding a discussion" was the most noble and useful way to deal with a literary text. I got this attitude, I think, from attending an "excellent," high-toned college, Williams College, where discussions were taken with enormous seriousness. They were powerfully conducted, led, induced, orchestrated by dedicated and often brilliant teachers. These teachers usually had a plan for their discussions, but they didn't bulldoze; they worked with subtle finesse so that these discussions often led to lively eruptions of energy and interesting, surprising insights. (One other thing: I've been left with a kind of subliminal sense that a good discussion always starts with a particular word, intoned either with gravity or irony: "Gentlemen, . . .")

Maybe if I could pull off with my students what they did with us, I'd still think of discussions as the ideal—though I doubt it. Anyway, since I've been involved in writing and teaching writing, my sense of an ideal classroom has changed. I've come to want some kind of *workshop*. That is, my ideal act of teaching is to get people to have an experience, not just talk. In a sense, of course, I've just made a false dichotomy: Talking *is* an experience; everything we do is an experience—even listening to a lecture. But that's a theoretical point and it involves taking the concept of experience in its broadest sense. As we normally talk and feel things, most students in most lectures and discussions don't in fact experience much: what is said doesn't matter or doesn't affect them much. I want a classroom where more happens, more matters—and where, in a literature class, the texts we read make a difference to students.

This essay was published in 1995 in *When Writing Teachers Teach Literature*. Eds. Art Young and Toby Fulwiler, Boynton/Cook Heinemann.

Having come to this pass, I now consider the following four activities as central in the teaching of any text—literary or not. I can't do all four in a fifty-minute class, but I could in a two-and-a-half-hour seminar. And I don't intend for these activities to *replace* discussions, just augment them. I guess I actually do want to replace lectures.

Helping Students Take Possession of the Territory Before They Read the Text

The usual pattern in literature classes—indeed in almost any kind of class in any kind of school—is to read a text first and then write afterward in response to it. And even if the text we read is imaginative, the writing is usually expository and critical. I hear two messages in this conventional arrangement. First, "The role of writing is to serve reading." Second, *"We* cannot enter the same discursive territory that the 'literary artist' occupies." I want to jostle these assumptions, and it is not hard to do so, by putting writing *before* reading and giving ourselves permission to write imaginatively. (I'm indebted to Jane Tompkins for the apt phrase, "taking possession of the territory." For more on this approach to texts, see my "Questioning Two Assumptions of the Profession," and "The War Between Reading and Writing—and How to End It" in this volume.)

Before I ask students to read the text, I like to ask them to write on the *theme* or *issue* that is central to the text. I try to give students a choice between a broad invitation to the general terrain ("Write about a time of being in love"), and something more narrowly focused on the particular approach of the poem or story we are going to read: "Write a declaration of love"; "Write a complaint about rejection"; "Write a 'Dear John/Jane' poem"; "Write a persuasion to bed." Some students benefit from a broad choice, but others have an easier time getting going if there is a narrower constraint. (Sometimes the constraint helps by providing something to resist. I seem to need the narrower constraint to get going—but then once going, I often need to violate it.) I invite students to write from their own experience, but also invite them equally to make something up: "Feel free to take on another voice and *imagine* someone persuading someone else." If we're reading a poem, I invite but don't push students to use some kind of verse: "Try writing in some kind of verse form—perhaps free-floating lines. But it's okay to use prose too." (I learned this whole approach from Charles Moran who pioneered using writing in this way.)

Once when I was teaching *The Tempest* I was struck with how the students couldn't enter into the play at all. In particular, I could tell that they were irritated at Prospero, but because they felt he was the "hero" of a "great work," they tended either to defer to him and point out "virtues" in him that they didn't really believe—or else just rail against him. The next time I taught the play, I asked students, before we turned to the play at all, to write two or three pages at home about the longest grudge they have been holding: "With whom? About what? What does it feel like? Can you imagine being over it? What would it take?" This led to interesting and satisfying pieces of writing; students got involved and enjoyed hearing some of each others' pieces. When we turned to *The Tempest,* suddenly they took Prospero much more seriously; they had a much more complex relation to him. They saw what they didn't like, but they also identified with him. Obviously, this writing activity didn't bring out all the important things in the play, but I didn't try to pretend that this issue was *the* central one (though it seems to me what James would call the *donnée*). I was simply trying to *open the door* to the play so that students would *experience* the text in a way that they didn't before. Having done this, I could move on to other issues in the play.

Sometimes I'm completely frank about what I'm doing and why. "Before we turn to ——— by —————, I want us all to do a piece of writing on a theme in that work. I'm doing this because I've discovered in my past teaching that students sometimes treat literary texts as 'objects under glass'—as 'museumified'—and then you don't get much from them. I think you get the most out of literary texts when you come to them as fellow writers—when you can turn to Shakespeare's play and say, 'Oh, I see you are writing about jealousy. I know something about being jealous—and even writing about being jealous. I may not have experienced it as Othello did or written about it as well as you did, but we are working in the same world here.'"

But sometimes I'll just jump in with no explanation. Perhaps even start off the semester writing on a theme of a work that won't come up for a number of weeks. That is, I think it helps their reading and discussion most if they write about it without being under the shadow of the "great writer"—without a sense that some "author" "owns" this territory. I'm trying to send the message that it's everyone's territory. I find this particularly useful when we are dealing with canonical texts—texts that the culture has already put under glass. But this kind of writing is also very gratifying with unknown and unhallowed texts: Students sometimes feel more on their own footing with them.

"But their writing is so paltry compared to Shakespeare!" I don't find it a problem that young students are not great writers. I'm not asking for fine works of art. Indeed, I usually ask for fast first drafts—even uncompleted sketches. In short, no one is pretending here. We're trying to get the feel of a territory. I'm also—and perhaps this is more important—trying to set up the conditions where students will risk *having* an experience. (Thus it's important that I take the risk of writing my sketch too—and sharing it.) What's striking to me and to students in the room is not that they have failed to turn out great literature, but that many of the pieces are remarkably satisfying to hear or read, and even effective informal pieces of writing in their own right.

Because these assignments can seem intimidating to some students, I tend to start them in class—sometimes giving a few prompts and spending up to twenty minutes writing. It often helps to ask three or four students to share just a few lines or snatches of what they have written after five or ten minutes. Hearing these rough bits of writing serves to prime the pump for others. "Oh, I see.

That's not great writing, but it's fun. I could do that." I've learned that people are braver about jumping in if the spirit is playful and we are often settling for short, incomplete pieces. But it's nice to ask people, by the end of the semester, to choose a couple of these sketches to revise into something more finished.

Of course, I can't grade these pieces, but I can insist that students *do* them under heavy penalty of downgrading. I usually find some class time to hear at least a few of them, and I encourage but don't require students to share their pieces with at least one other student in pairs or small groups. I find it a pedagogically helpful enterprise to *require* things that I don't grade.

Helping Students Notice and Articulate Their Perceptions, Reactions, and Responses to a Text

Because of the emphasis on process in composition over the last twenty years, it's become much easier to dispel the myth that texts are magically produced by means of genius or "knack"—the myth that real writers find or create great meanings in their heads and then clothe these meanings in text. We've been able to show how most writers engage in a process that students too can participate in: starting with incomplete pieces of feeling, impulse, meaning, and intention—and gradually building them into completed texts; letting the process of writing itself lead them to ideas and structures they hadn't planned at the start. And there's always negotiation with oneself—and often with others.

But it's still difficult to see this process in *reading:* to see how readers, too, actively create and negotiate meanings in texts; how the meanings of texts are not just found as right answers sitting there hidden in the text or in teachers' minds or in works of authoritative criticism. The reading process seems more hidden and magic—and sometimes *seems* instantaneous. When we pass our eyes over easy and unambiguous words and phrases, their meanings seem to appear instantly in mind. Students often feel that teachers and critics, "good" or "authoritative" readers, have a genius or a "knack" for "finding" the right meanings in hard texts—while they themselves as students can't find the meanings because they haven't got this genius or knack.

Reading may look passive: We sit quietly and let the image of the words print itself on our retina and thus pass inward to our brain. But of course reading—indeed all meaning-making—is a deeply active process of exploration. In fact, when students have trouble reading it's often because they've been mistakenly *trying* to be passive—trying to make themselves like good cameras, that is, trying to become perfect little photographic plates on which the meanings on the page *print themselves* with photographic accuracy. Because reading doesn't work that way, their performance suffers when they try to operate on that model. "Hold still. Don't jiggle." Good advice for old cameras; not good for seeing or reading. The more jiggling, the better.

It's fun to point out the findings of cognitive psychologists: Any act of seeing or "making sense" of what is around us is always a process that occurs in stages—through the passage of time—not instantaneously like an image passing through a lens. In the first stage, our mind takes in the first pieces of information—the first trickles of electrical impulses—and quickly makes a guess, a hypothesis, or a "schema" about what we might be looking at. Then the mind repeatedly checks this guess against further information that comes in. Often we have to change our guess or hypothesis as new information comes in—before we "see what's really there." If plain seeing and hearing are such time-bound, exploratory processes, so much the more so for reading. It's obvious that we cannot take in any text all at once. Thus, when we read words or hear them, we *understand what we expect to understand*—till evidence forces us to revise our expectation. Thus the huge effect of culture, gender, race, class, sexual orientation, and so forth on our reactions to a text.

I used to make this case conceptually to students. I thought I was convincing, but I gradually saw otherwise. What I've discovered (or rather rediscovered from my writing workshops where I stress "movies of the reader's mind" [see *Writing With Power* 255ff.]) is a way to help students *experience* this crucial bedrock fact about reading. I can help students abandon their magical model of the reading process by actually demonstrating to them experientially how all readers gradually construct the meaning of the text over time—just as writers do.

I create a laboratory of the reading process. I present a text to students one portion at a time and ask them to attend to the process by which they gradually construct the meaning. In effect, I am using a slow-motion camera to show how we all tend to make hypotheses and then change our minds in the act of reading further. That is, if we only see the first few lines or paragraphs of a text and we take the trouble to articulate what reactions, meanings, and expectations occurred in us, and if we go on to succeeding pieces of the text and do the same thing, we notice that later pieces of text force us to change our reactions and interpretations of earlier bits. Unless we go through this admittedly artificial, slow motion exercise, we often forget about those earlier reactions, meanings, and expectations because we revised them so quickly. Indeed, those earlier responses were often subliminal.

Therefore, I often cut up a text and pass it out, one section at a time. I ask students to take a few minutes to write out as full and accurate an account as they can of *what was happening* in their mind as they read each fragment—to "give movies of the mind." I need to encourage them not to leave out mental events that might seem stray or irrelevant; otherwise, they may only write down things they associate with English classes—and leave out odd memories and associations or even daydreams. The point is not to worry about the relevance or usefulness of the reaction: If it happened, write it down. *Nihil humanum. . . .*

This exercise helps students come into better possession of their own perceptions and responses—before there is much discussion and conclusion-drawing. Sometimes I ask for some sharing and discussion of reactions before students have seen the whole text—especially in pairs or small groups; sometimes I hold off any sharing or discussion till the end. I love seeing the play of divergence and convergence: Sometimes it seems like all idiosyncrasy—as though no one is reading the same text; sometimes there is amazing commonality. Usually, there's an interesting mixture of the two.

Obviously, certain students are better than others at making sense of hard texts (and of seeing rich implications in easy texts), but what less-experienced students see is that the *process* used by skilled students is not magic. Movies of skilled students' minds are usually movies of people making multiple starts, multiple hypotheses, being playful, and being flexible about changing their earlier ideas on the basis of later input. In fact, skilled readers often have more "wrong answers" in that they have more associations, more hypotheses to start with, and therefore end up abandoning more. And it's palpably obvious that when skilled readers engage a text, they do not enter some "other" "literary" world or "artificial space"; they attend to and consider *lots* of feelings and reactions and memories that unskilled readers often push away as "inappropriate" for "literature."

I'm trying to inject a spirit of *charitable empiricism* into the process of responding to literature (as I've been trying to inject it into the process of responding to the writing of colleagues in writing workshops). "We are not looking for what's right but for what *happens*. Eventually, we can talk about which larger interpretations seem more persuasive or plausible. But for now we're trying to learn to attend better. This is all about paying better attention." I'm trying to help students see that the human mind is never stupid or random. Every reaction, response, and interpretation that occurs makes perfect sense in the light of whatever else is in our mind (and *not* in our mind). I try to help students see how all their reactions make sense—however idiosyncratic they are.

This process leads to interesting discussions about cultural issues. When students pay better attention to the small details of their actual responses, they can see more vividly the powerful influences on their minds. Not just the influence of media and common cultural conventions and clichés, though these are important. The same image may trigger very different responses according to gender, class, race, or sexual orientation.

Obviously, this process enriches the discussion. It gives enormous particularity to responses and gets us beyond *global* responses like "It was scary/ironic/beautiful/sad." Or, to get down to a crass but nitty gritty reality of teaching, it gives students too much to talk about rather than too little—for any subsequent discussion or writing assignment. It helps students and the class become awash in very particulate literary data.

Someone might object, "You are inviting students to drift completely away from the text and attend only to their own reactions. This is not practice in reading, only in self-absorption." I suppose this is a danger, but it's not hard to avoid. I need to remind students to keep reading: "Read it again. See what happens when you read it again." Someone might also object, "You are sending the message that it's fine to be lazy about reading; that there's no need to work, think, struggle, analyze; that it's enough to relax and just notice what happens." It's true that I'm happy to help students not to *clench* as they read and not to feel they should go into some special or artificial "interpretive gear." I want to teach them that the process of responding and interpreting is built out of the everyday operations of the mind. But the process does not militate against thinking and work. The noticings *lead to* thinking—especially in the discussion where people compare responses. And I'm not saying, "Notice what happens when you relax lazily with a text," but rather, "Notice what happens when you struggle to figure it out." Actually, one of the issues that often surfaces is talk between students as to whether they experience this as "school thinking" or "regular thinking"—and the mental differences involved.

Sometimes students themselves object, "But this is so artificial! It makes me think of things in reaction to the text that I never would have thought of if I'd read it normally." I love to respond to this. "Reflect," I say, "on those things you thought of that you wouldn't 'normally' think of. Did I or the exercise *put* anything in your head that wasn't there already? I didn't add *anything*. Any 'new' or 'odd' reactions, feelings, thoughts, or memories were already in your mind anyway. I merely interrupted you and made you pause so that more of what was in your mind came to conscious awareness. The whole point of the exercise is to notice things that were already influencing your 'normal' fast reading—but doing so in ways that are below the level of awareness. What's new are not those 'odd' reactions, feelings, thoughts, and memories; only your awareness of them. There are no meanings *in* words, only meanings people bring *to* them. And the meanings people bring are their own meanings—amalgams of their own individual experiences."

I also find it helpful to go through this process with a text that *I* haven't yet seen (having a student choose a text, divide it into sections, and bring in copies for all of us to work on). This lets students see me having initial reactions, responses, and interpretations that later turn out to be inappropriate or plain wrong. It is important to engage in this exercise a number of times—starting early in the semester. Students get better at it.[1]

---

1. Numerous important voices are telling us how important it is for students to understand the actual particulars of what happens when we read a text—to see in some detail the phenomenological experience of the *process* of reading. Linda Flower and her colleagues have gone on from their talk-aloud writing protocols (to tell as much as possible about what goes on as someone engages in writing) to get equally useful insights from talk-aloud reading protocols (538–41). Sometimes she interrupts readers at various points in their reading—especially if they stop giving "movies of their mind." She cites a classic experiment by Asch to illustrate how deeply our processing and understanding of a text is influenced by whatever expectations and prior knowledge we might have. Asch (422ff.) had two groups read the same essay that began with the words, "I hold it that a little rebellion, now and then, is a good thing." But one group was told that the essay was by Jefferson, the other by Lenin. Readers had strikingly different responses to the same text.

Deborah Brandt, in her impressive book about literacy, argues that "the key to becoming literate is finding out how other people read and write and how print relates to what people do when they read and write" (9):

Asking Students to Render, Enact, or Perform the Text

What do we mean by skill in reading? At one level, we mean skill in getting meanings from the text ("decoding"). But at another level, we mean more—we mean *experiencing* those meanings or feeling some relationship or involvement with the meanings. Or to put it negatively, there are two problems in reading: not getting it and not "getting" it. No doubt, the first problem of not figuring out the meaning is more serious than the second one. When we suffer only from the second problem, we can understand the text, we know what it says, we can summarize it and perhaps even answer some analytic questions about it; but we are not making any contact with it or letting it make contact with us, not getting a felt experience from the words, not being able to feel any sense in which the words make a difference.

Interestingly enough, those students who tend to have difficulty with the first problem often do fine with the second one: *if* they get it, they "get" it. That is, once they manage to *understand* the text, they naturally make contact, they let the text touch them, they can invest. But students who have *no* difficulty with the first problem of merely understanding meanings often suffer badly from the second one—not "getting" it. This is not really surprising. For the fact is that the best way to understand lots of meanings as quickly and efficiently as possible is to remain relatively uninvested and untouched by them. In short, sometimes students find that they do better in school if they don't take texts too seriously or feel their impact too strongly. To *experience* texts often slows them down and makes it harder for them to "cover" everything the teacher wants them to cover—and sometimes even leads them to resist the interpretations that the teacher wants them to make.

We've long understood in writing classes that students often get more benefit from feedback when they read their text out loud than when they just hand it to readers on paper. It's a simple fact that when we read a text out loud we almost inevitably *experience* more richly and fully the meanings of the words we ourselves wrote. Indeed, the act of reading a sentence out loud (unless we are repeating the words in a rote, meaningless way), tends to make the mind *create* meaning and coherence. Reading out loud helps with *both* getting and "getting" the text. Many poets have long insisted that poems need to be read out loud, not silently.

For many years, then, I have stressed the reading out loud of texts in writing—and literature classes too. But in the last few years, since I've become particularly interested in the role of the human voice in language, my goal has

---

But writing (or reading) is a here-and-now enterprise, always occurring in the present tense. It unfolds as a cognitive process as evanescent as speech, erased and usually forgotten in the act of being accomplished. While research indicates that readers have somewhat better recall of "the very words" of a text than listeners do of "the very words" of conversation, process research shows how writers and readers easily forget the routes they have taken to arrive at "the very words" and their meaning. 35–6.

escalated. I can't help thinking about the voice as physical and part of the body. I've come to think that the ideal classroom somehow involves some kind of embodying and enacting. I've come to find it profitable to set students the task in small groups of finding a way to present or render or enact or embody the text (or part of the text if it is longer than a page or two). I steer away from the word "perform"—not only because it often makes students feel more nervous, but also because it stresses the theatrical more than I care to.

It helps when I lay out for students a range of concrete possibilities or options. "If you want to cop out, you can just persuade one member to read it— or just do a choral reading. If you want to be really adventuresome, you can give a completely wordless version in movement or dance or gesture. After all, it's not really necessary to utter the words; the audience already knows the text. Between these extremes there are a rich assortment of other possibilities: use different speakers for different parts—perhaps to enact a kind of dialogue between different parts of the text so as to show how different sections or dimensions or voices in it are responding to each other; 'double' certain words, lines, or sections of the text with extra voices in order to produce certain emphases; repeat certain words or sections over and over as a kind of 'ground bass' underneath a reading of the whole; read the text so that certain lines or sections overlap or are heard against other parts, as when singing a round."

I make it clear that it's perfectly fine to rearrange the words—creating different orders among words or sections. (What do we notice if someone reads it backward?!) It's alright to add or weave in other pieces of language that are *not* part of the text: bits of translation or adaptation; bits of other texts or pieces of one's own responses to the text that somehow seem illuminating or interesting; bits of discourse or language that this text might be responding to (*a la* Bakhtin).

I invite a loose and playful approach. I want to allay nervousness and I actually enjoy getting away from a reverent stance—from an attempt to "do justice" to the text. Students throw themselves into these renderings with gusto. It's true that this approach opens the door to the parodic. (This was when I learned that most of Emily Dickinson's lyrics can be sung to "The Yellow Rose of Texas"!) But in fact I don't mind an element of parody, especially when texts are "high literature." In a sense, I want students to "domesticate" these high works, take them off the pedestal, treat them familiarly. Since we get a range of renderings of the same piece, I don't mind if some are funny. But I know some drama teachers who make performance central to their teaching and give a somewhat more serious air to the enterprise. They get excellent results. (They have theater training and I do not.) Sometimes I give students just fifteen minutes of class time to prepare a quick version of something short. But when I give groups more time—for example, by asking them to meet in small groups outside of class—they often achieve something more ambitious.

I like to ask everyone in the class to work in groups on the same text—or different parts of the same text. I want us to see multiple renderings of the same text. (If the class is too large, I can have groups present their renderings to only a few other groups; or I can enlist only three or four groups on a given day and use other groups on another day.) The process shows in the most concrete and experiential way how texts naturally yield different emphases, different centers, different interpretations, different voices or tones. Even though some performances are playful, some are seriously moving. And throughout, the process is enjoyable and creates community.

This approach often brings out the literary and creative skill of certain students who didn't look strong before—students who are good at banter, speech, gesture, and the performative—who seemed unskilled when bare silent textuality was the only medium in the room. And those very students often become more skilled at silent textuality when they see that they have more literary sophistication than some of the students who *looked* more sophisticated on paper.

I love the way text-rendering makes the text more "felt" and memorable to students. In addition to gaining richer reactions and more developed feelings about the text, students often end up with a kind of physical or kinetic experience of the text in their limbs or bodies.

Helping Students Respond as Writers: Helping Them Write Their Own Piece of Imaginative Writing—Using the Text as "Springboard"

After we've worked on a text I like to ask students to do a piece of *imaginative* writing. The request would be too difficult or intimidating for many students if I made it at the start, but at this point we have internalized some of the *spirit* or *energy* of the piece. In addition, the other activities have given students practice at being both brave and playful.

I ask students to use the work we have studied as a kind of *springboard* for writing a work of their own. I pick out a few formal or structural features or some linguistic details in the work that could serve as germs or incentives to write—that is, to help us *bounce off of* the work or to *take a ride on* it. In short, I'm inviting students at this point—after having put energy into trying to hear and understand Shakespeare or whomever—to turn away from Shakespeare and write their *own* piece. Students can write about the same theme or even reply to the work, but I specifically invite students to concentrate entirely on the structural or linguistic features I've chosen and allow the topic to be entirely different.

For example, if we had been studying Shakespeare's sonnet 73, "That time of year," I might say, "Try writing a poem that starts out mentioning a season or time of year, and that also mentions a time of day and some common everyday process (the poem's fire glowing on its ashes). You might want to restrict yourself further with some of the following features: Use the first word or phrase of each quatrain and of the couplet ("That time . . . , In me . . . , In me . . . , This . . .); start each line with the first word in each of Shakespeare's lines; try sonnet form; make it some kind of love poem."

The possibilities are endless. And it's fun playing with different "extracts" from works of prose or poetry. For some reason, helpful generative and creative energy seems to derive from the borrowing of certain initial *words* or *syntactical features* (e.g., "Get a list of four adjectives in the first sentence"; "End with a question"; "Start with a quotation"). I enjoy using James Wright's poem "Lying in a Hammock at William Duffy's Farm in Pine Island, Minnesota" and asking students to pick a moment where they were at the home of some particular person and describe everything they can see and hear at that moment (as Wright does); and then end with a final line that is a large generalization that *seems* unrelated to the preceding lines (Wright ends with "I have wasted my life"). Frost's invitation poem is another natural—where each stanza ends, "You come too." We can similarly borrow formal features from fiction: "Write about an event in flashback form"; "Tell something through the eyes of someone who doesn't quite understand what really happened"; "Tell a story using almost entirely dialogue."

In borrowing certain features of structure or voice or architecture as aids in getting going, I've learned from the suggestions of poets like Kenneth Koch and Theodore Roethke. Koch, for example, suggests springboards as simple as this: After having students read and work on Blake's "Tyger, tyger" ask them simply to choose an animal and write a kind of poem of direct address—starting by repeating the name of the animal. Roethke made much more complicated problems for students such as laying out a long list of seemingly random words they must use and fit into a tightly defined stanza pattern. He insisted that we make better poems if our minds are so occupied with craft problems that we don't have much attention left for our "theme or message." (On Roethke, see Balaban and Hugo.) What's pleasing about this approach to writing imaginative pieces is that somehow the prior text we worked on and the artificial constraints seem to lead us to write pieces that say things we didn't know we were going to say—but that it turns out we seem to want to say.

In effect, I am asking students to borrow or take a ride on some of the imaginative energy or the linguistic and even syntactical juice of what we've been working on. To many of us teachers, this sounds like a scary enterprise, but it turns out that students are willing and able to do this better than most of us are, and usually they are grateful for the chance.

But it's not just presumption and playfulness that I am after. This kind of writing functions as an act of "interpretation"—an act of "replying" or "answering" the text—which is really the most natural and human way to "study" a work of literature. Students understand the work better after this writing.

From Harold Bloom I take this lesson: that one of the most natural and instinctive ways to produce our own writing is to "bounce off of" the works of other writers: to misread them. In short, in this stage of the game, I'm inviting students to function like writers—which means caring more about their own writing than about the writing of the "great figure"—and taking whatever liberties they might like. Using it, borrowing, stealing. I like to invoke Eliot's dictum that amateurs borrow, professionals steal.[2] I believe that proceeding in this way—taking these liberties and insisting on space for student writing—leads in the end their being *better* readers and critics. They come back to the texts of others as more interesting, interested, and invested readers.[3]

I'm grateful to people I've worked with in using and playing with these approaches: most of all to my students, but also to Nona Feinberg, Charles Moran, Jane Tompkins, and Betsy Wallace.

Works Cited

Asch, Solomon. *Social Psychology.* NY: Prentice Hall, 1952.

Balaban, John. "South of Pompeii the Helmsman Balked." *College English* 39.4 (December 1977): 437–41.

Bloom, Harold. *Anxiety of Influence.* NY: Oxford UP, 1973.

Brandt, Deborah. *Literacy as Involvement: The Acts of Writers, Readers, and Texts.* Carbondale IL: Southern Illinois UP: 1990.

Elbow, Peter. "Questioning Two Assumptions of the Profession" *What is English?* NY: MLA and Urbana IL: NCTE, 1990. 179–94.

———. "The War Between Reading and Writing—and How to End It." *Rhetoric Review* 12.1 (Fall 1993): 5–24.

———. *Writing With Power: Techniques for Mastering the Writing Process.* NY: Oxford UP, 1981.

Elbow, Peter and Pat Belanoff. *A Community of Writers: A Workshop Course in Writing* 3rd ed. NY: McGraw Hill, 1999.

Flower, Linda. "The Construction of Purpose in Writing and Reading." *College English* 50.5 (April 1988): 528–44.

Hugo, Richard. "Stray Thoughts on Roethke and Teaching." *American Poetry Review* 3.1 (1974): 50–51.

Koch, Kenneth. *Rose, Where Did You Get that Red? Teaching Great Poetry to Children.* NY: Random House, 1973.

———. *Wishes, Lies, and Dreams: Teaching Children to Write Poetry.* NY: Chelsea House, 1970.

Moran, Charles. "Reading Like a Writer." *Vital Signs.* Ed. James. L. Collins. Portsmouth NH: Boynton/Cook, 1989. Earlier version: "Teaching Writing/Teaching Literature." *College Composition and Communication* 32 (February, 1981): 21–30.

Wright, James. "Lying in a Hammock at William Duffy's Farm in Pine Island, Minnesota." *Collected Poems.* Middletown CT: Wesleyan UP, 1970. 114.

2. Nowadays we tend to assume that the goal of translation is to get present readers to enter the language and culture and world of the original text: to be "true" to the original. But for most of the history of our culture (e.g., in the eras of Chaucer, Shakespeare, and Pope)—and for many more cultures than ours—the goal of translation was quite opposite: to transform the language and culture and world of the original text into those of our own.

3. Many of the activities I've described here are spelled out in more pedagogical detail in "Workshop 13: Interpretation as Response," in Elbow and Belanoff.

18

Using the Collage for Collaborative Writing

Plenty of people have celebrated collaborative writing (e.g., Ede and Lunsford; LeFevre), so I can invoke the medieval trope of *occupatio:* I will *not* give all the reasons why collaborative writing is a good thing; I will *not* talk about how frequently it occurs in the world and therefore how our students should learn to use it; nor about the collaborative dimension of writing we think of as private; nor about how collaborative writing helps students learn better because of all the pooling of information, ideas, and points of view; nor about the students who have hated writing because it makes them feel lonely and helpless but who come to *like* it when they write with others; nor will I cite the much-cited Harvard research showing how students who study together get better grades (Light).

But I will mention in passing one interesting benefit of collaborative writing that I've noticed but found undercelebrated. When people write alone, they make countless simple and complex writerly decisions *tacitly,* instinctively—without articulating the reasons for them (e.g., to start with this idea, or to move that point later in the paper, or to change a word or phrase to modify the voice or the relationship to the reader). And that's as it should be: tacit decisions are quicker and the writer is going by feel, by ear. As Polanyi reminds us, our tacit knowledge always outstrips our conscious and articulate knowledge. But the process of writing with someone else forces us to put many of these decisions into words. If I say to my partner, "Let's start with this point," I usually have to say why—especially if I am proposing a change. And if my partner disagrees with me, he or she will naturally give

This essay is based on a paper I gave at a session on the collage that I organized at the annual convention of the Conference on College Composition and Communication in 1992. It was published in *Composition Studies* (formerly *Freshman English News*) 27.1 (Spring 1999).

reasons for the resistance. In short, the process of collaborative writing forces students to become more conscious and articulate about rhetorical decision making.

But what I find underrepresented in our professional literature about collaborative writing are the *problems*. First, collaborative writing is difficult and often unpleasant. When I used to force students to write pieces in pairs or groups, at least half of them would say at the end that it was the worst experience of the semester. And when I gave them the choice, relatively few took it. Collaborative writing may be jolly and social, but it takes a long time and leads to disagreements. Is there anyone who has not vowed never again to engage in a piece of committee writing?

Second, the writing that results from collaboration is often pretty bad. It is likely to be bland because the parties have to agree and they can only agree on lowest-common-denominator thinking. And there is often a dead, "committee" voice—no energy or presence. The surest proof of the existence of God is the King James translation of the Bible: only divine intervention could have permitted a committee to produce such wonderful prose.

Third, the collaborative process often silences weaker, minority, or marginal voices. The assertive and entitled tend to carry the day. Whenever there is a need for consensus in group work, there is great danger of silencing weaker voices (see Clark and Ede; Trimbur).

In order to deal with this perplexity—that collaborative writing is at once so valuable, so important, and yet so problematic—I've come to use the collaborative collage. Where the solo collage can serve as a bridge to regular essays, the collaborative collage can serve as a bridge to full collaboration. But like the solo collage, the collaborative collage is valuable in its own right. It can be as nice to stand on the bridge as on the other shore. (Readers not familiar with written collages will probably get a pretty good picture from what follows. But for a full and direct description of written collages, see "Collage: Your Cheatin' Art" in this volume, and also the first workshop in Elbow and Belanoff.)

The procedure for creating a collaborative collage is so easy and simple that it will make some people nervous. Let me lay out the directions I give to pairs or small groups working together:

- Individually, write as much as you can about the topic. Write your own thoughts. It's fine to use rough, exploratory writing. Try to exploit the insights, language, and energy that come from moving fast and getting caught up in your thinking and feeling.
- There is an alternative first step you can use if you prefer. Each person writes for ten or fifteen minutes—however he or she wants to start. Then people switch papers for the next piece of writing so that what is written is some kind of response to what the first person wrote. And so on. This method adds more of the quality of dialogue—thought answering thought. But by the same token, it can reduce the amount of sheer diversity in the collage, because the writers are more in touch with each other. In the first, nondia-

logical method, writers might well be in entirely different ball parks—which can be a genuine advantage.

- Individually, go back over what you yourself have written and choose the bits and sections you like most. Some might be a page or more, others very short. Choose at least twice as much material as you'll need for your contribution to the finished collage. Clean them up enough to share, but there's no need to spend too much time on the job.
- Together in your pair or group, read your individual pieces to each other. (Or share them through silent reading.)
- Together, agree on which pieces should be chosen for the collage. (Ground rule: no fair leaving anyone out—or letting anyone dominate the final version.)
- Together, give some feedback and suggestions in response to those pieces you have chosen. But there's no need for agreement in your responses. Just let everyone throw in their two cents. (You'll also have to agree on whether the final revising and polishing of bits should be done by the original authors or by means of trading pieces with each other.)
- Together, decide on a sequence for all the pieces you've chosen.
- Together, as part of this discussion about sequence, you may well decide you need some new pieces. Good new ideas might have come up in discussion; or you might realize that something important is missing.
- Individually, write any necessary new pieces; and revise and polish the chosen pieces.
- Together, look at what you have produced and decide whether to call it finished or to carry on with more work: for example, reordering of parts; revising of parts; writing new parts. This decision is collaborative, but further work can be individual.

Note that some of these tasks require agreement, but many do not. That is, there is genuine collaboration going on here—but only to a limited degree. This makes it much easier on participants than full collaboration and gives them a good bridge from individual work to group work. That is, participants *don't* have to agree on their ideas, thinking, conclusion, or thesis. They *don't* have to agree on language, wording, or phrasing. There are none of those awful tippy-toe discussions or time wasting arguments about how to phrase something. Nor about the voice or tone. At every moment, individuals are entirely in charge of every piece of writing with respect to thinking, wording, and voice—though of course these decisions are often influenced by comments and feedback from others.

Yet genuine collaboration is also going on—in fact two levels of collaboration:

- *Weak collaboration:* members read their writing to each other and give and receive individual responses from each other, and thereby *influence* each others' thinking and writing; this collaboration has a substantive effect on the final outcome. Yet this degree of collaboration is easy and nonstressful because participants don't have to agree.

- *Strong collaboration:* participants have to agree on which blips to use; they have to agree on what order to put them in; they have to agree on who does the revising; they have to agree on whether more revising is needed or whether to call it finished. Strong collaboration is harder because it requires agreement or consensus. But the scope of what people have to agree on is pretty limited.

Thus the collaborative collage speaks to the first problem of collaboration: difficulty or unpleasantness. But can it deal with the other two problems—weak or bland writing and the stifling of minority ideas and voices? Obviously, it can.

The collaborative collage invites all participants to stay entirely in charge of their own writing, and as a result, the final product is richer and more complex than most collaborative writing. (Even if members decide to revise each others' pieces, single individuals are in charge of thinking and language at any given moment.) The final product contains multiple points of view, multiple voices, multiple styles—and as a result, more tension and energy. Minority ideas and thinking have not been left out. In a collage, contrasts are a benefit, a source of energy that stimulates thinking in readers. The collaborative collage is a gathering of pieces each written from an "I" point of view—for the sake of a "we" enterprise.

The process I've described so far usually results in an *open* collage—a collage with multiple and conflicting points of view. If the students need to produce a *focused* collage, they must carry their partial collaboration a few steps further. They needn't leave out any of the conflicting material, but they need to spend additional time discussing the thinking in their open collage and find a way to agree on a conclusion or at least a common point of view. And then they need to write, add, arrange, or revise bits—again not taking away any of the contradictory material—in order to make the whole collage end up saying or implying their collaborative conclusion or point of view. They can even stop short of full agreement if they can agree on where they disagree and articulate that meta-agreement—further spelling out the implications of the various views and explaining what would need to be decided in order to settle their disagreement. But it's important for students to realize that even though they reach ultimate agreement on a conclusion or point of view, the focused collage still can and really ought to contain wildly divergent and contradictory pieces.

Learning to Make Space for Other Voices

Let me briefly suggest three additional methods for helping solo writers begin to get comfortable collaborating with other writers. These activities can serve as a bridge or introduction even to the mild collaboration I've already described.

1. The student writes a draft alone, but then shares that draft with one or

more others and invites them to write out some of their own thoughts in response: new thoughts on the topic itself or thoughts about what the writer
has said—perhaps even how it was said. These responses go to the original
writer who then gets to incorporate some passages from them into his or her
piece. The writer can put these passages in quotation marks, or in a different
type face, or even in a separate column running alongside the writer's own
text. Thus the single writer stays in complete charge of his or her text—but
incorporates the voices of others.

2. The student is writing about a topic while also doing lots of reading or
interviewing about it. The student is asked to produce not a conventional,
connected research or documented essay, but a collage that contains extensive
and extended quotations from the reading or interviews. Again, the inter-
jected material might be in long block quotations, in separate typefaces, or in
a parallel column or two. The goal here is to help students "place" their own
thoughts and voices in authoritative dialogue with the voices of others, especially of published writers. That is, this procedure can help prevent two common problems in research or documented essays by students: (a) essays where
the writer says almost nothing and merely wholesales the ideas and voices of
others; (b) essays where the writer brings in nothing but perfunctory
"quotes" to back up what is essentially his or her own monologue.

3. Students work in pairs (or trios) and start by writing a "real time" dialogue: they simply pass a sheet of paper back and forth to each other so each
can write a response to the previous turn. (The process is even easier in an on-
line classroom.) If they want to avoid one writer having to wait while the
other one is writing, they can get two dialogues going on two different topics.
This procedure can seem odd and artificial at first, but students get comfortable pretty quickly if we help them see that they are simply putting on paper
what they do naturally and comfortably in spoken conversation. They usually
benefit from being encouraged to let the dialogue go where it wants to go,
even if it wanders. It's a voyage of thinking and discovery. Then the students
read over what they have created, and they collaborate on revising it into a
satisfying and coherent dialogue. This doesn't mean the organization or sequence of ideas has to be neat and tidy. Think about Plato! Thus the students
have to agree about what the main line or direction should be, which parts to
keep and discard, and how to arrange or rearrange. But they each get to revise
their own contributions.

These three processes help students get used to making good texts out of
multiple thoughts and voices.

Using the Collaborative Collage as a Bridge
Back to Better Solo Writing

The collaborative collage can guide students not only toward better full collaboration, but also toward better solo writing. That is, the experience of writing and sharing collaborative collages—and seeing the unexpected virtues of

them—can help students learn to get into their solo pieces some qualities that are rare and precious in writing: conflicting ideas, multiple points of view, perplexity, tension, and complexity of structure. The larger principle of learning that operates here (as articulated by Vygotsky and Mead) is that we eventually learn to do by ourselves what we first learned to do socially in interaction with others. We internalize the social process.

That is, much *solo* writing suffers from the same weakness that is found in much collaborative writing. Many student writers, feeling a pressure always to have a clear "thesis," end up settling for the lowest-common-denominator point that the various parts of the self can agree on. They are tempted to stop writing when they feel perplexed or come across conflicting feelings and ideas—nervously sweeping complications under the rug. Students have somehow been led to think that writing should always "flow"—a favorite word of praise—and thus that the texture should be seamless. They don't realize the pleasure and energy that come from *bumps*. In truth, most good solo writing represents a single writer having some internal dialogue with herself—having more than one point of view and using more than one voice. Writing needs the drama of thinking and the performance of voices.

All these virtues can be summed up in the catchword that we've taken from Bakhtin's mouth: "dialogic." Fair enough. But it's fruitful to encourage some notes of overt *dialogue* into solo writing: passages where the writer actually breaks out into a different voice and point of view. It's not hard to create such passages by using launching pads like these: "Notice the complications we must consider, however, when we listen to the thoughts of someone who disagrees: '. . .'" Or, "There are some serious objections, however, to what I have just been saying: '. . .'" Or, "But wait a minute. Let's look at this issue from a contrasting point of view: '. . .'" In each case, the writer can carry on for a paragraph or longer speaking in a different voice from a different point of view. Of course it's hard to get full rhetorical control over multiple voices and points of view, but even when students don't handle the richness and complexity so well, they almost always gain powerful benefits to their thinking. (Teachers have often found ways to give better grades to papers that fall down—when their downfall stems from the attempt to deal with complex thinking—than to seamless papers that settle for simple, obvious thinking.)

I'm fascinated by the literal ability to talk to oneself—to give voice to the multiple views and consciousnesses that inhabit us. The ability to have thoughtful dialogues with oneself may be one of the most important goals of schooling. It is surely the mark of educated or developed persons to be able to engage in thinking and dialogue when there are no others around who are interested in their topic or interested in talking to them. One of the biggest difficulties for adolescents, in particular, is that they feel so vulnerable to their peers and therefore find it hard to delve very far into issues or feelings or points of view that their peers ignore or scorn as weird. One of the main things I want to teach my students is that they can pursue their ideas, even when they feel alone and can't get others to listen.

To sum up. My goal in this teaching activity is to make collaborative writing not only easier and more inviting, but also more complex and conflicted. And in the end, the more lasting goal may be to get richer thinking and more voices into solo writing as well.

Works Cited

Clark, Suzanne and Lisa Ede. "Collaboration, Resistance, and the Teaching of Writing." *The Right to Literacy*. Ed. Andrea Lunsford, Helene Moglen, and James Slevin. NY: Modern Language Association, 1990. 276–87.

Ede, Lisa and Andrea Lunsford. *Singular Texts/Plural Authors: Perspectives on Collaborative Writing*. Carbondale IL: Southern Illinois UP: 1990.

Elbow, Peter and Pat Belanoff. *A Community of Writers: A Workshop Course in Writing*. 3rd ed. NY: McGraw-Hill, 1999.

LeFevre, Karen Burke. *Invention as a Social Act*. Carbondale IL: Southern Illinois UP, 1987.

Light, Richard J. *Harvard Assessment Seminar: Explorations with Student and Faculty about Teaching and Learning and Student Life*. Cambridge: Harvard Graduate School of Education, 1990.

Mead, George H. *Mind, Self, and Society*. Chicago: U of Chicago P, 1934.

Polanyi, Michael. *Personal Knowledge: Toward a Post-Critical Philosophy*. New York: Harper and Row, 1958.

Trimbur, John. "Consensus and Difference in Collaborative Learning." *College English* 51 (Oct 1989): 602–16.

Vygotsky, Lev. *Mind in Society: The Development of Higher Psychological Processes*. Ed. M. Cole, V. John-Steiner, S. Scribner, and E. Souberman. Cambridge: Harvard UP, 1978.

Being a Writer vs. Being an Academic

A Conflict in Goals

Perhaps David and others can persuade me that I am wrong, but I fear that there is a conflict between the role of writer and that of academic. I wish there were not. In this essay I will explore how this conflict plays out in a first year writing class. But it will be obvious that I see the issue lurking in a larger dimension—even autobiographically. I am an academic and I am a writer. I've struggled to be able to make both claims, and I am proud of both identities—but I sometimes feel them in conflict. Thus I'm talking here about the relationship between two roles—two ways of being in the world of texts. It is my wish that students should be able to inhabit both roles comfortably.

Note that I'm talking here about roles, not professions. That is, I'm not trying to get first year students to commit to making their living by writing—nor to get a Ph.D. and join the academy. But I would insist that it's a reasonable goal for my students to end up saying, "I feel like I *am* a writer. I get deep satisfaction from discovering meanings by writing—figuring out what I think and feel through putting down words; I naturally turn to writing when I am perplexed—even when I am just sad or happy; I love to explore and communicate with others through writing; writing is an important part of my life." Similarly, I would insist that it's a reasonable goal for my students to end up saying, "I feel like I *am* an academic. Reading knowledgeable books, wrestling my way through important issues with fellows, figuring out hard questions—these activities give me deep satisfaction and they are central to my sense of who I am." In short, I want my first year students to feel themselves as writers and feel themselves as academics.

Of course, these are idealistic goals; many students will not attain them. But I insist on them as reasonable goals for my teaching, because if I taught well and if all the conditions for learning were good, I believe all my students *could* achieve them. I don't mind high or distant goals. But I'm troubled by a sense that they conflict with each other—that progress toward one could un-

David Bartholomae and I agreed to give papers for the same session at the 4Cs convention in 1994 (The Conference on College Composition and Communication). We wrote our papers independently, but then shared them and wrote responses. Our papers and responses were published in 1995 in *College Composition and Communication* 46.1 (February): 62–92. What follows here are fragments from my paper and from my response. (I rescued the last short fragment from the cutting room floor; there wasn't room for it in the original publication.) When I speak of "David" and "you," I am referring to David Bartholomae.

dermine progress toward the other. A distant mountain is a good guide for walking—even if I know I won't get to the top. But I feel as though I am trying to walk toward two different mountains.

. . .

• Sometimes I've felt a conflict about *what we should read* in the first year writing course. It would seem as though in order to help students see themselves as academics I should get them to read "key texts": good published writing, important works of cultural or literary significance; strong and important works. However, if I want them to see themselves as writers, we should primarily publish and read their own writing.

In my first year writing class I take the latter path. I publish a class magazine about four times a semester, each one containing a finished piece by all the students. (I'm indebted to Charlie Moran for showing me how to do this—supporting the practice with a lab fee for the course.) We often discuss and write about these magazines. This may be the single most important feature of the course that helps students begin to experience themselves as members of a community of writers.

But on reflection, I don't think there is any conflict here. It's not an either/or issue. To read both strong important published texts and the writing of fellow students serves both my goals. Academics read key texts and the writing of colleagues; so do writers. In short, I think I could and probably should read some strong important published works in my first year course. I would never give up using the magazines of students' own writing, but that needn't stop me from also reading at least some of the other kind of texts.

• Just as I see no conflict about what to read in my first year course (with regard to the roles of writer and academic), so too about *how to read* these texts. Whether I want my students to be academics or writers, it seems crucial to avoid coming at key texts (or at student texts) as models. That is, I must fight the tradition of treating these readings as monuments in a museum, pieces under glass. We must try to come at these strong important texts—no matter how good or hallowed they may be—as much as possible as fellow writers—as fully eligible members of the conversation: not treat them as sacred; not worry about "doing justice" to them or getting them dirty. To be blunt, I must be sure not to "teach" these texts (in the common sense of that term), but rather to "have them around" to wrestle with, to bounce off of, to talk about and talk from, to write about and write from. Again: not feel we must be polite or do them justice. In taking this approach I think we would be treating texts the way academics and writers treat them: using them rather than *serving* them. (I take this as one of the lessons of David's *Facts, Artifacts, and Counterfacts.*)

. . .

• How shall I teach my students to *place themselves* in the universe of other writers? Insofar as I want them to internalize the role of academic, I shouldteach my students always to situate themselves and what they have to say in the context of important writers who have written on the subject: to see the act of writing as an act of finding and acknowledging one's place in an ongoing intellectual conversation with a much larger and longer history than what goes on in this classroom during these ten or fourteen weeks. In short, I should try to enact and live out in my classroom the Burkean metaphor of intellectual life as an unending conversation. This is what we academics do: carry on an unending conversation not just with colleagues but with the dead and unborn.

But the truth is (should I hang my head?) I don't give this dimension to my first year writing classroom. I don't push my first year students to think about what academics have written about their subject; indeed, much of my behavior is a kind of invitation for them to *pretend* that no authorities have ever written about their subject before.

It might sound as though I invite only *monologic* discourse and discourage dialogic discourse. That's not quite right. I do invite monologic discourse (in spite of the current fashion of using "monologic" as the worst moral slur we can throw at someone); but I invite and defend dialogic discourse just as much. That is, I encourage students to situate what they write into the conversation of other members of the classroom community to whom they are writing and whom they are reading. Let me mention that the regular publication of the class magazine does more for this dialogic dimension than any amount of theoretical talk. I often assign papers *about* the class magazine. In short, I find it helpful to invite students to see their papers as parts of a conversation or dialogue; and I also find it crucial to assign dialogues and collaborative papers. My point here is that both academics and writers seem to me to engage in both monologic and dialogic discourse.

In short, the real question or point of conflict here is not so much about whether I should get my first year students to feel their writing as monologue or dialogue, whether to get them to speak to other voices or not, or to recognize their own positions or not. I'm working for both sides in each case. Rather it's a larger more general question: whether I should invite my first year students to be self-absorbed and see themselves at the center of the discourse—in a sense credulous; or whether I should invite them to be personally modest and intellectually scrupulous and to see themselves at the periphery—in a sense skeptical and distrustful. I recently read an academic critique of a writer for being too self-absorbed, of reading his subjectivity too much into the object he was allegedly examining, of being imperial, arrogant—practicing analysis by means of autobiography. I have to admit that I *want* first year students in my writing class to do that. I think autobiography is often the best mode of analysis. I'm afraid that I invite first year students to fall into the following sins: to take their own ideas too seriously; to think that they are the first person to think of their idea and be all wrapped up and possessive about it—even though others might have already written better about it. I invite them to write as though they are a central speaker at the center of the universe—rather than feeling, as they often do, that they must summarize what others have said and only make modest re-joinders from the edge of the conversation to all the smart thoughts that have al-ready been written. (By the way, I was trained by good New Critics in the 1950s who often tried to get me to write as though no one else had ever written about the work I was treating. Therefore, we cannot call this intellectual stance "nonacademic." New Critics may be out of fashion but no one could call them anything but full-fledged academics—indeed, their distinguishing mark in comparison to their predecessors was heightened professionalism in literary studies.)

. . .

• A last brief point of conflict between the role of writer and academic. We all know that when students write to teachers they have to write "up" to an audience with greater knowledge and authority than the writer has about her own topic. The student is analyzing "To His Coy Mistress" for a reader who understands it better than she does. (Worse yet, the teacher-reader is often looking for a specific conclusion and form in the paper.) Even if the student happens to have a better insight or understanding than the teacher has, the teacher gets to define her own understanding as right and the student's as wrong. Thus the basic subtext in a piece of student writing is likely to be, "Is this okay?"

In contrast to students, the basic subtext in a writer's text is likely to be, "Listen to me, I have something to tell you," for writers can usually write with more authority than their readers. Therefore, unless we can set things up so that our first year students are often telling us about things that they know better than we do, we are sabotaging the essential dynamic of writers. We are transforming the process of "writing" into the process of "being tested." Many of the odd writing behaviors of students make perfect sense once we see that they are behaving as test-takers rather than writers.

How about academics on this score? It would seem as though they would have at least as strong an authority stance as writers do. After all, the acade-mic in her writing has done a piece of research or reflection as a professional and is usually saying things that her readers do not know. But look again. I think you'll notice a curious resemblance between how students write to their teacher-readers and how academics write to their colleague-readers—even if the academic is a tenured professor. Yes, the academic may have data, findings, or thoughts that are news; yet the paradigm transaction in academic writing is one where the writer is conveying those data, findings, or thoughts to au-thorities in the field whose job is to decide whether they are acceptable. These authorities get to decide whether the writing counts as important or true—whether it is valid—and ultimately whether it counts as knowledge. Have you ever noticed that when we write articles or books as academics, we often have the same feeling that students have when they turn in papers: "Is this okay? Will you accept this?" But damn it, I want my first year students to be saying in their writing, "Listen to me, I have something to tell you,"—not "Is this okay? Will you accept this?"

Of course, some academics manage to send the strong perky message, "Listen to me, I have something to tell you." But the structure of the academy tends to militate against that stance. And of course the structure of the classroom and the grading situation militate even more heavily against it. Therefore, I feel I have a better chance of getting my students to take that forthright stance toward readers and their material if I do what I can to make them feel like writers, and avoid setting things up to make them feel like academics.

Utopias and Freewriting

You write in your essay that the classroom is "real space, not an idealized utopian space (66)." You seem to be insisting on two things here: that a classroom cannot be utopian, and that utopian spaces are not real spaces. Here is a crucial difference between our positions.

Let's look at a micro-utopian space that I love and that seems to preoccupy you: freewriting. This is an activity that permits a classroom space to be at once utopian and real. (Were not Fruitlands or Summerhill real spaces?) Note that freewriting does not involve trying to hide the teacher or her authority. Indeed, using it tends to make our authority more naked. Why else would students do something so odd and unnatural as to write for ten minutes—without stopping, no matter what—trying not to worry about the conventions of writing and also assuming that the teacher who orders it won't see it and is urging them not to show it to anyone else?

Nor does freewriting pretend magically to reveal one's pure natural essential self or to escape the effects of culture and the past. Far from it. People who use freewriting tend to notice immediately that it shows more nakedly than other kinds of writing all the junk that culture and the past have stuffed into our heads. Nothing is better than freewriting at showing us how we are constructed and situated. Another way of saying this is that freewriting is the opposite of an attempt to preserve the idea of a self-generated autonomous author. Rather it is an invitation take a ride on language itself, and (insofar as the phrase has any meaning at all) to "get out of the self": to relinquish volition and planning and see what words and phrases come out of the head when you just kick it and give language and culture a start.

So does freewriting pretend to be free? Yes and no. It is not free from the teacher's authority (until a person takes it over by choice), nor from the forces of culture and language. But it does create freedom in certain crucial ways. It frees the writer from planning, from meeting the needs of readers, and from any requirements as to what she should write about or how her writing should end up—for instance, as to topic, meaningfulness, significance, or correctness of convention.

Freewriting then is a paradigm of the real and the utopian: an example of how we can use our authority as teachers in our institutional settings to create artificial spaces that can heighten discovery and learning. It is a way to take ten minutes of a classroom and make certain things happen that don't usually happen given the institutional and cultural forces at work. Students discover that they can write words and thoughts and not worry about what good writing is or what the teacher wants; they discover that their heads are full of language and ideas (sometimes language and ideas they had no idea were there), and they discover they can get pleasure from writing.

This line of thought suggests that many of my other activities could be called utopian. Sometimes I get students to write something for me to read but not comment on; or I give them only uncritical feedback (response but no criticism or advice); or I get them to read their work to each other—and just listen; or I get them to give only uncritical feedback to each other. In every case I am using my authority to create an artificial situation where people respond to a text differently from the way they usually respond in other classrooms or outside the classroom. Is this escaping history or culture? I don't think so, but it does involve a kind of forcible "time out" from normality—a kind of pretending or play-acting or imaginative creation of different space.

Don't you do the same thing in your classroom?—use your authority sometimes to do what is artificial or different from cultural habit in order to heighten learning? You don't call it utopian, but that's only because you insist on associating utopian activity with not planning, not thinking—being naive, sentimental, and blind. Aren't *you* being naive in your unexamined use of the word "utopian" to mean that *I'm* not thinking about what I do, but *you* are thinking about what you do?

Admittedly, my utopianism often takes a different direction from yours—a direction that troubles you, namely, toward noninstruction. You say there is no writing without teachers not only in school but even out of school. I would acknowledge that there is no schooling without teachers, no assigned writing without teachers, no teaching without authority, and indeed little human interaction anywhere without unequal power or authority. But surely there is plenty of writing without teachers not only outside the academy but also inside. I'm thinking about all the writing that students do unrelated to their schoolwork: diaries, letters, notes, stories, poems, newspaper writing. Isn't language, above all, the realm where people most blatantly *do* learn without teachers? Children learn more grammar by age five than linguists can yet fully explain—and get very fluent in its deployment—all without teachers. (If you say that all children have "teachers" in the person of their parents and playmates, you are just aggrandizing a term to destroy it, since then there would be no way to distinguish between teaching and nonteaching.) The most striking fact about language acquisition is the absence of teaching. What people need for acquiring language is not teaching but being around others who speak, being listened to, and being spoken to.

It may be utopian to carry this principle of learning without teaching from speech to writing, but that is just what I and many other teachers and students have found useful. (An odd, minimal kind of utopianism: simply trying to stop teaching now and then—trying to cultivate in the classroom some tufts of what grows wild outside. But there is plenty of research about how tiny children learn not just to speak but to write before school—by being around writing.) Above all, it is empowering (another word that gives you trouble) for students to discover that they can learn so much without instruction.

Real and Unreal Genres

You write that no genre is more real than any other (68). You seem to accuse me of denying this—of thinking that personal or "natural" writing is more real. But I don't. What we're really talking about are two venerable human impulses with language: using language to dress up vs. using it to be naked; using it to sell the Brooklyn Bridge vs. using it to tap on the wall of the prison cell to see if anyone else is there.

Just because I celebrate a kind of nakedness and tapping on the wall— presence rather than absence (though I still love artifice and irony and communicated self-consciousness—as I think my writings will show), does that mean I am blind to genres? That I don't know that people have been using language these ways since the beginning—and that nakedness can be the most artificial of costumes? Even though I think it's possible actually to *make* contact by tapping on the wall, that doesn't mean that I'm blind to genre or that I think this kind of writing is more "real" than other kinds of writing. *You* are the one, really, who drifts into assuming that one genre is more real than another. You write that sentimental realism means "making the world conform to one's image (67)." Why do you say this of sentimental realism and not your prose? Look at your language. You imply that what I write are "tropes of freedom," "figures," "myths," "lies" ("Why should I . . . tell this lie, . . . this myth . . . ?" you ask [70].) But it's your prose, more insidiously than that of sentimental realism, that pretends to make the world conform to your image of it because you arrogate to yourself foundational knowledge as to what are myths, lies, and tropes—and you imply that what you write escapes myth, lie, and trope. You don't even bother to argue it, you simply imply it with what I might call the trope of sophisticated weariness in the face of unending sentimental naivete.

Separating Teaching from Certifying

Open admission universities and external degree universities are here.[1] Since they are meant to teach anybody, perhaps they will teach conventional universities. Certain lessons are clear: anybody should be able to work toward a college degree: enrollment in courses and presence on campus should not be required. But there's a less obvious lesson which I take as the theme of this essay: *It would help to separate the teaching and certifying functions of higher education.*

Imagine a state motor vehicles agency that wouldn't tell you the skills required for a driver's license and would only give you a license if you took its long, expensive driving course. This is how most universities do it: to get a degree you must buy the four-year preparatory package deal because the degree *is* the four-year preparatory package deal, namely, four years of course-passing.

· · ·

The common degree requirement of swimming a pool's length should be the model of an exam. It is the ideal combination of hard-nosed and soft-nosed. It is hard-nosed because it demands the ability to do the thing itself and won't accept substitutes, such as trying hard, serving time, following directions, or being acquainted with the concepts. But it is soft-nosed because there is no penalty for taking a long time or an unorthodox route; and it is used to demonstrate only whether the student can do the thing, not where he ranks on a continuum of better-than and worse-than. Thus the swimming test involves certifying but not ranking. This distinction will settle many of the debates about grading: let's grant the university's right to give or withold its "yes" as to whether a student can do whatever-it-is; but let's deny institutional expression of that itch to rank people first-, second-, third-, fourth-, and fifth-rate. It is no accident, by the way, that there is such a widespread tendency for teachers to rank students. It's not just invidiousness. Ranking scores or grades along a continuum turns out to be a way for the teacher to avoid the fact that he has not clearly specified the knowledge or competence he is trying to teach, and thus, naturally enough, cannot answer at the end of

These are passages from "Shall We Teach or Give Credit? A Model For Higher Education," *Soundings,* Fall 1971. A first version was published in *The Justice,* the Brandeis University newspaper, Spring 1969, while I was a graduate student there. This essay is about both teaching and assessment and so serves as a kind of transition to the next section.

1. The City University of New York has open admissions; the New York State Regents has started a program to give degrees by examination alone (no attendance required); an external degree university in England opened in January 1971 with 25,000 students enrolled. These developments have been preceeded by other experiments.

the term the simple question, "Can the student do the thing? Does he know the thing that your course set out to teach?"

If exams are used well (as swimming tests are used) they can be excellent ways of learning. A student might take a major exam every week starting when he arrives. After each try he would be given the papers of those who passed and be given citations of revelant books, tests, labs, etc. An extreme route, perhaps, but not really such a bad way to learn.

Of course exams would have to be better than many that are now given. Less trivial, and in fact harder. This doesn't mean teachers will have to strive for exams of ever greater byzantine complexity (though oblique, creative, and metaphorical exams might find their place) but rather that exams will become simpler and more staightforward. The teacher must simply ask the student to do or explain the thing itself—not ask for catchwords, phrases, or answers which can be given in ignorance. There's no reason why exams couldn't be posted ahead of time. Any exam which doesn't work if the student knows what's on it ahead of time is either asking the student for trivial learning or asking the teacher to judge it on a trivial level. It's interesting to ask how teachers have fallen into the habit of trying *not* to tell students what's on the exam. The reason is that higher education has come to focus almost entirely upon small-scale units that can be "crammed" for (i.e., most courses)—instead of focusing on completed, demonstrable skills or competencies themselves. Most college exams are too easy because teachers know that if they asked for deep competence in the thing itself, most students would fail. Most would have to take the exam seven or eight times before they could pass it. But that is precisely what is needed.

. . .

In separating certification from teaching, the important thing will be to make clear to students from the beginning exactly what is required. And then require it. The university can be hard-nosed when it provides many paths to the degree, allows theses and exams to be failed any number of times, and thus stops militating against unorthodox students and students who start from behind. When the university has finally separated certifying from teaching, it can say to potential students:

> It doesn't matter who you are: how well or badly you are trained, how far ahead or behind you start, how quickly or slowly or erratically you learn. We will award you the batchelor degree when you attain, (a) expertise in one area, (b) some competence in three others, and (c) a basic skill in writing. If you already have these attainments, you may have the degree right now. If you don't, you may get them however you please. (If you want to know precisely what we require, you may look at our file of completed exams, projects, and theses to see which ones were judged successful.)
>
> We also offer the following teaching and learning procedures which you may find helpful: . . .

Teaching

Teaching will benefit when it is separated from certifying. The teacher will no longer have the dual role which makes him both ally and adversary of the student—which makes him try to police the student while also trying to help him. Even if the teacher has somehow learned to keep his role as guardian at the threshhold from interfering with his efforts to help everyone enter, nevertheless, the conflict of roles is apt to be just as destructive in the eyes of the student: no matter how the teacher *actually* behaves, the student is apt to see him as the enemy—the person to be tricked, fooled, deceived.

The separation of teaching and certifying will help break down this adversary relationship, but the resulting relationship of helping need not be merely sweet and sentimental. The teacher will actually have to produce results: demonstrable competence. Or rather he will actually have to help the *student* produce demonstrable competence. Merely being entertaining, fun, or kindly will not be enough, as it now is in a structure which gives no more encouragement to a course where everyone learns than to a course where few learn (after all, it's just a matter of "serving time" or chalking up credit").

A refreshingly crude market economy will operate. A student will have no reason to spend time, effort, and money on a teacher unless he is really getting something out of it. Since he will no longer take courses or anything else "for credit," that is, in order merely to be done with them, he will be vigilant to see that he is making progress toward producing a satisfactory project or exam. If he thinks the teacher's efforts are a waste of time, he will do himself and the teacher the favor of not coming. Of course he is liable to be wrong about whether a course or teacher is a waste of time. After many attempts to pass projects or exams, students will grow shrewder about what kinds of courses or teaching are effective. This process of misperception and slow correction about how to learn is probably the most important learning there is. This complex feedback will also encourage teachers to grow shrewder about which of their behaviors are useful to students.

Teachers will have to admit what many are now reluctant to admit, namely, that they are in business to sell a service and can be judged accountable as to whether the service works. But though the arrangement will tend to be tough-minded with regard to *results*, it will not be restrictive with regard to *style* or *mode* of teaching. I had started to write that teachers will have to take the client into their confidence and try to explain why and how the service works (no doubt because I personally favor this style). But I wrote too hastily. The truth is that a market economy will *not* necessarily favor the style I favor. For although, on the one hand, business may be improved if the seller is pleasant to his client, takes him into his confidence, and makes the service enjoyable, all of these considerations are outweighed by results. For example, in the field of self-employed music teachers, a field where a market economy now operates, a teacher who gets results can use any style he chooses, however dictatorial. In a market economy, the benefits of an informal, jolly desk-side manner are balanced by the fact that most clients think they are getting more from a teacher who maintains his professional authority and distance.

. . .

My guess is that there will be just plain *less* teaching per cubic centimeter of learning attained. This guess is partially based on my experience teaching for the past two years in an experimental freshman program at M.I.T. (The Experimental Study Group), in which there has been a substantial separation of teaching and certifying: the student doesn't have to have any dealings with a teacher in preparing to be certified in some subject. The first thing we felt as teachers was how difficult teaching is in this setting. But then slowly it became clear that we were merely having to look naked upon the near-impossibility of any teaching. In the conventional arrangement, this dismal view is decently covered: the student works with the teacher and a course, the student and teacher come together regularly in class, various transactions occur, and then at the end there are rituals which permit both parties to believe that the student was taught. I believe more firmly now something I've long suspected: deep down, everyone *does* realize the ineffectuality of most teaching; it is so depressing to confront this ineffectuality that universities persist in confusing teaching and certifying in order partially to veil it.

. . .

It has recently been said that teachers teach subjects, not students—they teach students only by grammatical ellipsis. The assertion is elegant, but the fact remains that unless a teacher feels almost as strongly for his subject matter, there is little to counterbalance his inevitable annoyance at trying to teach it to people who don't understand or care about it as he does, and therefore he is more apt to produce repulsion than attraction between the student and the subject. It is just as well not to flinch from the fact that the teacher is a kind of pandar paid to share the object of love with clients who must inevitably seem insufficiently appreciative.

Why wax metaphorical, a reader is bound to ask, about the difficulty of teaching when it is already self-evident to everyone? But though the difficulty of teaching is assumed to be self-evident, many teachers show by their statements and their behavior that they have been tricked by our present structure into confusing teaching with certifying. It is very common for university teachers to say they like teaching but can't stand their present students because they are so unprepared or unintelligent or uncaring. (Teachers' condescension and scorn for their students is growing these days when the job market is tight and so many feel they are teaching below their station.) What they are really saying in most cases is, "I *hate* teaching, but I'd love to have a job as certifier for well-taught students," that is, a job pointing out to them what they are supposed to know and then examining them to see whether they have learned it.

. . .

But though the separation of teaching and certifying will not remove the difficulties of teaching, it will permit teaching to flourish uncontaminated by certifying. For in the present state of confusion, many of those who *are* in fact good teachers are mistakenly accused of being bad teachers when in reality they are merely bad certifiers. There is a type of good teacher, for example, who is called "easy," "sloppy," or "unprofessional" because he does not, as a certifier must, devote himself to being constantly vigilant against incompetence. He is accused of "letting the second-rate get by him," when in fact he is not interested in trying to stop anyone at all from "getting by him" since he has, consciously or not, refused the role of certifier. When he receives a piece of work or an utterance from a student, he feels that his primary responsibility is *not* to evaluate its competence but to speak to it, respond to it, reply to it, engage in interaction with it. (This involves the *skill* of seeing what's good even in a weak piece of work.) An evaluation tends to stop potential interaction ("I think Oedipus is really free." "B plus. Good job."); whereas a reply or response prolongs an interaction and adds new energy to it. When this sort of teacher takes his main responsibility to be to respond to a student's work, he is not thereby trying to *suppress* the question of the competence of the work: he simply lets it come out in its own way, which it always does sooner or later. It is simply not what seems important to him as a teacher.

Learning

Just as the separation of teaching from certifying will clarify the teacher's role, so too will it help students. The new arrangement will reward the student as well as the teacher for working out a cooperative relationship and discourage a useless adversarial one. Just as with teaching for the teacher, it will reward genuine learning for the student and discourage merely going through the motions or serving time. And as with teachers, it will be painful for many students through bringing out into the open more of the inherent difficulties of the enterprise. Although a few students will find it easy simply to be told what they must learn for a degree and then be allowed to learn it however they please, most will require help, guidance, time, and support—especially time and support while they go through the "floundering" that is involved in discovering that an act of responsibility must underlie any real learning.

This need for the student to learn responsibility will provide an interesting and healthy leveling influence: the so-called disadvantaged student may well begin to learn more quickly than the well-prepared student what is after all the main thing in learning: that no one can do it for you; you are stuck; you won't learn till you invest your own commitment and decide for yourself to do it. If I am not mistaken, many "advantaged" students will be slower to give up the opposite frame of mind which so often blocks learning: if you perform certain tasks or activities which feel like "doing what you are supposed to do" (taking certain courses, passing your eyes diligently over certain hundreds of pages and so on) and making certain kinds of internal gruntings and strainings that feel like "trying your best," then learning is guaranteed and the degree will be given to you by right, by obligation, because you deserve it.

. . .

When certifying and teaching are separated, a university can serve the whole community—all ages, races, and classes. If more students want to attend than can fit, decisions will be made on the basis of eagerness to learn and willingness to work for a degree. The university will discriminate no longer in favor of training but rather in favor of drive for a goal. Admittedly, this may mean discriminating against students without a solid drive for a goal—and there are many of them. For example, some disadvantaged students are so deeply discouraged by their lack of opportunities that they have effectively lost any strong goal they are willing to work for. The system proposed here will not help them directly; but when such a system has functioned successfully for a few years, and when the many disadvantaged students who *have* strong goals are well served by it, the others will learn that it is not necessary to stifle their aspirations, and they will develop goals they are willing to work for.

There are, of course, at least as many privileged students who are immobilized by the lack of any solid drive for a goal. Without doubt, immobilization will remain an unavoidable and even productive way of responding to an ambiguous or contradictory environment. Most people have been there. No system should permanently filter out persons with this response. But the last thing they need is to sit around campus feeling guilty, as they do now, because they somehow cannot manage both to be productive and to have fun in a setting that seems ideal for both. If attending university could be the flexible procedure suggested here, these students themselves would be the first to make available to others their time and space on campus, for they could easily return when ready. But the way things work now, a student feels afraid to leave without a degree. He exercises squatter's rights for four years because he was in a position to garner the credentials necessary for admission. (One of the functions of experimental independent-study programs in many universities is to let some students approximate the condition of not being in college without having to quit. One of the students in our program put it bluntly: "Why am I coming to this university and paying vast sums of money to do independent study, when I could be doing it on my own, for free, and without having to worry about all sorts of silly rules?")

. . .

What Kind of Leadership Is
Best for Collaborative Learning

I write this section out of some perplexity about how you wielded authority in the Institute. One of your main overall points is that collaborative learning helps a leader let go of some authority so that members of the group can invest more in each other. . . . Participants agree that they had more authority and invested more in each other than usual. But at one point in my discussion with them, they also seemed definitely to agree that you hadn't let go of one jot of authority and that in general you excercised a great deal of it very firmly.

This is a matter that interests me. Your formulation about "letting go of some so that they have more" suggests a model where there is a constant amount of authority available in a given situation. But the group's perception of the situation suggests that somehow more authority had come into existence. This makes me think of a corollary state of affairs: There have been times when it seemed to me I'd taught ineptly in such a way that I'd relinquished substantial authority and yet students hadn't ended up with any more. Perhaps less.

This leads me to suggest a different model involving the law of the nonconservation of authority: Certain subtle factors can make for an increase or decrease in the total amount of authority or control available in a situation. I was forced to reach exactly this conclusion when I was trying to analyze authority and control in the situations Chaucer portrays (especially marriages) in some of his poems—he being someone intensely interested in the importance yet slipperiness of authority. (See my *Oppositions in Chaucer* Wesleyan UP, 1975.)

On the one hand I can clearly see how appropriate it is for you to wield that strong authority. This—and the way you devise ahead of time such intelligent tasks for the group to do (clearer and better tasks than participants could devise collaboratively): all these things play a big role in making your Collaborative Learning Institute run so well. You are very separate from the group, but I can see how powerful that is. It is all summed up symbolically in that decisive moment when you walk out the door and leave them alone. (Participants were somewhat preoccupied with what you do when you walk out.) You are modeling for participants how a teacher of peer tutors might teach—and modeling in particular that a teacher of peer tutors is not a peer with them.

. . . [here I omit some lengthy description and speculation]

Yet I remain perplexed on this matter. I am not satisfied with a model that

In the summer of 1981, Ken Bruffee asked me to be an outside evaluator for his five week summer Institute for Collaborative Learning, a program for college teachers. I print here from my report a short section where I explore a matter that has continued to perplex me over the years.

starts off with such strong non-collaboration. I think it's at the beginning that people most need to learn how to collaborate at a gut level and thus most need to see it modeled by someone in authority. I finally arrive at the question I guess I've been circling around: *What mode of leadership is most appropriate for collaborative learning?* For collaborative learning, shouldn't we have some kind of teacher-student relationship which, though it reflects authority, nevertheless reflects collaboration too? I'm not sure whether or not you set up a relationship of this sort in the Institute. I need to know more about this subtle matter.

But because of our differences in temperament, I can point to some procedures or modes I have gradually worked out that are different from yours. I sometimes let myself satirize myself as merely a bumbler and too indecisive in my authority [which I did in the omitted pages], but in all honesty, when I look back at my struggles to find a satisfactory way of teaching and leading workshops, I think I am seeking, in a slow, intuitive, sometimes painful process, for ways of being a leader appropriate for collaborative learning.

As I look back I see three tendencies: one that seems right, one that seems wrong or unhelpful, and one that perplexes.

What seems right is a practice I've evolved of always using myself as model or guinea pig whenever I want to introduce a difficult or potentially threatening procedure. I make sure I freewrite with students or workshop participants; I introduce reading outloud by reading something of mine first; I introduce feedback by first offering something of my own for response; and I soon model the process of giving feedback. I used to worry that I would just intimidate them "because I'm so much better than they," but it turns out not to be a problem. I've discovered these practices illustrate the *similarities* between me and the group and serve to *include* me in the group, and thus tend to prevent my alienation from it. I am joining them in the process. And by always breaking the ice first myself—doing it honestly means risking myself or letting down some of my defenses—I think I manage to make things safer for others and make others more willing to risk honesty. It's not that I'm letting go of authority; I'm very much in charge when I do these things. But I feel I am collaborating with them in an important sense by sharing some of myself with them, and also helping move them toward collaboration by showing them how to be honest and nondefensive—and that it's safe to be that way.

What seems clearly unhelpful, on the other hand, is when I am sometimes too timid or unsure of my own authority, not able to trust myself enough. It always feels to me as though I have to get permission from people to be in charge—not just of adults but of young people too, perhaps even more so of young people. Even though it must be true, in the last analysis, that good leaders get permission, strong ones probably get it after the fact.

The third tendency is perplexing. I've never used this phrase till now when you are making me so much more conscious about issues of collaboration, but I think I have a kind of itch to try to *collaborate with those I lead*. I am still unclear about the extent to which this is a good thing. Could this be a groping toward the future? I certainly feel a need for new models of leadership in which there is more authority for members but also more support for the leader and less alienation or separation of the leader. Or is this a bad thing—a failure to wield my full authority and thereby also a tendency to inhibit the group from doing the authority business of making its own authority—a process you give such good attention to?

I am perhaps hypersensitive to being alienated from a group I am trying to teach or lead: I so hate having them mad at me. And I do much better with my style of leadership with adults and teachers than with adolescent students. How is it with you?

Anyway, I think I've finally hit on the right question to ask here: what mode of leadership is most appropriate for collaborative learning? Presumably, as in matters of "voice" and parenting, there is no single right answer. So much depends on one's being true to one's temperament. But all these ruminations drive me to feel that it must be possible to be very strong in leadership and also, somehow, to collaborate or to model collaboration.

Part VI

EVALUATION AND GRADING

*P*eter, you are just hung up by your old bad feelings as a student—and your problems with your authority as a teacher. You just don't want to get your hands dirty. You are trying to run away from necessary and useful work. Assessment and grading will simply go on whether you do it or not.

I've heard this charge before. It was when I was gradually thinking my way through to being a conscientious objector during the Vietnam war. "If you get *yourself* out of the draft, that will just make a place for some other poor guy who is almost certainly less privileged than you are." This was a painful charge to fight because it was absolutely true. No way to wriggle out of it. I could only get unstuck by putting aside the pragmatic question about the *effects* of my action, and insisting instead on a more internal and personal question: "What is right? What can I do—or not do—in good conscience? What am I willing to go to jail for?" (In the end, my draft board rejected my application—yet didn't draft me because by then I was too old.)

But I'm not a conscientious objector to assessment or even grading. *Sometimes* I want to wipe all assessment and grading off the face of the earth—but I don't trust that feeling. I *am* willing to evaluate, judge, and assess the work of students. And if I'm teaching in a conventional institution that links credit to grades, I am willing to give course grades. I'll even try to make my grades fair—not random or arbitrary. (For a while at M.I.T. during the Vietnam War, I and many others gave As to all students as a matter of principle. I'm not doing that now.)

What I'm trying to do with the essays in this section is *not* to run away but to think more carefully about evaluation and grading. I've found it interesting and satisfying to try to be dispassionately analytic (well, analytic anyway) about something that is troubling and perplexing. I've included a lot of my writing here, but in fact it's less than half of what I've published in the area.

It's good to come at evaluation and grading from the realm of *writing*. The evaluation of writing highlights problems inherent in most evaluation, but which people often overlook when, say, they are grading a calculus test (problems involved, for example, in choosing and phrasing the problems on the test).

It's hard for most of us to think clearly about evaluation and grading because of strong feelings we experienced as both receivers and givers of grades. I find it is important to distinguish clearly between three things that are often smudged together: *feedback, evaluation,* and *grading* (or holistic scoring).

The classic example of *feedback* is bumping into a chair in the dark. When someone misunderstands something I've written, their misunderstanding provides me with an important piece of feedback—even though they never offered me any evaluation at all. We get *highly* useful feedback on our writing simply by hearing our writing read outloud—either by ourselves or someone else. As I describe in the first essay of this section (and in "A Map of Writing in Terms of Audience and Response" in Part I), there are lots of useful feedback responses we can give to student writing that are not evaluative.

Evaluation invites responses among multiple dimensions (the thinking, the clarity, the spelling, and so forth). Thus there are lots of useful evaluative responses we can give that are not one-dimensional *grades* or holistic scores. The most vivid way to distinguish between evaluation and grading is to separate them by means of a grading contract. In this situation, evaluation flourishes because it is decoupled from the grade. I can write evaluative comments more easily and students can read them more productively because they are irrelevant to the grade. (More on contracts in the first chapter of this section.)

If our goal is learning, then grading is not necessary—though of course people often learn when they are graded. Nor is evaluation necessary for learning—though it often helps. It is *feedback* that is indispensable for learning. Notice the hierarchy of categories here. Feedback is the largest category. Evaluation is one kind or subspecies of feedback. One-dimensional grades are, in turn, a narrow subspecies of evaluation.

Feedback and evaluation of writing can come from many sources, not just teachers: from peers, from self, and from circumstances. If our goal is learning, our task is to figure out which forms of feedback, evaluation, and grading are most useful toward that end. This is the project I address in some of these essays. Evaluation for the sake of learning or improvement is technically called *formative evaluation*.

But of course learning is not the only goal for evaluation and grading. Sometimes we have to decide whether to give credit to someone, or whether to admit them to a course or a program or a school, or whether to give them a scholarship. Or we have to tell employers or parents how well someone did. In these situations we need verdict-giving or *summative evaluation*. Official or institutional verdict-giving usually takes the form of grading along a single scale.

What strikes me most in our current cultural moment is how preoccupied people are with institutional evaluation, assessment, and testing of all sorts, and how much one-dimensional scores and grades are a tail that wags teaching and learning. Teachers often write comments to justify their grade rather than writing comments they most want the student to hear and think about for the sake of learning. Students often get so dependent upon grades that they feel grades are the only reason to write—sometimes even refusing if there is no grade. These attitudes and behaviors are understandable—not a reason for blame. But they are a problem and a reason for change. More about this in some of the essays.

But I need to repeat that I am not a conscientious objector. I acknowledge that sometimes we really need the fairest and most accurate one-dimensional *verdict* we can get, as to how much or how well someone has learned—even if this gets in the way of someone's desire to learn. Therefore it is not my goal in these essays to get rid of grading or summative evaluation, but rather to make them more effective in two ways: (1) to make them do as little damage as possible to teaching and learning; (2) to make them as fair and as accurate as possible. Portfolios (only one topic among the many treated in this Part VI) can be a big help in making summative evaluation fairer and less damaging to learning. In addition, I have found portfolios to provide a useful lens for thinking about all kinds of larger problems of evaluation.

I have heard myself sometimes described as someone who looks at assessment only from the point of view of the classroom. When people say this, they are often also saying, "But there's a big tough world of assessment outside our classrooms, and your soft and utopian ways of thinking about evaluation in a classroom have no relevance to that toughminded world." Of course the classroom remains a focus of my interest, but I think the essays and fragments printed here will show that my focus is also much wider. I start off this section with a first essay that focuses on grading in a classroom. Then I slightly enlarge the focus, both in the next essay (on the development of a program-wide portfolio system at Stony Brook) and in the first fragment (on liking rather than evaluating). All the rest of the fragments and the final essay focus on issues of larger scale assessment or assessment theory. In addition, readers will notice another progression in these essays. I start off with my focus on short-term needs: finding ways to *get along* with the conventional grading situation that most teachers find themselves in. But in the later pieces, my focus is on the longer term: finding ways to *change* the practices that people too often accept as normal or inevitable.

19

Getting Along Without Grades— and Getting Along With Them Too

In this paper I am driven by the utopian impulse but also the impulse to tinker. On the one hand, I insist on the possibility of large change: grading is neither natural nor inevitable; we can avoid grading; we can step outside the mentality of evaluation; we can even change systems. Yet on the other hand, I insist on the importance of small, pragmatic changes—what some might call mere fiddling. Indeed, most of what I suggest here can be used within a conventional grading system. After all, most of us are obliged to do our evaluating within such systems (for now), and the human tendency to evaluate is inevitable. The utopian and the pragmatic impulses may seem at odds, but the common element is an insistence that things can be better. Change is possible.

My focus is on pedagogy, practice, and by implication, policy. My method is simply to try to think through my own evaluative practices since they are the practices all teachers engage in; this is a report on experience and thinking rather than on research.

When I speak of grades, I'm speaking of the quantitative, official grades that teachers commonly put on papers—and also the course grades we give at the end of the term and the holistic grades we use in large-scale writing assessments. I mean to distinguish between grading (quantitative marks)

I created this essay by working together two published essays: "Taking Time Out from Grading and Evaluating While Working in a Conventional System (*Assessing Writing* 4.1, 1997) and "Changing Grading While Working with Grades" (*Theory and Practice of Grading Writing: Problems and Possibilities*, eds., Chris Weaver and Fran Zak, Albany NY: SUNY Press, 1998). The present essay focuses primarily on classroom assessment. For the relevance of the principles here to the realm of large-scale assessments, see my "Writing Assessment: Do It Better, Do It Less," in *The Politics and Practices of Assessment in Writing*, eds., William Lutz, Edward White, and Sandra Kamusikiri, NY: MLA, 1996. (A fragment of that essay is printed later in this section.)

and the much larger and more various and multidimensional activity of evaluation.

This essay is in three parts: first, suggestions for how to step outside of grading; second, suggestions for how to step outside of the very mentality of judging or evaluation; and third, suggestions for how to *use* grades more effectively.

1. Ways to Step Outside of Grading

If I am suggesting ways to step outside of grading, I suppose I'd better summarize my reasons for *wanting* to do so. Grades seems to me a problem for these reasons:

- They aren't trustworthy.
- They don't have clear meaning.
- They don't give students feedback about *what* they did well or badly.
- They undermine the teaching-and-learning situation in the following ways:
  - They lead many students to work more for the sake of the grade than for learning.
  - They lead to an adversarial atmosphere; students often resent or even fight us about grades; many students no longer feel the teacher as ally in the learning process and try to hide what they don't understand. (Think of patients hiding symptoms from doctors.)
  - They lead to a competitive atmosphere among students themselves.

- Figuring out grades is difficult, and the task often makes us anxious because fairness is so hard to achieve.

Conventional grading is so ubiquitous that people tend to see it as inevitable and to feel hopeless about making any changes. Therefore, it's important to realize that grading is not built into the universe; grading is not like gravity—not "natural" or inevitable. If that sounds utopian, I can point to The Evergreen State College. I taught there for nine years. Since it started in 1971, faculty have given narrative evaluations instead of grades. The system works fine on all counts, including success in helping students enter high quality professional and graduate schools. Where Evergreen is a nonelite state college in Washington, Hampshire College is an elite private institution here in Amherst Massachusetts that also has a solid history of success with no grades. So we mustn't forget that educational institutions *can* get along just fine without grades. The pressure for grades is probably greatest at the secondary level since grades seem so central to the college admissions process; yet there are secondary schools that prosper without grades.

But discussions of institutions like Evergreen and Hampshire tend to trap people into either/or thinking: whether or not to have grading at all; whether or not to transform the entire curriculum as they've done at Evergreen or Hampshire. Let's wrest the discussion out of this binary rut. Instead of fighting about *Yes* or *No*, let's discuss *When?* and *How much?* I am interested in exploring temporary time-outs from grading, even while operating under a conventional grading system.

And let's jump from the largest scale to the smallest: *freewriting*. To freewrite for ten minutes is to step outside of grading for ten minutes. When I get students to freewrite, I am using my authority to create unusual conditions in order to contradict or interrupt the pervasive feeling in the air that writing is always evaluated. What is essential here are the two central features of freewriting: that it be private (thus I don't collect it or have students share it with anyone else); and that it be nonstop (thus there isn't time for planning, and control is usually diminished). Students quickly catch on and enter into the spirit. It's sad if teachers use freewriting in thoughtless or mechanical ways: just ten minutes now and then for no good reason—and sadder if teachers call it freewriting but collect it and read it. Still, most freewriting is a common instance of a kind of writing that is not really so rare: *nongraded* writing.

Every time teachers get students to do nongraded writing, they are inviting students to notice that the link between writing and grading can be broken: it is possible to write and not worry about how the teacher will grade it; it is possible to write in pursuit of one's own goals and standards and not just someone else's. When teachers assign journal writing and don't grade it, this too is an important time-out from grading.

A bigger time-out from grading is the single *nongraded assignment*. These can be "quickwrites" or sketches done in class or for homework; sometimes they are simply "ungraded essays." In either case they are usually unrevised. These writings carry more weight than freewritings if the teacher reads them or asks students to read them to each other, but still they break the link between writing and grading. (It helps to say out loud to the students that this writing is ungraded. Occasionally, students write *as though* it were a graded exercise. And indeed, many students have had the experience of being *told* that something was ungraded and then being surprised.)

These are small time-outs—ten minutes, one or two hours. What if we have *ten days of nongraded writing?* We can do that and still work solidly within a grading system. Many teachers start the semester with this kind of orgy of nongraded writing, and it has a deep effect on students' and teachers' relationship to writing. It improves students' fluency and enlivens their voices on paper; it helps them learn to take risks in writing; and it permits us to assign *much* more writing than we usually can in two weeks.

Portfolios. Portfolios are a way to refrain from putting grades on individual papers: for a while we can just write comments and students can revise. Grading can wait till we have more pieces of writing in hand—more data to judge. By avoiding frequent ranking or grading, we make it *somewhat* less likely for students to become addicted to oversimple numerical rankings—to think that evaluation always translates into a simple number. Portfolios permit me to refrain from grading individual papers and limit myself to writerly evaluative comments—and help students see this as a positive rather than a negative thing, a chance to be graded on a body of their best work that can be judged more fairly. Portfolios are particularly helpful as occasions for asking students to write extensive and thoughtful explorations of their own strengths and weaknesses.

Contracts for a grade. For the last few years, this has been my favorite way to step outside of most grading while still working within a regular grading system. Contracts provide a way to avoid trying to *measure* the quality of work or learning and yet still arrive at a grade for the course. A contract says, "If you do x, y, and z, you can count on such and such a grade." For me, the pedagogical principle in using contracts is this: I don't trust my efforts to *measure* learning or quality of writing, and I hate pretending to do so. I'd rather put my efforts into something I do trust and enjoy: trying to specify activities and behaviors that will *lead to* learning and good writing.

Most often I have used what might be called a limited or impure or timid contract—a contract that spells out the many, many activities that seem most central to producing learning for the course, and then says, "If you do all these, you are guaranteed a course grade of B." But the contract goes on to say, "If you want an A, I have to judge most of your papers or your portfolio to be excellent." Thus I am not getting rid of all official measurement of quality. But I am vastly reducing it.[1]

Contracts highlight the distinction between evaluation and grading. My contract minimizes grading (and a full contract eliminates it altogether), but in doing so it *helps evaluation to be more effective.* That is, even though a contract permits me to cut back on evaluation when I find that helpful, I continue to give lots of evaluation, and the contract permits me to make blunter criticisms or pushier suggestions and have students listen to them better. They know that my responses have nothing to do with their grade (up to a B). Students needn't go along with what I say in order to get a good grade. I've set up the contract so that they cannot refrain from making significant revisions, but I emphasize to them that they can revise entirely differently from how I might have suggested or implied—and they don't have to make their revisions necessarily better, just substantively different. In short, by decoupling evaluation from grading, I think we can make it healthier and more productive.

I like the learning situation my contract puts my students into: they have to listen to my reactions, evaluation, and advice, yet they get to make up their own mind about whether to go along with what I say. Their decision will have no effect on their grade (up to a B). This means they have to *think* about my response on its own terms—listen to me as reader and human being—instead of just reacting to me in the thoughtless and habitual ways in which so many students understandably react to teacher feedback. That is, students too often

1. Perhaps I should say that I am still grading, but that my only grades are *excellent, acceptable,* and *not acceptable for the terms of the contract,* but the procedure feels more like not grading. Perhaps, in addition, I should not use the word "contract" since I impose this policy unilaterally rather than letting students have a choice about whether to enter into it; and I don't ask students to sign anything. But the word is a convenient shorthand that suggests the general approach. (See the appendix for examples of my current contract—and some discussion of specifics.)

feel, "Of course my teacher is right," or else, "Well that's the kind of junk that *this* teacher wants, so I guess I'll do it for my grade." Either way, these students don't really wrestle in their minds with the crucial question of whether my reactions or comments actually make sense to them. In the end I think my contract gets students to listen to me better. (Of course, students occasionally tell me that they *feel* pressure to go along with my comments—even though they can see that it really won't help their grade. This provides fruitful occasions for me to help students explore their learning process and how they deal with the role of being a student: how they tend to feel and react to teacher comments and grades.) So whereas some people say that teachers are evading their intellectual responsibility if they don't grade, I would argue that we can create *more* intellectual engagement by minimizing grades and highlighting evaluation.

I hear an objection:

> But we need grades for motivation—to get students to work hard.

But notice how *indirectly* grades motivate students. The causal link between grading and student work is very tenuous. We hope that by awarding fair grades, we will cause students to exert themselves to engage in the learning activities we want them to engage in. But our hope is dashed as often as it is fulfilled. Some students get good grades without much work; some have given up trying to get good grades; a few don't care what grade they get; still others work only to psych out the teacher rather than to learn (and a few of these even cheat or plagiarize). I prefer the way a contract is more direct and simply requires the activities I think will lead to learning. I'd rather put my time and effort into trying to figure out which activities will in fact help them learn and grow rather than into trying to measure the exact degree of quality of the writing they turn in and hope that my grade leads to effort.

Do I find that using a contract makes everything perfect? No. I think my contract leads to a bit *more* work from the class as a whole, more tasks accomplished by more people. But I think it also leads to a bit *less* pushing, struggle, or strain from a number of students. This disappoints me, but I have to accept the fact that my real goal is not struggle for its own sake but struggle that comes *from them*—from intrinsic motivation. When students are habituated to struggling mostly or even only for grades, it's not surprising that they have a hard time coming up with this rarer and more precious kind of struggle. Gradually, pieces of self-motivation begin to kick in, and when that happens it's very exciting for both them and me. But I have to settle for less.

2. Ways to Step Outside of the Mentality of Evaluation

I want to up the ante. If we step outside of grading, we may not be stepping outside the mentality of evaluation or judging. After all, we sometimes read an ungraded assignment and say, "I'm sure glad I don't have to grade this because it really stinks." Is it *possible* to stop judging or seeing writing in terms of quality? Yes. In fact, it's not so unusual. That is, even though it is inevitable that humans *often* look at things through the lens of judgment or quality, sometimes they don't.

The most obvious example is when we like or love. Sometimes we like or dislike a person, an object, a work of art—and more to the point here, a piece of writing—without any judgment of its quality. We know this can happen because sometimes we are even aware of the two mentalities at once: we like it but we know it is not good—or we dislike it but we know it is good. We often love someone or something because we "value" them, not because we "evaluate" them. The loving or "valuing" is something we do or give or add; we don't necessarily base it on our judgment of the "value" or "quality" of the person or object.

I'm not saying that we always take off the judging lens when we like or love, for sometimes our liking or loving is indeed based on our evaluation of quality. ("It's so great I love it.") I'm simply insisting that liking or loving *can* operate outside of judging—and often do. When I began to realize this, I found myself liking more often—students and students' writing—without wearing my judging hat. Thus we can get better at liking students and their writing; it's a skill. (See the first fragment from "Ranking, Evaluating, and Liking," (excerpted in the Fragments section of this Part.) My main claim, then, is limited, but important: I'm insisting on the empirical observation that it is not unusual for us to spend some time outside the evaluative mentality.

I find it a great relief to do this now and then. It seems to me that these time-outs from the evaluative mentality help my teaching. I think they foster an atmosphere of support and appreciation that helps students flourish, think well, and stretch themselves.

I am not denying that there is a different and more obvious kind of stretching that comes from the opposite atmosphere of judging, evaluating, and criticizing. Many people testify with appreciation to how a tough teacher's evaluative criticism made them stretch. But this stretching-through-evaluative-criticism does not negate the quite different and more delicate kind of stretching that can occur when we reduce or remove the pressure of judgment and evaluation. Sometimes people don't take risks or try out their own values or start to use their own internal motivation until critical thinking is turned off and even nonsense and garbage are welcomed. In such a setting people sometimes think themselves into their best thinking or imagine themselves into being more of who they could be. Nonevaluative support and acceptance are common in the family, especially toward infants and young children, but the evaluative mentality is pervasive in school and college settings. Of course, banishing evaluation does not always lead to this delicate stretching—but then neither does evaluation always lead to that other kind of stretching.

This talk of liking and loving tends to sound soft, fuzzy, and unintellectual. I don't want to run away from that most dreaded indictment, *soft*! It's time to insist openly that there's nothing wrong with time-out zones from what is critical, hard, cool, and detached—not just in elementary school but in higher education. We need it, even for good thinking.

Nevertheless, I want to cut through the shallow-minded association between not being evaluative and not being intellectual. That is, we can have time-outs from the evaluative mentality itself and still operate in a fully intellectual, cognitive, academic spirit. We can do so through the use of certain questions about texts—especially about student writing.

Admittedly, the questions we most often ask of student writing are quality questions: "How good or bad is it? What are its strengths and weaknesses? How can it be better?" But these are not the only questions to ask of a text, and indeed they are not the most common questions we ask of important texts in literature, history, biology, or physics—whether in teaching or scholarship. In studying important texts we tend to ask questions like these:

> What does the text say? What does it imply or entail? What are its consequences? What does the writer assume? What is the writer's point of view or stance? Who does the text speak to? How does the text ask me to see the world? What would I do if I believed it?

Nothing should stop us from using these questions on student writing. They are simple, obvious, and important questions that have no inherent connection to quality or value. They are all requests to summarize, explicate, or extend the paper (or, carried one step further, to play the "believing game" with it).

Admittedly, when we use these questions on professional writing, we tend to *assume* value—sometimes even that these are "great works" and so don't need evaluating. And with student writing, many of these neutral questions have taken on evaluative freight. "What is this paragraph saying?" often means, "I don't think it is saying anything" or "You are confused."

But we don't *need* to use these questions in this way, and it's not hard to answer them without saying anything about a paper's quality. A careful summary of a bad paper need not reveal anything of its badness. Yes, we *can* summarize a paper by saying, "It says X—which is absurd," or "It says both X and not-X—which is self-contradictory," or "It says X and P and there is no relation between them." But we don't need to put a judgmental spin on summaries. For the fact remains that plenty of *excellent* papers say things that seem absurd or logically contradictory or seemingly unrelated. Some people can't summarize without praising or criticizing, but that's because they've never practiced.

There is one kind of badness that might seem unavoidable in a summary: if a paper simply doesn't say much at all, a careful summary will contain damningly little. But even this kind of badness will not show up when we answer the other questions: "What does the paper imply or entail, what does the writer assume?" Besides, some *excellent* papers say remarkably little.

So if we learn how to answer these kinds of questions about our students' writing without a habitual edge of evaluation (and it's not so hard) and if we train our students to answer them about each others' writing, we will be doing something perfectly intellectual, academic, cognitive, hard, and detached. We will not be giving in to the dreaded disease of "softness." Yet we will still be stepping outside of the mentality of judgment. Most of us have done this if only now and again, perhaps inadvertently. As with loving and liking, these questions don't *force* us out of the mentality of evaluation, but they *invite* us—if we are willing—to take off the lens of judging for a while. We discover it is possible to have long discussions of the meaning and implications of a paper and find we have wholly forgotten about the question of how good it is.

The same goes for other interesting questions we can ask of any text:

- How does the paper relate to other events or values in the culture? How does it relate to what other students are writing—or other texts around us? How does this text relate to other things the student has written?

There are related questions that, interestingly, we can't usually answer without the writer's help:

- How does the paper relate to events in the writer's life? Why did the writer write these words?

Yet these questions are no less intellectual or analytic or interesting. We often ask published writers to answer them. Why not ask our students too?

It's a bit harder to strip away our habits of judgment from some of the most interesting and pointed questions about craft and structure in a paper:

- How is the text organized or put together? How does the text function so as to say what it says and do what it does?

But even these questions *can* be answered in a non-evaluative fashion.

Finally, I would call attention to the most bluntly simple, obvious, and frequently asked question about a text, and insist that it is also, in fact, entirely irrelevant to quality:

- As reader, what are my thoughts on the topic? Where do I agree or disagree?

For even if I disagree completely with everything the paper says, it does not follow that I consider the paper bad. We often disagree with excellent writing. Even more frequently, we agree with terrible writing. It turns out not to be so very hard simply to talk about our agreement or disagreement and to give our thoughts, and not enter at all into the realm of judgment. If I simply *engage* the issue of the paper and tell my thoughts, I need not be playing the quality game.

Many students have never had a teacher take their message seriously enough to engage with it by saying, "Here are *my* thoughts about your issue." For this reason, students will often *infer* value judgments even if we are not making them. But they can gradually catch on to this more frankly intellectual way of talking about texts—and will be grateful to do so. When teachers talk only about how good or bad a paper is or talk only about its strengths and weaknesses, making suggestions for improvement, this can function as a way to *avoid* engagement with the topic or the writer.

None of these analytic, academic questions are inherently evaluative, yet they are much more intellectually interesting than questions about quality. In the end, then, I conclude that the *least* interesting questions we can ask of any text—by students or by published authors—are questions of quality or evaluation. The most intellectually interesting work comes from asking and answering many of our most common analytic and academic questions— questions that invite us (though they do not require us) to step outside the mentality of evaluation.

3. Ways to Use Grades More Effectively

I turn now to the nitty-gritty: grading itself. The essential fact about grades is that they are one-dimensional. Grades are simply numbers and the essence of numbers is very austere: N is wholly defined as "greater than N−1 and less than N+1." B has no other meaning than "worse than A and better than C." Conventional grades demarcate ten or eleven levels of *"pure quality"*—wholly undefined and unarticulated. We can visualize the one-dimensional essence of grading quite literally with a simple vertical line. Such a line is pure verticality; it is entirely lacking in the horizontal dimension.

This pure, numerical, one dimensional verticality—no words or concepts attached—is the main reason why conventional grades are untrustworthy if they are used as descriptors for *complex* human performances—and thus why grading leads to such difficulty and dispute. We see even more unrelenting verticality when faculty members grade essays on a scale of 1 to 100 (which is, amazingly, not so uncommon, for example, in some law schools).

In this section, I am suggesting two ways to deal with this unrelenting verticality: (A) reduce it somewhat by using fewer grades—what I call "minimal grading"; (B) add a bit of the horizontal dimension by using criteria.

(A) Minimal Grading—Reducing the Vertical

We can reduce the verticality of conventional grades by simply using a scale with fewer levels. Most of us use minimal grades when we make low-stakes assignments and grade them pass/fail or else use √ and √+ and √-. But we tend to assume that if an assignment is important and we want students to take it more seriously and work harder on it, we should use conventional grades with their ten or more levels of quality.

But this assumption is misleading and counterproductive. It rests on a failure to distinguish between *stakes* and *levels*. Every act of grading involves two very different questions: "How much credit is at stake in this performance?" "How many levels of quality shall I use on my evaluation scale?" When students take an assignment more seriously and work harder, it usually has little to do with our having added levels to our grading scale, and much more to do with our having raised the stakes and made the assignment *count* for more of the final grade. Few students will struggle hard for an A that doesn't count much for their final grade. (A few students have become obsessive about *any* A; a few others will struggle on a low-stakes assignment—not for the grade but because they are particularly interested in the issue.)

Thus the most reliable way to use grades to make students work harder is to raise the stakes—as long as we make the passing level high enough. Even a two-level scale can be very demanding if we put the bar at a high level. At M.I.T. for the last twenty years or so, faculty have given nothing but Pass and Fail as final grades to all first year students in all courses. The stakes are very high indeed and so are the standards, but only two levels are used. We need only increase the number of levels to three or four if we want to give less-skilled students a goal of "pretty good"—or to spur those students who are hungry to distinguish their work as superior. If we use three levels, we have even more scope for making strategic decisions about where to place the bars.

But there *is* something we reliably achieve by increasing the number of grading levels: we make *our* work harder. Think of the difference between reading a stack of papers in order to give them conventional grades, versus reading them so as only to pick out those that stand out as *notably weak* or *notably strong*.

I'm suggesting, then, that we can get what we need from the grading of important or high-stakes assignments if we use just three (or at most four) levels and make *pass* hard enough to get. Most of our difficulties with grading come from having too many levels—too much verticality:

- The more levels we use, the more untrustworthy and unfair the results. We know what the history of literary criticism has shown (along with informal research by students turning in the same paper to multiple teachers): good readers do not agree in their rankings of quality. Your A paper is liable to become a B in my hands—or vice versa. (Diederich provides the classic research on this matter.)
- The more levels we use, the more chances students have to resent or even dispute those fine-grained distinctions we struggled so hard to make in the first place. (Think of the resentment-laden arguments that occur about a plus or a minus!) Thus the more levels we have, the more we slide toward an adversarial student/teacher relationship and consequently the more damage to the teaching/learning climate. Yes, as long as there are *any* distinctions or levels at all, *some* students will be disappointed or resentful at not getting the higher level they were hoping for. But fewer levels means fewer borderline performances.
- The more levels we use, the more we establish a competitive atmosphere among students and a pecking order culture.
- The more levels we use, the more work for us. It's *hard* making all those fine distinctions—say between A and A minus or B plus and B. If we use just three levels, all we need to do is pick out papers that *stand out* as notably strong and notably weak.

In short, boundary decisions are always the most untrustworthy and arguable. Fewer boundaries mean fewer boundary decisions (see the highly useful pieces by Haswell and Wyche-Smith).

Let me consider some objections to minimal grading.

> But how can we compute a final grade for the semester using eleven levels, if our constituent grades use only three levels?

This is a problem if we only have a couple of constituent grades to work with at the end of the semester, for example, one paper and two exams. But if we have a fair number of papers, exercises, quizzes, or tests on a three-level scale, we can use some mathematical formula to calculate the final grade by simply counting up points (perhaps with different weightings according to how important the assignments are): 3 for a Strong, 2 for Satisfactory, and 1 for Weak. Alternatively, if there are a lot of low-stakes assignments graded Satisfactory/Unsatisfactory, we can decide that students with Satisfactory on all their low-stakes assignments start off with a foundation of B. Then their final grade is pulled up or down by Strongs or Weaks on their high-stakes assignments. Or vice-versa: we can average the high-stakes pieces, and if the result is some kind of "satisfactory" or "2"—let low-stakes pieces decide the gradations between C and B. A multitude of scoring systems are possible—and I haven't even mentioned other factors that most teachers count in their final grading, such as attendance, participation, effort, and improvement.

> We already use minimal grading: most faculty already give nothing but As and Bs.

Yes, many faculty have fallen into this practice. When some faculty members give a full range of grades and others give mostly As and Bs, we have a situation of semantic chaos. The grade of B has become particularly ambiguous: readers of a transcript have no way of knowing whether it denotes good strong competent work (many college catalogues define it as an "honors grade") or disappointing, second-rate work. C might mean genuinely satisfactory work or virtually failing work. Critics of "grade inflation" charge that even "A" has lost its meaning of genuine excellence (though some research undercuts that charge, see U.S. Department of Education). If instead of using symbols like A, B, and C, teachers used meaningful words like "excellent," "honors," "outstanding," "strong," "satisfactory," "weak," "poor," "unsatisfactory," all parties to grading would have a better understanding of the message.

> Some teachers will probably still give mostly Excellent or Strong.

Inevitably so. But the point here is to have teachers take responsibility for signing their names to *words* rather than to completely ambiguous letter grades. And in truth it can happen that most of the performances on an essay or even for the whole course are indeed genuinely excellent or strong, and therefore, we want to sign our name honestly to that assertion. But with conventional grading, when a teacher gives mostly As and B pluses, no one knows whether she is saying, "This was a remarkable outcome" or "I just don't want to make it too hard to get a good grade in my course."

I actually have some hope that we'd see a bit less grade inflation in a three-level scale, where teachers had to use a word like "excellent" or "honors" for the top grade rather than just A- or A. If a program or school really wanted to get rid of too many high grades, they could even insist on a term like "top 10%" or "top quarter" for the top grade.

And surely the *worst* grade inflation is at the bottom, not the top. Most teachers give passing grades and even Cs to performances that they consider completely unsatisfactory. Grades would be much more meaningful if we had to decide between the categories of "satisfactory" vs. "unsatisfactory" or "unacceptable."

> But minimal grading won't solve the problem of meaninglessness. Grades are just as ambiguous if most students get Satisfactory.

Not really. That is, even though minimal grading will probably give most students the grade of Satisfactory, we will have *clearly communicated* to readers, by the fact of our three-level scale and the use of this word "satisfactory," that this single grade *is* being used for a wide range of performances. This result is *not* so ambiguous as with conventional grading, where no one knows whether B is being used for a wide range or a restricted range of performances.

> But you're still evading the main problem of all. Sure, sure, it may be technically "unambiguous" to give most of the class a grade like Satisfactory, but the term still remains empty. It doesn't tell us enough. It's too unsatisfying to leave so many students in one undifferentiated lump.

Yes, "unsatisfying" is exactly the right word here. For it's a crucial fact about minimal grades that they carry *less information*: conventional grades record more distinctions. By sorting students into more groups that are thus more finely differentiated, conventional grades give students a sense of seeing themselves as better and worse in relation to more of their peers. Conventional grades *feel* more precise than minimal grades at the job of telling students exactly how well or how badly they did.

Thus students will tend, at first anyway, to experience minimal grading as *taking something away from them*, and they will be correct—even though what is being taken away from them is bad information. Information itself feels precious; distinctions themselves feel valuable; even spurious precision is missed. When students contemplate moving to minimal grading, they often put out of their minds what most of them actually do know at some level: that this information was bad and this precision was spurious. People are easily seduced into wanting to see themselves sorted into levels—*even* people who have a pretty good idea that they will find the information painful. "Doctor, I need you to tell me if I have cancer." "Teacher/examiner, I need you to tell me *exactly* how bad my paper is." There may be trustworthy precise knowledge about the cancer, but there can be no trustworthy *precise one-dimensional, numerical* knowledge about how bad a paper is. (Consider further that there often is *not* trustworthy knowledge even about the cancer. Thus, if we *really* want accuracy and precision in grading, perhaps we should make grades more analogous to the outcomes of much medical evaluation: "Based on my long training in composition and my extensive experience in teaching writing and my careful examination of your paper, I feel quite confident in saying that there is a 70 percent likelihood that it is a C plus.")

Even if the additional information and precision of conventional grades were entirely trustworthy and accurate, there would still be serious problems. Neither the students nor any other readers of the grades would benefit from the potential information carried by this precision unless they saw all the grades for the whole class. "B minus" means virtually nothing unless we see what grade everyone else got. In addition, that precise, accurate, and trustworthy grade would tell the students nothing at all about *what it is* they did well or badly.

(B) Using Explicit Criteria in Grading—Adding the Horizontal

I turn now to the second suggestion I am making in this essay. When I argued above for minimal grading, I might have seemed to be pleading for less information. No. I was arguing for less *bad* information. If the only grades we can give are purely one-dimensional or vertical, the only honest recourse is to cut back on information and go for minimal grades. But minimal grading is not our only option. My larger purpose is not to reduce information but to increase it. In this section I want to show that when we take away *bad information* from students by moving to minimal grading, we can give them *better information* in return. We can make minimal grades *more* full of meaning than conventional grades if we find a way to tell students what they are actually weak, satisfactory, or excellent *at*. To do so, we need to work out the *criteria* for our minimal grades.

That is, up till now I've been arguing only for less verticality. But using criteria, we can add a crucial *horizontal* dimension to grades. By spelling out the various features of writing that we are looking for when we grade, we are saying that "quality in writing" is not a single, monolithic, one-dimensional entity. And, of course, we are giving more information and meaning to our grades and making them less mysterious.

How do we name criteria? The simplest criteria are the traditional and commonly used pair, *form* and *content*. The distinction is surely useful in grading. Despite some criticism of the distinction as old fashioned or even theoretically suspect, students obviously benefit from knowing our different judgments about these two general areas: ideas-and-thinking versus clarity-organization-mechanics. Almost as commonly used in evaluating is a more elaborated set of criteria with elements like these: *ideas, organization, syntax/wording, mechanics.* Furthermore, many teachers like to specify in their evaluation the intellectual operation that is most central to a particular assignment by using criteria like these: *analysis, details, persuasion, research, documentation.* I have been naming textually oriented criteria. But some teachers use some rhetorically oriented or even process-oriented criteria like these: *connecting with the sub-*

ject, connecting to an audience, voice, substantive revision. The important principle here is that we do well to *name* and *acknowledge* and *communicate* the features of writing that influence our judgments. Since scholars and critics have failed to agree on what "good writing" really is, we get to decide what we are actually looking for and admit it openly to our students.

If we have a large number of papers to grade and we are assigning lots of papers—or if we are teaching a large class that doesn't center on writing and we have little or no help in grading—we probably need to resort to the simplest, least time-consuming way to use criteria: just give one overall grade (or perhaps form/content grades)—yet nevertheless, spell out explicitly for students the other features or characteristics of writing that we are looking for when we grade. Thus we might announce, "In grading this set of papers I will try to count these four criteria equally: . . ." Or "I will grade most on the strength of your argument, but I'll also take some account of these other three criteria: . . ." If our criteria are at all complicated, we can explain and describe them in a handout. And in order to help students do the best job of *meeting* our criteria, we need to announce them when we announce the assignment—before they write—and not wait till afterward when we hand back the graded papers.

The point is that even if we give nothing but a single minimal grade, we can make that grade carry much more information and meaning if we spell out our criteria in public. And using criteria even in this minimal way helps us grade more fairly. For the process of figuring out criteria and announcing them publicly renders us less likely to be unduly swayed if one particular feature of the writing is terrible or wonderful. For example, teachers often get annoyed by papers that are full of grammar and spelling mistakes and non-mainstream dialect, and consequently overlook virtues in information, ideas, or reasoning in such papers—and give them unreasonably low grades. We are less likely to slip into this unfairness if we have specifically announced our criteria.

However, we get the most benefit from criteria if we can actually give a grade on each one. We tell each student how well we think he or she did on each of the features of writing we are looking for. In doing this we are making *multiple vertical judgments* of quality.

But this will make grading too much work!

The principle of minimal grading comes to our rescue here. For just as it isn't so hard to read through a set of papers and merely note the ones that stand out as weak or strong, so it isn't so much harder merely to notice if an essay seems notably weak or notably strong on the criteria we have named as important. We hold each criterion in mind for a moment and see if that feature of the paper stands out for being strong or weak. In my efforts not to make it too onerous to use criteria, I even announce to students that Satisfactory is the "default" grade and so I will make a notation *only* if I find something notably strong or weak. If we use criteria in this more complete fashion, we have a kind of grid, and our "grade" on a paper might look something like this:

WEAK	SATISFACTORY	STRONG	(Note: No check means "satisfactory.")
			Genuine revision, substantive changes, not just editing
		✓	Ideas, insights, thinking
✓			Organization, structure, guiding the reader
			Language, sentences, wording
✓			Mechanics: spelling, grammar, punctuation, proofreading
✓			Overall

This is the form a grid might take when I photocopy a set of blank ones and make check marks. I often write a comment in addition: something more "readerly" and less evaluative—some comment about the responses and reactions I had at various points in reading. I think these discursive comments actually do more good in the long run than quantified evaluations. Indeed, I came to use grids when I gradually realized that my readerly comments were leaving students too dissatisfied, but I didn't want to give a regular grade. Grids were a way to give a bit of quantified evaluation but not on just one dimension.[2]

When I write comments on a computer—as I now prefer to do—I put the grid on a tiny file or even a "macro." Then, when I start to write a comment, I bring in the file or macro. This way I can write in little comments about a criterion. If I were using my computer on the same paper as above, my grid response might look like this:

GENUINE REVISION, SUBSTANTIVE CHANGES, NOT JUST EDITING:

IDEAS, INDIGHTS, THINKING: *Strong. I liked the way you complicated things by exploring points that conflict with your main point.*

ORGANIZATION, STRUCTURE, GUIDING THE READER: *Weak. I kept feeling confused about where you were going—though also sensing that my confusion came from your process of complicating your thinking. This confusion would be good if it weren't a final draft.*

LANGUAGE, SENTENCES, WORDING:

MECHANICS: SPELLING, GRAMMAR, PUNCTUATION, PROOFREADING: *Weak. Because of all the mistakes, this paper doesn't fulfill the contract and is not acceptable. I'll call it acceptable this first time IF you give me a fully cleaned up version by next class.*

OVERALL: *Unsatisfactory for now.*

---

2. Unfortunately, the spatial orientation of my grid works at crosspurposes with my metaphor of vertical and horizontal, but it's easier to represent quality horizontally from left to right if we want to use words to name criteria.

And of course I might write an additional discursive comment at the end.

When we use criteria in this fuller way and make *multiple judgments,* we finally make our grades carry explicit meaning—rather than letting them remain mysterious or magical. And we finally give students some valuable feedback on the particular strengths and weaknesses in their writing—feedback that they don't get from conventional grades. Indeed, mere checkmarks on a grid (perhaps with a few short comments) are sometimes clearer and more useful to students than the longer comments we write in our unrevised prose—especially when it's late at night and we are tired.

Grids are particularly useful for responding to a revised final version when we have already given plenty of feedback to a draft. After all, extended commenting makes more sense at the draft stage: we can give encouragement ("Here's what you need to work on to make it better") instead of just giving an autopsy ("Here's what didn't work"). For the final version, we can read through quickly and then check off criteria on a grid and give no comments at all. We give students better help if we assign papers and give full feedback on drafts and only grid check marks on final versions, than if we assign fewer papers and give full feedback on both drafts and revisions.

Let me explore the interesting issue of figuring out one's criteria. When students ask me, "What are you looking for?" I sometimes feel some annoyance—though I don't think my reaction is quite fair. But I enjoy it when *I* ask the question of myself: "What actually *are* the features in a piece of writing that make me value it?" If I try to answer this question in an insecure, normative way, I tie myself in knots: "What *ought* I to value in student essays?" But we are professionals in our fields and so we get to ask the question in an *empirical* way: "What *do* I value in writing?" For there *is* no Platonic correct answer to the question, "What is good writing?"

This process of empirical self-examination can be intellectually fascinating. We learn to notice more clearly how we read—and this can even lead to some *change* in how we read. For example, some faculty members discover that they are giving more weight than they realized to certain criteria (e.g., to matters of style or correct restatement of textbook and lecture material or correct mechanics)—and this realization leads them to attend more to other criteria. Or they discover that they use different criteria for student writing than for professional writing (e.g., that in student writing they disapprove of the use of first person writing or personal anecdote, but in published professional writing in their field they value it).

The use of criteria has a powerful added benefit because it helps students engage in valid and productive *self-evaluation.* When we ask students to give or suggest a conventional grade for themselves, we are putting them in an unhelpfully difficult spot. There are too many unstated criteria to sum up into one number and it's hard for them not to translate the question into characterological and almost moral terms: "Am I an A person or a B person?" It's much easier and more valid for students to grade themselves with a system of minimal grades and multiple criteria. When they rate themselves as strong, satisfactory, or weak on a wide range of skills or abilities, their answers are more likely to be honest and accurate. I ask such questions at the beginning of the semester ("As we start this course, do you rate yourself Strong, OK, or Weak on the following skills or abilities or areas of knowledge?"). This helps them set goals. I ask the questions again at midsemester. Most important, I ask them at the end ("Do you think your performance has been strong, satisfactory, or weak on these criteria this semester?") Also, I find it very productive to ask students themselves to generate the criteria that they think are important—again at the beginning, middle, and end of the semester.

The Institutional Dimension

In the third and final section of this essay, I've suggested two ways to make grades more trustworthy and meaningful—while still working within a conventional grading system: using minimal grades as a way to reduce the bad information in conventional grades; using multiple explicit criteria as a way to make grades more informative and useful as feedback.

But minimal grades and explicit criteria are not just useful *within* a conventional grading system. They could vastly improve institutional grading itself. At present, a transcript consists of countless single letter grades that no reader can trust since faculty members have such different standards. When a student gets a B, it can mean anything from good honors work to disappointing work. Nor can readers translate those grades into meaningful or useful information. Even when a student gets an A, we don't have any idea what skills or kinds of writing the student is good at—and inevitably, not so good at.

Transcripts would be much more useful if they represented a different deployment of energy and ambition. On the one hand, we should be *less* ambitious and stop pretending that we can reliably sort students into eleven vertical levels of quality—or that the sortings would mean the same thing in different teachers' hands and in different readers' minds. Transcripts would be more honest, accurate, and trustworthy if we settled for recording only three levels, say, *Honors, Satisfactory, Unsatisfactory* (or at most four: *Honors, Strong, Fair, Unsatisfactory*).

But on the other hand, it is feasible to be far *more* ambitious where it counts, and to give grades on *criteria* for each course. Thus, at the end of a course, we would provide the registrar with a small grid of grades for each student. There would be a grade for the student's overall performance—using three or at most four levels. But we would also list the three to six criteria that we think are most important, and for each we would tick off whether we thought this student's work was satisfactory or notably weak or notably strong.

Faculty members need not be forced to use the same criteria. There could be a large list of criteria to choose from: textual criteria like *clarity* and *organization;* process criteria like *generating, revising,* and *working collaboratively;* rhetorical criteria like *awareness of audience* and *voice;* and genre-related criteria like *analysis* and *argument.* Teachers could even create their own criteria. Indeed, there's no reason why teachers should be obliged to use the same criteria for every student in a course. After all, we might want to bring in certain criteria only for certain students (*creative* or *diligent*—or *unable to meet deadlines*) yet not want to speak about these criteria for all students.

This procedure sounds complicated, but given computers, it would not be hard to manage—both for giving course grades and in producing a transcript. (Elementary school report cards have long used this approach; and many high school teachers now have a list of fifty or more criteria they can add electronically to grades on report cards.) Readers of the transcript would finally get useful information about substance and be spared the untrustworthy information about levels of quality.

I have been suggesting a visual metaphor: Minimal grading asks for less of the vertical; using criteria means more of the horizontal. But my suggestions also imply a move away from the tradition of *norm-based* or *measuring* assessment toward the tradition of *criterion-based* or *mastery* assessment. Norm-based or measuring assessment involves making single, complex, all-determining decisions about each student: all are strung out along a single vertical line—each at an exact distance above or below every other student. Criterion-based or mastery assessment, on the other hand, implies multiple simpler decisions about each student: all are placed in a complicated multidimensional space—each student being strong in certain abilities, okay in others, and weak in yet more, with different students having different constellations of strengths and weaknesses. (See D. C. McClelland for the classic formulating essay in the criterion-based tradition. This tradition is also represented in the "New Standards Project," for which see Myers and Pearson.)

In this paper I am trying to get outside the either/or debates around grading. We can look for ways to step temporarily outside of grading and even of the mentality of evaluations; and we can look for better *ways* to grade and not grade. We can make small pragmatic improvements, but also push for large utopian change. The human impulse to judge or evaluate is inevitable and useful, but we also need to find ways to bypass that impulse. It won't be so hard, really, to have assessments that lead to a healthier climate for teach-ing and learning, and that give us a more accurate picture of student achievement.

Appendix: Examples of Examples of Grading Contracts

[*The terms of these contracts change from semester to semester as I constantly fiddle—often in cooperation with colleagues.*]

Example of a Contract for a Grade of B

Dear students in my first year writing course,

Imagine that this weren't an official course for credit at UMass, but instead that you had all seen my advertisement in the paper and were freely coming to my home-studio for a class in painting or cooking or computers (and paying me). We would have classes or workshops or lessons, but there would be no official grading. Of course, I'd give you evaluative feedback now and then (or often—depending on my style), pointing out the good things you do and pointing out places where something doesn't work or where you don't seem to be getting it. And I'd give suggestions for improving your work. But I wouldn't put grades on your individual paintings or give you an official grade for the course.

Notice how different that evaluative situation would be from what we have in this course—where many of you are *not* here by choice and I am obliged to give an official University grade. Surely that home-studio situation is more conducive to learning.

My goal in this course, then, will be to *approximate* the evaluative conditions of a home-studio course. (Ask me later about the fee schedule!) That is, I will try to create a *culture of support:* a culture where you and I function as allies rather than adversaries and where you cooperate with classmates rather than compete with them. Conventional grading can lead you to think more about grades than about writing; to worry more about pleasing me or psyching me out than about figuring out what you really want to say or how you want to say it; to be reluctant to take risks with your writing; sometimes even to feel you are working *against* me or having to hide part of yourself from me. I taught for nine years at Evergreen State College where no grades were given—just written evaluations. The system worked fine and was a benefit for both teaching and learning.

Therefore, I am using a kind of contract grading system in this course. I will give you feedback on much of your writing. Sometimes my comments will be nonevaluative; sometimes they will be frankly evaluative—telling you what I think works well and not so well. But I will not put grades on your papers and these evaluative comments of mine will have no effect on your final grade for the course—up to the grade of B. For the policy on higher grades, see below.

You are guaranteed a B for the final grade if you meet the following conditions:

1. Don't miss more than one week's worth of classes.
2. Don't be habitually late. (If you are late or miss a class, you are responsible for finding out any assignments that were made.)
3. Don't have more than one late major assignment and one late smaller assignment.
4. Keep up your journal assignments.
5. Work cooperatively in groups. Be willing to share some of your writing, listen supportively to the writing of others and, when they want it, give full and thoughtful responses.
6. Major assignments need to meet the following conditions:
   - Include a process letter, all previous notes and drafts, and all feedback you have received.

- *Revisions.* When the assignment is to revise, make it more than just a correcting or fixing. Your revision needs to reshape or extend or complicate or substantially clarify your ideas—or relate your ideas to new things. Revisions don't have to be better but they must be different—not just touched up but changed in some genuine way.
- *Mechanics, copy-editing.* When the assignment is for a *final draft,* it must be well copy-edited—that is, free from virtually all mistakes in spelling and grammar. It's fine to get help in copy-editing. I don't ask for careful copy-editing on early and midprocess drafts, but it's crucial for final drafts.
- *Effort.* Your papers need to show solid effort. This doesn't mean that you have to suffer; it's fine to have fun and even fool around with assignments. It just means that I need to see solid work.
- *Perplexity.* For every paper, you need to find some genuine question or perplexity. That is, don't just tell four obvious reasons why dishonesty is bad or why democracy is good. Root your paper in a felt *question* about honesty or democracy—a problem or an itch that itches *you.* (By the way, this is a crucial skill to learn for success in college: how to *find* a question that interests you—even in a boring assignment.)
- *Thinking.* Having found a perplexity, then use your paper to do some *figuring out.* Make some intellectual gears turn. Thus your paper needs to *move* or *go somewhere*—needs to have a line of thinking.
- Please don't panic because of these last three conditions. I recognize that if you emphasize effort, perplexity, and thinking, you will have a harder time making your papers intellectually tidy and structurally well organized. It's okay if your essays have some loose ends, some signs of struggle—especially in early drafts. But this lack of unity or neatness needs to be a sign of *effort,* not lack of effort.

Your final grade will fall rapidly below a B if you don't meet these conditions.

About Getting an A/B or A

My feedback on your papers will often talk about issues of quality, but in order to get a grade of B, you don't have to worry about or agree with my judgments at all. You can go entirely against any advice or judgment that I give—as long as you *do the activities* required by the terms of the contract.

But for grades of A/B and A, my judgments of quality come into play. That is, you can earn a grade of B on the basis of behaviors; but you can't earn a higher grade except on the basis of *quality of writing.* For an A/B or an A, you need to have a midsemester portfolio and a final portfolio that contain mostly excellent writing. But also, over the course of the semester, I will tell you if I consider your individual drafts and revisions to be excellent. We'll talk in class about criteria for excellent drafts and excellent final papers.

Final Thoughts

I hope you like this system. It will let you experiment and take chances in your writing and you can't lose (as long as you don't cop out). I will give you honest feedback and tell you where your writing seems strong or weak or doesn't work for me, but that will be feedback, not grading—up to the level of B. You can experience me as a coach and ally rather than someone to psych out or con, because my criticism will not count against you. You can learn and benefit from any criticism I give you without feeling threatened by it.

But you don't have to like the system. Some students don't. You will probably have to work harder for a B here than in certain other courses—where if you are good at the subject you can just skip class, browse the textbook, and then show up for the exams. But I'm not asking for any more work here than I asked for when I graded in the regular way—and no more work than other ENG 112 and 113 teachers ask for. We in the Writing Program see no reason why this course should be less demanding than, say, math or physics. After all writing is probably more important in its payoff than math or physics, since writing has been shown to be the major ability that correlates with success in college. In other words, even though I'm hoping this will be a "nice" system for you, I'm not pretending to wield less power or authority than if I graded in a conventional way. My goal is to use and focus my authority in a more productive way.

You will probably understand me and my teaching better if I spell out my ultimate goals as a teacher. I'm trying to provide a foundation of support and safety so you can

- put in a lot of work but not have to worry about the grade or about pleasing me—so you can explore and develop your *own* judgment and standards;
- explore and develop your ability to motivate yourself;
- learn to *like* writing and learn to use it as part of your lives—not just for academic duties;
- learn to use writing to help you with hard thinking—stretch your minds, wonder and question, and try to figure things out.

Sincerely yours,

Example of a Contract for the Grade of A

[*This contract simply builds on the contract for a B. But instead of the final section about high grades, I substitute the following:*]

You are guaranteed an A if you do the following things:

1. Fulfill the contract for a B.
2. In your process writing for the final draft of each paper, show
   (a) a good picture of the structure or organization of your paper;

(b) show how your paper pursued a line of inquiry and thinking—didn't just describe a static opinion.

3. At some point, during each major writing assignment, get an additional person's feedback on your midprocess or final draft (additional to what I set up as part of the regular class procedure). For this extra response, you can use someone in this class or outside. On one occasion before midsemester, make this a "skeleton feedback," and on another occasion, a "descriptive outline" (I'll have a handout describing these). The rest of the time you can get whatever kind of feedback you find most helpful, as long as it is thoughtful and substantive, not perfunctory. Please show me this feedback in writing: a good page long, at least—though informal is fine. (It's okay a couple of times to get oral feedback and write up a summary for me.)

4. At some point during each major assignment, *give* extra feedback to someone else—someone in this class or not. (Same guidelines or conditions as in no. 3.)

5. At some point around the middle of the semester, take a paper you've already written for this course or for another course and make a major, substantive revision of it. Include with this paper a write up of substantive feedback you've gotten from someone else and a descriptive outline of the revised version. Also, some process writing about the changes you've made.

6. Make a good effort to get something published. Send out something in good shape to a suitable place. Possibilities: a letter, essay, or feature story to a local paper or campus paper; an essay, story, or poem to a magazine or journal.

7. Make some genuine efforts to help others learn and to help the class go better. Possibilities: help bring out the thinking of others, especially people who are not being heard; listen well to others; set an example of being open and honest in class—without hogging the floor; help your peer group work better. Drop me an informal note at midsemester and at the end, explaining or exploring ways you have tried to fulfill this admittedly fuzzy condition.

[*I end with the "Final Thoughts" paragraphs of pep talk and exhortation as in the contract for a grade of B.*]

Works Cited

Belanoff, Pat, Peter Elbow, and Sheryl Fontaine. *Nothing Begins with N: New Investigations of Freewriting*. Carbondale: Southern Illinois UP, 1991.

Diederich, Paul. *Measuring Growth in English*. Urbana, IL: NCTE, 1974.

Elbow, Peter. "Ranking, Evaluating, Liking: Sorting Out Three Forms of Judgment." *College English* 55.2 (February 1993): 187–206.

Haswell, Richard and Susan Wyche-Smith. "Adventuring into Writing Assessment." *CCC* 45.2 (May 1994): 220–36.

————. "A Two-Tier Rating Procedure for Placement Essays: Washington State University." *Assessment in Practice: Putting Principles to Work on College Campuses*. San Francisco: Jossey-Bass, 1996. 204–07.

Lakoff, George and Mark Johnson. *Metaphors We Live By*. Chicago: U of Chicago P, 1980.

McClelland, D. C. "Testing for Competence Rather than for Intelligence." *American Psychologist* 28 (1973): 1–14.

Myers, Miles and P. David Pearson. "Performance Assessment and the Literacy Unit of the New Standards Project." *Assessing Writing* 3.1 (1996): 5–29.

U.S. Department of Education. *The New College Course Map and Transcript Files: Changes in Course-Taking and Achievement, 1972–1993*. Washington, DC: Office of Educational Research and Improvement, 1996.

20

Starting the Portfolio Experiment at SUNY Stony Brook

Written with Pat Belanoff

We seek here to give an accurate and practical description of a portfolio-based evaluation system we have just instituted. But we can be more accurate and practical if we avoid giving a static picture and instead suggest the inevitable historical flux: the experiments that preceded this system and the countless opportunities for modification in the future.

An Instructive History of Writing Evaluation

In the early years of the university (less than thirty years ago) the writing requirement at Stony Brook was a two-semester freshman course taught almost entirely by faculty members in the English department. Then, in the late 1960s, the requirement was reduced to a one-semester course. With the rapid expansion of the university—and one thing and another—that course began to be taught largely by graduate students. Before long, the limit of twenty students per section in writing courses was raised to twenty-five. All the while, writing skills of entering freshmen were probably declining.

Though portfolios have probably been used as long as teachers have taught, the essay printed here has often been credited with initiating widespread experimentation with *program-wide* assessment with portfolios involving *collaborative-grading*. However, I've recently discovered a 1971 article describing the use in a small religious college in Hawaii of exactly the same *kind* of portfolio assessment system—though the spirit behind that earlier system was rather forbidding. (See Charles J. Fox and Robert Tippets, "A Portfolio Program for Teaching English Composition." *TESL REPORTER* 4.3. English Language Institute, Church College of Hawaii: 1–2.) Pat Belanoff's and my essay was originally published in *New Methods in College Writing Programs: Theory into Practice*. Eds. Paul Connolly and Teresa Vilardi. NY: MLA, 1986. It was reprinted in *Portfolio Grading: Process and Product*. Pat Belanoff and Marcia Dickson, eds. *Portfolio Grading: Process and Product*. Portsmouth NH: Boynton/Cook, 1991.

Throughout this period, the crucial evaluative decision about proficiency in writing was in the hands of individual teachers—first faculty members, then TAs. It was assumed that teachers would not pass students who were not proficient—who could not write well enough for college work or well enough for other university writing assignments.

In the mid-70s, faculty members from around the university began to complain that students came to them who had passed the required writing course but who nevertheless were unable to write acceptably. In response to this problem, the University Senate put in place a proficiency exam in 1977. Passing the course no longer satisfied the writing requirement; the requirement was to pass the exam. With this change, the crucial decision about proficiency in writing was taken out of the hand of the individual teacher and given to examiners who did not know the student.

The goal of the proficiency exam was not just to reduce inconsistency in grading but in particular to keep up standards—or even push them up. Proficiency exams are inevitably attempts at quality control aimed not just at students but also at teachers. The Stony Brook exam, still a requirement for juniors and seniors who entered the university under that legislation, gives students two hours to write a persuasive or argumentative exam from a choice of three questions.

Though the exam was instituted as a move toward increased rigor, the legislation allowed students who passed it on entrance (it was given as a placement instrument) to be exempted from taking any writing course. Thus ironically, over the years (because of various factors, some of them economic), the exam ended up serving to exempt more and more students from any instruction at all in writing.

Standing back and looking at this story, we are struck with the idea that perhaps there would never have been a need for this added assessment (a procedure in addition to individual teachers giving grades), if the university had still provided two semesters of instruction—particularly if they were taught by faculty members. Might this be true generally? That we get more evaluation of writing as we get less instruction?

Problems with Proficiency Exams

As so many schools are discovering, proficiency exams have problems. First of all, there is serious doubt as to whether they do the very thing they are supposed to do, that is, accurately measure proficiency in writing. The research movement that gives high marks to holistic scoring for validity (but see Charney) also shows that no matter how accurately we may evaluate any sample of a student's writing, we lose all that accuracy if we go on to infer the student's actual proficiency in writing from just that single sample. We cannot get a trustworthy picture of a student's writing proficiency unless we look at several samples produced on several days in several modes or genres. That is, not only may students not perform up to capacity on any one occasion, there is no one generic thing we can call "writing" (see Cooper). Besides, faculty members continue to complain about the lack of skill in students who pass the exam.

And even if proficiency exams gave a perfectly accurate measure of writing proficiency, they seriously undermine, by their nature, our teaching of writing and send a damaging message about the writing process. A proficiency test tells students that they can do their best writing (demonstrate their proficiency) with fifteen minutes of thought on some issue just sprung on them, followed by writing, followed (sometimes) by some cosmetic revising and copyediting. No drafts, no discussion of the issue with others, no trying out drafts on readers, no getting responses. Surely few of us ever write anything that matters to us in this fashion. But students who pass are encouraged to believe that they can write anything this way, and students who fail are encouraged to believe this is the process they need to learn.

In addition, when a proficiency exam embodies a university requirement, the whole university can be seen as saying to students, "Here's a serious matter (single-parent families, care of the elderly, the relation of books to the real world). Tell us what you think about it in approximately five hundred words; we know you can give it the attention it deserves; and then you can go home." The writing is unconnected to the study of any material and cut off from connection with any ongoing conversation. Is that how we want students to approach serious intellectual issues?

In short, our experience as teachers and our knowledge of recent research in the field made us uncomfortable with the proficiency exam we found in place here. We also began to notice at conferences that others, too, often introduced accounts of their proficiency exams with a disclaimer and some slight gesture of embarrassment.

Thus we began to experiment with portfolios to evaluate writing—portfolios prepared in a writing class but read by outside readers. We were looking for a kind of quality control—not only to avoid inconsistency but to hold up standards (for we do not disagree with this goal behind proficiency exams)— yet also for a way to avoid the problems of proficiency exams. For four semesters we experimented with a relatively small number of sections. In the fall of 1984, along with a new university writing requirement we'd been working for, we made portfolios an official procedure in all sections of EGC 101. The new requirement says that every student must get a C or higher in 101 or else take it again. The portfolio system says that no students can get a C unless their portfolios have been judged worth a C not only by their teacher but also by at least one other teacher who does not know them.

Brief Overview of the Portfolio System

Our handout for all students in 101 is useful here for an overview:

> The portfolio system gives you a chance to satisfy the University writing requirement on the basis of your best writing, writing you have had a

chance to think about and revise, and it helps us increase consistency in grading.

At the end of the semester you will submit a portfolio of writing from the course: three revised pieces and one in-class piece. These will be judged by examiners who don't know you: 101 teachers other than your own. In order to get a C or higher in the course, your portfolio must pass. You must repeat the course if you do not get a C or higher. (Note that you are not *guaranteed* a C if your portfolio passes; your grade may be pulled down by other factors such as missing classes, or missing deadlines, or consistently unsatisfactory work on assignments.)

At midsemester you get a chance for a trial dry run on one paper. If it passes, that counts: include it in your final portfolio as it stands (though you may revise if you wish). If it fails, you can revise it and resubmit it in the final portfolio.

Each paper must have an informal but typed introductory cover sheet that explains what you were trying to accomplish and describes some of your writing process, for example, what feedback you got and what changes you made in revising.

Portfolios will fail if they contain more than a very few mistakes in grammar, punctuation, spelling, or typing. You will also fail if you have more than a few sentences that are so tangled that the meaning is unclear to a general reader on first reading. This level of correctness and clarity may be harder for some of you to achieve than for others—especially those of you who come to English as a second language. But we insist on it because you all *can* achieve it: you all have a chance for feedback and careful revising.

The examiners must be confident that the work you submit is really yours. This is why we ask for an in-class piece of writing on which you've had no help. Instructors will not forward portfolios to the examiners unless they are confident it is *your* work—and thus will insist on seeing lots of your in-class writing and also insist on seeing the successive drafts of all your writing. They won't accept new pieces on new topics at the last moment that you haven't worked on earlier as part of the course.

The Three Revised Pieces

1. A narrative, descriptive, expressive piece, or an informal essay. The emphasis is on writing from your own experience. (Fiction is fine, not poetry.)

2. An academic essay of *any* sort—except for one restriction: the essay must be organized around a main point, not just organized as a narrative or description or a rendering of experience. Thus, for piece no. 1, you could write an informal essay that just tells a story with a "moral" added at the end—or just describes a scene with a brief conclusion at the end. Such essays can be excellent writing, but for category no. 2 we are insisting on a different kind of essay—one that most university professors require when they assign writing in a subject matter course: an essay organized in terms of an idea (such as a claim you are arguing for) or an intellectual task (such as comparing, contrasting, defining, or analyzing).

3. An academic essay which analyzes another essay; that tells *what it is saying* and *how it functions* or *how effectively it says it*. You might analyze a newspaper editorial, a published essay, an essay written by someone in your small group, or you might even analyze one of your own essays. This is practice in close reading and in being able to explain how prose works on readers.

Modes of Writing

We've continually adjusted and tinkered with the kinds of writing we ask for, trying to embody the commitments we stand for as a program, yet trying not to hem in teachers too much.

Modes 2 and 3 above obviously represent our commitment to academic discourse, to the kinds of writing that other faculty members will assign. Indeed, we suggest that teachers might want a paper that students could use in another course for mode 2.

Mode 1 represents our strong commitment to imaginative or expressive writing—writing that tries to render or communicate one's own experience rather than explain or analyze it. We feel this mode of writing is currently under attack as inappropriate at the university level. But as Britton shows, expressive writing is the matrix from which skill in other modes derives; English departments are committed to the *study* of imaginative writing as perhaps the best expression of the human spirit; and personal or creative writing is the only mode through which most students can become sufficiently excited with writing to keep it up when not obliged to write—which is the only way they'll ever become genuinely skilled. If we don't give students practice in this kind of writing, no one else in the university will.

We've had some misunderstandings about the distinction between the kind of informal essay acceptable for mode 1 and the more formal one required for modes 2 and 3: teachers occasionally tell students that an essay fits the latter categories when portfolio examiners feel it does not. We've been reluctant to emphasize words like *formal* and *academic* because of what they often do to student prose. Probably we should talk more about audience and the discourse of various communities.

Some teachers like to use category 1 for the midsemester dry run: they want to start with what is easier and more fun and build up to what is harder. Other teachers use category 2 or 3 for the dry run in order to get an early start on what usually needs more work and to prevent overconfidence about midsemester results. Out of this dilemma rise some current experiments in using more than one dry run piece.

We decided not to evaluate the cover sheets: they must be there but students are not penalized if they are done poorly. We made this decision because we are committed to the usefulness of the process writing or "metawriting" called for by cover sheets, yet we don't want to emphasize it too much for students or teachers who hate it. Also we want to reduce as much as possible what readers have to evaluate. Cover sheets are more for students and teachers than for outside readers—though when the writing is borderline they can help readers decide.

Similarly, poor in-class writing does not count against a student (though we don't much talk about that to students). It represents a symbolic guard against plagiarism. Our main guard is that the individual teachers should not forward portfolios they do not trust were written by the student him- or herself. Again we let the in-class writing count favorably in borderline cases. This decision represents our desire not to penalize students for writing they've not had a chance to revise (though some would say that our view does not pay enough heed to "exam writing" as an important mode that students need practice in).

The Evaluation Process

At midsemester teachers meet to discuss sample papers and agree on some verdicts—a "calibration" session. Then teachers distribute their students' actual midsemester dry run papers to each other for a reading. The judgment is a simple binary Yes or No, Pass or Fail, worth a C or not. No comments or marks are made on the papers (except to circle unambiguous mistakes in mechanics—especially if a paper fails for that reason). A brief comment is paperclipped to failing papers—usually only a few sentences. (It is not the job of readers to diagnose or teach—only to judge. It is the teacher's job to interpret these comments to the student when necessary.)

If the teacher agrees with the verdict, the process is finished—and this is the case with most papers. But a teacher who disagrees can ask for a second reading from another reader. If that second reading is the same, the teacher can either go along with the two readers or else seek a third reading to validate his or her perception. However, the stakes are not high at midsemester. A failure doesn't count against anyone, as this is a time for teachers and students to get used to the process; in fact, teachers tend to prefer stern verdicts at midsemester to make sure students are not lulled into false security.

At the end of the semester the evaluation process is repeated but with full portfolios: the calibration meeting with sample portfolios; first, second, and occasionally third readings; comments only on failed portfolios. Again judgments are binary, and we treat portfolios more or less as a whole instead of making separate verdicts on each paper. (We say that a portfolio shouldn't pass if one paper is definitively weak, even if the others are very strong, but we purposely leave this matter somewhat inexplicit, believing that there needs to be room for judgment here.) But this time the gun is loaded: a student whose portfolio fails must repeat the course. Nevertheless, if the two concurring readers agree that the portfolio warrants it, the student may revise that paper and resubmit the portfolio. We treat the inevitable appeals to our office from students the way we treat appeals about grades. That is, we consent to hear stories or read papers when it seems important, for we feel we must be as loyal to students as to teachers. On those occasions when we see something genuinely out of line (rather than just a reasonable verdict that we might have called differently), we go back to the teacher or reader or group and ask them to look again—perhaps saying nothing more, perhaps telling our sense of the difficulty.

Note that though there is a lot of machinery, we try hard to keep it as quick and simple as possible. Because judgments are only Yes or No (instead of 1 through 4 or 6 as with most holistic scoring), because we read portfolios as a whole giving only one verdict, and because there are no comments except brief ones on failing portfolios, readings are surprisingly fast. Many strong portfolios can be read very quickly—some of the papers even skimmed.

An Emphasis on Small Collaborative Groups of Teachers

Small groups of teachers are presently the main vehicle for the functioning of the portfolio system. We invite teachers to form into their own groups of four or five according to friendship or interest (and we group those who prefer random groupings). These groups meet to read papers from each others' classes at midsemester and portfolios at the end of the semester. They decide on their own specific deadlines and on which of the three kinds of paper should come in at midsemester (or decide to disagree—allowing a mixed bag of genres). Some groups decide to require a second dry run paper three-quarters through the semester—or to ask for two papers at a slightly late midsemester date (in an effort to give students more sense of how they are doing).

A few teachers have complained that we give too much autonomy to the small groups—in particular that the crucial evaluative decision is too exclusively rooted in the small face-to-face group. They would prefer more work in larger groups (as, for example, when Elbow treats the Teaching Practicum as one large portfolio group for the fifteen or so new TAs each fall who are teaching in the program for the first time). This complaint stems from a justifiable nervousness that different groups will evolve different standards (and a couple of groups have gotten the reputation among teachers of being "harder" or "easier"). More pointedly, there is the fear that standards will be compromised because readers in a small group will often know who the teacher is for a particular paper and therefore may feel pressured to pass it if they know the teacher wants it passed—because the teacher is their friend or is particularly defensive or edgy. (We both know from experience with the system that it hurts when your own student's portfolio is failed and you think it deserves to pass: you are deeply involved with this student and gratified by his or her enormous progress.)

These are serious worries raised by conscientious teachers, and we feel them ourselves—though the majority prefers the emphasis on small groups. (In fact, we suggested having a larger group this last time and only five volunteered.) Did we start off giving too much autonomy to small groups because of our strong predilection for giving teachers their head and because of Stony Brook's strong tradition of total teacher autonomy? Perhaps. Anyway, we've made three policy changes this year that provide somewhat greater commonality or corporate functioning to the portfolio system:

1. We now have large meetings in the middle and at the end of the semester to read sample papers or portfolios. All teachers must attend. We agree on, or negotiate verdicts for, sample papers or portfolios. The change helps keep standards more consistent since formerly we left this calibrating function to individual groups.[1]

2. We are now instituting a programwide response sheet to attach to all failing dry run papers and all failing portfolios. These forms will present, as it were, a common voice of the program to augment the more local voice of the reader or small group and will have checkable boxes that represent programwide categories as to weaknesses in portfolio papers—though of course individual readers will also write a short comment in a space provided. (We have seen occasional comments that were *too* cryptic or idiosyncratic.)

3. Portfolios may now be revised if they fail with only one weak paper. The old policy increased pressure on readers not to fail an unsatisfactory portfolio if it somehow seemed clear from internal evidence or from special pleading from the teacher that the student was really quite skilled and diligent and should not have to repeat the course. Our new policy makes it easier to stick by tough standards—to say, "This isn't good enough"—but still give students a chance to redeem themselves. (This rewrite policy represents a compromise between those who wanted to allow *all* failing portfolios to be revised and those who wanted to stick with our original no-rewrite policy.)

In effect, these additions of programwide consistency are designed to save our emphasis on small collaborative groups for evaluating writing proficiency. Perhaps in the end we will conclude we should jettison that emphasis altogether and use an evaluative mechanism that is more "pure" or ETS-like—less messy. But we would find that sad.

For one thing, we want these small groups to have a prominent place in our program so they can function in other ways too—not just for portfolio business. We encourage groups to form around an interest in a particular technique or approach to teaching, even to do a bit of research. We think teachers

---

1. Within a year or two of writing this article, we made what I feel is a crucial change in this process. We stopped trying for agreement on a single verdict. Instead, we chose borderline examples and asked the group first for as many reasons as possible for passing it, and then for as many reasons as possible for failing; we explicitly asked everyone to play the believing and doubting games with the portfolio—trying to see the writing through different lenses. Then we took a straw vote. We made this change because we noticed that the pressure for agreement on an official verdict tended to make people dig in their heels more and sometimes even to degrade the nature of the discourse. We realized that absolute agreement was impossible, and that our real goal was to create a cohesive evaluative community and that the best way to get there was to create a nonadversarial process where members of the community were helped to see how various members of the community read and judged portfolios—and helped to try to see portfolios through the eyes of others. See our later essay, "Using Portfolios to Increase Collaboration and Community in a Writing Program" in *WPA: Writing Program Administration* 9.3 (Spring 1986), particularly pages 31 and 32.

need small groups to discuss other teaching matters and for just plain gossip and support. Most teachers like them.

As for impurity in evaluation, we could take a kind of amateur "aw shucks" line and say that we don't need perfect evaluation; we care more about teaching than about evaluation; we're satisfied that this evaluation is much more consistent than the grading of individual teachers and so we don't worry that it is less consistent than some God- or machinelike objectivity. But our reading and talking with others in the field of evaluation and our experiments over more than three years tempt us to take a more uppity line. We suspect that this "impure" process may in the end represent better evaluation.

That is, on the one hand, we obviously seek a kind of objectivity and quality control—we seek an evaluation process that involves outside readers with negotiated common standards. But on the other hand, because of our lively sense of the imperfections in the science of evaluating writing proficiency, we seek frankly *not* to seal off entirely the possibility of "leaks" or "pollution" into the evaluative procedure from the teacher who knows the student.

Yes, the whole portfolio system makes for messes—since it puts "objective" examiners in the same room with the student's own teacher and gets them tangled up in discussions of specific papers where the teacher may be personally involved. The system thus makes trouble. (Though in fact we've had little rancor.) But this is nothing but the trouble that results from putting out on the table what has always been in the closet in programs that evaluate with proficiency exams or leave evaluation wholly in the hands of the individual teacher. It helps to have some of these messy discussions in large meetings led by the directors of the program, but there is something to be said for letting some of them also go on in more private small groups, where of course there is some impure negotiating. We think this allows for more growth in teaching in the long run.

A Different Model of Evaluation

About half the midsemester papers fail. At the end of the semester about 10 percent of the portfolios fail, but that goes down to about 5 percent after some are rewritten. (The number of students who must retake the course is slightly higher because a certain number of them fade away toward the end of the semester and don't complete the course—or fail for other reasons.)

We see the portfolio as a way to ask for better writing and to get more students to give it to us. By giving students a chance to be examined on their best writing—by giving them an opportunity for more help—we are also able to demand better writing. For example, in our first semester of small-scale experimenting, we discovered that when we only explained the system to students and waited till the end of the semester to evaluate (no dry run), many of them failed who obviously didn't need to fail. They hadn't put in enough time or care because they clearly hadn't understood or believed that we were requiring good writing to pass—better writing than writing exams tend to ask for, perhaps better writing than their teachers had required for a C. (We noticed an interesting difference between the experience of reading a failing proficiency exam and a failing portfolio: the failing proficiency exam tends to make us sad that perhaps the student "couldn't do it"; the failing portfolio tends to make us mad that the student didn't put in enough time and care.)

This sounds like raising standards and raising the passing rate at the same time. Something fishy here. But evaluation by portfolio sets aside the traditional model of evaluation or measurement (norm-referenced) that leads us to assume that grades should ideally end up distributed along a bell curve. This traditional model of measurement aims to rank or differentiate students into as many different grades as possible, for it is a tradition of "measuring" minds; the ideal end product is a population distributed along a bell-shaped curve (as in IQ scores or SAT scores). Our portfolio process, on the other hand, builds on a different model of evaluation or measurement (criterion-referenced or mastery-based or competence-based evaluation). This more recent tradition assumes that the ideal end product is a population of students who have all finally passed because they have all been given enough time and help to do what we ask of them. (See McClelland on competence testing; also Grant et al.; also Elbow on the effects of a competence approach on teachers.)

Problems

We keep hoping that all problems can be tinkered away through further adjustments but no doubt many are inherent in the approach.

- The system makes more work for teachers. We have done all we can to keep readings from being too onerous or time-consuming: judgments are only yes/no, portfolios are judged as a single unit, cover sheets and in-class writing need not be read (usually), and comments are given only to failing portfolios—and then only brief ones. But the work remains.
- It puts more pressure on teachers and makes some feel anxious—especially those using it for the first time. If your student fails a proficiency exam, it's easy to say, "Well, I'm not teaching exam writing," but if your student fails the portfolio you are liable to feel—at first anyway—as though *you* have failed.
- Some teachers feel it dominates the course too much: as though they are having to "teach to the portfolio," as though it is too much in their minds and their students' minds, as though they are reduced to spending the whole semester on three main pieces and therefore narrowing their focus. We try to avoid this, we want an evaluation system that one can "teach to" without having to change or "pollute" one's teaching at all, a system that lets you teach almost any course. This feeling of constraint is felt most by teachers the first time they use the system, but it is also felt by a few very experienced and competent teachers.

- Some teachers feel that our reliance on groups puts strains on their relations with other teachers in the group when they disagree over verdicts.
- Some teachers feel that the emphasis on revising—and especially the opportunity to revise some failed portfolios—babies or coddles students too much and lets lazy students get by with help and nagging from teachers and help from peers.

Strengths

But the program continues to present more advantages than problems:

- The portfolio process judges student writing in ways that better reflect the complexities of the writing process: with time for freewriting, planning, discussion with instructors and peers, revising, and copy-editing. It lets students put these activities together in a way most productive for them. And it doesn't insist that students be judged on all their efforts.
- The message to students is that thinking and writing are enhanced by conversation with peers and teachers—and that first responses, although valid, need not be final ones. It also tells them that their reactions and opinions about serious matters deserve time and attention.
- It makes teachers allies of their students—allies who work with them to help them pass. Teachers become more like the coach of the team than the umpire who enforces and punishes infractions. One teacher commented, "They don't blame me for the standard they've been asked to reach. I think because of this I have a very good relationship with my students and I'm more comfortable in the role of helper than that of judge" (see Elbow, "Embracing Contraries").
- It draws teachers together, encourages discussion about ways to help students and about standards. Inevitably, this makes standards more consistent and teachers more conscious of their teaching methods.
- It emphasizes some important complexities of audience—showing students, for example, that we usually write for more than one reader and often for readers who do not know us. Many students come to college convinced that English teachers are hopelessly idiosyncratic and rarely agree—that one teacher's rules and expectations rarely match another's. We want students to realize that teachers can agree on evaluations even if their criteria may be somewhat different. We all write for audiences of individuals who agree on some things and disagree on others—"interpretive communities." Both students and teachers need more experience and talk about this crucial issue.
- Thus the portfolio addresses a critical, profession-wide problem in evaluation that most teaching sweeps under the rug. That is, to grade a paper is to interpret and evaluate a text, yet our profession now lacks (if it ever possessed) a firm theoretical discipline-wide basis for adjudicating between different interpretations or evaluations of a text. No wonder we are uneasy in

our grading. In this situation, the only source of at least some trustworthiness in grading comes from the kind of negotiation in a community that the portfolio procedure sets up. Such negotiation of a text helps teachers make connections between the teaching of writing and the study of literature.

Experiments with the Placement Exam

It was interesting for us, without special training in evaluation and testing, to find a proficiency exam in place, to go to meetings of the National Network on Testing and read its newsletter (and other material on testing), and gradually to conclude that no one really had the answer about the evaluation of writing. This realization was empowering and gave us courage to experiment.

Having done so with the portfolio and lived to tell the tale (so far, anyway), we are now experimenting with the placement exam that all students take on entrance to the university. Instead of giving students two hours for one essay as we have done in the past, we are now asking for four writing tasks: (1) twenty minutes of exploratory writing or freewriting about an extended quotation; (2) a one-sentence summary of the quotation; (3) a one-hour essay on the topic of the quotation; (4) twenty minutes of informal, retrospective process writing about the writing the student has already done on the exam.

We find this approach serves the two goals of testing that we're also trying to serve with the portfolio process. First, it improves trustworthiness of evaluation, since the readers can base their judgment on more than one piece in more than one mode. Second, it sends the message we want to send to students about the richness and multiplicity of writing as a process.

In the end, we see the portfolio system as a way to try to serve two contrary but desirable goals. On the one hand, we want some programwide commonality, not only in the evaluation of proficiency but also in getting teachers to work together under some common guidelines. On the other hand, we want to provide as much autonomy as possible to individual teachers and small groups of teachers.

Works Cited

Britton, James et al. *The Development of Writing Abilities (11–18)*. Urbana IL: NCTE, 1975.
Charney, Davida. "The Validity of Using Holistic Scoring to Evaluate Writing: A Critical Overview." *Research in the Teaching of English* 18 (February 1984): 65–81.
Cooper, Charles R. *The Nature and Measurement of Competency in English*. Urbana IL: NCTE, 1981.
Elbow, Peter. "Trying to Teach While Thinking About the End: Teaching in a Competence-Based Curriculum." *On Competence: A Critical Analysis of Competence-Based Reforms in Higher Education*. San Francisco: Jossey-Bass, 1979. 95–137. Reprinted in *Embracing Contraries: Explorations in Learning and Teaching*. NY: Oxford University Press, 1986.
————. "Embracing Contraries in the Teaching Process," *College English* 45 (1983): 327–39.

Grant, Gerald, Peter Elbow, Thomas Ewens, Zelda Gamson, Wendy Kohli, William Neumann, Virginia Olesen, David Riesman. *On Competence: A Critical Analysis of Competence-Based Reforms in Higher Education.* San Francisco: Jossey-Bass, 1979.

McClelland, D. C. "Testing for Competence Rather Than for Intelligence." *American Psychologist* 28 (1973): 1–14.

Problems with Grading

To grade reliably means to give the single quantitative grade that readers will agree on. But readers don't agree.

This is not news—this unavailability of agreement. We have long seen it on many fronts. For example, research in evaluation has shown many times that if we give a paper to a set of readers, those readers tend to give it the full range of grades (Diederich). I've recently come across new research to this effect—new to me because it was published in 1913. The investigators carefully showed how high school English teachers gave different grades to the same paper. In response to criticism that this was a local problem in English, they went on the next year to discover an even greater variation among grades given by high school geometry teachers and history teachers to papers in their subjects. (See the summary of Daniel Starch and Edward Elliott's 1913 *School Review* articles in Kirschenbaum, Sidney, and Napier 258–59.)

We know the same thing from literary criticism and theory. If the best critics disagree about what a text *means*, how can we be surprised that they disagree even more about the quality or value of texts. And we know of nothing in literary or philosophical theory to settle such disputes.

We know too much about the differences among readers and the highly variable nature of the reading process. Supposing we get readings only from academics, or only from people in English, or only from respected critics, or only from respected writing programs, or only from feminists, or only from sound readers of my tribe (white, male, middle class, full professors between the ages of fifty and sixty). We still don't get agreement. We can sometimes get agreement among readers from some subset, a particular community that has developed a strong set of common values, perhaps one English department or one writing program. But what is the value of such a rare agreement? It tells us nothing about how readers from other English departments or writing programs will judge—much less how readers from other domains will judge.

Students have shown us the same inconsistency with their own controlled experiments of handing the same paper to different teachers and getting different grades. This helps explain why we hate it so when students ask us their

From "Ranking, Evaluating and Liking: Sorting Out Three Forms of Judgment," published in *College English* 55.2 (Feb): 187–206.

favorite question, "What do you want for an A?": it rubs our noses in the un-reliability of our grades.

Some teachers might take a worldly wise view of my skepticism:

> So what else is new? Of *course* my grades are biased, "interested," or "situated"—always partial to my interests or the values of my community or culture. There's no other possibility.

But how can people consent to give grades if they feel that way? A single teacher's grade for a student is liable to have substantial consequences—for example, on eligibility for a scholarship or a job or entrance into professional school. In grading, surely, we must not take anything less than genuine fairness as our goal. When I am dismayed at the strong attraction for large-scale assessments that legislators and members of the public seem to feel, I pause and think about a simple fact: virtually *everyone* carries long-lasting resentment about some grade they experienced (perhaps justifiably) as unfair and inaccurate.

It won't be long before we see these issues argued in a court of law, when a student who has been disqualified from playing on a team or rejected from a professional school sues, charging that the basis for his plight—teacher grades—is not reliable. I wonder if lawyers will be able to make our grades stick.

Grading often forces us to write comments to *justify our grade*—yet these comments are often not the ones we want to write to help the student write better. "Just try writing several favorable comments on a paper and then giving it a grade of D" (Diederich 21).

Grades and holistic scores give too much encouragement to those students who score high—making them too apt to think they are already fine—and too little encouragement to those students who do badly. Unsuccessful students often come to doubt their intelligence. But oddly enough, many "A" students also end up doubting their true ability and feeling like frauds—because they have sold out on their own judgment and simply given teachers whatever yields an A. They have too often been rewarded for what they don't really believe in. (There's probably more cheating by students who get high grades than by those who get low ones. There would be less incentive to cheat if there were no ranking.)

We might be tempted to put up with the inaccuracy or unfairness of grades if they gave good diagnostic feedback or helped the learning climate; or we might put up with the damage they do to the learning climate if they gave a fair or reliable measure of how skilled or knowledgeable students are. But since they fail dismally on both counts, we are faced with a striking question: Why has grading persisted so long?

There must be many reasons. It is obviously easier and quicker to express a global feeling with a single number than to figure out what the strengths and weaknesses are and what one's criteria are. As C. S. Lewis says, "People are obviously far more anxious to express their approval and disapproval of things than to describe them" (7). But perhaps more important, we see around us a deep *hunger to rank*—to create pecking orders: to see who we can look down on and who we must look up to, or in the military metaphor, who we can kick and who we must salute. Psychologists tell us that this desire for pecking orders or ranking is associated with the authoritarian personality. We see this hunger graphically in the case of IQ scores. It is plain that IQ scoring does not represent a commitment to looking carefully at peoples' intelligence. When we do that, we see different and frequently uncorrelated *kinds* or *dimensions* of intelligence (Gardner). The persistent use of IQ scores represents the hunger to have a number so that everyone can have a rank. ("Ten!" mutter the guys when they see a pretty woman.)

Because ranking or grading has caused so much discomfort to so many students and teachers, I think we see a lot of confusion about the process. It is hard to think clearly about something that has given so many of us such anxiety and distress. The most notable confusion I notice is the tendency to think that if we renounce ranking or grading, we are renouncing the very possibility of judgment and discrimination—that we are embracing the idea that there is no way to talk about *quality* or about the difference between what works well and what works badly.

The main point here, then, is that *I am not arguing against judgment or evaluation.* I'm just arguing against that crude, oversimple way of *representing* judgment—distorting it, really—into a single number, which means ranking people and performances along a single continuum.

In fact, I am arguing *for evaluation.* Evaluation means looking hard and thoughtfully at a piece of writing in order to make distinctions as to the quality of different features or dimensions. For example, the process of evaluation permits us to make the following kinds of statements about a piece of writing:

- The thinking and ideas seemed interesting and creative.
- The overall structure or sequence seemed confusing.
- The writing was perfectly clear at the level of individual sentences and even paragraphs.
- There is an odd, angry tone of voice that seems unrelated or inappropriate to what the writer was saying.
- Yet this same voice is strong and memorable and makes one listen, even if irritated.
- There are a fair number of mistakes in grammar or spelling: more than "a sprinkling" but less than "riddled with."

To rank, on the other hand, is to be forced to translate those discriminations into a single number. What grade or holistic score do these judgments add up to? It's more likely, by the way, that readers would agree with those separate, "analytic" statements than they would agree on a holistic score.

Works Cited

Diederich, Paul. *Measuring Growth in English*. Urbana: NCTE, 1974.
Gardner, Howard. *Frames of Mind: The Theory of Multiple Intelligences*. NY: Basic Books, 1983.
Kirschenbaum, Howard, Sidney Simon, and Rodney Napier. *Wad-Ja-Get? The Grading Game in American Education*. New York: Hart Publishing, 1971.
Lewis, C. S. *Studies in Words*. 2nd ed. London: Cambridge UP, 1967.

The Conflict Between Reliability and Validity

Portfolios improve validity by giving a *better picture of students' writing abilities*. Most of us sense what research shows (Cooper), namely, that we can't trust the picture of someone's writing that emerges unless we see what he or she can do on various occasions on various pieces. And if we want to know about a student's *general* or *overall* writing ability, rather than just her skill in narrative or argument, we need to see her writing in various genres. Thus most exams give us only the most blurred or distorted picture of the student's actual writing capability. Think about what happens when a student has a bad day or the test question touches a nerve or seems completely boring. Think how much more we can trust the picture we get from three to a dozen pieces done in different genres on different occasions.

Indeed, the use of portfolios throws an interesting light on the very process itself of measurement or evaluation. For portfolio assessment occupies an interesting in-between area between the clean artificial world of carefully controlled assessment ("Take out your pencils. Don't turn over your books till I say 'go'") and the swampy real world where people actually write things for a purpose and where we as actual readers look at texts and can't agree for the life of us (for the hiring or the tenure of us) about how good they are. Or to put it differently, the use of portfolios highlights the interesting tension between *validity* and *reliability*. Let me explain.

When a portfolio increases validity by giving us a better picture of what we are trying to measure (the student's actual ability), it tends by that very act to muddy reliability—to diminish the likelihood of agreement among readers or graders. That is, if we are only looking at single pieces of writing by

---

This is taken mostly from the Foreword to *Portfolios: Process and Product*. Eds. Pat Belanoff and Marcia Dickson. Heinemann Boynton/Cook, 1991. A few passages are taken from "Reflections on an Explosion," in *Situating Portfolios: Four Perspectives*, Eds. Kathleen Blake Yancey and Irwin Weiser. Logan, UT: Utah State UP, 1997.

students—all written under the same conditions, all in exactly the same genre, all answering the same question—we are much more likely to agree with each other in our rankings than if we are looking at portfolios containing three or a dozen pieces by each student—and all of them different kinds of writing written under different conditions. When all the writing is alike, it's easier to agree about it.

Thus portfolio scorers have more trouble agreeing than scorers of single samples. "Training" doesn't seem to work as well. When portfolio scorers see multiple pieces by one student, they tend to have more trust in their sense of that student. As a result, they tend to fight harder for their judgment. In conventional single-sample tests, they are more liable to feel, at least unconsciously, "Why fight for my judgment, when I have no evidence that this text is typical of the student's other writing—especially the writing she does in more natural writing situations." (For three recent and vivid studies of actual scoring sessions that illustrate this interesting difficulty that portfolio scorers have in trying to reach agreement, see Broad; Despain and Hilgers; Hamp-Lyons and Condon. Vermont is being asked to rethink its statewide portfolio assessment procedures because testers can't get the inter-reader reliability score high enough.) In short, portfolios seem to kick back when people try to pin single numbers on them.

Even if we are not trying to test for that large dubious entity, "writing ability in general," but only for a small local skill such as the ability to write clear sentences, testers still run into the same problem: a one-shot exam helps scorers agree, but they are agreeing about an untrustworthy picture or sample. A portfolio of multiple pieces gives a more trustworthy sample, but that very trustworthiness often involves a mixed bag of both clear and unclear sentences—and so scorers have trouble agreeing.

What a mess portfolios make, then, for psychometricians looking for reliable scoring. What a problem for holistic testers who've been trying to impress administrators and professional psychometricians with good reliability scores on holistic readings.

Yet this very conflict and confusion gives us a more accurate picture of the student's writing ability. That is, the only accurate answer to the question, "How well does the student write?" is something like this:

> It depends. He's pretty good if you mean his playfulness and creativity. But he's pretty bad if you mean his ability to marshal evidence or think logically. He's pretty good in mechanics and usage when he takes the trouble and perhaps gets some help. Bad when he's careless or in a hurry. He's pretty good in the view of Reader Number One—who cares most about creativity and liveliness. He's pretty bad in the view of Reader Number Two— who likes a much more organized, controlled, polished kind of writer.

Any other answer would be skewed. If we "trained" the readers, we might get them to agree, but we would have a correspondingly *less accurate* decision about the value of that student's writing (that is, how it is actually valued by readers as they normally read). Thus holistic scoring locks us into giving scores that are inherently untrustworthy.

So in this very *difficulty* about reliability we see another benefit—another reason why portfolio assessment appeals to many thoughtful people. For the truth is that many of us can't help feeling that if reliability is high—if readers all agree about the worth of a piece of writing—something must be fishy. One of the main findings in literary theory and composition theory in recent years is that when people disagree in their interpretations or evaluations of texts, as they consistently do in normal settings, we have no agreed-upon basis for settling such disputes (see Smith). Neither literary theory nor philosophy gives us grounds for deciding on right or even better readings of texts. The very fact that carefully run holistic scoring sessions achieve high inter-reader reliability scores is simply an indication that all these people are not reading the way they normally read. "Good" holistic scoring usually means that readers must park their own standards at the door. Thus the sardonic comment I once heard from a scorer: "I'm bringing a peculiar reading process to bear on a peculiar writing process." (This situation makes me want to suggest a new piece of testing jargon: "reverse validity" or "mirror validity." Where a test with good normal validity would give a good picture of what we are trying to look at, good "mirror validity" would give us a good picture of how we do our looking—that is, it would do justice to the way readers actually read.)

So if assessment is to bear any believable relationship to the actual world of readers and responders—then reliability *should* be under strain. Given the tension between validity and reliability—the trade-off between getting good pictures of what we are trying to test and good agreement among interpreters of those pictures—it makes most sense to go for good pictures and let the interpreters fight, that is, to put our chips on validity and allow reliability to suffer. Notice how conventional writing assessments take exactly the opposite tack: they give us lots of agreement among readers, but it's agreement about a faint, smudged, and distorted picture of the student's writing ability.

Works Cited

Broad, Robert. "'Portfolio Scoring': A Contradiction in Terms." *New Directions in Portfolio Assessment: Reflective Practice, Critical Theory, and Large-Scale Scoring.* Eds. Laurel Black, Don Daiker, Jeffrey Sommers, and Gail Stygall. Portsmouth NH: Heinemann/Boynton-Cook, 1994. 263–76.

Cooper, Charles R. *The Nature and Measurement of Competency in English.* Urbana IL: NCTE, 1981.

Despain, LaRene and Thomas L. Hilgers. "Readers' Responses to the Rating of Non-Uniform Portfolios: Are There Limits of Portfolios' Utility?" *WPA: Writing Program Administration* 16.1–2 (Fall/Winter 1992): 24–37.

Hamp-Lyons, Liz and William Condon. "Questioning Assumptions about Portfolio-Based Assessment." *College Composition and Communication* 44.2 (May 1993): 176–90.

Smith, Barbara Herrnstein. *Contingencies of Value: Alternative Perspectives for Critical Theory.* Cambridge: Harvard UP, 1988.

How Portfolios Shake Up the Assessment Process and Thereby Lead to Minimal Holistic Scoring and Multiple Trait Scoring

Portfolios have put the assessment process in a pickle. They finally give more trustworthy pictures of ability, making us realize how little we could trust those old conventional, single-sample pictures, but with the same stroke portfolios take away the trust we used to have in the numbers we pinned on our pictures. Of course, people have been calling into question holistic scoring, grading, and single-dimension ranking for a long time. But portfolios have managed to make this critique stick with many more people.

The trouble is, sometimes we *need* a single number or a single dimension— a single "bottom line" verdict or holistic score. That is, in certain situations, we need to decide which students should be denied a place in our course or institution if we have limited resources—or denied credit, or made to repeat a course, or required to take a preparatory course. Sometimes we also want to exempt students from a course or pick students for an award or scholarship. We don't need *most* of the scores we normally get from holistic scoring, but sometimes we need some, and we can't just beg off and say, "Our readers won't agree because they finally see that ability is not one-dimensional."

Portfolios turn out to suggest a surprisingly workable way to deal with the very problem that they created: lack of agreement among readers. What about a full and rich portfolio where readers *agree* that most of the pieces are excellent? Are we not more than usually justified in giving this portfolio a score of *excellent* or *notably strong for this population,* or some such label? Similarly, what if most readers agree that most of the pieces are weak or unsatisfactory? Are we not more than usually justified in giving a score of *unsatisfactory* or *failing* or *notably weak*? In short, portfolios lead to the concept of *minimal* or *limited* holistic scoring.

At first glance, this procedure seems odd. For one thing it might seem theoretically scandalous to give holistic scores to a minority of portfolios at the margins and no scores at all to the rest. And the result is liable to involve an unsettlingly large group of portfolios in a middle, more or less acceptable, default range. But we would insist, on the contrary, that the real theoretical scandal comes from continuing to give that spectrum of holistic scores across the middle range: those scores where readers disagree are indefensible because they are simply the accident of compromise among readers or unilateral judgments decreed by the people who made up the scoring rubric.

This is a section that I wrote in an essay that Pat Belanoff and I coauthored: "Reflections on an Explosion," published in *Situating Portfolios: Four Perspectives,* Eds. Kathleen Blake Yancey and Irwin Weiser. Logan, UT: Utah State UP, 1997.

It's not our claim that minimal or limited holistic scoring—picking out the best and worst portfolios—is *truly* or *completely* trustworthy. We're claiming only that minimal holistic scoring involves making *fewer* dubious judgments and making only those judgments that are most needed. Fewer border decisions means fewer wrong decisions. In short, the principle here is the same as for surgery: since *every* operation carries a risk, we should operate only when there is a genuine need and a likely chance of success. Most holistic scores of writing are neither needed nor trustworthy.

Now just as it's cheaper to avoid surgery, it is cheaper to avoid all those unnecessary and untrustworthy holistic scores. Thus minimal holistic scoring recoups much of the extra cost of going from single-sample assessment to portfolio assessment. With minimal scoring, most portfolios can be read in just a couple of minutes: they soon establish themselves as too good for *unsatisfactory* and too flawed for *excellent*. Portfolio reading is faster and cheaper still if we don't need to identify top-rated portfolios. So if portfolios are used as an exit test—or if they are used for a placement procedure where students are not exempted, *only* poor portfolios need to be identified.

Most large-scale writing assessments are designed to sort students—not give feedback. But what if we actually wanted to give students some feedback—to use assessment to increase learning! Portfolios come to the rescue again and show us how to give more sophisticated and useful feedback on an exam. Since portfolios are mixed bags, they invite us, by their nature, to notice *difference:* strengths and weaknesses *within* a portfolio—whether between different papers in the portfolio or between different writing skills or dimensions.

Once we get interested in differences rather than just single numbers, we realize that it's not so hard to communicate these differences in scoring so that the student at last gets a bit of substantive feedback from the assessment process. For this feedback we don't need traditional analytic scoring—that elaborate process in which various writing dimensions or features are scored on a scale of four or six and these subscores are added up into a holistic score. No, it's much more feasible and trustworthy to use something much simpler and more minimal: readers score a writing trait or dimension or paper *only if* they feel it is notably strong or weak. Thus there are only two scores, *strong* and *weak,* along with a third, default middle range. The traits might be traditional ones, such as *ideas, details, organization, clarity of syntax, voice, mechanics;* or rhetorical features like *finding a subject,* or *making contact with readers;* scores might even note individual papers in a portfolio as particularly strong or weak. (See Broad, Figure 20-2 for a long list of features that readers can quickly check off as notably strong or weak while they read a portfolio—features that Broad derived from actual scoring and anchoring sessions.)

Obviously, we are no longer saving time and money if we decide to give this kind of feedback to portfolios. But there is a compromise that we used at Stony Brook: we gave this kind of analytic feedback only to *failing* portfolios. This didn't take much time—since readers already had to read failing portfolios more carefully. And of course it is the failing students who most need this feedback.

Works Cited

Broad, Robert. "'Portfolio Scoring': A Contradiction in Terms." *New Directions in Portfolio Assessment: Reflective Practice, Critical Theory, and Large-Scale Scoring*. Eds. Laurel Black, Don Daiker, Jeffrey Sommers, and Gail Stygall. Portsmouth NH: Heinemann/ Boynton-Cook, 1994. 263–76.

Multiple Trait Scoring as an Alternative to Holistic Scoring

Multiple trait scoring adds an element of description to the mere "yea/boo" of holistic scoring or grading. Thus it has the enormous advantage of giving at last some useful feedback and meaning to the audience of students, teachers, parents, administrators, legislators, employers, and others. Even though some students will complain if their bottom-line score is *neither excellent nor poor,* most of them will receive in return something more useful and descriptive than the B- or 4 they are more accustomed to: some indication of particular strengths and weaknesses in various dimensions of their writing. Even students with an *excellent* will almost invariably see features they still need to work on. And students with *unsatisfactory* or *failing* will almost invariably get some much needed encouragement by seeing some features or pieces that readers did *not* rate as unsatisfactory. Moreover, these failing students will see more clearly the *basis* of their failure, not just get an empty low number.

Finally, multiple trait scoring can sometimes even increase fairness by increasing agreement among readers. The point here is that even though much disagreement among readers is inevitable, some disagreement comes needlessly from the process of holistic scoring. For example, imagine a portfolio full of strong, interesting thinking, clear focus, and pertinent examples and reasons—but much unclear language and many surface errors. Imagine two scorers with different tastes: one of them cares more about the thinking and focus and less about unclear language and mistakes; the other has the opposite values—caring more about clear, idiomatic, and correct language and worrying less about writing that says little or says what is foolish. If these two readers score this portfolio with conventional holistic scoring, they will almost inevitably disagree about the score—despite their training (especially since most scoring guides don't give much help on writing that mixes strong and weak features). But they use multiple trait scoring, they have a good chance of agreeing that the thinking is strong and the language is weak. They may still disagree in their bottom-line score—perhaps one of them calling the portfolio

From "Writing Assessment: Do It Better, Do It Less," published in *The Politics and Practices of Assessment in Writing*. Eds. William Lutz, Edward White, and Sandra Kamusikiri. NY: MLA, 1996. 120–34.

strong and the other calling it merely satisfactory. But readers will be able to see the *grounds* for any bottom-line holistic score. If the language is judged weak and the thinking is judged strong and the bottom-line score is *strong*, the readers can tell that the scorer valued thinking more than language. When the values of scorers are not hidden, outside readers have a better chance of making their *own* informed decision about the student's actual abilities—for example as potential employees. (Freedman provides evidence that analytic scoring gives higher reliability.)

People often assume that multiple trait scoring is unfeasibly expensive. But when I last checked, the following states were using some form of analytic or multiple trait scoring for their statewide tests: Colorado, Georgia, Illinois, Indiana, Louisiana, Maine, Oregon, Texas, West Virginia. In addition, the switch from full holistic scoring to minimal scoring will produce savings.

Answering two objections to multiple trait or analytic scoring.

1. Readers will always see individual traits or analytic features through a holistic halo or lens. When they like a portfolio or paper as a whole, they will see the language and ideas as strong; when they hate it, they will see the same language and ideas as weak.

Yes, this is a problem. But what it highlights is something larger—a pervasive *bias toward holism* in the very process of human perception. The path of least resistance in human information processing is always to sort things into binary piles of like/dislike, friend/enemy, us/them, familiar/other. This is why people fall so easily into snap judgments. Hamp-Lyons and Condon found that holistic scorers often decided on a score very early in their reading of a portfolio.

What looks like a problem, therefore, is really the strongest argument *for* multiple trait scoring. Multiple trait scoring is an attempt to *fight against* this pervasively reductive tendency in human perception or information processing. Of course, the attempt must always fail to some degree, but that's all the more reason to persist with it.

2. Where the first objection was that multiple trait scoring doesn't work, the second objection is that it works too well. This objection might be put as follows:

> When readers judge by multiple traits or analytic features, they tend to miss the *essential* quality of the paper. In fact, the whole is always more than the sum of its multiple parts—thus the need for something "holistic". Analytic reading is completely artificial and fails to capture the real reactions of real readers. For example, multiple trait scoring tempts readers to give good scores to papers that are proper or conform to all the specified criteria, but which real readers find flat, unsuccessful, or even repellent; and to give poor scores to papers that fail the criteria, but which real readers find satisfactory or effective.

Yes, this too can happen. But let's pause and analyze why. The problem occurs when the analytic traits or criteria don't include those dimensions of the writing that may be subtle but which have powerful effects on readers. For example, when traits like "voice" or "effectiveness of examples and anecdotes" are not specified, the actual effect of a text on readers often slips through the analytic net. A paper might be weak in ideas, organization, and even clarity, but if the voice wins the reader's identification and the examples capture the reader's imagination, the paper is liable to be holistically experienced as satisfactory or downright effective by many real readers.

But here again, this problem is not an argument against multiple trait scoring. It's an argument for learning to specify better the traits or criteria that actually affect readers. Surely the main job in both the testing and teaching of writing is to figure out what features or criteria *do* affect how readers react and judge.

Furthermore, as we get wiser about why readers actually value writing and what actually goes on as they read, we may see other benefits of using multiple traits. For example, students who are tired of schooling and testing sometimes write prose that is subtly or overtly angry—prose that in effect gives readers the finger. Scorers often react negatively to such writing, and only an analytic process can help them notice some genuine skills or strong traits hidden in this sullen or irritating performance. Readers also sometimes grade papers down disproportionately if they have lots of surface mistakes or have lots of Black English. If it requires the minor "artificiality" of multiple trait scoring to see genuine skills in such texts, so much the better. (For a careful study of how readers are more critical when writers are not sufficiently deferential, see Freedman.)

Works Cited

Freedman, Sarah Warshauer. "The Registers of Student and Professional Expository Writing: Influences on Teachers' Responses." *New Directions in Composition Research*. Ed. Richard Beach and Lillian Bridwell. New York: The Guilford P, 1984.

Hamp-Lyons, Liz and William Condon. "Questioning Assumptions about Portfolio-Based Assessment." *College Composition and Communication* 44.2 (May 1993): 176–90.

Tracking Leads to a Narrow Definition of Intelligence

Tracking or "ability grouping" tends to favor only certain *kinds* of intelligence. Let me look at three ways this happens.

1. *Tracking favors quickness in learning.* When students learn quickly they look smart. When students learn slowly, they look stupid. "Slow" is the word

From a column I published in the *Amherst Bulletin*, Jan. 7, 1994.

everyone uses for unintelligent: "slow" children, the "slow" track. If you are slow, you get there more slowly, you are held back, and thus you are retarded.

But what's so bad about being slow to learn? When people learn slowly, it usually means that they have a different way of seeing things; that they have a different set of experiences and assumptions and don't take for granted what everyone else takes for granted; that they have to mull something over before it makes sense; that they are skeptical about accepting what teachers or text-books find obvious. Yet tracking almost inevitably rewards speed and punishes slowness. Slow students tend to be seen as unintelligent, yet they might be just as smart if not smarter than those chosen for higher tracks. We've all known smart people who are slow. Einstein had trouble in school.

2. *Tracking favors verbal learning.* Schools tend to ask for *words*—reading, writing, discussion. But what about the different kinds of intelligence mani-fested by artists, musicians, dancers, athletes, mechanics? Howard Gardner wrote an important, well-respected book (*Frames of Mind: The Theory of Multiple Intelligences*) showing that there are something like eight kinds of intelligence—none inherently better or "smarter" than the others.

Yes, verbal learning is a good thing. Schools do well to take it seriously, perhaps even to emphasize it. But the important point is that we don't have to neglect other kinds of learning as we emphasize verbal learning. Other kinds of learning can *lead to* verbal learning—sometimes even to better verbal learning. That is, artists and athletes often have insights that people don't get to by purely verbal learning. A frequent problem in classrooms is too many words—nothing but words unconnected to felt or lived experience—words ungrounded in common sense or street smarts.

I'm a writer. But I got interested in writing because of my difficulties with words. I've always been a bumbler and fumbler in my speech; always at a loss for words. And in graduate school I found I couldn't write: I couldn't find words, control them, organize them. I had to drop out before they kicked me out. I finally learned to be a writer—but I did it by learning to welcome the nonverbal, the inchoate, the mess. What I've had to learn is that if I want to find more and better words, I've got to stalk inarticulate hunches and pursue feelings that I can't put into words.

My point is that someone who is nonverbal and inarticulate is liable to be *very* smart—perhaps smarter than the quick verbal students in honors tracks.

3. *Tracking favors compliance.* "Follow directions. Do what the teacher asks." It's not that I'm arguing for *noncompliance* or disobedience. I'm a teacher. I love it when students do what I want. It makes my life much easier and it helps them learn what I'm trying to teach. Yet I've learned over the years that my *uncompliant* students are often smarter than my compliant ones. As I pay better attention to their writing and their behavior, sometimes I no-tice the rich complexity of what they are giving me. Often they are not just giving me the finger (it's interesting to see the subtle and interesting ways that students give teachers the finger); they are also often giving all of us some insights we've been lacking.

Let me point to a specific case where compliance hinders learning. Researchers in my field are discovering that people who are seriously blocked in their writing are often the ones who carefully follow all the steps and directions that teachers told them to follow: "Start by making an outline. Put each point on an index card. Have a topic sentence for each paragraph," and so on. In contrast, many of those who have no trouble writing don't do what they were told, and they say, "Well I know I'm going about this all wrong, but I just can't seem to write the way I'm supposed to write."

We can get a wiser view of schools, universities, and society when we realize how many people have been tempted to confuse quickness, verbal facility, and compliance with intelligence.

The Benefits and Feasibility of Liking

Liking and disliking seem like unpromising topics in an exploration of assessment. They seem to represent the worst kind of subjectivity, the merest accident of personal taste. But I've recently come to think that the phenomenon of liking is perhaps the most important evaluative response for writers and teachers to think about. In effect, I'm turning another corner in my argument. In the first section of my essay [not printed here] I argued against ranking—with evaluating being the solution. In the next section [also not printed here], I argued not *against* evaluating—but for no-evaluation zones in *addition* to evaluating. Now I will argue neither against evaluating nor against nonevaluation zones, but for something very different in addition, or perhaps underneath, as a foundation: liking.

Let me start with the germ story. I was in a workshop and we were going around the circle with everyone telling a piece of good news about their writing in the last six months. It got to Wendy Bishop, a good poet (who has also written two good books about the teaching of writing), and she said, "In the last six months, I've learned to *like* everything I write." Our jaws dropped; we were startled—in a way scandalized. But I've been chewing on her words ever since, and they have led me into a retelling of the story of how people learn to write better.

The old story goes like this: We write something. We read it over and we say, "This is terrible. I *hate* it. I've got to work on it and improve it." And we do, and it gets better, and this happens again and again, and before long we have become a wonderful writer. But that's not the true story of what usually happens in those circumstances. Yes, we vow to work on it—but we don't.

From "Ranking, Evaluating and Liking: Sorting Out Three Forms of Judgment," published in *College English* 55.2 (Feb): 187–206.

And the next time we have the impulse to write, we're just a *bit* less likely to start.

What really happens when people learn to write better? The story is more often like this: We write something. We read it over and we say, "This is terrible. . . . But I *like* it. Damn it, I'm going to get it good enough so that others will like it too." And this time we don't just put it in a drawer, we actually work hard on it. And we try it out on other people too—not just to get feedback and advice but, perhaps more important, to find someone else who will like it.

Notice the two conflicting stories about improvement—two hypotheses.

(a) "First you improve the faults and then you like it."

(b) "First you like it and then you improve the faults."

The second story may sound odd when stated so baldly, but really it's common sense. Only if we like something will we get involved enough to work and struggle with it. Only if we like what we write will we write again and again by choice—which is the only way we get better.

This hypothesis sheds light on the process of how people get to be published writers. Conventional wisdom assumes a Darwinian model: poor writers are unread; then they get better; as a result, they get a wider audience; finally, they turn into Norman Mailer. But now I'd say the process is more complicated. People who get better and get published really tend to be driven by how much *they* care about their writing. Yes, they have a small audience at first—after all, they're not very good. But they try reader after reader until finally they can find people who like and appreciate their writing. I certainly did this. If someone doesn't like her writing enough to be pushy and hungry about finding a few people who also like it, she probably won't get better.

It may sound so far as though all the effort and drive comes from the lonely driven writer—and sometimes it does (Norman Mailer is no joke). But, often enough, *readers* play the crucially active role in this story of how writers get better. That is, writers often *learn* to like their writing by the grace of having a reader or two who likes it—even though it's not good. Having at least a few appreciative readers is probably indispensable to getting better.

When I apply this story to our situation as teachers, I come up with this interesting hypothesis: *good writing teachers like student writing*—and like students. I think I see this born out, and it is really nothing but common sense. Teachers who hate student writing and hate students are grouchy all the time. How could we stand our work and do a decent job if we hated their writing. Good teachers see what is only *potentially* good, they get a kick out of mere possibility—and they encourage it. When I manage to do this, I teach well.

Thus, I've begun to notice a turning point in my courses—two or three weeks into the semester: "Am I going to like these folks or is this going to be a battle, a struggle?" When I like them everything seems to go better—and it seems to me they learn more by the end. When I don't like them and we stay tangled up in struggle, we all suffer—and they seem to learn less.

So what am I saying? That we should like bad writing? How can we see all the weaknesses and criticize student writing if we just like it? But here's the interesting point: if I *like* someone's writing, it's *easier* to criticize it.

I first noticed this when I was trying to gather essays for the book on freewriting that Pat Belanoff and Sheryl Fontaine and I edited. I would read an essay someone had written, I would want it for the book, but I had some serious criticism. I'd get excited and write, "I really like this, and I hope we can use it in our book, but you've got to get rid of this and change that, and I got really mad at this other thing." I usually find it hard to criticize, but I began to notice that I was a much more critical and pushy reader when I liked something. It's even fun to criticize in those conditions.

It's the same with student writing. If I like a piece, I don't have to pussy-foot around with my criticism. It's when I don't like their writing that I find myself tiptoeing: trying to soften my criticism, trying to find something nice to say—and usually sounding fake, often unclear. I see the same thing with my own writing. If I like it, I can criticize it better. I have faith that there'll still be something good left, even if I train my full critical guns on it.

Liking is not the same as ranking or evaluating. Naturally, people get them mixed up: when they like something, they assume it's good; when they hate it, they assume it's bad. But it's helpful to uncouple the two domains and realize that it makes perfectly good sense to say, "This is terrible, but I like it." Or, "This is good, but I hate it." In short, I am not arguing here *against* criticizing or evaluating. I'm merely arguing *for* liking.

Let me sum up my clump of hypotheses so far:

- It's not improvement that leads to liking, but rather liking that leads to improvement.
- It's the mark of good writers to like their writing.
- Liking is not the same as evaluating. We can often criticize something better when we like it.
- We learn to like our writing when we have a respected reader who likes it.
- Therefore, it's the mark of good teachers to like students and their writing.

If this set of hypotheses is true, what practical consequences follow from it? How can we be better at liking? It feels as though we have no choice—as though liking and not-liking just happen to us. I don't really understand this business. I'd love to hear discussion about the mystery of liking—the phenomenology of liking. I sense it's some kind of putting oneself out—or holding oneself open—but I can't see it clearly. I have a hunch, however, that we're not so helpless about liking as we tend to feel.

For, in fact, I can suggest some practical concrete activities that I have found fairly reliable at increasing the chances of liking student writing:

(a) I ask for lots of private writing and merely shared writing, that is, writing that I don't read at all, and writing that I read but don't comment on. This makes me more cheerful because it's so much easier. Students get *better* without me. Having to evaluate writing—especially bad writing—makes me more likely to hate it. This throws light on grading: it's hard to like something if we know we have to give it a D.

(b) I have students share lots of writing with each other—and after a while respond to each other. It's easier to like their writing when I don't feel myself as the only reader and judge. And so it helps to build community in general: it takes pressure off me. Thus I try to use peer groups not only for feedback, but also for other activities too, such as collaborative writing, brainstorming, putting class magazines together, and working out other decisions.

(c) I increase the chances of my liking their writing when I get better at finding what *is* good—or *potentially* good—and learn to praise it. This is a skill. It requires a good eye, a good nose. We tend—especially in the academic world—to assume that a good eye or fine discrimination means *criticizing*. Academics are sometimes proud of their tendency to be bothered by faults that others overlook. Thus I find I am sometimes looked down on as dumb and undiscriminating: "He likes bad writing. He must have no taste, no discrimination." But I've finally become angry rather than defensive. It's an act of true discrimination to see what's good in bad writing. Maybe, in fact, this is the secret of the mystery of liking: to be able to see potential goodness underneath badness.

Put it this way. We tend to stereotype liking as a "soft" and sentimental activity. Mr. Rogers is our model. Fine. There's nothing wrong with softness and sentiment—and I love Mr. Rogers. But liking can also be hard-assed. Let me suggest an alternative to Mr. Rogers: B. F. Skinner. Skinner taught pigeons to play ping-pong. How did he do it? Not by moaning, "Pigeon standards are falling. The pigeons they send us these days are no good. When I was a pigeon. . . ." He did it by a careful, disciplined method that involved close analytic observation. He put pigeons on a ping-pong table with a ball, and every time a pigeon turned his head 30 degrees toward the ball, he gave a reward.

What would this approach require in the teaching of writing? It's conceptually simple . . . but not so easy at first. Imagine that we want to teach students an ability they badly lack, for example, how to organize their writing or how to make their sentences clearer. Skinner's insight is that we get nowhere in this task by just telling them how much they lack this skill: "It's disorganized. Organize it!" "It's unclear. Make it clear!" Notice how much more practical and helpful it is to say, "Do *more* of what you're doing here," than to say, "Do something *different* from what you're doing here.

No, what we must learn to do is to read closely and carefully enough to show the student little bits of *proto*-organization or *sort of* clarity in what they've already written. We don't have to pretend the writing is wonderful. We could even say, "This is a terrible paper and the worst part about it is the lack of organization. But I will teach you how to organize. Look here at this little organizational move you made in this sentence. Read it outloud and try to feel how it pulls together this stuff here and distinguishes it from that stuff there. Try to remember what it felt like writing that sentence—creating that piece of organization. Do it some more."

When academics criticize behaviorism as crude, it often means that they aren't willing to do the close careful reading of student writing that is required. They'd rather give a cursory reading and turn up their nose and give a low grade and complain about falling standards. No one has undermined behaviorism's main principle of learning: that reward produces learning more effectively than punishment.

(d) I improve my chances of liking student writing when I take steps to get to know students a bit as people. I do this partly through assignments I give. That is, I always ask them to write a letter or two to me and to each other (e.g., about their history with writing). I base at least a couple of assignments on their own experiences, memories, or histories. And I make sure some of the assignments are free choice pieces—which also helps me know them.

In addition, I make sure to have at least three conferences with each student each semester—the first one very early. I often call off some classes in order to keep conferences from being too onerous (insisting nevertheless that students meet with their partner or small group when class is called off). Some teachers have miniconferences with students during class—while students are engaged in writing or peer group meetings. I've found that when I deal only with my classes as a whole—as a large group—I sometimes experience them as a herd or lump—as stereotyped "adolescents"; I fail to experience them as individuals. For me, personally, this is disastrous since it often leads me to experience them as that scary tribe that I felt rejected by when *I* was an eighteen-year-old—and thus, at times, as "the enemy." But when I sit down with them face to face, they are not so stereotyped or alien or threatening—they are just eighteen-year-olds.

Getting a glimpse of them as individual people is particularly helpful in cases where their writing is not just bad, but somehow offensive—perhaps violent or cruelly racist or homophobic or sexist—or frighteningly vacuous. When I know them just a bit, I can often see behind their awful attitude to the person and the life situation that spawned it, and not hate their writing so much. When I know students I can see that they are smart behind that dumb behavior; they are doing the best they can behind that bad behavior. Conditions are keeping them from acting decently; something is holding them back.

(e) It's odd, but the more I let myself show the easier it is to like them and their writing. I need to share some of my own writing—show some of my own feelings. I need to write the letter to them that they write to me—about my past experiences and what I want and don't want to happen.

(f) It helps to work on my own writing—and work on learning to *like* it. Teachers who are most critical and sour about student writing are often having trouble with their own writing. They are bitter or unforgiving or hurting toward their own work. (I think I've noticed that failed Ph.D.s are often the most severe and difficult with students.) When we are stuck or sour in our own writing, what helps us most is to find spaces free from evaluation such as those provided by freewriting and journal writing. Also, activities like reading out loud and finding a supportive reader or two. I would insist, then, that if only for the sake of our teaching, we need to learn to be charitable and to like our own writing.

A final word. I fear that this sermon about liking might seem an invitation to guilt. There is enough pressure on us as teachers that we don't need some-one coming along and calling us inadequate if we don't *like* our students and their writing. That is, even though I think I am right to make this foray into the realm of feeling, I also acknowledge that it is dangerous—and paradoxical. It strikes me that we also need to have permission to hate the dirty bastards and their stupid writing.

After all, the conditions under which they go to school bring out some awful behavior on their part, and the conditions under which we teach some-times make it difficult for us to like them and their writing. Writing wasn't meant to be read in stacks of twenty-five, fifty, or seventy-five. And we are handicapped as teachers when students are in our classes against their will. (Thus high school teachers have the worst problem here, since their students tend to be the most sour and resentful about school.)

Indeed, one of the best aids to liking students and their writing is to be somewhat charitable toward ourselves about the opposite feelings that we in-evitably have. I used to think it was terrible for teachers to tell those sarcastic stories and hostile jokes about their students: "teacher room talk." But now I've come to think that people who spend their lives teaching *need* an arena to let off this unhappy steam. And certainly it's better to vent this sarcasm and hostility with our buddies than on the students themselves. The question, then, becomes this: Can we help this behavior function as a venting so that we can move past it and not be trapped in our inevitable resentment of students? Or do we tell these stories and jokes as a way of staying stuck in the hurt, hos-tile, or bitter feelings—year after year—as so many sad teachers do?

In short, I'm not trying to invite guilt, I'm trying to invite hope. I'm trying to suggest that if we do a sophisticated analysis of the difference between lik-ing and evaluating, we will see that it's possible (if not always easy) to like students and their writing—without having to give up our intelligence, so-phistication, or judgment.

21

Writing Assessment in the Twenty-First Century

A Utopian View

How shall we deal with what lies ahead? In his essay Edward M. White warns us of future dangers and urges us to steer away from them. I will point to future ideals and try to get us to steer closer.

It makes me mad when people criticize me as utopian. Surely there is something misguided when the term "utopian" is used to criticize and is taken to mean "unrealistic" and "unsophisticated." We need the utopian or visionary impulse to keep from being blinded by what seems normal—to help us see that what is natural is constructed, not inevitable. When I get stuck I can often help myself by asking, "How *should* things be?" This helps me pry myself loose from the web of assumptions we live in.

What if we had a regular state college without grading? It sounds utopian, but teaching nine years at The Evergreen State College in Washington showed me it could be normal. Evergreen is a good-sized non-elite state college. It has the same teacher/student ratio and faculty salaries as the other colleges in the state system. It has proved that students with narrative transcripts and no grades at all can get into good graduate and professional schools and get good jobs.

What if we could write without being careful, without planning, without thinking about readers, without coherence or correctness or even a topic? Sounds utopian, but freewriting is exactly this kind of writing. Freewriting is a prime utopian move: an act of breaking out of the "nature of things." Visits to the utopian "nowhere" of freewriting have concretely helpful effects on our "normal" writing under conventional constraints.

This essay was published in 1996 in *Composition in the 21st Century: Crisis and Change.* Eds. Lynn Bloom, Don Daiker, and Ed White. Southern Illinois UP. 83–100.

So let me suggest four utopian models for assessment in the twenty-first century.

Portfolios

What if we did not make any serious assessments of someone's writing unless we had multiple samples: multiple genres produced on multiple occasions and most of them produced in natural writing conditions? The point is that we cannot get a trustworthy picture of someone's writing ability or skill if we see only one piece of writing—especially if it was written in test conditions. Even if we are only testing for a narrow subskill such as sentence clarity, one sample can be completely misleading.

Since the explosion of interest in portfolios, this principle does not feel very utopian any more. After all, a significant number of massive assessments use portfolios, for example, those at Miami University and the University of Michigan. Yet notice how most writing tests are based on single samples, and parents and the news media seem to take single-sample scores with complete faith.

"What about statewide tests? They could not use portfolios." But they could. Vermont and Kentucky already do. And statewide tests could use portfolios more easily if they did not try to test every student but rather tested more selectively. Selective testing, if it were more trustworthy through the use of portfolios, would serve the goals that are reasonable for such huge tests: to identify which schools need extra resources to bring more students up to par and to provide samples of unsatisfactory and exemplary portfolios for teachers—samples they could use for more local assessment at the school or regional level in order to give some genuine feedback to every student.

An Alternative to Holistic Scoring

What if we finally admitted the problems with holistic scoring and did something about it? Holistic scoring sometimes feels to people like the normal, accepted, "default" mode for evaluation—even the desirable mode. (And historically, holistic scoring helped us push for direct rather than indirect tests of writing.) But in fact, many people have been pointing out serious problems (see my appendix of works that question holistic scoring), and there is considerable exploration of alternatives. Here is a quick summary of problems with holistic scoring.

1. Holistic scores are not fair or trustworthy. They score complex, multidimensional performances with single numbers along a single dimension. More important, readers simply do not agree on holistic or single scores. The high levels of alleged inter-reader reliability that testers sometimes brag of for holistic scoring are the artificial effects of "training": getting readers to ignore their actual responses and values as professional readers. Portfolios have high-

lighted this reliability problem because they are so rich and complex that no single-dimensional score is adequate. Thus, portfolio scorers are turning out to be more resistant to "training" and peskier about sticking to their disagreements. (For three empirical accounts of these difficulties in portfolio scoring sessions, see in my appendix Broad; Despain and Hilgers; Hamp-Lyons.)

2. Holistic scores give no feedback to the learner or teacher. A holistic score is nothing but a single point on a "yea/boo" applause meter and provides no evidence as to why readers shouted "yea" or "boo." Sometimes testers provide a "scoring guide" along with holistic scores. But these Platonic descriptions cannot be used for feedback to students because they so seldom fit actual papers.

3. Holistic scoring feeds the dangerous assumption that there is a "true score" for any piece of writing (or even portfolio). Ed White addresses this danger directly: "When we evaluate student writing . . . we sometimes find differences of opinion that cannot be resolved and where the concept of the true score makes no sense. . . . Some disagreements (within limits) should not be called error, since, as with the arts, we do not really have a true score, even in theory" ("Language and Reality" 192).

4. Holistic scoring fuels what is probably the biggest enemy of thoughtful evaluation: judgment based on holistic, global feelings ("I like it/I don't like it") rather than judgment that tries to describe and to discriminate strengths and weaknesses.

5. Holistic scoring similarly feeds the cultural hunger for ranking and evaluation—the feeling that evaluation is not "real" or honest unless it comes in the form of a single number. Too many students assume that everything must be evaluated—indeed, that the *point* of writing is to be evaluated.

A truly utopian impulse would prompt us to ask why we need numerical scores at all. Why not make do with readers' descriptive accounts of what they see as strengths and weaknesses? This would be the most trustworthy evaluation because it would give the most valid picture of how readers actually read and value texts.

In fact, we *could* get along with nothing but that kind of writing assessment if we made some institutional changes. But I want to back down from the full utopian impulse and give in somewhat to pragmatic and institutional pressures as they now exist. That is, I want to acknowledge that we sometimes need, given present institutional realities, a bottom-line verdict. We need to know which students to admit or refuse, which students to pass or to oblige to repeat a course, which ones to give a scholarship to or not. Nevertheless, we do not need all those holistic scores from 1 to 6. We could just as well use what I call "minimal holistic scoring" or "bottom-line scoring." For example, in many situations we could give only two scores: Unsatisfactory and Satisfactory. Sometimes we might want to give a third score: Excellent or Honors. Minimal or bottom-line holistic scoring might seem theoretically odd, designed to offend both those who love holistic scoring and those who hate it. In fact, however, a version of minimal holistic scoring is being used in the writing programs at many places, for example, at SUNY at Stony Brook

(Elbow and Belanoff), Pittsburgh University (W. Smith, "The Importance"), Washington State University (Haswell and Wyche-Smith), and University of South Carolina (Grego and Thompson). The theoretical principle behind it is simple, crude, skeptical, and pragmatic and could be stated as follows: single-number scores for complex performances are inherently untrustworthy (especially for things as rich and complex as portfolios), and so we should make as few as possible. Therefore, let us figure out what minimal scores we *need* and make only those judgments. If we only need to know which students should get extra help, score only that one category.[1] (Notice also how so-called real-world scoring tends to be a form of minimal or bottom-line holistic scoring: you are hired or fired; your manuscript is accepted or rejected; your grant proposal is funded or not.)

Minimal scoring is much easier and cheaper. It costs a lot of money to score every paper or portfolio from 1 to 6. Minimal scoring is also more trustworthy, if only because it produces radically fewer untrustworthy scores. Yet it still gives us what we need.

It also leads to a significant and interesting psychological benefit: an emphasis on what might be called "good enough writing." (I adapt the concept from D. W. Winnicott, an interesting British psychoanalyst who coined the term "good enough mother." He was trying to question the emphasis on a kind of ideal mother who is always active and attentive to the baby and who makes everything happen right. He showed in the most concrete way how babies and toddlers need a mother who is *there* and available by not paying too much attention or doing very much for the child—a figure whom the child can move away from on longer and longer forays and always find there on return. He showed the importance of a certain kind of wise neglect. I pass over the fact that he framed all this in terms of the mother only.)

I have found the concept "good enough writing" useful in my teaching where I use minimal grading in conjunction with a contract. Students are not sweating their precise grade or score so much because they know that I will notify them if I see their work as not satisfactory—or as excellent. Those who do genuinely poorly get pushed; those who are hung up with winning push themselves for scores of Excellent—they "write to win." Most students can rest secure that the piece of writing they turned in is, overall, "good enough" and can thus think more productively about the nonholistic or analytic feedback they get from me and their peers about what happens in readers' minds during reading and what readers see as particular strengths and weaknesses. (Formerly, students were too preoccupied with whether the grade was B or C, and I was having to gear my comments toward justifying my often dubious choice.) Most of all, this emphasis on "good enough writing" helps students

---

1. Someone might object, "But we need more than those minimal scores because we could never get the scorers to give us exactly the number of basic writing students that we can afford to teach. We need a range of scores so we can make the students and the dollars match each other." But this very problem should lead to a sound assessment practice: compiling one list of failing students about whom all readers agreed, and then one more list of students about whom readers disagreed.

begin to pay more attention to developing their own criteria for writing and to become less dependent upon teacher evaluation.

Let me emphasize that by "good enough writing," I do not mean mediocre writing with which we cannot be satisfied. But I do not mean excellent writing, either. Some people believe we must never be satisfied with anything but excellence; the notion of "good enough writing" will be offensive to them. In my view, the concept is particularly appropriate for required writing courses where many students are there under duress and are more interested in satisfying the requirement acceptably than in achieving excellence. (Can we hold that against them?) Yet in elective writing courses, "good enough writing" is also appropriate because students there are more ready to develop their own autonomous standards.

An Alternative to Basic Writing

Let us question the pervasive assumption here: that if we want to give unskilled or inexperienced writers the help they need, we must give all students a placement test in order to identify the problem students ahead of time and put them into separate "basic writing" courses where they have no contact with the rest of the students.

In the Spring 1993 issue of the *Journal of Basic Writing,* there are three essays that question basic writing itself. David Bartholomae suggests that basic writing is a cultural construct that leads to institutional structures which "reproduce existing hierarchies" in a dangerous way (14). Peter Dow Adams investigates the records at his community college and is alarmed at how few basic writing students make it through the regular 101 course. He wonders whether these basic courses might actually impede rather than help the students placed in them. William Jones argues that basic writing courses often function in a racist way.

Furthermore, in a piece of extensive research that won the 1991 Braddock Award for the best essay in *College Composition and Communication,* Glynda Hull, Mike Rose, Kay Losey Fraser, and Marisa Castellano show how easy and natural it is for teachers of basic writing to mistake difference for deficit. They give us a helpful and detailed picture of how a basic writing teacher—a good and smart and caring one—comes to perceive a basic writing student as having a serious cognitive deficit when in truth the student's problem seemed to be that she engaged in discussion and conversation in a way that the teacher found inappropriate and indeed annoying. (In fact, part of her problem seemed to be that she was "too" assertive and behaved too much like a peer— she was not sufficiently deferential. This recalls the research by Sarah Freedman on how teachers respond negatively to student writing that is not deferential.)

The authors do not paint the teacher as incompetent or prejudiced—in fact, they imply that all of us would probably be embarrassed at what came to light if our teaching were examined and analyzed so closely. That was their point:

circumstances tempt all of us into misguided behavior. For it was the student's placement in a *basic* class that tempted the teacher into seeing a cognitive deficit where there was just an odd or even annoying way of talking. If the setting had been a regular course, the teacher would have probably just seen the behavior as "behavior." And imagine if the student had been in an honors section: "Lord, aren't these smart kids *pushy!* Sometimes I just get tired of them interrupting all the time and trying to steer the conversation their way."

These critiques of basic writing are tricky and debatable—indeed inflammatory.[2] Bartholomae and Adams tread very gingerly in their doubts about whether basic writing courses are worth having. Hull, Rose, and their colleagues do not question basic writing courses per se (though I think their findings do, along with the title of their article). Therefore, I will not push a negative argument—that basic writing programs do not work or do harm. Surely they often work well, and I would like to assume for the sake of this paper that they *always* work well.

But I can still pursue a *positive* argument. I want to propose a picture or model of how things *could* be, in the belief that this picture will attract us so much that we will want to move in that direction by the twenty-first century—even if all our present basic writing courses work well.

Let me try to give a concrete vision of how we might arrange things if we decided to skip all this placement testing and temporary tracking or segregating of basic students. All entering students would be placed into the regular first-year course. The only ones excluded would be those who cannot put down on paper in English the words they find on their lips or in their heads—students who cannot blurt words on paper. They would not have to be able to spell those words well or get them into correct or even clear sentences; they would simply have to be able to put much of their speech on paper. Thus the population of the first-year course would be very mixed indeed: very skilled writers cheek by jowl with extremely poor ones.

> What a mess! And what about poorly prepared, frightened students who need help to survive? You are just inviting the bad old days where universities accepted these students and gave no help—so they soon flunked out.

The important thing here is to notice the stranglehold link in our current thinking between *helping* unskilled writers and *segregating* or quarantining them into separate basic writing courses. We need to break that stranglehold

---

2. Arguments against basic writing courses often talk about tracking. But in all fairness, a distinction needs to be made. In the worst form of tracking, targeted students are put on a separate track in order to ship them to different final destinations—so the different populations never meet. In the typical university writing program, however, the tracking is less noxious: basic students are segregated on a separate track, but the goal is eventually to move them to the same station that all the others students reach—and with full integration during the last leg of their journey. In the end, I believe basic courses are a *kind* of tracking. Singling students out and separating them surely has an effect on their motivation and self-image. But it not the kind of tracking we see in many schools that shunts off—"cools out"—the allegedly less-skilled students so they do not have a chance to reach the desirable destination. Perhaps we should call it "temporary tracking."

and notice that there are a multitude of ways to give these students supplementary help without trying to identify them ahead of time and separating them from the rest. As long as they get help, unskilled and inexperienced writers can benefit from working along with more skilled students—and the more skilled ones will benefit, too.

What I am suggesting builds on a crucial pedagogical consensus that has been developing in our field: that instruction in composition does not depend on everyone having the same knowledge or skill and that the same instruction should go on in basic classrooms as goes on in regular ones. Indeed, most of the problems with the teaching of basic writing come from too much emphasis on how basic writers are a different breed of people and on how basic courses should provide a homogeneous, lockstep kind of teaching that consists of drills or other instruction requiring all students to be at the same skill level. Staunch defenders of basic writing such as Karen Greenberg agree that the main problem in basic writing classes come from thinking too much in terms of "levels" and assuming a deficit or cognitive deficiency when the students are just unskilled:

> Despite critical insights into basic writing gained from research in composition in cognitive psychology, and applied linguistics, too many basic writing courses are still based on a remedial model, and too many basic writers are still subjected to skills/drills content and to pedagogies that conceptualize writing as a set of subskills that must be mastered in a series of steps or stages. Finally, many programs continue to define student writers as "basic" based on their ability to identify and correct errors in someone else's sentences or texts. ("Politics")

In short, the kind of instruction we want for first-year students of all abilities is exactly the kind of instruction that would be forced on us if we had classrooms with extremely mixed abilities. We would have to focus on the nitty-gritty essentials: having students write, share their writing with us and with each other, and get feedback from us and from each other.[3]

> But Peter, you are just being hopelessly utopian.

Having learned to expect this criticism, I have prepared two replies.

First, think back to the problems Karen Greenberg just described as common in the teaching of basic writing courses: the tendency to teach to a deficit. Is it not just as utopian to think that we could change this tendency in the teaching of basic writing as it would be to move in the heterogeneous direction I am suggesting? Think of all the structural pressures that lead to the problems that Greenberg describes: basic writing teachers have rooms full of students culled from the general population because they are alleged to be

---

3. It is true that certain "instruction" depends on homogeneity or prior knowledge. In mathematics, you cannot learn Y unless you understand a particular X that precedes it. Yet look at how even mathematics has a long tradition of heterogeneous classrooms where individual students follow particular paths at different speeds working in small groups or individually and using workbooks or computer-aided instruction.

poor writers; basic teachers often get less recognition and reward than "regular" teachers; and sometimes, unfortunately but understandably, the weakest or most inexperienced teachers are given this usually uncoveted assignment. In short, we are stuck having to work toward one utopia or another (unless we want to continue to cheat these students). Surely my utopia is as feasible and more exciting.

My second reply must begin with a confession: I have tried to play a trick on you. That is, this seemingly utopian approach is currently being used with success (Grego and Thompson). At the University of South Carolina, the first-year writing course that serves about 1,700 students is entirely heterogeneous (except for some English as a Second Language classes). They have no placement exam, though students bring a portfolio of prior writings to their regular writing class for their teacher to look at. On the basis of this portfolio and lots of additional writing during the first week, teachers identify students they think will need supplementary help, and these students join what Grego and Thompson call the Writing Studio.

Writing Studio students meet weekly in groups of four with instructors. In these sessions, the students get practical help with the specific tasks of the regular 101 course for that week, but they also do some ongoing work on their relationship to writing (involving work on memories and feelings about writing). Students so placed are obliged to go; thus, there *is* some stigma. But they do not get any extra work—indeed, the Writing Studio gives them help with the regular work. These meetings probably get them through their regular homework a bit more quickly than if they did not attend.

After the first year of using this approach, Writing Studio students accounted for only about 6 of 75 or so students who failed 101 (and those few tended to fail many or most of their courses, so it probably was not a writing difficulty that held them back). And many Writing Studio students did well in 101.

The University of South Carolina has now completed its second year (1993–94) of applying this program to the entire entering class, and they are even more pleased about it. None of the Writing Studio students failed the course. I have met a number of times with Rhonda Grego and Nancy Thompson, who designed and run this program (and with the director, Tom Waldrep, and with a number of teachers and tutors, some of whom teach in both the regular course and the Writing Studio). They have an interesting story to tell. When teachers worked in the previous, conventional system (using a placement exam and basic writing classes), they were accustomed to thinking in terms of this creature call a "basic writer." The goal of the placement test was to identify basic writers and put them in the basic course. That same mentality persisted somewhat into the first year of their new heterogeneous system. That is, they were still trying to identify basic writers, but this time for placement into the Writing Studio—and individual teachers were making these decisions from within the 101 classroom. But still they tended to think in terms of "basic writers," and not surprisingly, the emphasis still tended to be on problems with syntax and mechanics.

During the second year, they have found that the concept of basic writer is beginning to dissipate. The teachers are beginning to think more in terms of a wide range of *different difficulties* that students have. Individual teachers are beginning to acknowledge more clearly how each of them is better at dealing with some of these difficulties than with others. For example, some teachers are not bothered by severe problems with syntax and mechanics, and so these teachers are not tempted to place students with these problems into the Studio; they feel confident they can help them. But other teachers feel quite the opposite and do send such students to the Studio. Similarly, some teachers do not mind working with deeply tangled, incoherent thinking—but some do. Some teachers don't sweat massive blockage and fear—but others do. In short, teachers are beginning to make more nuanced judgments than they used to make about which students to send to the Writing Studio. And they are beginning to realize that they do not always use the same criteria. Thus, they do not so much think of these students as "basic writers" but simply as writers who need a kind of help that they themselves cannot give.

In short, Grego and Thompson are noticing a profound change in mentality. Members of the writing program no longer view the world of students so much through the lens of basic/nonbasic; they do not so much see a world of sheep and goats. Instead, they are beginning to see a range of students with particular locations in a complex universe of strengths and weaknesses. This is exciting to me.

By the way, they are also finding some students joining the Writing Studio voluntarily—and often good students (for example, some pre-med students who have been told that writing skills will matter for their entrance assessments).

This interesting experiment in South Carolina is not a fluke. Berea College has also set up a heterogeneous first-year reading and writing course where students whom teachers identify as needing extra help are obliged to meet in small groups with faculty tutors. Interestingly, these students can cycle in and out fairly briefly when they demonstrate they understand what they were sent to work on; that is, they are not obliged to stay for a whole semester. California State University at Chico has been experimenting on a small scale and has instituted a full change since 1994 (see Rodby): all students are placed in the regular English 1, but those judged as needing extra help take a series of four-week workshops. Students meet weekly in groups of ten with an instructor. The first workshop is an exploration of the students' literacy history and practices; for the second and third workshops, the student has a choice among various topics (for example, understanding the assignment, narrative, research, and citations); and the fourth is on preparing a portfolio (which is the final assignment for all English 1 students). Washington State University has been using a one-credit supplementary course for students who need extra help and has now gotten rid of all basic writing sections (see Haswell and Wyche-Smith). New York University has long had a one-credit tutorial that students could take as a supplement to the introductory writing course. Johnson C. Smith University, a historically black institution, reports success in getting rid of remedial or basic courses in all subjects and moving to heterogeneous courses: "In addition to retaining more students, we are increasing student achievement as indicated by both internal and external measures" (Kidda, Turner, and Parker 22). No doubt there are other examples I do not know about where schools are exploring this kind of approach.

We can also see around us examples of the larger general principle involved here: that heterogeneity is an advantage; that instruction will permit and perhaps even benefit from difference. This was Bartholomae's point in "The Tidy House," calling on the work of Mary Louise Pratt, and he could also have called on Mikhail Bakhtin. Bartholomae and Pratt argue that linguistic homogeneity is the exception rather than the rule. Many elementary and secondary schools are getting rid of tracking, even though many people thought it was impossible. Also, we see lots of "mainstreaming" that was hard to imagine before. All the peer tutoring we see in schools and colleges is built on this same principle: bringing students of different skills together rather than keeping them apart. But we must remember that this approach is not an *alternative* to giving extra help to inexperienced or poorly prepared writers; it is a different *way* to give extra help and instruction. That is—and this is crucial—we do not get to save all the money now spent on teaching basic courses: much of it is needed for a different deployment of extensive support.

Objections to This Heterogeneous Approach

1. You are attacking basic writing programs just when they most need defense. Administrators and legislators are looking at basic writing programs with a hungry eye. They are saying, "Why should we pay for learning that students should have done before they came to college? Let unprepared students go back to high school or night school and prepare!" Administrators or legislators have already taken credit away from many or perhaps even most basic writing courses. They are now threatening the next step: to take away funding itself and simply drop basic courses altogether. There is lots of money to be saved.

So am I just playing into the hands of such administrators with my suggestions? No. The real problem for unskilled writers is the *present* system with its emphasis on assessment and on labeling students as basic writers and putting them in separate courses. This sends a very dangerous message: "These students are not yet ready for a regular college writing course." What I am proposing is a structure to send a very different message: "These students are bona fide college students. They have been accepted by the admissions process. They *are* ready for the regular college writing course. Of course, we provide extra help for some students—as we have always done."

2. But poorly prepared writers themselves will feel uncomfortable, intimidated, and humiliated by having to work in the same class with the regular students. Most of these students *want* to be held apart in a separate and protected situation.

No doubt a certain number of students do feel this way, so in fact it makes good sense to have a conventional basic writing course for those who want it. But let us ask them and give them a choice instead of deciding for them. (See Royer and Gilles on their remarkable experience with "directed self-placement" at Grand Valley State University.) Thus, students would only be in basic writing by choice; and they probably ought to be free to drop it when they decide it is no longer helpful. (No doubt some students would take this course when we would not have placed them in it.)

This principle of respecting students' own sense of what they need in order to succeed is one of the main arguments in favor of heterogeneity. One of the main products of the present basic writing system with its limited tracking is student anger and resistance. An enormous amount of the slow learning and nonlearning we see in school is really a result of resistance more than of inability. Listen to this student writing about her experience: "The first day of school when my friends and I were discussing our schedules, I found that I was the only one taking Basic Writing. . . . The day came for me to go to Basic Writing for the first time. I went to class that day thinking that maybe no one knows that this is a basic class. The work 'basic' just makes me think of dumb, and the fact that there were less than ten of us really did not help." Is this an attitude that will maximize learning? What kind of proof do we have that students are wrong when they say, "I don't belong in this dummy class"? We have enough evidence that some so-called basic writing students can function satisfactorily or even well in a nonbasic course. Maybe others could, too, especially if we give them lots of extra help while they are there. We need more exploration.[4]

Another product of the present system is student self-blame, lack of confidence, and consequent low motivation. Think how much these attitudes slow down learning. Listen to this student in a classic statement of self-blaming: "Before closing I have to comment on my teacher. Mrs. Chamberlain is a good and caring teacher and she is teaching this course well and if we fail a test or quiz it's not because it wasn't taught to us well but because we fail to meet our potentials." (These statements were written by students to me as an outside visitor, in confidence from the teacher.)

3. But our basic writing classes are *better* than our regular 101s—and these students need and deserve better writing classes.

---

4. Let us think for a moment about all the students who fail the regular writing course who were not placed in basic writing. They take longer than one semester to reach acceptable levels of writing. Perhaps their placement test was read badly; perhaps their placement writing really did look stronger than their characteristic ability; perhaps they did not work hard enough; perhaps they drank too much. Whatever the reason, we must indubitably say about them what we indubitably say about those who fail the placement test: these students were "not ready for success in the first-year writing course." Should we give a placement exam for motivation? Such tests exist, and they are at least as trustworthy as our writing placement exams. Or should we perhaps give all students a chance to make it in one semester—with extra help for those who look as though they need it.

Basic writing classes *are* better at many campuses, including my own. They can be better in various ways: they can have better teachers and curricula and can provide better support, more sense of community, and a richer, more productive cultural mix. But are they really better if they insist by definition on holding the students back a semester or two, costing them time and money? If the basic course is really better, why cannot a student satisfy the writing requirement with it? In short, if we really want to treat these writers well, why can't we explore the model they are developing in South Carolina and Cal State Chico? That is, why can't we continue to give these students all the advantages we currently give them (better teachers, curricula, support, and culture) but *not* give them those two dubious "advantages": being kept out of the regular course and being prohibited from satisfying the writing requirement as quickly as everyone else? (Northeastern University has a freshmen program for basic writers that, though it segregates them, does not cost them more time.)

I fear I have drifted into using a more pugnacious voice because of the adversarial structure I have used (answering objections). I do not want to be dogmatic about something we understand so little. What we clearly need is more exploration and trial. We have plenty of experience with quarantining students who do poorly on placement tests. What we lack is experience with heterogeneous courses where we nevertheless give lots of special, supplemental help to those who need it.

Implications for Assessment

It is important to recognize that the present basic writing system is deeply complicit or symbiotic with large-scale testing. Placement testing for basic writing is now the most frequent kind of writing assessment in higher education. (This is the finding of three research reports—CCCC Committee on Assessment; Greenberg, Wiener, and Donovan; and Lederman, Ryzewic, and Ribaudo—cited in Greenberg, "Validity" 17.) It eats up more money than any other kind of assessment. Because it is so expensive and yet seldom trustworthy or fair (usually being based on single samples written in artificial conditions), I resent it. I am looking for ways to save that money for teaching—and also get away from the labeling and segregative structure of most first-year writing instruction.

And really, all this basic writing assessment is part of a much larger problem: simply too much assessment, too much preoccupation with evaluation and measuring. Schools and colleges and legislators are more willing to spend money for testing than for teaching and teachers. We are dominated by a cultural assumption that our problems in education will be solved by more testing, more standards. We accede too often to a general tendency to mistake assessment for education, to feel that if we get the testing right, students will finally learn. The explorations I have engaged in here and the successful experiments at the University of South Carolina, Berea, Cal State Chico, and Grand Valley State University, suggest some very concrete changes we can make by the twenty-first century in our assessment practices.

We can avoid the large-scale assessments that basic writing programs have tended to foster—assessment detached from instruction—and get the assessment we need with small-scale, local assessments rooted in instruction. In South Carolina, it is the teachers themselves who make the placement decisions, and they make them in terms of which kinds of students they can deal with. William Smith has developed an interesting placement process at the University of Pittsburgh on this principle, as has Washington State University (Haswell and Wyche-Smith). The fact is that large-scale testing plays into the hands of administrators who want to cut programs by means of simplistic judgments about ability.

We can avoid entrance testing and use exit testing instead. That is, we are misguided if we try to decide ahead of time whether someone will benefit from regular writing instruction. We are not justified in setting up barriers to entrance, but we are perfectly justified in setting them up at exit. If we are more open and welcoming at first, we surely have to be tougher about not giving students credit for the regular first-year course until they produce a portfolio of "good enough writing"—not a shoddy minimal competency but rather something of genuine substance.

The Yogurt Model

Utopian thinking does not try to be realistic; it tries to provide visions or models. But I have been toying with the utopian genre in order to show repeatedly how something that looked utopian was in fact feasible under normal conditions. What looked like a vision was something we could see with our two eyes.

But let me turn a corner and talk about something I *have not* seen. I want to extrapolate principles from what we have already seen and push toward a utopian model that could guide our future planning. The essential principle in the yogurt model is the *mixing of cultures:* we benefit from the presence of an older, developed culture present whenever we are trying to teach a newer or inexperienced culture.

Let me describe what a first-year writing program would look like that built on the principle of mixed cultures. All students would be required to take the same three-credit writing course, but the course would be structured in a somewhat competence-based or outcomes-based way. When students produce an acceptable portfolio, they would get three credits and could leave. Thus, skilled students could get finished more quickly than unskilled ones. However, even very strong writers would have to stay at least half a semester, for the requirement would also try to ensure that students learn a process, such as the skills of generating, revising, and working with peers. Unskilled students would not just languish, however: they would also get lots of supplemental help—which might be obligatory for some, voluntary for others.

Because there would be no barriers to entrance and students could leave sooner or later according to their accomplishments, the stakes would be higher than usual on assessing final portfolios. Programs might want to put in some guidelines like these: portfolios would have to contain writing of different, roughly specified sorts and genres, illustrating various dimensions of the writing process. Portfolios would have to be ruled satisfactory by one other teacher in addition to the student's own teacher. (To help guard against plagiarism, perhaps students would have to include a paper or exercise or two produced wholly in a classroom workshop setting over a number of sessions so that they have plenty of opportunity for reflection, conversation, feedback from peers and teachers, and revision but not opportunity for taking these particular pieces home.)

Notice how this yogurt model makes us reimagine our conception of a "course." A course would no longer be a voyage where everyone starts out on the ship together and arrives at port at the same time; not a voyage where everyone starts the first day with no sea legs and everyone is trying simultaneously to become acculturated to the waves. It would be more like the Burkean parlor (Burke 45)—or a writing center or studio—where people come together in groups and work together. Some have already been there a long time working and talking together when new ones arrive. New ones learn from playing the game with the more experienced players. Some leave before others. People continually trickle in and trickle out, but they work and talk together while they are there. Unskilled writers would be there longer, but for that reason, they would often function as veterans, experts, elders, carriers of the culture. They would be better than the hotshot students at the writerly processes of sharing, cooperating, feedback, even revising. Thus, teachers would no longer have what seems to me the hardest job in teaching: starting out each course each semester with a room full of students who do not know how to function as members of a writing workshop—trying to build a culture from scratch.

At the very beginning, we would start out with only half the regular number of students, so we could work closely and pay lots of attention to them for about three or four weeks to build a strong writing culture. As we and they build the culture and get better, we would bring in new students, so that the new ones join into groups with the experienced ones and get acculturated. From that point on, there will always be veterans with the new ones, always new ones joining veterans. We would get to keep the culture over the semester breaks—even over the summer. We would always come back to the new semester with a class of two-thirds veterans who already know how to function as writers. Notice, by the way, that this is how most real-world learning groups work: there are always veterans around when new people join.

This vision of students trickling in and out rather than remaining a stable population might make us fear that everything will be chaos, impermanence, and lack of community: just a kind of "commuter culture," where students care only about their own progress and do not connect with others. But don't lose sight of the fact that most students would be there for 14 weeks; and for every student who gets out early, others would be there for longer than 14 weeks. For this model would lead to fairly tough standards. The conventional "time-serving" model of a course often functions as a way to permit lots of students to get by with writing that is *not* "good enough." Many of us cannot bring ourselves to fail students who come to class and turn in all their assignments for 14 weeks—pieces of writing that more or less follow the assignment but are really not good enough. After all, the conventional system sends everyone in 101 the following message: "These students passed the placement test; all they need is 14 weeks of dutiful treatment. Then you can let them go." It is hard for teachers to be demanding about what they require for a passing grade.

I am influenced here by my three years on a research team looking at competence-based programs in higher education. (See Elbow, "Trying to Teach," and the essays in Grant et al.) A competence-based, yogurt structure creates more incentive for students to invest themselves and provide their own steam for learning—learning from their own efforts and from feedback from teachers and peers. For the sooner they learn, the sooner they are free to get credit and leave. Instead of resenting the need to revise (as so many first-year students do), they would soon see that revising makes the biggest difference to how soon they can leave. They are not stuck for a prison term of 14 weeks. (By the way, some people might think that the administration of this kind of flexible system would be impossible. But competence-based programs managed to do it—*with much less time, expense, and complication than it currently takes to administer huge placement tests.* Imagine if you had never heard of placement testing and someone proposed setting it up.)

Notice finally how this approach reshapes what is probably the main influence on learning—the dimensions of freedom and coercion. This approach says all must take writing. But what counts is learning and results, not putting in time. Though no one is forced to take a "baby" or "dummy" course, no one is exempted.

Given this structure, I suspect that a significant fraction of skilled students will in fact stay for longer than they have to when they see they are learning things that will help them with other courses—*and* see that they enjoy it. It will often be their smallest and most human class, the only one with a sense of community like a Burkean parlor. But, and here is the point, they would no longer be there against their wills: they would be doing it by choice. The presence in a classroom of even two or three skilled writers staying longer by choice will have a significant effect on the culture.

What is so sacred, inevitable, necessary, or natural about our default models for teaching and learning—in particular, our model where we assume 20 or 25 students must stay and learn together in a room for 10 or 14 weeks? Utopian thinking helps us see that what looks natural is really a historically based construction. So while we are exploring heterogeneous grouping and variable lengths of stay in a class, let us also explore out unthinking assumptions about size. That is, we could have a similar kind of "course" where students did not meet in whole classes—only in groups of five or six. These small groups would meet once a week with an instructor for an hour or so; and then meet for two hours a week or so on their own at a time and place of their own choosing. Or perhaps one of these hours would be with an undergraduate tutor. (See Nelson for explorations of how teaching and learning can be structured around small groups rather than whole classes.)

Conclusion

My theme is that we need to honor the utopian impulse. What looks at first like unrealistic utopianism can turn out to be realistically feasible; what looks like a "nowhere" (what "utopia" literally means) can turn out to be a somewhere. Fredric Jameson speaks of the difficulty of utopian thinking in our era. He speaks of modern readers whose "fantasy tolerance is . . . modified by a change in social relations: so in the windless closure of late capitalism it [has] come to seem increasingly futile and childish for people with a strong and particularly repressive reality-and-performance principle to imagine tinkering with what exists, let alone its thoroughgoing restructuration" (Ruppert xiii–xiv). In our culture, people tend to have a powerless feeling that no major changes are possible. When I published *Writing Without Teachers* in 1973, teacherless groups or peer feedback groups were accused of being hopelessly naive and utopian. But we have seen the practice become commonplace. Who is to say that some of the utopian visions I have described here will not become commonplace as well?

Appendix: Works that Question Holistic Scoring

Belanoff, Pat. "The Myths of Assessment." *Journal of Basic Writing* 10.2 (1991): 54–66.

Broad, Robert. "'Portfolio Scoring': A Contradiction in Terms." *New Directions in Portfolio Assessment*. Eds. Laurel Black, Don Daiker, Jeff Sommers, and Gail Stygall. Portsmouth NH: Heinemann, Boynton/Cook, 1994. 263–76.

Buley-Meissner, Mary Louise. "Reading Without Seeing: The Process of Holistic Scoring." *Writing On the Edge* 4.1 (Fall 1992): 51–65.

Charney, Davida. "The Validity of Using Holistic Scoring to Evaluate Writing: A Critical Overview." *Research in the Teaching of English* 18 (February 1984): 65–81.

Despain, LaRene and Thomas L. Hilgers. "Readers' Responses to the Rating of Non-Uniform Portfolios: Are There Limits of Portfolios' Utility?" *WPA: Writing Program Administration* 16.1–2 (Fall/Winter 1992): 24–37.

Elbow, Peter. "Foreword." *Portfolios: Process and Product*. Eds. Pat Belanoff and Marcia Dickson. Portsmouth NH: Heinemann, Boynton/Cook, 1991. ix–xvi.

———. "Ranking, Evaluating, Liking: Sorting Out Three Forms of Judgment." *College English* 55/2 (February 1993): 187–206.

———. "Will the Virtues of Portfolios Blind Us to their Potential Dangers?" *New Directions in Portfolio Assessment*. Eds. Laurel Black, Don Daiker, Jeff Sommers, and Gail Stygall. Portsmouth NH: Heinemann, Boynton/Cook, 1994. 40–55.

Freedman, Sarah Warshauer. "The Registers of Student and Professional Expository Writing: Influences on Teachers' Responses." *New Directions in Composition Research*. Eds. Richard Beach and Lillian Bridwell. NY: The Guilford P, 1984. 334–47.

Gorman, Thomas P., Alan C. Purves, and R. E. Degenhart. *The IEA Study of Written Composition I: The International Writing Tasks and Scoring Scales*. Oxford: Pergamon, 1988. Vol. 5 of *International Studies in Educational Achievement*.

Gould, Stephen Jay. *The Mismeasure of Man*. NY: Norton, 1981.

Hamp-Lyons, Liz. "Scoring Procedures for ESL Contexts." Ed. Liz Hamp-Lyons. *Assessing Second Language Writing in Academic Contexts*. Norwood NJ: Ablex, 1991. 241–76.

Hamp-Lyons, Liz and William Condon. "Questioning Assumptions about Portfolio-Based Assessment." *College Composition and Communication* 44.2 (May 1993): 176–90.

Hanson, F. Allan. *Testing Testing: Social Consequences of the Examined Life*. Berkeley: U Cal P, 1993.

Huot, Brian. "Reliability, Validity, and Holistic Scoring: What We Know and What We Need to Know." *College Composition and Communication* 41 (1990): 201–13.

Lucas, Catharine Keech. "Toward Ecological Evaluation." *Quarterly of the National Writing Project and the Center for the Study of Writing* 10.1 (1988): 1+.

———. "Toward Ecological Evaluation." *Quarterly of the National Writing Project and the Center for the Study of Writing* 10.2 (1988): 4–10.

Scharton, Maurice. "Models of Competence: Responses to a Scenario Writing Assignment." *Research in the Teaching of English* 23 (1989): 163–80.

Smith, Barbara Herrnstein. *Contingencies of Value: Alternative Perspectives for Critical Theory*. Cambridge: Harvard UP, 1988.

Works Cited

Adams, Peter Dow. "Basic Writing Reconsidered." *Journal of Basic Writing* 12.1 (Spring 1993). Special Issue: 4th National Basic Writing Conference Plenaries: 22–36.

Bakhtin, Mikhail. "The Problem of Speech Genres." *Speech Genres and Other Late Essays*. Eds. Caryl Emerson and Michale Holquist. Tr. Vern W. McGee. Austin TX: U Texas P, 1986.

Bartholomae, David. "The Tidy House: Basic Writing in the American Curriculum." *Journal of Basic Writing* 12.1 (Spring 1993). Special Issue: 4th National Basic Writing Conference Plenaries: 4–21.

Benesch, Sarah. "Ending Remediation: Linking ESL and Content in Higher Education." Washington DC: TESOL, 1988.

Burke, Kenneth. *Rhetoric of Motives*. Berkeley CA: U Cal P, 1950.

CCCC Committee on Assessment. *Post-secondary Writing Assessment: An Update on Practices and Procedures*. (Spring 1988). Report to the Executive Committee of the Conference on College Composition and Communication.

Elbow, Peter. "Trying to Teach While Thinking About the End: Teaching in a Competence-Based Curriculum." *On Competence: A Critical Analysis of Competence-Based Reforms in Higher Education*. Eds. Gerald Grant et al. San Francisco: Jossey-Bass, 1979.

Elbow, Peter and Pat Belanoff. "State University of New York: Portfolio-Based Evaluation Program." *New Methods in College Writing Programs: Theory into Practice*. Eds. Paul Connolly and Teresa Vilardi. NY: MLA, 1986. 95–105. Reprinted in *Portfolios: Process and Product*. Eds. Pat Belanoff and Marcia Dickson. Portsmouth NH: Heinemann, Boynton/Cook, 1991.

Freedman, Sarah Warshauer. "The Registers of Student and Professional Expository Writing: Influences on Teachers' Responses." *New Directions in Composition Research*. Eds. Richard Beach and Lillian Bridwell. NY: The Guilford P, 1984.

Grant, Gerald et al. *On Competence: A Critical Analysis of Competence-Based Reforms in Higher Education*. San Francisco: Jossey-Bass, 1979.

Greenberg, Karen. "The Politics of Basic Writing." *Journal of Basic Writing* 12.1 (Spring 1993). Special Issue: 4th National Basic Writing Conference Plenaries: 64–71.

———. "Validity and Reliability: Issues in the Direct Assessment of Writing." *WPA: Writing Program Administration* 16.1–2 (Fall/Winter 1992): 7–22.

Greenberg, Karen, Harvey Wiener, and Richard Donovan. "Preface." *Writing Assessment: Issues and Strategies*. Eds. Karen Greenberg, Harvey Wiener, and Richard Donovan. NY: Longman, 1986. xi–xvii.

Grego, Rhonda and Nancy Thompson. "The Writing Studio Program: Reconfiguring Basic

Writing/Freshman Composition." *WPA* (Journal of Writing Program Administrators). (Fall/Winter 1995): 66–79.

———. "Repositioning Remediation: Renegotiating Composition's Work in the Academy." *CCC* 47 (Feb 1996): 62–84.

Haswell, Richard and Susan Wyche-Smith. "Adventuring into Writing Assessment." *CCC* 45 (May 1994): 220–36.

Hull, Glenda, Mike Rose, Kay Losey Fraser, Marisa Castellano. "Remediation as a Social Construct: Perspectives from an Analysis of Classroom Discourse." *CCC* 42.3 (Oct 1991): 299–329.

Jones, William. "Basic Writing: Pushing Against Racism." *Journal of Basic Writing* 12.1 (Spring 1993). Special Issue: 4th National Basic Writing Conference Plenaries: 72–80.

Kidda, Michael, Joseph Turner, and Frank E. Parker. "There *Is* an Alternative to Remedial Education." *Metropolitan Universities* 3.3 (Spring 1993): 16–25.

Lederman, Marie Jean, Susan Ryzewic, and Michael Ribaudo. *Assessment and Improvement of the Academic Skills of Entering Freshmen: A National Survey*. NY: CUNY Instructional Resource Center, 1983.

Nelson, Marie Wilson. *At The Point of Need: Teaching Basic and ESL Writers*. Portsmouth NH: Heinemann, 1990.

Pratt, Mary Louise. "Linguistic Utopias." *The Linguistics of Writing*. Eds. Nigel Fabb, et al. Manchester: Manchester UP, 1987.

———. "The Arts of the Contact Zone." *Profession 91*. NY: MLA, 1991.

Rodby, Judith. "Testing Our Ideas of Literacy." Unpublished MS. Department of English, California SU, Chico.

Royer, Daniel J. and Roger Gilles. "Directed Self-Placement: An Attitude of Orientation." *CCC* 50.1 (Sept 1998): 54–70.

Ruppert, Peter. *Reader in a Strange Land: The Activity of Reading Literary Utopias*. Athens: U of Georgia P, 1986.

Smith, William. "The Importance of Teacher Knowledge in College Composition Placement Testing." *Reading Empirical Research Studies: A Rhetoric of Research*. Eds. John R. Hayes et al. Hillsdale NJ: Erlbaum, 1992.

White, Edward. "Language and Reality in Writing Assessment." *CCC* 41 (May 1990): 187–200.

———. "Writing Assessment Beyond the Classroom: Will Writing Teachers Play a Role?" Eds. Lynn Z. Bloom, Donald A. Daiker and Edward M. White. *Composition in the Twenty-first Century: Crisis and Change*. Carbondale Il: Southern Illinois UP, 1996.

Published Works by Peter Elbow

Books

Writing Without Teachers. Oxford University Press, 1973. 2nd ed. 1998.

Oppositions in Chaucer. Wesleyan University Press, 1975.

(With Gerald Grant, David Riesman, and five others) *On Competence: A Critical Analysis of Competence-Based Reforms in Higher Education.* Jossey-Bass, 1979.

Writing With Power: Techniques for Mastering the Writing Process. Oxford University Press, 1981. 2nd ed. 1998.

Embracing Contraries: Explorations in Learning and Teaching. Oxford University Press, 1986.

(With Pat Belanoff) *A Community of Writers: A Workshop Course in Writing.* McGraw Hill, 1989. 2nd ed. 1994, 3rd ed. 1999.

(With Pat Belanoff) *Sharing and Responding.* McGraw Hill, 1989. 2nd ed. 1994, 3rd ed. 1999.

What is English? Modern Language Association and National Council of Teachers of English, 1990.

Edited Books or Collections

(With Pat Belanoff and Sheryl Fontaine) *Nothing Begins with N: New Investigations of Freewriting.* Southern Illinois University Press, 1990.

Pre/Text: An Interdisciplinary Journal of Rhetoric 11.1-2 (1990). (A special issue devoted to personal and expressive writing that do the work of academic discourse.)

Voice and Writing. In the Landmark Essays series, Hermagoras Press (now Erlbaum), 1994.

(With Mary Deane Sorcinelli) *Writing to Learn: Strategies for Assigning and Responding to Writing in the Disciplines.* (A volume in the series, *New Directions for Teaching and Learning.*) Jossey-Bass, 1997.

Essays, Articles, Reviews

(*Items marked with an asterisk are found in the present volume.)

"Two Boethian Speeches in *Troilus and Criseyde* and Chaucerian Irony." *Literary Criticism and Historical Understanding.* Ed. Philip Damon. Columbia University Press, 1967.

"A Method for Teaching Writing." *College English* 30.2 (Nov 1968). (Followed by, "Reply to Donald Hassler" 30.8 (May 1969).

"What is a Conscientious Objector?" *Christian Century,* Aug 1968.

"The Definition of Teaching." *College English* 30.3 (Dec 1968).

"More Accurate Evaluation of Student Performance." *Journal of Higher Education* 40 (Mar 1969). (Also in *Embracing Contraries.*)

"Exploring My Teaching." *College English* 32.7 (Apr 1971). (Also in *Embracing Contraries.*)

"Real Learning and Nondisciplinary Courses." *Journal of General Education* 23.2 (1971). (Also in *Embracing Contraries.*)

"Shall We Teach or Give Credit? A Model for Higher Education." *Soundings* 54.3 (Fall 1971).

"Teacher Power." (Invited essay-review of *Pygmalion in the Classroom.*) *Elementary English* June 1971.

"Concerning the Necessity of Teachers." (Invited response.) *Inter-Change: Journal of the Ontario Institute for Studies in Education* 2.4 (Winter 1971).

"Oppositions in *The Knight's Tale.*" *The Chaucer Review* 7.2 (1973).

"The Pedagogy of the Bamboozled." *Soundings* 56.2 (Summer 1973). (Also in *Embracing Contraries.*)

"The Doubting Game and the Believing Game." *Goal-Making for English Teaching.* Ed. Henry Maloney. National Council of Teachers of English, 1973 (reprinted from appendix, *Writing Without Teachers*).

"Trying to Teach While Thinking About the End: Teaching in a Competence-Based Curriculum." *On Competence: A Critical Analysis of Competence-Based Reforms in Higher Education,* Jossey-Bass, 1979. (Also in *Embracing Contraries.*)

"Why Teach Writing?" and "What is Good Writing?" *The Why's of Teaching Composition,* Washington Council of Teachers of English, 1978.

"Quick Revising." *Washington English Journal* 2.1 (Fall 1979).

"One to One Faculty Development." *Learning About Teaching: New Directions for Teaching and Learning* 4. Ed. Jack Noonan. Jossey-Bass, 1980.

"Taking the Crisis out of the Writing Crisis." *Seattle Post-Intelligencer, 1 Nov 1981.*

"Learning and Authentic Moments." *New Perspectives on Teaching and Learning: New Directions for Teaching and Learning* 7. Ed. Warren Bryan Martin. Jossey-Bass, 1981.

"About Resistance to Freewriting and Feedback Groups." *Washington English Journal,* Winter 1982.

"Comments on Kavanaugh." (Invited response.) Little Three Symposium on "Metaphor and Representations," Jan 1982, Wesleyan University. *The Berkshire Review* 17 (1982).

"The Doubting Game and the Believing Game." *Pre/Text: An Inter-Disciplinary Journal of Rhetoric* 3.4 (Winter 1982).

"Teaching Writing by Not Paying Attention to Writing." *Fforum: Essays on Theory and Practice in the Teaching of Writing.* Ed. Patricia Stock, Boynton/Cook, 1983.

"Embracing Contraries in the Teaching Process." *College English* 45 (1983). (Also in *Embracing Contraries.*) Followed by "Reply to Ronald Scheer and to Abraham Bernstein." *College English* 46.5 (Sep 1984).

"Spilt Milk." (Poem) *Soundings* 20, SUNY Stony Brook (Spring 1983).

"Teaching Thinking by Teaching Writing." *Change Magazine,* Sep 1983. (Also in *Embracing Contraries.*)

"In the Beginning Was the Word." Review of *Before the First Word,* a video cassette published by Encyclopaedia Brittanica Educational Foundation. *Change Magazine,* June 1984.

"The Challenge for Sentence Combining." *Sentence Combining: A Rhetorical Perspective.* Eds. Don Daiker, Andrew Kerek, and Max Morenberg, Southern Illinois University Press, 1985.

*"The Shifting Relationships Between Speech and Writing." *College Composition and Communication* 36.2 (Oct 1985). (Braddock award for the best essay of the year in that journal.)

*(With Pat Belanoff) "State University of New York: Portfolio-Based Evaluation Program." *New Methods in College Writing Programs: Theory into Practice*. Paul Connolly and Teresa Vilardi. Modern Language Association, 1986.

(With Pat Belanoff) "Using Portfolios to Increase Collaboration and Community in a Writing Program." *WPA: Journal of Writing Program Administration* 9.3 (Spring 1986).

(With Pat Belanoff) "Portfolios as a Substitute for Proficiency Examinations." *College Composition and Communication* 37.3 (Oct 1986).

(With Jennifer Clarke) "Desert Island Discourse: The Benefits of Ignoring Audience." *The Journal Book*. Ed. Toby Fulwiler. Boynton/Cook 1987.

*"Closing My Eyes as I Speak: An Argument For Ignoring Audience." *College English* 49.1 (Jan 1987).

Review of *Reclaiming the Classroom: Teacher Research as an Agency for Change*. Eds. Dixie Goswami and Peter Stillman. *ADE Bulletin* 87 (Fall 1987).

"A Remarkable Consensus." *Massachusetts English Teacher* 3/88.

"Getting More Discussion into MLA Convention Sessions." *Modern Language Association Newsletter* 19.4 (Winter 1987).

"To the Troops in the Trenches" and "Skeleton-Making Feedback and the Teaching of Thinking" and "A Note about Collaboration" and "A Moment from the Meeting." *Teachers and Writers* 19.4 (March–April 1988).

"My Vision for Writing and English Faculty." *Colleague* 5 (Winter 1988).

"The Pleasures of Voices in the Literary Essay: Explorations in the Prose of Gretel Ehrlich and Richard Selzer." *Literary Nonfiction: Theory, Criticism, Pedagogy*. Ed. Chris Anderson. Southern Illinois University Press, 1989.

"Foreword." Alice Brand. *The Psychology of Writing: The Affective Experience*. Greenwood Press, 1989.

"Response" to David Bleich's review of my *Embracing Contraries*. *ADE Bulletin* 93 (Fall 1989).

*"Toward a Phenomenology of Freewriting." *Journal of Basic Writing* 8.2 (Fall 1989). (Also in *Nothing Begins with N: New Investigations of Freewriting*.)

"Foreword: Expressive Academic Discourse." *Pre/Text* 11.1-2 (1990).

*"Reflections on Adacemic Discourse: How it Relates to Freshmen and Colleagues." *College English* 53.2 (Feb 1991).

"Some Thoughts on *Expressive Discourse*: A Review Essay." Review of *Expressive Discourse* by Jeanette Harris, SMU. *Journal of Advanced Composition* 11.1 (Winter 1991): 83–93.

"Foreword." *Portfolios: Process and Product*. Eds. Pat Belanoff and Marcia Dickson. Heinemann, Boynton/Cook, 1991.

"Polanyian Perspectives on the Teaching of Literature and Composition." *Tradition & Discovery: The Polanyi Society Periodical* 17.1-2 (1990–91).

"Writing Assessment: Do It Better, Do It Less." *Adult Assessment Forum* 2.4 (Winter 1991).

"Making Better Use of Student Evaluations of Teachers." *ADE Bulletin* 101 (Spring 1992). (Reprinted in *Profession 92*, Modern Language Association.)

*"Freewriting and the Problem of the Wheat and the Tares." *Writing and Publishing for Academic Authors*. Ed. Joseph Moxley. University Press of America, 1992. 2nd ed, Lanham MD: Rowman & Littlefield, 1997.

"Using Low-Stakes Writing in Judgment-Free Zones." *Writing Teacher* May 1992.

*"The Uses of Binary Thinking." *Journal of Advanced Composition* 13.1 (Winter 1993). (Edited version, in *Taking Stock: The Writing Process Movement in the 90s*. Eds. Lad Tobin and Tom Newkirk. Heinemann Boynton/Cook. 1994.)

*"The War Between Reading and Writing—and How to End It." *Rhetoric Review* 12.1 (Fall 1993). (James A. Berlin award for the best essay of the year in that journal.) Reprinted in *Critical Theory and the Teaching of Literature: Politics, Curriculum Pedagogy*. Eds. James Slevin and Art Young. National Council of Teachers of English. 1996.

*"Silence: A Collage." In *Presence of Mind: Writing and the Domain Beyond the Cognitive*. Eds. Alice Brand and Richard Graves. Heinemann/Boynton-Cook, 1993.

"Response to Glynda Hull, Mike Rose, Kay Losey Fraser, and Marisa Castellano, "Remediation as a Social Construct" (*College Composition and Communication* 42, Oct. 1991). *College Composition and Communication* 44.4 (Dec 1993).

"Ranking, Evaluating, and Liking: Sorting out Three Forms of Judgment." *College English* 55.2 (Feb 1993). Followed by a reply to four responses 56.1 (Jan 1994).

*"Voice in Literature." *Encyclopedia of English Studies and Language Arts*. Ed. Alan Purves. National Council of Teachers of English, 1994.

"Freewriting." *Encyclopedia of English Studies and Language Arts*. Ed. Alan Purves. National Council of Teachers of English, 1994.

"Will the Virtues of Portfolios Blind Us to their Potential Dangers?" *New Directions in Portfolio Assessment: Reflective Practice, Critical Theory, and Large-Scale Scoring*. Eds. Laurel Black, Don Daiker, Jeffrey Sommers, and Gail Stygall. Heinemann/Boynton-Cook, 1994.

*"To Group or Not to Group: System Leads to Narrow Definition of Intelligence." *Amherst Bulletin* 25.50 (7 Jan 1994).

"Advanced Classes Destructive of Motivation and Curiosity." *Amherst Bulletin* (18 Nov 1994).

"Group Work: Sharing and Responding." *Notes in the Margin*. Fall 1994. (Published by the Stanford University Writing Program.)

*"Introduction: Voice and Writing." *Voice and Writing*. Hermagoras Press, 1994. (A shorter version is published as "What Do We Mean When We Talk about Voice in Writing?" in *Voices on Voice: Perspectives, Definitions, Inquiry*. Ed. Kathleen Blake Yancey. National Council of Teachers of English, 1994.)

"How Portfolios Show Us Problems with Holistic Scoring, but Suggest an Alternative." *Assessment Update* 6.4 (July–August 1994).

(With Kathleen Blake Yancey) "On Holistic Scoring and the Nature of Reading: An Inquiry Composed on Email." Invited essay for inaugural issue of *Assessing Writing* 1.1 (1994).

(With Kathleen Blake Yancey) "An Annotated and Collective Bibliography of Voice: Soundings from the Voices Within." In *Voices on Voice: Perspectives, Definitions, Inquiry*. Ed. Kathleen Blake Yancey. National Council of Teachers of English, 1994.

"Being a Writer vs. Being an Academic: A Conflict in Goals." *College Composition and Communication* 46.1 (February 1995).

"Response to David Bartholomae." *College Composition and Communication* 46.1 (February 1995).

*"Breathing Life into the Text." *When Writing Teachers Teach Literature: Bringing Writing to Reading*. Eds. Art Young and Toby Fulwiler. Heinemann Boynton/Cook, 1995.

"Principles that Underlie My Teaching" and selected responses to student papers. *Twelve Readers Reading*. Hampton Press, 1995.

*"Writing Assessment in the Twenty-first Century: A Utopian View." *Composition in the 21st Century: Crisis and Change*. Eds. Lynn Bloom, Don Daiker, and Ed White. Southern Illinois University Press, 1996.

"Writing Assessment: Do It Better, Do It Less." *The Politics and Practices of Assessment in Writing*. Eds. William Lutz, Edward White, and Sandra Kamusikiri. Modern Language Association, 1996.

"Speech and Writing." Essay for *Encyclopedia of Rhetoric*. Ed. Theresa Enos. NY: Garland Publishing, 1996.

(With Pat Belanoff) "Reflections on an Explosion: Portfolios in the '90s and Beyond." *Situating Portfolios: Four Perspectives*. Eds. Kathleen Blake Yancey and Irwin Weiser. Utah State University Press, 1997.

*"Introductory Essay: High Stakes and Low Stakes in Assigning and Responding to Writing." *Writing to Learn: Strategies for Assigning and Responding to Writing in the Disciplines*. Eds. Mary Deane Sorcinelli and Peter Elbow. (A volume in the series, *New Directions for Teaching and Learning*.) Jossey-Bass, 1997.

"Grading Student Writing: Make It Simpler, Fairer, Clearer." *Writing to Learn: Strategies for Assigning and Responding to Writing in the Disciplines*. Eds. Mary Deane Sorcinelli and Peter Elbow. (A volume in the series, *New Directions for Teaching and Learning.*) Jossey-Bass, 1997.

*"Taking Time Out from Grading and Evaluating while Working in a Conventional System" *Assessing Writing* 4.1 (1997).

*"Changing Grading While Working with Grades." *Theory and Practice of Grading Writing: Problems and Possibilities.* Eds. Chris Weaver and Fran Zak. State University of New York Press, 1998.

*"Illiteracy at Oxford and Harvard: Reflections on the Inability to Write." *Reflective Stories: Becoming Teachers of College English and English Education.* Eds. H. Thomas McCrakin and Richard L. Larson, with Judith Entes. National Council of Teachers of English, 1998.

New Introduction for the 25th anniversary new edition of *Writing Without Teachers.* Oxford University Press, 1998.

New Introduction for the 17th anniversary new edition of *Writing With Power.* Oxford University Press, 1998.

*"Collage: Your Cheatin' Art." *Writing On the Edge* 9.1 (Fall/winter 1997/1998).

*"In Defense of Private Writing." *Written Communication* 16.2 (1999): 139–69.

*"Inviting the Mother Tongue: Beyond 'Mistakes,' 'Bad English,' and 'Wrong Language'." *Journal of Advanced Composition* 19.3 (Summer 1999): 359–88.

*"Using the Collage for Collaborative Writing." *Composition Studies.* Spring 1999.

"Individualism and the Teaching of Writing: Response to Vai Ramanathan and Dwight Atkinson." *Journal of Second Language Writing* 8.3 (September 1999).

"Independent Writing and the Implications for our Model of Writing." Submitted for publication.

Interviews

"When Teachers are Writers: Interview with Peter Elbow." *Writing Teacher,* January 1992.

"Going in Two Directions at Once: An Interview with Peter Elbow." John Boe and Eric Schroeder. *Writing on the Edge* 4.1 (Fall 1992).

"Peter Elbow on Writing." Videotape. Media Education Foundation, 1995.

"An Interview with Peter Elbow." Jeff Siegel, *Editor and Writer,* July/August 1997.

"An Interview with Peter Elbow." Kelly Peinado. *Teaching English in the Two Year College,* October 1997.

Informally Published Works

"Thoughts About Writing Essays." pamphlet handbook, Franconia College Press, 1965.

(With Bill Aldridge and Margaret Gribskov) *One-to-One Faculty Development.* Unpublished MS distributed by Evergreen State College, 1978.

"A Competence-Based Management Program at Seattle Central Community College: A Case Study." *On Competence: A Critical Analysis of Competence-Based Reforms in Higher Education.* Two-volume report put out by the Fund for the Improvement of Higher Education. Ed. Gerald Grant et al., 1979.

"Midstream Reflections." *Moving Between Practice and Research in Writing: Proceedings of the NIE-FIPSE Grantee Workshop.* Ed. Ann Humes. SWRL Educational Research and Development, Las Alamitos CA, 1981.

"Critical Thinking is Not Enough." *Critical Thinking/Critical Writing.* University of Northern Iowa, 1983.

"The Foundations of Intellectual Combat and Collaboration" and "Reply to Stanley Fish." *Proceedings of the Conference: Collaborative Learning and the Reinterpretation of Knowledge.* New York (John Jay College), 1986.